D0297194

Ghost Train to the Eastern Star

On the tracks of
The Great Railway Bazaar

PAUL THEROUX

HAMISH HAMILTON
an imprint of
PENGUIN BOOKS

To Sheila, with love

HAMISH HAMILTON

Published by the Penguin Group
Penguin Books Ltd, 80 Strand, London WC2R ORL, England
Penguin Group (USA) Inc., 375 Hudson Street, New York, New York 10014, USA
Penguin Group (Canada), 90 Eglinton Avenue East, Suite 700, Toronto, Ontario, Canada M4P 2Y3
(a division of Pearson Penguin Canada Inc.)
Penguin Ireland, 25 St Stephen's Green, Dublin 2, Ireland (a division of Penguin Books Ltd)
Penguin Group (Australia), 250 Camberwell Road, Camberwell, Victoria 3124, Australia
(a division of Pearson Australia Group Pty Ltd)
Penguin Books India Pvt Ltd, 11 Community Centre, Panchsheel Park, New Delhi – 110 017, India
Penguin Group (NZ), 67 Apollo Drive, Rosedale, North Shore 0632, New Zealand
(a division of Pearson New Zealand Ltd)
Penguin Books (South Africa) (Pty) Ltd, 24 Sturdee Avenue, Rosebank, Johannesburg 2196, South Africa

Penguin Books Ltd, Registered Offices: 80 Strand, London WC2R ORL, England

www.penguin.com

First published in the USA by Houghton Mifflin, New York 2008
First published in the UK by Hamish Hamilton 2008
1

Copyright © Paul Theroux, 2008

All rights reserved

The moral right of the author has been asserted

Except in the United States of America, this book is sold subject
to the condition that it shall not, by way of trade or otherwise, be lent,
re-sold, hired out, or otherwise circulated without the publisher's
prior consent in any form of binding or cover other than that in
which it is published and without a similar condition including this
condition being imposed on the subsequent purchaser

The lines from *L'Homme qui regardait passer les trains* © 1938 Georges Simenon Ltd, a Chorion company,
all rights reserved. Excerpts from 'Aubade' and 'Water' from *Collected Poems* by Philip Larkin, by kind
permission of Faber and Faber, Ltd. The extract from 'plato told' is reprinted from *Complete Poems 1904–62*
by E. E. Cummings, edited by George Firmage, by permission of W. W. Norton & Company.
Copyright © 1991 by the Trustees for the E. E. Cummings Trust and George James Firmage. The lines from
'Tom O'Roughley' by W. B. Yeats used by kind permission of A. P. Watt Ltd. on behalf of Gráinne Yeats.

Set in 11/13.5 pt Monotype Bembo
Typeset by Rowland Phototypesetting Ltd, Bury St Edmunds, Suffolk
Printed in Great Britain by Clays Ltd, St Ives plc

A CIP catalogue record for this book is available from the British Library

ISBN: 978-0-241-14253-0

www.greenpenguin.co.uk

Penguin Books is committed to a sustainable future
for our business, our readers and our planet.
The book in your hands is made from paper
certified by the Forest Stewardship Council.

Ghost Train to
the Eastern Star

Dear Helen

With best wishes
for a very happy
40th birthday

Fiona

Books by Paul Theroux

FICTION

Waldo

Fong and the Indians

Girls at Play

Murder in Mount Holly

Jungle Lovers

Sinning with Annie

Saint Jack

The Black House

The Family Arsenal

The Consul's File

A Christmas Card

Picture Palace

London Snow

World's End

The Mosquito Coast

The London Embassy

Half Moon Street

O-Zone

My Secret History

Chicago Loop

Millroy the Magician

My Other Life

Kowloon Tong

Hotel Honolulu

The Stranger at the Palazzo d'Oro

Blinding Light

The Elephanta Suite

CRITICISM

V. S. Naipual

NON-FICTION

The Great Railway Bazaar

The Old Patagonian Express

The Kingdom by the Sea

Sailing Through China

Sunrise with Seamonsters

The Imperial Way

Riding the Iron Rooster

To the Ends of the Earth

The Happy Isles of Oceania

The Pillars of Hercules

Sir Vidia's Shadow

Fresh Air Fiend

Dark Star Safari

Ghost Train to the Eastern Star

That feeling about trains, for instance. Of course he had long outgrown the boyish glamour of the steam engine. Yet there was something that had an appeal for him in trains, especially in night trains, which always put queer, vaguely improper notions into his head.

GEORGES SIMENON
The Man Who Watched the Trains Go By

Contents

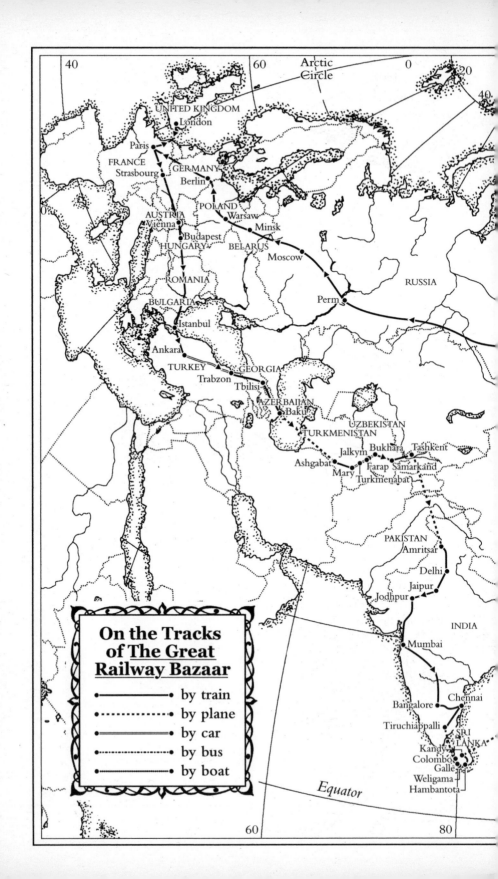

On the Tracks
of **The Great
Railway Bazaar**

• — • by train
• ---- • by plane
• ══ • by car
• ···· • by bus
• —— • by boat

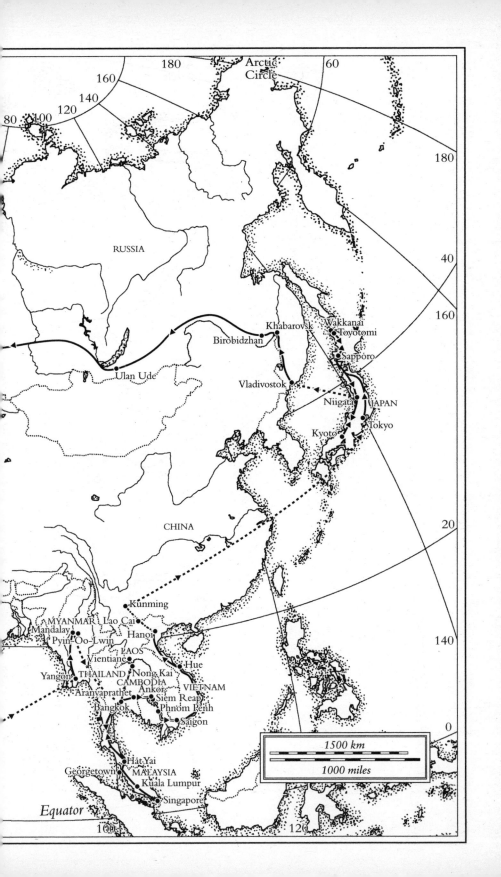

1. The Eurostar

You think of travellers as bold, but our guilty secret is that travel is one of the laziest ways on earth of passing the time. Travel is not merely the business of being bone-idle, but also an elaborate bumming evasion, allowing us to call attention to ourselves with our conspicuous absence while we intrude upon other people's privacy – being actively offensive as fugitive freeloaders. The traveller is the greediest kind of romantic voyeur, and in some well-hidden part of the traveller's personality is an unpickable knot of vanity, presumption and mythomania bordering on the pathological. This is why a traveller's worst nightmare is not the secret police or the witch doctors or malaria, but rather the prospect of meeting another traveller.

Most writing about travel takes the form of jumping to conclusions, and so most travel books are superfluous, the thinnest, most transparent monologuing. Little better than a licence to bore, travel writing is the lowest form of literary self-indulgence: dishonest complaining, creative mendacity, pointless heroics and chronic posturing, much of it distorted with Munchausen syndrome.

Of course, it's much harder to stay at home and be polite to people and face things, but where's the book in that? Better the boastful charade of pretending to be an adventurer:

> Yes, swagger the nut-strewn roads,
> Crouch in the fo'c'sle
> Stubbly with goodness,

in a lusty 'Look-at-me!' in exotic landscapes.

This was more or less my mood as I was packing to leave home. I also thought: *But there is curiosity.* Even the most timid fantasists need the satisfaction of now and then enacting their fantasies. And sometimes you just have to clear out. Trespassing is a pleasure for some of us. As for idleness, 'An aimless joy is a pure joy.'

And there are dreams: one, the dream of a foreign land that I enjoy at home, staring east into space at imagined temples, crowded bazaars and what V. S. Pritchett called 'human architecture', lovely women in gauzy clothes, old trains clattering on mountainsides, the mirage of happiness; two, the dream state of travel itself. Often on a trip, I seem to be alive in a hallucinatory vision of difference, the highly coloured unreality of foreignness, where I am vividly aware (as in most dreams) that I don't belong; yet I am floating, an idle anonymous visitor among busy people, an utter stranger. When you're strange, as the song goes, no one remembers your name.

Travel can induce such a distinct and nameless feeling of strangeness and disconnection in me that I feel insubstantial, like a puff of smoke, merely a ghost, a creepy revenant from the underworld, unobserved and watchful among real people, wandering, listening while remaining unseen. Being invisible – the usual condition of the older traveller – is much more useful than being obvious. You see more, you are not interrupted, you are ignored. Such a traveller isn't in a hurry, which is why you might mistake him for a bum. Hating schedules, depending on chance encounters, I am attracted by travel's slow tempo.

Ghosts have all the time in the world, another pleasure of long-distance aimlessness – travelling at half speed on slow trains and procrastinating. And this ghostliness, I was to find, was also an effect of the journey I had chosen, returning to places I had known many years ago. It is almost impossible to return to an early scene in your travelling life and not feel like a spectre. And many places I saw were themselves sad and spectral, others big and hectic, while I was the haunting presence, the eavesdropping shadow on the ghost train.

Long after I took the trip I wrote about in *The Great Railway Bazaar* I went on thinking how I'd gone overland, changing trains across Asia, improvising my trip, rubbing against the world. And reflecting on what I'd seen – the way the unrevisited past is always looping in your dreams. Memory is a ghost train too. Ages later, you still ponder the beautiful face you once glimpsed in a distant country. Or the sight of a noble tree, or a country road, or a happy table in a café, or some angry boys armed with rusty spears shrieking, 'Run you life, *dim-dim!*' – or the sound of a train at night, striking that precise musical note of train whistles, a diminished third, into the darkness, as you lie in the train, moving through the world as travellers do, 'inside the whale'.

Thirty-three years went by. I was then twice as old as the person who had ridden those trains, most of them pulled by steam locomotives, boiling across the hinterland of Turkey and India. I loved the symmetry in the time difference. Time passing had become something serious to me, embodied in the process of my growing old. As a young man I regarded the earth as a fixed and trustworthy thing that would see me into my old age; but older, I began to understand transformation as a natural law, something emotional in an undependable world that was visibly spoiled. It is only with age that you acquire the gift to evaluate decay, the epiphany of Wordsworth, the wisdom of *wabi-sabi*: nothing is perfect, nothing is complete, nothing lasts.

'Without change there can be no nostalgia,' a friend once said to me, and I realized that what I began to witness was not just change and decay, but imminent extinction. Had my long-ago itinerary changed as much as me? I had the idea of taking the same trip again, travelling in my own footsteps – a serious enterprise, but the sort of trip that younger, opportunistic punks often take to make a book and get famous.*

The best of travel seems to exist outside of time, as though the years of travel are not deducted from your life. Travel also holds the magical possibility of reinvention: that you might find a place you love, to begin a new life and never go home. In a distant place no one knows you – nearly always a plus. And you can pretend, in travel, to be different from the person you are, unattached, enigmatic, younger, richer or poorer, anyone you choose to be, the rebirth that many travellers experience if they go far enough.

The decision to return to any early scene in your life is dangerous but irresistible, not as a search for lost time but for the grotesquerie of what happened since. In most cases it is like meeting an old lover years later and hardly recognizing the object of desire in this pinched and bruised old fruit. We all live with fantasies of transformation. Live long enough and you see them enacted – the young made old, the road improved, houses where there were once fields; and their opposites, a good school turned into a ruin, a river poisoned, a pond shrunk and filled with

---

* The list is very long and includes travellers' books in the footsteps of Graham Greene, George Orwell, Robert Louis Stevenson, Leonard Woolf, Joseph Conrad, Mr Kurtz, H. M. Stanley, Leopold Bloom, Saint Paul, Basho, Jesus and Buddha.

rubbish, and dismal reports: 'He's dead,' 'She's huge,' 'She committed suicide,' 'He's now prime minister,' 'He's in jail,' 'You can't go there any more.'

A great satisfaction in growing old – one of many – is assuming the role of a witness to the wobbling of the world and seeing irreversible changes. The downside, besides the tedium of listening to the delusions of the young, is hearing the same hackneyed opinions over and over, not just those of callow youth but, much worse and seemingly criminal, the opinions of even callower people who ought to know better, all the lies about war and fear and progress and the enemy – the world as a wheel of repetition. They – I should say 'we' – are bored by things we've heard a million times before, books we've dismissed, the discoveries that are not new, the proposed solutions that will solve nothing. 'I can tell that I am growing old,' says the narrator in Borges's story 'The Congress'. 'One unmistakable sign is the fact that I find novelty neither interesting nor surprising, perhaps because I see nothing essentially new in it – it's little more than timid variations on what's already been.'

Older people are perceived as cynics and misanthropes – but no, they are simply people who have at last heard the still, sad music of humanity played by an inferior rock band howling for fame. Going back and retracing my footsteps – a glib, debunking effort for a shallower, younger, impressionable writer – would be for me a way of seeing who I was, where I went, and what subsequently happened to the places I had seen.

Since I will never write the autobiography I once envisioned – volume one, *Who I Was*; volume two, *I Told You So* – writing about travel has become a way of making sense of my life, the nearest I will come to autobiography – as the novel is, the short story, and the essay. As Pedro Almodóvar once remarked, 'Anything that is not autobiography is plagiarism.'

The thing to avoid while in my own footsteps would be the tedious reminiscences of better days, the twittering of the nostalgia bore, whose message is usually *I was there and you weren't*. 'I remember when you could get four of those for a dollar.' 'There was a big tree in a field where that building is now.' 'In my day . . .'

Oh, shut up!

What traveller backtracked to take the great trip again? None of the good ones that I know. Greene never returned to the Liberian bush, nor to Mexico, nor to Vietnam. In his late fifties, Waugh dismissed modern travel altogether as mere tourism and a waste of time. After 1948, Thesiger did not return to Rub' al Khali, the Empty Quarter of Arabia. Burton did not mount another expedition to Utah, or to substantiate the source of the Nile – at my age he was living in Trieste, immersed in erotica. Darwin never went to sea again. Neither did Joseph Conrad, who ended up hating the prospect of seafaring. Eric Newby went down the Ganges once, Jonathan Raban down the Mississippi once, and Jan Morris climbed Everest once. Robert Byron did not take the road to Oxiana again, Cherry-Garrard made only one trip to Antarctica, Chatwin never returned to Patagonia, nor did Doughty go back to Arabia Deserta, nor Wallace to the Malay Archipelago, nor Waterton to the Amazon, nor Trollope to the West Indies, nor Edward Lear to Corsica, nor Stevenson to the Cévennes, nor Chekhov to Sakhalin, nor Gide to the Congo, nor Canetti to Marrakesh, nor Jack London to the Solomon Islands, nor Mark Twain to Hawaii. So much for some of my favourite authors.

You could ask, 'Why should they bother?' but the fact is that each of these travellers, grown older, would have discovered what the heroic traveller Henry Morton Stanley found when he recrossed Africa from west to east ten years after his first successful crossing from east to west from 1874 to 1877 – a different place, with ominous changes, and a new book. Richard Henry Dana added a chastened epilogue to *Two Years Before the Mast* when, twenty-four years after its publication in 1840, he returned to San Francisco (but no longer travelling in the forecastle) and found that it had changed from a gloomy Spanish mission station with a few shacks to an American boom town that had been transformed by the Gold Rush. Dana was scrupulous about reacquainting himself with people he'd met on his first visit and sizing up the altered landscape, completing, as he put it, 'acts of pious remembrance'.

Certain poets, notably Wordsworth and Yeats, enlarged their vision and found enlightenment in returning to an earlier landscape of their lives. They set the standard in the literature of revisitation. If it is a writer's lot to repeat the past, writing it in his or her own way, this return journey might be my own prosaic version of 'The Wild Swans at Coole' or 'Tintern Abbey'.

My proposed trip to retrace the itinerary of *The Great Railway Bazaar* was mainly curiosity on my part, and the usual idleness, with a hankering to be away; but this had been the case thirty-three years before, and it had yielded results. All writing is launching yourself into the darkness, and hoping for light and a soft landing.

'I'm going to do a lot of knitting while you're away,' my wife said. That was welcome news. I needed Penelope this time.

Though I had pretended to be jolly in the published narrative, the first trip had not gone as planned.

'I don't want you to go,' my first wife had said in 1973 – not in a sentimental way, but as an angry demand.

Yet I had just finished a book and was out of ideas. I had no income, no idea for a new novel, and – though I didn't know what I was in for – I hoped that this trip might be a way of finding a subject. I had to go. Sailors went to sea, soldiers went to war, fishermen went fishing, I told her. Writers sometimes had to leave home. 'I'll be back as soon as I can.'

She resented my leaving. And though I did not write about it, I was miserable when I set off from London, saying goodbye to this demoralized woman and our two small children.

It was the age of aerograms and postcards and big black unreliable telephones. I wrote home often. But I succeeded in making only two phone calls, one from New Delhi and another from Tokyo, both of them futile. And why did my endearments sound unwelcome? I was homesick the whole way – four and a half months of it – and wondered if I was being missed. That was my first melancholy experience of the traveller's long lonely evenings. I was at my wits' end on the trip. I felt insane when I got home. I had not been missed. I had been replaced.

My wife had taken a lover. It was hypocritical of me to object: I had been unfaithful to her. It wasn't her sexual exploit that upset me, but the cosy domesticity. He spent many days and nights in my house, in our bed, romancing her and playing with the children.

I did not recognize my own voice when I howled, 'How could you do this?'

She said, 'I pretended you were dead.'

I wanted to kill this woman, not because I hated her, but (as homicidal spouses often say) because I loved her. I threatened to kill the man who, even after I was home, sent her love letters. I became an angry brute, and by chance I discovered a wickedly helpful thing: threatening to kill someone is an effective way of getting a person's attention.

Instead of killing anyone, or threatening it any more, I sat in my room and wrote in a fury, abusing my typewriter, trying to lose myself in the book's humour and strangeness. I had a low opinion of most travel writing. I wanted to put in everything that I found lacking in the other books – dialogue, characters, discomfort – and to leave out museums, churches and sightseeing generally. Though it would have added a dimension, I concealed everything about my domestic turmoil. I made the book jolly, and like many jolly books it was written in an agony of suffering, with the regret that in taking the trip I had lost what I valued most: my children, my wife, my happy household.

The book succeeded. I was cured of my misery by more work – an idea I had on the trip for a new novel. Yet something had been destroyed: faith, love, trust and a belief in the future. After my travel, on my return, I became an outsider, a ghostly presence, with my nose pressed against the window. I understood what it was like to be dead: people might miss you, but their lives go on without you. New people take your place. They sit in your favourite chair and dandle your children on their knees, giving them advice, chucking them under the chin; they sleep in your bed, look at your paintings, read your books, flirt with the Danish nanny; and as they belittle you for having been an over-industrious drudge, they spend your money. Most of the time, your death is forgotten. 'Maybe it was for the best,' people say, trying not to be morbid.

Some betrayals are forgivable, but others you never quite recover from. Years later, when my children were out of the house, I left that life, that marriage, that country. I began a new life elsewhere.

Now, thirty-three years older, I had returned to London. To my sorrow, about to take the same trip again, I relived much of the pain that I thought I'd forgotten.

Nothing is more suitable to a significant departure than bad weather. It matched my mood, too, the rain that morning in London, the low brown sky leaking drizzle, darkening the porous city of old stone, and because of it – the rain descending like a burden – everyone was hunched, their wet heads cast down, eyes averted, thinking, Filfy wevva. Traffic was louder, the heavy tyres swishing in the wet streets. At Waterloo Station I found the right platform for the Eurostar, the 12.09 to Paris.

Even at Waterloo, the reminders of my old London were almost immediate. The indifference of Londoners, their brisk way of walking, their fixed expressions, no one wearing a hat in the rain yet some carrying

brollies – all of us, including honking public school hearties, striding past
a gaunt young woman swaddled in dirty quilts, sitting on the wet floor
at the foot of some metal steps at the railway station, begging.

And then the simplest international departure imaginable: a cursory
security check, French immigration formalities, up the escalator to the
waiting train, half empty on a wet weekday in early March. In 1973 I
had left from Victoria Station in the morning, got off at the coast at
Folkestone, caught the ferry, thrashed across the English Channel,
boarded another train at Calais, and did not arrive in Paris until midnight.

That was before the tunnel had been dug under the channel. It had
cost $20 billion and taken fifteen years and everyone complained that it
was a money loser. Though the train had been running for twelve years,
I had never taken it. Never mind the expense – the train through the
tunnel was a marvel. I savoured the traveller's lazy reassurance that I
could walk to the station and sit down in London, read a book, and a
few hours later stand up and stroll into Paris without ever leaving the
ground. And I intended to go to central Asia the same way, overland to
India, just sitting and gaping out of the window.

This time, I had been refused a visa to enter Iran, and civilians were
being abducted and shot in Afghanistan, but studying a map, I found
other routes and railway lines – through Turkey to Georgia and on to
the Islamic republics. First Azerbaijan, then a ferry across the Caspian,
and then trains through Turkmenistan, past the ancient city of Merv,
where there was a railway station, to the banks of the Amu Darya River
– Oxiana indeed – and more tracks to Bukhara, Samarkand and Tashkent,
in Uzbekistan, within spitting distance of the Punjab railways.

After that, I could follow my old itinerary through India to Sri Lanka
and on to Burma. But it was a mistake to anticipate too much so early
in the trip, and anyway, here I was a few minutes out of Waterloo,
clattering across the shiny rain-drenched rails of Clapham Junction,
thinking: I have been here before. On the line through south London,
my haunted face at the window, my former life as a Londoner began to
pass before my eyes.

Scenes of the seventies, along this very line, through Vauxhall, and
making the turn at Queenstown Road, past Clapham High Street and
Brixton and across Coldharbour Lane, a name that sent chills through
me. Across the common, in 1978, there had been race riots on Battersea
Rise, near Chiesman's department store ('Est. 1895'), where clerks sidled

up and asked, 'Are you being served?' I bought my first colour TV set there, near the street on Lavender Hill where Sarah Ferguson, later the Duchess of York, lived; on the day her marriage to Prince Andrew was announced, my charlady, carrying a mop and bucket, sneered, saying, 'She's from the gutter.'

We were travelling in a deep railway gully, veering away from Clapham Junction, and from the train I got a glimpse of a cinema I had gone to until it became a bingo hall, the church that was turned into a daycare centre, and beyond the common the Alfarthing Primary School, where my kids, all pale faces and skinny legs, were taught to sing by Mrs Quarmby. These were streets I knew well: one where my bike was stolen, another where my car was broken into; greengrocers and butcher shops where I'd shopped; the chippie, the florist, the Chinese grocer; the newsagent, an Indian from Mwanza who liked speaking Swahili with me because he missed the shores of Lake Victoria; the Fishmonger's Arms – known as the Fish – an Irish pub where refugees from Ulster swore obscenely at the TV whenever they saw Prince Charles on it, and laughed like morons the day Lord Mountbatten was blown up by the IRA, and where, every evening, I drank a pint of Guinness and read the *Evening Standard*; this very place.

From scenes like these I had made my London life. In those days I prayed for rain, because it kept me indoors – writing weather. So much of what I saw today was familiar and yet not the same – the usual formula for a dream. I looked closer. The trees were bare under the grey tattered clouds, and most of the buildings were unchanged, but London was younger, more prosperous. This district that had been semi-derelict when I moved here – empty houses, squatters, a few ageing residents still holding on – had become gentrified. The Chinese grocer's was now a wine shop, and one of the pubs a bistro, and the fish-and-chip shop was a sushi bar.

But the wonderful thing was that I was whisked through south London with such efficiency, I was spared the deeper pain of looking closely at the past. I was snaking through tunnels and across viaducts and railway cuttings, looking left and right at the landscapes of my personal history and, happily, moving on, to other places that held no ambiguous memories. *Don't dwell on it*, the English say with their hatred of complaint. *Mustn't grumble. Stop brooding. It may never happen.*

I loved the speed of this train and the knowledge that it wasn't stopping anywhere but just making a beeline to the coast, past Penge, Beckenham,

Bromley – the edge of the London map and the old grumpy-looking bungalows I associated with novels of the outer suburbs, the fiction of twitching curtains, low spirits and anxious families, especially *Kipps* and *Mr Beluncle*, by the Bromleyites H. G. Wells and V. S. Pritchett, who escaped and lived to write about it.

In the satisfying shelf of English literature concerned with what we see from trains, the poems with the lines 'O fat white woman whom nobody loves' and 'Yes, I remember Adlestrop' stand out, and so do the trains that run up and down the pages of P. G. Wodehouse and Agatha Christie. But the description that best captures the English railway experience for me is Ford Madox Ford's in his evocation of the city, his first successful book, *The Soul of London*, published a hundred years ago. Looking out of the train window, Ford speaks of how the relative silence of sitting on a train and looking into the busy muted world outside invites melancholy. 'One is behind glass as if one were gazing into the hush of a museum; one hears no street cries, no children's calls.' And his keenest observation, which was to hold true for me from London to Tokyo: 'One sees, too, so many little bits of uncompleted life.'

He noted a bus near a church, a ragged child, a blue policeman. I saw a man on a bike, a woman alighting from a bus, schoolchildren kicking a ball, a young mother pushing a pram. And, as this was a panorama of London back gardens, a man digging, a woman hanging laundry, a workman – or was he a burglar? – setting a ladder against a window. And 'the constant succession of much smaller happenings that one sees, and that one never sees completed, gives to looking out of train windows a touch of pathos and of dissatisfaction. It is akin to the sentiment ingrained in humanity of liking a story to have an end.'

'Little bits of uncompleted life' – what the traveller habitually sees – inspire pathos and poetry, as well as the maddening sense of being an outsider, jumping to conclusions and generalizing, inventing or re-creating places from vagrant glimpses.

It was only twenty minutes from soot-crusted Waterloo to its opposite, the open farmland of Kent, many of the fields already raked by a harrow, ploughed and awaiting planting in this first week of March.

'Will you be having wine with your lunch?'

A woman in a blue uniform brought me a bottle of Les Jamelles Chardonnay Vin de Pays d'Oc 2004, praised on the menu for its 'subtle vanilla from the oak and a buttery finish'.

And then the lunch tray: *terrine de poulet et de brocoli, chutney de tomates*, the main course a fillet of lightly peppered salmon, with *coupe de chocolat* for dessert. This was, superficially at least, a different world from the one I had seen on the Railway Bazaar, that long-ago trip to Folkestone, and then standing at the rail of the ferry, feeling guilty and confused, eating a cold pork pie.

The tunnel was a twenty-two-minute miracle, the ultimate rabbit hole, delivering me from my English memories, speeding me beneath the channel to France, where I had only superficial and spotty recollections, of pleasures and misunderstandings, of eating and drinking, of looking at pictures, or hearing oddities, like that of the young pretty French woman who said to me, 'I am seeing tonight my fiancé's mistress. I seenk we will have sex. I love stupid women.' And then she said, 'You are smiling. You Americans!'

After the tunnel, rain falling from the French sky on the tiled roofs and the tiny cars driving on the right, but apart from that it could have been Kent: the same smooth hills and chalky plateau, and the same blight, the same warehouses, the low industrial outbuildings and workshops, the rows of bare poplars in the misty mid afternoon.

It was such a swift train trip, and so near was France to England, that it was hard to think of it as a separate country, with its own food and its peculiar scandals and language and religion and dilemmas. Enraged Muslim youths setting cars on fire was one of the current problems; only one death but lots of blazing Renaults.

Why is the motorway culture drearier in Europe than anywhere in America? Perhaps because it is imitative and looks hackneyed and unstylish and ill fitting, the way no European looks quite right in a baseball cap. While the petrol stations and industrial parks matched the disposable dreariness of American architecture, set against a French landscape they looked perverse, with Gothic spires and haywains and medieval chalets in the distance, like a violation of an old trust, the compact villages and ploughed fields and meadows set off by ugly roads and crash barriers.

Because of what Freud called 'the narcissism of minor differences', all these open fields, battlegrounds since ancient times, were the landscapes of contending armies, a gory example of civilization and its discontents. And so whatever else one could say, it was a fact that the route of this railway, once soaked in blood and thick with the graves of dead soldiers

– millions of them – had been serene for the past half century, perhaps its longest period of peace.

We crossed a river with a tragic name. One day in July ninety years ago, where the soft rain fell on the lovely meadows and low hills, in sight of the distant spires of Amiens on one side of the train and the small town of Péronne on the other, the valley of this river, the Somme, had been an amphitheatre of pure horror. On that first day of battle, 60,000 British soldiers were killed, plodding slowly because of the 66-pound packs on their backs. They advanced into German machine-gun fire, the largest number of soldiers killed on one day in British history. In the four months of this bloodbath, the first battle of the Somme, which ended in November 1916, more than one million soldiers were killed – British 420,000; French 194,000; German 440,000. And to no purpose. Nothing was gained, neither land nor any military advantage, nor even a lesson in the futility of war, for twenty-five years later – in my own lifetime – the same armies were at it again, warring in these same fields. All of them were colonial powers, which had annexed vast parts of Africa and Asia, to take their gold and diamonds, and lecture them on civilization.

The colours and clothes of the pedestrians on the streets nearer Paris reflected French colonial history – Africans, West Indians, Algerians, Vietnamese. They were kicking footballs in the rain. They were shoppers in the street markets, residents of the dreary tower blocks and tenements, the public housing at the edge of Paris that the Eurostar was passing and penetrating. We entered the city of mellow cheese-like stone and pitted façades and boulevards. London is largely a low city of single-family homes – terraces, cottages, townhouses, mews houses, bungalows, semi-detached villas. Paris is a city of rococo apartment buildings, bosomy with balconies, not a house to be seen.

With my small bag and a briefcase I looked such a lightweight that the porters at the Gare du Nord ignored me. I passed through the station to the front entrance, in the floodlit glow of the lovely façade with its classical-looking statues representing the cities and larger towns of France. They were sculpted in the early 1860s by (so a sign said) 'the greatest names in the Second Empire'.

The streets were thick with unmoving cars and loud honking and angry voices. I asked a smiling man what the problem was.

'*Une manifestation*,' he said.

'Why today?'

He shrugged. 'Because it's Tuesday.'

Every Tuesday there was a large, riotous demonstration in Paris. But for its size and its disruption this one was to be known as Black Tuesday.

2. The Other Orient Express

A national crisis is an opportunity, a gift to the traveller; nothing is more revealing of a place to a stranger than trouble. Even if the crisis is incomprehensible, as it usually is, it lends drama to the day and transforms the traveller into an eyewitness. Purgatorial as a crisis sometimes is for a traveller, it is preferable to public holidays, which are hell: no one working, shops and schools closed, natives eating ice cream, public transport jammed, and the stranger's sense of being excluded from the merriment – from everything. A holiday is an occasion for utter alienation; a crisis can be spectacle, seizing the stranger's attention.

The reason Paris has the luminous quality of being a stage set is that it was redesigned with that theatrical aim in mind, around 1857, by Georges Haussmann (hired by Louis Napoleon, calling himself emperor), who destroyed its houses and slums in mass evictions, flattened its alleyways and lanes, and gave it wide boulevards, soaring mansion blocks, monuments and fountains, and the big-city conceit of seeming to be at the centre of the world. The city was remade in a single style.

Paris's ornate backdrop of beautiful biscuit-coloured buildings and extravagant arches and obelisks – the imperial city, complete with floodlights – is so fixed in people's minds, especially people who've never seen it, that describing it is irrelevant. And anyway, who bothers? In the fiction of Paris, it is enough for the writer to state the name of a boulevard or a district. Take Simenon. I happened to be reading his novels, for their portability and their oddness. 'He returned to Rue des Feuillantines by a long detour in order to go to Montsouris Park' – no more than that; the place is taken for granted, as fixed as a picture on a calendar. The mention of evocative names is description enough. Nothing to discover, nothing to show; the city looms, but instead of feeling dwarfed, the big-city dweller feels important.

Yet this apparent familiarity, one of the powerful attractions of Paris, is an illusion. '*Couleur locale* has been responsible for many hasty appreciations,' Nabokov once wrote, 'and local color is *not* a fast color.' The brilliant Parisian stage set has a long history of insurrections, mob violence, unrest and the extreme humiliation of foreign occupation – in the experience of many Parisians alive now, the memory of Germans in charge, the betrayals, the shame of surrender. Once a city's boulevards have been marched by triumphant Nazis, they never look quite so grand again. Like many of its decorous women, Paris, while appearing inviolate, has had a turbulent past, been raped and pillaged and bombed and besieged, and has gone on changing, like its sister city, London, and the other cities on my itinerary: Vienna, Budapest, Bucharest, Istanbul, Ankara, Tbilisi, Baku and the rest of the glittering anthills of Asia, as far as Tokyo.

I seldom feel uplifted in a city; on the contrary, I feel oppressed and confined. In my travels I have been more interested in the places that lay between the great cities than the cities themselves: the hinterland, not the capital. It is my suspicion that people who are glamoured by big cities and think of themselves as urbane and thoroughly metropolitan are at heart country mice – simple, fearful, overdomesticated provincials, dazzled by city lights.

So the car burnings of a month before and the present crisis in Paris were revelations. I don't believe in the immutability of cities. I think of them generally as snake pits, places to escape from. But this *manifestation* – a huge noisy mob at (so the smiling man had told me) the Place de la République – had brought the city to a halt. Perhaps something to see – certainly a rowdy mob was more of a draw than anything I might look at in the Louvre.

I found a taxi. The driver was sitting comfortably, listening to the radio, his chin resting on his fist.

'Place de la République,' I said, getting into the car.

'Not easy,' he said. 'It's the *manifestation*.'

'What's the problem?'

'They're angry,' he said, and he mentioned the debonair prime minister, who wrote and published his own poetry, and who wanted to change the labour laws.

More minutes passed, during which the driver made a call on his mobile phone. Predictably, he reported that he was stuck in traffic.

'Also, it's raining.'

Recognizing a fellow taxi driver, he leaned out of the window and began bantering. Then he interrupted himself, saying to me, 'And there's road-works on the Boulevard Saint-Germain.'

When we had gone nowhere and the meter showed 10 euros – $13, for about fifty yards – I said, 'Then I think I'll go to the Gare de l'Est.'

'Better to walk there – it's just past that street and down some steps.'

I got out, walked back to the Gare du Nord, bought a newspaper, and saw signs to the Gare de l'Est. Crossing the street, I was distracted by a pleasant-looking restaurant, the Brasserie Terminus Nord, the sort of warm, well-lit, busy eatery that made me hungry on this cold wet day.

I told myself that this was a farewell meal, and ordered a half bottle of white burgundy, salad and *bouillabaisse marseillaise* – a big bowl of fish, mussels, large crabs, small toy-like crabs and prawns in a saffron-tinted broth, with croutons and *rémoulade*. The waiters were friendly and went about their business with efficiency and politeness and good humour.

Noticing my bag, one said, 'Taking a trip?'

'Going to Istanbul. On the train.' And I thought: also Turkmenistan and Uzbekistan and onward . . .

'Nice trip.'

'To Budapest tonight, then tomorrow night to Romania. I have a question.' I tapped the newspaper. 'What is the meaning of *licenciement*?'

'It means losing your job.'

'That's what the *manifestation* is about?'

'Exactly.'

He explained that the prime minister proposed changing the law to make it easier to fire workers who, in France, had jobs for life, since firing them was almost impossible. But the young people had risen up against the change – as did the unions, the communists and workers generally, because job security was considered sacred. If French jobs were not protected (it was argued), they would be taken by immigrant Poles and Albanians, leaving the social order in tatters and cultural life under siege by foreigners.

I finished my meal, talked with the waiters, and made a few notes. From these few hours in France I could conclude that French waiters are friendly and informative, French food is delicious, French taxi drivers have a sense of humour, and Paris is rainy. In other words, generalize on the basis of one afternoon's experience. This is what travel writers do: reach conclusions on the basis of slender evidence. But I was only passing through; I saw very little. I was just changing trains en route to Asia.

I continued on my way, walking to the Gare de l'Est, found a steep old staircase that was cut into the slope of the narrow road. A stencilled sign in French on the pavement said, THE GREATEST DANGER IS PASSIVITY.

Inside the station, at the far end of this road, a milling crowd with upturned faces searched the departure board for platform assignments. I saw my train listed – to Vienna. This information was confirmed by a voice on the loudspeaker: '*Platform nine, for the Orient Express to Mulhouse, Strasbourg and Vienna.*'

My train was called the Orient Express? I was surprised to hear that. All I had was a set of inexpensive tickets: Paris–Budapest–Bucharest–Istanbul, necessitating my changing trains in each city, three nights on sleeping cars. There are two ways by train to Istanbul – my rattly roundabout way, on three separate trains, and the luxurious way. It so happened that the luxury train was at an adjacent platform, its sleeping cars labelled COMPAGNIE INTERNATIONALE DES WAGON-LITS, a grand send-off, with an old-fashioned limo parked on the platform lettered PULLMAN ORIENT EXPRESS – POUR ALLER AU BOUT DE VOS RÊVES (to take you to the limit of your dreams).

This waiting train, which was not my train, was the sumptuous, blue and gold Venice Simplon-Orient-Express, which had run from Paris to Istanbul from 1883 until 1977. It was a ghost of its former self (one sleeping car, no dining car, grouchy conductor) when I took it in 1973, and it was cancelled altogether four years later. Its rusted and faded carriages were offered at auction in Monte Carlo, and all of them, all its rolling stock, bought by an American businessman. He ploughed $16 million into restoring the carriages and bringing back the lustre. He bought a version of the name, too, and restarted this luxury train in 1982. It has been a success with the nostalgic rich.

It was not my train because, one, it was too expensive: it would have cost me around $9,000, one way, from Paris to Istanbul. Reason two: luxury is the enemy of observation, a costly indulgence that induces such a good feeling that you notice nothing. Luxury spoils and infantilizes you and prevents you from knowing the world. That is its purpose, the reason why luxury cruises and great hotels are full of fatheads who, when they express an opinion, seem as though they are from another planet.

It was also my experience that one of the worst aspects of travelling with wealthy people, apart from the fact that the rich never listen, is that they constantly groused about the high cost of living – indeed, the rich usually complained of being poor.

I was on the other Orient Express, travelling through eastern Europe to Turkey. The total was about $400 for the three days and three nights, not luxurious (from the looks of the train at the Gare de l'Est) but pleasant and efficient.

'You will take this seat,' the conductor said, indicating a place in a six-seat compartment. 'You will change at Strasbourg for the sleeping car.'

Only one other passenger so far, an elderly woman. I sat down and drowsed until I was woken by a few toots on the train whistle, and off we went, this other Orient Express, pulling out of the Gare de l'Est without ceremony. After a mile or so of the glorious city, we were rushing through a suburb and then along the banks of the River Marne, heading into the hinterland of eastern France in the lowering dusk.

Travelling into the darkness of a late-winter evening, knowing that I would be waking up in Vienna only to change trains, I felt that my trip had actually begun, that everything that had happened until now was merely a prelude. What intensified this feeling was the sight of the sodden, deep green meadows, the shadowy river, the bare trees, a chilly feeling of foreignness, and the sense that I had no clear idea where I was but only the knowledge that late tonight we would be passing through Strasbourg on the German border and tomorrow morning we'd be in Austria, and around noon in Budapest, where I'd catch another train. The rhythm of these clanging rails and the routine of changing trains would lead me into central Asia, since it was just a sequence of railway journeys from here to Tashkent in Uzbekistan.

A lovely feeling warmed me, the true laziness of the long-distance traveller. There was no other place I wished to be than right here in the corner seat, slightly tipsy from the wine and full of *bouillabaisse*, the rain lashing the window.

I did not know it then, of course, but I would be travelling through rain and wind all the way through Turkey, on the Black Sea coast, through Georgia, and as far as Azerbaijan on the Caspian Sea, and would not be warm – would be wearing a woolly sweater and a thick jacket – until I was in the middle of Turkmenistan, among praying Turkmen, mortifying themselves and performing the dusty ritual of waterless ablutions, called *tayammum*, also on a train, but a dirty and loudly clattering one, in the Karakum Desert, where it never rained.

The little old lady caught my eye, and perhaps noticing that the book I had in my lap was in English, said, 'It's snowing in Vienna.'

With the pleasant thought that I would be in Istanbul in a few days, I said, 'That's all right with me. Where are we now?'

'Château-Thierry. Épernay'.

French place names always seemed to call up names of battlefields or names on wine labels. The next station was Châlons en Champagne, a bright platform in the drizzle, and the tidy houses in the town looking like a suburb in Connecticut seen through the prism of the driving rain. Then, in the darkness, Nancy, the rain glittering as it spattered from the eaves of the platform, and a few miles further down the line, clusters of houses so low and mute they were like the grave markers of people buried here.

Somewhere a woman and two men had joined the old woman and me in the compartment. These three people talked continuously and incomprehensibly, one man doing most of the yakking and the others chipping in.

'What language are they speaking?' the old woman asked me.

'Hungarian, I think.'

She said she had no idea, and asked why I was so sure.

I said, 'When you don't understand a single word, it's usually Hungarian.'

'It could be Bulgarian. Or Czech.'

'Where do you live?' I asked.

'Linz,' she said.

'Isn't that where −?'

Before I finished the sentence she laughed very hard, cutting me off, her eyes twinkling, smiling at what we both knew, and said, 'It's a charming little city. About a quarter of a million people. Very clean, very comfortable. Not what you might think. We want to forget all that business.'

'All that business' meant that Adolf Hitler, the Jackdaw of Linz, had been born there, and his house still stood, some deluded people making pilgrimages, though all the symbolism and language of Nazism was illegal in Austria. Just about this time, the writer David Irving was given a jail sentence and punished for making the irrational claim in print that the

Holocaust had not happened. It was as loony as saying the earth was flat, but in Austria it was unlawful.

'They're coming back in France,' the old woman said.

'Nazis, you mean?'

'My daughter says so. She lives in Paris. I go to visit her.' She looked out of the window – nothing to see but her own reflection.

'I take this train all the time.'

'You could fly, maybe?' I asked, only to hear what she would say.

'Flying is horrible. Always delays in this weather. This is much better. We will be in Linz early tomorrow morning, and I will be home for breakfast.' She leaned over again and whispered, 'Who are they?'

She was perhaps seventy-five or so, and had lived (so she said) her whole life in Austria. Next door to Hungary all that time and she didn't have a clue about this just-over-the-border language, could not even identify Magyar-speakers, which they were – I asked them on the platform at Strasbourg, where we waited for the sleeping car.

Ten o'clock on a cold night in March, the rain smacking the rails; some carriages slid along the platform on creaking wheels, with the welcome word SCHLAFWAGEN on the side, lettered in gilt. Why was it I felt no excitement entering a great hotel on a rainy night like this but was thrilled to climb up the stairs of a sleeping car and hand my ticket to a conductor and be shown a couchette? The bed was made, a bottle of mineral water on a little shelf; a sink, a table, a ripe orange on a plate.

I read a bit of Simenon, snuggling under my quilt, as the train pulled out of Strasbourg in the streaks of rain that sparkled, seemingly crystallized by the lights of the city. A few miles further on, the darts of rain pocked the surface of the Rhine. And I slept – it had been a long day, beginning at Waterloo, and all those memories of London. I was glad to be in a strange land, in dramatic weather, headed for places even stranger.

In the grey light of early morning, near a station called Amstetten, the snow was like the dirty snow in the Simenon novel I was reading, 'piles of it that looked like they were rotting, stained black, peppered with garbage. The white powder that loosed itself from the sky in small handfuls, like plaster falling from a ceiling.' But it was much whiter at a later station, Purkersdorf Sanatorium, its hundred-year-old hospital an architectural oddity, cubist in design. The snow was deeper further east, where villas stood by the line, stately chapels, sheep in muddy fields, and cemeteries dense with pious statuary. The Austrian houses looked bomb-proof, indestructible, with gardens of black saplings in the drifted snow.

Vienna for me was just its station and the very platform where Freud diagnosed his own *Reisefieber* – the anxiety of travelling by rail. He was so fearful of missing a train, he would arrive at the station an hour early, and usually panicked when the train pulled in. Here I got another train, slightly shabby, probably Magyar, for the leg to Budapest, where we were to arrive at noon. Even the landscape was shabbier, flatter, the snow thinner and lying in filthy twists as we rumbled over the border at the Hungarian frontier of Győr, which was a set of solid buildings dating from the time when this was one of the rusted folds in the Iron Curtain, factories and stubbly fields, bare trees and the late-winter farmland scored with plough marks and skeletal with ribs of snow. 'Farmland' seems a pastoral and serene description, but this was the opposite, so dark and dreary, with burst-open barns and broken fences, it looked less like farmland than a sequence of battlefields in a long retreat, the evidence of ambushes in a rear-guard action that ended in a smudge at the horizon, which grew and became human, a yokel on a bicycle.

Blackbirds streaked low across the winter sky over the thick Hungarian hills and ditches and brown copses that were all smeared with discoloured snow like stale cake icing, the dark landscape of early morning in eastern Europe, jumping in the train window like the tortured frames of an old movie.

The appeal of travelling through this wintry scene, just a few people on the train, the flat open land – What do they grow here? I wondered – the pleasure of it was its stark and rather romantic ugliness, and the knowledge that I was just passing through. I'd be in Budapest in a few hours, Bucharest tomorrow, Istanbul the next day. This sort of travel, an exercise in sheer idleness, was also a way of wallowing in the freedom of this trip.

Thirty-three years before, I had been anxious. Where was I going? What would I do with the experience of travel? I was oppressed by the sense that the people I loved most disapproved of my going. *You're abandoning us! I don't want you to go. You'll be sorry!*

In that mood of reproach, feeling scolded, I had looked out of the window of a slightly different route – Yugoslavia – and hated what I saw, feeling futile among the muddy hills and resenting every obstacle, as though the trip I'd chosen to take was just an elaborate encumbrance. But I was happy now, and happiness lends, if not enchantment, then a merciful detachment. I did not see the route I was travelling as enemy territory. It looked dishevelled and mild and a bit forlorn, but I didn't take it personally.

The lesson in my Tao of Travel was that if one is loved and feels free and has got to know the world somewhat, travel is simpler and happier. I thought that anyone who has lived through the latter half of the twentieth century is unshockable, and so has a better time of it, with lower expectations, a contempt for political promises. After a certain age the traveller stops looking for another life and takes nothing for granted.

And this time my wife was on the phone. She had prevailed on me to bring a hand-held device that doubled as mobile phone and Internet receiver. I had resisted. I had travelled for more than forty years without feeling the need to be in close touch. And I hated the sight of people using mobile phones as much as I hated the sight of people eating and walking at the same time – the unembarrassed indulgence, making a private ceremony into a public act, almost as a boast, braying into the damned thing and to the world at large: *Hey, honey, I'm on a train! Pretty soon I'm going to be in a tunnel!*

I had forgotten I had the instrument. I switched it on and got a screen message, *Welcome to Hungary*, and soon after that it rang again.

'I miss you,' my wife said. 'But I want you to know that I'm on your side. I know you have to take this trip.'

'How's the knitting?'

'I haven't started. I'm still looking over the patterns.'

I found her procrastination oddly reassuring, and we talked a little more, she at home and I on a train, looking out at the snowy fields outside a city of factories and tenements called Tatabanya, less than an hour from Budapest.

The sight of the old pockmarked city of puddles, smutty under the snowmelt, Keleti Station looming like a Hungarian madhouse in the rain, the slushy streets and muddy pavements, defrosting and dripping after the long winter – all of it made me hopeful. I wasn't looking for glamour or a version of home, but rather something altogether different, as proof that I'd covered some distance. Grim-faced women in old clothes, carrying shopping bags, scuffing through the slush in dirty boots, held out signs lettered ZIMMER, offering their houses or apartments for home stays, to make a little money in an economy that had tanked so badly that people were leaving in droves – mobbing Keleti Station for the trains going west to Austria and Germany and Britain. I was crowded by taxi touts and pimps, not pestiferous but merely desperate for money.

I dumped my bag at Left Luggage – my train to Romania was not due to leave until late that evening – and walked out to look at the grandiose edifice of the station, with its statues and winged chariot, stallions and feather-and-floral motifs, dated 1884, an Austro-Hungarian extravaganza, grandiose and pompous, seeming to mock the weary travellers in wet raincoats and the footsore pedestrians with shopping bags.

'How's business?' I asked a woman at a bookshop.

'Is bad,' she said.

I kept on asking as I strolled from the station, through the city to the Danube, for the pleasure of taking it all in, with the confidence that in eight or nine hours I would be back at the station to claim my bag and board a new train for Bucharest, the continuation of my own Orient Express.

It was about this time in my previous trip that I'd met the travelling companion I called Molesworth. He was a theatrical agent and *bon vivant*, unmarried, and his being a little fruity and familiar added to his twinkle. His clients had been some of the acting Cusacks and Warren Mitchell. A former officer in the Indian army, he had travelled widely in Asia. He winked into a monocle when he read a menu, and had a gentle habit of calling every man 'George', as when speaking to the Turkish conductor: 'George, this train has seen its better days.' After my book came out, he said people recognized him in the text, even through a pseudonym. I saw him now and then in London and invited him to parties, where he made himself popular with his theatre stories, all about luvvies, and afterwards my friends would say, 'Terry is splendid.' Before he died, he said the trip in 1973 to Istanbul was one of the best he'd ever made, and often added, 'You should have mentioned my name.' But his real name was too good to be true: Terrance Plunkett-Greene.

I trudged through the downpour with all the other trudgers until I came to a plausible-looking hotel called the Nemzeti, and went in, just to get out of the rain.

The restaurant was empty except for two women, wearing leather coats and smoking.

Wasn't I hungry? the pale waiter asked me. Wouldn't I be happier sitting in the warm restaurant and having the lunch of the day?

I agreed. Goulash was on the menu.

'Foreign people think goulash is stew. No. Goulash is soup.'

'But what does the word mean?'

'I don't know in English. But a *goulash* is someone who looks after sheep.'

'Red ink!' Plunkett-Greene would have said of the Hungarian wine. 'Peasant fare! Beans!' he would have crowed over the food here at the Nemzeti.

The women left. A youngish man took their place. As he was the only other person in the restaurant, we fell into conversation. His name was Istvan. He was in Budapest on business. He said that some European companies were relocating to Hungary because of the cheap labour and the well-educated (but poverty-stricken) populace. I was to hear this description all the way through Asia, especially in India. His own business concerned small engines.

'How is the government here?'

'Terrible,' Istvan said. He detested Hungarian politicians and their policies. 'They are socialists. They are left. I am right.'

This led to a discussion about the American government, which he also detested.

'Bush is dangerous, arrogant – not intelligent. And now we have to worry about what he'll do in Iran.'

I should have guessed then that I was to hear this opinion in almost every casual conversation for the next seven months, whenever I revealed myself as an American: that our president was a moron and his policies were diabolical and he was controlled by dark forces. That America, for all its promise and prosperity, was the world's bully.

I would then say, as I did to Istvan, 'Would you emigrate to the US if you had a chance?' And they would say yes, as Istvan did, not because they had the slightest notion of American culture, politics or history, but because they were passionate to get a job and make money, to own a car, a house, and flee their precarious hand-to-mouth existence to become Americans.

Istvan was fairly intelligent, but there were others, and the most un-settling thing was that the worst of them, the most brutish, would surprise me by praising the US government for its militarism. I was somewhat apprehensive because I would be travelling through at least six Muslim countries. But all of them were tyrannies, more or less, and I took heart in knowing that when people are badly governed, they seldom hold you personally responsible for the decisions of your own government.

I wished Istvan luck and plodded on, making a detour at a sex shop. Acting on my theory that a country's pornography offers the quickest insight into the culture and inner life of a nation, and especially the male character, I went in and assessed the goods. It was grubby stuff, which included bestiality (dogs and women), very fat people, very hairy people, a sideline in gay cruelty and every German perversion.

Like Czechoslovakia, Bulgaria, Poland, Romania and the other countries formerly in the Soviet shadow, when Hungary liberalized its policies in 1989 the immediate effect was the sanctioning of what had been regarded as antisocial behaviour – porn, loud music, vocal complaints and graffiti, which had been obvious from the walls I had seen on the outskirts of Budapest. Some of these promiscuous outbursts could have been dismissed as rising from irrational anger, but not porn. Pornography is specific, particular in its rituals and images, and it can't be gratuitous or faked or cooked up for its shock value, or else it won't sell. Shelves of videocassettes and DVDs of bestiality – women canoodling with dogs and horses, pigs and goats – meant that there was a market for it.

In the sleety rain and wet snow of the decaying city, amid shuffling boots (down at the heels in the most literal sense), wet faces and stringy hair, there was no sensuality, certainly no temptation for me to linger. Nothing looked sleazier to me than another imperial city overlaid by decades of Soviet style. Yet everyone I spoke to – for I was constantly asking directions – was polite to me, every one of the fatigued, greasy-haired people, scruffy in the late-winter drizzle. I seem to be criticizing, but I liked Budapest for being in a time warp and looking left behind.

I could not identify a Hungarian face – not a national face. The heavy jaw and wide forehead and close-set eyes were not enough; yet it seemed a monolithic culture – no ethnic people, no minorities in evidence, just a lot of weary white people, relieved that Hungary had been admitted to the European Union so that they could leave and find work elsewhere and maybe never come back, as a man said to me at a café in Keleti Station when I went to reclaim my bag.

'You're going where?' he asked.

I told him Romania, and he made me repeat it because he found it so funny. He laughed a big, mocking belly laugh.

From Hungary onward, it was clear to me that very few people are looking east. There were no tourists, and the only travellers were ones going home – reluctantly, because the great wish was to travel west, to leave home. The east represented hopelessness, poverty, failure, more excuses. Most of the travellers at Keleti Station wanted to go west, even the ones who were headed east. And no one was going to Turkey.

With the drunks, the drifters, the flinty-eyed evangelists looking for sinners to convert, the moneychangers, the lurking youngsters who might have been druggies or hookers or both, and the burdened old women heading to the countryside on commuter trains, the people who held my attention at Keleti Station were the chess players. They stood at a long marble pedestal near the bumpers, in the middle of the crowd of commuters waiting for their trains to be announced. Or perhaps they weren't going anywhere: a train station is a little democracy in which everyone has a right to exist on the presumption that he or she might be waiting for a train. These men were studying the chessboards, clawing at their hair and their beards, now and then making a move – the slow and graceful logic of chess at the centre of railway pandemonium.

The passengers who boarded the Euronight, the express to Bucharest, were Romanian – I was travelling against the prevailing current of people headed west. Who would take the train to Romania if they didn't have to? I was told that in recent years foreigners who wished to adopt Romanian orphans took this train from time to time, but because so many adoption agencies were fraudulent, fewer outsiders were willing to risk what might prove to be a disappointment.

I liked the way this train journey was removing me from things I knew, replacing them with the distortions of the foreign – the dream dimension of travel where things are especially strange because they look somewhat familiar. Fewer people, too, as though no one wanted to go where I was going, especially now, in the muddy landscape of Hungary, the drizzle crackling into the wet clumps of snow by the tracks.

Even here, still in Europe, I sensed an intimation of Asiatic ambiguity in the cat-stink of the sleeping car, the unsmiling crowd suffering in second-class hard seats, the clutter of the dining car: piles of fluorescent tubes in cardboard boxes and coils of wire stacked on the tables, with

sticky cruets of vinegar and bottles of sinister sauce, their caps clotted
with spilled and dried gunk.

*Racing into the darkness and the downpour, dramatic weather smothering the
tracks, whistle screaming, this train is perfect, this sleeper is a cozy throwback*, I
was writing in my notebook. It reminded me pleasantly, in sepia tones
and inexpensiveness (about $100), of my previous trip. I had taken a
diesel through Belgrade and Nis and Sophia before, but so what? This
was not much different – sullen men in tracksuits, women in shawls,
tired glassy-eyed children shivering in small wet shoes.

As on the previous night en route to Budapest, the sleeping-car
conductor punched my ticket, brought me beer, made my bed, and
reminded me that we'd be in Bucharest around nine the following
morning.

'Why you go Bucharest?'

'To look around,' I said. 'And then leave.'

'You aeroplane home?'

'I change trains. To Istanbul.'

'Istanbul very nice. Good business. Good money.'

'What about Bucharest?'

'No business. No money.' The conductor made a clown's mocking
face.

'Is there a dining car on this train?'

'Everything – for you!' When he winked at me I could see that he
was tipsy.

Rain was smacking on the window, the train swaying as most trains
do, seeming to describe an elaborate detour around the back of the world.
I was going the old way, as I had long ago, and there was hardly any
difference – Budapest had had the strained and uncertain and unstylish
look of the seventies.

Even though no one advertised a trip like this, it had not been much
trouble to find this antique railway experience – railways and buses were
how the poor travelled in much of eastern Europe. Most tourists going
to Romania, if they went at all, would take a short-hop plane. European
airfares were very cheap because they were based on fuel that was sold
untaxed. Someday soon a fuel tax would be imposed, airfares would
reflect their true cost, and this train would be valuable again. Well, it
was valuable now – the sleeping car almost full and the rest of the train
crowded.

A sudden station loomed, blobs of fluorescence in the darkness, the storm sweeping down, bursting in oversized drops on an unsheltered platform, the right texture of raindrops for this dark, creaking night train. The weather looked old-fashioned, so did the leaky roof of the station, the puddles in the ticket lobby, the wet benches, the utter emptiness. No one got on or off: just a station sitting in the dark – I saw it was Szolnok, on the Tisza River – and after that we were really benighted.

Remembering the conductor's wink, I went in search of the dining car, walking through the passageway of the dark tipping train making anvil clangs in the night.

And when I found it I thought: just at the point in my life when I'd imagined that all travel was a homogenized and bland experience of plastic food and interchangeable railway cars and waiters in fast-food caps, I stumble into the dining car of the Euronight to Romania and find three drunken conductors and a man (who turned out to be the chef) in a greasy sweater with a torn bandage unravelling on his hand, all of them playing backgammon in the bad light, drinking beer and smoking. No one was eating, and when the chef blew his nose messily he looked as if he were using a rag that had just wiped a dipstick.

Nor had the boxes of fluorescent tubes and coils of wire stacked on the tables been moved or tidied. They crowded the gunked-up sauce bottles.

At the sight of this filth and disorder, my spirits rose. It was easy to prettify a nation in an airport, but on this train travelling through the provinces of a hard-pressed country I felt I was seeing the real thing, a place with its trousers down. I didn't take this personally. I was grateful that no one had gone to any trouble for me, that I was not getting red-carpet service.

The chef did not even look up from his backgammon board when he said, 'Eat!'

Another, the man who had winked, said, 'Sit! Sit! You want chicken?'

'No.'

'Only chicken. Sit!'

He pushed some coils of wire to the far side of one of the tables – I was apparently the only diner – and then the lights went out. When the lights came on again there was a bowl of bread crusts in front of me, which seemed a neat trick.

'*Salade?*'

'No.'

I was served a bowl of dill pickles. I thought: who could invent this? Merely to live here was to experience satire.

Tipsy though he was, the conductor was able to form the words 'You lock couchette?'

'How could I lock it? I don't have a key.'

Without a word, in a kind of reflex of drunken panic, he ran out of the dining car. I followed him, and when he got to my compartment he motioned for me to check my bag. He gave me to understand, in gestures, that there were thieves on the train and that I must be very careful (wagging his finger, then touching it to the side of his nose).

The lights went out before we got back to the dining car, but came on again in time for me to see the man in the filthy sweater (and now I knew why it was greasy) standing over a frying pan, holding a cleaver, and sending up sparks and spatters. He could not remove the cigarette from his mouth, because he was holding the frying pan with one hand and smacking at a piece of meat with the other. His smeared glasses were slipping down his nose; he pushed them up with a deft nudge of his dripping cleaver.

He yelled at the others, one of whom relayed the message to me: '*Gratin?*'

'Okay.'

Then the backgammon players began bantering with each other.

When the plate was put before me I marvelled at the man serving me: his sticky glasses, his drooping cigarette, his dirty sweater and bandaged hand. The fried potatoes were coated with cheese. I picked at it, grateful for the reassurance that in this corner of the world nothing had changed in decades. And the next time someone praised the Hungarian economy or talked optimistically of Romania's imminent entry into the European Union, I could reflect on the revelation of this disgusting meal.

While the rest of the world was bent on innovation and modernization, looking for salvation on the Internet, things here were pretty much what they'd always been. Speaking of time warps, Hungary was about to elect another socialist government. For some reason, perhaps the sheer perversity that finds absurd logic still alive in the world, this pleased me. It reminded me of the time I'd spent in Vanuatu, in the western Pacific. One rainy day I saw some people on the island of Tanna standing and squatting, bollock naked, wearing only penis sheaths and refusing to listen to some missionaries who had come across the ocean to convert them. These God–botherers had then trekked twenty miles down a muddy path to share their Good News Bibles. The people on Tanna sent them away, saying they had their own gods, thanks very much.

Stubborn seediness has great appeal, and this ramshackle railway had not changed in thirty-three years. It was, if anything, worse, almost a parody of my previous experience. The Hungarian border was farcical too, the customs and immigration people tramping through the carriage in wet boots and ill-fitting brown uniforms. The Romanian border at Curtici was even grimmer, as though another act in the same farce: big beefy-faced brutes with earflaps and gold braids, a dozen of them swarming over the train demanding passports, opening bags.

One of the customs men went through my books, the Simenons and some others, and selected Nabokov's *Invitation to a Beheading*. He squinted at it. Did he guess that this novel is about injustice in a nightmarish police state?

'Where you going?'

'Istanbul.'

'What doing? You tourismus?'

'Me tourismus.'

Turning the pages of my passport, he put his fingers on the visas. 'Azerbaijan! Uzbekistan! Pakistan! India!'

'Tourismus.'

He flipped his big fingers at me. 'Heroin? Cocaine?'

I laughed, I tried to stop laughing, I laughed some more, and I think this idiotic laugh convinced him of my innocence. His comrade joined him, and together they searched my briefcase. I stood to one side, and when they were done they welcomed me to Romania.

Their baggage fondling was no worse than the TSA's at any American airport. In fact, it was a lot simpler and less invasive.

Just behind these customs men was an attractive woman wearing an ankle-length leather coat and high shiny boots, another figure from the past, a suitable introduction to Transylvania, where we were headed, and like a character in the Nabokov novel, which could have happened in a place like Bucharest.

★

The rain was still falling as, with howling brakes, the train came to a
dead stop at Baneasa Station in the centre of Bucharest, where I was to
change trains – the next one, for Istanbul, leaving later in the day. The
rain spattered on the oily locomotive and the platform roof and the
muddy tracks. But this was not life-giving rain, nourishing roots and
encouraging growth. It was something like a blight. It spat from the
dreary sky, smearing everything it hit, rusting the metal joints of the
roof, weakening the station, fouling the tracks. It lent no romance to
the decaying houses of the city; it made them look frailer, emphasized the
cracks in the stucco, turned the window dust to mud. There was something
so poisonous in its greenish colour, it seemed to me like acid rain.

Pale, pop-eyed Romanians had a touch of Asia in their dark eyes and
hungry faces, and almost the first people I saw were two urchins, very
skinny boys not more than ten, in rags, looking ill, both smoking
cigarettes and pretending to be tough. They had tiny doll-like heads and
dirty hands. They fooled among themselves and puffed away, and when
they saw me they said something, obviously rude, and laughed.

Only pale, underfed faces – now and then one of a girl that was
porcelain-pretty; skinny girls, fat women, tough-looking men, most
people smoking foul cigarettes – no foreign faces, none that I could see
at the station. Why would anyone come here? Romania was a world
few people visited for pleasure, and that was evident in its abandoned
look, its wrecked buildings, its mournful people. It seemed lifeless, just
hanging on. A great melancholy in the houses with cracked windows,
the broken streets, the bakeries where every pastry looked stale.

I went to make sure that the train to Istanbul, the Bosfor Express,
would be leaving on time. A young man standing near the information
booth said he hoped it would – he was taking it.

'I'm going to a conference in Turkey,' he said. He was an academic,
named Nikolai, teaching at a university in Bucharest.

He showed me where the Left Luggage window was – he was leaving
bags there too. On the way, I mentioned that I hadn't seen any foreigners
– none of the Asians or Africans or South Americans I'd noticed from
London to Hungary.

'Some Americans come here. We have bases.'

I might have known. Romania was in the news as America's friend
in the war on terrorism. Its right-wing government, desperate for money,
eager to join the European Union, had approved the imprisoning and

interrogation of suspects. The process, called extraordinary rendition, meant that a man like the one described in the *New York Times* in July 2006 from Algeria, who was picked up by American agents in Tanzania, would be blindfolded and sent to a third country to be questioned – and questioning always involved some sort of torture, ranging from sleep deprivation, to the suffocation and simulated drowning called water-boarding, to being hanged by the wrists against the wall of a cell, all these methods going under the Orwellian euphemism 'enhanced interrogation techniques'. I never heard that expression without thinking of a prisoner being kicked in the balls.

America's prisoners from across the world were shipped off to, among other places, jails in Romania, where humane conventions did not have to be observed and torture was allowed. But the incarceration and interrogation had been instigated by the United States and paid for by American taxpayers. The programme was so secret that it was only when, after two or more years, a prisoner was released and interviewed by a newspaper (as several had) that the despicable programme was revealed. Poland was also mentioned as a country of interrogation under torture.

Nikolai said he had things to do but would see me on the train. I had the feeling I'd made him uncomfortable with my questions and that he simply wanted to get away.

The largest, weirdest building in Europe – perhaps the world – the Palace of Congresses, is in Bucharest. I had thought it was within walking distance. I ended up taking a taxi – or perhaps not a taxi but a volunteer driver eager to make a little money.

The building was an impressively ugly and gigantic example of mega-lomaniacal architecture.

'Is amazing, eh?'

'Amazing.'

'You have zis in your country?'

'Nothing like it.'

On the way, we had passed many casinos. They were the only splash of colour in the brown city, along with smoky bars and massage parlours. It was a city of sullen, desperate vice. The driver gave me a copy of *What's On in Bucharest*. This guide offered tips on how to find sex. Avoid pimps, it said; you will probably get robbed. 'Better you ring the number of the escort agency, almost all of which can deliver ladies to your hotel room within half hour.'

An entrepreneur, identified as 'Arab businessman, Zyon Ayni', was opening a new nightclub in Bucharest, offering lap dances, fifty strippers and 'dances in private rooms'.

'"I sell fantasies. This is my business," synthesizes Ayni. If you want to go on a cruise with the company's yacht, accompanied by a very beautiful woman, the company also offers this service. Ayni's company owns twenty-five yachts but also planes, for those who are seasick.'

One club had opened, and 'unique at this moment in Romania, on Tuesday night, the international porn star, Quanita Cortez'.

As for drinks: 'A selection of drinks carefully picked on the taste of the most pretentious clients.' At the Harbour Restaurant 'you can have reinless fun with all your friends'. And the Culmea Veche Restaurant advertised itself as an 'above average Romanian restaurant'. Don Taco's boast was 'The only Mexican restaurant in Bucharest'.

They were empty. A few businessmen in Bucharest had money, and what foreigners there were making deals knew that Romanians were ripe for exploitation. The sale of orphans and newborn babies is one of the brisker businesses, followed by the traffic in women for the sex trade. When I rolled my eyes at the dereliction here, Romanians said, 'It used to be worse' – they meant the nightmare under Ceauşescu. It has been seventeen years since he stood to give a speech in the main square and people began to chant, 'Rat! Rat! Rat!' – and he looked cornered and crept away before being captured and shot like a rat.

The Third World stink and disorder were strong in Bucharest, its suburbs looked blighted, its farms muddy and primitive. Romania was another country people were leaving, all of them headed west. The look of Bucharest was desperate and naked, that look which is without shame or self-consciousness: everyone struggling, everyone dressed as though for a hike on a rainy day or dirty job.

No one I spoke to made any money. Nikolai, the university teacher – assistant professor – earned the equivalent of $200 a month. That is exactly what a clerk at a fast-food pizza restaurant told me he earned. His name was Pawel and his English was better than Nikolai's. Neither man had been out of the country. The average national wage was $100 a month. No wonder that Romania, like Albania, is furnishing western Europe with factory workers, hookers and car thieves.

*

'Mister Pawel' – it was Nikolai, hailing me on the platform. He introduced me to the people seeing him off, his university colleagues, threadbare scholars.

'What is your business?' one asked.

'I'm retired,' I said.

'Many retired people come here!' he said, being hearty. What did that
mean?

'Would you like to be going to Turkey with us?' I said.

'We would rather be going there,' one said, and pointed to where the
sun, like a coddled egg, was slipping through the sooty sky in the west.

Apart from Nikolai and a big grouchy-looking man with a moustache
like a small animal attacking his nose, there was a mother and small
daughter – the mother shaking her head and saying 'Bulgaristan', because
we had to pass through this (she said) unfriendly place. Clearly the route
of the Bosfor Express was not popular; I kept noticing that few people
wanted to travel east.

Seeing no dining car, I hurried back to the station lobby and bought
beer, bottled water and sandwiches. And then I found my sleeping
compartment and watched Bucharest recede from view.

We travelled across the flat plain that is the southeast of Romania,
through the immense fields of wheat that, besides orphans, is Romania's
only export. The farming villages could have been illustrations from
Grimm's Fairy Tales – cottages, huts, outbuildings, barns, all of them
aslant, surrounded by fields, no trees, the occasional flock of ducks or
turkeys, and the only human a hurrying man who, seeing a cast-off
plastic bottle, drank from it – the dregs someone had left – and flung it
away when he saw another one, which he snatched and drank from, and
tossed to the ground, where he pounced on another and greedily drank.
But in a huge homogenized world, this seemed like a novelty, because
it was a throwback to a much earlier time: nothing happening except
the rain falling on the desperate man and the village in the background,
beyond the railway ditch, the witch's house, the woodchopper's hut,
the Grey Dwarf's cottage.

Just at dusk the border, Giurgiu Nord: a decayed façade of a station
that turned out to have nothing behind it but wasteland, some leafless
trees, a snippy immigration official, and a miserable three-legged dog.

Giurgiu is a river town at the edge of the great flat Danubian Plain,
which is the southern third of Romania. The Danube River (second

only to the Volga in length) has a different name in each country it flows through; it's called the Dunav here. Past a settlement of filthy apartment houses, a rubbish dump next to them heaped with plastic bottles and blowing plastic bags, then a truck depot.

The edges of countries are often visual facts. The southern plain of Romania ended at the river, which was the border, but for greater emphasis the other side, the south bank of the Danube, was high ground, a long irregular bluff, which was the edge of Bulgaria, like a castle wall straggling to the horizon east and west. Across the river we went, the flow a hundred yards wide at this point, into Russe, the big river port of Bulgaria – power plant, cranes, chimneys, much bigger and more prosperous than any city I saw in Romania, new tenements as well as grotty ones, buildings in much better condition. Even the railway station was big and solid, unlike the purely symbolic one on the other side of the river in Romania.

One polite and one silly Bulgar examined my passport, and when they left my compartment an old man and three nasty-faced boys leaped into view and rapped on my window, making begging gestures, hand to mouth.

'You don't see this in airports,' I said to Nikolai, who stopped by to see if the Bulgars had searched me. He too called it Bulgaristan. He said you'd never find people begging like this in Romania, but I knew for a fact he was wrong.

· The border guards hadn't searched me. No one had taken an interest in my bag since I'd entered Romania, and that had been perfunctory, just a sniff-and-sort routine to satisfy a deprived and underpaid border guard. I'd hardly been searched since leaving London and had changed trains five times so far.

The train lost itself in the Bulgarian plateau and the higher ground south of the river, among the hills, where trees were like a sign of wealth, not needed for farmland or fuel, and the stations sheltered little clusters of pale Bulgars, scowling men, moustached old women. And then long sweeping hills, startling, lovely, because I had been expecting more Romanian decrepitude; finally sunset over Veliko Turnovo, and more beer.

I was woken by a sudden knock at two thirty the next morning. I sprang awake, still half drunk, and a slight but fierce Bulgar woman shone a flashlight in my face.

'Pusspoot.'

But that was all there was to the Bulgarian border. In the past, the passports were handled by the conductor, who then demanded a tip at the end of the journey. I didn't mind the interruption; I found it revelatory and vaguely exciting: a fierce foreign woman in a peaked cap and leather coat and boots appearing in the middle of the night at the foot of my bed, insisting that I obey her.

Half an hour later we were at the Turkish border, in a town called Kapikule, the heavy rain lashing the open platform and the glittering lights. The night was cold, and big shrouded Turks marched up and down. Three in the morning and all the officialdom of Kapikule had turned out to greet the train. In spite of the score of policemen and soldiers, only one man was processing the train passengers who were entering the Turkish Republic: he sat in a little lit window while we stood in the rain. I was last, Nikolai next to last. And now I could see the passengers: Romanians, Bulgars, Turks, big families, children in modest clothes, small Slavic boys no more than ten with moustaches as visible as those of their grannies, beetle-browed men – no tourists. With the driving rain, the old train, the intimidating border guards and the shadowy town behind the prison-like station, it could have been forty years ago, all of us squeezing into the far edge of Turkey like refugees, soaking wet.

Nikolai said, 'Is not modern!'

'Why are you going to Istanbul?'

'Attending conference on European enlargement. I am reading paper.'

'Romania's being allowed to join, right?'

'Will join in January 2007.'

'But not Turkey?'

'Turkey is problem. Human rights.' He shrugged, rain pouring down his face.

'Romanian human rights are better?'

'Improving now, because we want to join EU.'

'America is capturing people in places like Tanzania and Albania and sending them to Romania for interrogation.'

'Who tell you this?'

'It's called extraordinary rendition. They can be tortured in Romania.'

'We are friendly with America now. Also with Britain. We have US military bases. Romanians are against the war in Iraq, but we like Americans.'

'What is Romania's main industry?'

'Agriculture.'

'Nikolai, agriculture isn't an industry.'

'We have much wheat and maize.' He thought a moment, then said, 'Ceauşescu ruined the country. He destroyed it and tried to rebuild it. He put up ridiculous buildings.'

'I saw the Palace of Congresses.'

'Ha! A monster! His daughter wants his body to be dug up so they can identify him. It's not him, she says.'

'Do you remember when he fell?'

'I was seven in '89 when he was overthrown, but I remember the excitement. My grandparents lived with us. They were so happy. They always said, "The Americans will come." Meaning – will save us. They said it after the war. My parents said it. They said it in the 1950s. During Ceauşescu. "The Americans will come." After Ceauşescu. "The Americans will come." We hated our government. We wanted to be saved.'

'How do you know this?'

'One of my projects is oral history. I interviewed many people, not just my relatives but people from all over Romania. One man was in solitary confinement for seventeen years, for a petty offence. Another man I spoke to was walking down a street in Bucharest. He was carrying a French book – literature, maybe Flaubert. The police stopped him. They seized the book and they framed it as "antisocial". He got a year in prison – this was in the 1980s!'

'Weren't people angry, being treated like this?'

'They said, "The Americans will come. They will save our soul."'

'Has it happened?'

'We have a right-wing government. It is opportunistic. We have US military bases, and the people approve it. We have seen worse, much worse.'

Eventually we got to the window. I bought a Turkish visa for $20 and we had our passports stamped. Then, completely wet and very cold, I reboarded the train and went to sleep. It was then around four-thirty, and by the time I woke, dawn had broken and we were passing the Sea of Marmara, muddy fields on one side, ships beyond the tracks, the big bold city of domes and minarets in the distance.

Nikolai had crept out of his compartment, his face pressed to the window. He had never been to Turkey before; he had never been out of Romania. He looked alarmed.

'What do you think?'

'More modern than I thought.'

He was dazzled and swallowing hard, for it was not just the enormous mosques and churches that were impressive but the density of the building in these southwestern suburbs of Istanbul. I was impressed too, as much by the extent of the new construction as by its modernity. It made Romania seem the muddiest Third World backwater.

I said, 'Isn't it unfair that Turkey can't join the EU for another ten years or more?'

Nikolai said, 'They have problems with human rights of the Kurds and the Armenians.'

'The Kurds want to secede and start their own country, which is a little unreasonable. And the Armenian business was a hundred years ago. Look at this city – imagine the power of this economy.'

'But in the countryside is different. Poor people,' Nikolai said, thinking of the poverty in rural Romania.

'You've seen them?'

'No.'

'What about the Gypsies in Romania?'

'Is a problem. How integrating? We don't know. Some live in tents. We call *zidane*,' he said, using the Russian word for the people, called Rom or Romany all over Europe.

'What's the biggest problem in Romania?'

'Maybe Gypsies. Maybe poverty.'

'What's the cost of living?'

'Is the same as Toronto. My uncle lives there.'

He was appalled by what he was seeing, Istanbul rising all around us, the train screeching past the old city wall and new tenements. We were racing towards Seraglio Point and the sight of the Bosporus – Asia looming on the far side.

Nikolai was speechless. It was obvious that he had prepared himself for a shabby Asiatic city of oppression and torture, crumbly mosques and fez-wearing Turks and backward-looking Muslims. Instead he was greeted by a grand and reimagined city of laughing children and beautiful women and swaggering men which had been ignored by Europe and sneered at by the Islamic republics. It was a city of ancient gilt and impressive modernization. He could see that the old city had been preserved – we were passing through it, approaching Sirkeci Station in the old-fashioned but carefully preserved quarter of Sultanahmet; and beyond the Golden Horn were the bluffs of Beyoglu and the tooting ferries to the Asian side, which was lined with magnificent seafront houses, the villas they called *yalis*, and the rain still coming down hard. Nikolai shrivelled into a country mouse and, with his forehead pressed against the train window, looked as though he were going to weep with frustration.

3. The Ferry to Besiktas

Istanbul is a water world, and your first view of it, stepping out of Sirkeci Station, is the pin-cushion profile of minarets on domes seeming to rise from steep dark islands, turbulent ocean all around, the Sea of Marmara to the right, the Golden Horn to the left, the Bosporus straight ahead. Walk forward, walk anywhere, and you approach water splashing at the shores of the city, which is spread across three distinct promontories. Across the Sea of Marmara, dappled with raindrops this afternoon – past the ferries and cargo ships and fishing boats, those silhouettes of battlements and villas – is the shore of Asia, the twinkling edge of the Eastern Star.

To the southeast is Haydarpasa Station, looking like a dark waterside cathedral. Thirty-three years before, I had boarded an express to Ankara and Lake Van. Changing trains, taking buses, I had travelled overland to Iran and India and beyond. Things were different now: the Iranians had turned down my visa application, and war had brought anarchy to Afghanistan. I would take another route this time, head through Turkey and then hope to detour around Iran by changing trains in Georgia and rolling onward, through the Stans: Azerbaijan, Turkmenistan, Uzbekistan – places that had been forbidden to me all those years ago – and into India.

After three night trains I needed a breather in Istanbul. A short walk from Sirkeci Station was the ferry terminal. I took the ferry to the landing stage at Besiktas and strolled to the Ciragan Palas. This hotel was part of an old and elegant Ottoman palace, and was as welcome a hotel as the Pera Palas had been in the past. It was expensive, but it was at the edge of the Bosporus and easy to get to, a 20-cent ride on the ferry.

Since the mid nineteenth century, the Istanbul ferries 'were such a part of everyday life that they assumed an almost totemic importance'. The ferries dip and roll; the best way of admiring the vast, separated city is from the rail of a boat. 'The ferries' great gift to the skyline is the smoke from their chimneys.'

The words are those of Orhan Pamuk, the distinguished novelist and Istanbullu – he seldom left the city of his birth and said he had never been tempted to live elsewhere. Thirty-three years before, I had happened to meet Yashar Kemal, the novelist and political tub-thumper. He was still alive at the age of eighty-two, but was out of town. I decided to go in search of Pamuk and to see what the decades had done to Istanbul. For Pamuk, it is a city of joy and also of 'overwhelming melancholy', and yet the Bosporus is 'the font of our good health, the cure of our ills, the infinite source of our goodness and goodwill that sustains the city and all those who dwell in it'.

In his unusual chronicle of his life in the city, *Istanbul: Memories and the City*, Pamuk describes his childhood, his fractious family, his chronic ennui, his self-imposed solitude, his daydreams, his love of the side streets and the ships and the preoccupations that are peculiar to Istanbul. This is one of my favourite city books because it is written by a native son, a keen observer who knows all his city's faults as well as its virtues. It is right that it is also a family memoir, because his relationship with Istanbul is familial, the city like an uneasy relative, a funny uncle or an eccentric granny who provides him shelter. Such a book might be written by a New Yorker or a Parisian, but it would not be so persuasive, because New York is a modern city with a thin substratum and Paris is an artefact if not a confection. And a Turk is someone with deep roots, not a mere urbanite or transplant. For a Turk, Istanbul is an extension of Turkish culture and the Turkish personality, reflecting its conflicts, obsessions and character traits. Its complex and glorious history is evident in many of its buildings, glimpses of Byzantium and Constantinople above the heavy traffic and the teenyboppers on mobile phones.

Istanbul is ancient, and Istanbullus carry its old-fangledness in their heads – Pamuk is the proof of that. What do you think of us? the Turks often ask of strangers. New Yorkers and Parisians never ask such things, nor do Londoners, who take the view that strangers are the ones to be assessed or mocked, certainly not themselves. In most cities, the inhabitants are too busy and hard-pressed to care. But Turks are different, self-conscious of their longitude on the map, straddling Europe and Asia.

'To some degree, we all worry about what foreigners and strangers think of us,' Pamuk says. 'My interest in how my city looks to Western eyes is – as for most Istanbullus – very troubled; like all other Istanbul writers with one eye on the West, I sometimes suffer in confusion.'

'To see Istanbul through the eyes of a foreigner always gives me pleasure,' Pamuk goes on. Flaubert, Gide, Nerval, Knut Hamsun and Hans Christian Andersen all visited Istanbul and recorded their impressions, and in most instances what they saw was a fading Orientalism that ceased to exist as soon as it was described – the harem, the grotesque and the picturesque, dervishes, hubble-bubble pipes, the slave market, Ottoman clothing, floppy sleeves, Arabic calligraphy and, he says, the *hamals*, the porters, though such men can still be seen, heavily burdened with huge loads on wooden pack frames, trudging up and down the cobbled streets of the old city. Whenever I began to generalize about Istanbul's modernism, I encountered an exotic vignette – a shroud, a fez, a minaret, a veil, a donkey or someone grilling fish over coals by the roadside.

But Pamuk's book, like all passionate books, is a bewitchment. Once you've read his *Istanbul*, you have been persuaded to see the city with his eyes – a gloomy, smoky warren of narrow lanes and conflicted families, serene, half fictional, like a city in a dream.

I find most cities nasty, but I can see that Istanbul is habitable, a city with the soul of a village. Unless there is a bomb in the bazaar, or a Kurd-related outrage, there is never news of Istanbul in the Western press. To say it is beautiful is so obvious as to be frivolous, yet the sight of its mosques and churches can be almost heart-stopping. I am impervious to its charm, even the word 'charm', but I admire Istanbul for its look of everlastingness, as though it has always existed (it has been a noble city since its first incarnation as Byzantium 1,700 years ago, and looks it in part). Most of all I like the city for its completeness and its self-sufficiency: it is a finished work, distinctly itself. Of course, you can buy gold and carpets in the Grand Bazaar, or jewellery and leather goods in the Egyptian bazaar, but everything else is available throughout the city too, because Turkey makes everything – stationery, cheap clothes, computers, knives, cigarettes, refrigerators, furniture. Heavy industry flourishes. The newspaper business is lively and competitive, book publishing is energetic, Turkish literacy is high, and book sales are brisk.

Given the fact that Turkey shares borders with Iraq, Iran, Syria, Armenia and Georgia, as well as Greece and Bulgaria, it could be a cockpit, yet it is a generally calm and self-assured place.

Istanbul now was vastly more prosperous in the look of its spruced-up buildings and well-dressed inhabitants. The ferry to Besiktas was proof of that, with its Sunday-serene passengers: little families holding hands, groups of muttering boys, smiling girls with their eyes downcast for modesty's sake, elderly women in shawls, bearded mullahs, shrouded wives in black burqas, every gradation in the chairs and pews of the ferry, from defiant unbeliever to scrupulous Koran reader.

The city is dramatic in its vistas, its spaces, its mixed population, and for appearing to accommodate everyone, but it is too big and sprawling to be definable. Yet because it is whole and coherent, self-sufficient, with an impressive profile of domes and spires, it is an easy city to visit, allowing the traveller to be presumptuous. The formalities of Turkish life, the elaborate courtesies of the Turkish language, encourage politeness.

The massacre of Armenians a century ago, the later expulsion of Greeks, and the Kurdish outrages and Turkish reprisals are lamentable facts of Turkish history; still, no city in Asia is so self-consciously reform-minded. And it is lucky in its writers, who are public intellectuals in the European mode – Orhan Pamuk was one of many who denounced the downplaying of the Armenian slaughter. He represented a public conscience. Yashar Kemal had played that role, as had his near namesake Yaya Kemal. All such people – public speakers, makers of statements, sometime journalists, polemicists with their passion and daring – were almost unknown in the countries I'd just passed through: Hungary, Romania, Bulgaria. A young woman novelist, Elif Shafak, was also out-spoken against excessive Turkification and in defence of Sufism. Many of the writers were in hot water when I arrived, but they seemed (as Turkish writers frequently do) to regard hot water as their natural element.

That it is one of the most easily negotiated and hospitable cities in the world makes me a mild Turkophile. Although it's a frustrating city to drive in (the traffic moves at a crawl), it is full of alternatives – a metro, commuter trains, buses, dolmuses (minivans) – and it is one of the great cities for walking or taking a ferry from embankment to embankment. I had been too young and hurried to appreciate its virtues on my first visit. For one thing, Istanbul is a well-used city: its marvels are not mere artefacts and museum pieces. They are part of everyday life. The ancient mosques and churches, the bazaars, the bridges, the gardens, the promen-ades, the fish markets and the fruit stalls are busily patronized by Turks. Being a secular country, Turkey thrives on Friday, the Muslim day of prayer and rest, and the bazaars and shops are closed on Sunday, the Christian Sabbath.

Istanbul had an air of Sunday serenity and an off-season slackness.

Worry beads were not in evidence. It was only the next day in the empty bazaars that the hawkers were frowning, but when I remarked on the lack of customers, they said, 'The tourists will come next month, *Inshallah.*'

I was aware of being a solitary traveller on a long journey. With no detailed onward plans, I was not looking much beyond Turkey at the moment. The newspaper headlines were all about the Iraq War – it was a one-day bus trip to the Iraq border. The war was clearly unpopular, but no one singled me out or harassed me. On the contrary, I was welcomed in restaurants, and I delighted in the food: stuffed grape leaves, bluefish, cheese dumplings and an aubergine dish so delicious its name is a catch-phrase, *iman bayildi,* 'the imam fainted'.

In the rain and the raw March wind off the Bosporus, the streets were uncrowded. I walked from mosque to mosque, then made some calls, agreeing to give a talk at a local college, as I had done on my first visit. I was invited to a dinner party and asked if there was anyone I wished to meet.

'What about Orhan Pamuk?'

'He usually says no.'

The next day I gave my talk, at Bogazçi University, a former missionary college on the heights of Bebek, and this being hospitable Turkey, I was guest of honour at a lunch where all the other diners were women. One was an American who was writing a book on all the writers who had lived and written about Istanbul, among them Mark Twain, James Baldwin, Paul Bowles and a man I bumped into after lunch, John Freely, a New Yorker who has lived and worked here for thirty-five years, the author of many books on Istanbul subjects.

Since working women in male-dominated societies are often more forthright and funnier than women in more liberated places, this campus lunch was lively and pleasant. Afterwards, I spoke to an English literature class on the subject of time and travel, alluding not just to my return journey but (because the class was studying the Romantic movement) also to Wordsworth's 'Tintern Abbey'.

They were attentive students of the sort that used to exist on American campuses – modest, studious, intense, omnivorous readers, quoters of Byron, admirers of Shelley, note takers, listeners, not intimidated by esoteric Romanticism. They happened to be reading *Northanger Abbey* – a copy on each desk. They were aware that because they were Turks studying English classics they had to try harder; they had something to prove. And they easily understood what I was saying about my return trip to Turkey and my memories of my long-ago journey, because they got the drift of 'Tintern Abbey', where it was and what it stood for:

> These beauteous forms,
> Through a long absence, have not been to me
> As is a landscape to a blind man's eye:
> But oft, in lonely rooms, and 'mid the din
> Of towns and cities, I have owed to them
> In hours of weariness, sensations sweet . . .

Though they hadn't been born when I was last here, these students, because of their learning, could relate to my sentimental journey: we had Wordsworth in common.

From the class on Romanticism, I went to look at the hotel I'd stayed in my first time, the Pera Palas. The building that had once seemed glamorous to me now looked elderly and neglected, and after one drink in the bar I left it and walked along the drizzly boulevards towards Taksim Square.

One of the compelling features of Istanbul is that minutes from a palace or the holiest mosque or the most respectable neighbourhood are their opposites – the dive, the hovel, the lower depths. The density of the city allows this proximity. The big-city conceit of the snob is the notion that sleaze is elsewhere, but it is usually only a few streets away.

So there I was, after leaving the Pera Palas, in the twinkling of an eye, in a dingy downstairs bar, the Club Saray, among mostly empty tables, greeting Marjana, who had just joined me.

'You buy me drink?'

'Of course.'

She was blonde, starved-looking and sullen. She might have been ill, but what struck me about her was that of all the girls in the bar, dimly lit though it was, she was reading a magazine. Though she had just folded it into her bag, I could see that it was not Turkish but Russian. She had been so engrossed in it, she was the one woman who had not looked up when I'd entered. What was a Russian woman doing here?

'What are you reading?'

That was when she'd put it away. She smiled, and after she'd sat down she said, 'Pop stars. Music. Money.'

'You're Russian?'

'I live Ukraine' — but it might have been 'leave'.

'Kiev?'

'No Kiev. Small village.' She was sipping a glass of raki.

'Nice place?'

'Not nice. Small!' She shook her head, struggling for words. 'No life. No money.'

'Chickens?'

'*Da*. Chickens!'

'You come to Istanbul to make money?'

'You have money?' She was thin, with delicate hands and a hungry mouth, and she said 'money' like a famished person using a word for food.

'Plenty,' I said, and made the money sign with my fingers.

'So buy me another drink.'

'You didn't finish this one.'

I knew the routine. The conventional view is that these women are idle sauntering floozies, killing time over a drink, frittering the day away on a bar stool. No, they are strict and even terrifying timekeepers, especially when they have a pimp to answer to. And it's odd, because 'Hurry up', which is their mantra, is not an aphrodisiac and hardly an endearment.

The meter was running. Time is everything to a prostitute. As clock watchers they are keener than lawyers, though the term 'solicitor' applies to both, and they share the concept of billable hours, every minute needing to be accounted for in these foot-tapping, finger-drumming professions.

The prostitute also shares the lawyer's fake sympathy, the apparent concern for your welfare, the initial buttonholing how-can-I-help-you? clucking, the pretence of help that is a way of ensnaring you and making you pay. In both cases, as long as you go on paying you have their full attention, but they are always in charge.

Marjana, I could tell by her sideways glances, was getting signals from a Turkish man, probably her pimp, his heels locked on to the rungs of a chair as he rocked back with a drink in his hand.

'So we go?'

'Where?'

'Not far. Near this place. I like you.' The second drink was set down. 'I think you are strong man. You are from what country?'

'America.'

'Big country. Lots of money. I want to go to America.'

'How did you get here, to Turkey?'

'My friend tell me I can make money here. She say, "Work in café." Good work.' Marjana looked a bit rueful, pursing her lips as she sloshed the raki in her mouth, then swallowed.

'You came – how? Bus? Plane?'

'I fly in plane. Is little money.'

'Who's your boss? Ukrainian man?'

'Turk man.' She glanced to the side, where the man was still glowering, and she pressed her lips together. Then, with a toss of her head, 'We go?'

'Let's talk.'

'Talk, talk,' she said, irritated and impatient. She leaned over and tapped my knee. 'What about fuck?'

I palmed some Turkish lire and put the notes into her hand, a gesture that shut her up but did not calm her. She looked at me as though I might be weird, but the money was in the meter.

'You have family?' I asked. She nodded. 'Husband?' She nodded, but more slowly. 'Children?'

At first she simply stared; then she began to cry, pressing her knuckles against her eyes. She shook her head and looked miserable. I hung my head, and when I saw her shoes – high heels, scuffed and twisted and damp from the wet streets of Taksim – I felt miserable myself at the sight of her tormented toes.

A hard-faced woman loomed over her and began to mutter. She was plump, in a tight dress, and her potbelly was at the level of my eyes. I recognized the word *prablyema*. Marjana was still sniffling in sorrow.

'What you say to Marjana?' the woman demanded.

'Nothing,' I said lamely.

'She cry,' the woman said.

Marjana tried to wave the woman away.

'I didn't do anything,' I said, and sounded like a ten-year-old. But I had made her remember her small children.

The woman muttered again to Marjana. Tears, recrimination, defiance, accusation, more tears – this was as far from sex as it was possible to be. And at the periphery was a suggestion of violence in the smouldering gaze and threatening posture of the Turkish man.

The woman flicked her fat hand at me, grazing my face with her big fingernails. Though they were plastic glue-ons, they were sharp and claw-like, and could have served as weapons.

'Maybe you go, eh?'

Gladly, I thought. I stood up and backed away, a bit too quickly, but happy to go, saying goodbye. I had guessed that Marjana was one of many women lured to Istanbul and kept against her will – with a family elsewhere, unable to help her. I had wanted to talk, but in such circumstances, in most circumstances, talk is trouble.

I got more news of the dinner party: 'Pamuk said he's coming.' I was eager to meet him, not merely because of his well-made novels and his personal history in *Istanbul*, but because, as a passionate writer and self-described graphomaniac, he was probably eccentric, someone who lived at the edge of the world, the solitary soul that all writers must be in order to do their work and live their lives. Writers are always readers, and though they are usually unbalanced, they are always noticers of the world. From an early age I have not been able to rid myself of the notion that the best writers are deeply flawed heroes.

Among the Turkish guests at the party, some of whom were writers, all of whom were polite, patient and deferential, Pamuk was restless. Rather gangly and bespectacled, he thrashed around as he spoke. He reminded me of someone I knew. He was a taunter, hunching his shoulders, throwing his head back to laugh – and he had a loud, appreciative guffaw. He pulled faces, often clownish ones that his scholar's eyeglasses exaggerated. He was both a mocker and a self-mocker, a buttonholer, a finger wagger, and his consistent mode of inquiry was teasing. He was a needler, a joker, not a speechifier but a maker of deflating remarks in a smiling and mildly prosecutorial way, like a court-room wit.

I smiled when it dawned on me that he reminded me of myself – evasive, goofy, slightly moody, ill at ease in a crowd, uncomfortable at formal occasions. Latins look a lot like Turks: I felt he physically re-sembled me, and he had my oblique habit of affecting to be ignorant and a bit gauche in order to elicit information.

'What do you mean by that?' was his frequent question, demanding that you explain what you just said.

His mother loomed large in his life and in his Istanbul narrative. I asked him what she thought of the book.

'She didn't like my Istanbul book. Then I got a divorce.' He smiled. 'She wasn't happy about that. But I put her in a book – *My Name Is Red*. Then she was happy.'

'I put my mother in a book and she was very unhappy,' I said. 'She saw it as a betrayal. When my first book was published, almost forty years ago, she wrote me a long letter. I was in Africa at the time. She said the book was a piece of trash. That was her exact word. Trash! ' "Thanks, Mom!" '

Pamuk became interested. 'You must have been sad about that.'

'Strangely, no. I was energized. I think I would have been disturbed if she'd praised the book – I would have suspected her of lying. I thought: I'm not writing to please her. By the way, I kept the letter. I still have it. It was a goad to me.'

We were at the dinner table, being served a Turkish meal. While listening attentively to me, Pamuk was absorbing the reactions of the other people, his eyes darting.

'Why did you make a face?' he said to the woman next to me.

She denied she had made a face.

'Was it because we were talking about mothers, and you are a mother?'

'Of course not.'

'You did this,' Pamuk said, and squinted and showed his teeth and compressed his face into a comic mask.

He spoke about his years as a student, studying English, reading English books, and how as an anonymous Turk with a fluency in English he had taken Arthur Miller and Harold Pinter around Istanbul, pointing out the sights, explaining the history.

'I showed them the city. I was the translator. I was next to them, helping, listening. They had no idea who I was, but they were great writers to me.'

Talk of Arthur Miller turned to talk of Marilyn Monroe. I said that I had written an essay about the Sotheby auction of Marilyn's personal effects.

'Expensive things?' Pamuk asked.

'Everything – dresses, books, shoes, broken mirrors, her capri pants, a copy of *The Joy of Cooking* with her scribbles in it, her wobbly dressing table, her junk jewellery. She had a yellow pad of paper and, in her writing, the words "He doesn't love me." A cigarette lighter that Frank Sinatra had given her. Also her "Happy Birthday, Mr President" dress. And her toaster.'

Pamuk was delighted by the inventory. He said, 'I love catalogues of people's lives. Did you see the auction of Jackie Kennedy's possessions?'

'Yes, but no toasters in that one.'

He said he loved minutiae, the revelation in everyday objects. Not the treasures but the car-boot-sale items, always more telling. It was a novelist's passion, a need to know secrets, to intrude – without seeming to – on other people's lives.

Still eating, he sized me up and said, 'You went swimming with Yashar Kemal.'

'That's right – thirty-three years ago.'

'He is away, in south Anatolia,' the host said, because I had also asked how I might get in touch with him. 'He is sorry to miss you. He remembered you from that time long ago.'

It seemed to me amazing that he was alive and writing, at the age of eighty-two, this man who'd boasted of his Gypsy blood and his upbringing in the wild hinterland of Turkey among bandits and peasants. He had been inspired by Faulkner, another writer who boasted of being a rustic. But Pamuk was a metropolitan, a man on the frontier as all writers are, but essentially a city dweller.

'I read your book about South America,' Pamuk said. 'I liked the part about Argentina, especially Borges.'

Pamuk had much in common with Borges, not just his writing but his personality – an inwardness, a gift for the magical in his prose, wide and even arcane learning combined with a sense of comedy. Borges had been very funny in conversation, and often self-mocking, pretending to jeer at his own writing, insincerely remarking on how short his stories were – 'and probably full of howlers!' as he said to me of 'The Wall and the Books', his Chinese story.

The most endearing trait that Pamuk and Borges shared was a passion for the cities of their birth. Throughout Borges's writing is a nuanced history of Buenos Aires, and Borges would have nodded in agreement at Pamuk's judgement of a life in Istanbul, because it was so similar to that of a Buenos Aires person, a Porteño: 'When Istanbullus grow a bit older and feel their fates intertwining with that of the city, they come to welcome the cloak of melancholy that brings their lives a contentment, an emotional depth, that almost looks like happiness. Until then they rage against their fate.'

In his writing, Borges extolled the violence, the music, the steamy secrets of Buenos Aires while at the same time bemoaning its philistinisms and pomposities and backward-looking conceits. Pamuk, it seemed to me, was no different.

'You read to him,' Pamuk said. 'That was nice.'

'He enjoyed being read to. He had a little glimmer of eyesight – I mean, he signed a book for me – but he couldn't read.'

'Did he do this?' Pamuk shut his eyes and threw his head back in an imitation of Stevie Wonder lost in a rapture of appreciation, grinning and shaking his head. It was a sudden and unexpected turn. Everyone laughed.

'You're wicked,' I said.

'What do you mean by that?'

I said, 'He didn't wag his head. He sat there and often finished the sentences in the stories. He seemed to know most of them by heart.'

'Which stories? What did you read?'

'Kipling. He liked *Plain Tales from the Hills.* "The Gate of a Hundred Sorrows" – about opium smoking. "Beyond the Pale" – a doomed love affair. Borges was a connoisseur of unrequited love.'

'What else?'

'Parts of the *Arabian Nights* in the Burton translation. He owned a first edition, about twenty volumes.'

'Some of it is sexy. You read him those parts too, eh?'

Querying, mocking, needling, teasing, then all at once attentive. Pamuk approached a subject like a city dweller, darting up this alley and down that street, and then he was at an upstairs window calling down, raising a laugh, before his confrontation with a direct question. He also had a writer's gift for risking the sort of over-frank childish questions that can be disarming.

Talk of Borges and love led him to speak candidly about his father's mysterious other life and the loud battles between his father and mother: the turbulent household – evasive husband, agitated wife.

A woman sitting next to Pamuk said, 'My mother once bumped into my father when he was with his mistress.'

'That's a nightmare,' I said.

'Good answer!' Pamuk said, smirking at me.

His indirection, the manner of his teasing, his posturing and prodding, finishing with a trenchant remark, was proof of Pamuk's seriousness. I thought of how all writers, when they are alone, talk to themselves.

'When the inner history of any writer's mind is written,' V. S. Pritchett once said, 'we find (I believe) that there is a break at some point in his life. At some point he splits off from the people who surround him and he discovers the necessity of talking to himself and not to them.'

In *Istanbul* it is possible to observe this process taking place in Pamuk's restless mind, his discovering that his inner life is unknown to his family, his relief in talking to himself. He finds solace away from his family, in solitary walks and mumbling meditation, because, among others things – as a portrait of a city, about growing up in a conflicted family, the joy of reading, famous visitors, a love of solitude, the melancholy of an ancient place – the book is about how he abandoned all other ambitions to become a writer, or more than a writer.

He was in the news. This reclusive man seemed an unlikely hero, but a few months earlier he had been in court as the defendant in one of those national trials that is like a morality play, a lion being judged by donkeys. Around that time he wrote in *The New Yorker*, 'Living as I do in a country that honors its *pashas*, its saints, and policemen at every opportunity, but refuses to honor its writers until they have spent years in courts and prisons, I cannot say that I was surprised to be put on trial. I understand why friends smile and say that I am at last "a real Turkish writer".'

Outsiders complain that Turkey is repressive. Turks complain too. Every shade of Islamic opinion is present in Turkish society, ranging from the most benign to the most fanatical, and every shade of secular opinion as well. This, I think, is the reason every visitor to Turkey finds something to like in the country and always finds a Turk to agree with.

The odd but probably provable fact is that repression often has a salutary effect on writers, strengthening them by challenging them, making them resist, making their voices important, for at their best, writers are rebellious, and repression is the whetstone that keeps them sharp, even if the repression makes their lives miserable. A free country cannot guarantee great writing, and a public intellectual (albeit a reluctant one) like Pamuk hardly exists in Britain and the United States.

Pamuk's crime was his mentioning to a Swiss journalist that 'a million Armenians and thirty thousand Kurds were killed in this country and I'm the only one who dares to talk about it'. This remark resulted in death threats, newspaper attacks, vilification and a criminal charge of insulting the state. At his trial Pamuk faced a possible three-year sentence if he was found guilty, but the case was dropped. He was set free. He'd made his bones as a Turkish writer and he disappeared – Istanbul has that big-city quality of being a place in which you can vanish without a trace.

Pamuk does agree to be interviewed now and then. His voice is distinctive, his manner inimitable. Here is his response to a woman from a British paper badgering him on the subject of free speech in Turkey: 'Look,' he said to her, 'I never had any trouble writing novels. I talked about this with my publisher when we were publishing *Snow*, which was my own explicitly political novel – but then nothing happened to it. The only time I had trouble, I had trouble because of interviews, madam.' Then he waggled his finger at the woman and laughed.

He was waggling his finger now, at this dinner party, indicating one person, then another. 'What do you mean by that?' 'Why are you smiling?' 'I find that ridiculous.'

'How did you get to Turkey?' he asked me. 'Someone said, what, you took a train?'

'Train from London. Well, four of them. Via Romania.'

When Pamuk made a face he looked years younger, indeed like a disgusted child, his glasses shifting on his wrinkled nose.

'I was in Romania,' he said. 'A writers' conference, but on a boat – a sort of cruise. A whole week just sailing around with other writers.'

'It sounds awful.'

'Good answer!'

He smiled at the news that I had glided in from Bulgaria, through the boondocks of Turkey, habituating myself, and was planning to glide east again in a few days, to Ankara and Trabzon and Hopa to Georgia.

He said, 'I have read your book about Naipaul, *Sir Vidia's Shadow*.'

'What do you think?'

'A very affectionate book.'

'That's true, but not many people saw it.'

'Why not?'

'I don't know. Maybe quarrels are more interesting. People said it was cruel. I'd say unsparing. The quarrelsome part of it was played up as a writers' feud. But Naipaul was an important figure in my writing life.'

'How can we know what he thought of the book.'

'No way of telling. He's not talking.'

'I can't believe he didn't read it.'

'I don't think he did. His wife did, though, I'm sure of that.'

'The wife was part of your problem,' Pamuk said. 'Second wife, yes?'

'Right.'

Pamuk leaned over and looked across the top of his glasses and said, 'Am I a good reader of Paul Theroux?'

'Very astute.'

'And wasn't there another woman?'

'Naipaul's mistress of twenty-three years. He ditched her after his wife died and married a woman he had just met in Pakistan. It's a strange tale.'

'Maybe not so strange,' Pamuk said.

We talked about writers' lovers and pieced together the odd love life of Graham Greene, who remained married to a woman he had not cohabited with for sixty years or more, while chasing women and suffering through three or four grand passions, all of them with married women. His last affair was like a marriage. The woman visited him at his apartment every noontime and prepared his lunch, after which they made love. Then they had a drink, and at nightfall the woman returned home to her husband. This went on for years. The husband knew about it, but his wife said something like 'Don't make me choose.'

Pamuk said, 'It sounds perfect.'

'After Greene died, the woman divorced her husband.'

'Ah.' Pamuk looked happy, contemplating the complexity of this.

Over dessert, the other guests who were writers talked about the burden of being a Turkish writer abroad. Westerners whose knowledge of Turkey was limited to *Midnight Express* and doner kebabs would challenge them, saying, What about the Armenians? What about the Kurds? How come you torture people?

A writer named Yusof said that he had been an admirer of the Anglophile critic George Steiner.

'I was in London,' Yusof said. 'I had five books I wanted George Steiner to sign. I went to one of his lectures, and afterwards he took a seat at a table to sign people's books. He signed two of mine and said, "Where do you come from?" I told him Turkey. He pushed the rest of my books away – he wouldn't sign them. He said, "Go home and take care of your people." He meant the Kurds.'

On my way back to the hotel, it occurred to me that though the United States had supported the Kurds, tolerating Kurdish terrorism in both Turkey and Iraq, and were still fighting a war in Iraq, no Turk had blamed me for this slaughter, or even raised the matter with me.

The other writer I had wished to meet in Istanbul was Elif Shafak. We met at the Ciragan Palas, on another rainy day. She was so beautiful I forgot her books, writing seemed irrelevant, I was bewitched. I was reminded of the Kipling line 'Much that is written about Oriental passion and impulsiveness is exaggerated and compiled at second-hand, but a little of it is true,' and Elif Shafak seemed the embodiment of it. She was about thirty, with grey-blue eyes and the face of a brilliant child, which is also the paedomorphic face of a Renaissance Madonna, framed by wisps of light hair. All over her hands and fingers were thin silver chains, looped and dangling, attached to a mass of silver rings, as though she'd just escaped from a harem.

I found it hard to concentrate on what she was saying, so distracted was I by her loveliness. But her passion and impulsiveness were unmistakable, and I reminded myself that she had written five highly praised novels.

Unlike most other Turkish writers, she was cosmopolitan. She had either taught or studied, or both, in universities in Michigan and Arizona and at Mount Holyoke. Her mother had been a Turkish diplomat, so she had lived in many capital cities. Her father had vanished from her life; she was aware of his being present in Istanbul but never saw him. This absent father was the subject of her new novel, *Baba and the Bastard*, which was kept hidden in many Istanbul bookshops because of its racy title.

'Shafak' was an invented surname, the word meaning aurora or dawn in Turkish. The name suited her, since she glowed with life, and dawn in Asia does not come by degrees, the sky slowly lightening, but is like something switched on, filling the new day with a sudden brightness that seems complete. Elif Shafak had that radiance.

She was also unexpectedly combative – you don't expect such fight in a beauty, but it was attractive as, jingling the chains and silver filigree on her hands, she denounced various Turkish attitudes.

'Turkey has amnesia,' she said. 'Turks are indifferent to the past, to old words, to old customs.'

'I thought that Turkish reformers were generally a good thing.'

'No, they erased a lot that we need to know,' she said. 'The Kemalists and the reformers changed the culture. They threw away old words, they got rid of foreign words. But these words are part of who we are. We need to know them.'

I was transfixed by her eyes, by her slender fingers, a silver chain swinging from a ring on each finger.

'We need to know about the Armenians,' she said.

'You say these things in public?' I asked.

'Yes, though it's hard, especially for a woman here.'

'I'm interested that you have public intellectuals, speaking their mind. Most countries don't have them.'

'We have many. We fight and disagree all the time.'

'How do you get on the United States?'

'I like it, but I had to start all over there. I am someone here. There, I am no one.'

She talked about her studies in Sufi literature and culture, not the dervishes of Istanbul but the cults and practitioners in remotest Turkey. I offered her my memory of Sufis dancing at sunset at a mosque in Omdurman, in Sudan, one of the most dramatic encounters I'd had on my Dark Star Safari through Africa. Mine had been a happy accident, hers were both vivid and cerebral; Sufism was a study for her. I was nonetheless distracted – her beauty was like a curse that prevented me from understanding the nuances of what she was saying. Still, I felt that meeting Orhan Pamuk and Elif Shafak, I was looking at the future of Turkish literature.*

In a casual conversation with a Turkish scholar I mentioned how impressed I was with the work of writers like Pamuk and Shafak. And there were many others who'd not been translated. How to explain this literary excellence?

'Nomadism,' he said. 'The storytelling tradition is strong in Turkey because of our seasonal migrations. Iran has been settled for twenty-five hundred years. Greece is sedentary. But Turkish society has a dynamic structure. Because of this constant movement we became storytellers.'

All that remained, before I took the night express to Ankara, was a visit to the dentist. I had a loose filling, and fearing that the discomfort would only get worse over the next weeks or months, I asked for a recommendation.

---

* Later that year, Orhan Pamuk won the Nobel Prize for literature.

That was how I came to be sitting, canted back in a chair, being examined by Dr Isil Evcimik, who was a pleasant woman in her late forties with a reassuringly well-equipped office. Cuddly toys dangled nearby, to cheer up anxious children. They cheered me up too, and when Dr Evcimik told me that her daughter was at Princeton, on a full scholarship, I felt I was in good hands.

It seemed part of Dr Evcimik's technique to murmur a running commentary on what she happened to be doing at any given time. With a hypodermic syringe in one hand and a swab in the other she said, 'I will first swab' – and she swabbed my gums – 'and then we wait a little.' We waited a little. 'Then I put the needle in very slowly. Please tell me if it hurts.' It didn't. 'Good. Now we wait a little more.'

Was the tooth cold- or heat-sensitive? she wondered.

I didn't know, but it was sensitive.

'Can be either. Can be both. But better if it's one or the other.'

She explained reversible sensitivity. That could happen to me. Or there was irreversible sensitivity. 'In that case, you might need a root canal. Where are you going to next?'

'Georgia. Azerbaijan.'

'A root canal in Azerbaijan? I don't think so.' She selected a drill, saying, 'Now I will drill amalgam.' She drilled the loose cement out of the tooth and said, 'This is amalgam.' She sprayed the tooth, she drilled some more. She then mixed a substance on a dish. 'This is composite. This will taste very bad. Please don't swallow any – it's not poison, though.'

I sat, mouth agape, listening.

'Now I will fill.' She tamped the composite into the hole. 'This' – with a flourish of a tool – 'is a bonding agent. We will apply. And then' – a flash of silver – 'a collar. Like a belt around the tooth, so you can floss.' More manipulation. 'Not done yet. It's high. I will smooth it.' She did so. 'Please bite on this.' I did so twice. 'How is it?'

'Better.'

'I don't like "better".'

She buzzed it some more, she perfected it, she told me that she had always wanted to visit Hawaii, and to this end she gave me her bill, a bargain at the Turkish equivalent of $153.

When I told Dr Evcimik I was taking the train that night to Ankara, she said, 'That's the best way to go. The plane is expensive and lots of trouble. The airport is far and there are always delays. When I go to Ankara myself I always take the train.'

It was still raining in Istanbul. The rain had followed me from Paris, and it had defined each city – making Paris glisten with scattered light; giving the Budapest streets a slop of snow and mud and darkening the mildew on its buildings; muddying Bucharest and filling its potholes with black puddles. But in Istanbul the rain gave the roads a somnolent nobility, because it was a city of waterways and domes and slender minarets and towers that glowed in the diffused light of the downpour. The buildings were masterpieces, but what I remembered was how, at a distance, they were transformed by the rain.

4. Night Train to Ankara

The century-old station at Haydarpasa was floodlit and looked like an opera house on the night I crossed the Bosporus to take the night express to Ankara. 'A railway here in Asia – in the dreamy realm of the Orient . . . is a strange thing to think of,' Mark Twain wrote in *The Innocents Abroad*, when he was in Turkey. 'And yet they have one already, and are building another.' My night train was leaving at ten thirty, but I arrived an hour early, sliding to the pier on the ferry from the far bank. The whole station had been renovated. It was obviously regarded as a venerable building, worth preserving; the restoration had been extensive. Years ago, dark and decrepit, its days seemed to be numbered. Now that the train was the best way to go from Istanbul to Ankara, investment in the railways had increased.

The conductor in his new uniform was also an encouraging sign that Turkish railways were in good shape. He was standing by the stairs to the sleeping car. He greeted me, welcomed me aboard, and helped me locate my couchette. I saw that there was a dining car on this train. The carriages were new. All this was a kind of heaven – a private berth, a cosy cabin, a book to read (I was reading Elif Shafak's *The Flea Palace*), and twelve hours of comfort ahead of me. No border to cross, no interruptions. The other passengers were businessmen, wearing suits, carrying briefcases; a family with two children; and some shrouded women.

Turkish *manti* (dumplings) were on the dining-car menu: flour cubes, cheese, meat and spices, served with lentil soup and a glass of wine. After eating I turned in, read a chapter of *The Flea Palace*, and, rocked gently by the movement of the train, hearing the rain lashing the windows, fell asleep.

I awoke eight hours later in bright sunshine, the first rainless day since leaving London, in the dry rough hills and the gravesites and tumuli of Gordion, about sixty miles west of Ankara, where Alexander had slashed the hard-to-pick knot.

Nearer Ankara were new houses, gated communities, college campuses, rows of tenements – the building boom that seemed to be general around the growing cities of Turkey. On my first trip I had summarized Turkey as a peasant economy with colourful ruins, but modernized, mechanized, it had undergone a transformation: it was an exporter of food, literacy was high, and the trains had improved, though most people took buses because the roads were so good.

There was no train to Trabzon; I'd have to take a bus, I was told as soon as I arrived in Ankara and announced my intention of travelling northeast to Georgia and Azerbaijan. My plan was to circumvent Iran while staying on the ground.

I'd been invited to give a talk in Ankara, and it was hinted to me that the setting would be formal. That meant I'd need a necktie, an article I did not possess. I bought one for a few dollars, and that night, to the invited guests, I enlarged on my theme of the return journey, how it reveals the way the world works, and makes fools of pundits and predictors. How it showed, too, the sort of traveller I had been, what I'd seen, what I'd missed the first time. I was not in search of news – had never been, I said. I wanted to know more about the world, about people's lives. I wasn't a hawk in my travels; more a butterfly. But revelation was granted to even the most aimless traveller, who was happier and more receptive to impressions.

'An aimless joy is a pure joy,' I said, quoting Yeats.

> And wisdom is a butterfly
> And not a gloomy bird of prey.

Ankara, which had seemed to me long ago a dusty outpost at the edge of the known world, had become a thriving city, important for its manufacturing, bright, youthful, sprawling across the dusty hills and ravines, with three large universities at its periphery. Culturally it had reclaimed its past, the golden age of bull worshippers and philosophers who had flourished thousands of years before, to the west of Ankara at Hatusa.

Mingling with the people who'd attended my talk, many of them academics or politicians, I was told in confidence by a whispering man that they were against the war in Iraq and wished the United States had never invaded.

This moustached man tapped the air with his finger and said to me, 'Not

a single person in this room is in favour of what America is doing in Iraq.'
Perhaps self-conscious of his generalization, he turned to look at the hundred or so people in the room he had just characterized, and noticing some Americans, he added, 'The Turkish ones, anyway. All of us are against it.'

'We were a Turkoman family in Iraq,' a woman said to me, and introduced herself as Professor Emel Dogramaci of Çankaya University. 'We were powerful in Kirkuk.' By powerful, she meant wealthy. The family had become philanthropic in Ankara, having departed Kirkuk, a Kurdish area now. 'We left because we were not happy with Saddam.'

'Were you glad to see him overthrown?'

'Of course, but not at the cost of this war,' she said. 'This war is dreadful. It will not help. We don't see when or how it will end. The only certainty is civil war. Well, that is happening now, isn't it?'

I said, 'The depressing thing is that it could go on for years.'

'I dislike Bush. I prefer Clinton, for all his failings,' she said. I admired her confidence, her fluency, her style. She was a woman of a certain age, well dressed, glittering with jewels, opinionated and forthright. 'Bush doesn't know anything, but who are these people who are advising Bush? They gave him very bad advice. Did they know what they were doing?'

'Rumsfeld was one of them.'

'We know Rumsfeld!' the woman said, snorting at the name. 'He was supporting Iraq during the Iran–Iraq War. He was supporting Saddam! He was telling us to do the same!'

From their home in Kirkuk her family had observed Donald Rumsfeld paddling palms and pinching fingers with Saddam, and selling him weapons, among them land mines. The Iranian response was to send small children – because children are numerous, portable and expendable – running, tripping into the minefields to detonate the bombs with their tiny feet, to be blown to pieces.

'This is not political. It is not about oppression. It is a religious war – Sunnis against Shiites,' Professor Dogramaci said.

'Which one are you?' I asked.

'I am a cultural Muslim,' she said. 'I don't go to mosque. But Islam is in my past and my personal history.'

'Maybe Iraq will just break up into separate states – Kurdish, Shiite, Sunni,' I said.

'That could happen – a sort of federation. But I tell you this,' she said, and she faced me full-on, looking darkly at me, and her dress of watered silk, her lovely necklace and her glittering rings only made her more menacing. 'The oil does not belong to the Kurds alone. It belongs to the people of Iraq. If there is a Kurdish state and they claim the oil, and the others are left behind' – she raised her hand, her sparkling fingers – 'then I tell you there will be trouble.'

'What kind of trouble?' I asked.

'I cannot be specific,' she said, and looked like a fierce grandma. 'But we will not stand aside and watch it happen.'

Inclining her head, listening to this conversation, was Mrs Zeynep Karahan Uslu, a member of parliament for the ruling AKP, the Justice and Development Party. She was attractive, in her mid-thirties, and had the same independent air as the professor.

Noticing her, the professor's mood lightened. She said, 'You see? This woman is a parliamentarian. She has a child. She is from Istanbul. That is her husband, Ibrahim.' Ibrahim, watching us, began to smile. 'He follows her here to Ankara and looks after the child. Zeynep is a modern Turkish woman. I knew her father, a great scholar. I am so happy to see her!'

'Yes, it's not easy,' Zeynep said. 'Sometimes we sit in parliament until two or three in the morning. I leave and the police stop me. They see a woman alone in a car. They say, "What are you doing?" I have to say, "I have parliamentary business!" This would never happen in Istanbul, where people are up all night. But Ankara is a big, dull city.'

Not dull at Hacettepe University, though, where I was to speak the next day. Big posters greeted me: 'ABD! EVINE DÖN!'

'"USA – Go Back Home!"' my translator said.

'Is that meant for me?'

'No, no – it's for the demonstration on Saturday,' he said, intending to reassure me. 'The AKP is organizing it.'

Zeynep's party – and she had intimated that the city was dull?

The foyer of the building where I was to speak was hung with posters of Fidel, Che Guevara and Venezuela's Hugo Chávez. It was all like the sixties in the United States: inflammatory posters, yet the students were militant in a Turkish way, polite but firm.

Gory photographs along one wall showed Israeli atrocities in Palestine and massacres in Iraq – bombing victims, mass graves, blown-up houses, shrieking women, mourning families, children with arms and legs blown off, bloody bandages. And in large letters a declaration.

'What does that say?'

' "It is in our hands to stop all this!" '

At one table a pretty girl and a well-dressed boy, obviously students, were selling paper badges, disks trimmed in black ribbon, with a motto in the centre.

Before I could ask, my translator said, ' "We support Iraq resistance." '

It was an amazing display, even daunting: flags, bunting, denunciatory posters, angry images, and now that I understood the Turkish words for 'USA – Go Back Home!' I saw the demand all over – it followed me down the hallway to the university auditorium.

'Not a single person in this university believes the US is right in the war,' one of the teachers told me. 'Not one.'

Four hundred people were already in their seats. They were literature students. I told them that I was the same age as our bellicose vice president, but that was where our resemblance ended. After Dick Cheney graduated from college, he went to Washington to seek political power, and he never left. I joined the Peace Corps, to teach school in Africa. I distrusted politicians, and I avoided making friends with politically powerful people, because (I said) the nearer you are to such people, the more morally blind you become.

Then I talked about literature. 'People will tell you, "What's the use? What's the point of reading novels and poetry?" They'll tell you to go to law school or to be an economist or to do something useful. But books are useful. Books will make you thoughtful, and they might even make you happy. They will certainly help you to become more civilized.'

Afterwards I told them that I had been in Turkey thirty-three years ago, when the phones didn't work, and Turks in the hinterland had asked me to sell them my watch and my blue jeans. I could see from where I was standing that everyone had watches and wore blue jeans.

I asked how many of them had mobile phones. They all did. And to my other questions: all used the Internet, all used e-mail.

'How many are going to the demonstration on Saturday?'

All.

'Muhammad was illiterate. He had twelve wives and, let us say, a vivid sexual history,' another forthright Turkish professor was saying to me. I was in another part of Ankara, another campus, Bilkent University.

Muhammad the indefatigable womanizer: that is the way the Prophet is depicted by Neguib Mahfouz in his celebrated (but banned in every Arab country) novel *Children of the Alley*. So I wasn't shocked. But I said, 'Do you say these things out loud in Turkey?'

'Everyone knows my views,' he said and shrugged. 'But these are facts. Ninety per cent of what I say would be disputed by orthodox Muslims.' He smiled. 'Or would be considered heretical.'

He was Professor Talât Halman. As a former minister of culture in the Turkish government, and a scholar, writer and director of the Department of Turkish Literature at Bilkent, he had considerable authority. He had also taught a course at New York University on the history of Islam. He was in his late seventies, he was shrewd and funny, with the ironic and knowing manner of a confident scholar. Over lunch he told me much that I didn't know and had never, until now, inquired about.

'What do we know about Mecca at the time of Muhammad?' I asked.

'Mecca was mainly a pagan city, but with rabbis and priests here and there. The rabbis were suspicious of this new cult of Islam. They repressed it, or at least they tried to. That's why the Koran is full of battles – between Muslims and Jews.'

'Are there any historical documents that describe this early friction between Muslims and Jews?'

Professor Halman shook his head. 'Not many documents. That's the trouble.'

'Why were the rabbis suspicious?'

'They were alarmed by the new ideas and the way they were mingled with the traditional stories.' We were having big bowls of fragrant soup, but Professor Halman put his spoon down to explain. 'There is always tension present at the origin of a new faith. This has been true throughout history. There was lots of friction in Mecca at the time of Muhammad.'

'What is the significance of the Kaaba?' I asked, because the huge black cube of shining stone had always seemed to me an enigmatic symbol.

'The Kaaba in Mecca – it's a meteorite, of course.'

I hadn't known that, and said so.

'It is obviously a miraculous force of nature,' Professor Halman said. 'The Jews hadn't claimed it. No one had claimed it – so Muhammad did.'

I said, 'I'm interested in Joseph Smith, founder of the Mormons, which is an American religion. Columbus and the American Revolution were foretold in *The Book of Mormon*, translated from golden plates by Smith in 1827, so he claimed. When he was alive there were apparently lots of other American prophets like him, preaching and professing that God was directing them. Jesus had predecessors too. So how did Muhammad arise as a prophet?'

'There were no proto-Muhammads, as with Jesus and Joseph Smith,' the professor said. 'From the age of forty, Muhammad had these new ideas. He spoke. People wrote down his words. There's lots of apocrypha, too, especially the Hadith – wise sayings of the Prophet. About a million of them exist, but' – the professor smiled – 'who can establish their veracity? This number has been winnowed down to five thousand.'

'Can you quote a Hadith?'

He did so, promptly, with an irresistible one: 'The ink of a scholar is more holy than the blood of a martyr.'

I said, 'Jews don't proselytize, but Muslims do, and they make a lot of converts. What's the attraction?'

'At the time of Muhammad the converts were oppressed peoples. Islam gave them something to fight for – a great sense of victory.'

'But I'm thinking of now.'

'Even now, the traumatic experiences of colonialism and occupation, the memory of the humiliation of the Crusades. To a great extent, Islam was shaped by conquerors and colonialism.'

'So Americans fighting in Iraq will only make Islam stronger?'

'Yes, and bring about more suicide bombers,' Professor Halman said. 'Martyrdom is important in Islam. There are lots of mentions of martyrdom in the Hadith. There is quite a lot of militarism in the Koran.'

'But martyrdom is important in Christianity,' I said. 'That's one way of becoming a saint.'

'Yes. But unlike in Christianity, in Islam it is also good to aid and abet martyrdom,' he said. 'And giving away money is also a form of martyrdom.'

'What I don't understand,' I said, 'is why Muslims leave Islamic communities and emigrate to places like Germany and Britain, basically Christian countries. To live among Christians and Jews. And Muslims get fractious when they're told not to wear headscarves and so forth. Why bother to emigrate if it makes them so unhappy?'

'They emigrate because their countries are backward,' the professor said with superb good sense. 'Better to emigrate than to starve to death.'

'Muslim boys were burning cars in Paris a few months ago.'

He said, 'A North African has limited choices. He can only go to a Francophone country. He ends up in France and sees it is secular, and he objects. But you see Muslims are also reacting against political oppression.'

'Tell me how this applies to Iraq now.'

'American experts are the problem,' Professor Halman said. 'They were wrong about the Soviet Union and wrong about Iraq. They are academics and bureaucrats with vested interests.'

'Sinister forces?'

'Not sinister but obtuse. The ones who said the Soviet Union was strong were politically motivated, perhaps. They didn't know how weak the Soviets were.'

'So the US government gets the wrong advice?'

'Yes, and mainly from scholars. Scholars need to validate the status quo, or they will lose their funding.'

'The last time I took this trip,' I said, 'the shah was in power. Everyone said he was strong and progressive, though it was clear to me that the countryside was reactionary and orthodox Muslim.'

'That's a point. Advice-givers don't travel enough,' he said. 'Where are you going next?'

'Up to Trabzon, then Georgia, Azerbaijan, Turkmenistan, and –' I stopped; it seemed unlucky to mention more countries.

'That's good,' he said. 'Ankara is a dreary place.'

'But I've had an interesting time here.'

'It's a wasteland,' he said. 'And Turks are a melancholy people.' He pressed his fingers to his temples as though to accelerate his memory. 'I think there's been trouble in Trabzon. I can't remember what.'

So I headed out of Ankara intending to leave Turkey. Long ago, Turkey had seemed a distant and exotic country of frowning men and enigmatic women, with unreliable telephones and simple roads and a dramatic, confrontational culture. Now it had everything, it was part of the visitable world, but it was no longer the way to Iran and Afghanistan, so I headed north.

5. Night Train to Tbilisi

The trouble in Trabzon, on the Black Sea, where I found filthy weather, ugly rumours and ill tidings, was the incident that had slipped Professor Halman's mind: the murder a month before of an unbeliever in a fit of sentimental fury. This singular outrange – singular because such things seldom happened in Turkey – was the shooting of an Italian priest, Father Andrea Santoro, by an overexcited Islamist named Oguz intending to avenge the honour of Muhammad in a controversy over mocking cartoons of the Prophet that had appeared in various European newspapers. Oguz, who was sixteen, was caught the day after the murder, and Father Santoro's corpse was given a solemn send-off, attended by the highest Muslim clergy in Turkey, the muftis.

Symbolism is everything in religious strife, which is why it looks so logical, while being so stupid and brutal. The Catholic was singled out and shot for symbolizing the enemy, as any outsider might be, including me. The poor man had been praying in a back pew of the Santa Maria Church in Trabzon, where, on an average Sunday, there were no more than a dozen communicants. Rare as this murder was, it was so recent it concentrated my mind on leaving Trabzon. On arriving I'd asked, 'What are the sights?' and been told the ancient mosque was a must-see. It was a Friday, a day of prayer in this (so I was also told) pious city. I should add that not once in Turkey was I hassled for being an unbeliever, nor was the subject ever mentioned. But the rain got me down, so I began to look for ways to escape it.

Because there was no train, I had arrived on the night bus from Ankara, the Ulusoy coach – Greyhound standard – with frequent pit stops on the twelve-hour ride to the northeast, allowing passengers to get out and smoke, since smoking had been banned on Turkish buses. The exception was the bus driver, who could light up as much as he wished. These were also eating stops, at rest-area cafeterias, where the food was not bad: thick soup, trays of reddish beans, sinister slabs of meat drifting in black gravy, scorched kebabs and bread in round loaves the diameter of a steering wheel.

Over the mountains in darkness from Ankara, and still in darkness to Samsun and the edge of the Black Sea, we followed the coast road serenely until the day lifted. In the dreary, sunless dawn the towns on the shore, Ordu, Giresun, Tirebolu and nameless little settlements, looked ugly and lifeless, with hideous new buildings and ramshackle older ones on the barren coast. Yet the steep escarpment just behind the coast was beautiful, dark with wooded hills, and further back the mountains loomed in a tangle of rain clouds.

The sight of the Black Sea made the passengers happy. They were all Turks, clearly glad to be away from Ankara, which was overbuilt and modern, set in the dry hills; this was the drizzly shore of an inland sea.

'Karadeniz,' the old man next to me said when he woke and saw the water. I had once sailed on a Turkish ship called the *Akdeniz* – meaning the White Sea, which is what the Turks call the Mediterranean – so I understood this as the Black Sea. He marvelled, smiled, elbowed his wife in the ribs. Like the other men on the bus he wore a dark suit, a white shirt and a tie. In the course of the twelve-hour ride through the night, these men loosened their ties a little.

Judging from what I'd seen from Istanbul to Ankara to Trabzon, a building boom had overwhelmed Turkey, new houses everywhere, and the newer ones were dreadful, lopsided, misshapen, thrown together, and looked dangerously combustible; they were famous for falling down at the slightest earth tremor, of which seismic-prone Turkey had plenty.

But once I stowed my bag in a bus station locker and hiked to the foot of Trabzon's hill and up the steep winding streets to the middle of town, I changed my mind about the ugly houses. Trabzon was a pleasant place, even in the rain: a compact town centre, the usual Turkish shops selling food and clothes and sweets, but also something I hadn't expected: *banyos*, bathhouses. And I had the sense they were traditional baths and that this was not a euphemism for knocking shops.

I saw a man being luxuriously shaved in a barbershop, so I went in and, using grunts and signs, asked for the same. The whole process, with a haircut, took forty-five minutes; after the long bus ride I was restored.

Near the barbershop was a hotel that was undistinguished but clean. The room rate was $350 a night – who would pay that in Trabzon? Instead of checking in, I used the breakfast buffet in the restaurant, telling the clerk that I would pay for it. He said okay, so I idled over breakfast and tried to make a plan for my onward journey. I had seriously pondered my options: after weeks of travel I was still facing terrible weather, wet and cold, the north wind blowing off the Black Sea from Odessa; the recent murder of the Italian priest, for being Christian, was not encouraging; and the main point of interest in Trabzon was a mosque.

When I finished, deciding that I would head east, out of town, and took out my money, the clerk waved me away. I repeated that I was not a guest of the hotel. The clerk just smiled and said, 'No problem,' indicated that it was a slow day in Trabzon, and added, '*Beer-shay de-eel*' – You're welcome.

I walked back to where I had stowed my bag and on the way saw a sign advertising buses to the Georgia border and beyond: Tbilisi, Yerevan, Baku and other distant places. I went into a bus agency, and the door chime went *ding-dong*. Some women in black gowns were watching the Iraqi war news – scenes of American tanks – on a black-and-white television. They were eating pink popcorn out of a bag.

'Ticket, please?'

But the man at the desk scarcely looked up from his newspaper.

'Bus is fool.'

'Just one seat,' I said.

'Is fool.'

'Excuse me, *effendi*.' This politeness seized his attention. 'I have serious business in Teeflees,' I said, using the Turkish pronunciation. 'Very serious.'

He looked up at me and licked his thumb, manipulated a printed pad, and clicking his pen wrote me a ticket.

'Leaving at thirteen o'clock,' he said and went back to his newspaper. The shrouded women had kept their attention on the war news.

But in the event, the bus left at noon – good thing I was early, drinking a coffee next door to the stop. The bus was more than full: many people were sitting on the floor, on each other's laps, or strap-hanging. I could see no space at all. The driver poked my arm and said gruffly, 'You sit here,' and indicated a cushion next to him, on the step. 'In Hopa, many seats.' Hopa was near the Turkish border; the border post was a place called Sarp.

So I sat on a cushion on the floor of this crowded, beat-up bus, pleased with myself for being an older man, thus invisible, ghostly, grubbier than most of the bus passengers, some of them Turks going to Hopa, and the rest Georgians on their way over the border to Batumi. The Georgians were the ones with big black plastic sacks, bulging with Turkish goods that were apparently unobtainable in Georgia – children's clothes, toys, toasters, telephones, microwave ovens and boxes of biscuits. All this luggage boded ill for the upcoming customs inspection.

Only a hundred-odd miles to Hopa, but the entire coast road was being repaved, and we went so slowly and stopped so often the trip took five hours. I told myself that I was not in any hurry, and I smiled when I remembered saying to the ticket seller, *I have serious business in Teeflees*, because I had no business at all. This was one of those times when I was reminded again of how travel was a bumming evasion, a cheap excuse for intruding upon other people's privacy.

We passed some friendly looking towns, and stopped at many to pick up passengers. At Rize and Pazar we stopped for food. The hills beyond Rize were dark with tea bushes, and the Black Sea was motionless, as though we were at the shore of a glorified lake – no current, no tide, no chop or waves, more famous now for allowing prostitutes to be ferried across the water from Odessa to the Turkish shore.

We went through Hopa, where a two-mile line of trucks was parked, awaiting permission to go further. I got off the bus at the border, Sarp. The driver told me that we would all go through customs and immigration and then meet again and reboard the bus on the Georgian side. I thought: Not me, *effendi*.

One of the pleasures of such a journey is walking across a border, strolling from one country to another, especially countries where there is no common language. Turkish is incomprehensible to Georgians, and Georgians boast that there is no language on earth that resembles Georgian; it is not in the Indo-European family but rather the Kartvelian, or South Caucasian, one. Georgians triumphantly point out that their language is unique, since the word for mother is *deda* and the word for father is *mama*.

I paid $20 for a Georgian visa, got my passport stamped, was saluted by the soldier on duty, and walked into Georgia, where I learned there was a two-hour time difference from the other side of the border. It would be an hour or more before the bus passengers cleared their toasters and microwaves through Turkish customs. So when a Georgian taxi driver began pestering me, I listened – more than that, I offered him a cup of coffee.

His name was Sergei. We sat in a border café, out of the rain. He said business was not good. I looked for something to eat, but there were only stale buns and boxes of crackers. As soon as you leave Turkey, by whatever border crossing, the quality of the food plunges.

'You go Batumi?'

I said, 'Maybe. How much?'

He mentioned a sum of money in Georgian lari. I translated this into dollars and said, 'Ten dollars. Batumi.'

This delighted him. And Batumi was thirty miles away, so I was happy too.

'You get bus, Batumi to Tbilisi.'

'How long does it take?' I asked.

'Six o'clock. Seven o'clock.'

He meant six or seven hours. I said, 'Is there a train?'

'Yes, but train take nine o'clock, ten o'clock.'

'Sleeping car – *Schlafwagen*?'

He nodded, yes. So I threw my bag in the back seat of his car, got in the front with him, and off we went, dodging potholes and deep mud puddles. The road was empty. He said that in the summer people flocked here for a Black Sea holiday, but I found this hard to imagine: there were no obvious hotels; the houses were small and dark, as though mossy; the coastal road was in bad shape and, unlike its Turkish counterpart, was not being repaired.

Never mind, I was bouncing towards Batumi in a cold drizzly dusk – into the unknown, a place I'd never been. Its very dreariness and decrepitude were a consolation. I could see from the border, the roadside, Sergei in his old car and the men labouring with pushcarts that this was a benighted place, not expensive, and slightly creepy – wonderful, really, because I was alone and had all the time in the world. No sign of any other tourist or traveller; I had walked across the frontier into this wolfish landscape. And if Sergei was correct in saying that there was a night train to Tbilisi, it would be perfect.

It seemed to me that this was the whole point of travelling – to arrive alone, like a spectre, in a strange country at nightfall, not in the brightly lit capital but by the back door, in the wooded countryside, hundreds of miles from the metropolis, where, typically, people didn't see many strangers and were hospitable and did not instantly think of me as money on two legs. Life was harder but simpler here – I could see it in the rough houses and the crummy roads and the hayricks and the boys herding goats. Arriving in the hinterland with only the vaguest plans was a liberating event. I told myself that it was a solemn occasion for discovery, but I knew better: it was more like an irresponsible and random haunting of another planet.

Batumi was a low coastal town of puddly streets and dimly lit shops and Georgians in heavy clothes hunched over, plodding in the rain. On the outskirts were plump central Asian bungalows, and approaching the centre of town at dusk was like entering a cloudy time warp where it was permanently muddy and old-fashioned. In the 1870s it had been a boom town built on the oil fortunes of the Rothschilds and the Nobels.

'Football,' Sergei said.

We passed a muddy football pitch.

'Sharish.'

We passed a round church with an elaborate spire and a sharp-edged Christian cross on top.

'*Shakmat* club.'

Shakmat is Persian for checkmate: 'king death'. The chess club, a big building and one of the newest in Batumi.

We kept going, and Sergei conveyed to me in broken English that the train station was not in Batumi but further up the coast in a village called Makinjauri, where passengers boarded and tickets could be bought.

This, the last, westernmost stop on the Trans-Caucasian Railroad, was not a station but rather a rural platform under a grove of leafless trees and bright lights. Near it stood a ticket booth, the size and shape of one of those narrow little fairground sheds that offer tickets to the merry-go-round. I bought a first-class berth to Tbilisi for about $15 and felt I had lucked out, for the train was not leaving for hours. I paid off Sergei and enthusiastically tipped him for being helpful, then wandered around, looking for a place to eat.

Babushkas in aprons, bulky skirts, headscarves and thick leggings welcomed me into a cold, lamp-lit one-room restaurant, and one of them, explaining with gestures, made me a Georgian dish – a big round puffy loaf filled with cheese and baked in a pan, then cut into wedges. Peasant food, simple and filling. I drank two soapy-tasting bottles of beer and asked for more detail, which they cheerfully gave me: as we were in Batumi, this was *Adjaruli* cuisine – west Georgian style.

Some factory workers stopped in, and their English was sufficient for them to explain to me that they came here every evening at this time for the stew; so I ordered some of that, too, and like them, ate it with a wheel of bread.

'What country?'

'America.'

'Good country. I want to go!'

A sense of out of this world, I scribbled in my notebook between bites. *Cold, dirty room, old beaky women with raw hands in thick clothes; poor lighting, jumping shadows, a sputtering samovar, people talking in low voices; all weirdly pleasant.* At the ragged edge of Georgia – the ragged edge of Turkey, too – I was happy.

At some point the rain stopped. The darkness turned frigid, the night glistening with frost crystals that were star-like, and overhead, stars were visible above the Black Sea. At Makinjauri Station, on the exposed platform, a hundred or so people waiting for the train were stamping their feet and chafing their hands to keep warm, yawning because it was so late and so cold.

I had a compartment to myself. I bought some bottled water from a stall on the platform. Two blankets and a quilt were piled on my berth, and after punching my ticket the conductor gave me a sealed package: bed sheets with bunnies printed on them.

So I lay down and read the opening pages of Conrad's *The Shadow-Line* and fell asleep as we travelled north along the coast and then headed inland.

It was an old noisy train with clanging wheels, and couplings that banged as we went through the mountains; but it rocked like a cast-iron cradle, and I slept so well on the ten-hour trip I did not awake until we were almost at Tbilisi.

Even on the outskirts of the capital the full moon lit the huts in the hills, giving it all the look of a Gothic landscape, darkness and blunted shadow, and rooftops and hilltops bluey white from the cold moon. As I watched from the window outside my compartment, I nodded to another watcher, a man in a blue suit, plump, a head of white hair, a mobile phone to his ear, and when I smiled he sprang forward and shook my hand. The clamminess of his handshake made me guess that he was a Georgian politician. He acknowledged that he was, of President Mikhail Saakashvili's party.

Tbilisi Station was grim, poorly lit, stinking of ragged squatters, littered with blowing papers, and on a frosty morning in March not a place I wanted to linger. I took a taxi and, choosing a hotel at random, checked in and went for a walk.

In the course of idling there, I found that Georgians do not call their country Georgia. They give it its ancient name, 'Sakartvelo', after its legendary founder. 'Georgia' is from the Persian 'Gorjestan', Land of the Wolf. Armenians call the place 'Vir', another ancient name, a variation of 'Iberia'. But by whatever name, it was a supine and beleaguered country of people narcissistic about their differences.

I thought: if you simply flew into Tbilisi, you'd take this to be a pleasant if elderly-looking city of some lovely buildings and quite a few decaying older ones; of many – perhaps too many – gambling casinos; of boulevards and genteel tenements and ancient churches sited with emphatic plumpness on the rocky splendour of low hills; a presentable city divided by the gull-clawed Kura River. And you would be utterly deceived by this look of prosperity.

Overland from Turkey, through Hopa and Sarp and muddy Batumi, from the frosty platform at Makinjauri and onward, passing the towns and villages of Kutaisi, Khashuri, Kaspi and Gori – Gori, where Iosif Dzhugashvili, Joseph Stalin, was born in 1879, 'a lame, pock-marked, web-toed boy', urchin, street fighter and choirboy at Gori Church School, before going to a seminary in Tbilisi and becoming a gang leader and bank robber – the railway line showed that Georgia is essentially a peasant economy, struggling, backward-looking, Russophobic, mildly discontented, riven by dissent over the breakaway province of Abkhazia, and, in the raw dark days of late winter, proud but hard-pressed.

Many people in Tbilisi mentioned to me how, less than two months before, in one of the coldest winters in memory, the Russians had cut off Georgia's supply of natural gas. Within hours, the heat vanished from all households and factories, and a black frost descended. Other than firewood – and even that was in short supply in the deforested country-side – Georgia had no energy of its own. The country was without power, Tbilisi seized up, the traffic lights went off, businesses shut down, schools and hospitals were in darkness. The Russians claimed that terrorists had blown up the gas pipeline, but President Saakashvili loudly denounced the Russians, accusing them of deliberate malice – after all,

Ukrainians had not long before suffered the same frozen fate when their energy payments to Russia were in arrears.

Politicians in the Georgian cabinet ostentatiously handed out cans of kerosene. Less ostentatiously, trucks dumped loads of firewood on street corners for people to fight over. But the temperature remained below freezing, the river was iced over, the snow was deep, and fresh snowfalls blocked the thoroughfares.

'People were building fires in the streets to keep warm,' a woman told me.

Russophobia in Georgia reached new levels of intensity as the whole country shivered; and at last, after a week of suffering, Tbilisi looking as if doomsday had come – snowbound, frozen, corpse-like, frostbitten – the gas supply returned. But Georgia was reminded of its vulnerability, its poverty, its desperation, its dependence on Russia and its lack of adequate resources.

The weather was still cold and foggy when I arrived, but out of curiosity I decided to stay put for a few days. The hotel I'd found was near the centre of the city; I set off walking. I had arrived on a weekend, when people from Tbilisi and the suburbs hold a collective flea market on the streets near the river and across the bridge – and so I was able to see people parting with light fixtures and lamps, taps, postcards, plastic souvenirs, photographs, brassware, radios, candlesticks, samovars and religious paraphernalia, including crucifixes and paintings. Business was slow; there were many more sellers than buyers. The hawkers were older people, obviously trying to raise money, and it was obvious too that in many cases they were offering heirlooms for sale, literally the family silver – plates, spoons, salt shakers, teapots. The items that interested me were the icons, some of them silver or silver-plated, and after a few days of browsing, I bought a silver icon.

Big central Asian porches of shaped wooden gingerbread and carved screens jutted from some older buildings, and one whole district of traditional houses – and mosques, and a synagogue, too – had been renovated. But walking in a drearier part of the city, I passed a large crowd of people jostling on the pavement, an irregular line of contending humans in ragged clothes trying to squeeze themselves against a narrow door that gave on to David Agmashenebeli Avenue.

A young man appeared from inside the door and held up a square of cardboard with a number on it. I could read it: 471. As though she'd just won at bingo, an old woman, looking pleased, screeched and waved a scrap of paper – her number was 471 – and she pushed herself through the crowd and into the doorway.

This happened two more times while I watched. More numbers were announced – 472, 473 – and the winners admitted inside. The building had an air of elegance, though like many others in this district it had fallen into ruin. But there was no sign on the outside, only the crowd of people out front, each person waiting for his or her number to be called. What exactly was happening?

'Excuse me.' I followed the last people in. They were a small family – father, mother, child. They did not look distressed; they were warmly clothed, and the man had been bantering with the others left standing on the street corner, impatiently jostling.

What seemed to me an old haunted mansion had a lobby like a ballroom, with a high ceiling, leaded windows, some of them fitted with stained glass. Still, it seemed less like a mansion than a Masonic hall. No one challenged me, so I kept walking and looking around – the place was pleasantly warm and smelled of fresh bread. I followed the aroma and found two twenty-year-olds who were English-speakers, Marina and Alex.

'What's happening here?' I asked.

'This is the House of Charity,' Alex said.

Marina stepped back and gestured. She said, 'And this is the man.'

A pale, rather small man with a thin fox-like face and dark close-set eyes swept forward and stared at me, not in hostility but in a sort of querulous nibbling welcome. He wore a vaguely clerical outfit: black frock coat buttoned to his chin, an overcoat draped like a cape over his shoulders. Adding to his mysterious ecclesiasticism were his black boots, an occult-looking insignia on a heavy chain around his neck, and pinned to one lapel a ribbon-like adornment. He was about fifty, strangely confident for such a pale soul, and upright, with the messianic stare you find in people who have a sense of destiny, a belief that they are doing the right thing. In his heavy cape-like coat, his pasted-down hair, and his sallow, somewhat tormented saint's face, I put him down in my notebook in one word, *Dostoyevskian*.

'This – everything you see – was his idea,' Marina said.

'What do you do here?'

Instead of answering my question, Marina translated it for the man in black, and he replied in Georgian, which she translated back into English.

'We feed people,' he said. 'We feed all the people. Usually we feed about three hundred and fifty a day, but today is Open Door Day, so we will be feeding fifteen hundred people.'

'Are all of them poor?' I asked. This was translated.

'We ask no questions. Everyone is welcome. Some of them can afford to buy food, others are starving, but we make no distinction.'

'Is this part of some religion?'

The pale man smiled when he heard this. He had tiny, even teeth in his vulpine, small boy's face. He said triumphantly, 'No message! No religion!'

'So ask him why he does it,' I said to Marina.

She spoke for a while with him, he gave monosyllabic replies, and finally he shrugged and uttered a few sentences in Georgian.

'He says the reasons are too deep to discuss. It could take days to explain why he does this.'

Meanwhile, numbers were being shouted at the front door. Hungry people were hurrying in, smiling sated people were leaving, poking their yellow teeth with toothpicks.

'How about just a hint?' I asked, and Marina pressed him.

He replied, 'In 1989, many men were seeking power and had political ambition.' He meant at the time of the collapse of the Soviet Union. 'Georgia was free. I decided to do something different from that – maybe the opposite of seeking power, something humble and helpful, not political, not religious either. This was what I thought of.'

Now people were pushing past us to get to the dining hall, which had a number of tables big and small, about 150 places. When a person vacated a chair, a number was displayed outside and a hungry person tore in, scuffing in wet boots towards the smell of food.

We stepped back to let the traffic flow. I asked the man his name.

He was Oleg Lazar-Aladashvili, and he called this effort Catharsis. He had run it for the past sixteen years.

'Catharsis, in Greek, means spiritual cleansing through compassion,' he said. ('Spiritual renewal through purgation,' my dictionary also explains.)

'We have another house in Moscow,' he said. 'Our principles are charity, non-violence, and anti-AIDS. We also provide medical services and help to homeless people.'

'To anyone who asks?'

He became specific. He said, 'We provide help not as a gift but as a reward for work.' Everyone who was helped had to pitch in and do something – either assist in one of the programmes or be a caretaker in the building.

Oleg said that the building, this mansion that had confused me, had been the headquarters of the regional committee of the Communist Party of Georgia, but the party no longer mattered. People who'd benefited from Catharsis had helped paint and decorate it, made murals, tapestries and pictures. Wealthy families in Tbilisi had contributed jewellery, paintings, icons and antiques. Pope John Paul II had visited in February 1999 and donated a Bible. The Archbishop of Canterbury had also visited. Their signed pictures were hung in Oleg's office, which had an ecclesiastical atmosphere – heavy furniture, velvet cushions, gold tassels, a maroon carpet, stained-glass windows, leather-bound books, an enormous desk.

I gave Marina a $20 note and said that I would like to have a meal in the dining room.

'It is free,' Oleg said.

'But take the money anyway,' I said.

'Money makes no difference. The food is for everyone. We don't scrutinize the people we feed.'

Perhaps without realizing it, Oleg had paraphrased one of the precepts of the Diamond Sutra: *Buddha teaches that the mind of a Bodhisattva should not accept the appearances of things as a basis when exercising charity.*

'Please,' I said, and put the money in his hand.

'You must have a receipt,' Marina said.

'You can give it to me later.'

'No. The receipt must be given now.'

The special pad had to be found, then a pen, and finally a special stamp – the insignia of Catharsis, which was an upright bar with a diagonal crossbar and some squiggles. This took longer than I expected, and in their fuss to provide a receipt I began to regret my donation, pathetically small though it was. The laborious business to give me a receipt was like satirizing my twenty bucks.

Then they escorted me to the dining hall – one of the three dining rooms. After the religiosity of the office, this scene was almost Chaucerian, something medieval and bawdy about each heavily dressed, red-faced person gobbling at a big tin bowl of soup and a big bowl of bread – a whole round loaf cut into chunks – and a saucer of noodle salad sprinkled with oregano. The clank of spoons, the slurping of soup, the laughter, the yelling, children squawking, bowls being brought in on trays and banged down on the trestle tables: it was a rollicking scene of appetite and good cheer. And there were serving wenches – girls in aprons with mobcaps and billowy blouses, their faces glowing, perspiring from their work of wiping down tables and serving soup.

Isabella Kraft was one of them. She was from Cologne, Germany, from a large family – she had brothers and sisters. She was twenty, slightly built, blonde, very pretty, and looking overworked and earnest, ringlets of dampened hair adhering to her forehead.

'I've been here six months,' she told me. 'I'll be here for a year altogether. I finished school and I heard they needed people.'

All were volunteers, she said. She liked the idea that no questions were asked of the people, that no message was handed over other than the obvious charitable one.

'I do this in my spare time,' Isabella said.

'What do you do the rest of the time?'

'I work with handicapped children,' she said. She had the passionate intensity I had seen in Oleg's eyes, but she smiled, had a sense of humour; she was ardent, humble, unselfish, with no pretensions.

'Isabella! Stop talking and start working!' an old woman screamed.

'That is the supervisor,' Isabella said and laughed. She called back, 'He is from America!'

'Take me to America!' the toothless old woman next to me screamed, shaking her big soup spoon at me in a dripping demand.

Other diners at the long table began teasing and laughing. It was an unimaginably happy room of contented eaters with food-splashed faces, people with a hunk of bread in one hand and a spoon in the other, attacking bowls of thick beany soup.

None of the volunteers had anything to preach; no philosophy was imparted about what they were doing. They simply laboured without question. And because operating costs were low, practically the whole budget was used for food. Oleg later told me that he got money from local companies, Oxfam and various United Nations agencies, but that even without their help he would have continued to run the charity.

For the helpers it was a kind of inspired drudgery to which they brought humanity. Most of them were from other European countries, living frugally and far from home; they were uncomplaining, learning humility, but also in a position to understand the very heart of Georgia. I admired them for following the fundamental tenet of Buddhism, the key text of the Buddhist way, utter selflessness, perhaps without knowing any word of the Diamond Sutra.

Inevitably, a little later, on a nearby street I saw some Georgian youths skidding around corners too fast in their crappy cars and shouting out of the window, playing rap music much too loudly and being stupid.

Now and then you meet someone at a party or at a friend's house and he says, 'I'm from Tbilisi' – or wherever – 'and if you ever visit, you must look me up.'

And you say, 'Absolutely', but the day never comes, for why on earth would you ever go to Tbilisi? And usually the person is merely being polite and doesn't mean it. But Gregory and Nina, whom I had met a few years before in Massachusetts, seemed sincere.

And there I was in Tbilisi, under wintry skies, with time on my hands. And so I made the call.

'Are you going to be here tomorrow?' Nina asked.

'Oh, yes,' I said.

'Then you must come to the ballet.' Nina was a ballerina in the Georgia State Opera Company, and Gregory was her husband. 'It's the première of *Giselle*. Come to the Opera Theatre at seven. Ask for Lizaveta. She will have a ticket for you. We will meet you in the box.'

The Opera Theatre was a notable landmark of Tbilisi. I found it easily on foot. An imposing cheese-coloured nineteenth-century edifice on the main boulevard, Rustaveli Avenue, it was built at a time when Russia – which had annexed Georgia in 1801 – regarded an opera house as essential to the romantic idea of Georgia as one of the more picturesque regions of the Russian empire. Georgians were great agriculturalists, and their vineyards were renowned, but Georgians also danced and sang.

It turned out that Nina was not merely a prima ballerina but also head of the opera company. When I met her in the box, she had recently given birth to a little girl.

Gregory, who was a prosperous investor and also a doting husband and Nina's manager, said, 'But she will dance next year. She will prove that you can have a baby and also be a great ballerina.'

Other people – mostly friends and relations – were already seated.

Introducing me, Nina said, 'This is Paul. He went through Africa alone!'

'Is true?' a woman said.

'By autostop,' Nina said.

'Not really,' I said.

But the woman hadn't heard. She had turned to tell her husband that I had hitchhiked through Africa.

Then *Giselle* began. The title role was performed by a ballerina from the Bolshoi. The male lead, Prince Albrecht, was a local dancer who was only twenty-one. He was cheered when he appeared onstage. I had no idea what I was in for. I knew nothing about ballet, but it seemed to me a melodious way of spending an evening in Tbilisi.

After my rainy journey of bleak hills and foggy valleys and muddy roads, this packed opera house – warm and well fed – was the antithesis of Batumi: pale pretty sprites in tutus, men in tights, some of them spinning, some of them leaping, and an orchestra pit where men in dinner jackets scraped out mellifluous tunes and cascading harmonies.

I was sitting comfortably in a gilt chair, resting on velvet cushions, watching Prince Albrecht (in disguise) fall in love with the peasant girl Giselle. But there was a hitch: he had been betrothed to Bathilda, the Duke's daughter. Giselle also had another and very excitable lover. Lots of prancing and leaping and flinging of arms, and finally identities were revealed, sending Giselle off her head. Just before the prolonged and exquisite death agonies of Giselle, she heard the Wilis – 'the spirits of young girls who died before their wedding day', the programme said – and then she died.

Second act: Giselle was now transformed into one of the Willis. She was reunited with Albrecht and danced with him through the night. In so doing she saved his life, before she vanished at dawn. An angelic chorus line of flitting nymphs, eloquent mime, syrupy music, slender legs, graceful leaps and strange moves, especially Giselle's as she hopped on one toe while propelling herself by kicking her other leg, receiving wild applause and bravos.

This ballet induced such a feeling of well-being in me that I sat smiling tipsily at the big red curtain for quite a while after it fell.

And then I heard, 'This is Paul. He went through Africa by hitchhike!'

'Not exactly,' I said. 'Do you speak English?'

'As a matter of fact, yes,' the woman said. 'I'm British. I'm just visiting.'

She was, she said, a ballet correspondent for a London newspaper, in Tbilisi for the week. She would be writing about this.

Still besotted by the ballet, I asked, 'How do you even begin evaluating something as pleasant as this?'

'The corps de ballet needs work,' she said without hesitating, 'though they're about average for this part of the world, and if they keep working really hard they'll have a chance of being something watchable in about two years.'

So much for my angelic chorus line of flitting nymphs.

'The male lead, I'm afraid, doesn't really have what it takes,' she went on, 'though you can see the chap is trying his best.' She smiled grimly and dismissed him with a wave of her hand. 'That ballerina from the Bolshoi, Anastasia Goryacheva, is talented. She performed well, but she was terribly let down by the orchestra. They were just so plodding. They're all second-rate players, not real symphony musicians. I mean, they hardly seemed to care.'

So much for the mellifluous harmonies I'd heard.

Her criticism was probably accurate, though the audience had been more enthusiastic, had cheered the ballet all the way through, and had applauded numerous curtain calls. As for me, who had happened upon this spectacle and gaped like a dazed dog, I was grateful for the warmth and the music and the sight of the weightless legs of flitting nymphs moving to and fro on tiptoe.

A woman named Marika, who had also been at the ballet, offered to show me around Tbilisi – the parts that had been renovated, the districts that were still dilapidated, the ancient villas, the Soviet offices, the synagogues and mosques. But I found Marika more interesting than any of this real estate.

She was in her mid-thirties and, she said, from a noble family, large landowners, their ancestral home in Ratja. Both her grandfather and great-grandfather had spent time in Soviet prisons, thirteen years in her grandfather's case, for being members of the Georgian aristocracy and therefore counter-revolutionaries. One prison, part of the gulag in Kazakhstan, was a remote work camp near the city of Karaganda. Later, I read that Solzhenitsyn had spent a year in the same camp.

'You're a writer,' Marika said. 'You're lucky to be an American. Our writers were put into a prison in Mordva. It was a terrible place but had a nice name – White Swan Prison.'

In 2001, Marika worked for a while at the Ministry of Foreign Affairs in Tbilisi, earning 30 lari a month.

'That's not much, is it?'

'Fifteen dollars,' she said. She added that after various political upheavals, the most recent being the so-called Rose Revolution of 2004, which had been aimed at rooting out crooked politicians, government salaries had improved and she began earning $160 a month. She was now working for an insurance company, earning $200, and just getting by.

Gregory had told me that business was good, tourism was up, and the service industries – he did not specify which ones – were busy. Gregory also owned a vineyard, but said that though it was good-sized, wine-making was merely a hobby.

'Then what business are you in?' I asked.

'I'm managing Nina. But just for fun. I live on revenues and investments.'

So he was doing fine and was well connected. Marika had another story. She said that business was abysmal. Food was still cheap but salaries were pathetic. Most people her age spoke of emigrating to the United States. In this connection, she said that George Bush had come the previous year – in May 2005 – and had received a rapturous welcome. This had something to do with Georgia needing a powerful friend, for Georgia was, geographically speaking, in a bad neighbourhood, bordered by unfriendly Russians, the breakaway region of Abkhazia, the bandit-haunted valleys of Dagestan and the dangerous ruin of Chechnya, with its Islamic guerrillas and frequent bombings.

'What about emigrating to Turkey?'

'No,' she said, though some people would settle for a job in Europe.

We strolled, talking about the bleak, not to say obscure, future, and soon came to a restaurant.

'Have you had *khajapuri*?' she said.

'Yes. In Batumi.'

'Then you have to try Georgia's other national dish, *khingali*.'

This turned out to be a big bowl of broth with dumplings, some of them filled with meat, called *khafsuru*, others with greens, called *kalakuri*.

The restaurant was fairly crowded, mostly with families at the wooden tables, everyone eating dumplings with their fingers, Georgian style.

Marika wasn't complaining, but it seemed to me depressing that a university graduate with perhaps fifteen years' experience working in a big city should be paid so little.

On my previous trip I met many poorly paid workers, but they lived in an era of sealed borders and expensive travel. They expected no better and had no means to leave wherever they happened to be. But in these days of cheap travel, the world had shrunk, and anyone with access to a computer – which seemed to be most city people – knew that life was better elsewhere. The places I had known, of settled people in villages and towns, of working urbanites in big cities, with their civic pride and cultural pieties, these homebodies whose horizon was their national frontier, had all (it seemed to me) become soured and discontented. The world of settled people had evolved into a world of people wishing to emigrate. There was hardly any distinction, and not much romance, in being a traveller. It was now a world of travellers, or people dreaming of a life elsewhere – far away. *Please, take me to America!*

Some cultural pieties still persisted. Gregory and Nina invited me the next day to the christening of their daughter, Elena. The ceremony was performed in the district of Metekhi, in an old Eastern Orthodox church that had been built and rebuilt from ancient times. The church was dedicated to the Virgin Mary. More out of national pride than religious sanctimony, Georgians boast that Christianity was brought by Saint Nino from Greece in the fourth century (incidentally, at about the time it was spreading through Ethiopia). Saint Nino's image was everywhere.

Little Elena, just over a month old, pink-faced and beatific, was swaddled in a heavy blanket and wore a bobble hat. A very short priest chanted and made repeated signs of the cross. He had a bushy beard, an enormous nose and a hat shaped like a tea cosy, which gave him the look of a garden gnome costumed as a Smurf. Tapers were lit, candles were waved, icons were kissed, a profusion of genuflection and energetic idolatry. There were no pews – no seats at all.

We stood and watched the dwarfish bearded priest pressing his forehead against a saint's picture and murmuring prayers. The baby was being bounced: no sign of holy water.

Mobile phones also rang, men were chatting into them and making calls, other people were talking among themselves, laughing, greeting newcomers, inserting lari into the poorboxes, and some of them even praying.

Strangely, Gregory and Nina were excluded from the ceremony and stood some distance away, but watched eagerly as the godparents coddled Elena. I was excluded as well, but when I took too great an interest in a very shiny candle-lit icon, a man in a black smock hissed at me and indicated with angry gestures that I was standing too close.

'Up yours,' I said, smiling, and returned to the christening, which had become dramatic.

The baby was stripped naked, her bobble hat removed. And then I realized that the church was cold. Her skinny arms and legs began to thrash, and whimperings issued from her little red body.

The gnome-like priest adjusted his odd ecclesiastical Smurf hat and beckoned the godparents to the baptismal font, which stood like a large marble sink at the side of the church. He took the baby and immersed her in the cold water – totally, head to foot, as though he were rinsing a chicken. As he pronounced her new name and recited the baptismal formula ('and I renounce the devil and all his pomps'), baby Elena began to howl. She went on howling for quite a while, but who could blame her?

Then, as Elena was turning purple, the future ballerina was wrapped in her warm blanket, people kissed and shook hands, the mother and father received the priest's blessing, and sums of money were bestowed.

Aware of the superstitious sentimentality in such a rite, a number of opportunistic old women seized the chance to line the path that led down the hill from the church, and there they crouched, their confident hands extended for alms.

Some customs don't change. That baptismal ceremony had been performed in that very church since the early seventh century – indeed, the Byzantine era, before Arab caliphs took over in the year 654 and made Tbilisi an emirate.

When it came time for me to leave Tbilisi for Baku, I was offered a lift by one of Gregory's friends.

'It's no problem. I can take you to the airport,' he said.

'Railway station,' I said.

He scowled at me. 'You're going on the train?'

'That's right.'

'On the train?' he repeated hoarsely, in disbelief. 'Why don't you take the plane?'

Baku was an overnight trip from Tbilisi, not much more than the distance from Boston to Washington, but he had never taken the train. He had never been to Baku, in neighbouring Azerbaijan, though he had lived for several years in Moscow and had spent some months working in Germany.

It occurred to me that, though he was thirty-four and had grown up in Tbilisi, he had perhaps never been to the Tbilisi railway station – or not recently, because he seemed shocked at how haunted and dirty it was. He made a face, shrugged at me in helpless pity, wished me luck, and hurried away when he saw the elderly train standing at the platform.

6. Night Train to Baku
The Trans-Caucasian

A railway train in an old country seems to go backwards into the dark, simple and primitive hinterland that is the remote past. But that is an illusion. The train only appears to be a cruel artefact, as it crawls out of the huge neglected station crowded with passengers and rolls like a loud antique, looming rust-stained and sticky with grease, its bunks and seats obscured by dirty windows, the whole thing shaking from the whirrs of its clacking engine, spattering black oil on to the tracks as it makes its way on what seems a route into history. The train offers the truth of a place: horrible or savage as it may seem, the hinterland is also the present.

I always felt lucky on a train, as on this one. So many other travellers are hurrying to the airport, to be interrogated and frisked and their luggage searched for bombs. They would be better off on a national railway, probably the best way of getting a glimpse of how people actually live – the back gardens, the barns, the hovels, the side roads and slums, the telling facts of village life, the misery that aeroplanes fly over. Yes, the train takes more time, and many trains are dirty, but so what? Delay and dirt are the realities of the most rewarding travel.

Why don't you take the plane? The Georgian had asked me.

Because – I thought when I was in the corner seat of my railway compartment – aeroplanes are a distortion of time and space. And you get frisked.

Like a Soviet relic, complete with dented samovars in the vestibule and a very grumpy *provodnik*, a conductor in a stained uniform jacket, the Azerbaijani train was like something that had rattled out of bygone era. Even the platform at Tbilisi Station looked like a tableau from the distant past – old women squatting near big sacks of oranges and piled bags of dried fruit – from where? Azerbaijan, perhaps. Ragged children, old men in heavy boots sleeping against the sacks, young girls in long skirts holding babies. It was an unromantic view of peasantry, *Giselle* with scruffy costumes and no music. Many people I met in Georgia spoke of the modernity and promise of the country, even its alleged prosperity – 'And we can fly to Paris in a few hours.' But what I saw at Tbilisi Station could have been a scene from some dismal period in tsarist times. I felt it was a kind of luck for me to witness this.

It so happened that the railway tracks followed one of the roads to Tbilisi Airport. I could see a colourful hoarding on the widest thorough-fare that read (in English) *President George W. Bush Street*, a sign the visiting president could have seen, and read, on his visit to Georgia the previous year. With a vocal Muslim country on every border, Georgia was a natural ally of Bush's so-called war on terror, though I did not meet any Georgian who agreed with American policy, except in a shortsighted and self-interested way.

The outskirts of Tbilisi were dilapidated: tall dreary tenements on narrow potholed lanes, and beyond them ramshackle houses, small archaic-looking compounds – interconnected huts with courtyards, animal pens, stockyards. Peasant huts dominated – Asiatic jerry-building, a world apart from Tbilisi's casinos and city slickers and ballet and the velvety ritual of the christening.

After a while, the grumpy conductor in his soup-stained jacket and dented cap shoved open my compartment door.

'Ticket?' I asked.

'*Nyet, nyet,*' he said and pushed past me. He insisted on making my bed, and then – rubbing his fingers together in the money gesture – demanded 10 lari, about $5. This seemed steep, but when a big ugly man wearing a uniform in a foreign country asks for a small, specific sum, I usually hand it over.

The long-distance bus was the more popular way of going from Tbilisi to Baku. Not that many people took it: Georgia was westward-looking and Azerbaijan was to the east, at the edge of central Asia. But the bus was slower because the roads were so bad, and of course there were roadblocks, manned by soldiers. The train just rolled on, but the train was a revelation, the crummiest I'd been on so far. Nothing worked, neither the lights nor the locks. It was very grubby; it was an express yet it made lots of stops, the stations growing creepier and more ruinous.

Big shadowy Soviet-era apartment blocks stood in scrubby fields in the middle of nowhere. Compared to them, the huts and cottages further on were a relief for having a human scale. Old people plodded along dirt roads, like trolls vanishing into the growing dusk, which seemed to rise from the ground like dense fog. This twilight partially obscured Rustavi, a down-at-heel industrial city of steel mills and iron-works that had become antiquated. All this time we were following the winding course of the Kura River, which flowed through Azerbaijan and emptied into the Caspian Sea.

In the darkness of my compartment, rattling across eastern Georgia, I was thinking how my routines of travel were totally different from the routines of my writing life. The predictable regularity of humdrum domesticity is perfect for writing: monotony is the writer's friend. People said to me, 'You're always away!' But it wasn't true. I loved being home, waking in my own bed beside my wife, watching the news on TV, spending half the day writing, and then cooking, reading, swimming, riding my bike, seeing friends. Home is bliss.

This – the closed compartment on the old train to Azerbaijan – was something else. Travel means living among strangers, their characteristic stinks and sour perfumes, eating their food, listening to their dramas, enduring their opinions, often with no language in common, being always on the move towards an uncertain destination, creating an itinerary that is continually shifting, sleeping alone, inventing the trip, cobbling together a set of habits in order to stay sane and rational, finding ways to fill the day and be enlightened, avoiding danger, keeping out of trouble, and, immersed in the autobiographical, for my journal, writing everything down in order to remember, reflecting on where I am and what I'm doing.

Still being jogged in the dark compartment, I recalled the woman – where had I seen her? maybe Ankara? – who said, 'I want to live your life.'

And I had thought: Really! My nagged and scolded childhood, my undistinguished school career as a punk, no good at games, bewildered in college, terminated early from the Peace Corps, disgraced in Singapore when my contract wasn't renewed, hard up in London, refused a credit card by American Express at the age of thirty-two because I had no visible credit, divorced – oh, sorry, you mean all the books and the fun of travel!

A knock at the door: two soldiers with rifles slung at me. 'Gid owp.'

So I was interrupted in my reverie by gun-toting soldiers at the Georgia border, a gritty settlement called Jandari. They went through the motions of a passport check, perfunctory and simple; but the train was jammed full of people, and it was two hours before we started again.

The next stop came fifteen minutes later – the Azerbaijan border at Beakykok, with many more soldiers and an imposing railway station. The soldiers tramped through the train, scrutinizing passports. I was apprehensive because my visa specified 'Entry point – Baku'. I was more than 300 miles from there, but this didn't seem to matter to the soldier who licked his thumb and flicked through my passport. He took no interest in my bag or its contents, but he admired my shortwave radio, tuned to the BBC. *Fears of a civil war in Iraq are being expressed by officials at the highest levels*, a woman was saying on the news.

After midnight we were rolling again. I woke in the darkness, urgently, to use the lavatory but could not budge my door. It seemed I was locked in. The compartment was very hot and the train was moving fast, throwing me back and forth. It was too dark for me to see whether the lock was jammed. For five or ten minutes I struggled with the door in a cramped and growing panic – something I seldom feel. The light didn't work, but I dug out my BlackBerry and switched it on. No reception, but it proved a helpful flashlight illuminating my problem. At last, braced against the berth and kicking at the door, I managed to open it. The corridor was thick with Azerbaijanis gaping out of the window at shadowy Tovuz, in the western province, and some of them were staring at me, presumably because they'd heard me kicking the door, or maybe it was my odd-shaped flashlight. The toilet was unspeakable.

At dawn, nine hours past the border, I saw great flat plains with muddy patches, looking overgrazed by the flocks of nibbling sheep – hundreds of them, a clear indication of mutton stews and shish kebabs further down the line. The whole of the foreground was cropped flat, and in the distance were bare blue mountains.

On this great Gromboolian plain was a village of steep-roofed bungalows. Some of them had a graceful roofline, the curvature with a hint of Asia in the pitch. The landscape looked unfinished, like an Edward Lear watercolour – no trees, no people, the usual sheep, a few sketched-in paths, and I was reminded that I had not seen a tourist or a green leaf or any sunshine since leaving Paris.

Crossing the middle of this plain was a pipeline, like a snake or an above-ground sewer pipe. It was of course oil, the basis of Azerbaijan's wealth. In front of and behind the oil pipeline were more houses with those curved roofs, and muddy roads, and from the way the old women were dressed, in smocks and high boots, the way the shepherds stood like sentinels in the fields, I realized that I was in a different place altogether, not just the whiff of Asia in the appearance of things but a part of Asia I had never seen before, the on-ramp to the Silk Road.

In all this antiquity, an enormous floodlit oil depot gleamed on the plain, with flames whipping from tall chimneys, like a city of steel and fire.

Weather-beaten one-storey settlements gave on to more solid ones of two and three storeys, and towards noon a metropolis loomed in the distance, the city of Baku, the whole place floating on oil. After the bleak plains, the huddled settlements, the muddy villages and the muddier shepherds – the boom town. Baku was sited on a wide bay of the Caspian Sea, at the tip of a hawk-nosed peninsula, and believed by many of its inhabitants to be the dividing line between Europe and Asia. This belief was dramatized in the great Azerbaijani novel *Ali and Nino*, in which I'd first read the name Baku, a book so persuasive in its detail and mysterious in its origins it made me want to go there. By 'mysterious in its origins' I mean that its author, a Muslim named Kurban Said, was a man who had also used the Turkish name Essad Bey, and had been born a Jew in Baku, named Lev Nussimbaum.

No tourists stood in the train corridor gazing at the well-built suburbs of the capital, the look of prosperity increasing as we got nearer the station. All the passengers were Azeris – we'd picked them up at Ganca and Yevlax and Ucar and Kurdemir, and they seemed dazzled by the big city.

Baku doesn't need tourists. It is a wealthy place. The economy had grown 25 per cent the previous year, 2005, and was doing better this year – the fastest-growing economy in the world, exclusively from oil revenues. At the turn of the twentieth century, Azerbaijani oil was gushing from onshore wells, but now it is found mainly offshore, in the Caspian Sea, so that deep-water oil-rig specialists had to be brought in from Britain and the United States. These foreign oil workers swarm the bars, fill the hotels, and get into drunken brawls – exactly as I had seen in Iran in the early seventies, during its oil boom, which had produced xenophobia, notions of jihad and the Ayatollah Khomeini.

'Azerbaijan is a police state,' a Western diplomat said to me not long after I arrived. 'TV is controlled. Print media is somewhat free, but an opposition editor was gunned down last year.'

We were strolling through a plaza where some people were playing music. The spectators were surrounded by heavily armed police. The diplomat said, 'Wherever there's more than ten Azeris gathered you find a big police presence. This festival brings out the heavies.'

Two of the most appalling words a newly arriving traveller can hear are 'national holiday'. They send my heart into my boots. My train had stopped in Baku on the first day of spring, and this vernal equinox was celebrated by a festival called Novruz Bayram. *Novruz* – Farsi for 'new day'. Everything was closed, every shop shut, every market empty, the whole city, its harbour, its high road and back alleys; and I, who never planned ahead, had trouble finding a hotel room because all of Azerbaijan was enjoying a three-day holiday of general idleness and government-sanctioned frivolity. Nothing happened during the long festival of Novruz Bayram.

It is sometimes falsely stated that militant Islam has destroyed or displaced all the ancient pieties and rituals in the countries where it took hold, outlawing even the memory of these pieties. But Novruz Bayram was proof that some old rituals persisted, in spite of being heresies.

Rooted in Zoroastrianism, a creed much older than Islam and more than 1,000 years older than Christianity, Novruz Bayram is a festival of renewal, a time for buying new clothes, dusting the furniture, scrubbing the floors, planting flowers, and being happy for the onset of warmer and longer days, overcoming the chill and darkness of winter.

The prophet Zarathustra, who gave his name to Zoroastrianism, flourished and was persecuted perhaps 3,500 years ago in what is now Iran and Afghanistan. So Novruz Bayram is one of the oldest holidays on earth, and it has always had celebrants. Zarathustra preached monotheism, advocated the equality of women, scoffed at the notion of priests (because they were middlemen, easily corruptible), railed against animal sacrifice, evangelism and miracle-working. He denounced using the name of God to barter for power. He extolled the virtues of light and especially of fire. Novruz Bayram is a festival of springtime and sunshine.

The humane aspects of Zoroastrianism probably accounted for its diminution as a faith, if not its failure. A religion needs harshness and humbug to succeed, and all Zarathustra taught was understanding the earthly elements, the turn of the year, the one God. And three simple rules to live by: good thoughts, good words, good deeds. Also a belief in the purifying nature of fire, which was central to the faith and a symbol of the Almighty.

'The Persian word for fire is *azer*,' Tom Reiss wrote in *The Orientalist*, a book about Kurban Said, 'and since ancient times Azerbaijan's abundance of oil and natural gas, which led whole hillsides to naturally explode into flame, made it the center of Zoroastrianism.'

That was a few thousand years ago. Now only about 124,000 Zoroastrians remain – most of them in India, notably Mumbai, where they're known as Parsis. They are a dying breed, the last gasp of an ancient belief system. Novruz Bayram is not celebrated throughout central Asia – indeed, it is condemned in some Muslim countries as pagan – but vigorous celebrations in Azerbaijan and Turkmenistan make it one of the highlights of the year. Its old origins have been forgotten. It is an excuse to stop working, a respite from political strife, a few days of good feeling. I could see Azeris wearing their new clothes and going for promenades and eating the food associated with the festival, especially malt (*samani*) and eggs, because they represented fertility.

Most restaurants were open and, along with the malt and eggs, were serving other Azeri food: mutton pies, mutton wrapped in spinach, mutton kebabs, mutton balls, potato cakes, noodles and big stodgy desserts. Although businesses were shut, there was more street life, more vitality in the city because of the festival. Groups of musicians played to crowds of people in plazas and on the Caspian seafront – and at each gathering there was a large police presence.

In bars and cafés, people – usually young women, usually presentable, sometimes flirtatious – asked, 'What is your company?' because an American my age in Baku was probably in the oil business. Why else would I be in Baku?

'Just passing through,' I would say. 'To Turkmenistan.'

'They have gas.'

Baku got friskier at night, because the oilmen were typically roisterers, and I was assured that after midnight the roistering turned to debauchery, but I was asleep by that time.

Here on the shore of the Caspian Sea I wanted to find a ferry to take me to Turkmenbashi (formerly Krasnovodsk), on the western edge of Turkmenistan. From there by train via (so my map said) Nebitdag, Gumdag, and Gyzylarbat to Ashgabat, the capital, reputed to be one of the oddest places on earth because of the demented predilections of the current dictator, Saparmyrat Niyazov, who styled himself Turkmenbashi and renamed the port town after himself. I was eager to visit his country and ride the train through its deserts, eastward and into Uzbekistan.

But first I had to find a ferry. Because of the holiday, the ferry port was closed. The travel agencies were shut. No one in Baku had any information about the ferry, and when I went to the port and found a dockworker, he said the ferry had no schedule.

'When it's full, the ferry leaves for Krasnovodsk,' he said in Azeri, and this was translated by an English-speaking passerby, whose name was Ahmat.

'So I have to wait until it's full?'

'Yes. And maybe a long wait!'

'Why is that?'

'No one wants to go to Krasnovodsk.'

I said, 'I want to go.'

He muttered something and walked away.

'What did he say?'

'"Must be something wrong with you." He's joking.' Ahmat peered at me. 'You are from?'

'America.'

This fiercely moustached man, who was a civil servant on a holiday stroll, said he was well disposed towards Americans. He was aggrieved about the Armenians, who in the 1990s had captured the Azeri province of Nagorno-Karabakh, killing 20,000 Azeris and displacing a million more. The province is home to 100,000 or so ethnic Armenians. The UN Security Council had demanded the Armenian withdrawal in 1993, but the secessionists refused to comply. They were supported by many American politicians, whose efforts were greased by the Armenian lobby in the United States, which, like the Greek lobby, is small but wealthy and well organized. More than a hundred congressmen belong to the Armenian caucus. Until recently we had no embassy in Baku, and these days our relations with the country are poor. This is a pity, and shortsighted, since Armenia has carpets but Azerbaijan has oil.

Still, Ahmat said he felt friendly towards the United States and knew some American and English oil workers. Armenia was a problem, and so was Iran, he said.

From where we stood in Baku, the Iranian border was only about one hundred miles to the southwest. Ahmat said the Iranians were, in their way, a bigger problem than the Armenians, who didn't have much of an army. Culturally, Azerbaijan had little in common with Iran – much more with Turkey. Turkish and Azeri are almost the same language, and there was a move afoot to build a pipeline from Baku to Turkey, via Georgia. This would bypass Armenia and Iran.

In my quest to find a ferry, I met a voluble Azeri named Rashad, a man of about thirty, who said he would try to get me the ferry schedule.

'I like Bush!' he said when I told him where I was from. He began to laugh defiantly. 'I don't care about Iraq. Maybe it's good for those Iraqis,' he said, meaning the war. 'Maybe Bush gave them a chance. We have some soldiers there.'

I learned later that about 150 Azeri soldiers were stationed in Iraq, protecting a strategic dam.

'It's turning into a civil war,' I said.

'Because they're Shiites and Sunnis. But Bush! What I like is his talk about Iran – maybe a war!'

The American president had made ambiguous threats against Iran for developing a nuclear capability, although Pakistan, Israel, India and Russia – to choose a few neighbours at random – had the bomb.

'I want him to invade and destroy them,' Rashad said. 'Get rid of Ahmadinejad [the president of Iran] and make a lot of trouble.'

'You want America to do that?'

'We'll help. It's good for Azerbaijan. It's good for me. We will join NATO!'

He was smiling and punching the air.

'So Iran is your enemy.'

'Armenia is worse. Nagorno-Karabakh is the problem. They make Azeris into refugees – and it's our country. In football, Armenia is our enemy. In life, too.'

I had come to Azerbaijan because I couldn't get a visa to go by train from Turkey to Iran, as I had done before. But although it had been forced on me, this northerly detour was welcome because it allowed me to visit the setting of *Ali and Nino*. When I mentioned this to an American I met in Baku, he said, 'You have to meet Fuad Akhundov. He's done a study of all the places in Baku mentioned in the novel.'

The topography of literature, the fact in fiction, is one of my pleasures – I mean, where the living road enters the pages of a book, and you are able to stroll along both the real and the imagined road. A walking tour called something like 'Literary Landmarks' is not everyone's idea of fun, but it is mine, for the way it shows how imagination and landscape combine to become art: the Dublin pubs and streets mentioned in *Ulysses*, the railway in *Anna Karenina*, the towns on the Mississippi that are important in *Huckleberry Finn*, the marsh in *Great Expectations*, the Cairo streets that crisscross *Palace Walk*, the London of *The Secret Agent*, the Congo of *Heart of Darkness*, the Paris of *Tropic of Capricorn*, the Chicago of *Augie March* and – as I rehearsed earlier – Pamuk's cradle place of Istanbul.

So I was happy to meet Fuad Akhundov at the appointed spot, the main door of the Baku Philharmonic Society, built around 1910 by an Armenian architect to house the City Club, and mentioned in *Ali and Nino* as a casino. Because of Azeri wealth and Bakuvian pride, buildings like this one had been preserved and meticulously renovated over the past ten years.

'I am Bakuvian, born and bred. This is my city! Like Ali and Nino!'

Fuad wore, for effect, a red fez with a swinging gold tassel. He was tall, demonstrative, passionate and funny, given to the sudden oration, the startling declaration, the recitation of a rhyming poem, usually one of his own, often in archaic English. Under one arm he carried a plump picture album with an enormous archive of old photos of Baku that he'd found around the city. He was thirty-eight, and his day job was as a senior inspector for Interpol's National Central Bureau in Azerbaijan – good qualifications for a man in search of the truth behind the novel. He had also guided Tom Reiss in his pursuit of the real Lev Nussimbaum. As for Interpol business, smuggling was the problem – drugs, money, people. Fuad Akhundov was effusively talkative, and like most talkers, he rarely listened.

How talkative a non-listener was he? Well, the edition of *Ali and Nino* that he carried – a book he'd become obsessed by because it had explained his city, his culture, his past, his own nature; a book that he had read and underlined, with page markers and exclamation points – this book he had in his hand contained an appreciative essay by me, which I'd written four or five years earlier. I thought it would interest him that I was the same man as the one whose name was printed with Kurban Said's on the book: *With a new afterword by Paul Theroux*.

'That's me,' I said, touching my name.

'I want to show you something,' he said, deaf to my remark, whipping the book away and stabbing his finger at a dog-eared page.

He began to read: '"It was a big dusty garden with spare sad-looking trees and asphalt paths. On the right was the old fortress wall. In the center stood the City Club."' Fuad stood taller, waved his arms, became a manic weathervane, swinging his body around to point in four directions: 'The garden, there! The trees! The fortress wall! The City Club before us!'

I did not mention my name again. I hardly spoke, because Fuad was in full cry.

'Baku is not a melting pot – it never was,' he said. 'But we lived together. There was no Jewish ghetto, as in some places. The Jews lived beyond the Pale of Settlement, about five per cent of the population. They tended to be renters, not owners of real estate. Azeris owned the houses. So after the Soviets took over, the Jews moved on.'

I said, 'Nussimbaum was Jewish, but there are no Jews in the book.'

'Because it's a love story between East and West! Ali and Nino. Jews were lawyers and doctors. They occupied a totally different niche in Baku, not covered in this book. But we still have some Jews – in the town of Quba. Now look at this wall.'

We had walked downhill from the white building that had been the City Club and through the garden to get a better look at the fortress-like wall that divided the new city, where we stood, from the old city, West from East, Ali from Nino. Fuad said that it had been built in the twelfth century by Manuchehr II.

'Georgians always looked down on us,' Fuad was saying as we walked further into the garden. 'But we're closer because of shared problems.'

'What about the Armenians?'

'Great friendship, great hostility with Armenians,' he said. 'But I believe there are no permanent enemies. Armenians became hostages of the past, and so they deprived themselves of the future. We're overwhelmed by emotions! Armenians don't make any distinctions between Turks and Azeris. Hey, it's all about 1915. When I was at Harvard – visiting scholar, wonderful experience – I met Armenians from Yerevan and had no problems. But Armenians from Watertown were very belligerent.' Watertown, a streetcar suburb of Boston, was an Armenian enclave.

He hurried ahead, trotting past a low hedge to the centrepiece of a wintry garden of dusty ilex.

'Look at this sculpture.' As he approached a large, mottled sculpted head, Fuad's mobile phone began to ring. The ringing did not deter him from telling me that it was the head of the esteemed Azeri poet Vahid – 'real name Iskanderov, 1899–1965'. As he answered the phone, talking rapidly in Russian, he turned aside to translate the poem chiselled on the plinth from Azeri into English, ' "By fate's unfairness –!" ' and went on muttering in Russian.

Historically, Baku was full of proximities: mosque hard by church, Muslim adjacent to Christian, East near West, old next to new – as the book says, the old town in the new, like 'a kernel in a nut'. This persists into the present. The two schools mentioned in the novel still exist as schools, though no longer parochial ones. We walked up to the main road, Nikolayaskaya Street, towards the schools: Nino's, the Girls' Lyceum of the Holy Queen Tamar, actually St Nina's School; and Ali's school across the street, which was closed for the Novruz holiday. Nearby was the city hall and mayor's office, another seven-storey pile of ornate stone, built around 1900.

'This city was built by money, greed, and oil,' Fuad said. 'In 1901, half of the world's oil came from Azerbaijan. Look at this picture.' He flourished a page from the bulging album he carried. 'The first oil tanker in the world, the *Zoroaster*. Built by Alfred Nobel in 1880 – loaded in Baku, offloaded in Astrakhan.'

Walking along the city wall that divided Europe from Asia, the new city from the old – the old one twenty-two hectares, the same size it had always been – I was thinking of Fuad's enthusiasm for his city, his national pride, his love for a novel that he said meant everything to him. 'There is no other book in Azeri like *Ali and Nino*.' He was waving it. 'Not just because – yes! – it tells how Chaliapin visits Baku to sing, and Chaliapin really did come to Baku. But look at this mansion.'

We were in Sabir Square, beside the Muslim Charitable Society, a villa modelled after a Venetian mansion. The building, Fuad said, had been substantially destroyed in March 1918 in an Armenian uprising, when Armenians killed 30,000 Azeris (Armenian sources claim half that number). Built by one Musa Nagi, a wealthy man of the Baha'i faith, it had been rebuilt in the 1920s.

'Now we turn to chapter sixteen. Here is Musa Nagi,' Fuad said and began vigorously to read from the book.

I hate being read to. I hate the pauses. I hate the stammers and mispronunciations. Most of all I hate the slowness of it. I can read quickly and efficiently, and cannot stand someone taking charge and denying me the pleasure of reading the damned thing myself.

'Let me see that,' I said. 'Please.'

'No, no, this is the best part!' Fuad said and snatched the book away. And then he started to declaim it. I hated that, too.

'"I am an old man,"' he read, stabbing his finger at the page. '"And I am sad to see what I see, and to hear what I hear. The Russians are killing the Turks, the Turks are killing the Armenians, the Armenians would like to kill us, and we the Russians . . ."' He continued, reading very loudly and gesticulating, and when he saw my attention wandering, he stood in front of me and shouted, '"Our soul strives to go to God. But each nation believes they have a God all to themselves, and he is the one and only God. But I believe it is the same God who made himself known through the voices of all the sages. Therefore I worship Christ and Confucius, Buddha and Mohammad. We all come from one God, and through Bab we shall all return to him. Men should be told there is no Black and White, for Black is White and White is Black."'

'How true,' I said, hoping he'd stop.

But he wasn't finished: '"So my advice is this. Let us not do anything that might hurt anybody anywhere in the world, for we are part of each soul, and each soul is part of us."'

Fuad squeezed the book shut.

'Now I want you to look at the building again. You see how beautiful the façade. And there is Musa Nagi, the Baha'ist.'

Carved in the stone façade of the building was Musa Nagi's benevolent face.

Fuad's arms were crossed and he was reciting again, this time a poem:

> Every epoch has its face,
> Every epoch leaves its trace;
> Sometimes it is full of disgrace,
> And not just in this particular case.

'I wrote that myself,' Fuad said.

We continued through the square, which was named for Mirzah Sabir, a national hero who died in 1911. A statue of Sabir in the middle of the square depicted the man seated. It was, Fuad said, a visual euphemism, because 'getting him to sit' was a Russian expression for imprisoning someone, and Sabir, a writer and satirist, had been imprisoned.

'He derided mullahs,' Fuad said. 'Mirzah Sabir said, "I'm not afraid of a place of gods and devils. I'm afraid of a place with mullahs."'

We strolled in the old city and Fuad showed me Ali's house, just as it had been described in chapter one.

'You see the second floor? Ali's room! Where he looks out and sees' – now he read from the novel – '"the Maiden's Tower, surrounded by legends and tourist guides. And behind the tower the sea began, the utterly faceless, leaden, unfathomable Caspian Sea, and beyond, the desert – jagged rocks and scrub: still, mute, unconquerable, the most beautiful landscape in the world."'

He was moved by his own performance.

'Do you agree with Ali?' I asked.

'What about?'

'The sea. The desert. The most beautiful landscape in the world.'

'Yes, of course,' he said.

I heard an unstated *but* in his delivery. I said, 'But –'

'But I'm going to Canada,' Fuad said.

After all this nationalistic fervour and literary history, the civic pride, the declaiming, the quoting, the extolling of statues and mansions, the florid poems, his blazing eyes, his gestures, his red fez, he was bailing out.

'This government is making a mess,' he said, putting *Ali and Nino* into his briefcase. 'Tearing down lovely buildings and putting up shit. So I want to leave.'

'But this is a wealthy country, and you have an important job at Interpol,' I said.

'My son is six. I don't want to bring up my child in an atmosphere of hostility. I want him to have more chances.'

'What's the problem here?'

'Everything – the Russians mostly.'

Russia was behind all the secessionist movements, all the embattled and besieged breakaway republics, from Abkhazia and South Ossetia to Dagestan and Nagorno-Karabakh. When I asked what sense it made for the Russians to foment nationalist movements in these places, he said that of course there was no sense in it. It was perverse political malignity to make life miserable for Georgians and Azeris.

'No, no,' he said when I wanted to pursue this. 'Listen to my poem.'
And he recited again from memory:

> Baku is the place
> Where every stone
> Has a story of its own.

He crooked an admonitory finger in the air, sweeping the red fez off his
head. His voice broke slightly as he finished:

> And the stories could be magic
> Should they not end up so tragic.

' "Let's go to Fillifpojanz," ' Fuad said. He was quoting the novel
again, because the site of the Fillifpojanz coffee house still existed,
a bulky white-painted building on Barjatinsky Street, and was being
restored.

To get there, we passed the signs of Azerbaijan's prosperity: casinos
and bars, shops selling luxury goods, and Internet cafés where shaggy
youths were using video-mounted computers to speak with women –
wives and girlfriends. The good times were reflected in the Azeris
themselves, well dressed and busy, greeting the spring on this long sunny
holiday. Fuad had other plans. He wasn't very interested in describing
Fillifpojanz and was looking beyond *Ali and Nino* now. Having divulged
his plan to emigrate, he spoke of how happy he'd be, how hard he'd
work, when he got to Canada.

7. Night Train from Ashgabat to Mary

Turkmenistan, the Stan next door, was a tyranny run by a madman, Saparmyrat Niyazov, who gave himself the name Turkmenbashi, 'Leader of All the Turkmen'. He was one of the wealthiest and most powerful lunatics on earth and the ruler of an entire country. His people cringed at his name, his prisons were full of dissenters, his roads were closed to people like me. He had recently begun to call himself Prophet (*Prorók*), a harmless enough conceit if you're a civilian, but a pathological if not a fatal tendency in a despot. In support of his messianic claim he had written a sort of national bible, called the *Rukhnama* (The Book of the Soul), and he regarded himself as an accomplished writer, a clear sign of madness in anyone. Everything I had heard about this man and this country made me want to go there.

He treated the country as his private kingdom, a land in which everything in it belonged to him, including all of Turkmenistan's plentiful natural gas, much of which issued into the air from his own person in the form of interminable speechifying. Not long ago he prophesied that the twenty-first century was the golden age of Turkmenistan. I had heard that his insane schemes for promoting his image were on display all over the country, but especially the gold statues in the capital, Ashgabat. I was disappointed at not being able to take the ferry from Baku, but I was eager to see this jowly and vindictive potentate, who in word and deed was constantly paraphrasing Shelley – 'My name is Ozymandias, King of Kings: / Look on my works, ye mighty, and despair!' – in his desert wasteland.

For the first time on this trip I was airborne, on the fifty-minute flight from Baku to Ashgabat, and (so it seemed) travelling through the Looking Glass. The chummy term 'Absurdistan' did not begin to describe this geopolitical aberration – it was too forgiving, too definable, too comic. 'Loonistan' came closer, for it was less like a country than a gigantic madhouse run by the maddest patient, for whom 'megalomaniac' sounded too affectionate and inexact. Niyazov famously hated writers and snoopers, and Turkmenistan was one of the hardest countries in the world for a solitary traveller to enter. I might not have got into Turkmenistan at all. There were group tours: one day in Ashgabat, a one-day trip to the ruins at Merv, and off to Uzbekistan in a bus or plane. But I had a helpful, well-placed friend. I was grateful to be there.

Niyazov had recently built a vast space-age mosque and named it after himself, Saparmyrat Hajji Mosque, and encouraged his people to visit it annually, as a rewarding pilgrimage, a national haj. His portraits, some of them hundreds of square feet of his unappealing features, were everywhere. In some he looked like a fat and grinning Dean Martin wearing a Super Bowl ring; in others he was a nasty-faced CEO with a chilly smile, smug, truculent, defiant. One showed him as a precocious child of gold, seated in the lap of his bronze mother. The most common picture portrayed him, chin on hand, squinting in insincere bonhomie, like a lounge singer. Smiling was an important part of his political philosophy. He had Italianate features and was sometimes posed with a stack of books, like an insufferable author in a book-tour shot. He was sixty-five. He had declared himself 'Leader for Life'. It was the will of the people, he said. Everything associated with him told you he was out of his mind. He had banned beards, gold teeth and ballet.

Absolute ruler and head of state, and with much of the gas revenue in his own pocket, Niyazov was crazy in his own twisted way, and Ashgabat was an example of what happened when political power and money and mental illness were combined in a single paranoiac.

'He renamed bread after his mother,' someone had said to me before I went.

It was apparently true that he'd floated the idea, and he'd succeeded in something even nuttier. He renamed the twelve months of the year – January after himself, and some other months after members of his family. His mother's name, Gurbansultan-ezdhe, took the place of April. The days of the week were also new, his own innovation, and one was Mum's. In the purifying interests of nationalism, he abolished all non-Turkmen names and expressions, and decreed that the dictionary should be rewritten to reflect this.

One American I met there said, 'If you took Las Vegas and Pyongyang and shook them up in a blender, you'd get Ashgabat.'

'Like an underfunded Las Vegas,' another American said. He meant the white marble towers, the gold statues, the floodlights, the fountains, the empty spaces, the dead trees. Neither of these quips was quite right, because the place was uniquely weird. I knew that something was amiss as soon as I arrived. The gold statues and dead trees were just the beginning and were hardly the worst of it.

Apart from its gas pipeline, it was a country without a link to the world: no international telephones, no Internet, no mobile phones, no satellite hookups. Newspapers, radio and television were controlled; no real news at all and no access to the outside. My BlackBerry, which had worked in Baku and Tbilisi, went dark. The dictator had decreed that the Internet was subversive – and he was probably right. It was almost impossible to enter the country, and it was very hard to leave. Internet cafés had been closed for more than three years. People tended to whisper, and no wonder. In a typical case, reported by outside sources, a 58-year-old journalist – a reporter for Radio Free Europe – Ogulsapar Muradova, a mother of two, had been arrested, convicted (without a lawyer) in a secret trial, and given six years on a trumped-up charge. In September 2006, a month after she was imprisoned in Ashgabat, Muradova was found dead in her cell (she appeared to have suffered 'a head injury'), and her body was handed over to her daughters.

Turkmenistan's oddity was apparent from the outset, long before I saw the gold statues. Few planes ever landed at the casino-style airport, which was staffed by officials who had a very slim idea of how to do their jobs or make decisions – a characteristic of most dictatorships, in which fear of retribution created such rigidity that it bred incompetence. Men in handsome uniforms stood around, delaying the processing of passengers, most of them foreign workers – British, Malaysian, Filipino – in the gas industry. The officials grinned at each other, but when they met my gaze they glowered and looked fierce.

One of them, in a wide-crowned and shiny-visored cap, looked at me and sucked his teeth and said, '*Prablyema.*'

'What's the problem?'

'*Shto eta?*' He tugged at the T-shirt in my bag that held the offending object.

'Eekon,' I said. The silver icon I had bought at the pavement flea market in Tbilisi, with an oil portrait of Jesus staring from a lozenge at the centre, wrapped up so that it wouldn't get scratched.

'*Eta staroye,*' he said.

'No, it's new.'

'*Ochen dorogaya.*'

'Not really. It was cheap.'

'*Antikvarnaya!*'

'An antique?'

'*Da. Prablyema!*' he said. He showed me the flat of his hand. '*Zhdi zdyes.*'

I waited almost an hour. A team of men returned. One spoke English, while the rest of them clucked approvingly.

'Why you bring this eekon here?' he said slowly. 'Why you not bring it khome?'

'I *am* bringing it home,' I said.

He raised his hands. 'This Ashgabat, not khome.'

'I'm on my way home,' I said. Which was, in the larger sense, true. 'To give this to my mother.'

'*Mat*',' this man explained to the team. 'It is for his mother.'

Any mention of mother is useful, particularly in a country of tradition-minded desert folk whose leader, I was to discover, encouraged a cult of motherhood.

But the man was holding the customs form and looking baffled. I explained that, since a section of the form asked for *Description and Origin of Goods*, we could fill out that portion, and I would show it at the border, when I left, to prove I wasn't smuggling antiques. They seemed to think this was an appropriate compromise, and so after two hours I was riding into Ashgabat.

'He was on TV last night. Well, he's on almost every night,' the driver said. No one ever used Niyazov's name, not even the boastful 'Turkmenbashi', or if they did, it was in an undertone. 'He said, "If you read my book three times you will go to heaven."'

'How does he know this?'

'He said, "I asked Allah to arrange it."'

Niyazov's *Rukhnama* is a hefty-sized farrago of personal history, odd Turkmen lore, genealogies, national culture, dietary suggestions, Soviet-bashing, insane boasting, wild promises and his own poems, one beginning, 'Oh, my crazy soul . . .' The book contains more exclamation marks than a get-rich-quick ad, which it much resembles. He seemed to regard it as both a sort of Koran and how-to guide for the Turkmen people and a jingoistic pep talk, and though it is perhaps no odder, no more fabricated, than any other apocalyptic tome, it is strung on a very tenuous narrative – a blend of advice, his own speeches and potted history – and so it is little more than a soporific, 'chloroform in print', as Mark Twain described *The Book of Mormon*. I read it once. Niyazov would have to promise more than heaven for me to read his excruciating book two more times.

But it had immense value for the traveller passing through Turkmenistan, since all writing, even bad writing – especially bad writing – is revealing of the author's mind and heart. The ill-written *Rukhnama* is no exception. Early in the book, a hopeful Niyazov writes, 'The foreigners who read *Rukhnama* will know us better, become our friends faster,' though whenever I mentioned the *Rukhnama* to educated Turkmen, they rolled their eyes and looked embarrassed.

In his confused and patchy exposition, Niyazov reached back 5,000 years (so he said) and claimed, 'Turkmen history can be traced back to the flood of Noah.' In the aftermath, the receding of the waters, the original ancestor of the Turkmen, Oguz Khan, emerged. Oguz's sons and grandsons produced Turkmenistan's twenty-four clans. The figure of Oguz is one of the keys to the *Rukhnama*: Niyazov speaks of how the Turkmen called the Milky Way the Oguz Arch, and the Amu Darya River the Oguz River, and the constellation the Oxen was the Oguz Stars. Oguz also 'implemented . . . the use of the national Oguz alphabet'. His name was set upon many features of the earth and sky. Oguz also declared a golden age.

The subtitle of the *Rukhnama* (now referred to as *The Holy Rukhnama*) could be 'The Second Coming' – the actual subtitle is 'Reflections on the Spiritual Values of the Turkmen'. Niyazov emphasizes that he is a sort of reincarnation of Oguz Khan, just as powerful and wise, and to prove it he has named cities and hills and rivers and streets after himself. He meddled with the language in the manner of Oguz, ordering that Turkmen be written in Latin script, and claimed that because he had dedicated his life to making Turkmenistan greater, he would be its president for the rest of his life.

Niyazov was an orphan. Much is made of this in the book, and these descriptions have a clumsy tenderness. 'I have borne many difficulties throughout my life,' he writes, and tells how his father was killed in the Second World War, fighting for the Soviets in Ossetia. When he was a child of seven, his mother was killed in the earthquake that levelled

Ashgabat in 1948. Isolated, he was made strong, and he refused to mourn. 'When I considered my situation, I understood that I was not an orphan! How can someone be an orphan if he has a father like Oguz Khan?' Instead of natural parents, he had a nation and a cause and a father from history. And he incorporated his parents into the national fabric, naming the year 2003 after his father, Atamurat, and 2004 after his mother, Gurbansultan-ezdhe.

Later in the *Rukhnama* (oh, and 2005 was the Year of *Rukhnama*), he waxes emotional about his mother, and mothers in general. This turns into a programme to venerate motherhood. 'The mother is a sacred being . . . One can understand the value of sacred things only after one has lost them.' He goes on to explain that a father provides material support, but the mother supplies love. He recalls a Turkmen saying: 'Fatherless, I am orphan; motherless, I am captive,' and concludes, 'Fate decreed two pains for me. I was both an orphan and a captive.'

A lost childhood seems essential in a dictator's biography, an irregular upbringing being a determiner of a person's becoming a political tyrant. Niyazov's making a meal of his early suffering, and the existence of the Palace of Orphans in Ashgabat – there were similar institutions in other big cities – were evidence that one of his priorities was to make special provisions for abandoned or parentless children. Having no clan, no real family, though, was a unique political asset to him in this clan-dominated society. 'He has a feeling for orphans,' a Turkmen told me. This concern was as obvious on the ground as it was in the pages of the *Rukhnama*, where Niyazov describes how he lost his parents, how he was alone and destined to struggle.

In terms of abandonment complaints, the book sounds (sometimes word for word) like the upward climb of the Austrian paperhanger in part one of *Mein Kampf*, who wrote: 'In my thirteenth year I suddenly lost my father,' and 'When my mother died, Fate, at least in one respect, had made its decisions . . . The three-year-old child had become a fifteen-year-old despiser of all authority.' But the orphaning is sentimentalized in the *Rukhnama*, and there is much more – history, old saws, the promise of greater glory, the list of obligations and duties, of which the not exactly Hitlerian 'Maintain a smiling face' is one.

'Smile!' was an important Turkmenbashi command. He was as emphatic about Turkmen smiling as he was about work and worship. He wrote, 'As the old saying goes, "There will never be any wrinkles on a smiling face".' And he reminisced: 'I often remember my mother. Her smile still appears before my very eyes . . . The smile is visible to me in the dark of night, even if I have my eyes shut.'

A smile was powerful: 'A smile can make a friend for you out of an enemy. When death stares you in the face, smile at it and it may leave you untouched.' Even nature smiled: 'Spring is the smile of the earth.' Smiling could be a form of conversation: 'Smile at each other . . . Talk to each other with smiles.'

Pages and pages of this, most of it self-reverential. To his smile Niyazov owed much of his success as a national leader. 'That smile I inherited from my mother is my treasure.' This was perhaps why most of the portraits of Niyazov all over Turkmenistan showed him smiling, though he never looked less reliable, or less amused, than when he was smiling. His smile – and this may be true of all political leaders – was his most sinister feature.

At Niyazov's command, his book was studied in every school in Turkmenistan; a thorough knowledge of it was an entry requirement for all the colleges and universities in the nation and for advancement in the civil service. Those immigration officials who gave me a hard time had little idea of how to handle a simple customs matter but probably could have quoted 'A smile can make a friend for you out of an enemy' – though none of them smiled at me.

What Niyazov did not say in the *Rukhnama* was that after his education in Russia (he had studied electrical engineering), he had become a party hack. This was in the 1970s and '80s – Soviet times, when he rose through the ranks of the Politburo to become general secretary of the Communist Party of Turkmenistan. He was one of the educated provincials the Soviets (in this case Gorbachev, who had picked him, not knowing he was a loony) extolled as converts to Marxism and examples of the effectiveness of the system, and hoped might serve as agents of reform. Not mentioned in the *Rukhnama* is that he spent a great deal of time in Leningrad and Moscow; that he was married to a Russian – interestingly enough, a Jew – who chose to live apart from him, in Moscow; that he had two children, one of whom, Murat, hoped to succeed him.

Another significant omission in any subsequent edition of the book (of which more than a million copies have been printed, in more than thirty languages, including Zulu and Japanese) is any mention of the assassination attempt against Niyazov. In 2002, in what might have been a failed coup, he was almost killed when he was shot at as his motorcade sped through the city. This resulted in a wave of repression, the perpetrators and their helpers hunted down and either killed or imprisoned. Whole families were jailed, and nothing was heard of them afterwards. The word was that his own disgruntled and ambitious ministers had schemed to get rid of him, and the plan was that he would be kidnapped, taken hostage and deposed rather than knocked off.

Anyway, the caper failed, but understandably it confirmed Niyazov's paranoia, and his delusions of grandeur – evident throughout the country in the form of the gold statues – were now accompanied by delusions of persecution. He ordered a clampdown: no Internet, no telephones, total control of the media, of all comings and goings.

And that other inconvenient feature of tyrannies – roadblocks. These were installed throughout all cities and on roads leading out of the cities, about every four miles. In a twelve-mile journey to some nearby ruins I was stopped three times by the usual well-armed men in spiffy uniforms who did not have the slightest notion of what to do with the cars they stopped. They examined papers, they looked into the back seat of the car, they made scowling faces and shouldered their rifles; but really, they were foxed.

On that trip to see the ruins, I asked about Niyazov's passion for renaming. I was with two Turkmen – a man I shall call Mamed, whose English was shaky, and a woman I shall call Gulnara, who was fluent.

The funny part was that although Mamed and Gulnara had read about the renamings, there were so many changes they couldn't keep them straight.

'January is now Turkmenbashi,' Gulnara said. 'He named the first month after himself. Ha! February is Bayderk – the flag. March is Nowruz April is Gurbansultan-ezdhe – his mother. June is Oguz – our hero. But May is – what is May?'

Mamed said, 'May is Sanjar.'

'No, that's November.'

'Are you sure?'

'I know September is Rukhnama,' Gulnara said. 'What do you think, Paul?'

I said, 'It's every writer's dream to have a month named after his book.'

'August is Alp Arslan,' Mamed said. 'He was sultan.'

'You forgot July,' Gulnara said.

'I don't remember July. What is it?'

Gulnara shook her head. She squinted and said, 'Then there's October.'

Mamed said, 'Garashsyzlivk.'

'Independence,' Gulnara said.

They were just as vague on the days of the week, though Gulnara started confidently: 'Monday is Bashgün – Beginning. Tuesday is Yashgün, Young Day. Wednesday is Hoshgün.'

'Tuesday is Hoshgün,' Mamed said. 'Wednesday is Yashgün.'

'I don't think so,' Gulnara said.

Their confusion was funny but politically suspect, because the renaming was considered so important. By a government decree, all departments, all ministries, schools, colleges, the police, the army – all citizens – had to demonstrate a knowledge of the changes, and had to use them, too.

'What if people are talking in Russian?' I asked, which was common, since Ashgabat had a community of Russians who'd been there for many years, somewhat sidelined by Niyazov's nationalism, but too old to leave.

'Even speaking in Russian – although it would be normal to use the Russian names for months and days – they use the new ones. Which makes no sense.'

'Someone told me he renamed bread.'

'That was an idea,' Gulnara said. 'But he renamed ketchup. He made a big speech. 'Why do we say "ketchup"? This is a foreign word. We are Turkmen. We must have a Turkmen word for this!"'

'So what is it?'

'Ketchup is *uwmech*.'

'If I looked up *uwmech* in the dictionary, what would it say?'

'It would say "ketchup", except we don't have any new dictionaries in Turkmenistan.'

Mamed said, 'He got rid of them.'

All this talk of the obsessive president made Mamed and Gulnara self-conscious, and when they fell silent I said, 'Does it bother you that the president has made all these changes? Not just the renaming, but his mother's name, his father's name.'

'Most people don't think about it,' Gulnara said. She meant: don't want to think about it, because it will only make them miserable.

'What about the gold statues of himself he puts up?'

Mamed made a face, shook his head, became alert. It was said that hotel rooms and offices were bugged, to catch any subversive talk – surely this car could be bugged too?

But Gulnara had an opinion. She was confident and bright, qualities she shared with many of the Turkmen women I met. She said, 'The statues. The slogans. The five-year plans. We have seen this before. Stalin – and others.'

And it was true that for self-adulatory images and mottos on buildings, the Soviets had been almost unbeatable, with Lenin's gilded face everywhere, and the cities and towns with Lenin statues to which Stalin statues were added. It was not surprising that the aspiring S. Niyazov changed his name to Turkmenbashi (as Iosif Dzhugashvili had, to Joseph Stalin) and created a dictatorship, complete with a personality cult.

'This will pass away,' Gulnara said.

It was not just a wise observation but the right way to see what this autocracy was worth, for this hyperactive and domineering man would die, and since he was seriously afflicted with diabetes and had had at least one heart attack, it would happen sooner rather than later. And then the gold statues would come down.*

In the meantime, Turkmen, of whom there were five million, expressed their disaffection in jokes. One went, 'Why is Turkmenbashi the richest man in Turkmenistan?' Answer: 'Because he has five million sheep.' And they laughed recalling how Niyazov had suggested that his people chew on bones, because it was good for their teeth.

On our way to the ruins we had passed a number of state-owned vineyards – one of the other oddities of Islamic Turkmenistan was that it had a vigorous wine industry, for both export and local consumption. At the edge of the desert we approached some rising ground that was more a mound than a hill, on which there was a broken structure of mud bricks that was still recognizable as a mosque.

This was Anau, the ruins of a fifteenth-century mosque – not unusual in Turkmenistan, which saw its first Islamic evangelists in the seventh century; the Prophet himself had sent his messengers in this direction from Mecca, and the conversion rate was high. What made this mosque unusual was that architecturally it showed Chinese influence, features in

---

* 'He died in December 2006.

still bright mosaics that were almost unheard-of in mosques – images of creatures and portraits of humans, neither of them common in Islamic art, and over the archway of the entrance, shattered but sinuous dragons.

Much of Turkmenistan was desert wasteland, scrubby bushes and dusty boulders, an emptiness of lizards and a landscape like cat litter. In Soviet times its few towns and cities were outposts as benighted as in any imperial colony, where people in colourful clothes wove carpets and surrendered their reserves of gas and oil to the Russian overlords. This exploitation, one of the injustices denounced in the *Rukhnama*, had not always been the case. The dragons on the mosque were a reminder that this part of Turkmenistan was on the Silk Road, the route to China, and some of the toughest travellers, the greatest treasures, the boldest generals, the largest armies, had passed this way: Alexander the Great, the Parthians, the Arabs, the Mongols.

This mosque was a place of pilgrimage, because its grounds contained the tomb of Seyyed Jamaluddin, the father of a local governor from the fifteenth century. A dozen people, most of them women with their children, prayed at the pile of broken bricks that was his grave.

'They come here because he has good communication with Allah,' Mamed said.

There was another grave, the Tomb of the Unmarried Woman – though Gulnara said that 'unmarried woman' could also be translated as 'virgin'. Young women were praying here, and hundreds had come before: they had left tokens behind in the form of symbols for requests to be granted. Most were wishes to be blessed with babies. Bows were tied to the branches of a nearby tree, small carved cradles were unambiguous, and the sheep bones that were carefully piled, Gulnara said, indicated children too, since the bones were used as toys by Turkmen children. Hairpins meant girls, so did the patches of coloured cloth; little plastic cars meant a boy child was desired.

'In Islam, this is not usually done. You don't appeal to a dead woman,' Gulnara said. 'You're supposed to ask Allah. But this is a powerful woman.'

I mentioned that most of these appeals specified that boys were wanted.

She said, 'Women who give birth to girls have another special way of indicating that they want a boy. They will name the daughter Enough – Besteir – or else Fed Up – Bovduk. These are common names. I know many.'

About forty feet from the tumbledown mosque was another mound on which there were hundreds of toy huts made of broken clay tiles – propped-up walls, a lid for a roof – and some were slanted two-storey huts. It looked like a miniature city. A squatting man in a smock and a woman with a billowing headscarf were setting one up as we stood nearby.

'People praying for houses,' Gulnara said. The images represented the people – young couples mostly – who were living with their parents in crowded tenements or in poor villages just outside Ashgabat, who wanted homes of their own.

The cruelty of Niyazov's policies was obvious in this tableau of toy huts, which was a visible plea – not to Turkmenbashi but to Allah – for housing. Houseless people abounded in this fabulously wealthy country. In his role as city planner, Niyazov had ordered that houses be bulldozed, compounds flattened, neighbourhoods of Ashgabat dispersed, but he had not rehoused the people he'd displaced. They lived precariously in temporary huts on Ashgabat's outskirts. And where their houses had stood were gold statues, fountains, oversized white marble buildings and white marble apartment blocks of ludicrous aspect, risen like pillars of salt, with gold trim, all of them empty because they were, in their deluxe absurdity, unaffordable.

Islam was not one immutable thing but was subject to variations. In what anthropologists call syncretism – local customs or adaptations added to an imported belief system – Islam here took on a colourful form, like Catholicism in Sicily or the Congo. Here were the national saints and martyrs who might intercede, and also the fetishes. The toys and small-scale models and symbols set up in a beseeching way were an innovation. The symbolic naming was a way of gaining power over destiny. Appeals to spirits – not Allah. This sort of Turkmen-style praying, intending to control fate, was unusual among Muslims.

In the next few days, I reached the conclusion that Turkmenistan, perhaps because of its tyrannous history, was one of the most supersition-prone cultures I'd ever seen.

Because they were gilded and solemn, the statues in the Turkmen capital had an ecclesiastical aura. A leader on horseback, or one cast in bronze or carved in stone, was not quite the same as a leader shaped in gold. In all these statues Niyazov was El Dorado, the Man of Gold – all-powerful, all-knowing. You were not meant to gape at them but rather to venerate them. One statue, depicting Niyazov with his arm raised, rotated, turning to face the sun, seeming to guide it across the sky from dawn to dusk. Another, the Arch of Neutrality, stood atop a gigantic marble apparatus that looked like, and was locally known as, the Toilet-Bowl Plunger. Some gold statues showed Turkmenbashi sitting, others striding, waving, saluting and of course smiling a 24-carat smile. Many showed him as a precocious golden child.

He once said to a journalist, 'I admit it, there are too many portraits, pictures and monuments [of me]. I don't find any pleasure in it, but the people demand it because of their mentality.'

All of these statues and pictures were, of course, destined for destruction; their doom was spelled out in the gold lettering, in the gold gesturing. They were such hubristic conceptions, it was only a matter of time before they were pulled down. A statue of Lenin in Neutrality Square in Ashgabat was bronze and lifesize, its mosaic imitating the pattern of a Turkmen carpet, and its message, in Russian and Turkmen, read: LENINISM IS THE WAY FOR FREEING THE PEOPLES OF THE EAST. This was, by contrast, modest and charming, a far cry from the gold three-times-lifesize Niyazov statues, which looked like commands to submit to his insanities, and by implication would challenge future Turkmen to knock them down.

Although the city was made of white marble and gold, statues and tower blocks and ministries and amphitheatres, the whole of Ashgabat had the pompous and vulnerable look of a place defying the fates. If an earthquake didn't topple it, a coup d'état would, and all of it would be smashed to bits by the indignant citizens this spendthrift had cheated.

The irony of Ashgabat was that nowhere, among the gold statues and the white marble plazas with their fountains and the triumphal archways, was there a place to sit down. It was a city without benches, the subtle message being: *Keep walking.*

'I will build a forest in the desert,' Niyazov had promised. Turkmen said that he had loved the pine forests of Russia. He had been inspired by them; he missed them here among the stones and the dunes. Turkmenistan – its wind-scoured plains and ravines of sun-scorched rock – deserved a forest.

He had ordered the planting of hundreds of thousands, if not millions, of young trees; and although they were two or three feet high – the planting was still going on when I was in Ashgabat – the forestation plan was not a success.

Now, there are trees that are drought-resistant – certain cypresses, certain poplars, the low twisted trees you see in the parched ravines of Patagonia, the ones that somehow flourish in the howling wilderness of China's Xinjiang Uygur region. But the Douglas firs, white pines and arbor vitae, dear to the heart and memory of Niyazov, were doing badly. They had been planted in immensely long ranks and rows at the centre of Ashgabat, and on great swaths of dry land outside the city, as a sort of instant forest. Drip irrigation had been rigged to keep them watered, but they were the wrong species. They were baked by the sun, blown flat by the wind, and a full third of them had that peculiar rust-red hue, the vivid colour of an evergreen's death.

'They are called *arçabil*,' my new guide, Masut, said. 'He, um, likes them.'

I was waiting for someone to speak the leader's name. 'Turkmenbashi' was too pompous, 'Niyazov' too presumptuous and familiar. 'The President' and 'the Leader' were too formal, and 'the Prophet' was hard to say with a straight face. Later I learned that Turkmen usually referred to him as *mähriban ata*, 'dear father', or *serdar*, 'tribal leader'.

We were heading west, past signs saying PEOPLE–MOTHERLAND–TURKMENBASHI, scores of them, out of the city, where more forest had been planted and was seriously stunted and brown; some trees that had been secured by guy wires had toppled over. The trees had come from Russia and Ukraine – Bashi had swapped them for gas. The plantings looked like an enormous tree farm that had lost its lease.

On the side of a mountain, in large letters carved from marble blocks, was this sign in Turkmen: OUR HEALTH ROAD OF OUR GREAT ETERNAL LEADER. It was just the sort of clifftop message I had seen a decade before in Albania, and without doubt it would end up the same way, as a pile of rubble in the adjacent valley. This one was meant to encourage people to walk on the paved path that wound through the dying dwarf forest.

'He wants us to be healthy,' Masut said.

But it was questionable whether Niyazov did want his people to be healthy. He had closed all the hospitals outside Ashgabat, replaced thousands of healthcare workers with military conscripts, and instructed the country's doctors to pledge their allegiance to him, Turkmenbashi, and to the *Rukhnama* rather than taking the Hippocratic oath.

'Turkmen look healthy to me,' I said. 'They have a good diet. They don't smoke. They seem hard-working.'

'But he wants us to walk on the Health Road.'

That was the programme. Never mind that you were a nomad or a villager or a cotton picker, you had to do as you were told, healthwise: walk on the Eternal Great Leader's road, more than twenty miles of paved pathway traversing the mountainside. One of Bashi's many residences lay beyond that hillside, another palace. He claimed that the $100 million gold-domed, white marble presidential palace built for him was not of his choosing. ('All I wanted was a small, cosy house.')

'And many people don't have jobs,' Masut said. 'The figure could be sixty per cent unemployed outside Ashgabat.'

'I'm surprised people aren't angry,' I said.

'Some are angry. But we have cheap things, too. Natural gas for heating is free. Electricity is free. Petrol is three cents a gallon. I can fill the tank of this car for fifty cents.'

'What do you think are the problems here?' I asked.

'Yes, we have problems, but we can't address problems, because there are no problems,' Masut said and smiled at me, the smile that said: *Please, no more questions.*

Another day we went, Masut and I, to the big bazaar outside Ashgabat, which had two names: the Tolkuchka bazaar, from a Russian word that meant 'pushing', and the Jygyldyk bazaar, an onomatopoeic word in Turkmen that meant something like 'babbling' or 'jabbering'.

Turkmen have a horror of the evil eye, perhaps a lingering feature of the shamanism that has dominated the spiritual life in this region from ancient times, an anxious reflex that is apparent in every sphere of Turkmen existence. This aspect of superstition, combined with Islam, has produced holy-seeming paraphernalia for warding off the evil eye. These trinkets were on sale in many of the stalls in the bazaar, not just the staring glass eye or the carved wooden talisman, but a sheep-horn symbol that Masut said was effective against maledictions. This totemism was all part of the praying, the relic hunting, the tokens, the images, the bows and toy cars and dolls' houses that I had seen elsewhere. In a police state that had total control of all coming and going, a locked-down populace, it was rather touching to see people obsessed with dark magic and wicked forces.

It seemed that evil came as a weird and withering blast from thin air in the form of a diabolical death ray. The most common specific against this bedevilment was a charm that broke the force into pieces, a sort of prism made of coloured wool that one wore as a necklace or bracelet, or hung over a bed or a doorway. Some of these charms looked like the kind of multicoloured lanyards I had made in summer camp when I was a boy. But never mind how insubstantial they looked; the things worked, or so I was assured by Masut, who bought me a length of brown and red rope, an evil-eye deflector, to get me through to Uzbekistan.

'And this herb is so powerful,' Masut said, fingering a small sack of dried leaves, 'that it is known as Hundred Husbands.'

In most respects, the Tolkuchka bazaar on the outskirts of Ashgabat was greater, more vital and various, than its rivals – say, the covered market in Istanbul, the bazaar in Damascus or the Mall of America in Bloomington, Minnesota – with billowing marquees and curtains marking off the separate stalls. It was highly competitive and intensely local – not a tourist to be seen. It covered many acres, and the horse market occupied what could have been an entire fairground.

Buying a carpet or a melon or a sack of spices was only part of the interest of such a bazaar. A peripheral activity was the interaction of people – farmers from afar with their families, gawky boys, shy girls. The bazaar was a legitimate place for people to stare, to meet and, while not exactly to flirt, to exchange smiles. Country people travel for a day or two on an old bus or a night train to get to Ashgabat and meet city people; families rendezvous for picnics; men swagger and shout, and boys gape and seem to imitate them. This bazaar was a kind of vortex, drawing in Turkmen from all over in an ancient ceremony of encounter and negotiation, isolated people delighted to be in a big noisy crowd, with music playing and camels howling and hawkers shouting for customers.

Everything imaginable was on sale, not just Chinese clothes, shoes, belts and blue jeans, but rows and rows of locally made velveteen dresses and their detachable white hand-embroidered collars, yoke-shaped and lovely, that are unique to Turkmen women.

Besides the produce – tomatoes, carrots, potatoes, rice, herbs and fresh fruit, piles of it in stalls and on carts – were the traditional weavings of Turkmenistan: an acre of the bazaar devoted to rugs and carpets, most of them of a reddish hue but some of them green and yellow.

'You see these? They are fish,' Masut said, indicating the motif of fish bones on a large carpet. 'This one is from a clan that lives on the shores of the Caspian Sea, where fish are an important symbol.'

Brassware, samovars, silver spoons, silver dishes, the sort of flea market treasures I'd seen in Tbilisi – tables and tables of these. Russian stuff – belt buckles, military buttons, medals and campaign ribbons. And bronze artefacts, pottery from digs, some that looked genuine, others that looked fake. Stacks of coins, too, some of them roubles from the departed regime, and lots of them that the sellers swore were ancient – with a provenance that was Seljuk, Ottoman, Luristan, Gulistan, coins from the ruined cities in the desert, from the Gurly Turkmen of Afghanistan and India. How many of these were fakes? Probably many. But I found a man who swore that a coin I was flipping was actually gold, from Merv or Bokhara, and so I bought it for its portability, and its beauty, and the slipperiness of its head and tail.

Something else attracted me at the Tolkuchka bazaar: its multiracial shoppers and stallholders. Most of the people were obviously Turkmen, but there were many Russians, and some Persians, Azeris and Uzbeks, too. In the 1930s, Stalin decreed that the Soviet populations be dispersed, so that the pull of native peoples to be unified would be weakened, the colour of the population, so to speak, would be diluted. On the one hand, it gave republics like Turkmenistan and Uzbekistan the look of a melting pot; on the other hand, it made them tractable.

The farthest-flung ethnic group at the bazaar, and so in Turkmenistan, were the Koreans.

'Stalin sent you?' I asked.

'He sent my father and mother,' a woman said. She wore a white cap, like a nurse's cap, and a white apron.

There were several tables of Korean women, smiling, gold teeth glinting, shouting for attention, with trays piled high with pickled cabbage.

'*Kimchi*,' I said, the only Korean word I knew.

'Yes, yes! Try some!'

'It's cheap. It's the best. Buy some.'

'Take me to America!'

One afternoon in Ashgabat I caused a diplomatic incident – a common occurrence in Turkmenistan, but an inconvenience to a foreign traveller wishing for anonymity. Riling the government was one of the perils of life here, and was probably the reason Turkmen habitually kept their heads down and whispered.

I had agreed to give a harmless pep talk in Ashgabat to some writers and journalists. About thirty men and women showed up at a sort of boardroom in a hotel that the US embassy used as an annexe. This being Turkmenistan, they were of every physical type: stylish women in velvet dresses and white collars with the impassive faces of nomads, dark beaky men in heavy coats, younger moustached men in suits, Russian aunties in blue dresses and carrying satchels, some hefty warrior types braced behind their chairs with arms folded, a furtive man fussing with a big shoulder bag and two pale young women, slender Slavic beauties with lank blonde hair, standing shyly by the wall, staring at me with limpid blue eyes.

My topic was again the return journey, the pleasure of a traveller's growing older, how the passage of time reveals the truth of people and places. I spoke for about twenty minutes, with a young Turkmen translator who was fluent in English. At the end there was polite applause. The man who had been fussing with his shoulder bag had taken out an expensive camera and begun snapping pictures.

'Any questions?'

Hands shot up.

'What do you think of Islam?' one man asked.

I made a tactful reply, commending the verses of the Koran encouraging hospitality that I, a traveller among Muslims, appreciated, and quickly I moved on to the next question.

'I am a poet,' one of the Russian aunties declared. She went on to ask how she might get her poems translated into English and published in the United States.

I referred her to the fellow who had translated her question.

'How do you write a novel?' a young man asked.

I mentioned needing an idea, and characters, and a setting, and about two years of solitude.

'You are not here for very long,' another man said. 'How can you understand us in such a short time?'

'You're right,' I said. 'It's impossible. So what particular thing do you think it's important for me to understand about Turkmenistan?'

'Do you know about the pensions?'

'No, I don't. Tell me.'

'The government has reduced the state pensions for some people,' he said, his voice rising. 'In some cases, these were people who were granted pensions by the Soviet government, but when Turkmenistan became independent, these were eliminated. What do you think of that?'

As he spoke, the man with the camera leaned over and began snapping his picture.

He turned and snapped my picture as I said, 'We have a similar problem in the United States. A lot of older people will have to work longer because the government pension fund is running out of money. The qualifying age for Social Security is now almost sixty-six, and it's rising.'

'But what about us?' the questioner asked. Now his voice was strident. 'This situation is serious.'

The photographer positioned himself at the edge of the row of chairs and was clicking away.

'You're not getting your pension?'

'Many thousands of people are not getting it! They were workers. Now they're old and they have nothing to live on. This is a wealthy country, but they are poor. The government has done this to us. Why don't you write about that?'

'You're a writer – all you people are writers,' I said. 'You are the people who should write about it, not me. You have all the facts. So why don't you do it?'

'I am not a writer,' the man said. 'I am chairman of the Unity and Neutrality Party of Turkmenistan.'

Before this could be translated, the photographer leaped forward and snapped pictures from several angles, his shoulder bag bumping his side.

And then an American security officer took three strides towards the photographer and, approaching him from behind, grasped his coat in one hand and snatched the camera with his other hand. He frogmarched the man to the back of the room and outside. This all happened so fast, the photographer did not have time to protest, though I heard him howl as the door slammed.

'Do you write about love?' one of the pretty blue-eyed women asked.

Constantly, I said. I elaborated on this subject, and then declared the meeting over. The room emptied quickly.

But the harm was done. I had allowed a political dissident a forum. It turned out that this was the first anyone had heard of this underground party. And there was collateral damage, so to speak, for the writers and journalists who had been quietly invited (many of them unpopular with the government) had all been photographed. The photographer was a government spy, sent to make a record of the meeting and to report on what had been said.

'Not good,' said the young man who had done the translating.

'What just happened?' I asked the American security man.

I had been impressed by his deftness: without hesitating, almost without creating a scene, he had plucked the man and his camera from the room. Out in the corridor, the security man had popped out the camera's memory card and wiped it of its images as the photographer howled. The force of this expulsion came afterwards, like a shock wave, when it was apparent what had just occurred.

'Government guy,' the American said. 'He should know better. This is technically US government property. Can't take pictures here.'

'Is this going to be a problem?'

'We'll see,' he said. 'Hey, I liked your talk.'

The problem developed later that day when the photographer complained to his superiors at Turkmenistan's Ministry of Foreign Affairs. And the next day, the deputy chief of mission of the US embassy in Ashgabat was summoned to a meeting with the foreign minister.

Who is this Paul Theroux? she was asked. What are the details of his visa? Does he have permission to speak? When is he leaving? How is he leaving? What border crossing?

I had the answers to some of these questions. My visa was in order, and in a few days I planned to take the train to Mary, to see the ruins at Merv. Then the train to Turkmenabat and the Uzbekistan border at Farap, and then, I hoped, another train.

I spent the rest of my time in Ashgabat doing what Turkmen like doing most, sitting on a lovely carpet, eating my way down a spit of lamb kebab or through a mound of rice *plov*. Always there was hard bread, sometimes dumplings, tea and wine.

'Georgian wine,' one of my Turkmen hosts said. 'Stalin's favourite. He wouldn't drink anything else.'

Now and then these meals were served in homes that stood in empty fields, like the stage set for a Beckett play – a house in a wasteland that had been bulldozed to make room for a future prestige project or gold statue. Niyazov's people simply seized the houses and got rid of them, rarely compensating the owners. In the distance were the empty marble palaces and tower blocks, huge white follies trimmed in gold. Niyazov fancied himself a city planner, and he was obsessional, his megalomania on view for all to see. He had the dictator's most obnoxious trait of greatly resembling a dysfunctional person who had won the lottery.

Because I was now under a cloud, and being watched by the Ministry of Foreign Affairs, my position as an alien in Turkmenistan was explained to me. I had to be careful. But having Niyazov – Turkmenbashi, Leader of All the Turkmen – as an enemy was helpful, because when Western diplomats explained my predicament, they revealed Niyazov's quirks.

'He hates people meddling. He hates NGOs – in fact, he banned them,' one diplomat told me. He had banned human rights groups, religious groups and environmental groups. 'He allowed the Peace Corps in when they left Uzbekistan, but they can't work in any schools – they give language lessons mainly, and do what they can to make friends.'

'You see what you're up against?' another diplomat said. 'He's refused any help from the IMF or any loans from the World Bank, because if he accepted any money, he would have to disclose his own financial information. And that's his big secret. He considers most of these profits from gas his own, which makes him a billionaire many times over.'

A person who had spent some time with him in one of his palaces said, 'He's tease. He's a mocker. He banters with his ministers and humiliates them.'

'Of course his system's corrupt,' a student explained to me. 'You need to bribe a lot of people to get into college, but only Turkmen are allowed. A Russian or an Uzbek or a Korean wouldn't have a chance. They have no future here.'

'He stopped education at the ninth grade for most people,' a bureaucrat said to me. 'He was once asked about that by a foreign head of state. He said, "Uneducated people are easier to govern."'

Early one evening I took the night train from Ashgabat to the eastern city of Mary. When I found that the sleeper ticket cost $4, I became anxious: this was the price of six melons at the bazaar, and a ticket so cheap boded ill for a long journey. I guessed that the train would be dirty and crowded, a mass of people travelling in the light of a few 25-watt bulbs, and it gave me no satisfaction to be right.

The railway station itself was lovely, a classic Soviet building from the 1950s, very clean and patrolled by soldiers with machine guns. Yet no passenger was searched, and while all travellers on Turkmenistan's roads were subject to numerous roadblocks and the arbitrary search-and-seizure rules of the security forces, train travellers were blameless and carefree – another instance of railway passengers regarded as being beneath notice.

I sat in my four-berth compartment with a soldier in his dark uniform, a student of about twenty-two and a chin-bearded old man in traditional Turkmen dress – a cylindrical black lambskin hat, a long brown cloak over a smock, one of those national costumes that seem eternal and all-purpose and comfortable everywhere, in all seasons. He saw me and began to speak to the student.

'*Salaam. Dayf al-Rahman,*' he said.

'Welcome,' the student translated. 'You are a guest of Allah, the Merciful One.'

'Please thank him for me.'

The man spoke again.

'He has a question for you,' the student said. 'Will you answer?'

I heard the whistle blow. The train slowly left Ashgabat Station, and within minutes we were in the desert. The old man was monologuing to the student.

'He says that some years ago, an astronaut went to the moon,' the student said. 'He was from America. When he got to the moon, he heard a strange noise. It was an *azan*' – the call to prayer, usually chanted by a muezzin from a mosque. 'The astronaut recorded it. When he came back to Earth, the scientists in America analysed it, and they came to think that it was the voice of the Prophet Muhammad.'

'On the moon?'

'Yes. On the moon.'

The old man was still speaking, his chin beard swinging.

'Furthermore, he says that because of this, the astronaut became a Muslim and began praying five times a day.'

The old man was facing me, as though defying me to mock the story.

'I haven't heard this story,' I said.

'He says he believes it.'

'What does he think about it?'

When this question was translated, the student said, 'For him, it's good news.'

It seemed to me like a Turkmenistan version of a Pat Robertson*

---

* American Televangelist.

story: divine intervention in an unlikely place, resulting in a beatific conversion, the sun breaking through the clouds. Instead of Jesus speaking to a searcher, the speaker was Muhammad; but it came to the same thing. Muslims at the fringe always sounded to me like born-again Christians, literal-minded and impervious to reason. An Arabic scholar once told me that a persistent urban myth in the Middle East was that Neil Armstrong, sometimes confused with Louis Armstrong, converted to Islam.

But as all of us were going to Mary, the best tactic on this overnight train journey was to get along, perhaps keep off the subject of religion.

As I was thinking this, the old man was talking to the student.

'He asks if you believe in God.'

'I have a lot of questions on this subject,' I said.

'He asks, "But do you believe in life after death?"'

'I don't know about this. No one has ever come back from the dead to tell us anything, so how can we know?'

'The Holy Koran tells us.'

'I intend to read it when I have a chance.'

The old man, who was seated across from me, spoke directly to me in Turkmen and became very animated.

'He says: "The grass grows. Then the grass turns brown. Then the grass dies. Then it grows again. It turns green and gets tall."'

The old man was still staring, his face narrow, one skinny gnarled hand in his lap, the other gripping the long grey beard attached to his chin. His arthritic hands gave him an even greater look of piety.

'He says, "Life is like that, I believe."'

'Tell him I agree. Life is like that, even where I'm from.'

'Where are you from?'

'Tell him America.'

The old Muslim received this information with more interest than I had expected.

'He asks, "Do you have cotton in America?"'

'Lots of it.'

'Is it a good type of cotton?'

'Very good,' I said.

'He is wondering how many hectares of cotton are growing in America.'

'Tell him I'm not sure. Why is he interested?'

'He works in the cotton industry.'

'What does he do?'

When this question was asked, the man showed me his ruined hands, his twisted fingers.

'He picks cotton in the fields some distance from Mary – near Yeloten, south on the road to Afghanistan, where there are cotton farms.'

So he lived (according to my map) a few hundred miles from the Afghanistan border, a day's drive, not far from the ancient city of Herat, which I had visited on my first Railway Bazaar trip. Now Herat was dominated by a clan of well-armed warriors and a paranoid and vindictive warlord. A German traveller had been arrested there, tortured and shot as a spy just a month before, a fate I wished to avoid.

The old man's name was Selim. He told me his simple history. He had been born near Mary. He had not gone to school. As a boy he worked in the fields, and had picked cotton his whole life – mostly Soviet times. He had married a woman from his clan and they'd had four children.

'I think you are about sixty,' he said.

When I told him my age, he challenged me to guess his. He looked about seventy, so I guessed sixty. He laughed and said he was fifty.

At my Ashgabat farewell party in a Turkmen household, I had been given a bag of food for the train – spinach pies, mushroom turnovers, sticky buns, all wrapped in paper. In the dim light of the compartment I unwrapped the food.

'Ask them if they'll share my food,' I said to the student.

They nodded politely when the question was translated, and so I handed the food around – to Selim, the young soldier, the student and a hanger-on gaping in the doorway. Elderly-looking, grey-bearded Selim – could he really be fifty? – asked a question.

'He says, "Ask the American if we can say a prayer."'

'Of course,' I said and nodded to the man.

All Muslims wash before they pray. But in the desert, or when water is unavailable, they use sand or dust. If (as on a train) there is no sand, they perform the dry ablution called *tayammum*, making an elaborate business of rubbing the hands and wrists and arms, and slowly wiping the face, massaging the eyes, the cheeks, the jaw, then drawing the hands downward. Selim went through this ritual as the train rushed across the desert, rattling the windows and the door handles.

Then he prayed for almost a full minute, his eyes closed, speaking into the stifling air of the compartment. When he was finished I asked him what he had said – was it a standard prayer or had he improvised it?

He said it was improvised for the occasion. 'I thanked Allah for the food. I thanked the friend who brought the food and gave it to us. I wished the friend blessings on his journey.'

'*Sagbol*,' I said, and in thanking him, exhausted my knowledge of Turkmen.

'Do they pray in America at mealtime? he asks.'

'Many people do.'

'Do they pray at other times too?'

'Yes. Americans pray a lot.'

A knock at the compartment door: the conductor. He was handing out sheets for sleeping. The arrangement was that in return for our ticket we would be given a sheet. Tomorrow morning, we'd hand over the sheet and get our ticket back – we'd need it to pass through the station at Mary.

Though it was not late, the light was so bad there was nothing to do but sleep. The others, even the student, were early-to-bed people, I could see. So we turned in, each of us in a bunk. After the feeble light was switched off, I could see the dark plains passing, the low scrub, the boulders glowing, smooth and bluish in the moonlight.

Hours later, it was still dark as we approached the town of Mary. Another knock at the door, demanding the sheets, offering tickets. The others were awake and yawning.

I said to the student, 'Ask him if he's met any Americans before.'

'No,' Selim said. He thought a moment. He said, 'But I met an Uzbek once.'

Ashgabat had been hot and dry. Wishing to lighten my bag, I had given my sweater to Mamed and my scarf to Gulnara. Approaching Mary, I gave my heavy long-sleeved polo shirt to the student, who had been so helpful.

'It's a lucky shirt,' I said.

In return, he gave me another multicoloured cord to ward off the evil eye.

Selim said, 'I will wait at the station until eight o'clock. Then I'll get the bus to Yeloten. It costs five thousand manat. A shared taxi costs ten thousand manat. But I say, better to take the bus and give the extra money to my children.'

It was a lesson in rural Turkmen economics and paternal love: this man who'd just had a fitful night of sleep on the train would crouch in the darkness and cold of Mary Station and wait for three hours, wrapped in his cloak, to save 30 cents to divide among his four kids.

The conceit in the antique land hereabouts, Khorrasan, with its noble capital called Merv, was that it was once the centre of the world. In one extravagant metaphor, it was called 'the Soul of Kings'. It is almost axiomatic that such an oasis would eventually be turned into a dust bowl, and Merv had. But in its day, which is to say for thousands of years, it had been a marvel – an imperial metropolis, a centre of learning, a place of citadels, a walled city, or rather several of them. My interest was simply that of a wandering observer, seeing once again (as I had in the great Silk Road city of Turfan, in western China) that in the course of time, all great cities and their kings and their artefacts and their splendour and their pomps turn into dust. Looted of their treasures, their porcelains shattered into a million shards, their fortresses overrun and trampled, their people scattered, they remained a crumpled example of the vanity of human wishes.

Merv, what was left of it, lay in the hard glitter of the central Asian desert, about an hour up the railway line, near a town and station called Bayram Ali, which dated from 1887, when Tsar Nicholas II had planned to visit. A substantial villa was built for him in Bayram Ali, but in the event, his highness didn't show up, it wasn't used, and so it was turned into the sanatorium it is now, for people with heart and kidney ailments. Mary – the adjacent city and provincial capital – was the usual Turkmenistan artefact, half boom town, half slum: gold statues of Turkmenbashi, portraits of Turkmenbashi, the eternal slogan *Halk, Watan, Turkmenbashi* ('People, Motherland, Me'), white marble government buildings, prestige projects (an opera house, luxury hotels, a pointless flyover) and boulevards almost empty of traffic.

Off the big thoroughfares, on back streets, were low decaying houses and Soviet-era tenements. Some Russians remained – not many, though a small colony of hard-pressed Russian artists, voluntary exiles in a way, exhibited their work in one of Mary's neighbourhoods. The Germans whom Stalin had relocated here from the Volga region during the Second World War had all departed. I stayed in an inexpensive government hotel, where the other guests were Turkmen officials. Most people came to Mary to see the ruins at Merv, or the ones at Gonur Depe, also nearby. Either that or the cotton fields. On some of the side roads were bakeries and some joints roasting shish kebabs and serving piles of *plov* and chunks of bread.

One morning in Mary I met Evgenia Golubeva. A sturdy woman of about fifty, divorced, her daughters in Moscow, Evgenia was a third-generation Russian in Turkmenistan, well known locally, much loved and scholarly – she had studied the ruins here and in Gonur Depe in detail. As a Russian remnant, staying on, with nothing but praise for the Turkmen people ('so kind, so gentle, so hospitable'), she was a pleasure to spend time with, because she was knowledgeable and passionate about these flattened cities.

On the way to Mary, by the roadside, in the middle of a dusty plain, among thorn bushes and salty desert, I saw startlingly beautiful Turkmen woman – golden-skinned, with a sculpted face, wearing a fluttering cloak, standing gracefully next to a bundle, probably waiting for one of those small, dirty buses. Her beauty in this crusted wasteland was like a metaphor for Turkmenistan: lovely people, awful place.

Ancient Merv, to my fascinated and amateur eye, resembled many fabled cities I'd seen that had declined, all of them in deserts – the Chinese Taklamakan Desert, or the Nafud, or here in the Karakum wasteland. It had the appearance of sandcastles after the tide had brimmed and washed over them, simplified and smoothed their walls, flattened them, pitted their battlements and pillars – so that there was only the faintest suggestion of symmetry in the slopes of sand. As for elegance, you'd have to take the guide's or the historian's word for it. Basically you were looking at a lost city of millions that was now tumbled brick and blown dust and mud heaps.

But, as I kept thinking, this was a vivid metaphor for what happened to the hubristic world of wealth and power – indeed, the world of gold statues and marble palaces and vain slogans and upstart forests. The world of armies and conquest. The realm of generals and windbags. Ha! It all turned to sand and was overrun with rodents and lizards. Hawks flew over it, searching for vermin.

'This is Erk Kala, oldest part of Merv – from sixth century BC,' said Evgenia, indicating a wide low crater of dried mud.

This city, 'Merv, Queen of the World', one of the pearls of the Silk Road, had been an early centre of Zoroastrianism and been associated with Alexander the Great and Tamerlane. It had been mentioned by the Persians (it was once the capital of Persian Khorrasan); it was sacked by Tolui Khan, son of Genghis Khan, in 1221, and later visited by Marco Polo and Omar Khayyám. It had been Buddhist and Nestorian Christian. It is mentioned in Zarathustra's *Avesta* as a place of strength and holiness, of the 'good lands'. In its opulence, its only other rival had been Baghdad. Importantly, Merv had been targeted by Muhammad as the staging post for Islamic conversion. The Prophet himself had sent two of his closest disciples here to evangelize. 'My eyes in the East', he had called them; they were buried here.

And it was not one city but four or five, side by side, each of them distinct and from a different period, laid out over many square miles. The battered walls of some citadels still stood, with roughed-out rooms and the remnants of staircases, but it was all like a child's sand-pile simplification of splendour. You could wax poetic – some more recent travellers had done so, trying to give it life – but it was lifeless and pathetic, like all such desert ruins, not a vivid thing but rather a *Planet of the Apes* version of history, which is truer than most. You had to use your imagination.

At one of the old mosques, the graves of the seventh-century Muslim evangelists, Jaffari and Bureda, were marked by a marble slab with a long inscription. Evgenia translated: 'O traveller, you visit this place and you are lucky, because the people who are buried here are holy and close to God. If you have a problem, walk three times around the tomb and it will be solved.'

My problem, so I had been told, was that the Ministry of Foreign Affairs in Ashgabat was annoyed with me because of the uproar at my talk – specifically, the outburst by the dissident politician, but more to the point, the government's photographer had been frustrated in his spying, his memory card wiped clean of any images.

'You might have a problem at the border,' I was told. 'They might hassle you. They could seriously hold you up.'

So I walked three times around the tomb of Jaffari and Bureda.

What I liked of Merv was its innocence – no fences, no postcards, no pests, few signs, not even much respect. In this shattered and somewhat forgotten place in the desert, some visitors scrambled up and down the steep walls, kicking them apart, picking up pieces of broken pottery, and others picnicked among the crenellations. It was possible to see young

Turkmen boys genially pissing on the ruins. This was what became of pompous plans: the trickle of urine darkening the dust, the laughter of picnickers scattering crumbs and *plov* grains, spilling lemonade.

I was shown the old cistern and the Sassanid dome and the rebuilt ('Notice the squeenches,' Evgenia said) Sultan Sanjar Mosque ('Double dome, two khundred years before Brunelleschi designed Saint Peter's in Roma'), the third-century wall of Antiochus, the big ruined Buddhist stupa, the ice house, the site of the Mongol invasion where a million people were slaughtered, the ruined watchtowers . . .

And masses of tamarisks with purple blossoms graced the watchtowers. A sharp-angled falcon glided slowly above, circling, stalking. In the distance some men were grazing a herd of camels. Three small boys approached us where we stood. They were mounted on donkeys, yelling and galloping across an ancient wall, leaving hoofprints on it. They had no saddles, they held on to rope bridles, they kicked their skinny grey mounts.

'They are Beluchis, from Persia,' Evgenia said. 'They settled here many years ago.'

These human touches made the place real for me. Evgenia said that local people, superstitious about the aura of slaughter and conquest, avoided Merv and used it only to pasture their animals or to pilfer bricks. Goatherds huddled by the single remaining part of the exposed wall of the complex known as Gyaur Kala. The sun was setting on Merv. The shepherds' fire scorched the ancient bricks as they cooked their evening meal.

In Mary, over another mound of *plov*, a young Turkmen – formerly an exchange student in the United States, a recent university graduate, new to Mary – listed for me the problems in his country.

'First of all, it is a police state,' he said. 'We have secret police, we have spies, it is terrible. It is also a corrupt system. It is impossible to advance in any government job without bribes. Even going to a university requires bribing the admissions office. And if you are non-Turkmen, forget about it. You'll never get in.'

Unemployment was high, the teacher shortage was acute, salaries were low – a university professor pedalling his bike past the gold statues earned about $150 a month. The minimum wage was $20 a month; a cotton picker like Selim did not earn much more than that. Add to this the housing shortage, the potholes that characterized most streets, the interminable roadblocks and grouchy soldiers, the disgusting toilets.

'Many people are desperate.'

'Give me an example,' I said.

'Girls sell themselves on the street! Didn't you see them in Ashgabat?'

I had seen pretty girls on street corners – and by the way, all the major streets were named for members of Turkmenbashi's family – but how was I to know they were selling themselves?

'Where were you in the United States?' I asked, because he now and then mentioned his American host family. And he remarked on the fact that he had been twenty-two when he went to the United States but that this was his first time in Mary.

'Spokane.'

'After what you've told me about Turkmenistan, do you sometimes wish you'd stayed there?'

'No. I am a Turkmen. I love my country. I would only go to the USA in order to make money and send it to my parents.'

I met other former exchange students. They were cautious when they talked to me, for fear that anything they said would expose them to retribution.

But many of them said that life was hard, and it wasn't just the low salaries and the housing shortage. Because Turkmenistan was so near to the heroin-producing areas of Afghanistan, hard drugs were a serious problem in the country. Heroin addicts were numerous, and their need for money caused crime. Turkmenistan was also a trans-shipment route for drugs from Afghanistan to Russia. Afghan hashish was freely available.

In Mary I was told that the Ministry of Foreign Affairs was still watching me, and that this might be a good time to head east, to Turkmenabat and the Uzbek border. Someone would be sent to help me.

And one morning a man showed up at my hotel, the Margush. I shall call him Sedyk Ali. He said he had been deputized to accompany me to the border. He too had been an exchange student.

'What did you like about the States?'

'Good people. Clean conditions. No bribes.'

'Tell me what you didn't like.'

'The way that children treat their elders. Not good.'

What surprised him especially was the casual way that teenagers spoke to their parents – offhand, disrespectful, sarcastic, often talking to them as they walked away, with their back turned. It would never happen in Turkmenistan.

'My host family was very nice to me, but one day coming home from school the daughter was smoking a cigarette. I said her mother wouldn't like it. "My mother's stupid. Don't pay any attention to her." Imagine that.'

'What did you think?'

'I was shocked,' he said. 'A mother is holy!'

We drove through the prairie towards Turkmenabat, another renamed city – most people I met in Mary still called it by its old name, Charjou. In Ashgabat I had asked an American Peace Corps volunteer what this part of the country would look like. He had said, 'Looks like west Texas' – and it did. When we came to the inevitable roadblock in the middle of the scrub and the stony plain, there was a small settlement, called Rawnina, where some people were watching us, their cloaks drawn around them because the sharp wind was lifting the grit from the land and spraying it. The air was hot, the grey sky oppressive. Intending to further lighten my bag, I gave Sedyk Ali one of my cold-weather shirts.

He thanked me and, indicating the settlement, said, 'They are Kazakhs.'

A shrouded old woman squatted by the road with a pile of trinkets. Here in the middle of nowhere, a seller of amulets against the evil eye and against bad luck generally. It was said that in these wild and empty places you were likely to be harried by demons.

Sedyk Ali bought me an amulet on a multicoloured demon-distracting cord, thinking it might come in handy.

Perhaps it did. Our car dumped us in Turkmenabat, the driver saying he could not go further. But when we got another car, no sooner had the old man driving it pointed out the Amu Darya River – one of the wonders of this region for its ancient association, the fabled Oxus – than a roadblock appeared. The soldiers looked at Sedyk Ali's papers and told him to turn back.

Sedyk Ali wished me luck. I saw him through the rear window, standing in the empty road.

We came to Farap, the Turkmenistan border. I was apprehensive about the customs formalities, but there was no problem. I was searched, my bag examined, my icon remarked upon. My passport, too.

'You live Gawaii.'

'Yes.'

'Gonolulu?'

'That's right.'

'You stay Ashgabat?'

'Yes.'

'You see beeg beelding?'

'Yes.'

'Weech you like better?'

My favourite, I told him with absurd eagerness, was the big statue of Turkmenbashi on the giant marble toilet-bowl plunger. 'His arm is up' – I raised my arm in the same Sieg Heil way – 'and when the sun moves, the gold statue moves, like this. Beautiful. Gold!'

'Yes,' the border guard said, smiling in satisfaction. His interrogation over, he waved me through. 'You can pass. *Nyet prablyema.*'

So I walked past the barbed-wire fence on the dirt road through the desert towards Uzbekistan.

8. Night Train to Tashkent

Most travel, and certainly the rewarding kind, involves depending on the kindness of strangers, putting yourself into the hands of people you don't know and trusting them with your life. This risky suspension of disbelief is often an experience freighted with anxiety. But what's the alternative? Usually there is none. There was none for me here, at the edge of the Kyzylkum Desert, kicking through the gravel.

As I picked my way across the weeds and stones in the no-man's-land between the two frontiers, from dismal Farap in Turkmenistan to dismal Jalkym in Uzbekistan, it began to rain, not a downpour but desert rain, a bleak pattering that served only to moisten the dust and intensify the gloom. I came to a gate in a high barrier, the sort of fifteen-foot fence you see at the edge of a sports stadium car park, except that this one was trimmed with razor wire and enclosed nothing but a few low huts and stony desert. Not a car to be seen. The fence continued into the distance, the national boundary of Uzbekistan.

Some downhearted people were waiting by the gate, about twenty of them, their fingers hooked into the rusted chain-link fence, like captives, prisoners gazing mournfully through it. They were very wet. I took this to mean they had been there a long time. Obviously they were waiting to enter. But the gate was padlocked; no cars, no trucks, no camels, no traffic at all on the road.

Because even the most absorbing travel involves spells of tedium, it is boring to relate one's complaints about delays. This open-air border crossing took half a day – another rainy day. I was anxious, because I had checked out of Turkmenistan and could not re-enter. I could enter Uzbekistan only when I was allowed. But in the course of waiting in the rain to pass through the fence to the Jalkym customs post, I got acquainted with an old Turkmen who was travelling with his wife and daughter. He spoke no English, I had no Turkmen, and yet he grasped that I was going by road to Bukhara, and he gave me to understand that he was going to a village called Qorakol, about halfway there. Gesturing and grunting, he conveyed to me that we could go together.

I said, 'Okay.'

'Okay, okay.'

He was a powerfully built man in his fifties, wearing a lambskin cap and a heavy coat. Both of the women with him wore cloaks, and headscarves that were yanked forward to keep the rain off, so I could hardly see their faces; but I could tell that one woman was younger than the other. They were drenched, their boots muddy. In this group of people waiting to enter Uzbekistan there was very little chatter. I took this to mean that some were Uzbeks and the others Turkmen. They had the solemn patience of the poor in the presence of soldiers, with plastic bags for luggage and wet heads.

Hours of this. It was now mid afternoon. No signs of life on the other side of the fence. But then a soldier appeared. The Turkmen called out to him. The soldier walked away, into his shed. Half an hour later he emerged and walked the fifty yards to the fence.

The Turkmen said something to him, the soldier cracked open the gate, and then, in a paternal gesture, the Turkmen helped the two women through, and finally he pushed me through, while the others stared. We walked to the shed, but by the time I got there all I saw in the draughty open-sided structure were two soldiers at a table. I handed over my passport.

'America,' one said. He examined my passport, turning the pages slowly, wetting his thumb with saliva, and transferring the saliva to my passport.

The other soldier shrugged and stamped it and gestured for me to leave the shed in the direction of Bukhara, another empty stony road.

There on the road, standing near an old jalopy, a beat-up Lada with a broken windscreen, was the Turkmen and his two women. He beckoned to me. He introduced me to the driver, a small, sad-looking man in a dirty sweater.

'Bukhara,' I said.

'Qorakol,' the Turkmen said.

'Five dollar,' the Uzbek said and showed me five fingers.

I paid and, doors banging, springs creaking, tyres bumping, we began to race across the desert, the drizzle streaking the dust on the cracked windscreen.

The driver's name was Farrukh. He wasn't a taxi driver. He was one of the men you see at such places: he owned an old car, and he knew – as all such men know – that at borders like this he could find helpless people in need of a lift. Since so few people were allowed to leave Turkmenistan, and no one with any sense wanted to enter, business was slow.

I considered myself lucky, up to a point. There was always the chance – it had happened to me before – that the driver was an opportunist. Farrukh's first promising sign was that he asked for the $5 in advance. Dishonest drivers said, 'Pay me later,' and on arrival at the destination there would be threats and a shakedown. In another classic crooked manoeuvre, the driver might pull off the road, choosing a ghoul-haunted woodland, and tell me that he wanted more money, or else no more ride. There were more menacing ploys too, involving dire threats and lethal weapons.

After an hour we came to Qorakol, a town of low cement houses. The side streets were littered with baseball-sized rocks. Boys stood watching us, the only car. One yanked on a goat's tether, another kicked a tin can. The rain came down. The Turkmen in the rear seat gave directions and was dropped off at the gate of a high wall. He beckoned me out of the car – why? Yet I got out, and when I did, he embraced me in a big bear hug, as thanks for my paying, and then he wished me *salaam* and placed his hand on his heart, the most touching of Asiatic gestures.

'Bukhara,' Farrukh said.

It was another forty miles through the desert. Farrukh drove fast – it seemed he was not going to rob me. My bag was in his boot, my briefcase in my lap. From it I heard a familiar buzzing – my BlackBerry, which had not worked since Tbilisi, was alerting me to messages, now that we were in Uzbekistan and away from the enclosed world of Turkmenbashi.

A message from Penelope. She was worried. She had not heard from me for quite a while. Where was I?

We were passing a settlement of one-storey stucco houses, Farrukh slowing down for the potholes. I made a querying gesture, to ask the name.

'Jondor,' he said.

Passing through Jondor, on way to Bukhara, I typed with my thumbs. Then, succumbing to e-mail's narcissistic temptation to self-dramatization, added, *Racing in an old car into Uzbekistan . . .*

The outskirts of Bukhara looked seedier, poorer, dirtier, grubbier, more tumbledown than Turkmenabat, just over the border, which was merely ugly and strange. Farrukh was asking me a question with his hands.

'Hungry,' I said and accompanied this word with gestures of my own.

Farrukh indicated that he was hungry too. We drove down a back street, and he parked in front of a café.

We shared the meal: a bowl of cooked pigeon eggs, a bowl of meat dumplings, which Farrukh described using the Turkish word *manti* – but in this region everyone's *manti* were different – a wheel of hard bread, a pot of tea, and I thought, This is very nice. I think I'll stay in Bukhara.

'The difference between Turkmenistan and Uzbekistan is that Niyazov puts his opponents in jail and Karimov kills them,' an American in Ashgabat had said to me. This was a reference to the Uzbek dictator's suppressing an uprising in the city of Andijon in which several hundred unarmed demonstrators (but no one knew the exact number of casualties) were slaughtered by soldiers. This was in May 2005. A little over a year later, in September 2006, UNESCO awarded Islam Karimov the Borobudur Gold Medal for 'strengthening friendship and cooperation between nations, development of cultural and religious dialogue, and supporting cultural diversity'. So this hard-faced murderer and (until the massacre) solid ally of the United States now sported a gold medal from the United Nations.

The renewal and general fixing up of Bukhara had been one of the programmes for which Karimov had been rewarded. He was a murderer, but unlike Joseph Goebbels, when he heard the word 'culture' he did not reach for his gun. He had Bashi's obsession with the glorious past, and he too had lots of oil revenue. Most of the city in drizzly March seemed woebegone, but the restored part of Bukhara retained an atmosphere that was a mixture of the spurious and the authentic, half Disney, half Divanbegi – the bazaars, the mosques, the markets, the synagogues, the madrasas, the central pond and mausoleums, the ancient Ark.

I was inclined to stay because I liked the food, and I found a cheap hotel, where the news on TV was not of Uzbekistan but of the war in Iraq. Out of season, in the rain, the shops empty, it seemed I was the only unbeliever in this, the pillar of Islam.

The downside of being the only traveller here was that desperate hawkers implored me to buy carpets or samovars or silver jewellery; and because I usually walked away, a classic haggling technique, they offered excellent prices, and chased me, and reduced them even more.

'You buy this. Is beautiful,' a market seller said, showing me a silver dagger he had made. He demonstrated its razor-sharp blade by slipping it easily through a hunk of Uzbek bread he'd been eating.

I wasn't interested, but so as not to offend him I said, 'I'd never be able to travel with that.'

'No problem!'

'On a plane?'

'I wrap it in special way. I use folded metal. Put in your bag. When they x-ray, they see nothing. You take knife on plane!'

I bought a small icon and some old coins. I tried to engage various Uzbeks in a discussion about the massacre at Andijon, but no one had much to say. And by early evening the streets were empty. Bukhara was a city that emptied after dark – nobody on the street, not even much traffic.

Since Farrukh had kept his word on the $5 drive along the rutted roads from the border to Bukhara, I gave him another $5 to show me around the city, and to take me the next day to the outer suburb of Kagan, to buy a train ticket.

Kagan, a Russified town ten miles away, was Bukhara's train station – built there by a superstitious emir who considered railways a dangerous, possibly satanic innovation that had to be kept at a safe distance.

I was reassured by the ordinariness of the station, its busy lobby, the crowded waiting room, the sight of people boarding trains, and most of all by the tall board marked DEPARTURES in Cyrillic letters, the only destinations Самарканд (Smarkand) and Тошкент (Tashkent), because I was coming to the end of the line. Headed to India, I knew there was no overland route through the Hindu Kush mountain range that was open to me. In Tashkent, I intended to look for a flight to northern India; I'd heard there was a short flight to Amritsar in the Punjab, where I'd gone thirty-three years before, and could resume my sentimental journey.

'Tashkent,' I said to the woman at the ticket window, and pointed to the date on the calendar when I wished to go – the next day, at a quarter to five, the night train to Samarkand and Tashkent.

No berth to Tashkent, only Samarkand, the woman said.

Another $4 ticket. I used my time in Bukhara to write up my notes, and when Farrukh took me to the station to leave, I was so impressed by his dependability I offered him a tip. He said no, he would take only the agreed-upon amount, and with smiles and gestures he indicated that we were friends and that when I came back to Bukhara he would take me to meet his family – his wife, his two small children; we'd have a home-cooked meal. He already knew that I liked *manti* and pigeon eggs.

We hugged, we touched our hearts, we exchanged *salaams*, and I was off.

Even before the night train, the Bukhara Express, drew out of Bukhara Station, the two men in my compartment had settled themselves at the little table where I was writing and begun preparing their evening meal of tortured chicken and vodka. Without removing their heavy leather coats, they made ready. One twisted the top off a big bottle of vodka, the other unwrapped a roasted chicken and, using his hands as though shredding paper, tore the chicken into fragments, scattering bones and meat and grease on the table. He also unwrapped a package of grated carrot and a loaf of bread.

'*Woodka*,' the man with the bottle said, pushing it into my face. I could see that they were already drunk and would just get drunker.

'No thanks.'

But he insisted, so – to be companionable – I took a swig. And then I left the compartment and saw that we were moving slowly into the darkness.

The *provodnik* – why were they always such brutes? – demanded my ticket. With the two drunks in mind, I asked if he would sell me a ticket to Tashkent. We were due to arrive in Samarkand at two in the morning; if I changed my mind, I could simply stay aboard.

The train was technically full – the ticket seller at Bukhara had told me that. But *provodniks* are wily birds; they control all seats on the train; anything is for sale, at their discretion.

'Five dollars,' he said.

I paid up and he wrote me a ticket.

Back at my compartment, the two drunks had finished the grated carrot and the bread and the chicken – they had chewed and spat out the bones. They had nearly finished the bottle of vodka.

From time to time they sit beside me and put their faces against my notebook, marveling at the page of my writing, I wrote. And they stared crazily at me with the weepy boiled-looking eyes of drunks, trying to focus. They were so soused they did not bother to wipe their greasy cheeks, their food-spattered faces.

Because the crooked *provodnik* had sold more tickets than he had seats or berths for, the compartment began filling up with hopeful travellers. In addition to the two drunks, their leather coats gleaming with chicken grease, there was a pale young man, then two young women, also in leather coats, and a big boy in a baseball hat.

Farce, I wrote on the scrap of paper in my hand, a crossword puzzle I'd found in my briefcase, from an old Friday *Herald Tribune,* one of the harder puzzles I kept for my idle days. As there were now six other people in the four-berth compartment, and still a vodka bottle being passed around, I primly excused myself and slipped into the corridor, where I stood peering out through the windows at the ploughed fields, the cows, the sheep, the steppes of Gidjuvan.

Studying the clue *Keeping Don Juans at bay,* I worked out *Bucking the pass,* and I was nudged by one of the drunken Uzbeks, who had followed me and was staring over my shoulder. *Central Asian language* was another clue, five letters. I inked in *Azeri.* The man was breathing hard, but what could I do? Just look busy. *Finishing off a dressy outfit.* Ah yes, clichés in the form of spoonerisms. I wrote *Knotting the tie.* The man was still breathing hard, his alcoholic halitosis like car fumes. *Azeri* was wrong. I wrote *Uzbek,* and had the solution.

'*Krussvort,*' the Uzbek said, putting his face against the scrap of paper.

The same word in Russian, I later discovered.

At about ten o'clock I went back into the compartment. Now there were eight people, three of them sleeping stretched out, four of them jammed together on a lower berth (two were women), and one had tucked himself on the shelf of the overhead luggage compartment above the door. One, the upper berth, was empty – mine.

This was obviously the compartment where the *provodnik* stuck the extra passengers who had bribed him. He entered as I lay down on my berth and, pointing, indicated that in a few stations I would have to trade places with the man crouched in the luggage hole.

The drunks were snoring, the lights blazing in their eyes. The women had removed their leather coats and were wrapped in quilts. Soon everyone was asleep, even me.

Samarkand was a jolting stop at two in the morning. I could have got out and looked for a man with a jalopy, but I was half asleep and cold. The drunks, still drunk, were dragging themselves out of the compartment. Two more women got on. I glanced at the man in the luggage hole, and he waved an *I'm all right* signal to me and ducked his head, so I did not have to change places after all.

Nine of us in a four-person compartment, but it was orderly and safe nonetheless. Dirty, though, and smelly too – everyone sleeping in their clothes, the windows shut, wet boots steaming under the seats, stinky luggage, old leather jackets piled in a corner, chicken grease and bread crumbs and grated carrot littering the table. Filthy compartment, gracious people, no hassle: the railway experience of the Eastern Star.

The women were up early making breakfast – boiled eggs, pickled cabbage, chunks of hard bread. Did I want some? Yes, I said, and there we sat, rolling past Chinaz and Yangiyol, still nine of us, friends after a long night, entering the big city.

Shimoly Station – North Station – was one of the largest railway stations I saw on my entire trip, possibly the grandest, lovely even, and swept clean by old women with straw brooms. A ribbon of Uzbek motifs in bright mosaics ran around the top-storey façade of this palatial building, which the Soviets had built as a monument to their power and influence in this, the third-largest city in the Soviet Union, now the capital of independent Uzbekistan.

For me it was the end of the line, the first leg of my trip. From here to India or Pakistan, the only overland route crossed the most isolated mountain passes in the world and the antagonistic fastness of the Islamic valleys that produced Al Qaeda recruits and opium growers – perhaps a route to avoid, because it was off the map, beyond the reach of any government or any law but its own, a place of suspicious villages where every woman was veiled and every man armed. It was possibly the most inaccessible area on earth: the Pamir Valley, Waziristan, the North-West Frontier, where the Wali of Swat held court. Osama bin Laden was last seen there, but how would any outsider know more than that? There was no road, only a network of mountain footpaths. The nearest railway was the line in Tajikistan that went nowhere except from Dushanbe to Termiz on the border of Afghanistan – nothing helpful to me between Tashkent and Amritsar, though there was a short direct flight.

Spring had come to Tashkent: daffodils in the city gardens, pale sunshine, cherry blossoms, and, as in Georgia and Azerbaijan, people gathered in the parks and gardens, the men to sell the family silver and hawk postcards, the women to prostitute themselves.

'Take me,' a young woman said, and pursed her lips to make a kissing sound.

'Tomorrow,' I said, so as not to be rude.

On the next corner: 'Streep shaw, meester?'

'No, thank you.'

'Dreenks?'

'No, thank you.'

They were also selling old watches, chewing gum, bathroom fixtures, Soviet memorabilia, candelabra. A man from distant Chukchi offered me a walrus penis and some indigenous ivory carvings. Murat and Zahir specialized in Christian art; it seemed to be a niche market for enterprising Muslims. I bought another icon, for $100.

Rauf, at his stall of pirated videos, was studying English. Like Murat and Zahir and most other Uzbeks I met, he was eager to emigrate to the United States; like them, he hated the war in Iraq. Becoming an American did not interest Rauf much; he seemed to dislike America, but he wanted badly to go to America.

'Business very bad here, but worse in Samarkand,' he said.

He was filling in the blanks in an exercise book.

Beside *Can you swim?* he wrote slowly, *No, I cannot swim.*

I picked it up. I read the next question: 'Do you like to watch TV?'

'Yes, I like.'

'Like what?'

'Watch TV.'

'Yes, I like to watch TV.'

'Yes, I like to watch TV.'

I sat down. I read another one: 'What did you do last night?'

'With my friends, we listen the music,' he said.

'Do you own a car?'

'No, I am not have car?'

I pretended to read a question, saying, 'Do you like George Bush?'

'I am not,' he said, and stammered with fury, 'I am not like Meester Bush President.'

Rauf had a sister in Miami who had a green card. He lusted after one himself, and though he was hustling cheap videos and CDs at a stall, he wanted to get out of Uzbekistan and work in America. This eagerness

to emigrate to the West seemed to soften people's attitudes towards me
– I was never the object of personal hostility, except from the occasional
customs official.

It seemed I was the only foreign traveller in Tashkent. I was the only
guest in my huge hotel. I never saw another tourist in this vast city. And
when at last I went to Tashkent Airport for the flight to the Punjab, I
was the only person checking in, the only passenger boarding the plane.
It was the plane's one stop, the Uzbek Airways flight from Birmingham
to Amritsar, every male passenger a turbaned Sikh, every woman in a sari.

I left Tashkent feeling lucky that I had got here unscathed from
London, that my close encounters had been with good people. The
hassles and delays were part of all travel. The revelation was that the old
world still existed. The airport had been empty; but the marshalling yards
of Shimoly Station were busy with shunting trains, and the station itself
was crowded with people going all over the country, and they were
taking the train because they were poor.

As for me, here as elsewhere, I felt I was the fortunate traveller.

9. The Shan-e-Punjab Express to Delhi

Because it was a sacred city, a howling but deaf and discontinuous mob, mostly pilgrims, kicked along the streets and lanes of Amritsar. These sun-baked streets were thick with stinging dust and smelly traffic, and the traffic included sacred cows, three-legged dogs, old cars, twisted bikes, scooter rickshaws, pedicabs, the usual trotting two-wheeled pony carts – tongas and gharries – and rusted buses. There were heaps of sorted and pawed-through rubbish; the pavement overspill of fix-it men and their antique tools – spoke-shaves, chisels, cobbling awls, soldering irons, treadle-powered sewing machines; blue exhaust fumes, oily dirt, fresh dung, the fountain in the middle of the miserable road with its sign, AMRITSAR IMPROVEMENT TRUST, the temples so attractive to beggars because holy precincts encouraged the giving of alms; and loud noise trumpeting the simple but firmly held Indian delusion that honking horns sped the flow of traffic.

The point about the crowds of excited pilgrims in a sacred place is that they are giddy just from physically being there. Or more than giddy – chattering, skipping, giggling, goggle-eyed with rapture in this, the centre of Sikhdom, all of these turbaned men and fluttering women hurrying to the Golden Temple . . .

Welcome to India and the proof that, as Borges once wrote, 'India is larger than the world.' On the surface, nothing had changed in Amritsar. From what I could gather, the country was no different from what I had seen three decades before. This prospect delighted me. It was a relief, the mildly orchestrated free-for-all of India – something of a madhouse with a touch of anarchy, yes, but an asylum in which strangers are welcome, even inquisitorial ones like me; where anything is possible, the weather is often pleasant, and the spicy food clears your sinuses. Most of India embodies Blake's dictum that 'Energy is eternal delight.' All you need is a strong stomach, a little money and a tolerance for crowds. And a way of lifting your gaze upward and moving on, so that you don't see the foreground – in India the foreground is generally horrific. The reality was that Amritsar, like all Indian cities, looked as though it had been made by human hands, skinny ones, and so the result had a look of improvisation, faulty and fragile and somehow incomplete.

The horror is possibly true, or perhaps all illusion, as some Indians believe, smiling and saying, 'True and not true, sar. *Anekantavada*, sar. The many-sidedness of reality, sar.'

The austere torpor of the Stans had been wearing me down – the humourlessness and paranoia of a police state, no outward indication of struggle, a kind of beaten-down acceptance. Acceptance is not an Indian trait. In India, no one takes no for an answer: policemen are jeered at, authority exists to be defied, walls are erected to be defaced, and everyone is talking, often in English. Shoeshine boys, rickshaw wallahs, taxi drivers, beggars, businessmen, shopkeepers and Surinder ('I am agent, sar') Singh with his gimpy leg and his practised patter, all of them demanding attention. Surinder had assured me of a ticket to Delhi, though the train was full. He had connections, though his ragged clothes did not inspire confidence.

When I remarked that Amritsar hadn't changed, Indians clicked their tongues or sucked their teeth in annoyance. They insisted it had been modernized. I never saw where or how. It is a border city, only a few miles from the Pakistan frontier, and consequently not a place for investment. Besides, being a holy city in India is plenty, since Indians are instinctive pilgrims, liking the ritual, the spiritual boost and the companionship of a pilgrimage, which always involves a great number of people, a long train ride, loud music and platters of food.

I was at the main railway station with Surinder.

'How old are you?' he asked.

'Guess.'

'Please tell me, sar.'

'Go ahead, guess. What do you think?'

'No, this is very serious, sar,' he said, snapping at me for my face-tiousness. 'You must tell me now.'

I told him.

'You are lucky,' he said, sounding resentful. 'Very lucky today.'

'Why would that be?'

'You qualify for Old Age Exception.'

This meant 100 rupees off the 400-rupee fare to Delhi, $7.50 instead of $10, because I was over sixty. And a 25-rupee supplement for a seat, which required a large form to be filled out in triplicate – sticky blue copies and perforations. In the age of computers, which Indians excelled at – so I was told – many government forms were still filled out by hand in triplicate, on thick sewn-together pads, with flimsy sheets separated by carbon paper, using blunt pencils, following the printed direction PRESS HARD.

I searched for social changes. Joginder's greasy café and pastry shop was now Joginder's greasy Internet café and pastry shop and looked 200 years old. And the brick pre-war railway station, which I'd last seen in 1973, was seriously defaced by foot-high graffiti in Hindi and English. I recognized the word *Hartal* – strike, a commonly heard term in India – and was told the entire building had been scribbled on during the strike that had taken place a month before, but painted so professionally the angry slogans looked like advertising – which they were, promoting a mass sit-down. That had passed.

'But they will repeat it. So the writing will stay.'

In a world of change, India is exceptional. Everyone talks about India's great leap, Indian modernity, Indian millionaires and 'You must see the transformation of Bangalore.' 'The Indian miracle' was a boasting rant in every Western newspaper and magazine, but on the evidence of Amritsar this assertion was nonsense, not just a joke in bad taste but the cruellest satire. It seemed to me that little had changed except the size of the population, an unfeedable, unhousable, uncontainable 1.3 billion people, not many of them saying 'We are modern now' because more than a third of them were working for a dollar a day. Indians boast of the miracle, but when I mentioned to enterpreneurs the 400 million people living below the poverty line, they just bobbled their heads and hummed or else went silent, darkening in resentment that I raised the question and refusing to tell me what they paid their employees.

Yet the country still ran, in its clunky fashion, all its mends and patches showing, and what looked like chaos in India was actually a kind of order, like furious atoms spinning. Surinder Singh merely appeared to be a tout and an opportunist. In fact he was part of the complex system of Indian ticket buying. As I was congratulating myself on having secured a $10 seat on the express to Delhi, he showed up again, demanding the equivalent of an additional $10.

'What's that for?'

'*Baksheesh*, sar.' A bribe.

But he had kept his word.

No one succeeds in India without exploiting someone else, defrauding him, sitting on his head, twisting his arm, getting him to work for 12 cents an hour. The news is all about the winners – big business, call centres, manufacturing, textiles, all the rest of it. But for there to be big winners in India, there have to be bigger losers. It is the system.

Who shares in the wealth? In the Punjab, I heard of a powerful Indian lawyer who earned $1.5 million a year and still paid his driver $20 a week and got his shoes shined for 25 cents. Later in my trip I met a lawyer, a woman, who had been offered, by an American firm, a guaranteed $1 million a year plus profits on contracts, but she held out for more and eventually joined a rival firm that offered her almost $2 million. Nothing wrong with that, Indians say; it is an example of market forces, and the conventional Indian response is to say how such tycoons are great philanthropists. It is the Indian paradox: driving hard bargains, under-paying people, becoming a corporate slave driver, and later these same desperate employees will qualify for hand-outs.

The losers in India have their revenge, always, as I saw all over Amritsar: not just the strikes and sit-downs and go-slows to torment employers, but the visible fact that the biggest, fastest limousine is forced to travel at a crawl behind the pony carts and the skinny men on their bicycle rickshaws. That is the other truth about India, that so much of it is a moral lesson, a set of simple visuals; so much of it is vivid symbolism, the cows and the rickshaws and men pulling wagons, slowing the progress of limos and delivery vans. The van might be delivering computers, God knows, but the computers won't get through any quicker than the man with ten sacks of beans in his wheelbarrow.

By chance I met Amar Singh. He owned a car. He had functioned for years as a go-between for journalists. He said, 'We're a big power now.'

'In what sense?' I asked.

'Better than before. Much stronger.'

'Give me an example.'

'We're like America now,' he said.

In Amritsar this statement was debatable, but I was impressed by his confidence. No one would have said that thirty years ago. Yet in order to say such things you have to ignore the mangy cows, the stalled traffic, the squatters, the beggars, the crowds, the dirt, the squalor.

It was a relief to me that Amritsar was not very different. I liked it as it was – progressing, obviously, but so immersed in its past and its pieties that it could not change much. Because it was a holy city, its visitors put up with more inconvenience: dirt and distance and noise were the price of sanctity and blessings.

I had walked for quite a while, but then hailed a taxi, and it was Amar Singh who drove me slowly through the crowds. We passed a sign saying SERVICE TO HUMANITY IS TRUE SERVICE TO GOD.

I wrote it down in my notebook.

Amar Singh said, 'You're a journalist?'

'Sort of.'

We went to the Golden Temple, but the crowd was so large there was no way a car could get near. I left Amar Singh and walked the last half-mile with all the skipping pilgrims – good-humoured and frisky *yatris*, because they were near the object of their long *yatra*. Some were stepping out of their shoes and sandals and tiptoeing on the scalded bricks this hot day at the entrance to the temple; others were flinging scarves into a big barrel, or selecting scarves from it to put on their heads.

'What is this?' I asked.

'It is the system,' a man said.

'What is the system?'

'Cloth on head for temple.'

'No open head,' another man elaborated. 'No exceptions.'

He meant: no exceptions for *ferringhis* – foreigners. But I was wearing a hat.

A Punjabi woman interrupted to say, 'Your hat is acceptabubble.'

The label of my hat, a style called the Traveller, said LOCKE'S THE HATTER, ST JAMES, LONDON W1 – surely suitable headgear for the Holy of Holies?

I walked with a tramping crowd through a trough of water meant to purify our feet, but because it had been walked through by thousands of pilgrims, the water was foul – green and viscous, like swamp water. This was the usual thing – if a pool or a tank or a trough was considered sacred, it didn't matter whether it was stagnant. The holier the pool, the more foul-smelling it was.

Never mind. This was the India I remembered, and I was grateful to be here. The Golden Temple looked golder, brighter, more effulgent. I walked down the hot marble causeway with the happy pilgrims, but because I didn't have the faith, it was just a glittering palace of roistering Sikhs, a feature, a sight to see – the crowds interesting me more than the gold domes and chanting priests.

'Get over here!' and 'This is so neat, Ma!'

Sikhs with American accents, Sikhs with the west London whine, Sikhs from California, Sikhs from Scotland and Canada. I glided around the hot walkways for a while, made a circuit of the sacred pool, found my way back to the entrance and my shoes, and then hiked to the car.

'Do you know Mark Tully?' the driver, Amar Singh, asked.

Mark Tully, known in India as Tully Sahib, was for many years the BBC correspondent in India – a much-loved man for his sympathetic but scrupulous reporting, his truthfulness, his love for the country.

'I met him once,' I said. 'He's a great journalist and a friend of India.'

'I took him around here during the Blue Star action,' Amar Singh said.

So this taxi driver whom I had met by chance at the railway station turned out to have been one of the resourceful operatives during Amritsar's crisis in 1984.

Operation Blue Star was a military assault by the Indian army on the Golden Temple – an unspeakable, unjustified defilement of the holiest shrine in Sikhdom, Sikhs said. It was disastrous: heavy artillery in a small overcrowded town. It came about because Sikh militants had occupied the towers and cellars and kiosks of the temple. They were part of a revivalist movement that had also called for a separate Sikh state, to be named Khalistan ('Land of the Pure'). Led by a Sikh preacher named Sant Jarnail Singh Bhindranwale, this action was watched closely by Sikhs world-wide. Bhindranwale (a prophet to some Sikhs, a pest to nearly everyone else) was disruptive; he called for the murder of Hindus and moderate Sikhs. His beard reached to his waist, he was said to be charismatic, he was well armed, and he wouldn't budge from the temple he occupied with many of his followers and an arsenal of weapons in May 1984.

In June of that year, after some days of fruitless negotiation, Indira Gandhi, the prime minister, gave the order to dislodge Bhindranwale and his men. The army occupied Amritsar in large numbers, and black-suited commandos stormed the temple complex. They were cut down by machine-gun fire from Bhindranwale's men. Some soldiers fired from a distance, but succeeded only in killing civilians and wrecking parts of the temple. Indian army officers begged for backup, insisting they needed tanks. After initial refusals – because of the danger to civilians – permission was granted. Thirteen tanks were lined up and were met by a barrage of anti-tank fire and rocket launchers. Hundreds more died.

Still, Bhindranwale was trapped, and it was only a matter of time before he ran out of ammunition. He decided to go down in a blaze of glory. In the course of the siege he had become messianic, and in one version of the events he said to his men, 'Those who want to be martyrs, come with me.' He emerged from his hiding place firing his machine gun, and was mowed down with fifty of his men. Six hundred men on both sides had already been shot or blown up.

That was not the end of the business. Sikhs were furious that the Golden Temple had been desecrated by the assault, and Mrs Gandhi was blamed. Stories circulated that Indian soldiers who occupied the temple drank alcohol there and, much worse, smoked tobacco. Sikhs have a unique horror of cigarettes. Mrs Gandhi hunkered down, protected by a number of bodyguards. But Sikhs got their revenge four months later when, in October, Mrs Gandhi (who had ignored several warnings) was murdered by two of her bodyguards, who were Sikhs. One morning in Delhi, on the pretext of guarding her, they pulled out their service pistols and shot her dead.

With their obvious turbans, their full beards and their characteristic silver bracelets, Sikh males are among the most easily identifiable believers in the world. In the aftermath of Indira Gandhi's assassination Sikhs were singled out and set upon by Hindus – dragged from trains and buses, stabbed in bazaars, set on fire as they tried to flee in their cars. Perhaps 3,000 were killed – no figures are accurate, just round numbers of a tragic event that no one has forgotten.

'It was terrible,' Amar Singh said. 'So many people killed.'

'But it finished the problem of Bhindranwale, didn't it?'

'It finished problem, yes. But danger for us lurked everywhere.'

'What did you think of Mrs Gandhi?'

'A nice woman,' he said, but he was being polite. Even Indira Gandhi's closest friends would not have called this manipulative demagogue a nice woman.

'Do people still talk about Khalistan?'

'In villages, some people. Not city people.'

Nevertheless, Khalistan, 'an aspirant Sikh nation', has an office in Washington, which sends out press releases, campaign information, furious rants and images of the Khalistan flag.

That night I was making notes in my room in a cheap hotel in Amritsar, where there are no good hotels. It occurred to me why the Golden Temple looked golder and brighter and better kept than it had when I'd first seen it. Because of the damage of the siege and the reassertion of Sikh identity, the temple had been renovated, regilded until it dazzled.

I called Amar Singh the next day to get a ride to the railway station and to say goodbye. He mentioned the other journalists he had taken around. Besides Mark Tully, there was Satish Jacob, whom I had also met many years ago – Tully and Jacob had written the definitive account of the Blue Star operation.

'And David Brown from the *Guardian* – I drove him, too. He is now in Jerusalem. I helped him.'

Amar Singh said he still listened to the BBC. He followed world news and always looked for word of journalists he had driven. I complimented him on his curiosity and helpfulness.

'My aim is good service,' he said.

It could have sounded like a cliché, but it didn't. It was serious and sincere, and it touched me coming from this old driver who had a book and a newspaper on the front seat of his car, who lived at the periphery of journalism, who kept up with the news. That was part of the pleasure I felt being back in India again, where everyone seemed overqualified for whatever job they were doing. Though their talk could be maddening and their demands exasperating, I loved the fluency of Indians. The crowds of people seemed worse than ever, but I was pleased to be back in the Indian stew.

Amritsar Central Station had been built in 1931; the date was carved on its red-brick façade. The antique weirdness was another pleasure of India. Entering the station, I felt I could have been walking backwards into the past, passing the big gloomy station restaurant and its overhead fans, the urchins chasing each other on the platform, the Sikh in a brown suit and blue turban, the man in dusty pyjamas sleeping against a pile of burlap bags. And there were the station's hustlers, children mostly, selling bottles of pop they carried in a big bucket, or ice cream bars they hawked out of a wooden box, or with shoeshine kits slung over one skinny shoulder, all of them completely fluent in English but illiterate.

'What does that sign say?'

The boy was about thirteen, and I was pointing to one of the more dramatic-looking examples of railway strike graffiti.

'I don't know. I don't go to school.'

Half-naked sadhus, holy men with metal tridents and all their possessions in one small cloth bag; groups of women looking tidy and serene amid the squalor; a man hoicking just under a NO SPITTING sign; fierce moustached matrons and small girls, nearly all the women in saris or Punjabi dress, all the men in turbans. It could have been the 1930s; it could have been 1973, when I had been on the Railway Bazaar trip. Superficially, nothing had changed, and it was uplifting, as though time had stood still, as though I were young again.

'What is your bogie?' the conductor asked.

I told him and he showed me my seat. It was a day train, the seven-hour trip to Delhi, not as fancy or as fast as the Shatabdi Express, but comfortable, on time, with a meal service, and soon rolling and bouncing through the wheat fields of the Punjab—Pakistan just a few miles to the west.

I had thought of taking the train to Lahore, but the news from Pakistan discouraged me. Riots had recently taken place in many Pakistani cities, Lahore included, after this week's court case in which a man in neighbouring Kabul, one Abdul Rahman, was put on trial for converting to Christianity. The charge was 'apostasy'. One of the Hadiths specified death as the punishment for a Muslim who abandons the faith. But when the man's life was spared, riots broke out, huge mobs crying 'Death to Christians!'

'Death to America!' was another shout, and 'Abdul Rahman must be executed!' Meanwhile, court officials pondering the man's baptism said, 'Rahman's mental health will be evaluated.'

These Koranic laws were enacted in Afghanistan and Pakistan, which theoretically were our allies. But I knew it wasn't safe. The journalist Daniel Pearl had recently been abducted and beheaded in Pakistan, and Westerners were routinely harassed in the bazaars. This was the result of billions of dollars spent and many lives lost in the futile attempt by the US government to prop up the governments of these countries.

'This is a young democracy,' the American secretary of state remarked when Abdul Rahman's life was on the line for his crime of apostasy, and Afghanistan needed apologists.

So I didn't revisit Pakistan. Instead, I headed south and intended to keep going until I got to the southernmost tip of India.

Many people boarded the train at Ludhiana, among them Kuldeep and Kumar in the seats next to me. Neither wore a turban, yet I guessed they might be Sikhs – Westernized from their residence in England, where they said they lived, both in Ilford, Essex. Kuldeep had gone to England as a ten-year-old; Kumar had been born there. Both were visiting relatives in Ludhiana. Kuldeep was the more talkative of the two.

'Could you live here?' I asked him.

'I'm a Punjabi, I could live here easily,' he said. 'But my wife was born in England. She'd find it hard to adjust in a village.'

'What would it be like for her?'

'Maybe too quiet. But I tell you, village life is good. Plenty of food, cost of living is low, no stress. I don't need nightclubs. I'd like it.' He seemed a bit rueful that he was heading back to England. 'This India is different from the India I left. Some people are coming back.'

'Building houses?'

'Plenty. Big villas. Not many in Amritsar, because it's a border town. No one wants to risk living so close to Pakistan. But Ludhiana is quiet and safe. Jullundur, too. There, you see?'

We were passing a cluster of houses in a walled compound.

Kumar said, 'We have two growing seasons. You see all this wheat?' I did, it was unmissable, green and gorgeous, silky in the sunshine. 'This will be harvested in a few weeks. Then the rice will be planted, and the rains will come and fill the paddy fields.'

'This whole place is connected, too,' Kuldeep said. 'Those farmers look like rustics and hicks, but they all have mobile phones. Hardly anyone uses a land line.'

'What do they worry about?' I asked.

'They worry about democracy, as I do,' he said. 'The scheduled classes, for example.'

By scheduled classes he meant the lowest castes in India – the Dalits, the so-called Untouchables, whom Mahatma Gandhi called Harijans, Children of God. What Kuldeep was questioning was a system that had its American parallel not only in affirmative action programmes for minorities, but also in the stubborn resistance by the rest of the populace to the preferential fast track.

'They are now better-off than we are. They have so many advantages. These advantages were written into the law, to lift them up, and these laws have never been taken off the books. It's becoming a problem.'

'How many people are we talking about?'

'A big group – maybe thirty per cent of the population.'

'What else worries you?'

'The north–south divide – lots of friction. The Punjab and Haryana are feeding the whole country,' Kuldeep said. 'So much of the country's water comes from here. And what are we getting for it?'

Interesting, this man from Ilford, Essex, growing passionate and indignant about resources in the Punjab. He did not live here, but this was where his heart was.

'The pity of India is the bad roads – bad for so many reasons. We are not keeping pace with other countries with respect to roads. Corruption, mismanagement. It can take hours for a simple journey. Everything else is going ahead, but not road building.'

Kumar said, 'And there's the population. Look at this.'

The railway carriage was full – more than full: all the seats were taken, many people were standing, luggage was piled to the ceiling, and every time we rounded a sharp bend or stopped suddenly, passengers toppled and fell. The platforms of passing stations were jammed. People hung out of the windows. People jostled, and there may have been passengers on the roof – it was a common occurrence. Everyone was civil, but there was no escape from the mob.

And for all the talk of modernity, the train was in rough shape – very dirty, broken seats, filthy toilets, loose wires tangled in the passageways, chipped paint and the usual stinks.

Yet, amid the chaos and the crowds, life went on, the conductors punching tickets, passengers making phone calls, food sellers squeezing from carriage to carriage, calling out, 'Cutlet! Cutlet!' or 'Ess krim! Ess Krim!' or 'Jews! Mungo jews!' or 'Chicken rice!' or '*Pani*! Vutta! *Pani*! Vutta! Buttle vutta.'

'What's your biggest worry?'

'The division between rich and poor is growing,' Kuldeep said. 'It's huge at the moment and it's getting worse. Many people have everything, but also many people have nothing. How to fix?'

To change the subject, he said he was looking forward to the England–India cricket match in Delhi. 'It's tomorrow. You should go.'

'Maybe I will,' I said. 'Who should I be watching?'

'The bowler, Harbhajan Singh. They call him Bhaji – he's great.'

That was when I was certain Kuldeep was a Sikh. He had no beard, no turban, no steel bracelet. He had been Anglicized, but still he rooted for India, still was loyal to his race and religion: he mentioned the only Sikh player on the team.

Stretching my legs on the platform between coaches, taking the air, I struck up a conversation with Mohinder Singh. He was a businessman, living in Ludhiana, but on his way to Delhi. I mentioned that I had just come from Uzbekistan.

'We sell lots of woollen goods from Ludhiana to the Stans – Uzbekistan, Kazakhstan,' he said. 'Pullovers, scarves, mittens. They buy from us. We export everywhere. Bike parts. Ludhiana was in the *Guinness Book of Records* as one of the largest makers of bikes. Because of the successful bike industry, the motorcycle company Hero Honda located here.'

Jullundur was also a big maker and exporter of sports equipment. Footballs, cricket bats, cricket balls, hockey sticks. For religious reasons, many Hindus will not make anything involving leather, which they deem unclean. Sikhs, with no such sanction, have cornered the market.

He said, 'Lots of agricultural land is being converted into housing colonies. There's a big housing boom in the Punjab. Not just locals but non-resident Indians from Canada and the UK investing in property Small farmers sell up their land and use the money to send a son to the UK or Canada, to emigrate and make a go of it. Hoping he will succeed and send money back.'

He asked me if I had been in India before. I told him that I had last been in Punjab thirty-three years ago.

He asked, 'What do you think is the biggest difference?'

I said, 'What you're doing now. Talking about progress and praising India's economy. Confidence and self-esteem. I never heard that before.'

He agreed, saying, 'And phones. When we lived in Simla, my father was a paramilitary. Twenty years ago it was almost impossible to have a telephone. I remember the day we were notified that we could have a telephone. We rejoiced!'

'How long had you waited?'

'Two years!' he said. 'Now it isn't a mark of status. Even rickshaw wallahs have mobile phones.'

We were watchin the Punjab go past from the breezy passageway of the express train. With its fields of wheat, the women in shawls and the men in turbans, bicycles on the dusty roads, the countryside was unchanged from what I had seen all those years before. But Mohinder Singh's confident mood and the good humour of Kuldeep and Kumar were something new. My memory of India was of people looking to the past. What struck me now was meeting Indians who looked to the future.

I said, 'What do you think is India's problem?'

Mohinder Singh said, 'Crux of India's problem is overpopulation. As soon as we build any kind of infrastructure it becomes inadequate because of,' he shrugged, 'we have too many people.'

But after all the talk in the Shan-e-Punjab (Glory of the Punjab) Express of the success of India, the wealth of Punjab, the national renewal, all the optimists got off the train in the darkness at New Delhi Station to find the old India stubbornly clinging to life. A thousand passengers disembarked, burdened by bags, suitcases, sacks, children, old grannies and jerry cans of ghee, to find thousands more waiting for onward trains under the glaring lights – brighter in India than anywhere else I've been, the dazzling light that prevents you from seeing things.

The permanent residents of the station lay stretched out under sheets and blankets. Mark Twain, who saw such crowds of travellers and squatters, includes a satirical two-page description of a big-city railway station in India in *Following the Equator* (1897). And then he loses his jollity; he is baffled and disturbed by the squatters: 'These silent crowds sat there with their humble bundles and baskets and small household gear about them, and patiently waited – for what?' The squatters were still there, still waiting, the scene unchanged, Twain's words as true now as they had been a century ago. The people were sleeping, hundreds of them, completely covered, big and small, some like corpses in body bags, some like campers, some like mummies; lying in family groups under the lights at the Ajmeri Gate side of the station.

All the optimists from Punjab who got off the train with me walked past these hordes of homeless sleepers, beggars, squatters. The distressing scene, another fact of Indian life, was so obvious no one mentioned it, or even glanced at it.

In this dry season the Delhi air was a settled cloud of dust, of smoke, of car fumes, a fog of eye-stinging grit, and most of all a sweetish stink of too many people, the emanation of their outdoor habits that clots your nostrils. It is not a city smell but a suggestion of deforestation and desert and pulverized brick and wood-fuelled cooking fires, the odour of humanity, which is also an odour of death. Even in the pitch-darkness of one of the frequent Delhi power cuts, you would know you were in an overpopulated place that existed in a crisis of old-fangledness.

I stayed in the Delhi hotel where I'd stayed before. It was now luxurious. In a mood of self-pitying nostalgia I remembered how, long ago, I had tried to phone my wife in London from here and had met only frustration – her faint and evasive voice, not much warmth, and then a rising tide of static. 'Speak louder,' the hotel operator said over a sound like crashing surf on the line. Phoning was no problem these days. As the man had said, 'Even rickshaw wallahs have mobile phones.' From my window I could see that the dust cloud of the night had resolved itself into a grainy fog that hovered over the great horizontal city – no skyscrapers but many tombs, domes, monuments, mosques, temples, riverside forts, ancient walls and obelisks, wreathed in the vapour that had a human smell.

I got a box and filled it with my coat and gloves, my fleece vest, the icons I'd bought, and my maps of Georgia and Turkmenistan. I sent the stuff home, unburdening myself. Changing trains, I had found summertime; no more cold weather until Japan. With a lighter bag, just a change of clothes in it, and my small briefcase of papers, I was eager to move on.

Looking for onward train tickets, I went back to New Delhi Station and found the international booking hall. In the past, as in Amritsar, I had paid an Indian to stand in the queue for me. But this was well organized – not much of a queue, and I could pay in dollars. A proportion of railway seats were now set aside for foreigners, as a way of stimulating tourism, which in India is relatively small. The state of Hawaii has more than twice as many visitors (seven million) as the whole of India.

Seeing my application, Mr Sharma said, 'You're the writer.'

'That's me. Back again after many years.'

Leaping to his feet, he said, 'How can I offer you service?'

'Just looking for trains.'

I showed him an itinerary that would take me through old India, new India, poor India, India of the miracles, India of the maharajahs, India of *The Great Railway Bazaar*: Delhi-Jodhpur-Jaipur-Bombay-Bangalore-Madras-Rameswaram, from north to south.

'Please meet Mrs Matta, my boss.'

Mrs Matta was a middle-aged woman in a blue sari. She sat at a desk in a back office that was furnished in the Indian manner: a full PENDING tray, a cup of tea, photographs of smiling children and a framed one of the prime minister, a wall map of India showing all railway lines, and a shrine to the elephant-headed god, Ganesh, with a flickering vigil light in a yellow dish.

'Famous writer,' Mr Sharma said. 'Back again.'

Mrs Matta offered me a cup of tea and the visitors' book, saying, 'Please add your name. Write comments. Mention your satisfaction, if you please.'

I wrote, *India works because the railway works.*

I had believed that on my first visit; I still believed it. Because of the vast network of Indian Railways, I could go anywhere in the country. I could sleep on the train in comfort; I could eat on it, read a book, write my notes; I could talk with anyone. There are buses in India, there are taxis and limos. But as Kuldeep had told me on the train, *The pity of India is the bad roads . . . It can take hours for a simple journey.* There were many new airlines, but delays were a certainty, security checks were awful, and the airports were like garrisons, full of soldiers and impatient passengers, overcrowded and understaffed. Because they were an institution, Indian railway stations were well organized and efficient. And in India the train was the only way of being sure of leaving on time and arriving safely. The trains are slow, some people say, but in India being in a hurry is foolish and deluded – and often bad manners.

With a handshake from Mr Sharma and an approving head-wobble from Mrs Matta, I left the booking hall with all my tickets, chits, vouchers and supplementary fare receipts. The clutter and dusty pillars and uncomfortable chairs in an Indian office are no indication of its effectiveness. Out of the chaos of receipt books, carbon paper, flickering computers and fat files tied with faded ribbon arise decisiveness and clear results, even if you can't read the writing and your fingers are smudged with ink from handling them.

I marvelled at what I was able to accomplish in a morning in Delhi: the train tickets I needed, the very notebook I was looking for, some medicine for my gout (no prescription required in India for indomethacin), and the hottest ticket to be had, a seat at the England–India test match.

I had managed seventeen years of exile in England because I had not been an Anglophile – Anglophiles don't last long in England, and my detachment had kept me from being a cricket fan. I do not know the rules of the game, much less the subtleties, yet bowling, batting and fielding are easy-to-appreciate skills, pleasurable to watch. Most of all I wanted to go to this cricket match because it was the event of the week and because I wanted to see 50,000 Indians in one place.

I was glad I went. Cricket matches in England are famously sedate, characterized by limp hand-clapping, a yelp or two, the crack of the bat, the thump of the ball on the pitch, and now and then the bone-breaking sound of the collapsing wicket. But that was a world away from the pandemonium at Ferozeshah Kotla cricket ground in north Delhi – howling spectators, Indian flags, loud whistles, horns, flutes, trumpets, chanting. The Indian cricket crowd (so I learned) is noted for its barracking – hooting at errors, screaming at questionable decisions, and the occasional display of racial insensitivity, shouting 'Monkey! Monkey!' (*Bandar! Bandar!*) at black players on the British or West Indian teams.

The man in front of me had made a large Indian flag into a poncho and was wearing it. The man next to him was blowing a bugle. Everyone was howling. I had arrived after lunch. India had scored 209 and the sides had changed. It was England's turn to bat, and they had to better that score. They reached 124, with two of their best batsmen.

The fan next to me, Vikram – 'Call me Vicky' – told me this. He was nineteen and had called in sick at work like everyone else – Delhi businesses were quiet and understaffed as a result of this match. I remarked on the size of the cricket ground.

'It is capacious,' Vicky said. Another of the pleasures of India is hearing such words in casual conversation. 'That is Pietersen. He was hero of the Ashes series last summer.'

'Is he any good?' I asked.

'Power in hands is there. Timing is there.' Vicky was looking at the other end of the pitch. 'That is Flintoff. He is great batsman.'

'So England has a chance?'

'I think not. We have resourceful bowlers. See Bhaji Singh. He is magnificent.'

But the English batsmen were scoring runs. Vicky translated the Hindi chants: 'India will win!' and 'Blue is shit!' – the English strip was blue – and 'Bhaji–Bhaji–Bhaji!' The whole stadium was roaring, though some scattered claps accompanied a good hit from Flintoff. Even the most raucous football fans had nothing on this screaming mob, and the cricketers themselves, in celebration of a catch or a score, hugged and rolled on the grass of the pitch.

'It's a big day,' I said.

'Cricket is God in India,' Vicky said. 'More than God.'

And he went on narrating the match for me: 'See, careless half-controlled hoick off full toss . . . Ah, good catch in deep mid-viket . . . Flintoff tried an ill-advised sweep off a straight ball . . . He is out. Leg before vicket . . . Harbhajan will be Man of Match . . . See, player in crease.'

'Is it a sticky wicket?'

'A dicey pitch, you can say.'

To the cries of 'India will win!' I began to think that this was a manifestation of the new India. The vast stadium, the unanimous denunciation of England, the huge crowd and the confidence. It was also the commercial crassness of the new century, the players' clothing with advertising patches stitched on.

'India can win,' Vicky said as the afternoon wore on. 'We have to take five more vickets.'

Pietersen lofted a strong hit into the upper tier of the stands.

'That's a six-plus,' Vicky said.

But another of his big blows was caught at the boundary by an athletic fielder.

'Fare-thee-well!' Vicky shrieked.

The new batsmen faded fast: caught, blundered, leg before wicket, and soon it seemed certain the victory was India's. Assured that the match was in the bag, Vicky addressed other matters: Did I have children? What was my job? Did we have cricket in America? Did I like India?

Satisfied with my answers, he turned back to the match. And now I could see that India would win and that in a matter of minutes 50,000 triumphant cricket fans would be stampeding out of Ferozeshah Kotla cricket ground, looking for pale *ferringhis* like me to taunt with their victory. So I ducked out, hurried past security people, steel fences, metal detectors and ranks of cops holding lathis – long sticks for beating back a mob in what is known as a lathi charge. All these tough-looking men had gathered at the exits.

I was not the only person in a hurry. A stout, well-dressed Indian man in a white suit was steering his wife through a metal detector. He could have been a magnate, she a maharani. She set the detector buzzing, but she was waved on, towards a waiting limousine with a liveried driver – she was slow, heavy, trying to keep up with her tubby husband. She wore bangles, a thickness of necklaces and dangly earrings. The diamond in her nostril was as big as an acorn.

Outside the stadium, I could still hear the crowd. In a class-conscious country riddled by divisions, the whole cricket mob chanted as one, as though it was more than solidarity – an expression of self-esteem, joyous and assertive, pleased with itself, like a hoarse gloating echo of Amar Singh, who had said to me in Amritsar, 'We're a big power now.'

That evening, as if on cue, an American woman entered the lobby of my hotel with her husband, and I stepped aside to let them pass. They had just returned from a sightseeing tour of Delhi, which would have included Humayun's tomb and the Red Fort and the Qutub Minar and the sight of many Indians who had not shared in the country's economic miracle. Another reminder that travelling in India is not for the faint of heart, the woman's eyes were red from weeping, and she was sniffling, dabbing at her puffy eyes. She glanced tearfully at me, then looked away, muttering, 'I don't care. I'm not going out tomorrow.' Then, half actressy, half sincere, but certainly upset: 'Walter, it breaks my heart to see those people living like that.'

10. Night Train to Jodhpur
The Mandore Express

I knew without being told that the train to Jodhpur would be leaving from platform 16; it was obvious from the look of the waiting travellers. Most of the world dresses alike, in blue jeans, T-shirts and trainers. Rural India is one of the exceptions to this world-wide sartorial monotony, and Rajasthan remains outstandingly itself, self-possessed and multi-hued. At Old Delhi Station it was possible to see from the clothes of the women on the platform that they awaited the Mandore Express to Jodhpur.

Where else would they be going, draped and painted like that, dressed in yellow and red saris, russet shawls fringed with gold embroidery or ochreous borders, long saffron wraps, winking veils, heavy gold jewellery, ropes of knuckle-sized beads and heavy bangles, feet and hands painted with henna, the age-old plumage, brilliant and colourful? They were people of the vast desert state of Rajasthan, where the houses of Jodhpur are bright blue, the façades and palaces of Jaipur are pink, and men's turbans are crimson. As though to distance themselves from the dusty hues of their surroundings, Rajasthanis are emphatically adorned. But this is true of desert dwellers generally, for whom gold jewellery is wealth, and whose remarkable sense of colour seems a guarantee against ever becoming indistinguishable or lost.

The Mandore Express was an overnight train to Jodhpur – where I'd never been before – on my route to Jaipur, which I had written about long ago. Jodhpur is a city of weaving and furniture making, traditional crafts, and these included copying antiques. Indians know Jodhpur as a producer of deceptive fakes that are sent to all the markets and bazaars and to credulous museums abroad – terracotta, porcelain, brassware, statues, idols, swords and daggers. Jodhpur also had a Vatican-sized maharajah's palace that had been turned into a hotel, and the maharajah still lived there – rode polo ponies and rejoiced in the nickname 'Bapji'.

Fish-glued to the side of the train was the manifest, a list of passengers and berths for second-class AC. I found my name, but before the train drew out of the station I saw some vacancies in first. I appealed to the conductor to upgrade me. He took my money, made out an excess-fare receipt in triplicate, handed me a sheaf of chits, and showed me to a four-berth compartment. Two people had already seated themselves: a young man reading *Debonair* magazine and opposite him a young woman braying a mixture of Hindi and English into a mobile phone. The fierce-sounding woman had the humourless beaky face and cold eyes of a shrew. She was an example of how physically ugly a person's face becomes in the middle of delivering a loud complaint; she was a gargoyle in horn-rimmed glasses.

While she howled, Rakesh, the man opposite, told me he was a salesman and exporter of shawls and scarves. He was going to Jodhpur, where his cloth was printed and dyed with the vivid Rajasthani colours.

'I come on this train every few weeks,' Rakesh said. 'It's the best way. I arrive early in Jodhpur, do a full day's work, and head straight back on the night train. This saves me from having to pay for an expensive flight and a hotel room.'

He then offered me some of his food: spiced chickpeas, a bag of cashews, some obscure dumplings and deep-fried fritters.

'Must I repeat?' The young woman said, her eyes flashing. 'I am on train. And I am furious. They are all against us! Three ministries, three secretaries. Finance Ministry is worst.'

A scratchy reply from the phone had her scowling again.

'I don't give a fig! We must be strong!'

More babbling had her rolling her eyes and scratching her hairy arms.

'You did not see memo? It was audacious!'

I smiled, impressed, because I could not remember ever having heard the word 'audacious' used in conversation by an English-speaker in all my eavesdropping life.

Then she began to sound like a field marshal: 'But we can win! We must prevail! We will regroup. We will respond in kind. Never mind, I tell you!'

Clicking her tongue, she drowned out the reply.

'Enough, enough. You can find me in Jodhpur on my mobile,' she said, and silenced the thing with a stabbing finger.

It was an amazing display of unselfconsciousness. I often think that people shout into mobile phones in order to warn any casual listeners that they are to be reckoned with; that mobile-phone screaming is more a show of aggression to eavesdroppers than for the person at the other end of the line.

As a wanderer in India, I was grateful for anyone or anything that came my way as I went about casting strangers for roles in my narrative. Here, purely by chance, I was in a compartment with a sympathetic salesman who offered me food and with a hairy troglodytic woman shrieking abuse into her mobile phone.

'Do you mind?' she said sourly, twisting her beaky face at me. 'I've had a long day.'

She meant that the bench I was sitting on was her berth and that she wanted to turn in. I had been assigned the upper berth. This was one of the niceties observed on Indian Railways, especially in mixed compartments: I had to climb into my berth. It was early evening, and we had twelve hours of travel ahead of us, but she insisted on sleeping. Still, it was wonderful how by taking the train an idle traveller like me could penetrate to the sleeping quarters of a middle-aged native woman and (if I wished) could look down and observe her snoring and scowling in her dreams.

I obliged. I crept up the ladder to my berth and began reading Christopher Hibbert's fluent and well-documented account of the Indian Mutiny of 1857, *The Great Mutiny*. The uprising (bloodthirsty Indian troops) and its aftermath (bloodthirsty British troops) comprised one of the most violent racial convulsions in Indian history, yet the narrative was full of life and unexpected pleasures. An English notable and resident of Delhi named Thomas Metcalfe 'could not bear to see women eat cheese', and sent them out of the room to satisfy themselves with their cheddar; and Lord Macaulay summed up his low opinion of Indian achievements by saying, 'Medical doctrines that would disgrace an English farrier. Astronomy which would be ridiculed at an English girls' boarding school. History, abounding with kings thirty feet high, and reigns 30,000 years long. And Geography, made up of seas of treacle and butter.'

In the darkness, the train rattled fast through the cool desert night, clanging on the rails. I slept, seeming to rotate, like a person undergoing what a science-fiction writer would call 'matter transfer'. In the morning, seeing the foul-tempered woman again, yawning fangy and open-jawed like a jackal, I was reminded of another description in Hibbert's *Great Mutiny*, of a woman 'with large, dark and unforgiving eyes'.

But, this being Rajasthan, I was treated to a ravishing early-morning sight. We were drawing into a station where a stunning young woman, a purple sari fluttering around her slender body – a woman of film-star beauty, great glamour and poise – walked lightly on pretty feet past me on the platform, carrying a basket of fresh tomatoes. I got out to get a better look. I watched her cross the platform to another train to sell tomatoes, and then a smiling old woman approached me with a pitcher of milky coffee, poured me a cup, and I stood there in the golden morning, uplifted by all this. The train whistle blew and we were off again, and, passing the sign *Please Discourage Beggars*, I returned to my compartment.

The shawl salesman was still asleep, but the grouchy woman was awake and sitting, facing out of the window, her back to me. The rattle and clatter of the train crossing the desert contrasted with the scene: the lively sound, the vacant landscape. Skinny trees here and there like dead saplings stood in the rubble and dust of flat empty India.

I peered past the woman and said, 'This is lovely. After Delhi, the great emptiness.'

'It is not empty at all,' the woman said.

'It sure looks empty to me.'

'There are people everywhere, if you would look.'

I was looking, but there were none.

She laughed, forcing contempt through her impressive nose. 'You think it is empty. It is not empty!'

Believe me, it was the edge of the Marusthali Desert, in sun-baked Rajasthan, and it was empty.

But she said, 'It is intensively farmed. It is all cultivated.'

'Some of it is,' I said, seeing some furrows raked into a gully and some stalks of withered grass, perhaps wheat.

'All of it is! Don't you see?'

This was a very irritating woman, a scold, who at seven-thirty in the morning was shrieking in contradiction.

'What's that, wheat?'

She snorted and said, 'These people would not be so stupid as to plant wheat. They plant something that needs less water. They cultivate millet.'

'I see.'

'And those trees that you are ignoring. They hold the nitrogen in the soil. They are beneficial.'

'I see.'

Attempting a tone of haughty condescension, she merely sounded rude, and her rudeness was comically like self-parody. What she said could have been interesting, but her nagging tone made it abusive. I suspected the reason was that this Indian woman had assumed that she would be sharing the compartment with one other person, the shawl salesman, and what she found was a third person, a big tattooed foreigner from beyond the pale, glaring at her through sunglasses and scribbling in a notebook. Her intention was to make me feel unwelcome, and I mentioned this in my notes, adding that this was to be expected in the new robust and assertive India of peevish caste-obsessed bureaucrats.

'You're a lawyer?' I asked.

'I am a journalist. Environmentalist. I am going to a conference on water issues in Jodhpur.' She turned back to the window. 'Prince Charles is going to address our meeting about water conservation.'

'Prince Charles is in Jodhpur?'

'At Umaid Bhawan. As I said, to address our conference.'

That could hardly have been the reason. I had seen his name in the Delhi newspapers; he was on a private tour of India with Camilla, Duchess of Cornwall, formerly Parker Bowles, née Shand, and now Mrs Charles Windsor – her first visit to the country.

'Maybe you'll get a chance to meet the prince.'

She shrugged and made a face. 'I don't care.'

'It's a big deal, isn't it?'

Though she was grubby from a night on the train and was sitting in wrinkled pyjamas, she attempted to be haughty, saying, 'I've had enough of royalty.'

I could see she was simply trying to put me down, and that fascinated me. I didn't mind that she took me for a backpacker, a scrounging vagabond, an idle traveller – that much was true. What she didn't know was that, as she was faced away from me, I had just finished writing in my notebook, *Sourpuss – wrinkled pajamas – sunken eyes – I've had enough of royalty.* And since I was also planning to stay at the Umaid Bhawan Palace, perhaps we could all meet for tea – grouchy woman, Prince of Wales and me.

'What a coincidence. I'm going there too,' I said. This did not get a rise out of her. I asked, 'Who do you write for?'

She glanced over her shoulder, mentioned the name of her magazine, then turned back to the window, so that all I saw were her skinny shoulders and her rumpled clothes. Perhaps she suspected that I had leaned out of my berth during the night and peered down at her twisted form, as she emitted flutter blasts of halitotic snores.

When the shawl seller woke up, he looked out of the window and, seemingly on the basis of the telling contours of a few dusty hills, said, 'Half an hour to Jodhpur.'

We chatted while the woman sulked and muttered into her mobile phone. He too had been at the cricket match in Delhi. I said, 'Cricketers used to clap and look bored or phlegmatic. When did they start hugging each other and rolling on the ground?'

'About ten or fifteen years back,' he said. 'The Australians started it. They made it more American style. Changed the colours, made it commercial – changed the whole sport.'

'If you don't mind?' the woman said, pushing past us. We were entering Jodhpur Station, but she was in such a hurry to get out of the train that she was already thrusting her way – sharp elbows out – to the end of the carriage and to her water conference, though, looking at her, you would have thought she was headed to a witches' sabbath.

There is always a mob scene when a train arrives at a large station in India: the onrush of porters, coolies, men with wheelbarrows and luggage carts, water carriers, food sellers, taxi drivers, rickshaw wallahs, hotel and guesthouse touts. They pile on to the platform and block the doors so as to be first.

I allowed them to entrap the grouchy woman, and I slipped past, moving quickly to the taxi rank with my small unimpressive bag.

Near the middle of Jodhpur my car was surrounded by big serious men carrying brass plates. The plates were glittering and heavy, and the men lifted them, seemed to shake them at me, gesturing for me to roll the window down.

'Who are these men?' I asked the driver. 'What do they want?'

'It is Navratri, sar. They are celebrants.'

I opened the window, assuming they wanted some rupees for their brass plates, but no: one person stepped forward and, putting his thumb into red powder, applied a dot to my forehead.

On the way to the Umaid Bhawan, the driver told me that Navratri was just beginning – nine nights of fasting and praying, devoted to the goddess Durga. This mother goddess is one of the fiercest in the Indian

pantheon, easily recognizable from the weapons in her many arms and
her necklace of skulls – she is much fiercer than the male gods, and is a
power of both creation and destruction. Durga means 'the Inaccessible', I
was put in mind of the petulant woman on the train, a Durga incarnation
howling into her mobile phone, who throughout the trip was making
herself inaccessible to me.

'Also Navratri, very important to Surya,' the driver said.

I had been to Surya temples. Surya, the sun god in Hindu cosmology,
is worshipped more devoutly in Rajasthan than in other places because,
as I later found out, the royal Rajput family – the Rathore clan, rulers
of Rajasthan – are regarded as *suryavanshis*, descendants of the sun god.

An unlucky aspect of this year's Navratri and this sun imagery was
that a solar eclipse had occurred the previous day in this part of India,
and the darkening of the sun was clearly visible in Jaipur.

'It was not an auspicious day,' a woman told me at the Umaid Bhawan
Palace, and this was bigger news in Jodhpur than the arrival of Prince
Charles and his duchess. A solar eclipse during this religious holiday was
a bad omen.

This was in the lobby of the Umaid Bhawan (on whose walls and
platforms were more stuffed leopards and tigers than I'd ever seen
together in my life), where I had gone hoping to talk with the Maharajah
of Jodhpur. His grandfather Maharajah Umaid Singh had commissioned
this palace to be built in 1928. At the time, this part of Rajasthan, the
desert kingdom of Marwar, was beset by famine and drought, and the
idea was that this project, which took fifteen years to complete, would
be a way of occupying and employing his subjects, the desperate and
hungry Marwaris. It was one of the last palaces, and certainly the last
great palace, to be erected in imperial India. The finished building, of
russet Rajasthani sandstone and marble, set on a hill at the edge of
Jodhpur, is a vast roseate palace with a great glowing dome, with touches
of the Gothic and jocular art deco, with pinched Mughal turrets, elaborate porches and the weirdest architectural capriccios of Rajputana. It
may have been built to give Marwaris employment, but there it stood
to inspire awe.

The present maharajah lived decorously in one wing, designated as
the Royal Apartments. Prince Charles was upstairs in a large suite with
his last duchess, his entourage nearby. Upstairs too were the water
conference people, looking for answers to the inevitable ecological catas-

trophe in India — more drought and famine. In the luxury hotel wing were the other guests: honeymooners, tourists, Indophiles, the lucky few and, travelling light, an idle grinning note taker – me, talking to a helpful Indian woman.

'Bad omens. Time to burn joss sticks?' I asked.

'No, more serious than that. "Don't look at the sun," I was told by a member of the maharajah's family. "Don't go outside." I said, "But I have work to do!"'

She said that if I was interested, I could attend the elaborate ritual for Navratri at the Mehrangarh Fort on the other side of Jodhpur, above the blue-painted city, a hilltop garrison so imposing Rudyard Kipling called it 'the work of angels and giants'. The *puja* – prayer ceremony – would be led by priests and members of the maharajah's family, the maharani, and the maharajah himself.

'Essential to propitiate goddess Durga, because of solar eclipse,' the woman said.

The ritual would mark the start of the nine days of fasting and praying. And some people ('in the villages', as smug city-dwelling Indians liked to point out) would be sacrificing a goat.

'Burning it?'

'No. Cut off head of goat. Let blood flow.'

One very hot day in Jodhpur, I followed the procession of Rajput royalty to the steep-sided fort and across its ramparts. The Durga temple (the traditional family temple of the Jodhpur royals) at the fort was an old one – the fort itself dates from the mid fifteenth century – and it was mobbed with devotees and semi-hysterical subjects of the maharajah, a living connection to the sun diety.

Following him in the heat of this sun-struck fort was a shuffling mass of people with flutes, bells, gongs, drums and garlands of flowers, all of them chanting, '*Durga Mata ki jai!*' – Praise to Mother Durga.

Ritual is important to me, not for its dubious sanctity, but because it is a set of gestures that reveals the inner state of the people involved and their subtle protocol. From under an awning I strained to see the ceremony, the mutterings, the water splashings, the prostrations. The priests were both submissive and self-important, attending to the maharajah, who was performing the *puja* under the gaze of his loyal and chanting subjects. Here, an element of theatre was added to an element of devotion.

The most painful moment was the arrival of the maharajah's son Shivraj Singh, the Yuvraj of Jodhpur and heir apparent. There were whispers that he might at last show himself, and this stirred a great intensity of anticipation, because he was known to have been severely injured.

The yuvraj was thirty-one, very handsome, and for years had been a renowned polo player – a great rider, a high scorer – and a champion of the game at which Jodhpur had distinguished itself for centuries. But just a year before – in February 2005 – the yuvraj had been in a polo accident. As he attempted to turn his horse sharply, it had stumbled, the yuvraj had fallen to the ground, and the horse had landed on top of him. After lying in a deep coma for more than a month, the poor man at last flickered to consciousness. With a period of intense physiotherapy – his therapist was a young American woman – he had regained rudimentary use of his limbs, and here he was, in his first public appearance since the horrible accident.

In a turban, white jacket and trousers, draped with garlands of marigolds, with an attendant on either side of him, he struggled to stay upright, making his way to the temple through the thicknesses of rose petals that had been strewn on the ramparts. His faltering was hard to watch, yet he was a man who had come back from the dead.

What was touching about the Durga *puja* was that it marked the cycle of life and death, it celebrated rebirth, and so everything that happened here in the blazing sun of the fort, the ringing of bells and gongs and the Durga chants, mattered to this broken young man who was a living symbol of how the mother goddess could help.

The priests applied powder to his forehead, tied a sacred thread to his wrist, flicked water, and passed out sweets, all this to the shrieks of the chants and the sound of flutes and gongs.

'Durga Mata ki jai!'

The prince was led to a gilded chair under a white cotton canopy near the temple, the portly maharajah beside him, the maharani in purple silks, the retainers with trays of sweets, the priests and the hundreds, perhaps thousands of worshippers tumbling over one another for a glimpse of their semi-divine king.

I was standing behind the canopy, trying to keep my bare feet on the cooler, shaded part of the bricks. The yuvraj signalled that he wanted water. The heat was like a glittering hammer. I watched him make a great effort to hold the glass and tip it and drink. He was clearly in bad shape, yet he was determined to complete this act without help, and when at last he was led away, looking frail, determination was more evident in his movements. He was a man with inner strength; I felt that he had come a long way and that his willpower would take him further; in the course of this fragrant and harmonious ceremony his posture had become resolute and more certain.

There is something about the presence of royalty – it is a throbbing in the air, a vibrancy, a buzz – that sets people's pulses racing. Probably it is not much different from the excitement on the red carpet on Oscar night, but it is heightened by the religious fervour associated with ancient royalty. It was obvious here at the fort, with all the Jodhpur royals on view, looking pious and protective as the delighted people watched them – a kind of rapture inspired by the big reliable-looking maharajah, his lovely queen, his wounded son, the image of the mother goddess smeared with ritual paste, flames leaping from oil lamps, and the powerful chiming of gongs and bells.

I stayed in the hotel part of the Umaid Bhawan, hardly believing my luck at being a guest at such a place. I made a tour of the Jodhpur bazaar and the antique shops, looking for treasures and trying to sort the real from the fake. But it hardly mattered; what I liked best in an Indian market was simply walking from stall to stall, from shop to shop, threading my way among the plodding camels and the rickshaws and the browsing cows in a city where nothing looked modern.

A few days later, more regal vibrations set the Umaid Bhawan Palace buzzing: heightened activity, lots of breathless movement, a briskness I had not seen before. After lunch, I saw a long red carpet being unrolled.

'Prince Charles is leaving,' one of the carpet rollers said, kneeling on the polished marble floor of the outer lobby, straightening the edges of the thing.

I wanted to have a good look at Prince Charles's new wife, so I lingered by the great arch of the palace entrance.

'May I help you, sar?' It was a security man.

'I'm waiting for Prince Charles. I want to say hello.' The security man had a badge and a truncheon. I added, 'I met him once.'

I took my place at the very end of a line of people who were saying goodbye: butlers, cleaners, chowkidars, sweepers, syces, hotel staff, secretaries, menials and me.

All the hotel guests had gathered for the farewell; all the attendees of the water conservation conference were there too. I searched their faces and spotted the grouchy woman from the train. She was small, troll-like, round-shouldered, across the room. She did not see me until the prince approached my line, and when our eyes met I winked at her. Ha! She darkened in a way that I had come to recognize. I remembered how she had barked the word 'audacious' into her mobile phone.

The prince and the duchess made their way down the line, thanking each person, and when my turn came I said, 'Paul Theroux. You came to the première of the film of my book *The Mosquito Coast* in London twenty years ago. I'm sure you don't remember.'

'Of course I remember,' he said, smiling and snatching at my hand. He had a high pink colour and thinning hair, a correctness of posture, and the frustrated smirk of someone who believed he had never been taken seriously enough. He looked boyish and slightly sheepish rather than princely.

The duchess was just behind him, looking untidy, older and somewhat motherly in the faintly bawdy way of some doting mothers with big awkward sons: friendly, frumpy, a bit hunched, smallish and compact, potbellied in her tight combination of dark jacket and skirt – much too formal for this desert heat, more appropriate for a garden party in England, which she perhaps believed a maharajah's banquet to be the nearest equivalent. That was forgivable in someone who had never been to India before.

She touched the prince's arm and said in a vague and likeable way, 'Bother, I've forgotten my dark glasses.'

Someone overheard her and quick-marched to deliver the order that the glasses must be found.

Prince Charles said to me, 'What are you doing here?'

'Just travelling, sir. Heading south.'

'Are you writing, something?'

'Trying, your highness. Scribble, scribble.'

This made him laugh. 'I'm scribbling too. But not books. And not for publication, though I sometimes wish . . .' And instead of finishing the sentence, he laughed again.

The previous month, portions of the prince's Hong Kong diary had become public. He had printed it privately and circulated it among his friends. It was full of colourful observations and a few pointed ones, and the unexpected sharpness of these had made headlines in London newspapers. He had mocked the hand-over ceremony, called some of the Chinese notables 'waxworks', spoken of the Chinese president's 'propaganda speech', and scorned the goose-stepping Chinese soldiers. He also complained of being stuck in club class, rather than first, on his way out: 'Such is the end of empire, I sighed to myself.' What this proved was that though he may never be crowned king of Great Britain and Northern Ireland, he could still make a decent living as a travel writer with such breezy generalizations.

'Travel safely,' he said. Then a photographer caught up with him, and he was posed with the staff for a group photo. As the picture was taken he said into the dazzling flash of the camera, 'Are you absolutely sure you want me to do this?'

Then the duchess's dark glasses were found, and off the royals went to their private plane. They had an entourage of twenty-six people, including the prince's private chef.

'The prince apparently doesn't like your food,' I said, teasing a man who told me he had helped organize the royal visit.

'Oh, his highness is very particular about his meals,' the man said, suddenly fussed and stern, as though remembering. 'There was quite a hullabaloo here to find the ingredients for a certain kind of brown bread that the prince likes to eat. Certain herbs. They finally found them somewhere in the market.'

Another day, I had tea with Maharajah Gaj Singh II. The thirty-eighth Rathore Chief of Marwar and Maharajah of Jodhpur was fifty-eight but seemed older, with the weather-beaten air of an aged warrior. He had assumed the throne and had taken on the title of maharajah at the age of four, on the death of his father. He was well known for having no pretensions. He may have been descended from Surya, the sun god, but he urged everyone to call him 'Bapji' – Daddy Dearest. Just as well. The English had never allowed themselves to be impressed with semi-divine claims of ancestry. In Victorian times, the College of Heralds stated: 'The Aga Khan is held by his followers to be a direct descendant of God. English Dukes take precedence.'

Bapji had allowed part of the Umaid Bhawan Palace to be converted to a hotel, in much the same spirit as some of the hard-up English aristocracy with their castles and stately homes, turning them into museums and teahouses, fitting them for rose garden tours and game parks and croquet lawns, so that they could go on living in one wing and paying the bills. In the most heavy-handed way, by amending the Indian constitution in 1969, Indira Gandhi had stripped the Indian royals of their privy purses. In response, some maharajahs became businessmen, others became landlords, and many sold the family silver. Indian antique dealers were always unwrapping daggers or crystal goblets adorned with crests and saying, 'Royal family of Cooch Behar, sir. Deaccessioned, sir. I obtained the whole blooming lot, sir.'

Bapji had made himself popular as a member of the Indian parliament and as an ambassador. To raise funds, he had collaborated with the Taj Group in creating a luxury hotel. Over the years, it had fallen into disrepair, but it was restored to its former glory. It was also something of a menagerie of the moribund – toothy tiger heads on most walls, stuffed leopards in feline attitudes on plinths and above staircases, buffalo, antlered bucks, pairs of enormous elephant tusks in the game room and even in the private apartments – trophies of alpha males gathering dust, and photos of memorable days: upright hunters cradling rifles, with their boots resting on dead tigers and dead leopards.

'Welcome, please sit,' Bapji said when I arrived in his study. He was a stoutish man in a traditional Rajasthani outfit resembling white pyjamas, the long shirt called a *kurta* and tight trousers – jodhpurs indeed. And he was barefoot. The room was a repository of family photographs and books and files, and on the coffee table in front of me, videocassettes of *Godzilla*, *Great Journeys* and *Yes, Minister*. A cricket match was in progress on a television across the room, and it remained on, Bapji glancing at it from time to time throughout our conversation.

'Things have settled down. It was quite busy with the royal visit, as you can imagine. But it was a private visit.'

'What other kind is there?'

'A formal visit. In that case it would be state-sponsored. The prince would get one day off – the informal part of a formal visit, so to say. But this one he paid for himself.'

'He seemed pretty jolly.'

'He's happy. She's happy too.'

It seemed to me that Bapji and Charles were about the same age. I said, 'You weren't at school with him by any chance?'

'I was at Eton. Then Oxford – Christ Church, the first in my family to go to Oxford. He was at school at Gordonstoun.' Bapji smiled. 'A grim place – highly spartan. He would have been happier at Eton. His boys went there.'

'Had you met the duchess before?'

'I knew her brother, Mark Shand. And she has a sister, Annabel. I don't know her.'

A servant brought tea and biscuits. I asked Bapji about his ancestry – whether it was true, as I'd heard, that his family was descended from the sun deity.

'It's true, we're associated with Surya,' he said. 'There is no sun worship as such, but you know the yoga position, the *surya namaskar*. Our family goes back to the *Ramayana*. We are *kshattriya* – warrior caste.'

This was a delicate way of putting it: the family claims descent from Lord Rama, who is associated with the sun. By contrast, Lord Krishna is associated with the moon.

'This is all documented?'

'Oh, yes. Our family history is well recorded. My ancestors arrived in these parts in 1211. Prior to that, the grandson of Jai Chand ruled, so our family traces their relation to the Rashstra Kuta family, early in the tenth century.'

He was speaking of a family tree stretching back 1,000 years, from branches to roots.

'I seem to remember being in a sun temple.'

'There's one in Jaipur.'

It was at the height of Galta Gorge, near a temple I had visited long ago on the outskirts of the city.

'Are you fasting for Navratri?'

'I am doing my best. Fasting depends on choice. Some people eat nothing for nine days – take only water. Some eat one meal. Some eat fruit. And there are Rajputs who kill a goat – as a *prasad*, an offering. Alcohol is also offered. And, yes, some drink it.'

'I hadn't realized that everyone did something different.'

'I'll tell you,' he said.

'I hope you don't mind my writing this down,' I said. 'I find this interesting.'

He waggled his head in the Indian way, meaning okay. And now I realized what was lovable about him, what made him sound trust-worthy and unpedantic: it was his lips, a slight slushiness of delivery, a

lopsidedness in his jaw, which made him seem, in spite of his full
moustache, like a small boy.

'Each community assigns special values to certain foods. That which
makes you strong and excitable is forbidden to Brahmins, because theirs
is an ascetic tradition. But a sadhu might smoke hashish' – and he raised
his hand and puffed an imaginary joint. 'But *bhang* is not smoked. It is
powdered and made into milkshakes, called *thandhai*.'

'What's the mixture?'

'Milk, water, ground almonds and some other ingredients added to it.
And of course the *bhang* – you call it cannabis? It makes you pretty silly.'

'I must try it.'

'Some people start laughing. Some people pout,' Bapji said. 'Opium
eating is also part of our culture. That's become a ritual in western
Rajasthan. In the past it was common, eating opium.'

'No religious sanction against it?'

'No. It's a tradition. We *kshattriyas* can eat meat and drink alcohol,
though within the *kshattriya* caste there are some differences. Especially
at the two ends of the spectrum, you can say – the high castes at one
end, and the scheduled and tribals at the other end.'

'I thought vegetarianism was the norm,' I said.

'There is an untruth abroad that the majority of Indians are vegetarians.' He laughed in refutation and wiggled his toes. 'It's not true.
One Englishman made a study. He found that, on balance, there are
more non-vegetarians than vegetarians in India.'

'You eat meat, sir?'

'Us, yes, meat eaters! Hunting was part of our tradition. And there
was a tradition of a goat being slaughtered in front of the temple.' He
made a slicing, throat-cutting gesture with one hand. 'I saw you at the
puja the other day at the fort. Goat sacrifice would have been done there
some years ago.'

'How long ago?'

'In my lifetime,' he said. Not long ago – he'd been born in 1948. 'As
a young boy I saw it, the killing of the goat. It was very shocking to me.
But my mother said, "It is part of growing up. If the sight of blood
bothers you, you can't be a warrior."'

I loved his candour, his ability to talk about anything, his interest in
explaining the minutiae of drug use and goat sacrifice. He leaned forward,
eager with a new detail.

'There are subtleties, you see. Apparently, if the goat doesn't shudder, it won't be accepted as a sacrifice. The animal needs to be afraid, to be suitably terrified, to stand still but also to visibly show fear. If not, you take it away and put a ring in its ear. The animal is impure.'

Though Bapji did not say so, I later learned from pilgrims that at the Kali temples – deemed very sacred – in Kolkata and Gauhati, goats (always black ones) are beheaded and bled as sacrifices every day, sometimes as many as fifteen or twenty. The carcasses are later butchered, cooked in the temple kitchens, and served in curries to the poor.

Behind his head was a shelf of photographs. I recognized one as being the Rajmata of Jaipur, the former Gayatri Devi, a great beauty in her time. 'Rajmata' literally means queen mother. She had endured a number of hardships – not just the early death of her husband and eldest son, but a fairly long and vindictive imprisonment by Mrs Gandhi for refusing to knuckle under when the constitution was arbitrarily changed. A heavy smoker, known to be a connoisseur of single-malt whiskey, the rajmata lived in Jaipur much the way Babji did, in an annexe of her grand palace.

Bapji explained the connection: 'The first wife of the Maharajah of Jaipur was the sister of my grandfather. The deal was that his niece would also marry. So aunt and daughter' – that is, the sister and her daughter, I guessed – 'were both married to the same man. The aunt was eight or nine years older than he was – you see, he was only fifteen.'

I was somewhat lost in this explanation, and not sure of the dates, but it was so steamy in its complexity it didn't matter. I urged him to go on.

'His British guardian wouldn't let them cohabit. She came out of the bedroom in a huff. "What's the point of being married if I can't sleep in there?" Ha-ha!'

He got up and stretched, and we walked to the wide pink balcony that overlooked the palace gardens, a white marble pavilion shimmering in the distance on the green lawn. He said, 'I was born in this palace. This was my only home. How old are you?'

I told him.

'You look younger than me,' he said.

But then his life had been somewhat more eventful than mine, not just his glorious birth as a descendant of Lord Rama, the relentless rituals, the goat sacrifices and the prophetic assumption of his mother, the reigning maharani: 'You must be a warrior.' But his becoming a maharajah at the age of four, after his father, just twenty-eight, died in an air

crash. His princely world of privilege had been turned upside down by
Mrs Gandhi. Still in his twenties, he'd been a diplomat, the Indian high
commissioner to Trinidad. And there was his son's tragic accident,
something else to age him.

As if that weren't commotion enough, there was an unstable younger
brother – illegitimate and vindictive – who made several attempts to
behead Bapji. On one occasion, the film-maker Ismail Merchant, who
had made a movie at the palace, was present, and watched horrified as
the crazed brother blundered into a dinner party and swiped at the guests
with a sword. Ultimately, Merchant reported, this mad, disinherited
brother was himself beheaded and cut to pieces. All this Babji seemed to
bear with equanimity.

'Maybe I should do yoga,' Bapji said, clutching his belly through his
kurta.

'How did you like diplomatic life?'

'I enjoyed it. I got on very well with the Indians in Trinidad. They
were keeping the balance, and so was I. It was like walking a tightrope.
But I told them that I was not their high commissioner. They were
Trinidadians, weren't they? I made it plain to them that I was not batting
on their side.'

Probably it was the cricket match on television that brought back the
memory and the metaphor.

'My predecessor was an old Muslim gentleman who wrote a memo
to the effect that he wanted to ban cricket tours between India and
Trinidad because they aroused strong emotions.' He laughed recalling
it. 'A black Trinidadian came to me and said, "We want cricket tours!
We want to see Gavaskar!"' – a great batsman. '"What happens among
us is our problem!"'

Bapji broke off to watch the end of the cricket match, and when it
was clear that India could not be beaten, he talked about the military
tradition of his state. Celebrated in India, but unsung heroes everywhere
else, the Indian army had been heroic in both world wars. Bapji explained
that in a decisive battle in September 1918, the Royal Jodhpur Lancers
led the charge into Haifa with the Hyderabad and Mysore mounted
lancers on their flanks, surprising and defeating the German-Turkish
army dug in on Mount Carmel.

'They charged straight into machine guns. Uphill – great horseman-
ship, great valour. Dalpat Singh led the charge and died in the action.'

Bapji was gesturing again. 'Straight across, into the fire. Of course, many died, but they killed four hundred men and took Haifa. They were very brave.'

He was looking out of the window at the expanse of green lawn behind Umaid Bhawan. He straightened and twisted the ends of his moustache.

'My people have courage.' He nodded. 'Heroes.'

He asked how long I would be staying. I said that I was going to leave for the station soon and I'd be on the train that night.

'You'll see my grandfather there.'

He was not being enigmatic. He meant the equestrian statue of Umaid Singh in front of the Jodhpur railway station.

11. Night Train to Jaipur

Kapoorchand, a dignified man of about sixty, was doing exactly what I was doing, and for the same reason. He lived in Jodhpur; he needed to be in Jaipur. 'Train is best,' he said, slightly contorted, sitting cross-legged on his bunk, and when he saw me fussing with my bedding, he said, 'Don't do that. Coolie will take care of it. They have responsibilities. They must make your bed. They must wake you on time. They must bring you tea.'

His tone marked him as a man of picturesque outbursts. I waited for more. It seemed that we would be the only ones in the compartment. I put my things in order: water bottle, food I'd brought from the hotel, my notebook, that day's *Hindustan Times*, my copy of *The Great Mutiny* and an Indian Railways Concise Timetable.

The timetable impressed Kapoorchand. He said, 'Plane might not take off. Or it might drop you in Delhi instead of Jaipur. Or you might have to wait hours.' He smiled through the window at the platform of Jodhpur Station. 'Train will leave on time. It will arrive on time. I will do my consulting and I will get evening train back to Jodhpur.'

He gave me his business card, which indicated he was a chartered accountant with the firm of Jain and Jain.

'Are you busy?'

'Too busy. I have been all over India, but always train.'

I said, 'Gauhati?' It was in distant Assam.

'I have been there.'

'Manipur?'

'Yes.'

'Darjeeling?'

The answer was yes to the ten other remote places I mentioned. As we were talking about these far-off stations, a man in a soldier's uniform slipped into the compartment, said hello, and began chaining his suitcase to the stanchion on the upper bunk.

'Is that necessary?' I asked. As I spoke, the train whistle blew and we were on our way.

'It is precaution, so to say,' Kapoorchand said and consulted his watch, smiling because the train had left on the minute.

As the soldier climbed into the berth over my head – older passengers, like me, got the lower berths – Kapoorchand gave me a chain and padlock from his briefcase that he carried as spares. But I didn't use them. I had very little in my bag, and I usually tucked my briefcase under my pillow, because it contained my passport and credit cards and notebooks and about $1,500 in small notes.

'You know Jain religion?' Kapoorchand asked. 'I am Jain. I meditate three hours a day. But I will do more. I have two brothers who have renounced world. They wander. They use no shoes. They travel many kilometres together.'

'Does this sort of life attract you?'

'Very much indeed.' He was tall, friendly, silver-haired, obviously a businessman – Jains are noted for their business acumen and also for their spirituality. He was well dressed for a railway passenger, in a starched long-sleeved white shirt and blue trousers; he wore an expensive watch. He said he also wanted to renounce the world. 'I will do so in five or six years. I will wander. I will discover myself.'

'Where will you live?'

'I will live in my soul.'

He gave me a Jain pamphlet titled *Universal Fraternity*, which I flipped through as he sat and ate from his small box of food. The pamphlet was full of sage advice – humanistic, brotherhood of man, do the right thing. I read a bit, read the newspaper, and wrote my notes about my talk with Bapji. The soldier was snoring; night had fallen, though it wasn't late. Kapoorchand seemed eager to discuss the life of the soul. Perhaps because he had just finished eating, he talked about the spiritual aspects of food.

'Onions and garlic are worst,' he said. 'They make a desire for sex. And they cause angerness.'

'I did not know that.'

'My friend when he travels without wife never eats onions.' He was enumerating vegetables on his fingers. 'Carrots. Root vegetables. I don't eat, because it is killing the living plant. I eat tops only.'

'Potatoes?'

'Some people eat. But for me – no. So many live things can be found on a potato.'

'Live things, such as . . . ?'

'Bacteria and moulds. Why should they be killed because of me?'

For this reason, Jains habitually wore masks, so as not to inhale any gnats that might be hovering near their open mouths; and they swept at the surface of water to disperse – what? water bugs? mosquito larvae? – before they drank. It was a strict interpretation of the Do Not Kill stricture: nothing must be killed, and that included flies and mould.

'Fruit is good, but . . . bananas can be tricky. It depends on time of day.' Up went his admonitory finger. 'Banana is gold in morning. Silver in afternoon. Iron in evening. One should not eat bananas in evening. Also, no yoghurt in evening, but yoghurt in morning is beneficial.'

'Indian food is spicy, though,' I said.

'Not beneficial. Chillies and pickle make angerness. They increase cruel nature.'

I could see that he enjoyed putting me in the know, because there is a freight of detail in Indian life – an ever-present cargo of dogma, of strictures, of lessons, of distinctions – that turns Indians into monologuers. Their motive seemed pedantic, not to convert you but to exaggerate how little you knew of life.

I ate some of the food I'd brought and offered a bit to him. He looked confused, but took it. He said, 'I am so ashamed. I didn't offer you anything because you were writing. But now you offered. This is my fault. You set a better example.'

'That's a compliment.'

'Shake my hand,' Kapoorchand said suddenly. I leaned across the rocking railway compartment and did so. He said, 'You are generous. Good. I have many theories about handshakes. If you do it like this' – he extended a limp hand – 'you are not generous. You are a cheat. Or it might mean you have only daughters. I shook a man's hand like that once and asked him, "How many daughters?" He said, "Three." Then he said, "Why did you not ask about sons?"' Kapoorchand paused, allowing me to savour this moment. 'I said, "Because you have no sons." Man was astonished. "How did you know?"'

'What's the answer?'

'Handshake. Weakness. Weak sperm cannot make sons.'

'Any more theories?' I reminded myself that this man was a chartered accountant on his way to Jaipur to spend a day looking through the entries of a company's ledgers.

'Yes, many. Those who become angry but do not express their anger-ness get sick. Many die of cancer. They hold the angerness inside their body and it kills them.'

'Possibly.'

'Do you have theories, Mr Paul?'

'I have a theory that no house should be taller than a palm tree.'

'That is good. I have a *haveli* some distance from here. Modest size is there.'

'I also have a theory that nothing matters.'

Kapoorchand stared at me, looking dismayed.

Feeling that I had shocked him (I was simplifying something that Leonard Woolf had once written), I said, 'And I sometimes notice that when a man is looking at you and telling a lie, he touches his eye or his face.'

'That is so!' Kapoorchand said. 'There is so much untruth in the world. That is another reason I will become a sadhu. My brothers did so. My father became a saint.' He fumbled with his wallet and drew out a small faded photograph. 'Here is his picture.'

Even faded and in black and white, the photo showed a man with a kindly face, grey-bearded, a white turban on his head.

'First he waited for some years. When he saw that I was settled, he said that he would become a saint. He lived for fifteen years as a saint.'

'How did he go about this?'

'He came to me. He said, "Look after your mother." I did so. I do so still. He then renounced all worldly things. He gave up shoes, going bare-foot only. Sleeping on floor. Owning nothing. He became a sadhu, a holy man. He went about by walking in bare feet. Simple clothes, living in ashrams, going from place to place, sometimes walking fifteen kilometres a day. He could not visit me, but I could visit him, if he allowed it.'

'Was he happy?'

'Very happy.'

And Kapoorchand explained that another branch of the Jains, the Digambara sect, renounced clothes, too. They kept to the forests, living naked, appearing in public only every dozen years or so for the great spiritual gathering, with ritual bathing in the Ganges and other rivers, called Kumbh Mela.

'You mentioned that you meditate.'

'Three hours daily, in morning time. I recite Jain scriptures. I say prayers.'

'Tell me one. I want to write it down.'

He said, or rather intoned,

> I forgive all beings.
> May all beings forgive me.
> I have friendship with all,
> And vengeance with none.

He went to sleep soon after that, while I scribbled, thinking: This man is the perfect travelling companion.

Jaipur Junction Station in the middle of the night was crowded with people, though in India it was hard to tell the travellers from the squatters. Even in the dark hours of the morning there were chatterers and tea drinkers under the glaring lights, family groups huddled over pots of food, some people sleeping in heaps, stretched out like mummies, or like corpses in body bags. Others were haggling over tickets, and dawn was far off.

'Get a coolie' were Kapoorchand's parting words.

I left him to his arduous pursuit of virtue. I didn't need a coolie. I needed a taxi. A group of touts and drivers, tugging at my sleeves, followed me outside, and I chose the oldest of them, on the assumption that he would be the most reliable, and we settled on the fare before I got into his old car. He drove me into the darkness, but kept his word. And even at that hour I found a welcome at the hotel, and a glass of juice, and a cosy room; I slept soundly.

I had stayed in this hotel before, the Rambagh Palace, but it had been barer then, a big echoey place of marble halls. In the morning I saw it was now luxurious.

'I did not see the inside of a train station, I did not take a train or board a bus, until I was in my late teens,' an Indian woman told me at the Rambagh Palace.

She was in her early forties, a well-brought-up woman from a good family who had always gone to school in a chauffeur-driven car. 'I never saw a poor person. I never saw a slum. I never took public transport. I

didn't know how to buy a ticket. Home to school, school to home –
that was the routine. But one day I rebelled. I was about seventeen or
eighteen. I told the driver, "I'm walking home." He followed me in the
car. He was afraid for me, and afraid of what my father would say. But
walking home, and then taking trains later, I finally saw what India was
really like. And I was so shocked. I had no idea such poor people existed
in India.'

In the market and antique shops of Jodhpur I had seen a number of
reverse-glass paintings that had attracted me, and one had bewitched me.
This was a painting of an Indian Nautch girl – a dancing girl – caught
in a sinuous move, intentionally teasing, probably painted in the middle
or late nineteenth century, with Chinese characters in black brushstrokes
on the wood-slatted back, and set in a decaying frame. I wasn't sizing it
up. I was teased, indeed falling in love. It was an old feeling.

The collector's instinct, which is also a powerful appetite, begins
with a glimpse of something singular, and a smile of recognition. The
technique of painting on the back of a pane of glass, building up effects
that were visible when viewed from the front, was European in origin
(a cheaper and quicker version of stained glass); but the style of this piece
was Chinese, the subject secular and unusually sensual. Europeans in the
eighteenth century introduced this technique to India, where it
flourished. The Chinese had learned reverse-glass painting from early
Jesuits in China at about the same time or earlier, and some itinerant
Chinese artists eventually reached India, where they produced many of
these secular pictures. Portraits of royals and dancing girls and scenes
from the *Ramayana* had been painted, and Indian artists had begun
creating their own reverse-glass paintings – theirs were of Krishna and
Shiva, Ganesh and Hanuman – in brighter colours, with highlights of
gold and silver.

What entranced me was that, though these paintings were superb,
they were not treasures in the classic sense, not yet very popular with the
big-money buyers. They were beloved objects from a simple household,
created by an individual hand, someone with enthusiasm and vision.

I bought the painting of the Nautch girl (probably done by a Chinese
painter in Gujarat) and looked for more. It was not easy to find others,
but I was delighted by the variety I encountered – religious, mythical,
erotic – and by the out-of-the-way places where I found them.

Travelling with, say, something like glass painting in mind (it could also be lime pots, weavings, tribal earrings, Deccan daggers or the bestiary of moulded brass handles from palanquins), it is possible to make an amateur study merely by wandering in the bazaars. Yet another pleasure of travelling in India is the dawdling in antique shops, in markets and museums, talking to dealers and collectors and connoisseurs. After you've seen hundreds of the paintings, some dusty, some cracked, taken out of drawers and attics and cupboards, you begin to develop an eye, to distinguish the real from the fake, the good from the hastily contrived ones.

In the stifling attic of a shop in the Jaipur bazaar, near the pink façade of the Hawa Mahal, bristling with windows – the Palace of the Winds – Mr Kailash was showing me some glass paintings. They were too crusted and cracked and neglected-looking not to be genuine, but when I mentioned the cracks, the man began to hector me.

'Like human body, sar! You have feet and ankles and knees and elbows, all attached, but also all separate. Not true, sar?'

'True,' I said.

'God made us this way,' Kailash Sahib said, holding the painting in my face. 'The painting is like body. It requires – what? Yes, operation! It is normal, sar. And it is rare image. Without crack it would be lakhs of rupees, but this is small money.'

After some haggling I bought it, and Kailash Sahib said he would send it to me in a few months.

'You are lucky to find such beautiful painting piece. Please write in visitors' book.'

I wrote my name and, *We bargained. We both won.*

'You are also lucky that today is the first day of Gangaur festival. As you leave here you can see the procession. Go to City Palace, it will be wonderful.'

The Gangaur festival celebrates the union of Shiva and Parvati, whose marital bliss is an inspiration to Indian couples and who are also noted for 'lovemaking so intense that it shakes the cosmos, and the gods become frightened'. This celebration would unfold over eighteen days in this month of Chaitra (March–April). Most Indian festivals were no less noisy and disruptive than any other aspect of Indian life, so it was hard for an alien like me to tell when the pageant actually started or finished. The wonderful part of this one was that cars and trucks had been diverted from the route of the procession, so that the parade flowed uninterrupted past the Palace of the Winds, the ancient observatory, and the lanes and boulevards of the gated city.

Forty elephants, painted with flowers and Hindu symbols in coloured chalk, were draped in red banners, silk scarves fluttering from their tusks. There were dancers whose sensual movements and hip thrusts could be seen even through their billowing skirts; a boy on stilts fifteen feet in the air; a band playing Indian oompah music in syncopation with thumping brass; yoked bullocks pulling gun carriages mounted with cannons; and four camels with large-bore guns mounted on their humps. And landaus and painted carriages with flute players inside, and prancing horses, and more elephants and dancers and bands, and at last a palanquin with an image of Parvati ('she who dwells in the mountains') on top.

Onlookers began tossing coins at the image and the bearers of the palanquin, which was a litter ten feet long, two men supporting each of its four enormous handles. The men tried to shield their heads from the shower of coins, and as soon as they moved on there was a scramble for the coins that had bounced off Parvati and the heads of the bearers – another mob scene, adults shoving children aside to snatch at the coins in the road.

That was when I slipped away and began walking with the rest of the dispersing crowd on streets that were free of traffic. It was a pleasant and productive walk. I stopped and drank a Kingfisher beer as the evening coolness descended. And down one wide street I saw a pharmacy and bought vitamins and a bottle of sleeping pills and some more capsules for the gout that occasionally plagued me – total cost, 170 rupees, $4.20. A prescription is seldom necessary in India, where drugs are cheaper than sweets.

And after a mile or so a scooter rickshaw swept next to me and said, 'Get on, sar. I will take you home.'

It was dusk, and the buildings crammed into the Galta Gorge were darkening. A monkey chattered and leaped to a branch in a banyan tree above Mr Gopal's head, yanking the branch down and making a punkah's whoosh. We entered the gate and crossed the courtyard to some ruined buildings, with coloured frescoes of trees and people on their façades. Some had been raked with indecipherable graffiti and painted over; whole panels had been chiselled away . . . On the ornate temple walls, stuck with posters, defaced with chisels, pissed on and scrawled over with huge Devanagri script advertising Jaipur businesses, there was a blue enamel sign, warning visitors in Hindi and English that it was 'forbidden to desecrate, deface, mark or otherwise abuse the walls'. The sign itself had been defaced: the enamel was chipped – it looked partly eaten. Further along, the cobblestone road became a narrow path and then a steep staircase cut into the rock walls of the gorge. At the top of this was a temple facing a still black pool . . .

This paragraph, copied verbatim from *The Great Railway Bazaar*, doesn't need quotation marks around it because not much at the monkey temple in Galta Gorge had changed in the thirty-three years since I'd last seen it. It was larger but just as ruinous, looking ancient: that was the Indian way. Instead of Mr Gopal, I had Mohan with me. Mohan wanted to show me a miraculous image somehow imprinted in the rock face on a cliffside temple, high above.

A new pool had been dug, and now there were two, one for men and boys, the newer one a *zenana*, strictly for women wearing saris, for modesty's sake, but they were drenched and clingy, so the effect was the opposite. They splashed among naked girls of six or seven. Both tanks brimmed with foul-looking water in which the pilgrims thrashed, dousing themselves and drinking – more like a hot evening at a public swimming pool than a day at a holy shrine, all the boys laughing and splashing, jumping, diving, some of them swimming and gargling under a spout of water issuing from the mouth of a carved marble cow.

Seeing me writing in my notebook, one of the small boys hauled himself out of the tank and said, 'Please, sar. Give me pen.'

'Why do you want it?'

'I am schoolboy, sar.'

I gave him my cheap extra pen from the hotel and ascended the stairs, following Mohan.

'Monkeys,' I said. 'I hate monkeys.'

'Sacred monkeys,' Mohan said, as though this made a difference when they bared their teeth at me. Decades ago I had taken them to be baboons, but these were rhesus monkeys, big and small, with mangy fur and wicked eyes. Once, seeing monkeys like this, Paul Bowles had written that 'their posteriors looked like sunset on a grocer's calendar'.

The monkey god temple was a cave-like shelter at the top of the gorge. I climbed up, as I had all those years ago, and seeing a priest squatting nearby, I left my notebook and pen outside – it seemed sacrilegious to bring writing implements into the inner sanctum.

But no sooner had I gone inside than I heard, 'Sahib! Sahib!'

The biggest monkey had stolen my small notebook and pen. I shouted and the creature dropped the notebook, but he skittered about ten feet away and began gnawing the rubber plunger off the top of my pen.

I threw some peanuts at him. He flung the pen aside and went for them.

'Good karma,' Mohan said of my feeding the monkey. And he showed me a stain on the temple wall. 'Image of Hanuman is miracle. You see it is natural in rock.'

The lumpy rock wall, identified as a monkey's head and shoulders, had been outlined in orange.

'Six hundred years old,' Mohan said. 'Not less.'

From this height I could see that Galta was much bigger than it had been before; what had seemed to me a dusty shrine in a ravine was now a large complex of temples. Far above it on the ridge was a sun temple, for the Surya devotees. The spitting and splashing – explicitly forbidden before on a comical sign – was now tolerated, as was the screeching and swimming in the tanks, and the sight of women with wet clinging saris, and small naked girls laughing at the edge of the pool and poised like water sprites.

As I passed them again, the women were floating small waterborne dishes, each one bearing a candle flame – in Hindu belief, a *deepak,* or holy flame – as a white and brown heron stalked along a low shelf, from time to time dipping its beak in the water.

'Hanuman is my god,' Mohan said. 'I do *puja* every day at my temple before I go on duty. Also my wife. Also my daughter.'

Indians boasted of how much had changed in their country. It was modern, it was wealthier, 'even rickshaw wallahs have mobile phones' – all that. But in Galta Gorge I realized that nothing had changed. The place was bigger but just as dirty; more people, more monkeys, the same pieties.

And then, after lunch one day in Jaipur, I decided to leave. Thanks to the train, it was easy to do. I went to the station, where the train was waiting. I got on. The train left. I simply evaporated.

12. Night Train to Mumbai
The 'Superfast' Express

The lovely heart of Jaipur is what the tourist sees, a pink princely city of temples and palaces – painted elephants, the marvellous fort, all of it dusty but beautiful, like Rajasthani women in their gorgeous silks and gold-trimmed veils. But the train traveller sees a different Jaipur and begins to understand the city's true size. It sprawls to the horizon, a city of three million, mostly living in one- and two-storey houses. Thirty minutes after leaving the station, and way past the airport, we were still passing the outer suburb of distant Sanganer – decrepit, but even so, a town full of temples that was entered through a triple gateway. A few hours later, the train moved through a yellow plain, flat and dry as far as I could see, with a scattering of trees. Some of it was ploughed, awaiting planting, and flocks of goats browsed in the grass. But really it was a great expanse of wide-open country. In this nation of more than a billion people – utter emptiness.

'Superfast' might have been a misnomer for this train – eighteen hours of travel, a two o'clock departure from Jaipur, arriving in Mumbai at eight the next morning – but the euphemism was consoling. I had to catch up on note taking, and I was becoming absorbed in *The Great Mutiny*. It was a trip of 720 miles.

Mr Gupta, my compartment mate, was being transferred by his employer, a telecom company, to Mumbai.

'The transfer was unexpected and very stressful. I'm taking the train because I need a rest,' Mr Gupta said. 'Planes are a problem. You hurry and then you wait. Sometimes the plane is circling for half an hour. Ridiculous.'

'You have a place to stay in Mumbai?'

'I will stay in a hotel for one month. Then I'll find a place and my wife and children will follow.' He was making a call to his wife as he spoke, and when he hung up he said, 'So how do you find India? Mostly friendly?'

'Oh, yes. No problems.'

'This is Sawai Madhopur. There's a tiger sanctuary near here, at Ranthambore.'

'Sanctuary' might have been stretching it, I found out later: only about twenty tigers, a dwindling number because of persistent poaching. The area had once been the private game reserve of the Jaipur royals, and many of the animals had ended up stuffed and peering from the ornate walls of the Rambagh Palace and the Amber Fort.

We plunged into a landscape of long lumpy hills, brown and dry and treeless, at the edge of farmed valleys. Women in beautiful yellow and orange saris hacked at gardens with heavy hoes and carried water jars on their heads, as in the old aquatints, walking with stately grace down narrow paths, past goats and chickens.

Later in the afternoon groups of people were gathered in wheat fields for harvesting, some bent double to slash at the stalks, others tying them into bundles – not a single sign of mechanized intervention. It all looked ancient. And that was only a matter of miles from Kota Junction, for though the surrounding villages were among the simplest I'd seen in India, Kota itself was an industrial city, with an atomic plant not far away, and so modern as to be intensely polluted (guidebook: in 1992 'levels of radioactivity were way above "safe" levels'). That was part of the panorama: a long hot afternoon in rural India that included ancient ploughshares, wheat harvested by hand, water jars carried from the village well, and nearby an atomic energy plant leaking radioactivity.

We were soon among the ploughshares and the harvesters, and in the twilight a group of labourers in *puja* postures, an Indian version of Millet's *The Angelus*.

Mr Gupta said, 'People work very hard here.'

We passed a man ploughing. I said, 'They're looking ahead. "No man, having put his hand to the plough, and looking back, is fit for the kingdom of God."'

'Who said that?'

'Jesus. It's in the Bible.'

'Very nice.'

Night fell in the wide valleys, and here and there I could see candle flames in the little huts. A food seller came to the compartment and offered me the vegetarian special for 45 rupees – a dollar. So Mr Gupta and I each bought a tray. While we ate and talked, another traveller joined us and took a top berth. He was a shawl seller, on his way to Mumbai to take orders.

Mr Gupta's phone kept ringing. 'You will excuse me? Sorry for the disturbance, but my little girl, who is four, misses me greatly. I need to reassure her.'

He spoke to his little girl three more times before he turned in. He was another young man from the provinces joining the twenty million in Mumbai.

By the small light over my berth, I read *The Great Mutiny*, then fell asleep and thrashed in mutiny-inspired dreams of bloody mayhem, religious fanaticism, revenge and anarchy.

In the morning, Mr Gupta and the shawl seller were up and packed. They were getting off at Santa Cruz, while I continued the whole way, into the heart of the city.

The frenzied careerists of Mumbai seldom stopped talking about how the place was booming, as though having rid it of its old name, Bombay, they had founded a new city. Their obtuse pride was odd in a country infatuated with its past, obsessed with its own complexity, where nostalgia was a ruling passion. But the Indian craving to belong to the wider world is more than a billion strong – and not just to belong, but to have the world's good opinion of them, to impress with their history, their moralizing and disquisitional nature, their unembarrassed pleasure in speechifying, their love of the orotund and the sententious, and the enduring quaintness of their customs: how they avoided killing a flea, how they worshipped lingams ('It is penis, sar'), how they drank the river water from Mother Ganga, how they propitiated the goddess Lakshmi in order to acquire wealth, how they approved of the widow-burning practice of suttee and arranged marriages, while at the same time describing their progress in hedge funds, computer software, nuclear reactors or astrophysics.

'This is my husband, Arun,' an Indian woman said to me later in Mumbai, her eyes flashing with defiance. 'It was not a love match. Our parents arranged it. We hardly knew each other. We have been very happy. We have three children. We will arrange their marriages, after – of course – we have consulted astrologers.'

She was showing off, trying to bait me. I was on the point of saying, 'Funnily enough, I picked up my wife in a bar,' when her husband began boasting about how India led the world in corporate takeovers in the global steel sector. I did not say, 'Why hire market analysts in India when you can hire soothsayers and astrologers?'

Mumbai was India's boast, representing everything it wanted the world to admire. I could see the city was bigger. The limits of Mumbai had expanded for miles. They were around Mahim on my first visit; they were now at thirteen miles north of it, at Thana and Mahisa. But Mumbai the magnificent was also home to Asia's biggest slum. Commuters into Mumbai from the suburbs could spend hours on buses and trains. Both its airports had been swamped by this development, so their nearness to the centre of Mumbai actually distorted the size of the city, sprawling north and east in immense low suburbs, which rose from the huts of the outskirts to the busy district at Colaba, with its tall buildings, its churches and its municipal offices of the peculiar Indo-Saracenic architecture of the Raj, which was mocked as 'disappointed Gothic'.

'When I got back to Mumbai from New York last week I saw that a new building had gone up,' an American businessman said to me. 'It's not Shanghai, but it's growing fast. Basically a new building every week or so.'

It is a shock to travel from the countryside, especially the desert provinces of the north, to the biggest city in India and one of the biggest in the world. Out of the yellow plains and through the dust and tiny villages to this enormous port, packed with people, its dark streets jammed with honking cars. The official population is seventeen million; unofficially it is in excess of twenty million, and still growing; and because it is hot and so much of its life is outdoors, entirely visible, Mumbai is like a city without walls.

'Foreigners come and all they talk about are the poor people,' an Indian woman said to me. She was an executive with a large company. 'I want to say, "What about the poor people in your country? There's more to India than poor people."'

That's true, but there are quite a few poor people in India. Anyway, Indian statistics, like Chinese numbers, are stupendous and ungraspable. When an Indian says, as one said to me, 'There are two hundred and fifty million middle-class Indians, which is very nice, but four hundred million are living below the poverty line,' how do you respond? Two hundred years ago, the French aphorist Chamfort described Paris as 'a city of amusements, pleasures, etc., in which four-fifths of the inhabitants die of want'. You could say the same of any city in India.

If you dropped your gaze from the new hotel or the new call centre, India looked as poor as it ever had. I was reminded of V. S. Naipaul writing in *An Area of Darkness* (1964): 'India is the poorest country in the world. Therefore, to see its poverty is to make an observation of no value.' But that's no longer true.

It would be truer to say that poverty in India now represents a perverse kind of wealth: the half billion people earning a dollar a day are producing India's food surplus; the sweatshop factory workers are the backbone of its textile industry; and low-paid employees are the workforce of its high-tech sector. The whole Indian economy is driven by the poor, by low salaries, and of course by a tremendous work ethic, which in India is a survival skill and an instinct. 'The high standard of life we enjoy in England depends upon keeping a tight hold on the Empire,' Orwell wrote. 'In order that England may live in comfort, a hundred million Indians must live on the verge of starvation.' The desperation of the slum dwellers can be shocking; when Naipaul visited a *chawl*, or slum tenement, for a later book – *India: A Million Mutinies Now* (1990) – he wrote, 'I was so demoralized, so choked, driven so near to a stomach-heave, by the smell at the entrance, with wet mangled garbage and scavenging cats and kittens in a little patio, and then, in the sudden dark passage, by the thick warm smell, catching at my throat, of blocked drains . . .' And so on, making a meal of it. He is shocked, appalled, almost undone by what he sees, and seems to have changed his mind about discussing the Indian poor. But he is one of the few writer-travellers who in subsequent books on India retraced his own footsteps.

Unlike the poor in Europe or America or even China, the poor in India are a constant presence. Where else do people put up plastic huts on the pavement along a main road – not one or two but an entire subdivision of makeshift shelters? They inhabit train stations, sleep in doorways, crouch under bridges and railway trestles. They do it for safety and also con- venience, since they are not parasites nor lazy louts but underpaid workers, many of these squatters actually doing jobs in Mumbai. Among the poorest are the Koli people, descendants of the original inhabitants (the city takes its name from their patron goddess, Mumbai-Devi). Most of the Koli are fisher folk who live at the edge of the sea in black and battered shacks, near one of Mumbai's most expensive districts.

With poverty so obvious and unmissable, the foreigner sometimes bursts into tears, until he or she learns the Indian trick of looking only at the background, where all those new buildings are rising. While I was in Mumbai the municipal council launched 'a drive to clear hutments and shanties from the roads and footpaths'. On the first day 1,000 such shelters were pulled down and the occupants scattered. In one morning, more than 6,000 people were made homeless.

'Where will we go? The BMC has razed our houses,' one of the victims said.

'Our houses' was an interesting phrase. The structures were made of twigs, branches, waste timber, bits of string, plastic sheeting with taped seams, cotton cloth, blankets, cardboard, splintered plywood, threadbare canvas; each one with a flickering lantern and a cooking fire.

Squatters are so firmly established in every Indian city their seemingly makeshift camps are as deceptive as birds' nests, as well camouflaged, as tightly woven, and just as complex; and these people have counterparts in every city in the world. As the Indian woman said to me, 'What about the poor people in your country?' Well, yes. New Orleans is a vivid example of a place where the poor were either hidden or unapproachable. It seemed that until they were flushed out by the floodwaters of Hurricane Katrina no one knew they existed, nor knew what to do with them.

There is a depressing travel book to be written about the poor in America. The problem is, how to penetrate this world? The book is almost unwritable, except by someone who actually lives in such a place – though living in one slum does not license a person to live in or even visit another slum. The poor in America live in dangerous places; out of paranoia, or for protection, or because of neglect by the police or harassment by gangs, they have themselves mostly contrived this danger, to seal themselves off from authority, or from outsiders, anyone inquisitorial who would be regarded (with reason) as an enemy. I have never seen any community in India so hopeless or, in its way, so hermetic in its poverty, so blatant in its look of menace, so sad and unwelcoming, as East St Louis, Illinois, the decaying town that lies across the Mississippi from flourishing St Louis, Missouri. Yet I can imagine that many people from St Louis proper would weep at the sight of Indian poverty. They dare not cross their own river to see the complacent decrepitude and misery on the other bank.

The Indian poor are accessible, conversational, often congenial and friendly, and generally unthreatening. No one can travel among the American poor the way I could travel among the Indian poor, asking intrusive questions. What's your name? How long have you lived here? Where do you work? How much money do you make? – the usual visitor's questions. I got answers, and even hospitality. In the same sort of area in the United States – the decaying sections of Jackson, Mississippi, the Roxbury neighbourhood of Boston, the Anacostia district in Washington, DC and many other places – I would be threatened or robbed or sent away for daring to ask such things. *What do you want here?* It is an understandable response. But in India I was unexpectedly welcome in such places – the slums, the squatter camps, the stinking *chawls*, the reeking *bustees*.

'This is the biggest slum in Asia – it said so in the paper,' a young man named Kartik said to me in the area of Mumbai called Dharavi. The name is practically a synonym for desperation: 520 acres in the depths of the city, 600,000 inhabitants and grim statistics, though the celebrated Dharavi factoid of 'one public toilet for 800 people' – the vision of a very long queue of people hopping with impatience – is misleading, since it was malodorously clear to me on my visit that many people in Dharavi regarded a public toilet as a superfluous novelty.

Dharavi was in the news, because with Mumbai's new prosperity the slum land had become valuable. Mumbai is essentially the gigantic island of Salsette, and most of it had been claimed. There was a move afoot to tear down Dharavi and put up expensive houses for the rising class in the new Mumbai. The idea of demolishing Dharavi was an example of the cunning greed of property speculators, because 'slum' did not really describe it. Far from being a fetid precinct of despair, it was a self-sufficient part of the inner city, indeed a city itself, and parts of it did not look much different from any other part of Mumbai. The Chor bazaar district, for example, was just as ramshackle and grim, yet just as packed with thriving businesses and hectic households and the Indian mob. The Indian mob, here as elsewhere, was made up of shrieky young men and boys who seemed driven by a frenzy of sexual repression and high spirits – but sexual repression most of all, seeking release, with the grabby hands, squiffy eyes and damp eager faces of scolds and onanists.

Kartik's family history was typical. His father had come from the southern state of Tamil Nadu when he was fifteen years old. Some relatives lived in Dharavi. He shared a small room with five other boys and worked at a hotel, cleaning tables for the equivalent of $2 a month – this was, interestingly enough, at about the time I was on my Railway Bazaar trip, in 1973. After a year or so, Kartik's father got a casual job on Indian Railways, cleaning carriages and earning $4 a month. This led to a proper job and some training as a plumber and fitter, dealing with water tanks on the railway. He had started out earning 900 rupees a month (about $20) and now earned about 7,000 rupees ($150). In that time, over thirty years, he had married and raised a family, yet he had never moved from Dharavi slum.

'He is happy. He is getting food. He is not begging,' Kartik said. 'But we were poor, and we are still poor. My brother is unemployed. I got a job because I managed to pass my driver's licence when I was sixteen. There is plenty of work in Mumbai for a driver who is reliable and honest.'

We were sitting on stools in front of the shack his father had built against another shack. Kartik didn't want to show me the inside. He said he was waiting for some men to come and fix it, but I took this to mean that he was self-conscious about its size, just a hen coop really, with squalor all around it and an unbelievable racket that made its flimsy planking chatter and throb.

'But software engineers also live here in Dharavi slum,' he said. 'They work for IBM and earn forty thousand rupees a month' – $900. 'My friend is marrying a girl who is in the US. He is a Tamil, named Shekhar. She is from a wealthy family. Her dowry is one kilo of gold and two lakhs of rupees' – $4,500 – 'and a motorbike.'

'What about your marriage prospects?'

'None. I would like to meet such a girl.'

There are other consequences of living at such close quarters. According to the *Hindustan Times*, a recent study of 3,600 girls in Delhi concluded that one in eight had been raped by a family member, and three quarters of them feared being raped by someone in the family.

I left Kartik and walked towards the more salubrious part of Mumbai, keeping to back streets because of the crush of people and the traffic on the main roads. When I reached the Church Gate area, and was cutting through a wide lane that was closed to cars, an old woman in a blue sari walked quickly to keep pace with me and asked where I was from. When I told her, she said, 'Welcome.'

Three children walked along with her: a small girl of about ten, a boy of about fourteen and an older skinny girl, perhaps sixteen. They all looked undernourished; it was hard to tell their ages. The older girl caught my eye because she was graceful and was dressed in the thick gauzy skirts of a Gypsy. Most noticeable was the fact that her left forearm was missing.

'Maybe we can help you,' the old woman said. 'What is your name?'

'I'm Paul. Are these your children?'

'I am their auntie.'

I had a pretty good idea what that meant. It was early evening, a coolness and a darkness descending, and I wanted to know what she was offering. If there is a difference between being a tourist and a traveller, this was it. A tourist would have been at a temple or a museum; I had been in a slum, and out of curiosity was strolling along with the soliciting Mistress Overdone, the bawd, and her three depraved-looking youths.

'What do you want?' I asked.

'Just talk, sir.'

'Go ahead, talk.'

'Better we talk in there' – she indicated a teashop.

So she led the way to the shop, where I sat in a booth next to the skinny one-armed girl, with the old woman and the other two children on the opposite side of the table.

'*Chai, chai,*' she said to the waiter.

'Do you want anything else?'

The small girl wanted ice cream, the boy wanted a samosa, the one-armed girl said she was happy with tea, and she sipped it shyly, snuggling next to me.

'We live just near,' the old woman said and pointed out of the window of the teashop. 'Five minutes.'

I glanced at the one-armed girl, who was smiling anxiously at me. Her sunken eyes were strangely yellow, like those of a nocturnal animal, and the skin of her good arm, pressed against mine, was very dry and hairy, suggesting malnutrition.

It was perfect, this secluded place, with the insinuating old woman who was, I was pretty sure, pimping these children. It was one of the pleasanter districts in Mumbai, and she must have had luck buttonholing foreigners like me or else she would not have been so confident. I wanted her to tell me what she had in mind – what activity, what price, what length of time, what sort of promises she'd make.

She had told me how near she lived; now she began telling me how clean it was, how private. 'So quiet, sir. Very good building.'

I had many questions. But what kept me from asking them was the flow of people into the teashop. The shop was a kind of snack bar, with plates of food in glass cases – buns and samosas and sandwiches. We were sitting near the entrance, and every person who entered – mostly men – stared hard at me. It was about six-thirty in the evening. I was the only foreigner in the place, and here I was, in a booth with a procuress and two sallow and debauched-looking children and a teenage whore.

I wanted to ask, How much? And, What's the story?

I started to ask them their names, but I realized that if I did that, the people around me would hear and instantly know what was up. I tried to pretend we were old friends.

'He's really hungry!' I said. 'Want another ice cream?'

Three tough-featured young men walked past, then chose to sit in the booth opposite, where they could hear and see everything.

I cringed, thinking how I looked there. I wanted to say: I'm a traveller. I'm writing a book. I'm just asking questions. I have no designs on these young children!

'Let we go,' the old woman said, perhaps realizing how awkward I felt.

I said, 'Look, I'm going to be around for a week or so. I'm pretty busy right now. We can meet again.'

'When?' the old woman said. 'Where?'

'Anywhere,' I said evasively.

'Tomorrow,' she said. 'What time?'

'Any time. I'll find you – here,' and I put down 200 rupees. 'That's for the food.' And I whispered, 'I have to go.'

'Mr Paul!' the woman called out as I slipped past the booths. Now everyone was staring at me, thinking, He's a perv! And I hurried through the door, murmuring, 'Get me out of here.'

But for days afterwards, I kept thinking of the small children, the one-armed girl, how hungry they'd been, how they'd sucked at the tea and eaten with their heads down, in a concentrated and famished way, with animal delight. I did not see them again – I had looked. They'd probably found another foreigner.

★

Killing time in the Chor bazaar, the Thieves' Market, looking for reverse-glass paintings along Mutton Street, with its mainly Muslim dealers in glass and porcelain, silverware and lamps, I strayed into a narrow lane to look at some old coins and found a man who said he admired George Bush. Lingering and chatting, putting an antique dealer at ease, often had the effect of causing him to open drawers and cupboards and show me objects, not to sell them, but just for the interest, their curiosity value – an ancient piece of pottery, a glazed tile, a moonstone, a lime pot in the shape of a yoni, a monkey skull pendant from Nagaland, a human skull from Tibet.

'Look at this, from Persia,' Rajendra, the dealer, said, taking the lid off a narrow box.

He showed me a foot-long dagger, silver inlaid with gold, inscribed with a Farsi poem and elaborately engraved, with a thick ivory handle. Uncapping the handle, Rajendra withdrew a smaller knife – an ivory-handled shiv, also traced with gold.

'Damascus blade. Very old. Very rare. Very costly.'

One of the gorier bits of trivia regarding damascene blades was that after they were heated and worked they were quenched by being plunged into a living human, a man who died giving strength to the blade. I mentioned this to Rajendra.

'I know nothing about that, but . . .' He allowed the sunlight to dance on the details of the blade and the gold of the haft and the veins of ivory. 'Pure gold. Ivory from whale.'

'How much?'

'Crores! Crores! But not for sale,' he said, and leaned closer, sounding angry. 'I want to present it to the US ambassador in Delhi. He can put it into a museum, or give it to President Bush, or sell it and give the money to the families of the American soldiers who died in Iraq.'

'You want to give this dagger to Bush?'

'Bush is a great man.' He wielded the dagger. 'Bush was right! History will prove him right.'

'Right about what?'

'Islam! The brutalness of it!' He pointed outside, where the Chor bazaar was thronged with Muslim shops and secondhand dealers and car repairers and watch menders. 'Bush had to do that. Look at history. Aurangzeb killed his father.'

He also killed his brothers. He was a notorious bigot, a mosque builder, a warrior king. 'That was, what, about four hundred years ago?'

'They kill animals. They eat them. Have you seen them kill a goat? It is horrible.'

'Hindus in Jodhpur kill goats during religious festivals. They did it a few weeks ago at Navratri.'

'But Muslims bleed it while it is still alive!' Rajendra said. 'We have always had problems with Muslims. Look at Indian history! Twenty years ago a maharajah came to me to buy some things. I said to him, "Never mind these few things. You can have them. But I want to say to you that Islam will be the main problem in the world. The main cause of the world's troubles."'

'What did the maharajah say?'

'He didn't listen. But Bush knows better. People say – even my friends say – Bush is wrong. But no, Bush is pukka right. Without Bush the world would be finished!' He now held the dagger in both hands, as though offering it. 'I want to give this to those who have died. Maybe you can talk to someone.'

'There's an American consul general in Mumbai. Just call him and tell him what you want to do.'

Rajendra put the dagger back into its silk-lined box. He said, 'People will be angry with me if I do this, so I am hesitating. They will say, "Who is he? Just a *bunniah* [trader]," but I know I am right. I know that Bush is right.'

On my trip of 28,000 miles and hundreds of encounters, I met two people who supported the American president: the man in Baku who wanted the United States to invade Iran, and Rajendra. No one else.

Everybody in India – and in the States too – talked about outsourcing. India was making shirts and shoes and electronics, and the growth areas were IT (information technology), BPO (business process outsourcing) and KPO (knowledge process outsourcing). These were labour-intensive businesses that had helped swell Mumbai to its present size of twenty million, overfilled its trains with commuters, packed its hotels and restaurants, and impelled developers to look at Dharavi slum as a property development opportunity. Hundreds of millions of Indians lived below the poverty line – the suicide rate in rural areas was unusually high – but hundreds of millions were also making money.

'The Indian miracle, I tell you,' Indians said to me as we drove through the streets of Mumbai, past the slums, people sleeping on the pavements, the lame and the halt. Was the miracle, I wondered, just an illusion?

I badgered friends to connect me with some moneymakers. The biggest IT company in India was Tata Consultancy Services. In the month I visited the TCS office in Mumbai, the company was worth $4 billion. It had more than 80,000 employees in seventy-four cities world-wide, but this place in Mumbai was one of the largest, and since the Tata family is from Mumbai, this office was perhaps the firm's hub and headquarters.

Instead of taking the train, I allowed myself to be persuaded that a car would be quicker. But the car took twice as long – one and a half hours to get to Vikhroli, on Mumbai's sprawling outskirts. The company lay behind a high wall, traffic-choked and desperate on the outside, serene on the inside, tree-shaded and orderly, like a college campus. This was the Godrej and Boyce Industrial Garden, and though the Godrej Group manufactured soap, detergent, hair dye, hair oil, nappies, 'stylish wedding napkins', machine tools and furniture, its large tracts of available land also made it an outsourcing heaven. Dozens of American companies were located behind the walls of this shady compound.

'Welcome, sir,' said Mr Burjor Randeria, the CEO of this branch of TCS. He was sixty-one, a Parsi, very hospitable and helpful. He was a Zoroastrian – a flame flickered on a dish on his desk, where there was an image I took to be Ahura Mazda. 'We know him as Asho Farohar,' Mr Randeria said. Next to this bearded guardian was a portrait of the frizzy-haired guru Sathya Sai Baba, a small statue of the elephant god Ganesh and a Ganesh mantra box, about the size of a large matchbox, which cleverly buzzed with intoned mantras day and night.

'It creates vibrations of Ganesha,' Mr Randeria said. 'I have it on all the time.'

'But you're a Parsi.'

'I find this soothing.'

We talked about the Parsis. The Tatas were a Parsi family, noted for their philanthropy, having founded hospitals, schools, training colleges and orphanages. There were, Mr Randeria said, only 73,000 Parsis in the world, most of them in Mumbai. They were a dying breed.

'We marry late. We seldom have more than one or two children. And Zoroastrians don't convert others. You have to be born a Parsi.'

He had been born in Sanjan, Gujarat. This was where the first Parsis landed after Muslim persecution in various jihads from the eighth to the tenth centuries, which ultimately drove almost all of them from Persia. 'Parsi' means Persian.

After Mr Randeria worked for Swissair for a number of years, looking for places to outsource Swissair's revenue accounting – labour costs were much too high in Switzerland – in 1995 he founded a company that provided financial support services for airlines. Tata had a stake in this company, but then Tata had a stake or part ownership in many companies. The name Tata was stamped on the back of most Indian buses and trucks and cars. Tata owned Tetley Tea and many retail stores. Taj Hotels was owned by Tata, and its hotels included the Pierre in New York and what had been the Ritz-Carlton in Boston. Telecom, steel, software, utilities, Internet and insurance companies were all Tata enterprises.

One of the curiosities of the company, founded by Jamsetji Nusserwanji Tata (1839–1904), was that a sizeable portion of the immense Tata profits went to charitable groups. This was the case from the beginning, the company endowing research institutes and hospitals. Ratan Tata, the current CEO of the whole business, is a single man in his mid-sixties about whom very little is known, other than the fact that he lives rather modestly. He continues to build up his company, buying steel mills and telecommunication giants and, recently, producing affordable family cars – and, as always, looking for constructive ways to give most of his money away. In 2006, the year I poked my nose into Tata Consultancy Services, sales in the conglomerate brought in $24 billion.

Walking through the marble halls of the huge building, I asked Mr Randeria who his competitors were.

'Microsoft, Infosys, many others,' he said. 'But our motto is "Top Ten by 2010." We will get there by various ways. Growth both organic and inorganic. Code of conduct. Culture. Ethics. Expansion. Also acquisition – we recently acquired Pearl Insurance and the banking and financial giant Chile Comicron. We are very serious. We have an office in Budapest that caters to European languages.'

'I passed through Budapest. I had the idea that a lot of Hungarians were looking for jobs.'

'If they are willing to work and have skills, we will hire them.'

'Funny to hear that from an Indian company,' I said.

'But consider our advantages. English language, a legacy from British rule,' Mr Randeria said. 'And education. We are on the whole a very well-educated country.'

'So everything's rosy.'

He knew I was baiting him, but he took it well. 'No. I toe the line, but everyone knows there's corruption in India and that you can buy a degree. And there's our population. It's growing at a hectic pace.'

It was 600 million in 1973. It was now more than twice that. I said, 'What can you do about it?'

'You can only bring it down by education,' Mr Randeria said. 'Adult literacy. You see, if you have an education, you have many sources of pleasure and intellectual stimulation. Ways of using your time. Without education, it's only sex in the rural areas.'

'Do you remember what Mumbai was like before this population explosion?'

'Oh, very well indeed.' He smiled at the memory. 'When I was a boy in Jogeshwar, streets used to be deserted by seven or eight in the evening. It was dark. My parents wanted me home. We saw foxes and hyenas, and so many snakes. Now it's a very crowded place.'

Jogeshwar, once a remote area of Salsette and the site of a famous cave, was a large and congested population centre about ten miles from central Mumbai. Mr Randeria said that 400 families a day – an average of four people per family – migrated to Mumbai.

Swiping his security card from door to door, leading me into the call centre, he said, 'We are the call centre for' – he named an American retailer he made me swear I would not reveal – 'at levels one to four. If you have a problem with your electric drill, we will sort it out.'

He showed me the rooms where advanced classes in English language were taught (including American intonation), and the technical rooms where employees learned the inner workings of the products, so they could answer a flummoxed buyer's question or offer advice.

Please remove the chuck key from the pouch, insert it in the chuck of the drill, and turn clockwise to tighten the teeth against the bit . . .

That sort of sentence was practised and rehearsed in the classrooms and then recited over the phone by Indian employees, who gave themselves American names ('Rick', 'Andrea') and spoke in American accents.

Through soundproof windows, I could see the cubicles – sixty or eighty to a room – where Indian employees wearing headphones were speaking to American callers who had problems with their products. A large banner at the front of one room read, WHAT CAN I DO TO RESOLVE YOUR ISSUE TODAY?

These were voice-based technical supporters, whose accents and manner needed to be reassuring.

Just rotate the prahduct until the bahdum is verdigal, and look for the ten-digit serial number. It should start with B. B for Bahb.

In other departments, accents were less important. One room was staffed entirely by medical technicians and doctors, fielding medical questions from a Danish HMO. They were speaking to Danes in Esbjerg and Aalborg and Copenhagen, brainstorming problems pertaining to diabetes.

Another zone at TCS was devoted to number crunching: several thousand cubicles of clerks at computers helping to redeem frequent-flier miles, or deal with pricing, or explain other ticket matters for international airlines.

'You see this man,' Mr Randeria said. 'He is speaking to a ticket agent in – it could be New York, it could be Dallas – who has a problem with a ticket.'

The employees in this room didn't need American accents or names; they were providing backup, emergency service and tech support. The room was a racket of undifferentiated voices, like a cage of macaws.

'Airlines are some of our best customers. For them to get the maximum benefit from a flight, they need advice on space control and yield management.'

From ticketing to pricing to seating logistics (which is what I took 'space control' to mean), all this was managed by these techies in Vikhroli, who worked every day and every night of the year.

'It's stressful work,' Mr Randeria said. Because of that, TCS provided a gym, a cafeteria and a resident doctor. And all employees commuted to work by the company shuttle service, which stopped at various hubs in the city.

'Suppose there's a power cut?' I asked. Such things were common, and barely concealed under the euphemisms 'brownout', 'rolling blackout' or 'load shedding'. 'What happens then?'

'Last July we had power cuts. Ninety-three centimetres of rain in sixteen hours.' That was more than three feet of rain in a little more than half a day! But Mr Randeria was smiling. 'We had two hundred per cent redundancy backup. I'll show you.'

He took me to a towering building at the rear of the complex. 'This is the UPS – uninterrupted power supply. But we also have additional backup generators. In India these are essential.'

'This seems a success story,' I said.

'If IT and BPO hadn't happened, India would be twenty years behind. Look at China. China is already the leader in hardware and is attempting to be the leader in software. But we have the advantage of language.'

'Can China learn English fast enough to be competitive with India?'

'Time will tell,' he said. 'We put a big emphasis on training.'

It was obvious that such an enterprise succeeded because there was a large workforce of intelligent, polite English-speakers with a good education and a need for money; people who could not leave India; who, at an earlier time – as when I was here last – would have sought jobs as schoolteachers, civil servants, accountants, pen pushers and paper chewers; who filled the traditional Indian occupations for the educated, as pundits and *bunniahs* and box wallahs.

This was the cleanest and most orderly building I had so far seen in India, and even as I was leaving I was asking Mr Randeria questions about training and expansion and salaries.

'Mr Paul,' he said gently, 'what you should do is see our operation in Bangalore. Just Bangalore itself – you will be awestruck.'

13. Night Train to Bangalore

The Udyan Express

Early morning Mumbai was sunlit and damp and somewhat slimy from a night of condensation on the old dark paving stones, a city of empty streets, before workers and traffic hit town and the sun was at its worst. But now, at six or so, as I was hurrying to Victoria Station, the slime helped me remember the city I had seen long ago, a city of squatters and sweepers and rickshaws, with a ripe and reeking smell – of money and death.

Victoria had a new name. The grandiose, cathedral-like building (more 'disappointed Gothic'), commemorating the queen's 1887 jubilee and one of the grandest railway stations in the world, was now called Chatrapathi Sivaji Terminus, after the wily warrior king of the Marathas, who unified Maharashtra and battled the Mughals in the seventeenth century.

Because of my last-minute ticket, I was able to get only second–class AC: stalls in an ancient carriage, berths with curtains instead of doors, like a troop train in an old film, or the one in *Some Like It Hot*, with flapping, curtains. Passengers peered out of them like nomads peeping out of tents. On the outside of the next carriage, running its entire length, was a piece of denunciatory graffiti in tall and graceful white letters: THE MOST CORRUPT PERSON ON THE RAILWAY IS SHYAM PRAKASH. An aside in Hibbert's book on the 1857 Mutiny was the line 'One of those arcane statements, beloved by the wall defacer, whose meaning is usually known only to the cognoscenti.'

I was going to Bangalore because everyone talked about it as the site of the high-tech economic engine that was driving India's economy. And Bangalore was a stop on the way to Madras, where I had been before and wished to go again.

I was sleepy from the early start, and drowsed in my berth. When I woke up an hour or so later, we were in a landscape of blunt brown hills and deep ravines, tiny villages in the empty India of struggling farmers.

Away from the sea of people, this bulked like the mainland. The news about this agricultural part of Maharashtra was that deeply indebted and drought-stricken farmers were drinking rat poison, committing suicide in record numbers (almost 2,000 in the previous six years, and 800 of those in the year I passed through, the deaths accelerating in the first three months of 2006 to 'a suicide every eight hours').

We were headed southeast in a region of rock temples and deep, elaborate caves, dating from the first and second centuries BC, near the station at Lonavale and Malavli – a little under a hundred miles from Mumbai but a world apart, with a narrow muddy river further on, trailing through the small villages and offering a chance for women to do laundry in its opaque water. Fifty to eighty women at a time were thrashing clothes against rocks while their husbands laboured in the wheat fields, and their kneeling children formed cow shit into Frisbee-sized disks and dried them for fuel. This was not the Indian miracle. Less than three hours from Mumbai and its plutocrats and boasters, this was the India of the hut, the cow-dung fire, the bean field, the buffalo, the ox cart and the bicycle – of debt and drought and death.

Past Pune, in the early afternoon we came to Daund Junction, where a gathering of aged but highly ornamented women – 'tribals' – were waiting for a later train. Mirrors the size of silver dollars were sewn or woven on to their embroidered bodices, and each woman had a small filigreed ornament in the shape of a chandelier depending from her left nostril. They wore russet or yellow shawls, and veils and bangles, and the huddle of them, all in finery, about twenty altogether, could have been Gypsies. India is full of them; indeed, India is the origin of the Gypsy nation. It is a thrill to see people wearing traditional clothes, especially in a place where so many had become assertively Western in their dress. I always have a sense that where people wear traditional clothes they are keeping their folklore and the subtleties of their language alive as well.

So, the slow way to Bangalore ('like Silicon Valley!') revealed the eternal and stubborn and in some places desperate India. Crushed-looking villages where women squatted in fields of onions and stunted corn, planting or weeding. Nothing had changed for these people. I wrote in my notebook: *Flying over this I would have missed the splendor and the misery. When someone says 'India' I don't see one thing or even a hundred, but rather ten thousand images, and many stay in the mind. I keep noticing small children working at hard jobs, loading donkeys with sacks of gravel, or cleaning and mopping; or here at Daund boys hardly more than 9, scurrying around with big sacks, emptying trash bins.*

Indians in cities often wail, 'Too many people!' But these people in rural Maharashtra were growing their own food and drawing their own water and building their own houses and making their own fuel.

Their land had the flat and parched appearance of the African bush: low trees too thin to give any shade, dead grass, dusty paths. Even something African in the villages of stucco huts with verandas and tin roofs, the farm buildings with thatch roofs and walls of woven branches.

Hours passed, but the landscape of plains and ploughed fields did not change. A familiar melancholy descended on me, the effect of a long hot afternoon on a train rolling through a landscape of sparse trees and stricken fields. Near a halt in the middle of nowhere, a man was squatting on his haunches at a level crossing on a country road, and two men on bikes and an old red bus waited for the train to pass by. As the train continued across the great abdomen of India, I thought that if you didn't see this – the immensity, the destitution, the emptiness, the ageless solitude – you would know nothing of India.

The huts could not have been simpler: made of piled-up boulders, the roofs formed of bundles of straw. The crude plough was pulled by a bullock, a man guiding the animal and whipping it with a switch. To say 'Mumbai is in Maharashtra' is meaningless, because nothing could be less like Mumbai than this vast plain and its fields of lentils, a herdsman watching from an embankment as his twenty or so buffaloes bathed in a river. They rolled and wallowed, dipping their heads. Their horns were painted red.

The day was very hot, over 100 degrees, but the heat did not slow down the hawkers at Sholapur.

'Jews – fruity-fruity jews!'

'Mag-zeens, mag-zeens!'

'*Pani, pani, pani, pani* – vutta!'

'Biscuits, cheeps! Biscuits, cheeps!'

Seeing me, a man said, 'Luntz?'

'What have you got?'

He was dispensing dhal in cups. I bought some, and a bag of pistachios and a bottle of water, and ate and watched India pass. After eleven hours the landscape had hardly changed, flat to the horizon, fields ploughed by oxen, a gathering of women with brass jars at a well among grazing sheep, like a lithograph plate from the Old Testament – and even now, in the state of Karnataka, the villages seemed as remote and ruinous as any I had ever seen on earth, and many of them clearly visible to anyone travelling to the much-hyped city of Bangalore.

Towards the end of the afternoon, two young men joined me in my compartment. They were information technology employees, working in Bangalore. They spoke in what I took to be their own language – anyway, incomprehensible to me – for about fifteen minutes before I realized they were speaking English.

Rahul, the older of the two, complained that some IT workers in Bangalore were making the almost unheard-of sum of $30,000 a year, raising property prices.

The other young man, Suresh, talked about his travels, training IT people in places such as Singapore and Bangkok. He claimed that Indians were tormented by the police in both of those cities.

Just at dusk, at a stop in Dudhan, in the last light of day, a man with a withered foot and foreshortened leg limped with a stick, poling himself down the platform. Then the sun buried itself in the dust beyond the shacks. A woman approached the train, pleading for money, holding a skinny naked child, obviously ill, flies on its face and flies crawling between its lips.

The sight of these desperate wraiths stayed with me in the darkness. I slept. I woke to sunlight, the train gliding through palm groves, all the windows open, the fragrance of the countryside filling the carriage.

Small, sleepy, tree-shaded and bungaloidal Bangalore was so inconsequential at the time I crossed India on the Railway Bazaar that I didn't stop on my way to Madras. It was a town of retired people, many of them British, Indian army officers, fading God-botherers, with all that implied: gardening, bowling, cricket-watching, churchgoing, running Women's Institute jumble sales, among the clubbable and the soon-to-be-decrepit in the limbo of Staying On, the Indian equivalent of Cheltenham or Bognor Regis or Palm Beach. They could sit on the veranda, sipping cups of tea or *chota* pegs of locally distilled brain damage and moan how India was going to hell.

'It was pensioners' paradise, you can say,' an Indian told me soon after I arrived. His name was Vishad Gupta, and he laughed as he said it.

He was laughing because, about four or five years ago, a dramatic thing happened: Bangalore exploded, becoming the centre of India's high-tech industry. The placid city of fewer than a million inhabitants became a boom town of seven million.

'It happened for three reasons,' Vishad said, putting up one finger to indicate the first reason. Vishad's title was Director of Strategies and Business Initiatives for one of Tata's subsidiaries, in a new Bangalore business-only suburb called Electronics City Phase 2. Phase 1 was full. It was a short distance from the centre of Bangalore, but a long car ride because of the nightmarish traffic, which included bikes, scooter rickshaws, ox carts, sacred cows and hurrying pedestrians, all of them in the road – the broken, dusty road under construction.

'First reason, weather and climate. Nine months of moderate temperatures,' Vishad said, and put up another finger. 'Two, lots of educational institutions – lots of graduates, lots of talent. And lastly' – finger three – 'people are quiet and calmer, more relaxed. It is safer here. Delhi is aggressive. Mumbai is crowded and hot. This is the right place.'

And the government of Karnataka, where Bangalore is situated, introduced tax incentives in the mid-1990s; this gave benefits to start-up companies and attracted foreign companies, too. Language was another factor. Because there is no single dominant language in a babel of contending tongues (Coorg, Konkan, Tulu, Kanada, Hindi and others), English was widely spoken. The two men in my compartment said they spoke English at home, though theirs was almost an idiolect, or at least a variety of English that I did not find easy to understand, with the usual archaisms, of which 'thrice' and 'mountebank' and 'redoubtable' were just a few.

I took the very large number of Christian churches in Bangalore (I counted nine without going out of my way) to be a reflection of the culture of the British residents, whose retiring here was the penultimate stop on their way to salvation. Some quiet streets survived, with many old trees at their margins – unusual in India, where road-widening is a government policy. So some of old Bangalore remained, but it was overwhelmed by new buildings and construction sites: gated communities, new hotels, a property boom, speculation in land and housing, and the sort of eternal work in progress that I saw in every Indian city I visited.

'This will be our new flyover . . .'

I saw the thing everywhere. It was always under construction – people sleeping under it, cows congregating near it for shade, slogans painted on it. And I had the feeling that when at last the flyover was finished, it would be inadequate.

On my way to International Tech Park at Whitefield, at one corner of Bangalore, my driver said, 'You know Sai Baba? That is his ashram.'

So instead of going to Tech Park, I went to the ashram.

Bhagwan Sri Sathya Sai Baba was born not far away, at Puttaparthy, on the train line to Chennai; and he set up his ashram here for the same reason all the rest of the companies did – the agreeable weather, the shady streets, the gentle nature of old Bangalore.

The ashram sat behind a big wall, but the security guards welcomed me with *namastes*. LOVE IN ACTION was printed in big letters on the ashram's inner wall. A huge open-sided hall with a high roof housed the fresh-air platform where Swami held his daily *darshan*, or spiritual meeting, with his followers. To comprehend the Swami's teachings you had only to look at his symbol, which was a circle containing the emblems of the world's great faiths: a cross representing Christianity, a crescent for Muslims, the Zoroastrian flame, and so on for Judaism, Buddhism and Hinduism. Conflating all these faiths, Sai Baba had created a belief system that included almost everyone. But he seemed to reject the idea that he was leading a religion.

'"No religion, no prayer," Swami says.' This homily was from a volunteer caretaker wearing a badge with a Swami saying: WORK IS WORSHIP.

'Just follow your own religion. Love yourself.'

The unmistakable image of the Swami I had seen in many taxis, many homes, on many desks and office walls: the kindly smile, the frizz of hair.

The caretaker was Narayan. 'Swami says, "Heart to heart. No preaching. Only serve humanity with true heart."'

This sounded agreeable to me, so I decided to dismiss my taxi and look around the ashram. The Swami was not in residence. His art deco villa sat empty, in lovely gardens, behind a high fence.

I chatted with some devotees, but they were oblique and wouldn't linger or tell me their names ('Don't use my name, use Swami's'). They were emphatic in saying that Sai Baba had had no guru as a youth, though he did have a previous incarnation. And a new incarnation would appear in the near future – probably the year 2030.

Swami in recent pictures was smaller, slighter, older than his celebrated photographs suggested, the hair a less symmetrical frizz-ball, his smile more fatigued than impish. But he was eighty. His direct confrontation, his practical advice, his refusal to preach – the essential Swami appealed to these people.

'He will leave his body at ninety-six,' one devotee said. 'And after some eight years, the third and last incarnation will be born. Named Prema Sai. I wish to observe this.'

The non-Indian devotees had the least patience with my questions, but one of the Indian ashramites explained some of the subtleties of Sai Baba's thought. 'Swami teaches that there are four types of people. *Artha* type. Poor in all senses, scarred on the inside. *Arthathee* type. They want things. They seek to have things. *Jidnyasu* type. They only have questions. They need answers. And the *Jnani* type, who are enlightened. They know everything. They see a cloud and they know it will rain.'

I said, 'I think I'm a *Jidnyasu*. Just questions.'

'Yes. I can see.' I was taking notes – these were hard words to spell.

'Swami says, "I'm not here to preach new thoughts." '

That was a good approach.

'Don't search for God out there – search within yourself. Attain happiness. Search for *ananda*' – bliss or serenity.

I said, 'I've been trying.'

' "What is God?" Swami asks. And he answers, "It is experience." '

'I like that.'

'Believe in yourself.'

With that, the devotee left me to find my own path. I sat near the twice-lifesize statue of the tuneful goddess Saraswati, who was depicted playing her sitar. I remembered someone had told me that Sai Baba could work miracles, but lovable ones, such as producing chocolates in his hand for children.

'Yes, he does miracles,' another devotee said. 'But only to attract illiterates. *Chamatkara*, they are called. They are meant to astonish you.'

There were hundreds, perhaps thousands of accounts of Sai Baba's miracles, claiming they were proof of his divinity. These included making objects such as crucifixes and Bibles appear, multiple healings, miraculous messages, instances of translocation – the transfer of humans, some of them dead – and a celebrated manifestation of the Koh-i-Noor diamond when Sai Baba criticized an audience for being dazzled by the gem: 'Did any one of you even glance at me who created it, as you clamoured for a look at that piece of creation?' Many former adherents had come forward to denounce Sai Baba for faking his miracles.

But the basic philosophy emphasizes the inner light that people can find in their own hearts, and the power of practical work. *Hands that help are better than lips that pray* – one of the Swami's sayings would not have sounded strange if spoken by Lenin, Mao, Jesus or Jimmy Carter.

'People come here from all over,' the guard at the front gate said. 'Some imams from Iraq. And Ravi Shankar. Hillary Clinton wanted to come, but security was a problem, so she didn't come.'

Near this quiet compound of spiritual renewal – down the noisy congested road – was more of booming Bangalore. I walked outside the gate and took a taxi to International Tech Park. Its new buildings loomed in the distance, rising from watermelon stands, clusters of rickshaws, fix-it shops, juice stands and food stalls.

Behind the walls of Tech Park, among the towering glass-and-steel buildings with glittering signs – Infosys, Oracle, Disa, Think Inc. and others – was one for Perot Systems. I recalled the diminutive, quack-voiced, jug-eared Texan, Ross Perot, running for president of the United States on a platform called United We Stand America, which included the pledge to prevent jobs from being outsourced to places like India. Perot spoke of how we would hear 'a giant sucking sound' as American jobs were lost. Now, having failed in his bid for the presidency, the quacking tycoon had found that Indians in Bangalore would work for a fraction of what an American would earn.

Many of the jobs being done in the Bangalore call centres had once been performed in the United States by college students and housewives. All were part-timers. The work was tedious and poorly paid.

But around 2001, American companies – and there were now thousands of them in this city alone – discovered that young Indian graduates with good degrees, fluent in English, well mannered, patient and persistent, would do the same jobs, full time, for very little money. The city had become so widely recognized as a business alternative that in an April 2006 episode of *The Simpsons*, the town of Springfield outsourced the operation of its nuclear plant, and Homer Simpson went to Bangalore to find Indian employees for the plant. Bangalore was perhaps the best-known centre of cheap, trainable labour in the world. I wondered why, until I went there and found that at the time I visited the call centres, the entry-level employees (most of them university graduates) were earning less than $2,500 a year. Bangalore's prosperity rests on these people – their need for work, their high educational attainments, their skills, their good character, their prudent austerity, their punctuality, their humble status and most of all their willingness to work for low pay.

'Cannot proceed,' the security man at the gate in Tech Park said to my taxi driver. So I made some inquiries and got permission to visit another call centre, this one in yet another gated compound of big company offices, Electronics City Phase 2. This phase was only two years old but was already filled with flourishing businesses – that is, foreign businesses with Indian employees.

I went in the evening, because that was when the callers would be dealing with the western United States, California specifically. I was led through another gateway, another security fence, into a modern building with a few Indian touches – a shrine to the elephant god, Ganesh, god of new endeavours, and an artificial waterfall. I was given an ID badge for security purposes, I was signed in, and I was shown through the labyrinthine headquarters.

'Bangalore used to be quiet and sleepy,' Hardeep, the night manager, told me. 'It is now working day and night. It's cosmopolitan, people from everywhere. Less than thirty per cent of the people in Bangalore are local, because of IT growth.'

I said, 'The IT people in Mumbai said they were worried about Chinese competition.'

'Yes, the Chinese are trying to compete, but they have a different mindset. Ask a Chinese worker to tighten a screw, he will make three turns. The Indian will give an extra turn.'

'I'll try to remember that. What about money?'

'Our cost of business is going up, but we are still forty to fifty per cent more cost-effective. Now the IT industry in India is sixteen to eighteen billion dollars. By 2008 it will be sixty to eighty billion.'

'I meant what does a call centre worker earn?'

Hardeep hemmed and hawed, but I found out by nosing around that the answer was from $50 to $60 a week, often a fifty-hour week, and that might include a night shift that ended at three or four in the morning.

'We don't think about China – China is already playing a role. We think, What is the next India?'

'What's the answer?'

'Maybe Philippines. But political instability is there. Attempts have been made in Africa. Ghana was looked at, but no good results were found.'

I was impatient to see and hear Indians on the phone. I hadn't managed much of this in Mumbai. Hardeep said that he could show me those rooms but that I could not divulge the names of the companies involved. I said okay, though I recognized some of them – banking and mortgage groups, and the names of some airlines.

'This wing is tech support,' and he named a large airline. 'Let's say someone is processing a boarding pass anywhere in the world, doing a check-in, and they have a problem with anything. They call, and the call is answered by one of these tech people.'

'Can I listen?'

I cocked my head to the earphones and heard an American voice at the other end, perhaps in Los Angeles, saying, 'So do I just put that ten-digit code in?'

The tech person was a friendly looking man, about thirty, studying a computer screen as he helped the airline employee in an airport far, far away.

'This is internal organization support,' Hardeep said, 'not an end customer.'

'What's the difference?'

'End-customer support is voice-based, requires accent – US or UK. You are identified with a particular country. "Hello, I'm John . . ."'

'But it's really Mohun, isn't it?'

'For our purposes, it's John.'

We were passing down a corridor and into a new room with about a hundred cubicles and workstations. At each one sat a young Indian man or woman. They looked like students working late at the library, except that they were on the phone and the room was humming with their voices. The call centre employees worked from scripts, and all calls were recorded so they could be reviewed for effectiveness.

'The brand image from a consumer perspective should not change, or else the person on the phone in the US will think you're taking a job away.'

Which was exactly what was happening: an Indian helping an American to solve a problem with a computer or an appliance or an insurance form.

This fascinated me: Indians mimicking Americans, not just in the way they were dressed (short-sleeved shirts, blue jeans, trainers), but in the American jobs they were doing, using broad American accents. All had American first and last names.

I met 'Lynn Hayes', who was born Hasina, in Kerala, on the coast. She was twenty-two, unmarried, and worked from 5.30 p.m. until 2.30 a.m. at the call centre – the best time to call California. She was cold-calling contractors in the San Francisco area, to sign them up for a home warranty company that wanted its own fix-it men.

Listening in, I heard a blunt, 'Who's this?'

'Lynn Hayes,' Hasina said in a neutral, regionless American accent. 'May I please speak to the manager?'

'He's out.'

'When is he expected in the office, please?'

The accent was American, this politeness wasn't.

'I dunno,' the woman at the other end said.

'May I call you back?'

'Up to you. He's pretty busy.'

Lynn Hayes persisted until she was able to find a time when the manager of this firm of contractors might be in.

'We have to sign up two hundred and twenty-five American contractors a month for this company,' Hardeep said. 'They have to be involved in plumbing, electrical, building and so forth. It's almost impossible to find them in some states. New York is tough. Arizona is better. California is hard.'

'How does she know who to call?'

'We purchase telephone numbers.'

These were the leads – I thought of them as the Glengarry leads, and I imagined this room of callers fitting neatly into the plot of David Mamet's *Glengarry Glen Ross*, the definitive drama on cold-calling and rejection. The workers in Bangalore were not vying for bonuses or a set of steak knives, but every time one of them snagged a contractor, he or she got a gold star on the leader board.

'David Lewis' (Nitish Chandra) said, 'I make about one hundred and thirty calls a day. It's really hard. Every twenty calls we get to speak to a contractor. Out of, say, six interested, we sign up one.'

'Hello, this is Tina,' said Aisha, in an accent that was nicely nasal, and after a brief exchange, 'Can I leave my number?'

She dictated a number that was in the 212 area code – New York City – and when the person phoned back, from somewhere in the USA, the call would be routed to Bangalore.

As I was writing this down, someone called out, 'Chris just got another star on the board!'

'Chris Carter', who was Subramaniam to his parents and friends, had been working in the call centre for over a year and had a pleasant and persuasive manner. He also had mastered a forced but fairly convincing American accent – all of them had been drilled intensively.

'Do you say route or rowt?' I asked. 'Roof or ruff?'

Rowt and ruff, they said. And *in*-surance. And *ree*-peat. And minny for many, peenless for painless. All the pronunciations that I found annoying.

'This is Sean Harris,' Ramesh was saying, tapping his pencil on a scribbling pad. 'We require a contractor in the Santa Rosa area. We have minny jobs. May I kindly speak to the manager?'

This would go on until two or three in the morning, the whole room cold-calling California, doing the impossible, looking for willing plumbers. There were a hundred callers in this room, 1,000 employed by this firm, 10,000 callers in Bangalore – a figure that was expected to triple in the next few years.

It was difficult for me to get accurate salary figures from any of the managers – every one shrank at my question; it was a sensitive issue. Twenty-five hundred dollars a year was the lowest amount I heard for a newcomer; some earned $4,000. Someone at the top of the pay scale could expect to earn $30,000 or $40,000, which was a very high salary in India, and few achieved it. Most stayed at the bottom, averaging about $50 a week, but because of the stressful nature of the job, and the unsocial hours, there was a high dropout rate. Some techies and software support men I met at the company gym said they earned $6,000 or $7,000 a year, and some software designers earned $10,000 – more than enough to tempt them to stay, but a pittance to the American client. There was never a shortage of applicants: Hardeep said he was besieged by new graduates looking for work. Again I recognized the paradox, that India's poor were its wealth.

Since the time of the East India Company, in the seventeenth and eighteenth centuries, Indian labour had been exploited for its cheapness. Coolie labour was the basis of the British Raj, from the mid nineteenth to the mid twentieth century, whether it was growing cotton for the textile mills, or jute for rope, or tea to satisfy the imperial thirst, or (as in the 1850s) Indian opium for the purpose of weakening China, turning it into a nation of addicts, and enriching the British. Indians were still being exploited, but unskilled labour and muscle power had ceased to be of much use; the workers now were intelligent, educated, mostly young, a whole workforce of cultivated coolies.

One of the older municipal buildings in Bangalore was Mayo Hall. A two-storey ecclesiastical-looking structure built at the end of the nineteenth century, it was dedicated to the memory of India's fourth British viceroy, Lord Mayo. Lord Mayo's pomposities led him to make a ceremonial visit to a penal colony in the Andaman Islands, some distance from India's eastern coast, and there he met his end, a crazed convict knifing him to death. This same Lord Mayo once said, 'We are all British gentlemen engaged in the magnificent work of governing an inferior race.'

In my succeeding days in Bangalore, I met some of the dropouts. Vidiadhar and Vincent had managed one of the earliest call centres, processing mortgages for an Australian company, providing tech support, and selling software.

'It was fun for a while, but the hours were awful,' Vidiadhar said.

'The big problem was the perverts,' Vincent said. 'Aussies! They'd hear a woman's voice on the line and say, "Go out with me on a date and I'll buy everything you're selling."'

'Some would say, "What are you wearing?"'

'That was only the beginning!' Vincent said. 'It could get pretty rough. I'd rather not repeat it.'

Vidiadhar said, 'For the US customers we said, "We're in California" – well, the headquarters of the company *was* in California, so it wasn't really a lie. If we'd told them we're in India, they would have said, "How can an Indian understand the problems I'm having with my product?"'

They too said that they'd bought telephone numbers and customer profiles, which was reminiscent of the Glengarry leads.

'We had hot leads and cold leads. We paid a lot of money for some of them, but we knew so much about the people – their age, their address, if they'd refinanced their mortgage, what sort of credit rating and financial history.'

But the stress had got to them after a few years, and the women objected to the heavy breathers. So Vidiadhar and Vincent entered that other growth area in Bangalore, making deals in the American clothing market.

'Any labels I'd recognize?'

'Are you familiar with Kenneth Cole, Banana Republic and Tommy Hilfiger?' Vincent said.

The usual routine was that one of these companies would give them a specific pattern. The cloth, cotton or silk, was generally from India; the buttons and waistbands were from the United States. They would run up a sample, get it approved, and sign a contract for a certain number of units.

I said, 'Banana Republic sells a type of pyjama bottom that I usually wear on the train. Drawstring type with pockets. They cost about forty dollars.'

'We make them for seven.'

Vidiadhar said, 'Any US clothing company could sell their clothes for fifty per cent off and still make a good profit.'

The men and women who cut and stitched these clothes, the low-level tailors, earned $1,000 a year.

'That polo shirt you're wearing,' Vincent said. 'It looks familiar. I'm pretty sure it was made here.'

I found some glass paintings in Bangalore and got acquainted with the man who sold them to me, Mr V. K. Reddy, who said he dabbled in antiques. He was blimpish and backward-looking, opinionated and very funny in his conceits, with a big moustache, as outlandish as an actor's comic prop, that he continually twirled with his big blunt finger. He was stout, with a dyspeptic scowl, and his manner, his booming voice especially, was that of a former Indian army officer, which he might have been.

'What a lot of bosh!' he said when I told him that Bangalore was regarded as an example of the Indian miracle.

'What do you think it is?'

'This town was nothing, I tell you! Just little retired ladies and gents living out their days as pensioners. And now this! For the past three years!'

'Nightmarish traffic,' I suggested.

'You are naïve, my friend! Worse than nightmarish.'

'Noisy,' I said.

'Noisy is not the word, sir!' Mr V. K. Reddy said and worked on his moustache, tweaking its sticky tips. 'It is hellish din.'

'But you have your antique shop.'

'No more than a hobby.' He leaned forward and said, 'It so happens that I have in my possession Mother Teresa's personal rosary, with a letter in her own inimitable handwriting, testifying to its authenticity. I can offer this for your perusal, and should you purchase it, you would not regret it.'

'Must be unique,' I said.

'Of unparalleled interest,' he said, still plucking at his moustache. 'And don't forget spiritual value.'

If I should return to Bangalore, Mr Reddy said he would take me to lunch at the Bangalore Club. 'There you will see the old Bangalore. The old India.'

He meant the Raj, and the genteel and dusty Anglo-Indian aftermath of tiger shoots and high tea and polo matches and dented tureens of mulligatawny. But a day or so later, near where I sat, at breakfast in my hotel, a cup of coffee in one hand, the *Times of India* in the other, I read that at a local court four members of a family had just been given life sentences 'for abetting self-immolation'. Two were the sons of the victim; that is, to help in the ancient (and outlawed) practice of suttee, they had thrown their sixty-year-old mother on the funeral pyre of her husband, joining his burning corpse in death. Everyone talked about the new India, but the old India was never very far away.

14. The Shatabdi Express to Chennai

The longer I stayed in Bangalore, the less I liked it. Many of the Indians I met there wanted me to be dazzled by the changes, but I was more horrified than awed. What went under the name of business in Bangalore was really a form of buccaneering, all the pirates wearing dark suits and carrying mobile phones instead of cutlasses. The place had not evolved; it had been crudely transformed – less city planning than the urban equivalent of botched cosmetic surgery. The proud, tidy, tree-shaded town of the recent past was now a huge, unfinished and deforested city sagging under its dubious improvements, where it was impossible to walk without falling into an open manhole or newly dug ditch. Most of the pavements had been torn up and the trees cut down in the interest of street-widening. The bypasses and flyovers were all under construction, wearing a crumbled and abandoned look, and the skinny men working on them, poking the clods of earth with small shovels, suggested they'd never be completed.

In a few years you won't recognize it, the developers said, but was that a good thing? The whole place smouldered in the foul dusty air of a building site. I realized that what I had liked about Amritsar and Jaipur was that they hadn't changed much since my first visit. They were larger, of course, but they were finished and habitable. Mumbai and Bangalore were simultaneously being torn down and built up, works in progress, but Bangalore's distance from the sea, from any body of water, made it grittier and gave it a look of anguish. And there was something else: I attempted many times to walk in Bangalore, but the traffic was so bad I seldom succeeded in crossing the street.

So, one morning at five, while the city was still asleep, only the call centre shuttle buses and the temple monkeys and the sacred cows stirring, I slipped out on the express to Chennai, sliding through rice fields and palm groves to the coast. The train was fast: it was an eight-hour journey, short by Indian standards, and I arrived in time for a late lunch of Tamil food – steamed buns called *idlies, masala dosa* (a kind of crêpe), soupy curry, and spiced potato, coconut, and curd, served on a freshly picked palm leaf. The city I had known long ago as Madras had quadrupled in size and yet looked the same: mildewed colonial buildings, tropical gardens, the streets thick with traffic, and just to the east a long sandy shore and the sea breeze from the Indian Ocean, which was a relief.

I had planned, in retracing my steps, to take a train from here to Rameswaram, at the tip of India's nose, and then the ferry to Sri Lanka.

'But there is a trouble in Sri Lanka,' a travel agent told me.

'What kind of trouble?'

'A new offensive.'

Tamils were well up on developments in Sri Lanka, since they had a stake in the guerrilla war. He meant the Tamil Tigers – they had attacked some Sri Lankan soldiers. The train to the south, the night ferry to Sri Lanka, had been fairly simple, even pleasurable, thirty-three years ago, but no information about this route was available in Chennai. It was another obstacle, like the Iranian visa I'd been unable to get, the war (and the kidnapping and murder of Western travellers) in Afghanistan and the xenophobia in Pakistan. I was trying to follow in my own footsteps, but now and then I had to make detours.

The Chennai I had known as a city of around two million was now a sprawl of eleven million. Because Chennai had few tall buildings, it could grow only by spreading and overwhelming the surrounding villages, eating up the rice paddies and wheat fields, filling them with people and cars and hastily erected houses. Long ago, I had visited the outlying hamlet of Tambaram, beyond the southern outskirts of the city. Wooded, with tall trees and palm groves and gardens, a railway station, and a small college, Tambaram was now a crowded and urbanized precinct of Chennai, its rural atmosphere overwhelmed and altered. It was strange: as Indian cities underwent name changes – Bombay to Mumbai, Madras to Chennai – their character seemed to change too, as though they no longer had to live up to that old genteel image and could become nightmarish in new ways.

'Where going, sir?' said the doorman at my hotel.

'For a walk.'

'Take car, sir,' he said, and signalled for a taxi.

'Never mind.'

'Walking not possible, sir!'

My hotel was near Mount Road. I intended to walk west, perhaps to St Thomas Mount, a landscape feature mentioned by Marco Polo, where (so the story goes) the doubting apostle was martyred by a Brahmin wielding a lance. Both the lance in question and the remains of the saint were enshrined in San Thome Cathedral. I also wanted to stroll along Beach Road and look for evidence of the tsunami that had hit the year before.

'I'm walking,' I said, and kept going.

The main road, with its emporiums and bazaars, was just a few minutes away. I reached it and began to negotiate my way, but the crush of jostling pedestrians and broken pavements forced me into the gutter. I stumbled along at the kerb, bumped by rickshaws and spooked by honking cars. I kept this up for a hundred yards – hating it, growing frustrated, appalled by the huge number of people, their push and pull, shouldering me aside. I was bigger than any of these bandy-legged Dravidians, but it was all I could do to stay upright and moving forward.

I liked to think of myself as unflappable, but the simple walk gave me pause: the hot day, the mob, the car fumes; my making so little progress on what I'd intended as a stroll down Mount Road, which was memory lane. I did not look for pleasure in travel, and I expected nuisance and delay. But this was something else, pointless and unrewarding effort of a sort that no one wants to hear about.

Only the natural courtesy, good nature and geniality of the Tamils in the crowd kept me from being trampled – that was a discovery. Overpopulation was made bearable by politeness. But, trying to walk, I was getting nowhere, seeing nothing, merely protecting myself.

'You see, sir?' the doorman said, summing me up on my sudden return. 'Difficult.'

Difficult was not the way I thought of the mobbed streets in Chennai. They were something else – unendurable, pure horror, *cauchemardesque*. They were freaking me out.

'Walking is not possible. Take taxi.'

So I took a taxi to Beach Road and on the way reflected on the life of the expatriate American in India: the multitasking businessman or lawyer with his driver, his air-conditioned office and his secretaries – India is the land of retainers, gofers, body servants, door openers, waiters and flunkies. The spouse of such an expatriate is similarly elevated, transformed from a simple soul, possibly unlettered – who would have trouble finding India on a map – to a memsahib, the status of an important lady in society, with a cook, a cleaner, a *chowkidar*, a *dhobi* or launderer, and if she has a garden, she will have two gardeners.

Typically, this expat couple has limited interests, knows nothing about Indian history, does not speak Hindi. Their offspring may attend an exclusive school, catering to the children of wealthy Indians and diplomats, in which case the husband will be involved with the school and his wife busybodying with the other parents. They may talk about their hardship, but India has allowed them to taste power – the power of wealth and, even more beguiling, the power over servants and an ease of living that is almost unmatched in the world. In Bombay in 1860, the visiting Bostonian Richard Henry Dana recorded in his diary his surprise at the number of servants in English households (one modest house he visited had seventeen flunkies) and his shock at their low wages. 'Their pay is very small & they find themselves [their own] food, lodging and clothing.' Nothing had changed.

Inconvenient and grubby though India sometimes seems to the expatriates, it is preferable to being back home and having to drive their own car, cook their own meals, wash the dishes and do the laundry. The role of the burra memsahib (the great lady), the corrupt quest for cheap labour, the laziness and complacency of the life, the clubbing and party-going – all this was described in satirical detail long ago, as the dereliction of the British Raj, by Kipling, Orwell and other mockers. But in this high-tech-driven Raj, the sahibs were back – in Delhi, in Mumbai, in Bangalore, in Chennai and many other places. Most were Indians lording it over the cheap labour; many were Europeans, some were Americans.

Their counterparts in the old Raj hadn't walked; neither did these people. And now I was one of them, sitting in a taxi to avoid fighting the crowds. I did not like this at all. I did not approve of what I was doing.

I got to the beach – very hot, very dirty, like the wide flat foreshore of the beach at Santa Monica, but this one piled with wrecked boats, squatting fishermen near them fussing with nets at the tidemark. It was hard for me to imagine a worse life than being a fisherman on the beach at Chennai. Having been displaced by the tsunami, they lived in hovels – there were thousands of them – of crackling wind-blown plastic sheeting supported by stick frames of driftwood, two years after the seismic event. Many had drowned. The blue plastic tarps wore the stencilling of emergency services. Some men were offshore hauling nets; women were selling fish by the side of the road; small children were playing cricket using appropriately shaped bats and wickets of driftwood.

There was no shade. In the blazing sun the temperature was well over 100 degrees. It would be much hotter next month.

I talked to people with memories of the tsunami. One old man said, 'Full water, up to St Mary's' — and he pointed a quarter of a mile away, inland, across Beach Road.

'Boats, too. Full damage,' his son said.

These heavy twenty-five-foot boats, shaped like large fibreglass dories, had been lifted by the tidal wave and tumbled across the road on to the lawn of St Mary's College.

'Master,' one man said, tugging my arm. 'Help us.'

'You want money?'

'No money. You help pull boat.'

I surprised them by taking hold of the line, and they laughed as I joined them in pulling one of the fishing boats up the beach and away from the tidemark.

That was one of six boats named *Acts of Mercy*. Others were named *SOS Children's Village*. The names reflected the charitable agencies that had provided them after the disaster struck.

I hung around to see them unloading the morning's catch — three or four boats accounting for about fifty pounds of small elongated fish, like oversized sardines. Skinny children gathered near me and made pleas of hunger, gesturing to their mouths, rubbing tummies, and some of the men, too, asked for hand-outs.

'I'll buy your fish,' I said. I intended to give them money for their catch and then hand the fish back to them. 'How much for all of this?'

'No. Buyers are there,' the old man said.

'Money, money,' the younger men said.

I was backing up. I didn't want to show them any money. I said, 'You have fish. Fish is money.'

'Fish is little money.'

That was probably true. I said to one of the boys, 'You come with me,' and he followed me to Beach Road. I gave him some rupees, just to make a graceful escape from this crowd of twenty or more hungry and half-naked men, looking small and spidery on the hot white sand.

I walked up the scorching road by the beach, and after a mile or so I recognized an odd cylindrical building from my first trip, and from an old watercolour I owned. The painting's style, the art of it, was undistinguished – I had bought it cheap in London – but it depicted an unusual structure of this city. The title was *The Ice House, Madras*. I knew very little about the building other than that it had been put up to store ice that had been sent by ship from New England.

The building, with its single castle tower, which I had first seen in a state of disrepair, a ruin of flaking green paint, had been renovated and repainted. With wide verandas, arched windows and a bright, creamy façade, it looked smug and renewed in a compound behind a wall. Around it was a garden of purplish bougainvillaea, and in the driveway a statue ringed by flowering shrubs. The plaque at the gate said VIVEKANANDAR ILLAM.

Since I owned an old picture of this former ice house, I had wondered about the building for thirty years. Now it was open, one of the sights of Chennai, with its history displayed in its newly painted rooms. I went inside and bought a ticket and browsed. A little of its past was given, and I dug up the rest. It had been built in 1842 by Frederic Tudor, 'the Ice King', a merchant from Boston. Tudor had brought the first shipment of ice in 1833 from Massachusetts to Madras on the clipper *Tuscany*, and later built this storehouse. In the beginning, most of Tudor's ice came from ponds near Boston where I had skated as a boy.

From his cabin, Henry David Thoreau had watched the Tudor Ice Company cutting blocks of ice on Walden Pond in the winter of 1846–7. Impressed, Thoreau wrote about it in his journal, as well as in the 'Pond in Winter' chapter of *Walden*, estimating that on a good day the cutters could produce 'a thousand tons' of ice slabs. Knowing that the ice was being shipped to India provoked Thoreau to lyricism in his journal: 'Thus it appears that the sweltering inhabitants of . . . Madras and Bombay and Calcutta, drink at my well,' and 'The pure Walden water is mingled with the sacred water of the Ganges.'

Tudor continued to bring ice to India for the next thirty years, until he died in 1864. Later (so one of the captions in the Ice House said), 'the invention of the "steam process" of making ice ruined [the ice import] business.' The Madras Ice House became defunct, and in the 1890s it passed into the hands of an Indian businessman, who enlarged it, naming it Castle Kernan.

When Swami Vivekananda visited Madras in February 1897, the fanciful-seeming structure, cylindrical and strange, was regarded as suitable for his holy presence. The Swami stayed in the building, 'delivered seven electrifying lectures', and was urged to consecrate it as a spiritual centre. He agreed, and a few months later sent his disciple Swami Ramakrishna to spread the word. Ramakrishna lived a guru's life here, meditating and preaching spiritual renewal.

One day in 1902, while praying in the Ice House, Swami Ramakrishna heard 'a bodiless but familiar voice declaring "O Sasi [Swami R], I have spat out the body"' – and soon afterwards Ramakrishna received the news that Vivekananda had passed away.

Eventually the Ice House was bought by the Indian government. It was first used as the Brahmana Widows' Hostel, then a teachers' hostel, and then was left to rot. When I saw it in 1973 it was a semi-ruin. It was now a spiritual centre and a museum, a permanent exhibit of the life and work of Swami Vivekananda, an architectural curiosity and part of India's 'cultural heritage', so the sign said; but also, in its way, a permanent contribution to the Chennai skyline from a New England entrepreneur.

This little discovery and its history cheered me up, but when I left the Ice House and headed south along Marina Beach towards Mylapore and its churches, I was followed by a troop of ragged children, begging for money, asking for food, for anything; and by the time I had outwalked them, I was back in the crush of people and traffic.

In my Bangalore hotel I had found a discarded copy of *Dream Catcher*, by Margaret Salinger, a memoir of her experience growing up in the J. D. Salinger household. It was a humane and insightful account of a volatile man whose moods dominated the family. He was not lovable, vulnerable Holden Caulfield, but paranoiac and self-important, with an easily ruffled disposition. Margaret convincingly made the case for the Salinger household having all the traits of a cult and J. D. himself the severe attributes of a cult leader.

In the course of the book, Margaret mentions her father's interest in Raj Yoga and Sri Ramakrishna, who was Vivekananda's guru. She quotes from *The Gospel of Sri Ramakrishna*:

A man may live in a mountain cave, smear his body with ashes, observe fasts and practice austere discipline, but if his mind dwells on worldly objects, on 'woman and gold,' I say, 'Shame on him!' Woman and gold are the most fearsome enemies of the enlightened way, and woman rather more than gold, since it is woman that creates the need for gold. For woman one man becomes the slave of another, and so loses his freedom. Then he cannot act as he likes.

'The only thing worth reading' was J. D. Salinger's judgement on this bit of pompous misogyny. Swami Vivekananda was another story. He is praised by Seymour Glass in the Salinger short story 'Hapworth 16, 1924'. A scripture I found at the Ice House suggested why this might be so. The Swami said, 'Each soul is potentially divine. The goal is to manifest this divinity within by controlling nature, external and internal. Do this by work, or worship, or psychic control, or philosophy – by one or more or all of them. This is the whole of religion. Doctrines or dogmas or rituals or books or temples are but secondary details.'

I still wondered if I might find a ferry to Sri Lanka. Often, it was not until I was near a point of departure that I got reliable information. It was easy in Chennai to find out about flights to New York City; it was impossible to get a straight answer about ferries that departed Rameswaram, just down the line.

Chennai was listed among the cities described as being the engines driving the economy of the new India. Foreign companies relocated here to improve their profits, to manufacture clothes and electronics, to get their phone calls answered, to outsource their piece goods. Yet my being in Chennai only confirmed what I had felt in Bangalore, that the new India was rising on the backs of poorly paid (but well-educated) workers. Yes, it was better than their starving, and I admired their work ethic. But I had seen enough; it was another shocking and unfinished transformation, and I hated having to contend with the continuous struggle and non-consensual rubbing in this reeking sprawl of eleven million people, no matter how conscientious they were.

The beautiful thing about boredom or irritation in an Indian city was that it could be relieved by catching a train. I went to Egmore Station and bought a ticket for the morning train to Tiruchirappalli – 'Trichy' to most Tamils. It was less than a six-hour ride, with coconut trees and paddy fields the whole way. The man in the next seat introduced himself as Sathymurthy. He was a Tamil. I asked him if he knew anything about the ferry to Sri Lanka.

'Notwithstanding the present crisis,' he began, and then, in the mel-lifluous generalities I had come to associate with Indians who had no idea what they were talking about, he described the situation in the south. I was soon asleep. When I woke, he was gone and the train was pulling into Tiruchirappalli.

Trichy was everything I hoped for: small, dusty, mostly rickshaws, rising from the flat outskirts a vast rock fort with a temple on top, and further out an ancient, partially painted temple complex covering many acres. With this, cheap food and fruit juice, a small population and no traffic to speak of: the sort of country town that had hardly changed in thirty – or perhaps a hundred – years. No outsourcing here, no talk of the new India, no careerists, no techies, no industrial parks or call centres, and the best hotel in the place was a great bargain.

I visited the temples, taking my time – it was 95 in the shade – and tried to make plans to go further south. Rameswaram was only half a day from here.

'No ferry,' I was told by Mr Sundrum, a writer I met in Trichy who had recently been to Rameswaram. More mellifluous generalities. 'Fighting has flared up.'

I did not know it at the time, but this fighting was the start of a major offensive that had begun in the north of Sri Lanka by the group that called itself the Liberation Tigers of Tamil Eelam. At the end of it, more than 4,000 people would be dead.

Sundrum said, 'There are boats to Sri Lanka. The Tigers run them. They have their own transport system. They can take you across.'

But this would mean finding someone in the Rameswaram immi-gration office to bribe, so I could get an exit stamp in my passport. And then crossing the Palk Strait, which was heavily patrolled because of the recent killings and bombings. On the other side, I would be safe in Tamil-occupied territory, but entering Sri Lankan territory (picking my way through the land mines), I'd have to seek out a Sri Lankan immi-gration officer and bribe *him* for a stamp, because I had entered the country illegally. I expected the crossing to be a lot of trouble, but the danger of being killed was something else.

'It wasn't like this before,' I said.

'Fighting is there,' Sundrum said. 'Why don't you go to Chennai and look at the call centres and the new developments in IT? Trichy is nothing. Chennai is a leader.'

'I've done that. I want to take the ferry.'

Sundrum was rather proud of the fact that the Tigers were in control of the Palk Strait, that they ran a rudimentary ferry service. In their hearts all the Tamils I met wanted the Tigers to succeed, though they were a murderous lot who had blown up an Indian prime minister, assassinated Sri Lankans, displaced tens of thousands of people – Tamil and Sinhala alike – violated peace agreements and raised hell.

For the time being I stayed in Trichy, caught up with my notes, visited the temples. I liked walking in the town, which was not populous but covered a broad area, on both banks of the Cauvery River, wide and waterless in this dry season. And even in this heat, being a pedestrian was enjoyable most of the time.

Temples attracted beggars. I had seen this my first day in India, in Amritsar – the grovellers at the Golden Temple. But it had been true since Turkey: wherever there was a mosque, there were beggars; they hung around churches, they lined up at temples. I had seen them again in Tbilisi, in Ashgabat, in Bokhara and Tashkent. They were a feature of Indian temples, grizzling for rupees, whining, sometimes demanding; everywhere I'd gone they'd thrown themselves at my feet or pawed my sleeve. I'd usually surrendered something.

Indians were instinctive givers, especially the pilgrims and penitents, who built up good karma by giving. Because of Trichy's ancient and well-preserved temples, many pilgrims visited, and consequently so did many beggars. The beseeching poor were part of the Indian scene: the lame and the halt, the blind, the limbless, with outstretched palms or begging bowls, sometimes displaying a limp or a drooling infant, an ashen-faced tot with the pox.

I did not harden my heart against them. I handed over some rupees and moved on, pondering the Indian miracle.

A smiling boy in a school uniform approached me.

'Good afternoon, sir. Where do you come from?'

I told him, and complimented him on his fluency.

'I speak English well because I study it at school,' he said.

He was sturdy, about twelve or thirteen, his uniform spotless, though he wore no shoes. I asked him his name.

'My name is Murugam. India is my country.'

I thanked him and walked towards the temple gate.

'Give me ten rupees,' he said.

'Not today.'

'Buy me a Coca-Cola.'

'Sorry.'

'All right, give me five rupees.'

'Tell me why.'

'I come from a big family. Give me one rupee. Give me something. Give me your ball pen.'

He said that because I was writing in my small notebook: *Boy. Uniform. Murugam.*

As I walked away he began hissing curses at me, and he became loudly abusive when he saw me give some money to a crippled old woman who lay in a heap with her hand extended, palm upward.

Beggars I saw as part of life in India. How could you have 1.3 billion people and not have beggars? They went with the temples, they were part of the landscape – they weren't even the worst part. But they got me down. You could live a long time in India if you stayed indoors, bossing the servants, but I was outside most of the time, usually in the role of a pedestrian, and many other people were outside too.

My time was up: I had to move on to Sri Lanka. I admitted to myself that I was spooked and needed relief.

One day I saw a round rotted fruit by the side of the road. It was crawling with insects, alive with big ants, blackened by them. Was it a coconut or a durian? Whatever, it represented a little world of hunger obscured by its eaters.

I finally left Trichy, and India. What sent me away was not the poverty, though it was pathetic and there was plenty of it. It wasn't the dirt, though it sometimes seemed to me that nothing in India was clean. It wasn't the pantheon of grotesque gods, some like monkeys, some like elephants, some wearing skulls as ornaments, some in a posture of repose under the hood of a rearing cobra – terrifying or benign to the believers propitiating them with flowers. It was not the widow-burning or the child marriages or the crowds of the cringing and the limbless, the one-eyed, the stumblers, the silent ones who hardly lifted their eyes. An experience of India could be like entering a painting by Hieronymus Bosch – among the deformed, the fish-faced, the crawling, the flapping, the beaked, the scaly, the screaming, the armless and the web-footed.

Not the heat, either, though every day in the south it was in the high 90s. Not the boasting and booming Indians and their foreign partners screwing the poor and the underpaid for profit. Not the roads, though they were hideous and impassable in places. Not the fear of disease or the horror of the obscenely wealthy, though the sight of the super rich in India could be more disquieting than the sight of the most wretched beggar.

None of these. They can all be rationalized.

What sent me away finally was something simpler, but larger and inescapable. It was the sheer mass of people, the horribly thronged cities, the colossal agglomeration of elbowing and contending Indians, the billion-plus, the sight of them, the sense of their desperation and hunger, having to compete with them for space on pavements, on roads, every-where – what I'd heard on the train from Amritsar: 'Too many. Too many.' All of them jostling for space, which made for much of life there a monotony of frotteurism, life in India being an unending experience of non-consensual rubbing.

And not because it was India – Indians were good-humoured and polite on the whole – but because it was the way of the world. The population of the United States had doubled in my lifetime, and the old simple world that I had known as a boy was gone. India was a reminder to me of what was in store for us all, a glimpse of the future. Trillions of dollars were spent to keep people breathing, to cure disease and to extend human life, but nothing was being done to relieve the planet of overpopulation, the contending billions, like those ants on the rotting fruit.

I had not felt that way in India long ago, but I was younger then. I took the short flight over the Palk Strait to Sri Lanka, into a different world.

15. The Coastal Line to Galle and Hambantota

I stumbled into Colombo on my birthday. The winsome hotel clerk in the crimson sari knew this somehow. She said, 'Happy birthday, sir. Please call us if you want us to come up and sing to you.' That 'us' made the offer sound either wickeder or more chaste.

To give the day a meaning I went for a walk, marvelling at how thinly populated the city was compared to the ones I'd just left in India. The entire population of the Republic of Sri Lanka was the same as the population of the city of Mumbai: twenty million. And the placid and procrastinating Sinhalese were a reminder of how frenzied and loquacious the Indians had been, forever vexed and talkative. I found a barbershop and asked for a baldy and wound up with a crewcut. Then I had my picture taken by a pavement photographer. I bought a Sri Lankan notebook. The taxi driver who took me back to the hotel asked me whether I wanted to see anything special, and when I asked him what he meant by special, he gave me a fangy stare and said, 'Vimmin.' I said primly no. But the word stuck in my head. I remembered that Colombo had a reputation for debauchery. Perhaps I could find another taxi driver later on and indulge myself in birthday depravity among Sinhalese voluptuaries and lotus eaters.

Regarding my birthday as auspicious, and while it was still daylight, I sat in the garden of the hotel under a fragrant arbour, opened the new notebook, and began a story, 'The Elephant God': something to occupy my evenings later on and a way of venting my feelings about India. Darkness fell as I was writing. The garden was empty, the hotel was empty; no one wanted to come to Sri Lanka these days. The Tamil Tiger offensive was in the news: a mine in Trincomalee had exploded the day before and killed seven people, shootings in the north had claimed four lives, and suicide bombers were expected in Colombo.

In my room, I saw that a small cake, a bottle of wine and a birthday card were arranged on the coffee table. I yanked the cork on the wine and poured a glass. I sat down and sipped it. The room was still and hot and mostly dark. The wine was like purple ink. I drank some more of it and thought: Debauchery. Who would know? It's my birthday!

I ate a piece of the cake and was about to have more wine when my scalp shrank and my skull began to burn. I had a terrible headache from the first glass of wine. I fell asleep on the sofa, my own snores waking me around midnight, still snorting and drooling; then I pulled my clothes off and went to bed. In the morning, I woke up a year older and went in search of train tickets.

On my Railway Bazaar visit, I had wanted to see Sri Lanka's most celebrated alien, Arthur C. Clarke, who had settled here in 1956. But then, in the wake of his *2001* notoriety and the demands on his time, I hadn't managed it. Another lesson in the Tao of Travel is: wait long enough and all things are possible. This time I made a plan. I sent a message to him through a mutual friend and hoped for a favourable reply.

In the meantime, I went to the main railway station to buy a ticket to Galle, some way down the tsunami-ravaged coast.

'No advance booking,' the clerk said through the barred window that made him seem caged.

'How do I get a ticket?'

'Come before the train leaves.'

'Any reserved seats?'

'No. Just push.'

'How much does it cost to Galle?'

He made a face. 'A hundred-something for any ticket.'

A dollar to go anywhere on the train.

The next day, I had a message that Sir Arthur would meet me. His secretary said that he was not strong, that he was suffering from what she called post-polio syndrome, but that I could stop by tomorrow. This meant hanging around Colombo for another day. I was eager to meet him. Sir Arthur pops up in all sorts of contexts: sci-fi and real science, pulp magazines and scientific journals, astronomy and astrophysics and paranormal mumbo-jumbo, the earliest satellites, a paedophilia scandal (in which he was libelled), the space programme, Stanley Kubrick, celebrities, as a booster of Sri Lankan culture, as an early ecologist, a maker of documentaries and a TV pundit. He was a speechifier and a prognosticator and a prolific writer. He had been at it so long, many people (including ones I met in Sri Lanka) wondered whether he was still alive. But he was, nearing eighty-nine.

The Tamil Tiger secessionist war had had the effect of turning Colombo into a very quiet place, with few visitors and no tourists to speak of. There were not even many Sri Lankans on the pavements, except in the bazaar near the main railway station. A 'speak only Sinhalese' policy, which had been established in schools by the government in the 1970s, meant that so few Sri Lankans spoke English, they were unemployable by foreign companies looking for cheap labour in the IT industries. (On one occasion in the 1990s, 3,000 college-educated Sri Lankans showed up for call centre jobs; fewer than one hundred spoke English.)

Rebuffed by the high-tech employers, they were instead hired to make polo shirts and jeans and T-shirts and trainers in Sri Lankan sweatshops. The economy was in terrible shape, the war was picking up, the government was stumbling; but like many poverty-stricken tropical countries with an incompetent government and its army under fire in the provinces, Sri Lanka was old-fashioned and, except for the war zones, rather sedate, or at least quiet, like a place holding its breath.

I had lunch with a diplomat who filled me in on the Tamil Tigers. He told me that the secession-minded Tamils in Sri Lanka had been calling for their own state for the past thirty years. And not just giving speeches but fighting. The Tigers fought with single-minded savagery. At one time there had been dozens of Tamil organizations intent on secession – groups of all persuasions, some moderate, some conciliatory and some not fighting at all, but open to debate and compromise.

One by one, the leaders of these groups had been killed by the Tigers, their members ambushed, huts burned, women raped, soldiers scattered; now only the Tigers remained. I had been told in Trichy by a boasting Tamil that the Tigers pioneered the suicide bomb.

My diplomat friend said this was true.

When I challenged him, he said, 'Suicide bomb vest' – in other words, they invented the concealed bomb.

Not really. Just such a sinister device is described in Joseph Conrad's novel of London bombers, *The Secret Agent* (1907), in which a suicide bomb is worn by a cynical pest known as the Professor, who boasts that he can blow himself up whenever he feels like it. He regards it as a liberating contraption. He has a habit of 'keeping his hand in the left pocket of his trousers, grasping lightly the India rubber ball, the supreme guarantee of his sinister freedom' – a hard squeeze and the bomb explodes and Paradise Now. As one of his terrorist colleagues says later in the novel, 'You carry in your pocket enough stuff to send yourself and, say, twenty other people into eternity.'

But (so I was told) the Tamil Tigers – or rather the Black Tiger Suicide Squad, its subgroup of zealots, wearers of the self-destructing vest – hold the world record for suicide bombings. The official figure is 1,680 in the twenty years between 1980 and 2000, far more than Hamas and Hezbollah combined. One of the better-known Tiger victims was Prime Minister Rajiv Gandhi, who was blown up in Chennai in 1991 by a young Black Tiger woman, one of many Tigers who objected to Indian soldiers' joining the Sri Lankan army in ridding Sri Lanka of this ethnic violence.

The Tigers were tenacious and disinclined to bargain; when their leader, Velupillai Prabhakaran, was described as 'ruthless and elusive', I took this to mean stupid and stubborn, the sort of qualities that fuel the village fanatic's monomania. He was a grade-school dropout with a fifth-grade education, famously unreasonable, impervious to logic, unmoved by sending children to their death. A more literate or imaginative man would have given up or compromised long ago. He almost never showed his face. He had emerged in 1972, when he was just eighteen, energized the Tigers, and committed his first murder in 1975 – shooting a Tamil political leader for being too moderate. In the rare photographs of him, Prabhakaran was a tubby, moustached little man in too tight, too clean khaki fatigues who looked indistinguishable from any toothy bristling stallholder in the dry-goods section of the Chennai bazaar. All that was known of him was that he suffered from hypertension and high blood pressure, that he lived in an underground bunker in the north, and that he had never been to Colombo in his life.

'What are his beliefs?'

'Just Tamil, Tamil, Tamil,' my friend said.

Prabhakaran had no political philosophy, no economic ideas, and he stood for nothing except Tamil sovereignty and secession. The Tigers were well armed and well funded. The largest Tamil community outside India can be found in Toronto, and Canadian Tamils (and American and Australian Tamils too) are assessed a 'liberation tax' by collectors from the old country. Some are coerced, with threats to their families, but most pay happily, in the same spirit that the Irish in America gave money to Noraid, to pay for the bombs that blew up women and children in Ulster in the 1970s and 80s.

The Tamil convulsion, and all the deaths, had occurred after I had last visited, and because the violence had retarded Sri Lanka, I instantly recognized the place. It had hardly changed. Colombo was a forgotten city with little foreign investment and a failing economy, so while it was visibly faltering, it was not cursed with meretricious modernity. Because of the indifference of the money men and the speculators, Colombo's colonial buildings remained intact. No one could afford to pull them down or replace them. The sculpted stone on the shop fronts and emporiums of timeworn Victorian and Edwardian Colombo still stood, the wooden floors inside still creaked, the dust-coated ceiling fans still turned. The city was pretty much the one I'd seen three decades ago, and I spent my days before meeting Arthur C. Clarke walking its streets and browsing in its arcades and applying for onward visas.

I called Sir Arthur's secretary the following morning, as I'd been directed to.

'Sir Arthur will see you.'

I easily found his house. I'd been near it the day before, looking for a visa to Myanmar – the Myanmar embassy was down a nearby lane, and Sir Arthur's neighbours were the Iraqi embassy and a Sai Baba ashram. This quiet district was distinguished by its high walls and well-patrolled gates and security cameras and the occasional splash of someone diving into a pool I could not see.

Sir Arthur lived behind ten-foot walls, with wire mesh on top of them, in a big squarish house that was comfortable and spacious rather than luxurious. I announced myself, the gate swung open, and I was directed to a stairwell, its windows playfully decorated with bumper stickers from NASA, and one with a large vertical arrow and the message MARS: 35,000,000 MILES. I entered the working wing of the house, a lobby, the secretary's office with its file drawers and paraphernalia – fax machine, computer, phones. Documents framed and hung on the wall certified that Sir Arthur had become a member of one society or another, or had won a prize – lots of these; and plaques, trophies, ceremonial knickknacks inscribed to him. His was a well-rewarded career. He was a serious scientist as well as an ambitious and imaginative writer, anticipating possible futures. It was an old tradition. Writing enthusiastically about Ray Bradbury's *Martian Chronicles*, Borges claimed that Ludovico Ariosto and Johannes Kepler were early sci-fi dreamers and practitioners. In her memoirs, Doris Lessing (herself a science-fiction writer at times) praised science-fiction writers as visionaries.

'Hello!'

Sir Arthur appeared in a wheelchair, the familiar, smiling, bespectacled man; upright, balding, but rather frail, even in this heat with a blanket over his skinny legs. He looked like the sort of alien he had described in his prose fantasies. Men of a certain age, and some women too, often have the watchfulness, the pop-eyed, almost reptilian stare, the glowing dome and the bone structure we attribute to extraterrestrials.

He had that elderly and slightly unearthly appearance. The apparatus of his state-of-the-art wheelchair only emphasized his Martian look. He'd had polio about twelve years before and was suffering the serious aftermath that afflicts some polio victims years later – muscle weakness, poor breathing, cell degeneration. That too made him alien-looking, because he was cheery and welcoming.

'I'm feeling a bit cloud-nine-ish,' he said as he was wheeled into his study, where there were many more plaques and trophies, framed letters from heads of state and signed photographs – surely that beauty was Elizabeth Taylor, and wasn't that beaming fatty the late pope?

Sir Arthur's lopsided lips and slightly chewed pronunciation of the word 'cloud' was from the west of England. I asked him if he was from those parts. He said he'd been born in Minehead, on the Somerset shore.

'A lovely coast – long beaches, very pretty,' he said. He spoke slowly, a voice that was also whimsical and vague, with fluttery hands and an expressive frown that suggested memory loss. 'How'd you get to Sri Lanka?' he asked.

'I travelled through India,' I said, to spare him the details of Georgia and Turkmenistan. He didn't say anything, so I said, 'Do you have any thoughts on India?'

'India. Reaching critical mass.'

'Population, you mean?'

'Out of control. Too many,' he said.

He pulled out a diary as wide as a ledger, opened to the day's date. *April 12* was underlined, and beneath it, in a child's scrawl in big letters, *Titanic sank 1912.*

'Today is an important day,' he said and tapped the page of the diary with the yellow nail of a skinny finger. The *Titanic* was on his mind. 'Terrible thing! But is this the right day?'

'We can check,' I said. But of course he was an expert on the sinking: fifteen years before, he'd written a novel, *The Ghost from the Grand Banks*, about two expeditions competing to raise the wreck.

'Look at this,' he said and pushed a small silver tray across his desk. It was filled with little glass vials. He picked one up. 'Look.' The vial was labelled MOON DUST. 'Can you see it?'

It was pale grit, like the residue of stale celery salt in a spice jar. He chose another one.

'Look.' This one was labelled RUSTICLE – TITANIC. A small dark scab of fungoid iron that had been scraped from the hull and presented to Sir Arthur.

'What is this?' he asked me, lifting another vial, containing a whitish blob.

'Looks like a piece of popcorn.'

'It's a Styrofoam cup from the dive! Crushed by the pressure. Look how small it is.'

He smiled at the silver tray and sorted the other vials and defied me to identify their contents. They were filled with rare gravel and floating organisms and crumbled souvenirs from expeditions.

'What are you writing, Sir Arthur?'

'Nothing. A few notes. I've destroyed enough trees.'

'What about memoirs?'

'Done plenty of those,' he said. 'All my friends are gone. Look' – and he gestured to the wall of photographs.

This gave me a chance to rise and look at pictures and examine the signatures and inscriptions: a warm salutation from Liz Taylor, a scrawl from the pope, scribbles from Neil Armstrong and Buzz Aldrin, from smooth-faced smilers who might have been actors, from Stanley Kubrick and others, including Darth Vader.

'Wernher von Braun,' I said.

But he had gone back to tapping his diary. 'You see, the *Titanic* represented triumph and disaster.'

'Hubris, I suppose.'

'What's that?'

When I repeated it, he said in a quoting and declamatory voice, ' "Not even God can sink this ship!" Heh-heh-heh.'

Now I could see the whole message on the T-shirt he was wearing under a warmer shirt. It said, *I invented the satellite and all I got was this lousy T-shirt.* It was true that he had envisaged and described satellites circling the Earth long before they were made and blasted into orbit.

'You know *Metropolis*? Lovely film,' he said suddenly – by now I was getting used to his style of conversation, a kind of alienspeak: little bursts of talk, inspirational impulses, staticky delivery and explosive memories. 'What is it? Nineteen thirties? The image of a man holding the hands of a clock. Think of it – what that image says.'

'Oh, yes, I remember,' I said. I'd never seen it, but that didn't matter. He wasn't really listening; he kept talking. And he was still toying with the silver tray, squinting at the vials.

'One of the greatest films ever. I want to see it again.'

'Were you influenced by any films when you wrote the script for *2001*?'

'Loved films. Kubrick! I wrote the film, yes. Kubrick was all right.'

'Wasn't he difficult?'

'I don't recall any blood on the carpet,' he said. 'We had disagreements, but they were amicable. Did he die? I can't remember.'

'He died a few years ago.'

'Is Conrad Hilton alive?' Now he was tapping the vial of moon dust.

'I believe Conrad Hilton is dead.'

'Do you play table tennis? Table tennis is the one sport that I excel in. My greatest hobby, my only sport.'

'I'll play you any time, but I'm sure I'd lose.'

'Look,' he said. He had put the moon dust down and snatched up an old photograph. A woman with light hair and a pale dress, on a sunny day in a garden that was probably English, was surrounded by three androgynous children. 'That's my mother. Which one is me?'

I chose the wrong one. He was the more girlish and subdued child in the frilly outfit.

'That was taken in Taunton or Minehead. I was about six.' He smiled at this scene from the 1920s – the sunshine, the flowers, his beautiful mother.

I said, 'Is there a film of *Day After Tomorrow*?'

'I think so. I think I walked out.'

'*Childhood's End* is one of my favourites.'

'"Remember Babylon" is mine,' he said. 'Wonderful story. It won a

prize in *Best Ever*. Where is it?' He fossicked in a stack of books and
found a copy of his *Collected Stories*. 'In here somewhere. "Dog Star" is
another one I like.'

'*Childhood's End* could be a good film,' I said.

'Should be a film, but it's too downbeat from the human point of
view.' He was trying to find 'I Remember Babylon' in the thick book
of stories. In front of him, in all the clutter, was a typed poem, Shelley's
'Ozymandias'.

'I love this poem,' I said.

He put the *Collected Stories* down and picked up the poem. 'I wanted
to reread it.' He looked closely and read, '"Look on my works, ye
mighty, and despair!" Heh-heh.'

'Maybe the earth will end up like the scene in "Ozymandias".'

'If you wait long enough, oh, yes,' he said. Then he looked directly
at me and said, 'Did I mention how I saved the life of the man who
made the atom bomb? I'm trying to remember the details. And then
there's this other matter.' He pulled the diary out of the clutter. 'When
did the *Titanic* sink? Was it today? I think I wrote something about it.'

We found a reference book and the facts: the *Titanic* hit the iceberg
on the night of 14 April 1912, and sank early on the morning of the
fifteenth.

As I was noting this, Sir Arthur said, 'The plane came low down the
runway' – he was describing how he had saved the life of the man who
invented the A-bomb. After this scattered recollection, which I found
hard to visualize, he said, 'It should be in my biography. It's somewhere
in my writings. It's very spooky. And the other film I'd like to see again
is *The Lost World*, about 1930. First film I ever saw.'

The hero of that Conan Doyle story and some others ('The Day the
Earth Screamed') is Professor Challenger – bold scientist, man of action
and adventure. It was easy to imagine an aged and infirm Professor
Challenger as someone like Sir Arthur, surrounded by books and
trophies, faltering and fugitive in his memories.

'Conan Doyle, well, he went nutty,' Sir Arthur said. 'It was spiritualism.'

'Wasn't it the death of his wife that unhinged him?'

Sir Arthur was frowning. He said, 'I'm trying to remember the name
of the astronomer who said, "Flying is impossible. I've proved it beyond
all argument." And the Wright brothers had already taken off! Heh-heh.'

'What's the next big thing in science?'

He didn't hesitate. He said, 'Matter transfer.'

' "Travel by Wire" is one of your stories. That's matter transfer.'

'Did I write that? I can't recall.' He thumped the desk and became stern. 'What I need is to draw up a chronology! The main events. The books. The places. People. Friends. The scripts. See,' and now he leaned over and faced me, 'scriptwriting is not very inspirational. It's a hard slog.' He began trawling at the side of his desk. In a stack of books he found the one he was looking for. 'Here it is. *The Ghost from the Grand Banks. Titanic* – all of it.'

He turned the book over in his trembling hands.

'If she could be raised, what a tourist attraction!' he said.

I smiled at his sudden excitement. He was a scientist, but he was also a showman, and spectacle, the glamorous, the stupendous, the Professor Challenger exploits, were essential aspects of his literary imagination, and perhaps of his science too, wowing the reader, dreaming of the undreamed of, in the literature of astonishment.

Still holding his book, he said sadly, 'I'm spooked by the man in the lifeboat handing over his child. "Goodbye, my little son." ' He paused. He was tearful. He said, 'Died of exposure! Sister ship came along. Too late! Disaster!' After swallowing a little, he said tentatively, 'You wrote some books.'

'Yes. In one of them, *The Mosquito Coast*, there's an unattributed quote from you about technology and magic.'

'Clarke's Third Law!' he said and rubbed his hands. 'Any sufficiently advanced technology is indistinguishable from magic.'

'What is Clarke's First Law?' I asked.

'First Law,' he said, hardly hesitating. 'The only way of discovering the limits of the possible is to go beyond the impossible.'

'Second Law?'

'There is no Second Law, only first and third. Heh-heh.' He became playful and animated. He began to recite a poem he said he'd written long ago. Perhaps his numbered laws put him in mind of it.

> The two-legged lama's a priest,
> The four-legged llama's a beast.
> Alas, for cosmic melodrama
> There isn't any three-legged lama.

'I didn't realize you were a poet.'

'I write poetry occasionally,' he said, and then an expression strained his features. I had seen this off and on during my visit, his trying to remember something. He said with difficulty, 'Did I ever tell you the story of how I shared bed and breakfast with the tsar of Russia?'

He was addressing me as though speaking to an old and valued friend. I said, 'No. I'd love to hear it.'

'Oh, yes.' He smiled. 'We were only a few weeks old! You see –' He gripped his head with his fingers like a soothsayer trying to force a vision, and then in a convulsive way said, 'They were in exile in England in 1918. We had an English nanny, a Miss Hinckley, and she' – he paused and pressed his head again – 'she'd been to Russia.' His voice trailed off and he seemed out of breath. 'Royal family, yes.' He had lost the thread of the story and was murmuring Miss Hinckley's name. At last he said, 'What stories she could tell.'

He went silent, drifting into a private reverie. I sat wondering if I should excuse myself and leave, but Sir Arthur seemed content. I covertly made notes, a sort of inventory of the framed pictures and what trophies I could read. There was a shelf of model planes – jet planes and toy rockets.

'You asked if I wrote poems,' he said and brightened. 'I wrote a poem when I was young. It ended, "I rose and fled, afraid to be alone."'

He became sad, seeming to remember. I said, 'What were the circumstances?'

'I was being evacuated to America. Sent away.' He was staring into space. With feeling, he quoted again, 'I rose and fled, afraid to be alone.'

His secretary knocked and opened the study door. 'It's time,' she said. To me, she said, 'Sir Arthur's tired. He needs his lunch and his nap.'

But Sir Arthur was still in his posture of recitation, his back straight, his head upright. I thought he was going to say some more lines of his poem. He said, 'I dedicated it to the boy I was in love with.'

His secretary winced. She had started wheeling him out, but Sir Arthur was smiling wistfully, and I felt I'd had a glimpse of his passion and sadness.★

★

★ 'Sir Arthur died on 22 March 2008, as I was correcting these pages. He was buried in Colombo, his tombstone bearing an epitaph he wrote himself: 'Here lies Arthur C. Clarke. He never grew up and did not stop growing.'

The next morning I went to Fort Station in Colombo. The station had not changed, except that it was very crowded because of Avurudu, the Sinhalese New Year, the occasion of the full moon. Paul Bowles, who spent time on this coast, once wrote, 'New Years here is not a day but a season.' True – even a week later there were rituals and high jinks and reduced service on buses and trains, most people regarding the holiday as a reason to stay home, eating the specified meals and obeying the astrological directives.

This also happened to be an auspicious day to travel (once the head was 'anointed by the juice of the *nuga* leaves at 7.39 a.m. while standing on *karanda* leaves'), and the ticket queue was so long I simply pushed myself on to the train and got a seat. No one asked for my ticket. The train had not changed in all that time. It pulled out and rolled through the Colombo outskirts and down the coast to where the tsunami had hit.

I remembered this as one of the most beautiful journeys I'd taken on the Railway Bazaar – one of the loveliest railway lines in the world, at sea level, right next to the beach, travelling along the glittering shore, the blue sea and the palm groves, all the windows open, the ocean breeze blowing through the carriage. It could have been the same sunny day I spent on this train in October 1973: the same people, monks, nuns, families, children, old women in shawls, men in neckties, men in sarongs. 'The recommended colour of dress is blue,' the Avurudu astrologers had announced.

On a morning like this, on 26 December 2004, on this coast, the tide had ebbed dramatically. *The tide went out to the horizon*, Sri Lankans told me. *All we saw was mud and sand and distant rocks – no water at all.*

The weird sight of the water sucked off the ocean floor, the exposed sand gleaming in the bright sun, had attracted the villagers who lived by the shore. They had, many of them, run on to the sand and into this new land. Big fishing boats sat helpless in the middle of the strange waterless place.

And then the tidal wave appeared as a high wall of foam rushing towards them, and soon it was on them, on everyone, crashing on to the land, crushing houses, sweeping huts away, drowning cattle and people, hitting a train just like this one and knocking it sideways off the rails, drowning 1,500 of the passengers, almost everyone in the carriages.

The tracks had been hammered apart, even brick and cement houses tumbled and destroyed, foot-thick walls smashed to pieces. Yet, a kind of miracle, most trees – the palms, the bunches of pandanus with great stalking roots, the sweeps of mangroves – were left undisturbed by the same wave that swept away fortress-like walls and paved roads. Because of these tenacious trees the coast retained a look of serenity, not the knocked-flat aftermath I associated with a hurricane.

Many houses had been rebuilt – bright bricks, fresh cement, newly woven thatch and bamboo. There were new bridges and paved roads, and all along the rail line evidence of a massive rebuilding effort. The line itself had been repaired two months after the tsunami, but now, sixteen months later, I could see that many people still lived in emergency shelters, and here and there were signs with arrows saying TSUNAMI CAMP. Hundreds of thousands of people had lost their homes.

The most poignant sight, very common, was the many grave markers along the shoreline, as though the people had drowned on that very spot – and perhaps they had – the gravestones in the shape of Buddhist stupas, big and small, clusters of them on the beach, under the palms, dozens in some places. I began to associate the big stupas with adults, the smaller ones with children, and even infant-sized stupas, as though these poor people had been turned to stone by the horror of the sudden slap of the wave, and remained there, petrified on the beach.

My carriage was crowded, people sitting and standing, swaying as the train rounded the curvy shore, but freshened by the sea breeze.

'So glad to see you,' said the man next to me. 'Tourists are afraid to come here because of the troubles – the Tamil business, the tsunami, and what and what.'

'I was here a long time ago,' I said.

'It was different then,' he said.

'I think it was the same.'

'I mean, it was better.'

'Maybe.'

We were all headed to Galle this beautiful day, but all along the line was the evidence of tsunami damage. Where villages and houses had been rebuilt, roads repaved, bridges fixed, there were gravestones and stupas and plaques, with freshly chiselled inscriptions, commemorating the many thousands who had died.

After the clusters of palm trees and mangroves, Galle appeared suddenly, a town on a big blue bay, an old Dutch fort, and just outside the station, the market square. There were more people now, but the rest was as I'd remembered it: the bazaar, the ramparts, the scooter rickshaws, the hawkers' stalls selling cloth and kitchenware. In 1973 I bought an old dagger from one of these market traders, a nine-inch blade and an Asiatic lion's head carved on the bone handle. I carried it in my bag for the next two months, through Southeast Asia and Japan and onward through the Soviet Union. No one questioned it. I still have it. Over the years it became rusty and dull, but while working on this book I bought a whetstone and sharpened it, cleaned it, restored it, until it has become once again a glittering thing, good as new, a souvenir of another time.

'This was all underwater,' one of the market women told me. I could see some damaged houses, but the seventeenth-century fort was untouched. Children were playing on the walls of the fort.

I had been told the name of an inexpensive guesthouse in Galle. A man on a scooter rickshaw took me to the top of a winding road on the tallest hill in town.

That evening I sat on the rooftop veranda of the small, quiet Lady Hill Hotel, writing about my visit with Sir Arthur, my melancholy at seeing him so frail, so vague, his mind drifting. The town's lights twinkled through the trees, the sky was full of stars; from this vantage I could see the lamps of the fishing boats in the harbour. The air was fragrant with night-blooming flowers.

I considered this one of the best evenings of my trip: the muted buzz of the small seaside town at night, the soft air, the perfume of the blossoms. No event, no drama, just contentment, as though I had set off from London and travelled for months to be here, at this moment, sitting under the full moon of the Sinhalese lunar New Year.

All the talk the next morning was of five more casualties of Tamil Tiger ambushes, and another land mine, and an assault on a Sri Lankan army position. For the previous three years, there had been a ceasefire, negotiated by the Norwegian government, but this agreement was clearly falling apart, as Tigers claimed more lives. The deaths were shocking, violent and unnecessary. It was obvious that the Tamils would eventually possess part of the north of Sri Lanka. Already they had a de facto state, with their own Tamil schools and hospitals. And their army was notoriously full of child soldiers, kids between the ages of thirteen and seventeen (UNICEF put the figure at almost 16,000), who had been forcibly recruited or abducted from Tamil villages. After the tsunami hit, many children, orphans of the storm, were given guns and press-ganged into the Tamil Tigers.

There had been a famine in Sri Lanka when I'd last been in Galle. The harvest had been disappointing, and food was scarce. I wrote then: 'They had driven out the Tamils, who had done all the planting.' I had also written: 'But Galle was a beautiful place, garlanded with red hibiscus and smelling of the palm-scented ocean, possessing cool Dutch interiors and ringed by forests of bamboo. The sunset's luminous curtains patterned the sky in rufous gold for an hour and a half every evening, and all night the waves crashed on the ramparts of the fort.' That part was still true.

Walking around Galle in the morning sunshine, I remembered that, when I was last here, I had wanted to go to Hambantota. I hadn't done it, but I could do it now.

Most of the fighting was in northern and north-central Sri Lanka and along the upper part of the east coast. I was on the southwestern coast; Hambantota was in a safe place, at the southern tip of the island. It was the last post of Leonard Woolf, who was a British colonial agent in the town and who was the subject of an unusual in-the-footsteps-of book, *Woolf in Ceylon* (2005), by Christopher Ondaatje. On my first trip I had read Woolf's sombre masterpiece, *The Village in the Jungle*, and assuming it had been set somewhere down there, I had wanted to see that part of the island. Ondaatje, also an admirer of Woolf, had the same idea. But he had better credentials. The older brother of the novelist Michael Ondaatje, he'd been born in Ceylon of a burgher family. His ancestors were among the earliest settlers of the island, many of them eminent. His father was a tea planter, and like many men isolated on tea estates, peculiar and bibulous. In his footsteps book, Ondaatje revisited the scenes of his own early life as well as the key places in Woolf's colonial career. Along the way he answered all the questions that had arisen in my mind about Woolf's knowledge of Sinhalese life, his seven years as an officer, and the background of his writing. The book is a leisurely ramble around Sri Lanka, literary, archaeological, political and autobiographical. He spared me from having to find the settings of Woolf's underrated novel and of many of the short stories.

Heading to Hambantota, I took the train from Galle to Matara, another line along the coast, so close to the shoreline that the spray flung by the heavy rollers from Africa reached the broken windows of the battered carriages. The tsunami aftermath, large-scale destruction and small-scale rebuilding, was visible all the way. The footprints of houses, the cement slab or a row of boulders, were all that remained of many buildings on the shore – nothing else left except the coconut palms that had fed the vanished family.

We came to Weligama, a cove with – just offshore – a small green island piled with sculpted rocks and feathery trees and an alluring villa with a white plaster veranda. I first heard the name Weligama from Paul Bowles, who told me that in the 1950s he had sailed from Tangier to Colombo, to live on that offshore island, named Taprobane.

'Taprobane was the ancient Greek and Roman name for Ceylon, but this modern Taprobane is an island once owned by Count de Mauny, a somewhat louche Frenchman who claimed that he had inherited his title from his grandmother, though many thought it bogus.' This is from Ondaatje, who described the fraudulent count as a scandal-plagued pederast who'd found a happy refuge here in the 1920s.

But who wouldn't want to stay? The bay at Weligama is as lovely as any in the South Pacific and has the same limpid beauty, the blue sea and a white sand beach enclosed by groves of palms, clusters of bamboo huts and a sense that the world is elsewhere. 'The opportunities for happy living are greater in Ceylon than anywhere else I've been so far,' Bowles wrote in a letter to Gore Vidal in 1950. And a month later he pronounced it 'the best country to settle in, from all points of view'. He praised the courtesy of the people, their cleanliness, their hospitality and their skill as servants. He loved 'the ever present triumphant vegetation of the coast'. And he was bewitched by the notion of living on an island.

Bowles had glimpsed Taprobane first from this same train in 1949 and managed to buy it a few years later. He wrote his Tangier novel, *The Spider's House*, there, but not much else. And after an unhappy stay on the island in 1954, accompanied by his wife, Jane, and his Moroccan lover, he decided to sell it. Jane had hated it: large bats hung on the trees and flapped around, beating their wings, which were a yard wide. And Bowles needed the money.

About fifteen miles further down the coast was the town of Matara, an old railway station and the end of the line. I got out and walked to the bus terminal for the bus to Hambantota.

'This is the bus. Leaving sometime soon,' a man explained to me.

He was also going to Hambantota.

He said, 'This is the worst time of the year to be travelling. Everyone's going home for the Avurudu festival.'

It did seem that the train had been full, and this bus was filling up. I bought a bus ticket from the conductor – the fare was about 25 cents for the fifty-mile trip.

'You speak English,' I said. 'Not many people do.'

'They don't teach English in schools any more. But I studied it – older people speak it.'

That had happened after I'd been here; the Tamil insurgency had also happened; and as I'd seen in Colombo, both had, in their way, stunted Sri Lanka, kept tourists and investors away, while giving the island the look and feel of bygone Ceylon. But the small population and the old-fangledness were a relief: because business was terrible, the country was spared foreign exploitation and kept its soul.

The bus driver tooted his horn. Everyone got on and the bus circled the Matara clock tower and headed south along the coast. The man I'd spoken to at the station had taken a seat beside me. His name was Takil; he asked me where I was from, and when I told him he said, 'I've been to Miami.'

'What doing?'

'I was working for a Saudi sheik,' and he told me the sheik's name. The sheik was one of the thousand or so princes but was particularly well connected: his brother was a minister in the Saudi government.

This sheik had a $25 million mansion in Golden Beach, another estate in Los Angeles and houses elsewhere. I had never heard of Golden Beach, but Takil assured me that it was a wealthy community at the northern edge of Miami and that only billionaires lived there. Bill Gates, for one.

'He lives in Seattle, surely?'

'He kept a house in Golden Beach, near my sheik.'

I had to travel to Dikwella (which we were passing through) on an old Sri Lankan bus to find out these things about my country.

'He needed a big house,' Takil said. 'He had three wives and lots of children. He was only twenty-eight, though.'

'What did you do for him?'

'I waited on him. I served him his food.'

'You're a Muslim?'

'No. Buddhist. And I don't speak Arabic. Funny, eh? He spoke to me in English. This was back in the 1980s. I was only twenty myself. He trusted me, and I was good at my job. He kept me on for four years.'

'Was he a playboy?'

'Not really. He had married an actress but divorced her. He was looking for another wife.'

'In Florida?'

'Anywhere. He travelled a lot. He had lots of relatives living in America. He chartered a British Airways jet for his trips.'

'Oil money?'

'Yes. Lots of it – lots. But no interests. He took his children to Disney World, he took them to Los Angeles, and sightseeing. He didn't work. He did nothing.'

'Prayed, I suppose.'

'No. He wasn't particularly religious.'

I said, 'People wonder why Osama bin Laden hates the Saudi royal family and wants to punish the United States for being its ally. That sheik and people like him are the reason, and we're all paying a horrible price for it.'

We had passed Tangalla – its prison figures in Woolf's *Village in the Jungle*. We were coming to a river. Takil said it was the Ambalantota, and that we'd be in Hambantota pretty soon.

The land had flattened and become scrubbier and more thinly populated. It seemed to me that the tsunami had swept through and scoured it of its houses, but Takil said that we were looking at salt flats. For hundreds of years salt had been produced here by evaporation in the great flat enclosures and lagoons, called *lewayas*. Ondaatje explained that a century ago Leonard Woolf 'revolutionized salt collection' here by introducing a payment scheme that was fair and regulated, and that was closely supervised by him.

We went down a road of overhanging trees, lined by small villages, and were soon in the town square of Hambantota. Takil headed home to celebrate Avuruda, and I looked for a place to stay. I found nothing, but it was still only the middle of the afternoon, so I looked at the boats in the harbour and strolled through the town, then got a scooter rickshaw to take me to Woolf's government bungalow that Ondaatje had found. Throughout his book, Ondaatje repeats that the country had changed very little in the nearly one hundred years that had passed since Woolf was a colonial officer, and he quotes a Sri Lankan who, in a 2002 newspaper article, discussing the grim events and the hardships of peasant life recounted in *The Village in the Jungle*, said, 'It was an era when the jungle ruled the lives of the humble peasant as it does even now in remote villages scattered across the country.'

What is unusual about the novel, what gives it a weird nobility, is that, written by a young Englishman and published in 1913, its main characters are Sinhalese peasants. Its plot hinges on village marriage customs, traditional rivalries and peculiarly Sinhalese vindictiveness, passions and satisfactions. Rape, multiple murder and exploitation are central to the book, which stands out in my mind as having perhaps the most violent plot and depressing ending of any novel I've ever read. Just when you think that the last surviving character represents hope and possibility, she looks out of her hut one night and sees the glinting eyes of a pig – or demon – about to devour her.

For his pains, Leonard Woolf got very little for the novel. His friend Lytton Strachey said, 'I was disappointed to see that it was about nothing but blacks – whom really I don't much care for.' And although it was dedicated to her, Woolf's wife, Virginia, was indifferent to its merits.

As a despised and overworked expatriate employed by the Singapore government as a university lecturer in the 1960s, I found Woolf's five-volume autobiography in the college's library and read it all. The second volume, *Growing*, about his years as a despised and overworked colonial officer, gave me heart and helped me to become patient and sympathetic. In that book he describes the necessity of being efficient – replying to letters on the day they are received, keeping accurate notes, learning to be methodical, developing an interest in the culture. Taking his advice, I followed his example and became productive and a little happier as an alien in Singapore.

'Where staying?' the scooter rickshaw driver asked me.

I had no idea. It was now late afternoon, and the light would soon be gone.

'Any hotels here?'

'Hotel there,' he said and pointed up the road, east along the coast, the way I'd come.

That was how I found the small one-storey hotel, salt-crusted, flecked with mildew and sitting behind a sand dune, the pounding surf and a wild beach on the other side. A German tour group, just arrived, had already marked their territory, hogging the lounge chairs by draping towels on them – though all the chairs were unoccupied except for the towels. These Germans were perhaps the first tourists I'd seen on my trip – the first large group, anyway – and were on an Ayurvedic retreat. They were apparently unfazed by the news of land mines or talk of strife.

I stayed here a few days, made another trip into Hambantota, and continued my story 'The Elephant God', writing one day about the main character:

She had come to understand what the solitary long-distance traveler eventually knows after months on the road – that, in the course of time, a trip stops being an interlude of distractions and detours, pursuing sights, looking for pleasures, and becomes a series of disconnections, giving up comfort, abandoning or being abandoned by friends, passing the time in obscure places, inured to the concept of delay, since the trip itself was a succession of delays.

Solving problems, finding meals, buying new clothes and giving away old ones, getting laundry done, buying tickets, scavenging for cheap hotels, studying maps, being alone but not lonely. It was not about happiness but safety, finding serenity, making discoveries in all this locomotion and an equal serenity when she had a place to roost, like a bird of passage migrating slowly in a sequence of flights.

'Nice and quiet,' the hotel manager said, passing me one day. 'You can relax here.'

But I had not come all this way to relax. I told him I would be leaving the next day.

'Avurudu,' he said and smiled. 'Impossible. No buses.'

'I'll find a car.'

'No cars. Nothing. Everyone home with family. Not auspicious to travel.'

He showed me a prominent item in that day's newspaper. Favourable Avurudu times were listed, including this one: 'The auspicious time to leave home for work falls at 6.35 a.m. on Thursday, 20 April . . . Wear gold-coloured clothing and set off facing the North, after consuming a meal of moru and rice.'

That was three days away. The whole country was shut down until then. Nothing was running, no buses, no trains.

'Where you are going, sir?' the manager asked as I checked out the next morning.

When I said Colombo, he laughed, meaning 'impossible'.

I walked to the road and hitchhiked. An overcrowded van took me almost to Matara. I had to crouch in an uncomfortable position, with passengers' elbows in my kidneys. Finally, after more than four hours, I could stand it no longer. I got out, hitchhiking again, and after half an hour a man in a small car picked me up. Near Galle, at a bend in the road, I saw a large painted banner: WARM WELCOME FOR US—SRI LANKA FRIENDSHIP, and a great crowd of excited people awaiting their American visitors, on whom they would lavish Avurudu hospitality, garlands of flowers and baskets of fruit.

I saw no sign of the Americans nearby, but further down the road I heard the unmistakable *yak-yak-yak* of a helicopter settling to earth, somewhere out of sight in the jungle. Later I found out that the helicopter contained three US senators and their wives, who had come to visit a tsunami refugee camp. A junket: politicians picking up a family holiday, being personally thanked and rewarded for their country's generosity. There was no better example of official travel and unofficial travel: the swoop and buzz of the senatorial chopper overhead as I stood on the narrow road, bumming a ride.

16. The Slow Train to Kandy

One of the happier and more helpful delusions of travel is that one is on a quest. At the end of Avurudu, when the auspicious day for work, for travel, arrived, the one determined by the astrologers and soothsayers, I took the train to Kandy, the capital of the former kingdom, at the centre of the island, sitting at a high altitude, where in a famous temple a tooth of the Buddha was enshrined in a gold casket. It was a place of pilgrimage.

All the trains I took in Sri Lanka were small and slow, possibly the same rolling stock as those I'd taken long ago, but dirtier. Yet the routes were so dramatic, by the blue sea or the green hills, I hardly noticed the condition of the railway carriages or my hard bench. And it was only seventy-five miles to Kandy, the line rising from the coast, passing through the gardens and villages on the slopes, the rice terraces full of still, silvery water and mirroring the sky, the rock temples hacked out of cliffs, the monasteries at the higher elevations. Coconut plantations, vegetable farms, pineapple fields, markets overflowing with blossoms: the way to Kandy was strewn with flowers.

Into the cooler air and taller trees, past Ambepussa Station and Polgahawela Junction, with its Buddhist monastery and temple. In the middle of the steep ascent that began at a place called Rambukkana, it began to rain – the first rain I'd seen since Bokhara, over a month before. The train's windows were open, the rain spattered in, but there weren't many passengers, and there was enough room so that we could move to the drier seats.

An older man with a tightly rolled umbrella and a wide-brimmed hat and a briefcase made room for me on one of the benches.

'You are welcome.'

His name was Mr Kumara. He had been a clerk in the Department of Health and was now retired, living on a pension.

'And I have so many other interests.' He had a confident manner, and his hat, his umbrella and his briefcase gave him a look of authority. His calm smile seemed to invite questions.

'What sort of interests?'

'Palmistry and numerology. I make predictions.'

'What was your best prediction?'

'That Franklin Roosevelt would be assassinated,' he said, and before I could challenge this, he added, 'And that a certain woman would leave her husband – and she did.'

He asked me for some of my dates, of numbers related to my life. He took out a pad and did some calculations based on my birth date, covering the page with obscure mathematics and crossings-out until he arrived at a single number, which he circled.

'Your number is two,' he said. 'You look younger than your age. You will have a good sun line. I can tell you that without looking at your palm.' He then made a new page of calculations. 'Here are the years that fate has decided for you – the significant years. When you were twenty-three, thirty-two, forty-one and fifty.'

I considered these and thought: Africa, Railway Bazaar, disastrous affair, divorce – fateful years. Mr Kumara was looking at my palm.

'Sun line is there! See, I told you!'

Now, without anything to do except hold on to the stanchions and the straps, the other passengers took an interest and leaned over, as though to double-check the lines on my palm.

'Here is lifeline. You could live to eighty-two or eighty-five,' he said, manipulating my thumb flesh. 'This is Mount of Jupiter. You are stubborn, self-made man. Determined. Don't bend to anyone. You brook no interference from anyone. You live life by your own self. You are flirtatious, but not good at satisfying your sexual appetite.'

This drew murmurs from the other passengers, and I shook my head, trying to cast doubt on this assessment.

'You are a Jupiter, a leader among men,' he said, but stated it as a fact – he wasn't impressed. 'Your eyesight is bad, yet I see you don't wear glasses.'

'I had double cataract surgery.'

'What did I say?'

He was speaking to the onlookers.

'You are charitable, but you were cheated by the love of your heart,' he said. 'People abused your judgement in the past. Not true?'

'All true.'

He was on to my left hand now. He said, 'Your left hand is more interesting than your right.'

'In what way?'

'More irritated,' Mr Kumara said. 'You have won the battles with the enemy. In future you do not need to worry about the enemy.'

'That sounds good.'

'Very much foreign travel in your life,' he said.

'Are you saying that because I'm in Sri Lanka?'

'Your living depends on it,' he said, twisting my hand, peering at my palm. 'You will soon receive unexpected wealth in unexpected ways. And your career is good. Nothing bothers you. But you have bronchial problems and breathing problems.'

'That part isn't true.'

'They will come,' he said confidently. 'Before thirty-five you were very upset. Job, marriage, life – very bad.'

'That's a fact.'

'You will fall in love more than twice.'

'Twice more?'

'It seems so.' He looked me square in the face and let go of my hand. 'You are a judge, a lawyer, a writer. Maybe an ambassador.'

'If I were an ambassador, would I be sitting on this train?'

The passengers nearby looked at me for confirmation. I smiled. Apart from the insulting suggestion that I might be a lawyer, he was right on most counts.

I had got used to the tsunami damage on the coast, the ruins and the rebuilding. But inland, up these hills, the houses were whole and the villages intact, shining in the gentle rain, the dense green leaves of the foliage going greener in the drizzle.

'This is Peradeniya,' Mr Kumara said, getting up and unfastening the strap on his umbrella. He gave me his card – his name and address. 'When you come back to Sri Lanka, please call me. You can meet my family. My wife is an excellent cook.'

'And when I come back you'll be able to verify your predictions. "Unexpected wealth".'

'I tell only what I see,' he said. And stepping out of the coach he said, 'Lovely gardens here. You must see them.'

I planned to, by going from Kandy, which was only a few miles away. I felt it would be harder to get a taxi at the gardens.

At Kandy I walked from the station with a growing crowd of pilgrims to the Dalada Maligawa, the Temple of the Tooth, thinking about Mr Kumara's prophecies and palmistry. I had assumed that this Buddhist population of Sinhalese would be rational and compassionate. In some forms, Buddhism is like a vapour, an odour of sanctity, the minimalism of self-denial, not a religion at all but a philosophy of generosity and forgiveness.

Odd, then, to see Sri Lankans closely observing the bizarre Avurudu strictures ('Lighting the hearth should be done wearing colourful clothes and facing the south . . . juice of nuga leaves on the head at 7.39 a.m. . . . Set off facing the north . . .'); or being drawn to Mr Kumara's numerology – his addition and subtraction and his confident soothsaying. And now in Kandy the panoply of this thickly decorated temple, the gilded pillars, the ribbons and semi-precious stones, the shrouded statues and heavy-lidded gaze of a hundred gesturing Buddhas – and flowers, candles, fruit and flags, relics and flaming tapers, all the paraphernalia I associated with the blood and gold and organ pipes that epitomize the interior decoration of South American cathedrals and the wilder excesses of Catholicism, complete with a swirling fog of warm incense: 'That vast moth-eaten musical brocade, / Created to pretend we never die.'*

I kicked off my shoes and joined the queue of people eager to see the Buddha's tooth, which in this temple, in its gold casket, was like a saint's relic, Saint Francis's skull, a mummy in a catacomb, a splinter from the True Cross. The story of the Buddha's tooth dates from the fourth century AD, and there is some question as to whether this is a real canine or a replacement for the tooth (a fake one, said the Sinhalese) that the pious Portuguese burned in Goa as being wicked and idolatrous. The Portuguese who venerated splinters of the True Cross and the skulls of saints, who had all but destroyed Kandy in their time; and what remained of it when the Dutch conquered it, in the sixteenth century, the Dutch had pulled down, leaving very little for the British when they showed up in 1815.

The inner rooms of the temple were crowded and stifling, mobbed with Buddhists propitiating the impassive statues, prostrating themselves, waving lighted tapers, and making passes with their outstretched arms – as though practising to be Christians.

* Philip Larkin, 'Aubade'.

I walked outside and along the lake, liking this pleasant air at 1,600 feet, and then found a curry house (plate of rice covered with highly seasoned sauce, 75 cents), and sat reading the paper, about recent Tamil Tiger actions. In the place where I'd planned to cross from India to Sri Lanka, an armada of heavily armed Tiger watercraft, camouflaged as fishing boats, had attacked some Sri Lankan navy vessels. Eleven Sri Lankan sailors were either dead or missing, and in the retaliatory action, eight rebel boats were sunk, thirty Tigers dead. And in Colombo three Tiger commandos in diving gear, setting mines, had been captured; two of them committed suicide by swallowing cyanide capsules they kept handy for that purpose.

A Sri Lankan sitting near me struck up a conversation. Seeing the article I was reading, he said, 'Sixty-seven people killed in the last two weeks. And this is during a ceasefire!'

His name was Kaduwella. He had come to Kandy to see the sacred tooth. He said that the Tamil Tigers had attacked the temple.

Of course: a place of such serenity, such glitter and sanctity, it was inevitable that the Tigers would violate it. And why not? In a paragraph that reads like a historical free-for-all, Christopher Ondaatje describes the skirmishes over the Buddha's tooth going on for 1,000 years, how Kublai Khan tried but failed to capture it, how the Indians succeeded in snatching it in the thirteenth century but lost it to a Sinhalese king. When the Chinese failed in their attempt to steal the tooth, they took hostages instead – members of the royal family. The Portuguese were fobbed off with a fake tooth. So the Tamil Tigers were the latest in a long list of predators, poachers and violators of the Temple of the Tooth.

The Kaduwellas lived in Colombo. While his wife and children smiled shyly, Mr Kaduwella invited me to his house.

'We'll have a good meal,' he said with a glance at my plate, as though dismissing it, but he and his family were all eating something similar.

I asked him how to get to Peradeniya. He said it was too far to walk, and when we finished lunch he went out of his way to find me a taxi and negotiate the price. And as we parted he repeated his invitation.

In the past I might not have visited Peradeniya Botanic Gardens. More likely I would have visited the Peradeniya Bar and sat there most of the night. But these days, in travel, I seldom went out at night, and got up earlier, and often visited gardens – particularly the gardens that were devised by the British, in which many of the trees were ancient, and some of the specimens planted in the nineteenth century. I got interested in gardening only after I became a householder, and that was as a result of the windfall occasioned by the success of *The Great Railway Bazaar*. I used the money to buy a house, I planted shrubs, I planted flowers, and more recently have been planting various varieties of non-invasive bamboo.

The bamboo groves at Peradeniya were dense, many of the canes gigantic – even named *giganteus* on their labels. What happens to the clumping non-invasive bamboo after one hundred years? The clumps are twenty feet wide and the plant itself grows as tall as a three-storey house. The cycads were vast and feathery, the old palms stood tall; in a place like Sri Lanka, a land of procrastination and decline, these great gardens had ripened and flourished. I was reminded of the palms and mangroves on the coast – Bowles called them 'triumphant vegetation' – that had resisted the onslaught of the tidal wave and the fury of the flood, and stood, like these trees and ferns and bamboos at Peradeniya, not only unviolated but bigger and more beautiful.

Leonard Woolf had walked here, so Ondaatje said. He had spent a year in Kandy, at the law court, fascinated by the convoluted murder cases and the complex marriage disputes. He had so impressed his over-lords he got a better post in Hambantota, where, so he claimed, he would have been happy to spend the rest of his life.

It was easy to see how Sri Lanka could capture your heart, as it had Sir Arthur's. It was especially pleasant to be in a place where not much changed. Yet it was a violated place – the war, the tsunami, had held it back, kept it from improving in any way. The war of Tamil secession had probably had the greatest effect. War is weird in that way: time stops, no one thinks of the future but only of survival or escape.

I left Kandy. And a few days after I left Colombo, just down the street from my hotel, near a park I'd passed many times for its being so pleasant, a large group of pregnant women had lined up to be examined at a pre-natal clinic, the weekly 'maternity day' offered by the Sri Lankan army. Without warning, one of the women, a member of the Black Tiger Suicide Squad, pretending to be pregnant (her maternity dress bulged with a bomb), blew herself up and took six people with her into oblivion.

17. Ghost Train to Mandalay

My first reaction to Rangoon, now a sad and skeletal city renamed Yangon, was disbelief. The unreality of arriving in a distant modernized city cannot compare with the unreality of seeing one that has hardly changed at all. If a place, after decades, is the same, or worse than before, it is almost shaming to behold. Like a prayer you regret has been answered, it exists as a mirror image of yourself, the traveller, who has to admit: I'm the same too, but aged – wearier, frailer, fractured, abused, weaker, shabbier, spookier. There was a human pathos in a city that had faded in the years I'd been away, something more elderly, almost senile. So, adrift in the futility of being in a foreign city, woozy in the stifling heat, I fitted right in. After a day or so I took a horrid pleasure in being here, back in time, in the place I had remembered and had once mocked with youthful satire, a ghost town that made me feel old and ghostly.

The crumbling and neglected city seemed surreal, because the place was isolated under the Myanmar military dictatorship, and helpless and tyrannized. Soldiers were everywhere, even in the sepulchral back streets. It looked pessimistic, unlucky and badly governed. It had no bounce. It was a city without visible ambition: no challenge, no defiance. Being young here wasn't an advantage, nor was strength any use; brains just made you unhappy and a target for the secret police. Students and journalists were hated and abused. So were democrats: win an election here and the army put you in jail. But a reign of terror is seldom terror in the true sense; it is anxious boredom and suspense, and a kind of hopeless resignation bordering on despair, like a household dominated by the pathology of drunken or nagging parents.

The Burmese I met talked frankly about their fears and the political intimidation. They had the sullen defiance of people who were constantly bullied.

'They rule with the gun. They can come to your home at any time,

knock on your door, and take you.' This from a taxi driver, a man of
thirty or so, speaking in a whisper.

'Why would they want to take you?'

'For no reason!'

And another man, a trader in a market, said to me in the same kind
of cautious whisper, 'A prison sentence here is a life sentence. Many of
my friends have been taken away. I know I'll never see them again.'

The generals had been in power in the 1970s, when I'd been here
last. They were still in power, propped up by their control of the drug
trade and enabled, bankrolled, by the Chinese government, their biggest
trading partner, in exotic substances such as heroin and more mundane
items like watermelons. The United States and many other countries
refused to do business with Myanmar for ethical reasons. It was a pariah
state that had defied the democratic process by invalidating the 1990 general election and imprisoning the winner of it, Aung San Suu Kyi. Since
then she has been threatened, attacked, imprisoned, persecuted, widowed
and continually put under house arrest. I arrived in Myanmar at a time
when her sentence of house arrest was extended for another year, her
street barricaded with roadblocks and sentries. Not even the hungriest taxi
driver would dare to take me to her street, nor even speed me past it.

But so familiar was Yangon in its sameness and its smells that I easily
found my way around. To get my bearings I walked to the main railway
station, inquired about a ticket to Mandalay, and then strolled along the
streets towards the river, marvelling at the crumbling buildings, the old
cracked shop-houses, the hawkers squatting in the shade of the arcades
selling oranges and mangoes, the battered cars, the stinking monsoon
drains – nothing new. The pagodas were brighter, the stupas freshly
gilded, the walls newly whitewashed. Frustrated by the military repression, people seemed to take refuge in Buddhism, which preached
patience and compassion. Apart from the newly painted pagodas, the
city was ruinous, which was unique in the reinvented Southeast Asia.
Myanmar was exceptional in its decrepitude and low morale, its
inefficiency almost total.

The imperial city still remained, Victorian in its long colonnades and
narrow passageways. I marvelled at the existence of the broad and massive
buildings with their tall windows and balconies and porches, all of them
preserved by being ignored. Any of Rangoon's well-known colonials
would have found the place familiar. Had Rudyard Kipling, George

Orwell, and H. H. Munro (Saki) – all former residents – walked down Dalhousie Street towards Sule Pagoda and turned into Strand Road, they would have recognized the old Sailors' Home, the General Post Office and the Strand Hotel. And they could have negotiated the city using (as I did) an early edition of a *Murray's* guide.

The Strand Hotel was almost alone in having been extensively fixed up, restored to its former glory, with a palm court and ceiling fans and a spruced-up lobby, and flunkies wearing immaculate frock coats and white gloves. The Strand's fine-dining restaurant served 'grilled beef tenderloin "Mulwara" topped with foie gras' for $34. The price of that one dish fascinated me, because it so happened that in Myanmar, where education was despised and considered suspect, schoolteachers earned $34 a month. Only the army got richer; everyone else was struggling to get by, hustling and hawking and in the money-changing business – the official exchange rate was 300 kyats to the dollar, the black market rate five times that.

In this sort of tyranny, without any opposition, everyone was forced to wheedle and whine, negotiate, horse-trade and tell lies. But if the military in Myanmar was odious, the people I met were soft-tempered and helpful, and it was perhaps the only country I passed through where I met nothing but generosity and kindness. And the Burmese were the most ill-treated, worst-governed, belittled and persecuted of any people I met – worse off than the Turkmen, which is saying a lot.

I didn't stay at the Strand, though I had done so long ago. It was ridiculous to pay $450 a night for a single room. I found a perfectly adequate (which is to say somewhat dreary but cheap) $45-a-night hotel near the Shwe Dagon Pagoda.

'Train is full,' Mr Nay Aung, the ticket agent, had told me at the station. He suggested that I come back the next day.

I waited a day. I walked to the Shwe Dagon and around the city. I saw hardly any tourists, not much traffic, all the signs of a dictatorship: selfishness and paranoia clinging to power, epitomized by well-dressed soldiers in heavy boots, threadbare citizens in rubber flip-flops. I was full of admiration for my younger self. Yangon had been ramshackle then, but I had no money; I had succeeded by improvising, flying by the seat of my pants. One of the lessons of this second trip was that I had been a hardy traveller, and yet I knew it was not so much hardiness as a desperation to make the trip fruitful.

'You are so lucky,' Mr Nay Aung said to me the following day. 'We have a cancellation.'

He sold me a ticket to Mandalay: first class, but with four people in the compartment. The train would leave around one in the afternoon and arrive in Mandalay at three the next morning. This improbable schedule – only one train a day – Mr Nay Aung could not explain.

'Yes, it is not convenient to arrive at three o'clock. It will be so dark then.'

I remembered the Mandalay train as basic, the trip an ordeal. This train was in better shape, but it was no less a ghost train, a decaying relic of the past, taking me from the skeletal city haunted by the military to the northerly ghost town of Mandalay. I felt that strongly as we set off. I had no idea how accurate that vision of Mandalay was, as a city of wraiths and the living dead, of people being screamed at by demonic soldiers.

In the sleeping compartment a young Frenchman was lolling in his berth, his sinuous Thai girlfriend, in her teens, wrapped around him. I said hello and then went to the platform to buy some oranges.

A monk with a bundle slung over his shoulder was being pestered by a ragged Burmese man. The monk was speaking English and trying to give the man some money – some folded worn notes.

'No, two dollah,' the Burmese man said.

'This same, these kyats,' the monk said.

'Two dollah,' the Burmese man said again.

I said, 'What's the problem?'

The ragged man was a scooter rickshaw driver who had taken the monk to the station. He insisted, as many Burmese did of foreigners, on being paid in American dollars.

'Here,' I said, giving the man the two dollars. The man took them with both hands, fingers extended, then touched them to his forehead.

'You're a stranger,' the monk said. 'You don't know me.'

I had been reading a Buddhist text, the Diamond Sutra, as background for another Indian novella I was writing, 'The Gateway of India', so I was able to say, 'The Diamond Sutra says that you should give and not think about anything else. You don't speak Burmese?'

'I'm from Korea.' It turned out that he was on this train to Mandalay, the fourth person in my compartment. He said hello to the Frenchman and the Thai girl, and soon after, with a clang of couplings, the train started to move.

I looked out of the window and marvelled again, as I had on arriving in Yangon. Nothing had changed on the outskirts, either – after the decaying bungalows and creekside villages, it was just dry fields, goats cropping grass on the tracks, ducks on murky ponds, burdened women walking, looking haughty because they were balancing bundles on their heads, slender sarong-wearing Burmese and befouled ditches.

I dozed, I woke up; the Frenchman and his girlfriend had separated and were asleep in the upper berths. The monk sat opposite me.

He was a Zen monk, and his name was Tapa Snim ('Snim means monk in Korean'). He had just arrived in Myanmar. He was fifty. He had shifted his small bundle; it was now in the corner of his berth. He was a slender man, slightly built, very tidy, with clean brownish robes and a neatly shaved head that gave him a grey skull. He was not the smiling evasive monk I was used to seeing, who walked several inches above the ground, but an animated and watchful man who met my gaze and answered my questions.

'How long have you been a monk?' I asked.

'I became a monk at twenty-one,' Tapa Snim said. 'I have been meditating for twenty-nine years, but also travelling. I have been in a monastery here in Yangon for a few days, but I want to stay in a monastery in Mandalay.'

'How long will you be here?'

'Meditation for six months, then I will go to Laos and Cambodia – same, to meditate in a monastery.'

'You just show up and say, "Here I am"?'

'Yes. I show some papers to prove who I am. They are Theravada Buddhist. I am Mahayana.. We believe that we can obtain full enlightenment.'

'Like the Buddha?'

'We can become Buddha, totally and completely.'

'Your English is very good,' I said.

'I have travelled in fifteen Buddhist countries. You know something about Buddhism – you mentioned the Diamond Sutra.'

'I read it recently. I like the part of it that describes what life on earth is:

> A falling star, a bubble in a stream.
> A flame in the wind. Frost in the sun.
> A flash of lightning in a summer cloud.

'A phantom in a dream,' Tapa Snim said, the line I'd forgotten. 'That's the poem at the end. Have you read the Sixth Patriarch's Sutra?'

I said no, and he wrote the name in my notebook.

'All Zen Buddhists know this,' he said, tapping the name.

We travelled for a while in silence. Seeing me scribbling in my notebook, the Frenchman said, 'You must be a writer.'

He had a box of food, mainly potato crisps, pumpkin seeds and peanuts. He shared a bag of pumpkin seeds with us.

Up the great flat plain of Pegu Province, dusty white in the sun, the wide river valley, baking in the dry season. Small simple huts and villages, temples in the distance, cows reclining in the scrappy shade of slender trees. Tall solitary stupas, some like enormous whitewashed pawns on a distant chessboard, others like oversized lamp finials, under a blue and cloudless sky.

The bamboo here had the shape of giant antlers, and here and there pigs trotted through brambles to drink at ponds filled with lotuses. It was a vision of the past, undeveloped, serene at a distance, and up close harsh and unforgiving.

Miles and miles of drained and harvested paddy fields, the rice stalks cut and rolled into bundles and propped up to await collection. No sign of a tractor or any mechanization, only a woman with a big bundle on her head, a pair of yoked oxen – remarkable sights for being so old-fashioned. And then an ox cart loaded with bales of cotton, and across a mile of paddy fields a gold stupa.

I walked to the vestibule of the train, for the exercise, and talked awhile with an old toothless man going to Taungoo. When I asked him about the past, he seemed a little vague.

'I'm fifty-two,' he said, and I was reminded how poverty aged people prematurely.

When I went back to the compartment, Tapa Snim was rummaging in his bag. I watched him take out an envelope, and then he began knotting the two strands that made this simple square of cotton cloth into a sack.

'Do you have another bag?' I asked, because this one seemed improbably small for a long-distance traveller.

'No. These are all my possessions.'

Everything not just for a year of travel, but everything he owned in the world, in a bag he easily slung under one arm. True, this was a warm climate, but the sack was smaller than a supermarket bag.

'May I ask you what's inside?'

Tapa Snim, tugging the knot loose, gladly showed me the entire contents.

'My bowl, very important,' he said, taking out the first item. It was a small black plastic soup bowl with a close-fitting lid. He used it for begging alms, but he also used it for rice.

In a small bag: a piece of soap in a container, sunglasses, a flashlight, a tube of mosquito repellent, a tin of aspirin.

In a small plastic box: a spool of grey thread, a pair of scissors, nail clippers, Q-Tips, a thimble, needles, rubber bands, a two-inch mirror, a tube of cream to treat foot fungus, a stick of lip balm, nasal spray and razor blades.

'Also very important,' he said, showing me the razor blades. 'I shave my head every fifteen days.'

Neatly folded, one thin wool sweater, a shawl he called a *kasaya*, a change of clothes. In a document pouch he had a notebook and some papers, a photograph showing him posed with a dozen other monks ('to introduce myself'), and a large document in Chinese characters he called his *bhikkhu* certificate, the official proof he was a monk, with signatures and seals and brushwork. He also had a Sharp electronic dictionary, which allowed him to translate from many languages, and a string of beads – 108 beads, the spiritual number.

As I was writing down the list, he said, 'And this' – his straw hat – 'and this' – his fan.

'Nothing else?'

'Nothing.'

'What about money?'

'That's my secret.'

And then carefully he placed the objects on the opened cloth and drew the cloth together into a sack, everything he owned on earth.

'Tell me how you meditate.'

'You know the Japanese word *koan*,' he said. It wasn't a question. 'For example, in ancient China, a student asked an important Zen monk, "What is Buddha?" The monk answered, "One pinecone tree in front of a garden."'

Through the train window I could see a village set in a bower of dense trees, offering shade, scattered groves of banana and coconut, more lotus ponds, people on bikes. And here before me the shaven-headed and gently smiling Tapa Snim.

'I meditate on that. "One pinecone tree in front of a garden." It is a particular tree.'

'How long have you been using this *koan*?'

'Years. Years. Years.' He smiled again. 'Twelve hours a day.'

'Is it working?'

'I will understand eventually. Everyone has Buddha-spirit in their mind. By reason of sufferings and desires and anger we can't find it.' He rocked a little on the seat and went on. 'If we get rid of suffering and desire and anger, we can become a Buddha.'

'How do I get rid of them?'

'Meditate. Empty your mind – your mind must be vacant. Non-mind is the deepest stage of the deep stage.' He asked to borrow my pen and the little notebook I'd been using. He said, 'Every night I have a serious question in my head – every day and night. Look.'

He set down six Chinese characters, inscribing them slowly, each slash and dot. Then he poked at each of them, translating.

'Sun-faced Buddha, moon-faced Buddha,' he said. 'For twenty-six years I have thought about this. If I solve this, I will know truth. It is my destination, my whole life, to solve this problem.'

'But how did you happen to choose these images?'

'One day, a famous monk, Ma Tsou, was asked, "How are you?" This was his reply.'

'Why did you come here to meditate? You could have stayed in Korea.'

He said, 'Buddha travelled! So I travel. I am looking for enlightenment.'

'What do you think about Burma?'

He laughed and told me that on the day of his arrival he had gone to the railway station but the ticket window was closed. So he waited on a bench and, waiting there, had fallen asleep. When he woke up he discovered that the pouch at his waist had been razored open – literally, by a cutpurse – and some of his money stolen.

'But small money! Big money is in a secret place.'

'You've been to India?'

'India can be dangerous,' he said. 'But I have a theory about India.' He sat forward, eager to explain. 'I see many poor people there, and I think, What is their karma? They are the poorest people in the world. Why do they receive this big suffering? Eh?'

I said I had no idea, and that the people here – right outside the window – seemed miserably poor, living in bamboo huts and steadying wooden ploughs pulled by oxen, and labouring under the load of heavy bales.

'India is worse,' he said. 'This is my ridiculous thought. I know it is silly, but . . .' By 'but' he implied that it was not ridiculous at all and that I should not be too quick to judge him. 'Indian people have many bad karmas. In their history, they created violence; they destroyed Buddhist stupas and persecuted monks. They all the time blame Muslims, but Hindus have been just as bad. In my Indian travel I think this is the deep reason for the suffering there.'

'What about Korea – any suffering?'

'Suffering everywhere! In Korea we have mad crazy Christians, because we are under the influence of the United States.'

'Reverend Moon?'

'Many people like him!' Tapa Snim said. 'I am glad to be here.'

In the setting sun, the muted pinks and browns, the subdued light, the long shadows of the labouring bent-over harvesters. And in the dusk, the unmistakable sign of rural poverty: no lights in the villages, only the lamp-glow in small huts or the small flare of cooking fires at ground level, the smell of woodsmoke. All the train windows were open to insects and smoke and, passing a swamp or a pond, a dampness in the air, the malodorous uprush of the hum of stagnant water.

The last discernible station before darkness fell was Taungoo, a kind of boundary – it was all Upper Burma after this. While I'd been talking to Tapa Snim, the young Frenchman and his girlfriend had crept out. I asked Tapa Snim to watch my bag and walked through three or four carriages to the dining car.

Sitting there, drinking a tall bottle of Myanmar beer, I felt the kind of wordless bliss I'd experienced in Sri Lanka, at the little guesthouse in Galle, as though I'd come all this way to be uplifted by the night air, the breeze rushing through the train windows, tearing at the grubby curtains, the slopped and food-splashed tables where Burmese, propped on their elbows, were slurping fried rice and noodles, laughing and drinking, the darkness outside broken only by the occasional lantern or burst of fire or candle flame, illuminating nothing but itself, but 'a candle is enough to light the world'. Apart from that, nothing to report. I felt lucky to have met Tapa Snim, and I was thinking, Glad I came.

'May I sit here?'

I said yes, of course, there were very few empty seats in the car. He was a smiling man of forty or so, Oo Mindon. He said he was a merchant.

'I sell biscuits, noodles, cigarettes,' he said. 'Children's clothes.'

He owned a stall in the Myoma bazaar in Ye-u, a town northwest of Mandalay. It was a 150-mile journey, six hours by bus from there on bad roads, he said. All overland travel in Myanmar was slow and dirty, but though he did not complain about the difficulty, he clucked as he described the distances and the road conditions.

After the usual questions – country? wife? children? job? – he laughed and said, 'I like democracy.'

He was a stallholder in a small bazaar in a benighted corner of the country, north-central Myanmar, and he launched into a long denunciation of the government, the generals, the roads, the disrepair of the trains and the buildings. He travelled quite a lot, supplying outlying towns with biscuits and noodles, and he said the situation was terrible. He used all the old names: Burma, Rangoon instead of Yangon, Maymyo instead of Pyin-Oo-Lwin.

'The army is no good. They make trouble.'

'What's the answer?'

'We want elections,' he said.

'Didn't Aung San Suu Kyi win the last one?'

'Yes. She is good. She should be in the government. We like her.'

To bait him I said, 'Why do you want democracy?'

'Because life will be better. We will have development – not this, what you see, rich soldiers and poor people.'

A big boy joined us at the table, Oo Mindon's son, who was sixteen. He did not speak a word of English, though he was in high school. This was the next generation, the one that the generals had intimidated and shortchanged by limiting their education. Oo Mindon himself had studied English and had a secondary-school education.

'What does he do?' I asked Oo Mindon, of his son.

'He likes to play video games,' he said, and furiously manipulated his thumbs to illustrate the obsession.

I'd had no lunch, yet, hungry as I was, I did not want to risk the fried rice being jogged and swilled in a blackened wok by the churning wooden paddle of the chef in his sweat-soaked undershirt, a cigarette dangling from his lips – or was it the sight of the plates being dunked in the sludgy water of the washbasin?

Back in the compartment, seeing me hunched over my notebook, the Frenchman said again, 'You must be a writer' – the only words he spoke to me in fifteen hours.

Tapa Snim, the Zen Buddhist, was quietly sleeping in a small compact way, wrapped in his robes and pillowing his head on his bundle of possessions. I dozed but could not stay asleep. The problem was the over-bright fluorescent lights on the compartment ceiling that could not be turned off, which kept waking me from hectic dreams of persecution.

Towards four in the morning, lights flashed outside the train, the marshalling yards of Mandalay. My memory of the city was of air so dense that at twilight it resembled the fog of a London particular: furious dust clouding orangy bulbs, dimming them; air that had made me gag; a nebulous nightmare of swirling murk.

The air was just as thick with choking dust as I lingered on the station platform to say goodbye to Tapa Snim. And then I hurried out to the street, hounded by rickshaw drivers. I had the name of an inexpensive hotel. I singled out an elderly driver with a weary face and got in the back of his scooter rickshaw, and he drove me into the darkness.

The back streets of Mandalay were unpaved, rutted and irregular. There were no streetlights, the shops were shut, though some houses had glaring spotlights for security purposes. The air was foul, the night hot, the darkness oppressive. The invisible city stank, and even after fifteen or twenty minutes the old man was still jogging along, humping and bumping on the bad surface. It was four in the morning.

This knowledge that I was completely in the hands of a stranger was not something new. It had happened many times on my trip. A man representing himself as a driver offered me a ride in his jalopy several times in Turkey; again in Georgia; memorably, on the border of Turkmenistan and Uzbekistan I'd had to crawl through the passenger-side window before I was bounced to Bokhara; in India a number of times, by rickshaw wallahs. And there was my humbling hitchhiking experience in Sri Lanka, the rattletraps of Yangon, and now this, the scooter rickshaw in Mandalay darkness, no one awake. All these modes of transport counted as the Orient Express.

But this was the ghostliest experience I'd yet seen. The night-black streets of risen thickened dust, the dim lights, the smell of dead fires and cooling embers, the chatter and flap of the scooter, the stranger riding with his back turned to me – all of this filled me with the same surrealistic sense of being borne into the darkness by a skinny old man in rags, spirited into his world. I thought: I don't know who he is. I don't know where I am or where I'm going. I could not read a single sign, and there wasn't a soul around.

I was alone and apprehensive, with the traveller's awareness of having made a leap in the dark. This heightened my senses and gave a sharpness to every moment that passed, every smell, every flash of light. Afterwards, when I thought about my travelling in Upper Burma, my first memory was of this night ride in the darkness, the heat in my face. The reason is probably simple: I was alone, I was with a stranger, I had no idea where I was going, I was moving through inspissated blackness. It summed up what was most vivid in my travelling life, but especially on this ghostly revisit – rattling into the night in this phantom rickshaw.

The slowness of the scooter rickshaw exaggerated the distance, but even half an hour in the darkness of such a place was suspenseful.

I was surprised when I saw the hotel ahead, just off the road, the driver having kept his word. Before I paid him, I made sure a room was available. The building was locked, the door chained, but I woke the night watchman, and he unchained the door and brought me to a desk. A man lying supine on a blanket behind the desk had heard the knock and was waking and yawning.

On the sunny days that followed – only the nights were befogged – I saw that Mandalay hadn't changed much either. It had more hotels, including a luxurious one, Singapore-owned, within walking distance of mine, that seemed empty. But there was no other prosperity or newness in the great flat city on its grid of streets. One of the blessings of such poverty was the absence of traffic. Just a few cars, many motorbikes and scooters, lots of bicycles, and that relic of the old Burma, the bicycle rickshaw, or pedicab.

The beauty of the bicycle rickshaw is the breeze in your face, fresh air and a placid journey, travelling at almost a walking pace through the deep sand of the back lanes of Mandalay. I found a man to take me to Maha Muni Temple, less for the temple experience than to travel from the southeast corner of the fort, through the populous part of the city, to the complex of temples and the monasteries of the southwest.

The driver, a slender but sturdy older man, spoke English well. He said life was awful, and like many other Burmese who told me this, he spoke in a whisper and often looked around.

'I look back,' he said, turning his head, 'because someone might be listening.'

At Maha Muni a group of pretty girls beckoned me over to where they crouched in the temple garden under a tree. One of them held on her knees a basket of shivering sparrows.

'Good luck. You let one go. Five hundred kyat.'

For twenty-five cents I could give a bird its freedom. I gave her a dollar and she handed me one stupefied bird at a time, and off each one went, chirping as they soared away.

The sights of Mandalay – the gold temples, the multi-level Zegyo bazaar, the carved teak of Shwe Nandaw Palace, the busy monasteries, the fort with its ramparts and its moat filled with lilies, the hill to the north with more temples – none of these held my attention as strongly as the driver.

His name was Oo Nawng, and he had the broad, kindly-seeming Polynesian face of many Burmese. He was exactly my age. He had spent his working life, almost forty years, as a primary school teacher in a small town outside Mandalay, and had retired at the age of sixty-two. He had two daughters; one of them, married to a carpenter, had five children and lived in a village on the road to Pyin-Oo-Lwin. The other daughter was a tailor, a seamstress, who was in her late thirties. Oo Nawng had urged her to get married, but (although some men had expressed a romantic interest) she refused, saying, 'I can't get married. I have to look after my poor father and mother.'

In ragged shorts, a faded shirt and a woven bamboo pith helmet, Oo Nawng was poor in a vivid and easily explainable way. After he had retired from teaching, he lost the hut that went with the job. His pension was the equivalent of $2 a month. He had found a hut to rent on Mandalay's outskirts, 'a small bamboo house'. The rent was $4 a month. One of the reasons for his retirement was his kidney ailment, which required hospitalization. The cost of his medicine had emptied his savings, and though his daughter's sewing helped, he was struggling to get by.

The bicycle rickshaw on which he sat with dignity was the last resort. He was too old to get any other kind of job. He owned the bike, but the rickshaw itself, the seat, the wheel, the footrest, which was fastened to the bike by a clamp, was rented, 25 cents a day.

I found out all this, and more, by traipsing around Mandalay with him, because he knew the sights, he knew where good food could be found, he was openhearted and candid. I wanted to find the fish soup I remembered from long ago, spiced and creamy, with noodles. It was called *mohingas*, he reminded me, and took me to a place that served it. He had some too. He took me to a Muslim trader named Soe Moe, to a trader who sold old opium weights, to a Burmese man who made long trips into Nagaland – not the Naga Christians who were numerous on the Indian side, but animists, monkey worshippers and fetishists, living traditional lives in jungle clearings. The Burmese man had piles of weird artefacts: necklaces of monkey skulls and bison teeth and hornbill casques, antlers, masks, bone armlets, knives, swords, spears and textiles. In trade, the man gave medicines to the Naga people, because no government agencies ever went up the rivers and into the jungles that bordered India.

When I talked to Oo Nawng about the future, he laughed and said, 'What future? I'm old!'

'You're my age.'

Oo Nawng wrinkled his nose and said, 'I don't want to live a long time.'

'Because of your kidney problem?'

'No. Because I have no money. How long can I pedal a bike? Maybe two years more. If I get some money, I'd like to live a long time. But if not, I would prefer to die.'

All his years of studying, homework and teaching had allowed him to make this fatalistic statement in perfect English. That's what it came to: his intelligence and fluency gave him the ability to pronounce his own mournful epitaph.

He was one of the millions who didn't matter. He was old, he couldn't fight, couldn't work, wasn't important to the economy – a drain on available resources. The military men who ran Myanmar would have said that Oo Nawng was better off dead. Oo Nawng himself agreed. After a working life of educating children, he was a pauper.

At a fruit juice stand he said, 'Eighty-five per cent of people are against the government.' He sipped his juice. He said, 'The other fifteen per cent are government relatives. And Chinese.'

I had come across this hatred for the Chinese on my first trip. I heard much more of it this time, because the local Chinese were now able to make deals with the bureaucrats and traders in the People's Republic.

They were in the gem trade, the drug trade, in food and wood export. The mansions of Mandalay, in walled compounds, were mainly owned by Chinese merchants. The Sinocentric Singapore government, the People's Republic and India were supporters of the Myanmar military dictatorship, propping up the regime and its arrest and imprisonment of people for political crimes. A number of Burmese told me in whispers that the country was full of collaborators, informers and spies. Defying all the twenty-first-century trends of liberalization, Myanmar was going sideways and backwards.

The government that had held on for forty years was determined to go on holding on. Quite a lot of money was at stake, because as a well-educated Burmese man told me in Mandalay, 'The government is making a lot of money on drugs – on the opium trade. The generals here are all involved with the world drug cartels.'

I heard lots of praise for the United States in distancing itself from the regime, and lots of blame for China and Russia and Singapore in support- ing it – China especially. But China's prosperity, its need for oil and wood and food, had created a new dynamic. China had no interest in any country's developing democratic institutions; on the contrary, it was a natural ally of repressive regimes. When the World Bank withheld funds from an African country because it was corrupt and tyrannous, demanding that it hold an election before it could qualify for aid, China would appear with money – 'rogue aid', with no strings attached, and got the teak, the food and the drugs.

'We could have an internal coup, but it wouldn't change much,' one man told me. 'There are no liberals in this government.'

This man too had been reduced. 'My family had a Mercedes when you were here before. Now all I have is a Chinese motorbike.'

'What will come?' Oo Nawng said. 'More of the same.'

He said there weren't enough tourists, and the ones who visited were not interested in taking a bicycle rickshaw. They wanted a taxi. They spent money at the hotels. He was glad that I had hired him three days in a row, but I would go, and what then?

'I meditate twice a day,' he said, as though explaining how he made life bearable. He woke at four thirty in the morning and sat for an hour. After dinner, he did the same. 'My *koan* is "Buddha meditates monk". I pray and' – he shut his eyes and spoke with intensity – 'Buddha sits on my head.'

It was too complicated to explain, he said. Most of Oo Nawng's teeth were missing, and he was down to one good front tooth.

He seemed to represent the melancholy I felt in this return. He wasn't downhearted. He was realistic. He did not want to live well, only to have the meagre rent for his bamboo hut and some money for food. What was the point of living if you had no food?

He seemed to find it mildly amusing that I was shocked by his saying he'd rather die.

Oo Nawng preyed on my mind. Thinking about him, I could not sleep. I had visions of him in his battered pith helmet of sun-darkened bamboo, pedalling his rickshaw along the ruts of Mandalay's back streets. The little skinny man with his rusted bike and his rented rickshaw and his notebook. Like me, he too was a ghost – invisible, ageing, just looking on, a kind of helpless haunter.

People gave money to children in the Third World, to orphanages, to empower women, to clinics, to schools, to governments, but they never gave money to people who were simply old so they could live a little longer and die in dignity. Oo Nawng wasn't old – he was my age – but in Burma this counted as elderly.

The day before I was to leave for a trip to the north, a sentimental journey to Pyin-Oo-Lwin, I looked for him on his usual street corner, under the big shade tree. No sign of him.

I took the trip to Pyin-Oo-Lwin. On my return, I looked for Oo Nawng again on his street corner. The other rickshaw drivers said they hadn't seen him. I thought I might find him in the market, where a trader might know where he was – Oo Nawng had brought me here to look at tribal tattoo implements, little stilettos the Karen people used as finials for their tattooing needles. I asked Soe Moe, the Muslim trader I'd met earlier (his real name was Hajji Ali; the Burmese name was fanciful), whether he'd seen Oo Nawng.

'That old man who brought you here? No.' Then, without any prompting from me, he said, 'He is so poor.'

'I've been thinking about him.'

'He's a good man,' Soe Moe said. 'He has a good heart. He brings people here. I give him a little.'

Soe Moe meant that if a person bought something, he'd give him a tip.

That night I thought of Oo Nawng again, as a superior ghost, a *nat*, a Burmese guardian figure dressed in a long gold tunic, smiling, obliging, radiating goodness and protection. He reminded me of my father, the soul of kindness. And the following morning I went to Oo Nawng's street corner again and waited. No one had seen him. This seemed odd, given his punctuality. One man said, 'He's not coming today. It's Saturday.'

I went away, fearing that he was dead. Later in the morning I looked again – no Oo Nawng. I walked down a side street where men were selling oranges out of wheelbarrows, and others hawking onions and bananas. I kept walking in the noon heat, the sun beating on my head, thinking of Oo Nawng's battered pith helmet.

After forty-five minutes of useless kicking through the sand piles and gravel of these streets, I turned and – as in my dreams – saw Oo Nawng pedalling towards me, smiling.

'Get on, sir.'

I got on to the seat of the rickshaw.

'Where to today?'

'Take me to a quiet place where no one can see us.'

He pedalled a while, then stopped in the shade of a banyan tree at the opening to an alley.

'Quiet enough?'

'Perfect.' I then gave him an unsealed envelope.

He looked in. He did not seem surprised, though he touched the contents to his forehead. Then he frowned and said, 'We must go change it. You change it. They won't believe me – they'll say I stole it.'

So we went to a moneychanger, and the fat envelope of dollars was swapped for a big dirty brick of Myanmar kyats, secured by rubber bands.

'Let's get a drink.'

We drank lemonade, and he told me his full name, Oo Ng Nawng. He wrote his address, and after that, *trishaw driver, chair man*. As though thinking out loud, he said, 'I will pay my rent for a year, maybe two years. I will buy a secondhand rickshaw. Later, I can sell it. Yes, yes.'

'Good.'

'I'm happy,' he said. His smile, too, was almost unearthly, beatific, a ghost smile of reassurance. 'Now where do you want to go, Mister Baw?'

18. The Train to Pyin-Oo-Lwin

In the darkness of early morning in the train's ordinary class, all the windows open, nothing was visible except the blurred outlines of the low buildings. Mandalay, like a city sketched in charcoal, was little more than these soft tracings and its complex smell, of wood fires and dust, dog hair and blossoms, crumbled brick and incense, diesel fumes, stagnant water and the aroma of small fried cakes that the other passengers were wolfing out of fat-soaked wrappings of newspaper.

The way to Pyin-Oo-Lwin was the way to China. Nine hours north was the town of Mong Yu, on the border, with the Chinese town of Wanding on the other side. At the end of another day's travel, about 300 miles by bus over the mountain roads of Yunnan, was the provincial capital of Kunming. Myanmar's close relationship with China meant that the border was wide open. Myanmar trucks went north carrying vegetables, huge teak logs, crates of precious rubies and bales of opium; Chinese trucks came south with cargoes of rubber sandals and tin pots and cheap bikes, arms and ammo.

This train was so slow that the sun came up before we began the serious climb out of the flat river valley of Mandalay. As soon as we ascended the first hills, the air freshened with cooler aromas of vegetation, the yellow blobby flowers of the kasein trees, the canal odours with their hyacinths, which the Burmese feed their pigs. Ponds were layered with white lotuses, lovely orchards of plum trees spread out for miles, and fields bristled with onions. The recent rain had left a sparkle in the air – the sweetness still lingered.

The young teak trees here were spindly, with big fan-shaped leaves, lots of them beside the track.

'They are twenty-two years old,' Ko Tin said. He was on the seat beside me – upright, on cushions, like a booth in a diner, too narrow to recline on, too stiff-backed to be comfortable, but Pyin-Oo-Lwin was only five hours up the line.

'In Kachin there are teak forests, trees one hundred years old. The Chinese buy them.'

In the distance was a great blue humpbacked mountain, its scored and shoulder-like ridge extending for miles.

'We call that mountain "the Buffalo",' Ko Tin said. The name could not have been more apt. Once hearing it, I no longer saw a mountain but only a muscular animal.

I was inexpressibly glad to be heading this way on this creaky train – grateful that so little had changed, though I hated to think that the time warp was entirely due to the military dictatorship, which had kept Myanmar in a state of suspended animation. All that had changed was that the prisons were bigger, and the army was so huge it was like a parallel population – healthier, better dressed, better educated, feared and hated ('Soldiers here don't have to pay taxes!'). In a country where everyone else lived precariously, the military was secure. But because of their struggle, the Burmese were eager to talk, to help, to work, and in spite of the threats and dangers, willing to confide in a foreigner.

I mentioned the army and people said without prompting: We hate them. I mentioned the government and they said: They're corrupt, they're bad, they're destroying the country. I mentioned Aung San Suu Kyi and her fourteen years of house arrest and they said: We want her. Or: We want democracy. I asked questions about Buddhism and they said: The monks are angry too! When I raised these subjects I always got the same answers.

Ko Tin was no different. He said he hated the army, and 'I like democracy.' And he mentioned that anyone who criticized the government was imprisoned.

'Do you know people who've gone to prison?' I asked.

'I know many people who, one day, just disappeared. Here – then not here. Went away suddenly. That is what happens. You never know where they went. They go and never come back. You never see the police. It all happens in the dark.'

Now on the steepness of the mountain slopes, the train was in and out of tunnels and crossing the motor road. Convoys of trucks, tarpaulins lashed to their cargo, lumbered up the road.

One open-sided truck was filled with straw.

'Watermelons,' Ko Tin said, 'going to China.'

One flatbed truck with enormous shrouded figures.

'Carved Buddha images. We make good ones. The Chinese people buy them for their temples.'

Other trucks laden with rice, tomatoes, beans, onions, bananas, oranges, lemons, peppers – poor, hungry Myanmar supplying food to wealthy China. Myanmar was like a fiefdom of China, sending tribute, so that China could abandon its farms, build factories in its paddy fields, and spend more time developing its manufacturing and technology.

I had been wakeful at five a.m. when we set off, but a few hours later I was slumped in my seat, asleep. I woke in the chill of the higher altitude – about 3,000 feet – and saw coffee bushes, flower stalls and poinsettia trees seven feet tall.

Also army camps, many of them: big walled compounds, well-built houses and office buildings and barracks, the neatest landscaping, and one had its own airport. All of them were probably here because of the salubrious climate on the lower slopes of the Shan States.

Just before we got to Pyin-Oo-Lwin, the train passed the outer walls of what could have been a university campus – gates, archways, green lawns, flower beds – but was (Ko Tin told me) a large military academy and had a sign in Burmese and English: THE TRIUMPHANT ELITE OF THE FUTURE.

I had known Pyin-Oo-Lwin as Maymyo. All that had changed in thirty-three years was the name. Almost the first thing I saw were pony carts – the gaily painted tongas that resembled small wood-framed stage-coaches. I had taken one long ago to the old guesthouse Candacraig. In any other country the pony carts would have been a tourist lark, some-thing picturesque in which a visitor could sit for a photo. But no, here they were still used as public transport, the cheapest form, a short-distance conveyance to and from the bazaar.

The railway station was the same, probably from the 1930s, a Burmese man told me, though the simplicity suggested much earlier – one-storey, brick and timber, tin roof, the train schedules painted on to the white-washed wall. Beside the new name was the message 3506 ABOVE SEA LEVEL.

A train waiting in the station was due to leave shortly for Lashio, an eleven-hour trip, not far from the China border. I was happy to get out here and reacquaint myself. I had no desire to go further – didn't have the stomach for it. Once again, I was somewhat in awe of my younger self, that 32-year-old who sat on wooden benches in third class all the way to Naun Peng, just to see the all-steel Gokteik Viaduct that crossed a gorge in the upper Shan States. I had been hard-up and home-sick, with no idea of what lay ahead, worried about money, not sure of my route. I had been completely out of touch and – while tramping through the mud of Maymyo and hailing a pony cart to Candacraig – missing my wife and children.

'You know Candacraig?' I asked a man lingering at the station.

'I take you.'

He had a thirty-year-old Datsun. I had remembered Burma as a country of old cars, in some cases antiques, bangers and jalopies.

The driver's name was Abdul Hamid, a man perhaps in his seventies. He asked me where I was from, and was pleased when I told him.

'I like Texas,' he said.

'Why Texas?'

'Cowboys. John Wayne.' He drove a little, murmuring, then said, 'Gary Cooper. From films.'

Pyin-Oo-Lwin was frozen in time, which is to say it looked bigger and shabbier than before – the market, the shop-houses, the arcades, the bungalows, the clock tower in the town centre showing the wrong time and lettered PURCELL TOWER – 1936, perhaps the heyday of Maymyo.

As a British hill station it had been planned by Colonel James May, and for his pains, his urban planning, the British had bestowed his name on the town. Quite rightly, the Burmese changed the name back to that of the village it had once been, its only drawback being that Pyin-Oo-Lwin was hard to say without faltering.

But the villas of the Raj remained, the most amazing oversized bungalows and tin-roofed châteaux, many of them with a tower or cupola, a set of verandas and a *porte-cochère* for the carriage, and tall chimneys – the town was chilly in January. These houses were of wood with red or painted brick facings, still looking elegant and rather bizarre. In England they would have seemed like satirical versions of parsonages or vicarages or shooting lodges, but here they looked outlandishly, assertively handsome and spacious.

Some had twee Cotswoldish names like 'The Hedges' and 'Rose Manor', and others had Burmese names. Many locations had two names: Maymyo and Pyin-Oo-Lwin were interchangeable. Tapsy Road was now also Thiksar Road. Candacraig was the Thiri Myaing Hotel.

But Candacraig was the same place, a big imperial double-fronted villa with a tower. The only difference was that instead of standing at the end of a muddy road, in a damp sloping field among scrubby bushes, the building – freshly painted – was now set in gardens. The landscaping included some hopeful topiary and flower beds, a gravel walk and a fixed-up tennis court. The front walkway was lined with low trimmed hedges and clusters of pink and white impatiens. Just inside the front veranda was a foundation stone lettered CANDACRAIG, 1904.

It was a 'chummery', a sort of frat house of the Raj where young single men – someone like George Orwell, who was a policeman, or H. H. Munro, who was also in the police – would have gone in the hot season for a month of leave. The more established officers of empire, with wives and children, had their own bungalows or villas. The town had always had a large population of Indian descent, and many Nepalese too, descendants of the courageous and well-drilled Gurkha soldiers the British had brought to Burma.

I walked up the path and on to the veranda and inside the open door, into the past.

Here there was no let-down. The whole place had been restored: the big varnished staircase with its curved banisters, the teak railings running along the upper gallery as in an English country house, the vast entryway rising two storeys to the beamed ceiling and the stuffed buffalo head, and more trophies – small, sharp deer horns mounted on plaques in a long row.

I stood before the bare desk with its guest book open on it. The floor had been polished, the place was clean, with its tang of new varnish. Not a single guest in sight, no one at all, yet it was as warm and as welcome a destination as it had been thirty-three years before – more so, since it was for me, as some other places had been, a homecoming. It was full of memories, a ghost-haunted house in an unthreatening sense.

Though I had claimed in *The Great Railway Bazaar* to have encountered him on the train – I wanted to give my little trip some drama – it was here at Candacraig that I'd first met the hospitable Mr Bernard.

This kindly and dignified man had challenged me to guess his age, and when I guessed wrong, he told me he was eighty, saying, 'I was born in eighteen ninety-four in Rangoon. My father was an Indian, but a Catholic. That is why I am called Bernard. My father was a soldier in the Indian army. He had been a soldier his whole life – I suppose he joined up in Madras in the eighteen seventies. He was in the Twenty-sixth Madras Infantry and he came to Rangoon with his regiment in eighteen eighty-eight. I used to have his picture, but when the Japanese occupied Burma . . . all our possessions were scattered, and we lost so many things.'

Mr Bernard, a colonial from a transplanted family (he'd never been to India), was a link to the nineteenth century. His memory was wonderfully precise. He told me in detail about his working on the railway, his army career, his life as a chef and a steward. He had met Chiang Kai-shek and Lord Curzon and the Duke of Kent – all in Mandalay, where he served them six-course dinners at the officers' mess. He remembered the day Queen Victoria died, the day the Japanese invaded Maymyo, and he told me about his many children. I met a couple of them when they came to my room to bring me buckets of hot water for my bath and to build a fire in my bedroom fireplace.

Now I was back in this stately mansion, glad that it still existed and was in business.

'Yes?'

A man slipped behind the registration desk and twisted the guest book my way for my signature.

'Welcome, sir.'

He was a smiling slender Indian, about fifty or so, in a baseball cap and a jacket – he had just come from supervising some gardeners repaving a path. The clothes made him seem athletic.

I said, 'I was here once a long time ago. This place is in really good shape.'

'Recently renovated,' the young man said. 'New paint. New varnish. Better plumbing. When were you here, sir?'

'Thirty-something years ago!'

'A long time, sir.'

'I wrote about it – about being here, meeting Mr Bernard.'

'My father,' the man said. He looked at me narrowly, and then his smile brightened. He had beautiful teeth, a friendly face. 'You are Mr Paul Theroux.'

'That's me.'

'I'm Peter Bernard' – and he shook my hand. 'I'm manager now. I'm so glad to see you. We talk about you all the time. We have a copy of your book. You were up there in room eleven. Let me take you there.'

It is not often in life that you make a general travel plan and everything works out perfectly, but this was one of those times. And the best part was that, because perfection is unimaginable, there were limits to hopes. The rest came unexpectedly, unbidden, undreamed of.

'I remember you, sir!' he said.

It was more than I'd hoped for, and that was pure pleasure, a return to the past without an atom of disappointment – the past recaptured, like a refuge, everything that I'd wanted a homecoming to be but that a homecoming (at least in my case) never was. This was a wonderful way back, as though this man in his fifties, who'd been a teenager before, had been waiting for me to return.

'You came from Lashio on the train, on a pony cart from the station,' he said. 'You smoked a pipe. You wore a black shirt. Such a small bag you had.' We were in the room – spacious, with a fireplace and a view of the gardens. 'I saw you writing at the table here.'

So, at last, a witness to my long-ago misery, my loneliness, my scribbling. I said, 'Your father – what happened to him?'

'Dead, sir. Some years ago.' But he began to smile again. 'He read your book! A guest brought him a copy. He was so happy to read about himself. Everyone knew about it. He became quite well known. Because of what you wrote in your book, many people came here. They mentioned you.'

Peter Bernard showed me around the mansion – the floors were polished, the beds made, the fireplaces whitewashed, flowers in vases, the tables laid in the dining room. The light was exceptional, because all the rooms had large windows and each room its own balcony. Imperial architecture here, the villas and bungalows of the British colonial officers – Indian army, civil service – was deliberately roomy and comfortable, reflecting their pretensions to be considered upper class if not aristocratic. That was the imperial ploy: as soon as the British got to the colonies, they jumped up a class or two and put on airs and browbeat the underlings, the servants, the workers they referred to as dogsbodies. Kipling dramatized it, Saki satirized it, Orwell objected violently to it, E. M. Forster fictionalized it, J. R. Ackerley tittered over it. But Mr Bernard had stood and served; he was, after all, a Victorian, from a transplanted family, a loyal British subject.

His first name had been Albert. If I had known that, I would have remembered it; it was my own father's name. Mr Bernard had been chief steward of Candacraig, appointed in 1962 at the age of sixty-six summoned out of semi-retirement to straighten the place out. He'd been so old when I'd met him (he had stories of the First World War), he might have waited on the colonial policeman Eric Blair, who might have stayed here, before he left for London to become George Orwell. Mr Bernard had died at the age of ninety.

The portrait of Mr Bernard in my book had done what the written word sometimes accidentally does, worked a kind of magic. It had brought visitors, and it had given Mr Bernard 'face', which was so important in Burma, especially for a non-Burmese of Indian descent. I had mentioned in my book that his father had been in the Indian army. Peter told me that his grandfather had held the post of bandmaster in the Madras Infantry, and that he had never returned to India, nor had any other member of the family ever been to India, even for the merest visit.

'What's it like there, India?' Peter asked. 'So many people, eh?'

Later he invited me to his house – the family house, built by Mr Bernard for his nine children.

It was a sprawling bungalow called Newlands, at the end of a long driveway – the usual wall around it – and beneath a large banyan tree. I was greeted by two men in their sixties, Vincent and John, so delighted to be told who I was that they got my book from a back room and showed it to me. Mr Bernard's signature was on the front endpaper.

'He used to read it,' Vincent said. 'It made him really happy.'

Of the nine Bernard children, only two were married, John and Margaret. Victor – born in 1945, named for the victory over the Japanese – had died of heart failure.

'He was a priest, a Salesian father, with a church upcountry in Wa State.'

Wa State was distant and isolated, in the Shan Plateau, the poppy-growing and opium-exporting area, in the smoky mountains of the Golden Triangle. But Father Victor Bernard hadn't been fazed and had been popular in his parish, which included the main town of Pang Wai. The Wa people were darker than the Burmese, animist, jungle-dwelling. They were mainly poppy cultivators and had a high incidence of opium smoking. What made them especially attractive to Catholic and Baptist missionaries was their colourful paganism. Noted for their dog eating, their headhunting and their connoisseurship of skulls, they often set so many skulls on poles that they created (as Mr Kurtz had done in the Inner Station) what seemed avenues of human skulls in the jungle, aiming at purification, to drive evil spirits away.

The Wa denied they were cannibals, the Burmese historian Thant Myint-U claimed. It was only good fortune that they sought in their strenuous decapitations: 'a good skull or two would ensure all the maize and dog and good liquor (strong rice wine) they needed to be happy'. Wa State bordered China, and Pang Wai was conveniently near the Chinese town of Cangyuan, on the opium trans-shipment route. Even in a shrinking world, Wa State, east of the Salween River, was not just distant but almost inaccessible.

I sat in the Bernards' parlour drinking tea, catching up. Margaret now lived in Berlin. A German doctor who'd read my book had made a visit to Candacraig. A widower, he'd taken the trip for his nerves and had met Margaret, who was a receptionist at the hotel. He fell in love with her. They married here, garlanded with flowers.

In a country of slender, soft-voiced beauties with creamy skin, the loveliest smiles and the gentlest manner, the rest of the Bernard brothers had remained stubbornly single. This baffled me. Apart from Margaret, the sisters, too, had chosen spinsterhood. The better I got to know them, the more I felt that this was a comment on their happy household, the mutually supportive family Mr Bernard had fathered, and maybe an indication of how they had lived in Upper Burma, in a closed culture, Catholics of Indian descent among Buddhist Burmans. Pictures of Jesus, of Mary, of saints, were hung on the walls of the parlour. On the mantelpiece a gold chalice glittered among devotional tokens.

Their mother, Theresa Bernard, had been beloved and doted on; she'd died only a few years before, also at the age of ninety. It was as though they were all so content they couldn't bear to leave the serenity of the homestead. Margaret had left the country. Jane had recently visited her in Germany, and reported that she was happy in Berlin. Of the others, none had left Myanmar. They continued to live the provincial life of the small town, with occasional visits to Mandalay.

'I'm still waiting for my lucky day,' Vincent said of his marriage prospects. He was a powerfully built man who, with a Dutch partner, managed 2,000 acres of maize some distance from Pyin-Oo-Lwin.

John, whose nickname was Sunny, was a thin, watchful man. He sat sideways on a straight-backed chair, tremulous in the early stages of

Parkinson's disease. He said, 'I remember you so well, Mr Paul. You were in the corner room. You talked to us.'

'Your father was proud of you,' I said.

'Your wrote our names in your book!' Vincent said.

'Was your father strict?'

'He beat me twice a week,' Sunny said without rancour, smiling, widening his eyes.

Peter agreed: I had described their father's interesting career as a colonial servant, but I hadn't mentioned his severity. Well, how was I to know? Their father had been punctual, methodical, demanding, an early riser. Candacraig had been his entire responsibility, and the burden had come at the end of his career. He had supervised the place until his retirement. And, though it had been owned by the government, he had turned it into a family enterprise: all the children had worked here at one time or another.

Vincent said, 'People came holding your book, wanting to meet my father. Tourists from Britain. From America. Aussies, too. My father met them and talked to them and told them his stories.'

'He was eighty-one when he retired,' Peter said.

'Later, when they came, we informed them he was dead,' Sunny said. 'Some of them cried. They went away sad.'

They showed me family albums, memorabilia, a large studio portrait of their father, looking owlish in horn-rimmed glasses. And so I sat there, and drank tea, and was happy. It was a homecoming I had not expected, like a visit to generous grateful relatives I had not seen in decades. Nothing like this had ever happened to me among my own family. Was this a motivation, the embrace of strangers, in my becoming a traveller? It was all positive and pleasurable, the men I had remembered as eager polite boys; the women who'd just been names. The wonderful part was the continuity of it all, that life had gone on. Without daring to anticipate such an event, it was the sort of reunion I had hoped for when I set out to repeat my trip.

I looked at the bazaar and the Christian churches – Gothic in red brick – and spent a day at Kandawgyi, botanical gardens that dated from the first serious settlement of the town, when the railway had been finished in 1900. It was a beautifully landscaped area of more than 400 acres, with a pond and bamboo groves and endangered deer and a research centre devoted to growing mulberry trees for silkworms, as well as the raising of silkworms themselves. Walking along the flower-bordered paths I was reminded that at an earlier time I would have directed the rickshaw driver to pass the Kandawgyi Gardens and asked him to stop at the Kandawgyi Bar, if such a place could be found, and I would have stayed there, getting half drunk and homesick.

The night before I left, I did get half drunk at the Aung Padamyar, an Indian restaurant that Vincent recommended. It was run by one of his female cousins, for Mr Bernard's brother was also an old-time resident of Maymyo.

Dennis Bernard, another cousin, introduced himself. Another genial wraith from the distant past, he said, 'Remember me? I set the table for you at Candacraig.'

He was also in his fifties, semi-retired. He said that he had worked for Mr Bernard as a waiter and a cleaner.

'It wasn't easy,' he said. 'We had to get up at four in the morning to clean the dining room and set the tables. Empty the ashtrays. Sweep. Uncle Bernard insisted that we get there at that time. "Be very quiet, the guests are sleeping." He was so strict. He checked each table. "Don't hurry," he said. "Do it all correctly." And he could get really angry.'

'What made him angry?'

'If we left the spoon out of the sugar bowl.'

I went back to Mandalay. It was then that I searched for and found Oo Nawng and gave him the money. He said, 'I'm happy.'

Before I left, I made a visit to the Irrawaddy, just to see the river and the boats and the landing stage. It was too far for Oo Nawng to go in his bicycle rickshaw, so I took a taxi. On the way, we passed a big bold sign: THE TATMADAW WILL NEVER BETRAY THE NATIONAL CAUSE.

'What's the Tatmadaw?'

'Damadaw,' the driver said, giving it the correct pronunciation. 'Is the army.'

'Yes?'

'Stupid army.'

19. Night Train to Nong Khai

The great challenge in travel is not arriving at the glamorous foreign city, but solving the departure problem, finding a way out of it, without flying. Buses are usually nasty, and bus stations the world over are dens of thieves, cutpurses, intimidators, mountebanks and muggers. Hired cars are convenient but nearly always a rip-off, and who wants narration from the driver? The train is still the ideal – show up and hop on.

The express trains out of Bangkok were brand new and comfortable, yet Bangkok was hard to leave. I had thought I would breeze through, but found myself seated in a cool shadowy room with muted gong music playing and a Thai woman washing my feet. She called herself Sky, because her name (she said) was too hard for me to say. I was so moved by the foot-washing I wanted to weep. Then she had me on the table and was kneeling on the backs of my thighs and tugging the kinks out of my arms. They were sore from rocking up and down Myanmar on the ghost trains. She poked her elbows into the small of my back and did a sort of samba along my spine, digging her toes into my vertebrae, and I thought of my trip from Colombo to Galle. She punched my upper back, rubbing her knuckles in the recesses of my muscles, and I thought of the two drunks on the train from Bokhara, their hands in the remains of a torn-apart chicken, their eyes glazed with vodka, as I stayed in the corridor trying to remain upright. She worked on my arms, flexed one then the other, twisted them, and I saw the rigid posture of the Muslim sitting stiff-backed on the train from Ashgabat to Mary.

She straddled me, as though playing horsy. This was heaven, having her seated on my back like a child on a pony ride, her knees forward, using them to massage my kidneys as she hammered the kinks out of my back. I had seen horsemen sitting like this in the desolate fields of Romania, but I was the pony now, and she the rider.

She slipped back, gripped my legs with hers and pressed, a wrestling move, kneading my calves with her heels, and then she took hold of my feet, finding each joint, each muscle, rolling each toe – whose feet are ever venerated and squeezed and chafed in this way, even by a lover? I had a vision of all the people, in India and Sri Lanka and Myanmar, whom I had seen walking – their cracked and tortured feet in broken shoes and shattered sandals.

'Over, please.'

Then I was face-up, with a cloth mask over my eyes, as Sky knuckled and punched my legs and made a circular syncopation, open-handed against my inner thighs, playing a percussive tune. All this for almost two hours, a kind of bliss, some of it hurting badly, but when she stopped I wanted more. What lover ever spent that much time appeasing the tension in her lover's body?

Near the end she took my right hand. I write with this hand. It is cramped like a claw most of the time from holding a pen. She used her fingers to pry my hand bones apart, massaging my palm, bending my whole hand backwards, flexing my fingers, and then, finger by finger, cracking my joints, pulling each digit, until my hand stopped being a blunt instrument and acquired an elasticity, opening like a blossom.

'The children's hands bleed, sir!' a carpet seller had told me in Jaipur, unrolling a rug. 'Look at the tiny knots!'

And then fruit juice under the stars, and my thinking, I'll stay a little while longer.

The last time I had stayed at the Erawan Hotel – famous, venerable, atmospheric – it was full of American army officers and camp followers of the Vietnam War. There had been only two great hotels in Bangkok then, the other being the Oriental, just as venerable and luxurious. Now there were many posh hotels. Bangkok was a so-called spa destination, and the Grand Hyatt Erawan, on the site of the old hotel, had a whole upper level of spa bungalows, like a village for sybarites and lotus eaters on a high rooftop. My bungalow had its own massage room, steam room, veranda and bamboo garden. A swimming pool was just outside. Did I want another massage? Was I hungry? What about a cup of tea? How about a banana?

In a much too big, humid city, still with a traffic problem, even with most of the *klongs* (canals) and creeks paved over, and questionable sights – newly painted temples and the murky Chao Phraya River – the hotel had become the destination. People checked in and simply stayed for a week, being waited on and pampered, without leaving. The Oriental was more palatial, with its spa and cooking school in a villa across the river, its five gourmet restaurants. The same general manager, Kurt Wachtveitl, had been there all those years ago.

'Ten million tourists come here,' Kurt told me. 'But it won't be long before there are twenty million, because the Chinese are starting to arrive – to shop, mainly for gemstones.'

The city itself is still busy and bright, the side streets still sleazy, with grubby bars and brothels in the same districts as before. Tourists come to shop for silks and eat great meals. Some book buyers, too – the five-storey Paragon Shopping Centre had the best bookshop I'd seen since leaving London. Bangkok had been a destination for sex tourists and soldiers on R and R. Though the city is now prosperous from manufacturing – sweatshops and outsourcing – that rosy dimension remains. Pat Pong Road, which used to have a seedy charm, good natured in its pimping, is now just scuzzy, and raucous, with loudly contending whores.

I was on my way to see a tailor. The taxi driver said, 'You like sandwich?'

'I'm not hungry.'

'No. Sex – two women.'

'Sandwich?'

'One front, one back, very nice.' He found my face in his rear-view mirror. 'Or you want lady-boy?'

What I wanted was to buy a train ticket, be fitted for two shirts, get some film developed, buy a present for my wife's birthday and have my laundry done. When I marvelled to an American teacher in Bangkok that I managed all of these inside an hour, he said, 'But you probably got them all done at the same place, right?'

He was roughly my age, and that day he was in a hurry to get to his Thai girlfriend's birthday party.

'She's turning twenty,' he said, knowing I would ask.

'So you're in heaven.'

'Tell you a story,' he said in a cautioning voice. 'A *farang* met a Thai woman and fell in love with her. They got married. When the woman got her American visa, they moved to the States, to the guy's home town. They were really happy. The Thai woman learned English, got a job, and was a devoted wife. The ideal woman – the guy's dream. Like you said, heaven. This lasted five years.

'Then one day the woman says, "I have to go back to Thailand. My husband is very sick. I have to be with him." ' *Husband?* Yes, she explained. She'd been married before and had never got a divorce. But that was a detail.

' "When will you be back?" the guy asks.

' "I can never come back. I don't know how long he will be sick. Better to say goodbye now. If he dies, I'll have to look after his family." '

I said, 'And the moral is?'

'She was young, but there was a lot the *farang* didn't know.'

The youthfulness of Bangkok is a surprise: the bright faces, the smiling sylph-like beauties working as shop assistants, staffing hotels and restaurants, filling the new metro and sky train. It is a city of schools and colleges, and so a city of beautiful students. I found myself staring. The wok stirrer at the smallest noodle stall might be a ravishing woman, the more lovely for her strenuously paddling the noodles, her skin glowing from her effort, dampened and strangely lit by the cooking fire.

The bar girls were as fresh-faced as the college students, though most of them were a bit younger, more like artful schoolgirls, and just as casually dressed, their small breasts pressing against their T-shirts. The masseuses in the red-light district, in their efficiency and charm, were almost indistinguishable from the massage therapists in the spas. There was nothing particularly whorish-looking about the whores or meretricious-seeming about the tarts; any of them could have passed for bookshop staff at Paragon or salesgirls at Robinsons Department Store, and their English was as good. Hostesses in the wildest saloons were as demure as hostesses at the coffee shops in the great hotels. Bowing and politeness were common to all these women, not a sign of submission but a ritual show of respect, and self-respect. No matter their work, these women walked with upright and stately grace because Buddhists believe the head is sacred and should be held erect.

'Massage?' was the first question from every taxi driver. It was a question I was to hear hundreds of times over the next month in Southeast Asia from taxi drivers, rickshaw men, chair men, scooter boys, kids on the street, whisperers in bars and touts in hotel lobbies. But they didn't mean the sort of massage I'd had at the Erawan or the Oriental. A massage was a euphemism for sex, any kind of sex, agreed upon downstairs, then negotiated upstairs.

Nokh – it means bird in Thai – had worked at Robinsons. She told her family in Pattaya that she still worked there. Her father was a farmer. She went home once a month for a ritual meal and to pay her respects and visit the temple. She had lived in Bangkok for two years. She was the eldest of four children, had just turned twenty-five, and had responsibilities.

One of her responsibilities was to pay for the education of her younger sister Boonmah, who (unlike Nokh) had finished school and was attending college. Nokh and Boonmah lived together in a small room in a northern district of Bangkok, Nokh paying for everything.

Working in the women's clothing department paid so poorly that Nokh couldn't make ends meet. 'Small money,' she said. ('A lot of Thai girls work at Robinsons to meet marriageable *farangs*,' an American *farang* told me.) One of her friends told her she could earn more money in a massage parlour, so she gave it a shot.

'You should talk to her,' my friend said.

'Is she out of the ordinary?'

'No. That's why you should talk to her. She's typical. There are tens of thousands just like her.'

She was small, slim, doll-like, fragile-looking. What appealed to me immediately was that when I met her for our appointment she was reading a magazine, with much the same absorption as the bar girl I'd seen in Istanbul. She didn't look up. The sex worker is attentive above all, restless, with a bird-like alertness, partly to look for a mark, partly for self-protection. Reading was not only unproductive, but because it caused inattention, it was dangerous. She had been startled into anxious giggles when I interrupted her. I said that to talk to her, I'd give her what a customer would.

She laughed. She said, 'Customers give big man six thousand baht. Big man give me one thousand baht.'

That was $25, so I doubled it, and she was happy and forthcoming.

'Does your sister know where you work?'

'I tell her I work in a karaoke.'

'What about your parents?'

'I tell them I work at Robinsons. They be sad if they know where I work.'

'Why doesn't your sister work?'

'She does small work. But she has to study.'

'Is she pretty like you?'

'She very fat!'

'After she graduates, what will you do?'

'Save money. I want to have a coffee shop in Chon Buri.'

Nokh looked at her watch, but was embarrassed when I asked if she had to go. It was five in the afternoon. She was due at work at six, which meant that she would pin her disk to her blouse, displaying her number. She would sit behind a wall of glass, in the fish-tank arrangement of the Bangkok brothel, and would wait, smiling, until a man chose her. She passed the time this way until two in the morning. And the man who chose her might go later to a restaurant and for his meal choose a fish from an aquarium in just the same way.

'I read magazine!' she said, as though to reassure me that she wasn't killing time.

I found her situation depressing. Nokh was wasting her youth in a whorehouse, not for her own gain but, because she was the number one child, to support her sister. She was so small, so polite and pleasant, intelligent too. I asked a few more inconsequential questions and then off she went, into the cruel world.

Solving the problem of how to leave the enormous city, one night I took a taxi to the railway station at the centre of Bangkok. I had a ticket on the 2045, the night train to the Laotian border at Nong Khai. At the station there were no formalities, no security, no ticket check, no warnings, no friskings. I bought a big bottle of water and some beer, saw from the departure board that my train would be leaving from platform 3, found my sleeper, and climbed aboard. This was about thirty minutes before we left. I was seated, drinking a beer, when the conductor knocked on my door, said hello, and punched my ticket. Then he made my bed. And soon after, we slid away from the station, headed north.

I had found a Simenon paperback in one of the big Bangkok book-shops, *The Man Who Watched the Trains Go By*. I got into bed and enjoyed one of the most pleasant experiences I know in travel, tucked into a wide berth on an Asiatic train, in a private compartment, reading as the carriage gently rocks, and knowing that I won't have to stir for twelve hours, when I will be at the edge of another country, a new frontier.

At dawn, I kicked the shade up and saw flooded paddy fields and the great flat landscape of northern Thailand. I opened the window and the train stopped at a small station where there were handsome families, a smiling monk wrapped in his ochre robe, and pretty girls in T-shirts and white shorts – on this entire trip, Thailand offered me my first glimpse of women's bare legs. The stations were swept and tidy, no litter, everyone in clean clothes, children playing, and adding to the calmness and serenity there were plenty of benches and chairs where people waited for the next train. The cleanliness seemed to represent a kind of optimism and self-esteem, and all this order was framed by green fields and polyphonic birdsong.

I tend to evaluate places according to habitability – whether I can live in them. Passing an idyllic glade, I saw a hammock strung between two palm trees and myself swinging in it. This self-centred impulse I put down to my escapist fantasies inspired by distant places, but it's only human to look for an ideal location to live in, the great good place we all seek. A lovely landscape, I think, but if I am able to put myself into it, surely it is lovelier.

On the way to Nong Khai on this train I saw a sunlit bungalow on stilts on a side road, a hammock underneath it, some banana trees and chickens near it, a vegetable garden behind it, rice paddies beyond it, an ox in a meadow and low jungle all around, and I thought: Yes, it would be nice to live there. Except for a flicker of temptation in Sri Lanka, I had never had a serious thought of this anywhere else so far. But in the north of Thailand, I entertained the notion of simply dropping out of the world and fitting myself into this version of pastoral, walking up and down in my pyjama bottoms.

When I arrived in Nong Khai, on the Mekong River, as though to prove the validity of this impression, who should get out of the train but two big wheezy *farangs,* red-faced and chain-smoking, with their Thai wives and a sister-in-law. They had boarded the train some way down the line, perhaps at the very place I was having escape fantasies.

Miles was from England. He wore a heavy suit and tie in spite of the heat. Rudi – tattooed, quite fat, in a black T-shirt and boots – was from Rotterdam.

'We got on the train at Khon Kaen.'

'Visiting there?' I asked.

'We live there,' Rudi said.

'It's heaven,' Miles said. 'About a hundred expats – all good chaps. We look after each other. We're all brothers in Khon Kaen.'

Rudi said, 'But I go back to Holland.'

Miles was only half listening. He was speaking to the three Thai women, seeming to berate them, going, 'Bumpity-bump, bop-bop.'

'What are you saying?' I asked.

'You really should learn the language, old chap. Makes life so much easier. Kon-kap. Bop-bop. Bumpity-bip.'

Miles made it sound like Martian, pursing his lips, nodding, widening his eyes. His face was slick with perspiration.

The women smiled patiently and murmured among themselves.

I met the *farangs* again later on in the morning, nearer the river, in an open-fronted shed called Alex's Travel Service, where Laotian visas were being processed and sold. This was efficiently done – you could have your photo taken, or send a fax, or have a meal, for it was also a noodle stall. I had my breakfast noodles while my visa application was being initialled and stamped. Then I wandered outside.

'Is that your wife?' I asked Rudi.

'Yes,' he said. 'Well, not my wife but the woman I liff wiz.'

The three women were middle-aged, beginning to thicken, but with the warm Thai smile and the placid, self-contained serenity, talking among themselves, without complaint, and now and then acknowledging Miles's approximation of Thai.

'We have everything in Khon Kaen,' Miles said to me. 'Even a hospital.'

'I have to go back to Holland every muntz or so to collect my pension,' Rudi said. 'Dey won't send it to me. Also to see my grandchildren. But always I come back here.'

'Bumpity-bump,' Miles said, reddening.

'Beer is cheaper in Laos,' Rudi said. 'So we go dere. Go down the river. Drink beer. Eat sumsing. Ferry nice.'

'Pip-pip,' Miles said. He was dressed as though for an outing in Brighton with the bowling club, sweating profusely, smoke coming out of his ears and nose. He was a life-of-the-party type who told jokes in funny foreign accents. 'Sap-songg!'

He squinted as he twanged the words, straining and pursing his lips. Was this Thai? If so, his wife, or girlfriend, didn't get it. She smiled and twisted her face in embarrassment.

'Sip-bip-bip!'

Now she hid her face in her hands.

But Miles just snorted and puffed his cigarette and said, 'Can't beat it. Makes things so much easier. Kap-ko!'

He grimaced in the heat, dabbing at his dripping forehead with a grey hanky. His tight shirt collar was sodden. The Dutchman too was sweating in his T-shirt and black biker jeans. When Miles started up again, tittering and cheeping with his explosive syllables, the three women fled to the shade of a mango tree.

'Take my advice – what did you say your name was?'

'Paul.'

'Paul. You won't get anywhere if you don't bip-kai-bip, kap-ko.'

I had finished my noodles and was waiting for my passport, which Alex, in the shed, soon gave me.

'Is that *farang* speaking Thai?' I asked.

'A little bit. But it's rude to say kap-ko.'

My last time here I had walked down a path to the Mekong and been ferried over in a small sampan propelled by a farting outboard motor, and my passport had been stamped under a tree on the far bank. Today we were taken in Alex's van across the Friendship Bridge, from Thailand to Laos, over the wide river, and to the border post. There was hardly any traffic.

The decadent Vientiane of Vietnam War days, which had catered to servicemen on leave, had become a sleepy place, a capital yet hardly a city, more of a backwater than it could have been a hundred years ago. I remembered it as a wide-open town: whores gathered in hotel lobbies who greeted new arrivals by smiling and snatching at them. In Vientiane, the very word 'hotel' was a euphemism for a cathouse, and the debauchery in the bars was celebrated throughout Southeast Asia – the live sex shows, the nude dancers, the stark-naked waitresses who managed amazing feats with cigarettes. At the White Rose, the most notorious bar, I saw a drunken man flicking his Zippo and setting fire to a waitress's pubic hair. She slapped herself with one hand and pushed him away with the other, demanded a tip, then moved on to the next table.

Vientiane had not grown any bigger, yet the contrast could not have been greater. The change was a testament to what the Vietnam War had done to Laos. I saw Vientiane then (and described it) as the most corrupt and dissolute place I'd ever travelled to. Diminutive Laotian whores and big whooping American soldiers dominated the place. Drugs were easy to buy, and so was porn. 'Anything you want,' pedicab drivers said. 'What you want, Joe?'

But the riotous Americans who had sexualized the place, turning Vientiane into a fleshpot, had left, and it was now a sleepy town on the banks of the muddy river, famous for its cheap beer, attractive to backpackers. One of the characteristics of backpackers – careful with their money, socially conscious on the whole – is that they have sex with each other and resist the locals. Vientiane's streets were mostly empty, so were its shops, and its bars could not have been more sedate. Just 25-cent beers and $3 hotel rooms, pedestrian-friendly with quiet, hospitable folks, yet strangely colourless.

'Mistah?'

Two Lao girls approached me as I was taking an evening stroll by the river. They were so slender-hipped and grubby they might have been boys. They did not speak English except for one unambiguous verb.

'Where do you live?'

They giggled and tugged my arms and tried to tempt me by pointing to a grove of trees at the riverbank, an obvious haunt of rats and snakes.

They recognized the futility of tempting me and didn't persist. I kept walking. Vientiane still proclaimed itself a capital, yet it was no more than a dusty riverside town, with warm weather and friendly people and a government with obscure intentions. Its glory was its temples, dating from the early nineteenth century, not ancient but built in an ancient style, with bonnet-like triple-pitched roofs, sometimes five or six of them overlapping, and amateurish murals inside, in courtyards with glazed tile walls. Children played outside while their parents were inside, devout in their prostrations, imploring the gold Buddhas with incense sticks and flower petals.

After two days I had caught up my diary and finished my Simenon and was considering going to the Vientiane museum when I met Fiona, a backpacker. She was thirty, travelling alone, and like a lot of solitary travellers, resourceful, also shrewd, direct, opinionated and full of misinformation. She didn't read much, she said; she got her facts from other travellers like herself, on buses, in hostels, waiting under trees in the rain. She had just arrived in Laos.

'I'm a traveller. That's all I want to do. But I ran out of money,' she said. 'I have to go back to England, but I'm only going so that I can make some money. I want to come back here, or somewhere. I just want to travel. I don't want to do anything else.'

We were in a noodle shop. I offered to buy her a beer, but she said tea was fine.

'Thing is, when you're trying to save money, you need a flatmate. My last flatmate, Roger, was gay. When I say gay, I mean not just gay but, um, know much about S and M?'

'A little bit,' I said. 'Was that Roger's thing?'

'Roger's thing was parties. There are these S-and-M parties all over London. I went to some. The people were quite nice! Barristers. Company directors. Jobs in the City, stock market blokes. Roger was a clerk in chambers. But they have this one thing in common.'

'Pain,' I said.

'Not just pain. Spanking. Whipping.'

'Does nothing for me,' I said.

She wasn't listening. 'Roger had these two friends. One was really tall with a metal spike through his nose and tattoos and piercings. A bloke. The other was a very small frizzy-haired girl with Deirdre Barlow glasses. She was the weirdest of the lot.'

'In what way?'

'They all went to bed together. I called them the Circus People. "Circus people coming this weekend, Roger?" When they showed up, the flat stank. They didn't wash.'

'But weird in what way?'

'They got Roger into cutting and scarification. They took these sharp knives and cut him all around one leg. Roger said, "When they put the salt water on it, I was in heaven."'

I said, 'I'm losing my appetite.'

Fiona said, 'But it got me thinking. What about the people who are really in pain? Poor people. People in prison. That's a kind of insult to them in their suffering.'

'Good point.' I hadn't thought of that. I said, to change the subject, 'So you want to go on travelling?'

She said, 'Yes. My hero is Michael Palin. The BBC guy? He goes all over the world.'

I said, 'With a camera crew and someone to do his makeup and buy his tickets. He's got people who tell him where to stand!'

'He's a real world traveller. And he's funny, too.'

'I'll give you that. He makes jokes.'

'He's clever too!' She leaned over. 'I'd never heard of Lhasa until he went there.'

'Fiona, it's the capital of Tibet. I was there once.'

She didn't care. She said, 'I'll bet Michael Palin has been here in Laos.'

'Or maybe not.'

'That's what I want to do.'

'Be Michael Palin? That's your ambition?'

'Wouldn't you want to be Michael Palin?' she asked.

The next day, as I was having lunch at an outdoor café in Vientiane, an old American woman entered with two young men. They sat near me, and from their conversation I gathered that one was her son and the other his Indian lover. The woman sat queening it for a while, and the young men talked intimately. And then a waiter approached her.

'Ask them. They make all the decisions,' she said. 'I'm just along for the ride.'

Strange little dramas occurred, the glimpses I got as a traveller, not a short story but a fleeting look of something else. I always knew that there was much more, and so these people appeared like characters waiting for me, as some Americans had in India, to assign them parts in a bigger story.

I was satisfied that the depraved Vientiane of whores and stoners I had known was gone, replaced by a Vientiane of budget travellers and backpackers. Meanwhile the Laotians themselves did their best to escape across the river to Thailand, where there were opportunities for work and real money.

A pedicab, locally known as a tuk-tuk, passed me as I was walking down a street. The man said, 'Where?'

I thought that I might go to the museum or see some more temples. But I said, 'How much to the bridge?'

He named a price, and not long after that I was back at Nong Khai Station, waiting for the Bangkok train, thinking about the little dramas. A woman smiled at me.

'Anyone sitting here?'

'Be my guest.'

She was American, tubby and short, duck-bottomed, about fifty or so, in black capri pants, her hair drawn back but most of it fluttering around her sweaty face. She was pale, unnaturally so in this bright sunshine. She carried a misshapen duffle bag, which she unzipped, taking out a ten-inch baguette sandwich wrapped in paper. Pulling off the paper, holding the sandwich in two hands, like a tool, she tilted her head and began eating, working on it from its narrower end.

'Real good,' she said, chewing.

'What's in it?'

'Usual stuff. Mystery meat and salad.' She laughed. She seemed sure of herself, and here she was, alone in an empty railway station on the Thai–Laos border on a hot afternoon.

'You from the States?'

'Missouri. But I live in Khon Kaen.'

Another one. I didn't say anything for a while. I was content. I'd just had some noodles across the road from the station, and the Thai noodle seller had said I should stay, live here, lots of *farangs* had done that and were happy. Eating noodles on the border in a shady open-sided restaurant, waiting for the Bangkok train, was a kind of bliss. Plenty of women here would want to move in with you, he said, promising me romance too. Now I was on the platform with the fat woman from Missouri as she gnawed at her sandwich.

Nong Khai was perhaps the cleanest of any railway station I'd seen since I left London. Not a speck of litter on the platform or on the tracks, no one spitting, no graffiti, no one in rags, no beggars, the whole place swept and mopped, gleaming in the afternoon light.

This order, and the politeness and efficiency of the ticket seller, put me in an optimistic mood. Really, this seemed to me an almost unimprovable society of happy families and good roads and people in clean clothes. And their self-respect and innate propriety meant that they did not have to be tyrannized and fined in order to be tidy.

The woman was still noisily chewing, in a way that would have shocked a Thai. She was sweating in her tight jersey, her hair had come loose, she had a drop of mayonnaise on her nose and a smear of it on her cheek.

'What do you do in Khon Kaen?'

'Officially, I don't do anything.'

She looked at me meaningfully, still chewing.

'Unofficially, I'm a missionary.'

'Spreading the word?'

'You got it.'

'Quoting Scripture?'

'Absolutely.'

' "The letter killeth," ' I said. 'Who said that?'

'Paul. Corinthians. "The spirit giveth life." '

'They have plenty of spirit.'

'Not Christian spirit.'

'Like they need lessons in piety in Thailand?' I said, my voice cracking with impatience. And I thought of all the Thais I'd seen bringing flowers and incense to temples, their crouching and their prostrations, their faces glowing in the light of candle flames, the special quality of their beauty when they were in the act of praying.

'They need Jesus.'

I took a deep breath and said, 'What is it with you people?'

She just chewed defiantly.

'They need Almighty God.'

I said, 'If Almighty God had been an immense duck capable of emitting an eternal quack, we would all have been born web-footed, each as infallible as the pope – and we would never have had to learn to swim' – a quotation from Henry James's father that I find useful on these occasions.

Her eyes popped from her big mouthful, and her whole face was in motion as she chewed. She swallowed and said, 'I have a mission,' and it was no longer a Christian mission at all, but pure greedy appetite, as she took another bite, wagging her head, working her jaws, like an oversized mongrel worrying a bone.

Soon after that, the train to Bangkok pulled in. I found my compartment. I sat for a while. An old man joined me, and as though a living reproach to the missionary, he meditated for a long time, looking beatific. His name was Vajara. Night fell. He took the upper berth. He was gone when I awoke in Bangkok.

20. Night Train to Hat Yai Junction
Special Express

An enormous multicoloured portrait of Rama V, the great innovating King Chulalongkorn, hung above the waiting room at Bangkok Central – Hua Lamphong Station, built in 1910, the year the much-loved king died. He was the moving force behind the modernization of Thailand, introducing political reform, improving education and roads and the railway too, in 1891. He was also the king portrayed in the book that inspired the plonking musical *The King and I*, both book and musical loathed by all Thais, who see them as insulting falsifications poking fun at their revered monarch. Thais regard the king as semi-divine and Rama V (rightly) as especially benevolent and far-seeing, not to be spoken about casually, much less demeaned or criticized as a risible Siamese royal, waltzing or dallying with an intrusive *farang*.

On my previous trip I had asked an idle question about the present king. I had been in a sampan with a young Thai man and a Thai woman, the man a photographer, the woman a journalist. The man was teaching me how to scull with one oar, like a gondolier. We were in a klong, a canal sixty feet wide, not near any other boat or person. My harmless question produced a silence so deep it was as though I had not spoken at all.

Then the Thai woman looked down at the deck of the long boat and made a chirruping sound in her pretty nose. It meant *uh-oh!*

'You say one word about the king,' the Thai man said to me, in a voice more fearful than censorious, 'and it's your neck.'

I had asked about King Bhumibol Adulyadej, Rama IX, the one-eyed, unsmiling billionaire, also half god half man, the longest-ruling monarch in Thai history. He had reigned since 1950, and now, on my second visit, his eightieth birthday was coming up. Pictures of him were everywhere, and many Thais wore yellow T-shirts and yellow bracelets, because yellow was the royal colour.

It was Sunday, and a hot bright somnolence, with a hint of sadness, descended on Bangkok, reminding me of the oppression of empty Sundays when I was very young. If I stayed in the big city (I reasoned) I would be caught, and in the pleasantest way would procrastinate, happily pummelled by delicate little princesses in massage rooms, with gong music playing softly and candles burning. I might never leave.

Satisfied that Bangkok had got bigger but had kept its soul, I dragged myself away on a southbound express.

The talk was of Muslim insurgency in the south, secessionists' bombs in markets, sectarian throat-cuttings, local militia groups and mujahideen and mentions of Al Qaeda and the Muslim Brotherhood. There had been seven recent incidents, some deaths and torchings of Thai shops. The southern provinces, bordering Malaysia, had a Muslim majority, and there was talk of sovereignty and the introduction of sharia law and other repressions and archaisms. The Thai government hadn't had much success in pacifying the south, nor had the army managed to contain the bombers, whose numbers had grown in recent years.

'Maybe we should just let the Muslims down there have their province,' a Thai woman had said to me at a dinner party in Bangkok, speaking in a fatalistic way. 'Maybe they'll stop killing people then.'

Leaving Bangkok for the south, I felt more than ever like a romantic voyeur in a half-drowned world. The train made a great loop around tin-roofed settlements. 'There it was, spread largely on both banks, the Oriental capital,' Conrad wrote in *The Shadow-Line*, published a hundred years ago, his descriptions still ringing true: 'a vegetable-matter style of architecture, sprung out of the brown soil on the banks of the muddy river'. Then the train rattled across the river on a rusty bridge. 'Some of those houses of sticks and grass, like the nests of an aquatic race, clung to the low shores.' The embankment temples ('gorgeous and dilapidated') and the watercraft, some chugging boats, some sampans being poled; onward past coconut palms, banana groves, mango trees, ponds choked with lotuses. Green, low-lying, the vertical sunlight glittering on the swamps and stagnation, the slender women carrying heavy loads – it all made me sad.

It was a voyeur's ennui, the traveller's sense of being superfluous, just gaping and moving on; the sadness of seeing these graceful people in this big city – another big city – all their struggles, all their hopes. We rumbled past a suburban station, Bang Bamru, where women were washing clothes at a pump, their children splashing nearby. The women looked elegant even in their drudgery, and the sight of two small boys, hardly older than seven or eight, further on at Nakhon Pathom, one with his arm lightly around the other, made me inexpressibly melancholy. They each wore clean shirts and shorts and were barefoot. Why did neat, tidy, dignified, obedient, well-behaved poverty strike me as so sad?

At last, after an hour or more of the jungly countryside – of farmhouses, rice fields, bungalows, a family of four riding on a motorbike, browsing cows, a shrimp farm, a Christian school, a tall gold temple, a man setting off firecrackers in front of a crowd of people – I didn't feel so bad.

Then birds singing, dogs barking on dusty roads, tall trees surrounded by fields of lemongrass, mango orchards – and I felt even better.

And all the rest of the day, until nightfall, while I wrote more of my new story, 'The Gateway of India', there were rice paddies, soft green squares of them with raised edges, some of them new, just flooded, to the horizon.

In the compartment next to mine were two girls in their late teens and an older woman, whom I took to be Chinese. The woman had a broader face than most Thais, and she wore a cuff of gold bracelets and a gold necklace. The odd thing was that, though they spent most of the day sleeping, they left the compartment door open, and the woman always smiled when I went by, as I deliberately did, for her smile.

'Way you going?'

'Penang,' I said.

'We go Penang too.'

As often happens on long-distance trains, I kept bumping into them – at the window in the corridor, idling in the noisy passage between carriages, waiting to get into the lavatory.

'Where are we?' I asked the woman, seeing a temple at the end of a road.

'I don't know.' But I had broken the ice. The next time I saw her, she said, 'You business?'

'Me business.'

'What you name?'

'Paul.'

'Baw,' she said. She smiled and canted her head towards her compartment. 'My name Lily. Those my babies.'

Then I guessed she was a procuress, and wanted to talk to her more, but the next time I passed their compartment the door was shut.

Darkness dropped quickly, as it does on the equator, and in the morning I woke to golden clouds, a pinky-blue sky and jungle interspersed with rice fields like water meadows – the deep south of Thailand, near the Malaysian border, lush, deep green, thinly populated and some of it under siege.

At Hat Yai Junction I got out and was directed to a booth to buy an onward ticket, then I reboarded; only the front half of the train would go to Butterworth and the border. I looked for the procuress and her two girls but couldn't see them anywhere. Most of the seats were empty. I chose one in the open compartment and dozed. I woke twenty minutes later when the train got under way, passing among sudden boulder-shaped hills.

Two young women – English, from their voices – each with an enormous bulging backpack, sat across the aisle from me. Both were engrossed in books, the dark one reading a John Irving, the skinny head-scratching one *The Mosquito Coast*. For a pleasant hour or so I watched this second one, rapt – or nearly so – chewing her lips as she read.

From time to time they looked up and spoke.

'Seen the bog?' the first one said.

'Toilets are rank!'

'Should we wait till later?'

'Wrong question!'

'Bound to be loos at the border.'

'Tidy loos? Here? I don't think so!'

They went back to their reading. After a while the first one yawned and twisted the John Irving in her hands and said, 'This book is so dense!'

I waited for a response, but the second one didn't volunteer anything about me. She was near the end. I waited until she finished the book, and when she did, she placed it on her lap and took a deep breath.

'What do you think?' I asked.

'The book?' She made a face. 'Wasn't what I was expecting.'

She handled the paperback as if to grasp at a thought. 'All the bugs. All the jungle. It reminded me of when we were in Vietnam.'

'But the family in it,' I said, 'did they convince you, or is it just another story?'

She nodded hard and said, 'I'm like way convinced. Way, way.'

Satisfied, I revealed myself as the author.

'Was this a trip you took?' she said, tapping the book.

'No. It's a novel. It's a story. It's, um, fiction.'

She was smiling, as though she'd learned my secret. She said, 'So I guess – what? – writing's your hobby?'

This threw me, but I was also smiling.

She said, 'What do you do the rest of the time?'

'That's pretty much it. Scribble, scribble.'

The other girl said, 'Were you influenced by *The Poisonwood Bible*?'

'No. See, my book was published in 1981.'

'I wasn't even born then,' the first one said.

'I can't believe you're sitting right there,' the second one said. 'Hey, Doug!'

A young man a few seats away turned around and then came over. He was short, compact, and looked portable and somewhat satirical, being introduced by the pretty girls to this guy who wrote this book he had never heard of. She waved the battered paperback she said she'd stolen from a shelf in a youth hostel in Phuket. Doug had a small bag and wore sun-faded clothes and sandals. He said he had been travelling for three months. Apart from that he was noncommittal.

'Where are you going?' I asked.

'I'm not going anywhere,' he said. He looked me in the eye. 'Going nowhere.'

I liked him for his vagueness. The pen in his shirt pocket said something. He reminded me of the person I had been all those years ago, on this train from Bangkok to Penang.

He wasn't talking, and the backpackers just had questions, so I excused myself, and passing down the car saw Lily, the procuress, and her two girls in the last seat. The girls, on her right and left, were asleep, and she slumped to pillow their heads as if they were a pair of kittens.

'Baw,' Lily said and gestured for me to take the seat opposite. 'Sit here.' After I sat down she said, 'What kind business?'

'Book business.'

'That good!' She smiled. She had gold teeth to match her jewellery. 'What you country, Baw?'

I told her.

'America good!' She hugged the girls. 'You like them?'

'Yes,' I said.

'They sleep so much!'

It was true. I had seen them awake only once, the night before, in the train's corridor.

'Pretty, huh? Cue, huh?'

'Very cute.'

One of them stirred and yawned. The woman squeezed the girl's cheeks affectionately, and her eyes briefly opened.

'He business,' Lily said. The girl wrinkled her nose and went back to sleep. Then she winked at me. 'Penang nice place. Baw, you come visit me?'

Later in the morning we halted at the frontier station. It was the ideal border post, a long platform, Thailand at one end, Malaysia at the other. About twenty passengers entered, presented their passports to be stamped at each country's desk, and went through the last turnstile.

At a noodle stall on the Malaysian side I bought a bowl of *laksa*, one of the great soups of Straits cuisine – spicy, curried coconut soup with noodles and beansprouts. It is thick and rust-coloured from the chillies and its many ingredients – *laksa*, from the Sanskrit word *lakh*, for 100,000 (as Mr Kailash had said to me in Jaipur), is a Straits colloquialism for 'many'.

A doddery white man in a torn shirt and tennis shoes shuffled behind me. His laces were undone, his fly was half unzipped. He could have been eighty. He carried a small duffle bag. He was alone and hard of hearing – the immigration clerk had to shout – and squinted through thick glasses. What was he doing at this jungle border crossing? I was worried for him and watched him until he found his seat on the onward train, where he sat with his head in his hand. Travelling kids were everywhere, and it was rare, almost unheard-of, to see a frail man like this on his own.

Doug had seemed to me the person I had been, so I felt affectionate towards him. But I felt only sadness when I saw this old man; I felt protective, and fearful too. In a matter of years that wandering coot, the ghost whom no one noticed, would be me.

21. Night Train to Singapore

The Lankawi Express

When the train pulled into the station at Butterworth I felt ill – the *laksa*, I guessed. Greedy for the taste of it, I'd had seconds. I had not stopped at Penang on my previous trip. I might have passed by this time too, except that my guts were griping. I was dizzy and couldn't bear the thought of onward travel. So, bent double, I took the ferry across the harbour to Georgetown, got a taxi to the Eastern and Oriental Hotel, and curled into a ball, rising only to rehydrate with glasses of water fortified by a pinch of salt and a pinch of sugar. I felt so ghastly the next day I took a pill; when that didn't work I went to a Chinese herbalist down a side lane and got a potion. I stayed in bed. After three months of travel I was seriously laid low.

All that second night I heard loud music from the nearby streets – the bars, the clubs, the narrow lanes of massage parlours and neon signs. I had been sick only a few times on this trip, but this was by far the worst – cramps and nausea. My usual way of dealing with illness was to suspend all activity, find a good hotel, and sleep it off – eat nothing, keep drinking salted water. I did so here at the E & O.

Eventually I felt well enough to shuffle around the town on the sea legs of convalescence. With its colonial houses and covered walkways, its monsoon drains and narrow Chinese shops stacked high with goods, Georgetown (named for King George III) was a marvel of preservation. It looked much like the Singapore where I had worked in the 1960s. I had been to Georgetown once before, in 1970, on my way to a remote fishing village up the coast, Batu Ferringhi (Foreigner's Rock). Out of curiosity I went there again, in a taxi, and found that it had become a corniche of high-rise hotels and condominiums, luxury homes, big resorts and dreary tenements crowding the beachfront, a place of unparalleled ugliness.

Chandra, the taxi driver, was of Tamil extraction but born in Penang. He had never been to India. I asked him why. He said, 'Too many people.' He was married to a Chinese woman who had been a childhood neighbour and friend. They had two children. His sense of hospitality was such that he invited me to his house for tea, and when I commented on his addressing his wife in Tamil, he said, 'We always speak Tamil at home.' His wife was a Hokkien-speaker, and of course the national language was Malay, and he was fluent in English and knew 'a bit of German. *Danke. Guten morgen*'.

Many Germans had second homes here, he said. But mainly it was a resort for Arabs.

'Saudis – they have the money,' he said. 'But also Jordanians and Syrians. Their country is too hot – they have to leave, but they don't want to go to Europe or America. They know people hate them there. Americans say they're terrorists. They get double-checked at airports. And they don't want to be in a country where the women have to remove veil.'

'They wear veils here?' It seemed odd in a country where Muslim women were gracefully dressed in sarongs and tight-fitting blouses.

'The women eat like this,' Chandra said, and gestured, lifting an imaginary veil and sipping an imaginary drink. 'No man can look at their wife. Only them.'

'Lots of Arabs?'

'Thousands. Many thousands. Big planes, full of families – women in black, men in suits. Children. They can be very rude. They break things at the hotels and they fight when we ask them to pay. And rude when they talk to you. Sometimes they say to me, "We go"' – and Chandra flapped his arms – 'because they can't say "airport".'

'So what do you think?'

'I think if you're a good person, you don't need religion.'

'They've got a lot of religion.'

'They pray five times a day, and still they are terrible. So rude!'

Chandra took me to Penang's botanical garden so I could see the varieties of bamboo. I debated whether to look up the procuress Lily, but I was still convalescing. I felt too fragile to roam the streets at night. I found an old paperback of *The Great Railway Bazaar* in a Georgetown bookshop and read some of it and thought: I am not that man any more, nor do these places exist any more. I was impatient to get to Singapore, so I bought a ticket and returned to Butterworth on the ferry and got a night train to Kuala Lumpur, in a compartment that was jammed with so many cardboard boxes there was hardly room for me. My fellow traveller was a Malay salesman for a firm dealing in table fans.

'Samples-lah!' he explained, but he was gone, with his boxes, when I woke up.

Even in the dim early morning I could see that Kuala Lumpur's main railway station was a marvel of good design, with marble floors, efficient clerks and lots of trains to choose from. Any city in America would have been proud to have such a station. I bought a ticket on a later train to Singapore so that I could have my noodles here.

Pulling away from Kuala Lumpur, I could see the city like a mirage hovering at treetop level, a capriccio of spires – jungle and palms in the foreground, the other-worldly skyscrapers showing in the mist, silvery in all the green, a fantasy skyline. That sight was a reminder that Malaysia was an oil-producing nation; the beautiful railway station and this train were more proof of the country's prosperity.

In the seven hours through the jungles of southern Malaysia, the kampongs of graceful houses, the palm-oil plantations, I wrote more of my Indian story. The verdant zone was restful and reassuring. Approaching Johore Bahru and the border, I saw that all I had written in my notebook was *jungle – palms – muddy river*.

WELCOME TO SINGAPORE was the greeting at Woodlands Station, the customs post, and under it a warning: THE PENALTY FOR DRUGS IS DEATH.

Little tinky-winky Singapore was unrecognizable, the most transformed of any city I had ever known in my life, a place twisted into something entirely new; and the people, too, like hothouse flowers that are forced to grow in artificial light, producing strange blooms and even stranger fruit. But I was disarmed by the feline good looks of Singapore women, soft, pale, kittenish girls with skinny arms and fragile bones; vulpine women, fox-faced and canny, quick-eyed, tense with frustrated intelligence. In great contrast, the toothy men hurried clumsily after them, down futuristic streets, giggling into mobile phones, pigeon-toed in their haste.

No one was fat. No one was poor. No one was badly dressed. But many Singaporeans had (so it seemed to me) the half-devil, half-child look of having been infantilized and overprotected by their unstoppably manipulative government. The entirety of Singapore's leadership was personified by the grouchy, hard-to-please Lee Kwan Yew. This tenacious nag, it seemed, refused to go away: after forty-one years in the government, at age eighty-three, he was still micromanaging the place. The city-state showed his tweaked and tinkered-with look, and so did the people. I had lived and worked here, at the University of Singapore, for three years in the 1960s. Then I'd passed through on my Railway Bazaar in 1973. Now I was back again, and nothing was familiar.

I was disoriented as soon as I left my hotel near the city centre, a place I had once known well, at the top of Orchard Road. But it no longer looked like Orchard Road. The street names had stayed the same, which made it all the more confusing because the streets themselves had been redrawn. Singapore had been a tiny colonial city on a tiny island, with a hinterland. It was now a single modernized piece of geography – island, city and rural areas had been combined to form a city-state, with muddy shores. It was a thoroughly urbanized island, 270 square miles of it – about the size of the Spanish island of Menorca, but much smaller than New York City.

It was a place without solitude. Cameras everywhere, snitches too. You can be arrested and fined for being naked in your own house, if someone gets a glimpse of you through a window and reports you. This is an inconvenient law, because being a place with no privacy, Singapore is also a place of great loneliness and fear, the apprehension of people who know they are forever being watched. Singaporeans are encouraged to spy on each other; rats are rewarded.

Joseph Conrad would have been able to find his way around the Singapore of the 1960s. He described a walk through the city in his long story 'The End of the Tether'. But the old horizontal city of shop-houses and bungalows had become a vertical city of tall buildings, and because of intensive land reclamation, the whole of Singapore was bigger by forty-three square miles. What had been the waterfront was now far from the sea – Beach Road was nowhere near the beach. Restrictions and subways limited the traffic on this island of merchandise for sale, highly organized streets, clusters of housing estates and many mansions. Flyovers had replaced narrow lanes, parks had replaced slums and shop-houses. A city of restaurants and department stores. A city of frenzied shoppers, most of them young. What struck me was that, as an effect of living in this place, Singaporeans were strange without knowing they were strange.

'You are here at an auspicious time,' a Singapore friend said.

'I hear that a lot.'

'No, really. They just unbanned *Saint Jack.*'

My Singapore novel, published in 1972, was at last available in Singapore. And the film made from it in 1978, by Peter Bogdanovich, was being shown in theatres. It was the only Hollywood film ever made entirely on location in Singapore – but done by trickery, as the Singapore-based writer Ben Slater had revealed in his recent book, *Kinda Hot: The Making of Saint Jack in Singapore.* Bogdanovich had not revealed to the authorities that he was filming my banned book, and because of this deception, and the film's portrayal of the sex trade, the Chinese gangs and the more colourful neighbourhoods – such as Bugis Street, thoroughfare of transvestites – the film had been banned. Because the ban had been lifted, and I had just arrived, my friends alerted the press. I was interviewed. It was the first and last time on my trip that my face appeared in the local papers.

Four interviews, each posing the question (among others): 'What do you think of Singapore?'

Singaporeans, keenly aware that they live in a safe, very tidy, highly organized and generally unfree city-state, need to be reassured that it is Shangri-la. It didn't matter that I'd been in Singapore for only two days.

'It all looks absolutely marvellous,' I said.

Interviewers can encourage harmless self-glorification in their subject, or they can be obstinate and unimpressed, or devious. But they have their uses. A great way to find old friends in a foreign city is to be interviewed for the press. In Singapore I met many people I would otherwise have been unable to find: great friends growing old here, and even old enemies – enemies, after all these years! But a cruel and unforgiving government can make its citizens cruel and unforgiving. Several people who were informants for the interviewers said, in so many words, what a horse's arse I had been and how they hadn't liked me.

'I talked to two or three of your former students,' one interviewer said, clicking her pen over her stenographer's notebook. The open page was covered with neat handwriting.

'Let me say one thing,' I said, interrupting her. 'The university students I had in Singapore were the brightest, the best, the most hard-working of any students I'd ever taught. And they spoiled me. I never found students that good anywhere else, so I gave up teaching.'

'That's quite a compliment. What did you teach?'

'Shakespeare's contemporaries, like Middleton and Tourneur. The revenge plays of the Jacobean period. What else? I gave a series of lectures on *The Winter's Tale*, and tutorials on Conrad, Henry James and D. H. Lawrence — all the stuff on the Cambridge syllabus. *Great Expectations*.' She was writing this down. 'So what did they say?'

'They weren't very complimentary.'

'Really?' I was surprised. The head of the English Department, D. J. Enright, a highly regarded English poet and literary critic, much loved by the students, affected an air of bonhomie with them, while being something of a taskmaster with his staff. He was a hard worker himself, and he suspected me of being an upstart. His need to assert himself had turned him into an inveterate gossip, and his puritanical streak made him a retailer of steamy rumours. He held court in the Staff Club, where we all drank beer, moaned about the government and the weather, and speculated on campus adulteries. As the first American who'd ever taught in Enright's department, I had to prove I was a scholar. And I needed the job; I tried hard to impress him. I liked the diligent students, so I felt my effort was in a good cause.

'One of your students said, "If you can't say something nice, don't say anything. So I'm not saying anything."'

I swallowed and said, 'Go on.'

'Another one said you were arrogant. Does this bother you?'

'No,' I said. But it did. I saw my earlier self in my office, working my way through a stack of students' essays about *The Changeling*. I was twenty-seven years old. I was on the lowest lecturer's salary, earning the equivalent of $50 a week. I had a wife and two children to support. I was trying to write *Saint Jack*. I wasn't arrogant, I was desperate.

My novel was about a man of fifty, hard up in Singapore, with dreams of happiness. I was hard up; I felt fifty. I had dreams too.

'And another one . . .'

'Oh,' I said, because being belittled made me remember, 'I lived in a tiny house with no air conditioning.'

'This one said you were unapproachable.'

'I was in my office from nine to five — Enright insisted we keep office hours. "Where's Paul?" he'd say, even when I didn't have to deliver a lecture. Students dropped in all the time. I thought they liked me.'

She was still studying her notebook page. 'One described you as a "less than perfect teacher".'

'Less than perfect! Ha! Probably true.'

'Do you remember a student called Kirpal Singh?'

'Very well. A nice kid. What I remember was that he was poor and studious, odd man out – a Sikh among the Chinese. And the government took his scholarship away. The government's line was that studying English didn't build the nation. They wanted engineers and economists. Kirpal got screwed and so did lots of other scholarship students. More of Lee Kwan Yew's meddling.'

She was reading: ' "Singh recalls that Theroux would be late for class, not return assignments on time, and fail to give individual feedback, making him feel shortchanged as a student".'

'Are you going to print that?'

'I'm going to write a balanced piece.'

'Shortchanged?' I said, my voice becoming shrill. 'I stuck my neck out and complained to the vice chancellor when his scholarship was taken away!'

Several interviews were published, with the anonymous abuse and innuendo, and the one with Kirpal Singh's criticism. In that piece Kirpal, who was fifty-seven, was described as 'a poet and associate professor of creative thinking at Singapore Management University'.

I called his office. I said, 'Kirpal, this is Paul Theroux. Why are you saying these terrible things about me?'

'They misquoted me,' he said, and gabbled a little about his innocence. 'Want to meet for a beer?'

'Time for a Tiger,' I said.

Over fish-head curry at an open-air restaurant, Kirpal was shamefaced and apologetic. I smiled as he explained that he had said to the reporter I was *sometimes* late and *occasionally* didn't return assignments and *now and then* . . . He was bearded and grizzled, still wearing a turban, hot-faced, jolly and plump. His new wife was Chinese. They had a small boy. It was wonderful to see Kirpal, talking about his poetry, still alive, animatedly trying to convince me that he had not maligned me, while I laughed and drank Tiger beer.

'There should be a retraction,' he said, tugging his beard.

The other interviews rubbished me in the same way, not for being a bad writer but for having been a poor teacher, for my dubious character. In Singapore, a place that demanded absolute loyalty of its citizens, accusing someone of being unreliable or disloyal was much worse than saying his writing was bad.

An old colleague who got in touch after the interviews invited me to his club. He said, 'They were so unfair. You must be annoyed.'

'Not annoyed. Fascinated.'

One of the characteristics of autocratic rule, even a benign, well-intentioned autocracy like Lee's Singapore, was that whispers and betrayal, survival skills, had become modes of being. Wayward citizens were punished unmercifully: anyone caught with drugs was hanged, and even petty criminals were flogged with a *rotan*, a narrow rattan rod, sometimes thirty or forty strokes on the back or buttocks. What I have written so far here would be enough to get my arse whipped in Singapore.

Strange blooms, eh? Cruel and unforgiving government, eh? Drop your trousers and bend over, Mister Thorax! You're getting fifty cuts of the *rotan*!

An exaggeration? Not really. My friend Christopher Lingle, the scholar and journalist, wrote an op-ed piece for the *International Herald Tribune* in 1994 that mentioned 'certain south-east Asian countries . . . bankrupting the opposition by means of a compliant judiciary'. He did not mention Singapore by name, yet the Singapore government took umbrage. Lingle lost his job at Singapore's National University and was charged with contempt of court and violating a law against 'scandalizing the judicial system'. He was placed under house arrest, from which he cleverly escaped, doing a midnight flit out of the country.

I happened to see Lingle in Bangkok, on my way here. He is a serious and widely published political economist and university professor.

'Lee takes too much credit for Singapore's success,' Lingle had said. 'What has he actually produced? Seventy per cent of Singapore's businesses are foreign-owned.'

'Singapore is a success, though.'

'Cities are always places of high productivity. He wouldn't have been able to run Malaysia.'

'Tell me why.'

'Because he is articulate but incoherent.'

'How would you rate him?'

'I don't rate him at all. Singapore is an example of banal economic theory,' Lingle said. 'A monkey could do it.'

Punishment for not toeing the government's line was always on the Singaporean's mind. It shows in the Singaporean face, typically an anxious face – pouting kittenish women, frowning nerdish men. When I'd lived in Singapore – because of my writing, and for speaking my mind in lectures – I had not been popular with the government, and the government had not changed. After three years here, I was told by the new department head – a whiny, fretful-faced local man, politically connected – that my contract would not be renewed. I was fired for being a political liability. *You talk too much*, my colleagues said. *You tell too many jokes.* I published stories in *Playboy* magazine. So I left under a cloud of growing xenophobia. Thereafter, I became someone a loyal Singaporean could not praise, which was why, decades later, I was still being rubbished.

'If you play along, you advance here,' an Indian labour organizer told me. I had met him in the Indian district, on Serangoon Road. He was bringing me up to date. 'But if you criticize, the PM will crush you like a cockroach.'

'There is no other place like this on earth,' said my old club-going Singaporean friend, whom I will call Wang. He meant this in every possible sense. He was a citizen, and he spoke with the usual Singaporean ambivalence.

Nominally, Singapore is a democracy. In reality it is no such thing. Any critic of the government is subject to criminal proceedings, heavy fines, libel suits, threats or jail. The leader of the opposition party once said euphemistically that the government had engaged in shady dealings. A lawsuit followed. The Singapore technique is diabolically effective. Foreign critics like Chris Lingle are deported or placed under house arrest, and if they are journalists, their newspapers or magazines are sued. This has happened numerous times to the *Far Eastern Economic Review*, the *International Herald Tribune*, Bloomberg.com, and other news outlets. Singaporean critics or aspiring politicians are pursued through the courts with fanatical zeal, and sued with such severity they are bankrupted. Judges are appointed by the government and are indeed compliant. Destroyed financially, an opposition politician can't run for office – can hardly live.

'But he doesn't beat people in the streets,' Wang said, speaking of Lee Kwan Yew, who now held the title of 'minister mentor' and whose son is prime minister. 'He', in Singapore, always meant Lee.

I reminded Wang that Lee had famously praised the Chinese in 1989 for brutally suppressing, shooting and imprisoning the demonstrators in

Tiananmen Square, backing the Chinese government in the massacre of thousands. And Lee's uncompromising approval of this cruelty had frightened Singaporeans to such an extent that similar demonstrations had never occurred here, though individually critics had been persecuted.

'He's very shrewd,' Wang said. But Wang was also shrewd. He said, 'Think of the Machiavelli line about "economy of violence".'

'Kill a chicken to scare the monkeys, the Chinese disciplinarians say.'

Lee gave a rare press conference when I was in Singapore. I saw it on television. He had aged in a remarkable way, not just becoming white-haired but acquiring withered, almost simian features – not the thuggish scowl of a Triad chieftain he'd had when I'd last seen him, but a pinched and unforgiving look that I associated with unhappy captives, like a caged thing scowling through bars.

'I can't retire,' Lee protested at the beginning of this talk. And through-out it he kept up the tone of an old meddler who says, *Look what you're making me do!* He went on, 'There are things in Singapore that no other minister can do.' Even at the age of eighty-three, he refused to retire and play golf. 'I still have ideas. I want to tweak it a bit more.'

Lee's use of the word 'tweak' always meant meddle and micromanage and fiddle with people's lives.

'Why not leave that to younger politicians and leaders?' someone inquired.

'I'm the only one who understands what Singapore needs,' he snapped. 'Next question.'

A foreign journalist suggested obliquely that this was an arrogant way of governing – after all, he had been out of office for some years.

'If I were arrogant, would I be talking to you?' Lee said, and told the man to sit down, adding, 'There are very few things you can tell me about Singapore – what will work, what won't work. That's my value to the government.' He was annoyed at having been defied. Before he left the podium, he said, 'I know what will work here because I tweaked the system to get us here!'

'He's respected, he's somewhat admired, but not loved,' my friend Wang said. 'He knows that. He's rather sad that he's not loved.'

Lee is of course a cold and single-minded control freak, a puritanical, domineering know-it-all, oddly resentful in the things he says; and Singapore society reflects everything in Lee's personality. Not surpris-ingly, Lee's domineering father was a severe disciplinarian, who insisted his son speak English at home. Lee is a highly emotional man who has publicly sobbed, to his own shame and to the horror of his stoical electorate. People said, *I thought that was the whole point of him, that he didn't cry,* and yet there he was, on national television, blubbing his heart out.

Beware the blubbing autocrat, for he will make you cry. As a leader, Lee allowed his personal agonies to eat into people's lives, making Singapore a reflection of one man's anxieties. He famously hates gum-chewing, smoking, littering and nudity. Chewing gum is banned in Singapore, hardly anyone smokes, no one litters – the fines for them are severe – and *Playboy* has been banned for decades. Lee suspects he is being plotted against, so it is a society without any privacy and virtually without an opposition. Lee is xenophobic; Singaporeans likewise tend to be dismissive or sarcastic about foreigners, regarding them as decadent and disorderly. Lee is puritanical. So are they. Movies are routinely censored, TV shows too. *The Sopranos* was sharply edited and bleeped. *Deadwood* was so bleeped it became incomprehensible, and broadcasts were stopped. *Six Feet Under* was chopped to pieces for its sexual innuendo. Lee refuses to be challenged or questioned, much less criticized. Apart from anything else, this condescension and censorship are odd in a highly educated country, with one of the highest literacy rates in the world.

Virtually the only Singaporean who has dared to speak openly to the government is a fiction writer and former linguistics professor, Catherine Lim, a courageous woman in her mid-sixties. Unlike her imaginative and witty novels, her op-ed pieces read like stern memos. She asks for more transparency, more idealism, more heart, more sentiment. In a 2007 essay published in the *Straits Times*, she wrote: 'Even in a society often described as aggressively materialistic and coldly efficient, there are, fortunately, Singaporeans who believe idealism has a place, and that the fire, passion and commitment of the Old Guard, who saw Singapore through the difficult early years with little hope of financial reward, are still alive in some young Singaporeans.'

No sooner does one of Lim's pieces appear than it is jeered at by a government functionary, and Lim is put in her place. In any other country, she would be regarded as a caring, auntie figure. She is not so much a critic of the government as someone who is trying to define a national mood and suggesting modest proposals, but even so, such temerity in Singapore makes her sound like Thomas Paine.

Despising and belittling the electorate, intolerant of the political opposition, which he regards as riff-raff, Lee is as prominent now as he was forty years ago when I first arrived to teach at the University of Singapore – and was told by the vice chancellor to get a haircut. That was in 1968, not a notable year for barbershop visits by twenty-somethings.

On my return trip, I tried to talk to my interviewers and friends about Lee and his party and Singapore's political direction, but no one except my old friend Wang would discuss politics – and he did so in a whisper. For fear of being misunderstood or overheard, no one mentioned Lee Kwan Yew by name. He was like the Mafia capo who is never named. In the Genovese crime family, a soldier would refer to the boss, Vincent (the Chin) Gigante, only by touching his chin, never speaking the name. It was rare to hear anyone say 'Lee'. They said 'He' or 'LKY', sometimes 'the Old Man' or 'Uncle Harry', or they winked.

Because Lee shaped Singapore, the place bears all his characteristics and is stamped with his personality, his quirks, his crotchets. He has caused Singaporeans to take up golf. He has no sense of humour – laughs are rare in the city-state. Singaporeans' personalities reflect that of the only leader most of them have ever known, and as a result are notably abrasive, abrupt, thin-skinned, unsmiling, rude, puritanical, bossy, selfish and unspiritual. Because they can't criticize the government, they criticize each other or pick on foreigners. And in this hanging and flogging society they openly spank their children.

An expatriate woman from Europe who had lived in Singapore for many years said to me, 'Singaporeans have no grace. They are the rudest people I've ever met. I was pregnant with my second child. I had a tiny child by the hand. On a bus, no one would ever stand up to give me a seat.' A moment later, she added, 'But I love living here. I have a comfortable house. My children have good schools. It's well organized. It's safe.'

Lee, a Cambridge graduate, is a great admirer of the British. He has a prickly history with the United States – his socialist utterances in the 1960s provoked the CIA to subvert some people in his party with payoffs and intrusions. He has never forgiven America for this.

'He's a frank admirer of President Bush,' one of my Singaporean friends said. 'But he disliked Clinton for his irregular private life. Do you remember when that American boy damaged the car and was caned for it?'

This was Michael Fay, an eighteen-year-old who was stripped naked, bent over a trestle and tied, then arse-whipped with six strokes. He also got a heavy fine and four months in prison – this for spray-painting graffiti on cars in a Singapore car park. Fay was a punk who deserved to be disciplined. But whipped? Yet his punishment was mild, practically ridiculous, in comparison with the torture meted out to many others in Singapore's jails, whose cases never got into the newspapers: many more strokes, long prison sentences on political grounds or for thought crimes, or death by hanging for drug offences.

Wang said, 'Fay would not have been caned had Reagan been in power. Lee was trying to teach Clinton a lesson, showing Clinton that Singapore disapproved of him by whipping the American boy.'

Some US senators lodged a protest. President Clinton called the punishment 'excessive', though his outrage at the caning must be weighed against his unseemly haste just two years earlier, in 1992, to stop campaigning for president in New Hampshire and fly back to Arkansas to authorize the execution of Ricky Ray Rector, a mentally retarded black man.

The American reaction to Fay's punishment provoked Lee to reveal in an outburst what he really thought of American society and how he viewed Singapore. 'The US government, the US Senate, and the US media took the opportunity to ridicule us, saying the sentence was too severe,' he said in a television interview. The United States 'does not restrain or punish individuals, forgiving them for whatever they have done. That's why the whole country is in chaos: drugs, violence, unemployment and homelessness.'

Like the head of an isolated cult who preaches to his people that only they are pure in a wicked world, Lee actually believes that America is 'in chaos', and he enjoins Singaporeans to believe this nonsense and to count their blessings. We Americans are undisciplined and bestial, out of control and criminal. Singapore is the opposite, orderly and safe, non-violent and hard-working, and will continue to be so under Lee's leadership.

Some time ago, on a rare trip to Paris, so a well-placed friend told me, Lee was granted a meeting with François Mitterrand. Lee began lecturing the premier of France on governance. After Lee had left the room, Mitterrand said, 'Who is this ridiculous man who wastes my time? Running Singapore is like running Marseilles. I am running a whole country!'

Lee's Anglophilia is shared by Singaporeans, but it is based on a dated notion of English ways, a set of social snobberies – tea-drinking, cricket-watching and harmless affectations – and an over-formal way of dressing in the Singapore heat, turning up the air conditioning so they can wear tweeds and Burberry sweaters. Like Lee, Singaporeans are assiduous, honest, tidy to the point of obsessiveness and efficient. They also tend to be inflexible and stern. They are fluent in English, though with a small vocabulary, and in pronunciation and idiomatic bewilderments they have made the language their own. Their jaw-twisting yips and glottal stops are so sudden and glugging that some words can sound less like language than a gag reflex.

Lee is a vain and domineering patriarch, and with the passing years he sounds more and more like the head of a cult than a political leader. His son Lee Hsien Loong is prime minister, and a chip off the old block. Hsien Loong's wife, Ho Ching, is the executive director of the government-linked Temasek Holdings. The Lee family is the nearest thing to a political dynasty. Yet Lee never smiles. He is never satisfied.

'No one ever gets a compliment here,' a Singaporean woman told me. 'There is no flattery. People are suspicious of compliments or any expression of appreciation. Toughness is the style. Good manners are suspect.'

In a Singapore joke, a man goes into an antique shop and sees a lovely image next to an ugly one. 'I know that's Kwan Yin, the goddess of mercy,' the man says, 'but who is that ugly one?' The shop owner says, 'It's Kwan Yew, the god of no mercy.'

Singaporeans are intensely aware of their living like lab rats in this huge social experiment. It seems to make them melancholic and self-conscious and defensive.

Singapore is a real tinkered-with experiment – not the political con game of Turkmenistan, or the free-for-all of India, or the tyranny of Myanmar, or the muddle and make-do of Sri Lanka, or the neglect of Laos. Thailand seemed to me exceptional – a success because people were proud, loved their king, had a sense of unity and had never been colonized. Singapore came into existence because the British colonized the jungly place. Having made it a class- and race-conscious island of clubs and bars, the British kept it as an imperial artefact until the Japanese invaded, during the Second World War, little skinny soldiers riding in on bikes, capturing the island and humiliating the British for four years in diabolical prisons.

The Japanese demonstrated that British rule was hollow, self-interested and weak. After the war, the British looked impotent and lost their will to govern. Singapore was dominated by Islamic, Chinese-hating Malaya, which became the Republic of Malaysia in 1963. At last, in 1965, in a lachrymose display, weeping on TV (but he cries easily), Lee declared the island's independence. He was humbled, because he had believed his destiny was to be Malaysia's prime minister, not CEO of this tiny island, more a corporation or a cult than a country. But he reminded Singaporeans that they were surrounded by enemies, and he invited the world to do business in his city-state. Foreign companies relocated here, invested their capital and helped Singapore to become an economic success. It has flourished because it made itself useful to the great powers and to global business.

Because initiative is dangerous in an autocracy, Singaporeans are employees, not innovators. And because space is at a premium and the cost of living is high, Singaporeans marry late and, either through pessimism or procrastination, tend not to produce children. The birth rate fell so sharply in the early eighties that a government dating agency was started in 1984, to host matchmaking parties, to promote marriages and births. This agency, called the Social Development Unit, or SDU (known to Singapore wags as Single, Desperate and Ugly), was a failure. While I was in Singapore in 2006, it was disbanded.

Over the course of my week here, I reacquainted myself with old Singapore friends and heard their stories.

One said: 'My wife went to Australia. She was studying for a degree. But when she finished, she wouldn't come back. I went there and tried to persuade her. She said that she could never live here again, although she was born here. It wasn't a man. She just couldn't bear Singapore any more. So we got a divorce.'

One said: 'Your student [and he named him] killed himself. Your student [and he named her] also killed herself. Suicide is a Singapore solution.'

One said: 'We never go to Malaysia or Indonesia, although they're right next door. The Muslims are crazy. They want to overwhelm us. They deliberately isolated us.'

One said: 'Life here is shopping and eating. Also "What kind of car do you have?" and "Where are you going on holiday?" When women get together they talk about clubs, investments, money, stock tips and servants.'

One said: 'Do you remember [and he named two former students]? They got married, but when they split up she became a fanatical Catholic. She never goes out. She only stays in her flat and prays.'

One said: 'I bought a new car a few years ago. It cost me forty-five thousand dollars US. I first had to apply for a permit to buy it. In ten years I'll have to renew this permit, and that will cost money. Everything is regulated – buying the car, driving, access, parking. It's a fortune, and this is just a little Nissan sedan. But no one really needs a car here.'

One said: 'We never talk about politics, race or religion. We never talk about the prime minister. We never tell ethnic jokes. We hardly tell jokes. Joking can be dangerous.'

One said: 'Yes, we're pushy. There's a reason for it – the Hokkien expression *kia su*, "afraid to lose". No one wants to be seen holding the short straw.'

One said: 'Remember [and he named a Singaporean]? He still hates you!'

One said: 'Yes, it is a life without texture.'

One said: 'The big man [Lee] has erased the old Singapore. Singapore begins with him. He has obliterated the past. Though you can see the city had a colonial history, he has tried to erase it. That's your problem here, Paul – you're a ghost from the past.'

And here is the contradiction. Everyone I met in Singapore treated me with the utmost courtesy. I was fed the Singapore delicacies – chilli crabs and dumplings and steamed fish and bowls of *laksa*. I was invited to give a lecture at the new national library, and 400 people showed up. I was driven around by the sweetest, most solicitous people I'd met on my whole trip. They smoothed my way. What did I need? How could they help? Did I want something to read? Was there anyone I'd like to meet? Was I hungry? Was I tired? Was I having a good time?

I swore I would not carp. I had been sick on my trip, endured nasty governments and horrible hotels, drunk filthy water on dirty trains and eaten disgusting food and put up with drunks and thieves and pests. Here I was in a place where everything worked, everything was clean, everything was on time.

While I wrote my notes at night, my hand began to shake. It seemed ungrateful to be criticizing, yet it was horribly unfair that there was so little room for people to grow and be happy. The government's interest in the arts or culture was entirely fictitious, just another bid for control. For all the bright talk there was a reflex of pessimism when it came to action. No one wanted to have children in Singapore, not many people even wanted to get married. The city-state kept evolving, but because the rule was 'conform or leave', Singaporeans remained in a condition of arrested development, all the while being reminded that they were lucky to be governed by inspired leadership – in effect, the Lee family.

Lee was a social leveller, but like all levellers he had elevated himself, introduced contradictions, and created a society in which there were privileges for the few, monotony for the many. Lee and his planners were full of great ideas. The trouble was – and it seemed to me a fault of most repressive, power-hungry people – they didn't know when to stop.

But there is another Singapore. It takes a while to find, and you need someone in the know to help. One of my friends, 'Jason Tan', heard me denouncing Lee for sanitizing the place, and said, 'Give me a couple of days. I'll show you things that most people don't see.'

The first thing I saw, at midnight in the outer district of Geylang, was a skinny prostitute in a tight red dress, praying as she burned so-called gold paper (*kim chwa* in Hokkien) in a brazier on the pavement, a thick sheaf of gilt-embossed fake banknotes – quite a blaze, outside a noisy joint where other prostitutes (kittenish, vulpine) were groping men, who were standing at a bar.

'She is transferring gold,' Jason said, 'from this world to the souls in the underworld, who can spend it – like Western Union, into the next world.'

I liked this unusual Singapore sight: decadent beauty, obvious vice, ancient superstition, defiant litter, veneration, smoke and ashes. There was something about this intense little ceremony, being performed by a dusky dragon lady in a crimson dress, white-faced with makeup, red lips, with long fingernails and stiletto heels, that made it superb.

In a Singapore that had turned its back on the past, that never talked about having been part of the British empire, or despised subjects of the Japanese for four years of occupation, or as the setting for books by Joseph Conrad, Somerset Maugham, Anthony Burgess or even me – Singapore's history had started with Lee Kwan Yew – this prostitute praying in the open, using fake money and real flames, was a strange and wonderful thing.

Something stranger lay beyond her: twelve long streets of whore-houses, massage parlours, bars, knocking shops and love hotels. Local lady-boys – young men in makeup – were cruising and winking, and so were transvestites; streetwalkers were perched on benches or motor-cycles, looking decorous and making kissing sounds of invitation.

'How much?'

'Eighty dollah. Take me.'

That was fifty US dollars, and in Geylang it was the going rate for a short time.

'You want I come your hotel? Hundred dollah. Take me.'

Some slender women from China with snake-like features and long legs simply held their breasts and offered them in delicate eloquence, saying, 'No speak English.'

It was the old recognizable Singapore, but there was much more of it than before. Because Singaporeans were encouraged to put the best face on their city-state, and because (as I learned later) none of the sex workers were Singaporean, this wild side was never written about or advertised.

'See? See?' Jason Tan said. 'This is Lorong Four – all the even-numbered streets up to Lorong Twenty-four or Twenty-six are reserved for sex.'

Lorong is the Malay word for lane or small street, and we were walking up East Coast Road, which bisected the numbered streets, looking east down the *lorongs* where each shop-house held ten or fifteen prostitutes, some lolling on couches, others sitting inside glass enclosures like aquari-ums, each girl wearing a number and frantically beckoning as we came near.

'Does the government know about this?'

'Are you kidding? These are government-licensed whorehouses. The girls have medical cards. They have to get regular checkups.'

It was more than a few licentious streets; it was a whole district of crowded roads, each one like Gin Lane – noodle shops, open-air bars, brothels, cheap hotels, women sitting on kerbstones, teenagers gaping, groups of young men swigging beer; very busy on this hot night, very noisy, very lively. The pedestrians and gawkers were mainly locals – Chinese, Malays, Indians, with a smattering of bewildered *ang mohs*, the Singapore term for red-haired devils. Because Singapore was well policed, the district was safe; because Singapore is tidy-minded, there was no litter; and because of restrictions, there was hardly any traffic.

Just strollers, cruisers, touts, pimps and the usual selection of Artful Dodgers. The whole district was well organized while allowing freedom of movement. I didn't see any police, yet it was orderly, and I presumed self-regulated, probably by gangs, the Triads, the secret societies that have been enforcers in Singapore since the nineteenth century.

The love hotels – Hotel 81, Fragrance Hotel and others – were brand new, several on each street, with prices posted: $25 for two hours. They were staffed by young male clerks in uniforms, in contrast with the pimps and the brothel managers, who were tattooed and looked tough and gang-connected.

'If you just gonna look, lah, get out. You waste my time,' a thuggish man said to me, ordering me away from a fish tank full of numbered beauties.

'These guys are mostly ex-cons,' Jason said. 'Don't piss them off. They'll thump you.'

Inside the entrance of every brothel was a Chinese shrine, a Taoist niche, with a furious god, one of the Immortals, and a pot of smouldering joss sticks and some fresh fruit and a dish of money.

'You come here to talk-talk-talk, lah?'

'I was just wondering . . .'

He was a short but muscular man with a brutal haircut, a scarred face and badly inked prison tattoos. He darted at me and barked, 'Get out!'

The sex industry is fastidiously time-conscious, much more so than most other industries; the minute, not the hour, is the important unit. There is no clock watcher like a pimp or a whore, though given the large amount of time they spent idly awaiting a trick, this seems an unreasonable statement.

'Are these local girls?'

Jason said no. He had the subtle Singaporean eye for ethnicity and racial distinctions. The girls, he said, were Thai, Burmese, Malay, Indian, Cambodian, Vietnamese, mainland Chinese, Indonesian, Mongolian, Filipino. They were the nationalities that served as domestics in Singapore: the scrubbers, the amahs, the child minders, the house cleaners, the car washers. The word here was that no Singaporean girls worked as domestics. The same foreign nationalities were sex workers as well.

Like the stews and baths of Elizabethan London, teeming with fearless whores and promenading clients, drunks and lurkers, spitting and spewing, guzzling beer, slurping oysters, this part of Geylang, with its great sweaty vitality, was vicious too, the women like zoo animals, gesturing and pleading from cages, promising a good time, something special, a bath, a Jacuzzi, a massage, making unambiguous gestures and mouthing obscenities.

'Choose one,' the pimps cried. 'Hurry up.'

What made it unusual was that these women were not in bars, not dancing, not drunk. No strip clubs here, no shakedown. The brothels were arranged like Chinese shops, where instead of merchandise – but of course they were a form of merchandise – the women sat waiting for customers, hissing at them: Choose me!

Towards the end of one *lorong*, young prostitutes clutching handbags, wearing high heels, stood under the eaves of houses, smiling, or under trees, or near cars. When I approached them, fierce boys appeared, shielding them.

'Don't talk to the girls. Talk to us!'

'You hungry?' Jason asked me. 'You want noodles?'

We sat, each of us with a bowl of noodles and a beer, on a street corner at the edge of this floating world.

'There's Gerrie Lim,' Jason said. He had told me earlier that Gerrie might show up.

I had heard of Lim. A Singaporean, he was the author of *Invisible Trade*, about the sex industry in Singapore, not just the business of whorehouses and high-priced escorts, but also the trade in rent boys, lady-boys, male prostitutes. Earlier in his journalistic career Gerrie had had a monthly column in *Penthouse* magazine, writing about adult films. In the noodle shop he told me he was something of an authority on a famous Singapore porn star named Grace Quek, who in 1995, under the name Annabel Chong, had had sex with 251 men in about ten hours, setting a record (later broken). Annabel's feat had been filmed.

'Her mother saw the movie. Poor old woman cried.'

The pixie-faced 23-year-old's sexual athleticism, which was both rebellious and weirdly competitive, had a local angle. In a film of her life, she said she was rebelling against the typical Singaporean restraint, the stricture 'close yourself to the world'. And in an interview she gave in 2000, she had elaborated on this: 'I looked back on my entire life in Singapore and realized that all my life I had been processed.' Perhaps Singapore repression did inspire her joyless exhibitionism, but it seemed to me that Grace Quek's most Singaporean trait was her reflex to blame the little island for her wilful nymphomania. Blaming was a national vice. Singaporeans did not see themselves as individuals but rather as indistinguishable cogs in Lee Kwan Yew's experimental machine.

Gerrie Lim was noncommittal when I laid this out. His equivocation was also a Singapore trait and a survival skill. He was a slightly built but intense man in his late forties, with a polite manner. His over-large glasses made him seem scholarly from one angle, lecherous from another.

'What do you think of this?' Gerrie asked, and gestured to the activity around us.

'I wasn't expecting it. Maybe old Singapore didn't change. Maybe it just moved to Geylang.'

'This is the other Singapore,' Gerrie said. 'People don't believe it!' He said to Jason, 'You take him to Paramount Shopping Centre?'

'We go Paramount later.'

'You take him to Orchard Towers?'

'Later.'

'What's Orchard Towers?' I asked.

'Four floors of whores,' Gerrie said. 'You want to see an escort service? Russian girls, English ones. Big money.'

'Maybe later,' I said. I had finished my noodles. 'I think I'll just walk around here.'

I chose a *lorong* at random and walked down it, looking left and right at the glowing, freshly painted shop-houses, each with the front door open, getting glimpses of girls seated just inside; some had fish tanks of girls. Further down the *lorong*, the road narrowed; it was darker, the houses looked gloomier, but still their windows were lit, the distinct movement of women upstairs.

'That's all,' Jason said.

We reached the end of the *lorong*, where a dark lane intersected it. No streetlamps here, not even any shop-houses, only shadows.

'Might as well go back,' Jason said.

But I saw the lighted tip of a cigarette moving towards us, and the person who held it, a man in a white smock-like shirt.

'Good evening, gentlemen. Can I help you?'

'What have you got?'

'Come this way,' he said. He almost disappeared in the darkness, but because his shirt was white we were able to follow him. No lights burned anywhere here. From time to time I saw the red tip of his cigarette when he puffed it. When my eyes became accustomed to the darkness I saw that he was leading us between two low tin-roofed buildings through a wooden gate. I followed the scrape and scuff of his loose sandals. Because it was too dark to take notes, I said to myself, Chicken coop. Behind me, Jason was sighing, sounding anxious. The man was beckoning.

'What's your name?' I asked.

'My name is King. Come through here.'

He led us into a deeper darkness. No helpful sky or stars or moon here, just walls all around and a tin roof.

'In here,' King said.

I could not see anything at all. He shot a bolt on a door and felt for a light cord. In a sudden brightening, King jerked a light on and I saw four young girls come awake, to a sitting position, on a bare mattress. They wore T-shirts and shorts, but because of the dazzle of the bare bulb they squinted and made faces. They were secondary-school age and the room was like a crude bedroom, the girls blinking and covering their faces.

'Which one you want?'

I had been as startled as the girls. But they looked worried and unwelcoming, and who could blame them?

'Maybe we'll come back later.'

Sighing, King turned off the light and locked the door. When we were in darkness again, he said, 'Maybe you want something a little younger?'

He was leading. He scuffed on his sandals to another low tin-roofed hut and fumbled with a bolt, pulled the door open, switched on a bright light.

More blinking girls, like an apparition in the brightness, five or six of them squirming on a mattress that lay flat on the floor. Their blinking in the light made them look terrified – and they may well have been terrified, for none was older than fourteen or fifteen. They were Thais, with simple dignified faces, very skinny, almost frail, also in T-shirts and shorts, jostling.

King said something to them in their language. No sooner had he finished than they stood up in a little twitching group, their shoulders touching. They were at once fearful and eager, shy, looking pressured, like fourteen-year-olds in a gym class being hectored by a fierce coach.

'Which one you want?'

One thin-necked unsmiling girl, with pale skin and a fragile body, narrow shoulders and no breasts, tried shyly, turning sideways, to catch my eye. She was attempting to smile, but her eyes gave her away, for as she posed as a coquette, she seemed afraid that I might choose her. She was a soft pale thing with muscles like custard. Was I imagining that she was twisting a little stuffed toy in her hands?

'Maybe later.'

'I'll be here,' King said.

I got one last glimpse of the girl before he switched the light off. Her child's face stayed with me the rest of the night and saddened me.

We met Gerrie Lim back at the noodle shop. We left Geylang and went by taxi to Katong and the Paramount Shopping Centre, where energetic Filipinas howled when they saw us. This horde of clawing, screeching girls fell upon us and tried to drag us into one of the bars that lined the long hallway. We then went back to Orchard Road, where Gerrie brought me to an escort agency run by a lisping and unamiable Indian, who opened a fat album of photographs.

'Russian . . . Ukraine . . . Romania,' he said. They were hard-faced women, alluringly posed in expensive dresses. It could have been a clothing catalogue. 'This one works during day in estate agency . . . This one teacher . . . This one in shop. Booking fee three hundred. You work out the negotiation for whatever else.'

He was one of many, Gerrie said after we left. Twenty-four pages of the Singapore telephone directory were filled with escort services. We took a short walk up Orchard Road to a busy intersection at the corner of Scotts Road. In an earlier time I used to go to the nearby cinema I saw *Midnight Cowboy* here.

'What's this?' I asked, because we were right on Orchard Road, in the middle of one of the largest shopping districts. I had passed the building twenty times without knowing what was upstairs.

'Orchard Towers,' Gerrie said. 'Four floors of whores.'

We went to the top floor and worked our way down, from bar to bar, seeing the same ethnic variety we'd seen in Geylang – Thai, Burmese, Mongolian, Lao and all the others. The bars had themes. One was hard rock, another tropical decor. Gerrie's favourite was country and western; most of the girls were from Vietnam.

I bought some of the girls drinks. They smiled. 'Please,' they said. 'Take me.'

I said goodnight to Gerrie and Jason. Alone, I walked back to my hotel, which was surprisingly near. The face of the young girl who had been woken on her mattress by the over-bright light at Ah King's stayed with me. Sad, fearful, frail, her small breakable body and bright eyes. What haunted me about her was that she was obviously a recent arrival, not yet debauched, with a luminous innocence, the glow you see on the face of a child.

The next day I was in a taxi, going to a book sale, hoping to stock up for the next leg of my trip. I saw the driver's name on the identity disk on the dashboard: Wally Thumboo.

'Wally, can I ask you a question?'

'Can,' he said with Singaporean economy.

I mentioned where I had been prowling – Geylang, Katong, Orchard Towers, even Serangoon Road, where taxi drivers themselves paid for sex – Indian girls for a few dollars, the lowest of the Singapore stews.

'No Singapore girls!' he said to my reflection in his rear-view mirror. That was his boast, and it was perhaps the rationalization for all of it.

'Why not?' I asked.

'We no do, lah!'

And he began lecturing me on the vices of foreigners. It was his master's voice, like listening to Lee Kwan Yew denouncing the morals of Americans while at the same time justifying the red-light district. The place of piggy *lorongs* was regulated, it wasn't dangerous, and best of all it was sanctioned because it didn't corrupt Singapore women. These were all foreigners. Only foreign women did those things. Singaporeans were well educated and much too pure for that.

'It is shameful for our girls to do such things.' And he became sententious and preachy, boasting of Singapore virtue.

22. The Slow Train to the Eastern Star

Back in Bangkok, buying a train ticket to the border, I ran into a *farang* who advised me to take the bus instead. I could even buy a bus ticket here at the main railway station. He smiled when I said that I had wanted to take the train to Cambodia long ago, but that it hadn't been possible.

'When was that?'

'Thirty-three years ago.'

'Bus is quicker.'

'I'm trying to be consistent.'

The Cambodian border wasn't far, only half a day's journey. The beauty of it, and its singularity, was that the train tracks ran due east, an almost straight line to another twinkling point of the Eastern Star.

The train left at six in the morning and would be at the border town of Aranyaprathet in the early afternoon – plenty of time to struggle across the border and onward to Siem Reap. That was the other thing I'd wanted to do all those years ago, visit the Angkor ruins.

None of this travel had been possible before, and the Thai side of the border had been thick with refugees, because the whole of Cambodia was in the grip of the Khmer Rouge, ruled by the reclusive tyrant Pol Pot. The Cambodian nightmare had ended in the late 1980s, but there were plenty of people who said that Cambodia was still tyrannized and hopeless. Now at least I could get a train to the frontier, and probably a bus after that.

I was bleary-eyed in the pre-dawn darkness when I boarded the train, which was almost empty, except for a Thai family and some huddled women, and at the far end of the open carriage, an Indian, obviously a trader, travelling with cardboard boxes.

Indians were hated in Thailand, a Thai man had confided to me once when he saw an Indian standing on a street corner. I asked him why.

'Because he is a *kaek*.'

'What's a *kaek*?'

Ghost Train to the Eastern Star

'*Kaek* is Indian. Also Pakistan man: Arab. Sri Lanka,' the Thai man said. 'Dark face, round eye.'

In the land of smiles, the races didn't mingle as much as it seemed.

'We have a saying. If you see a snake and a *kaek* at the same time, kill the *kaek* first.'

The Indian got off at Chachoengsao Junction, about an hour into the trip. The train rattled eastward into the heat, past mango orchards and cane fields. I was happy being on the move again, with the pleasant prospect of crossing into Cambodia later in the day. All the way to the border were tidy villages and little shops, flags of royal yellow and portraits of the king, commemorating the sixtieth year of his rule. After high-density Singapore and Bangkok, this was sunny, empty country-side and fresh air. Here and there I saw a rural village that was like a village in my Asiatic dreams, pretty bungalows surrounded by fruit trees, bananas, coconut palms, vegetable gardens and browsing cows, in a wide-open landscape that ventilated my mind.

I did not need to be told that we'd arrived at Aranyaprathet: everything about it suggested that it was the end of the line. The little station was empty, the road leading from it to the few streets of shops was empty except for some tuk-tuks. The town itself, like all border towns, had an unfinished look, a bit lawless, fatigued, provisional, undercapitalized, exactly the way travellers feel when they arrive in such a place, weary and noncommittal. The businesses cater less to the people living there than to the ones passing through. No one ever intends to stay long in a border town, and this anti-romantic note makes them attractive to travellers, reflects their own restlessness.

In Southeast Asia it seemed there was always a noodle shop that served as an agency for dealing with border formalities; that took passport pictures; that provided visa applications; that also sold cold drinks and fried rice and beer and stringy chicken; that owned a van for ferrying people to the border; that probably did laundry, too. And had waitresses who flirted with the travellers, because it was harmless, a gratuitous gesture – the guys would be somewhere else in an hour or so.

I found the noodle shop in Aranyaprathet that provided all these services. I had my noodles and caught the next van to the border post, a mile or less from the town. I fell into conversation with an American backpacker, a recent college graduate, about the onward journey and Angkor. Somehow the subject of India came up.

'I heard India sucks,' he said.

At the frontier on this hot day, children and young boys waited with big rubber-wheeled wagons to take the travellers' luggage and boxes, since, as with most national boundaries, the checkpoints were far apart, a town on each side. In this case, the salubrious one of Aranyaprathet was here, and over there was the disorderly gambling-paradise-on-the-rise of Cambodian Poipet, a few new casinos amid the rubble and slums of the scruffy town.

I walked across carrying my small bag, finding it remarkable how similar this rural border was to others I'd crossed elsewhere in the under-developed world: the usual junk-filled creek, the usual touts and hawkers and moneychangers, the pests, the lost souls, the overburdened women with small children, the nervous-looking men.

Then the queue at Thai immigration, a little paperwork, a passport stamp, and out through the door and the long walk to Cambodian immigration, more paperwork, another stamp, and a gauntlet of touts and hawkers and moneychangers. The Cambodian side was dustier, poorer, noisier, much more chaotic than the Thai side, and something of a shock.

It is seldom necessary to look for transport in such a place. At most borders of this kind transport is looking for you – buses needing passengers.

'Battambang! Siem Reap! Phnom Penh!'

'Siem Reap,' I said.

I was hustled to a waiting bus, an old one, with weary faces at the windows. I handed over my $5. It was very hot inside.

The tout said, 'No a.c., but we can open the windows.'

When the bus started down the bumpy dirt road I thought, If the road is this bad so near this town, it must get much worse further on. This proved to be the case. The next 150 miles, from the border to Siem Reap, took six hours. Locals said that in the wet season it could take twelve hours, the unpaved road turned to sludge by big tottering trucks, buses mired behind them, sometimes tumbling over the edge into the storm ditch. Today it was only dust and slowness and one blown-tyre episode, near enough to a noodle shop to serve as a pit stop. On a wall of this shop was a poster that I was to see in fifty more places in Cambodia: a photo of an adult holding a child's hand, and in big black letters, SEX WITH CHILDREN IS A CRIME.

Jouncing along the rutted road, looking out at the hard-pressed villages – poorly built huts, littered paths, rice harvesters working in flooded fields, ox carts blocking our way, men on old bikes – I had a vision of northern Malawi, in central Africa: the same bad roads and rusty bikes, the same sunshine, the same weariness. And something else: a creepy feeling that I put down to bad vibes.

African landscape, I scrawled in my pocket notebook. It's impossible to write on a bus, so that was about all I wrote until nightfall.

The negative vibrations I felt were not imaginary. They were the effect of the battered fields and broken huts, but most of all they were the effect of people's faces, a distinct derangement of features. Often, in a poor country the faces of old men, and especially their eyes, hold a look of terror. It can also be a look of fatigue and resignation, and underlying that, a tortured face, one that has seen horrors. Old women's faces too, but women in such places are stoical and resigned to violence; the men seem weaker and more deeply wounded.

This feeling wasn't hindsight, though I learned later that a half dozen of the 167 torture prisons and killing centres of the Khmer Rouge regime were located along this route. The book that gave me this and much more helpful information for understanding Cambodia was Philip Short's *Pol Pot: Anatomy of a Nightmare*, which I bought and read after I got to Phnom Penh.

'The landscape . . . and the life style [of rural Cambodia] were, and still are, closer to Africa than China,' Short wrote in his book. Coincidentally, he had been a newspaper correspondent in Malawi for some years. I had worked in Malawi at about the same time.

'The resemblance to Africa is overwhelming,' he went on. 'Every village has its witch, or *ap*, and its *k'ruu*, or healer; each rural community its *neak ta*, the ancestor figure . . . who inhabits a stone or ancient tree and must be propitiated by offerings of incense and perfumed water. In the countryside, more murders are attributed to sorcery than to any other single cause.'

As in remote parts of Africa, the carrying of a talisman was useful for protection in Cambodia. A so-called 'passport mask' – a small beaded object, a dried monkey's paw, a lion's tooth or an elephant-hair bracelet – might serve to defy the foul fiend in Africa. In Cambodia, the strongest talisman was a foetus that had been ripped whole from its mother's womb and then killed and mummified. Called a *kun krak*, a smoke child, this piece of ghoulishness was the most prized of the magic talismans, and had been used by Khmer Rouge soldiers as well as by villagers.

On this trip I saw the truth of Short's saying that 'rural life in much of Cambodia is not essentially different from what it was five centuries ago'. So travelling down this road was like banging through Africa, and then night came, and we were banging through the darkness.

'See those blue lights?' the young Cambodian man next to me asked. He pointed to bluish fluorescent tubes that dangled near the huts in the villages (not many) that had electricity. 'Know what they're for?'

I said I couldn't guess.

'To catch cockroaches and crickets,' he said.

'Good idea.'

'Then they eat them,' he said.

Sometime after the sequence of blue lights flickering in the jungle, we came to the junction of a good road.

'This is the road to the airport,' the young man said.

Of course, the only paved road in this whole western province was the one that served the tourists who flew in, almost all of them foreigners; everyone else, the masses, bounced and rumbled on the bad roads, or sat in ox carts, or steered bikes around the potholes. And if I hadn't come this inconvenient but illuminating way, I wouldn't have known that.

Then – after the solemn and scarred countryside of weary farmers – bright lights, luxury hotels, casinos, girlie bars, strip clubs, fancy restaurants: Siem Reap and ancient Angkor.

The bus was still rolling. I asked the Cambodian man his name. He said, 'Saty.'

'Saty, I'm looking for a nice hotel that's not expensive.'

He said, 'I know one.'

I was thinking of Henry T. saying, 'I would rather sit on a pumpkin and have it all to myself, than be crowded on a velvet cushion.' That was how I happened to find Green Town Guest House, a Chinese-looking villa in a compound behind a fence, with a noodle restaurant in its courtyard, for $10 a night.

If luxury is, first of all, a high degree of comfort, this counted as luxury. The villa was clean, peaceful, friendly and well run. It was always easy for me to find a quiet table to write my notes. None of the sort of un-helpful suggestions and obsequious interruptions that, in more expensive hotels, are excuses for tips.

It took me a day to recover from the overland jaunt from Bangkok. I slept late, wrote notes, got laundry done – two pounds of laundry was $1. The temperature was in the nineties, and humid. I went to a barber and got a shave, and sitting there in the peaceful shop on a back street of Siem Reap, I was reminded of the early morning in rainy Trabzon when I'd been shaved by a Turk with a flashing razor – how it had set me up for the road ahead.

And I walked. Siem Reap was a little town until a few years ago, where people went for the Angkor ruins, which are a few miles to the north. Now it's sprawling city of a million people, of hideous hotels and expensive restaurants, a honky-tonk plunked down in the jungle.

No matter where I went here, I had a sense the place was haunted. I was creeped out – maybe an effect of my awareness of Cambodia's violent recent history, though I had not yet read the Pol Pot biography. The ghostliness was present even in the sunniest parts of town, a suggestion of the hideous past, of blood and unburied bodies, of torture, trickery, lies, punishment – like the darkness I had felt rising from the earth when I walked through Dachau, the stink of evil.

Most Cambodians have a memory of the bad years; perhaps they conveyed this sense of psychic trauma, carried it around with them. The hurt was apparent in their posture, in their voices, in their eyes. Another haunted landscape to suit me in my role of revisiting spook on the ghost train.

This hovering, heavy, oppressively haunted air was strongest in the jungle around Siem Reap, among the twisted lianas and dark leaves and sun-speckled shadows. It was like a foul vapour at the huge lake nearby, called Tonle Sap; it was palpable at Angkor, which was a place of both jungle and violated ruins.

Not just a temple, nor even a collection of them, Angkor is a ruined city. The name Angkor is derived from the Sanskrit word *nagar*, meaning city. It contains a royal palace, a set of sacred precincts, monasteries and residences, much of it surrounded by a wide stagnant moat and a perimeter wall. It lies brooding among tall trees, brilliant sculpted towers and high walls, many of the structures half strangled by vines. It seems as though the temples were built to mimic symmetrical mountains, and their looming aspect, which is an assertive Asiatic Gothic, lends them tremendous power – power magnified by the way they have been eaten away by time, pitted by centuries of bad weather and neglect, their roughened texture like the volcanic rock at the edges of high Pacific islands lashed by waves, hollowing it and sharpening it like coral and giving it archways and great delicacy. In sheltered porches and doorways, and under jutting eaves, masterpieces of Khmer sculpture still stand, garlanded with flowers, with vigil lights and incense sticks. Even with tourists in silly hats scampering on its steep stairways and yelling to each other from cupola to cupola, the ruins epitomize sanctity, harmony and radiance. At its peak in the early thirteenth century, Angkor covered one hundred square miles.

Almost as impressive as the monasteries and walls and temple complexes is the jungle – tall trees, miles of shaded paths and cool groves. The foliage is at one with the stone stupas, seeming to grow out of the holiest places, the roots twining over walls and bas-reliefs – thick, rounded and supple banyan roots like tentacles. The trees are part of Angkor, some destroying it, others helping to secure and keep whole the fragile walls. The narrower paths lead to isolated shrines with images of bulgy elephants and what seems the dominant totem of Angkor, the king cobra, Naga – cobras in the form of balustrades, cobras slithering on roof eaves or a single rearing cobra with its hood flared to protect the Buddha image.

Angkor is also a visual catalogue of smiles chiselled in sandstone. The most enigmatic – but serene at first glance, softening almost to mockery, becoming ambiguous – is the smile on the lips of the vast Buddha image at the Bayon Temple in Angkor Thom. Thousands of smiling images adorn the walls, from the thin smiles of praying monks to the happy-face smiles of bulb-breasted *apsaras* – half-naked dancing girls, demonstrating how the dance was part of Angkor ritual.

The look of the alluring women on the *wat* was an echo of the coquettish girls selling silks and postcards and soft drinks on the ruined walls, calling out, 'Come back – take me with you,' 'I will be your girlfriend,' 'Take me!' Just teasing to make the other girls giggle and smile.

The Khmer smile is not a mere expression of happiness but a representation of an assortment of moods as well as a sort of unreadable rebuttal. The great range of smiles is codified at Angkor, and it has been intensively studied. Philip Short cites Charles Meyer, a French adviser to Prince Sihanouk, on the subtleties of the Khmer smile, 'that indefinable half-smile that floats across the stone lips of the Gods at Angkor and which one finds replicated identically on the lips of Cambodians today'. It serves as an 'ambiguous and likeable' mask, but is also a smile that 'one erects between oneself and others . . . [like] a screen hiding an emptiness that has been deliberately created as an ultimate defence against any who might wish to penetrate the secret of one's innermost thoughts'.

Much of Angkor was broken – you can see it in its patches – suggesting not only the passage of time, perhaps 700 or 800 years of erosion, but also epochs of severe trauma. It was built in a succession of historical periods; it was damaged and much of it destroyed over time, too, shattered by the Siamese in the fifteenth century, subsequently by marauders, and as recently as twenty-five years ago, when it was besieged by the Khmer Rouge and the whole sacred city became a battlefield.

Angkor is also a place of human damage, crudely appropriate to the legless and armless statues and smashed images. I had hired a tuk-tuk – this one a motorcycle pulling a small two-wheeled carriage. It was mood-softening, breezy, slow going. The biker, Ong, didn't know much about Angkor, but he was patient and ferried me around all day. I had a guidebook and a map and made my own way.

I often came upon the victims of Cambodia's more recent violence – amputees, the land mine victims, human amputees among amputated statues. (Guidebook: 'Cambodia has more than 40,000 amputees, more per capita than any other country in the world.')

Deep in the jungle at Ta Prohm Temple, along the narrow grassy path, a whole orchestra of land mine victims played music on gongs and flutes and stringed instruments – music that tore at my heart, for its beauty and for its being played by blind men, and one-legged men, and men with missing fingers or burned and bandaged arms. With their prosthetic legs neatly stacked to the side, their twanging music rose in counterpoint to the forest screech, the ringing whine of cicadas, the loud peeping of insects, the squealing of bats.

Near another labyrinthine temple called Banteay Kdei, I was strolling along and saw what looked like a group of small schoolboys posing for a picture – or was it a choral group? There were thirty of them standing in three rows, the tallest boys in the back row, though none was very big. They stood straight, facing forward, smiling.

I said hello and asked the man near them who they were.

'Orphans, sir.'

The man, Sean Samnang, ran an orphanage in Siem Reap. He went in search of homeless children and orphans, and fed and trained them.

I had been encountering beggars in large numbers since arriving in north India. It was as though there were a whole underclass of people, millions, whose livelihood depended on begging. I wondered why these particular children were so affecting – and not just them but the amputees and the solemn women crouching near a basket of coins. Was it because they seemed so reluctant, such hesitant beggars? I would defy any passer-by to resist emptying his wallet, confronted by the sad smiles of thirty children standing shoulder to shoulder by the roadside, with the utterance 'Orphans, sir.'

Cambodians could be forthright, rude, conditioned by their harsh recent history – toughened and taught survival skills by the years of tyranny. Yet even these hardened people were no match for the wave of visitors, the sex tourists and predators, that were the reason for the many signs forbidding sex with children and warning of penalties for child rape. Throughout Angkor, all around Siem Reap, were signs saying REPORT SEXUAL EXPLOITATION.

I asked Ong, my tuk-tuk driver, if he knew anything about this.

Now and then, he said, men visiting from Europe would hire him as a driver and ask him to find them young boys.

'How young?'

'Just kids, little boys,' Ong said. 'But it's wrong. And I don't know any.'

'What about Cambodian men – do they ask?'

'Never. But one man from Switzerland ask me for a ride on my motorbike. He sit behind me and touch me – here and here. I was so frightened! I don't know what to do. He say me, "Come up my hotel room. I give you money." I say no. I no like to think about it. I so scare.'

I was not prepared for people so poor to look so beautiful. Maybe I was remembering the child prostitutes cooped up in the Singapore brothel. I had foolishly begun to associate poverty with ruin and bad health, and Cambodians were so hard-working it seemed outrageous that they were struggling just to eat.

And something else about their beauty. Even as beggars they had dignity. They weren't cringing or rapacious; they stared, they looked solemn, they hardly spoke. But most of all they were familiar. They looked like their own statues. The Cambodian face is also the face of a Khmer statue; their bodies are sculptural and finely made; they seem iconic, authentic, part of the culture, the slender boys like willowy Buddhas, the women like *apsaras* and angels.

Some of these *apsaras* and angels, these living sculptures, resided in the Old Market district on the east side of the Siem Reap River, where I idled in pyjama bottoms under the trees in the mellow guesthouse for $10 a day, plus noodles. It wasn't lechery; the gentleness of the people made it easy for me to linger. It was a pleasant stroll in the perfumed air to the riverbank. And now and then, seeing me walking blithely, a tuk-tuk driver would ask, 'You retired here?' because many grizzled men like me in faded T-shirts and pyjamas had hunkered down in Cambodia. At these prices I could stay until my visa ran out, months from now. It is sometimes that way in travel, when travel becomes its opposite: you roll and roll and then dawdle to a halt in the middle of nowhere. Rather than making a conscious decision, you simply stop rolling.

It had happened before, and I knew why. 'At a certain season of our life we are accustomed to consider every spot as the possible site of a house,' Henry T. wrote in *Walden*. For the traveller this season never ends. Yet I knew what I had to do.

23. The Boat *Sontepheap* to Phnom Penh

At the centre of Cambodia, in its enormous floodplain, lies an inland sea, Tonle Sap Lake, so broad in the rainy season that when you're on it you might be in a great ocean, no shores visible. It is not a big blue ocean but a brown one, the frothy chop beaten by the brisk wind to resemble the foam on a latte. It is not deep. Even in the middle it is full of mud banks and shoals, and in the unlikeliest places there are fish weirs and perhaps a narrow sampan sitting low in the water, two or three men and boys on board wearing lampshade hats, the whole scene in profile like an image of graceful brushstrokes on an ancient pot.

I took a Jeep about seven miles from Siem Reap to the low-lying and mucky north shore of the lake, a fishing village, Phnom Krom, where in the early morning one or two long and usually overloaded motorboats leave for Phnom Penh. They travel southeastward down the lake to where the Tonle Sap River begins its flow, and continue along the river to the jetties of Phnom Penh, about six hours, the water route to the capital.

The departure of the boats is an event in Phnom Krom and the nearby village of Chong Khneas, where the fishing families live in basketwork huts perched over the shore, the places busier at six in the morning than most other inland villages at noon. Apart from the outboard motors on a few of the sampans, the scene could not have changed in hundreds of years: naked children slapping at mud puddles, women selling bananas and rice, but most people mending nets, tending cooking fires and sorting fish in baskets.

Snakehead fish are caught here. They are the key ingredient in *amok*, one of Cambodia's delicious national dishes, the snakehead simmered in coconut milk with spices. Because the snakehead has natural enemies here, the fish grow to only a few feet and are not the monsters they've become in some places in the United States where they've been introduced.

I found the gangplank to my boat and was about to climb into the cabin when a big man in a Hawaiian shirt – obviously American – said, 'I wouldn't go in there if I were you.'

I smiled at him because he'd said it so confidently. I stepped back and let other passengers stream into the cabin.

'Look. There's only one way out,' he said. 'This thing capsizes and it's all over. How would you escape? You read about ferries that sink in places like this, and you wonder why so many people die.' He shook his head. 'Now I know.'

So we sat on the roof together and he introduced himself – Mark Lane, explaining that he was a mate on a ferry out of Homer, Alaska, making runs to the Aleutian Islands. He was taking a break from that cold work by spending a few weeks here in the sunshine.

We had pulled away from the bamboo pier and out of the inlet and were about a quarter of a mile into the lake when the boat slewed and tipped sharply and almost slid us into the water. There were howls from people down below, trapped in the cabin. The boat had snagged on a mud bank and yawed. For about fifteen minutes the slanted boat did not move but only sent up mud and bubbles from the churning screws.

'This might be a long trip,' Mark said.

But after we got under way once again, the boat went fast. The only other snag was a mud bank in the middle of the lake, out of sight of land, another slew and swerve and delay.

In stretches of the lake, floating villages were whole water-world communities of houseboats and buoyant huts, an economy of water people enclosed by the perimeters of their nets and bobbing net floats.

These fishing communities looked self-sufficient, orderly and discreetly territorial, far from government intrusion and regulation. Even before Pol Pot, the government in Cambodia, whether French colonial rule or American puppetry, had brought nothing but war and destruction, torture and death. Left to themselves, in the middle of this lake, the Cambodian water people functioned perfectly.

Sitting side by side on the roof of the boat, using our small duffle bags as cushions, Mark and I talked about Angkor and what we'd seen.

'I did something in Siem Reap I've never done before in my life,' Mark said.

'What a great opening,' I said.

'No, seriously,' he said. 'I had a tuk-tuk driver – my wheelman. He only had one eye, he's twenty-five, lives with his aunt – really nice kid. You know how it is. You spend a few days with these guys and you hear their story.

'His name was Sar. He didn't talk much about his past, just about his future. He had it all mapped out. His aim was to be an accountant. Ever heard anyone say that? "I want to be a doctor," yes. Or an airline pilot. Or an astronaut. But an accountant? So it seemed to me he was on the level. He had been to high school and done some courses, but to get his accountant's degree he needed college.

'He told me that there's a certain man in Siem Reap who's a well-known teacher of accounting and economics. This tuk-tuk driver Sar wanted him as a mentor and teacher. "So what's the plan, Sar?" I asked him.

' "The plan is that I earn enough money as a tuk-tuk driver to pay for my education. I live with my aunt. I study with this man. I get an accountant's degree and then a job in Siem Reap. All the new hotels need accountants. New businesses also need them. It's a perfect plan. But one thing – it's impossible."

'He's staring at me with his good eye, and he's smiling. I asked him why it's impossible.

' "Because I rent this motorbike. I can't make enough each day to pay rent and save money. So I'll go on driving, and first I'll make enough to buy a motorbike. Then I'll use the bike to make money, and I'll save some of that. When I have enough, I'll study to be an accountant. But that time is far away."

'I said, "Good for you." He took me to Angkor. He took me around town. I kept thinking about his plan. And by the way, he didn't ask me for money. I paid him the usual, ten dollars a day.

'Couple of days went by. I kept waking up at night – couldn't sleep. I was thinking about Sar and his plan. I also thought how, when I was sixteen, my father kicked me out of the house – "Get out of here. I don't want you." My father was a complete bastard. A man in the neighbourhood took me in and treated me as his son. He's my real father. He was a Navy SEAL. If he hadn't done that, I would have become a druggie, on the street, a lost soul. That helping hand made the difference. I thought about that a lot.

'Next day I met Sar as usual. I said, "Let's go to the motorbike dealer." I got all the prices and compared them. I put down eleven hundred dollars and he got the motorbike, a Suzuki 110 – just what he needs to be a tuk-tuk driver in Siem Reap and make some money.

'I said, "Okay, now it's up to you. It's not impossible any more." And I gave him my e-mail address. We'll see what happens. It might be interesting.

'Hey, it was the last of my money, but I didn't really need it. It might make the whole difference between success or failure in his life.'

'That's a good story,' I said. He wasn't boasting. It had just happened and he was still ruminating about it. He was a nice guy with a good heart, not a wealthy man but a hard-working mate on an Alaskan ferry, nearing retirement, with a modest income. He seemed something of a loner, but I could see he was energized by his good deed and eager to see how it would all turn out.

When I told him about my experience with the rickshaw driver in Mandalay, he said, 'The great thing is, it's not like foreign aid. Every dollar is being used. No middlemen!'

All this time we were travelling along the wide brown inland sea, under a cloudless sky, in sunshine that blistered my face and arms. My perch on the cabin roof was so bright and so blowy, I had given up trying to read – it was Robin Lane Fox's biography, *Alexander the Great*. A shore appeared to the south, and as we approached it, a shore to the north became apparent as a black line in the distance. Further on, the shores closed in, and houses on stilts teetered at their banks. In the distance was a large gold temple, and then we passed through a break in the shore that narrowed to a river. This was the Tonle Sap River, the major outlet from the lake, which joined the Mekong at Phnom Penh and continued south through Vietnam.

While the sun beat down on our heads, frying us on the boat's metal roof that was like a griddle, Mark told me about the storms on his ferry run to the Aleutians, the days of fog, the way the whole boat would ice up and freeze and become top-heavy and unstable. In the distance I could see some half-naked men tossing fishing nets and others pulling up crab pots.

Borne by the current, we passed higher banks, bigger houses, riverside settlements, fishing boats, motorboats and fortified embankments. The houses piled up and became more dense, and the city appeared as we approached the landing stages.

★

Phnom Penh had a scruffy, rather beaten-up look, like a scarred human face in which its violent past was evident; it was a city that had suffered extreme punishment of a kind that was impossible to conceal. It was a city under repair, which is also the look of a city falling apart, and there were very poor neighbourhoods, but unlike India, it was poverty without squalor. There are architectural marvels in Phnom Penh – the royal palace, residence of Sihanouk's successor, Prince Ranariddh (Cambodia had reverted to being a kingdom), the national museum with its imposing collection of Angkor treasures and statuary, some colonial-era villas, the main post office, the Grand Market, some temples – yet instead of raising the tone of the city, these dignified buildings only made the rest of it look worse.

Spelled out in pebbles underwater near a temple, I found the message IF YOU WANT A GOOD REBIRTH YOU MUST LIBERATE FROM THE DELUSIONS. It seemed to me that Cambodians had few delusions. Within recent memory, they had seen everything – terror, starvation, mass murder. They had needed to be tough to survive, so they did not have the geniality of Thais or the dreamy obliqueness of Burmese or the practicality of Singaporeans. But even the streetwise Cambodians in the city, who were direct and demanding, were capable of graceful gestures. With good reason, they had lost hope in the promises of government and justice. Once, in casual conversation with a Cambodian, I said I'd like to come back someday. He looked at me with disbelief. He said, 'Why you want to do this?'

It seemed incredible to him that anyone would want to return to this death-haunted country. He wanted to leave Cambodia; everyone he knew wanted to leave. Phnom Penh was thronged by pedestrians, by cycle rickshaws and scooters. No one had money for cars. That alone made it picturesque for me, trying hard not to be a romantic voyeur, though it was obviously a struggle for everyone else.

For superficial reasons, I was happy – happy in the way the big pink middle-aged men were happy in Cambodia, though most of them were in beach towns like Sihanoukville. It was one of the greatest places in the world to be a barfly. Cheap beer, good food, fine weather and any number of congenial companions – other barflies and beautiful women who, it seemed, had little else to do but watch you drink and smile.

On a side street of Phnom Penh, at Sharkey's bar, one of many such bars, big ugly Western men drank beer and played pool in the company of small pretty Cambodian women, who pawed them and poured their drinks. This arrangement is a kind of heaven for many men. It was the atmosphere of cheap beer and mild debauchery I had seen all those years ago in Vientiane. It wasn't outdated; it had just moved further down the Mekong River.

'What do you want?' the tuk-tuk drivers asked in Phnom Penh with a smile, confident that they could provide anything I named – heroin, a massage, a woman, a man, someone to marry, a child to adopt, a bowl of noodles or a souvenir T-shirt.

As in Siem Reap, the Phnom Penh hotels ranged from the luxurious to the basic. The sumptuously furnished and Frenchified châteaux like Le Royal, set in walled compounds with guards posted outside, had rooms for $500 a night; at the other end, the little side-street pension where Mark Lane was staying was $15 a night. But his room had no windows. I found a hotel overlooking the river for $25 a night, with breakfast. Since Burma, my usual morning meal had been noodles or a mound of rice with a fried egg on top.

I wanted to read about Pol Pot. I found a bookshop near the national museum and swapped my copy of Robin Lane Fox's life of Alexander for Philip Short's life of Pol Pot. On the shelves, to my surprise, were copies of my own books: bootlegged copies, smudgily printed, looking homemade.

'Where was this printed?' I asked, picking up a copy of *Dark Star Safari*.

'It's a photocopy,' the clerk said, though it was a chunky book, more like a bound proof copy than the finished article.

'Why do you go to all the trouble to photocopy this book?'

'Because it's a bestseller.'

'People read this guy?'

'Oh, yes, sir,' he began, but before he finished I took out my driver's licence and showed it to him. He held it in two hands, studied it closely, then shrieked – a gratifying reaction. Then he became anxious and said, 'Are you angry with me?'

'Of course not.'

His name was Cheah Sopheap. He asked me what I was doing in Cambodia. I took a bootlegged copy of *The Great Railway Bazaar* off the shelf and showed him the endpaper map. I had wanted to travel from Thailand through Cambodia in the early seventies, I said, but it had been impossible.

'It was a bad time then,' Sopheap said. 'The city was empty. All the people had been sent to the countryside.'

'So there was nothing here?'

'Just prisons.'

'And Pol Pot was making trouble for you?'

'Pol Pot was nothing,' he said. He made a face and flicked his finger as though at a gnat.

To the world, Pol Pot was a moon-faced monster, so this was a surprising answer. Sopheap explained, saying that before the coming of the Khmer Rouge, Cambodian society had evolved to the point where the rich were ostentatiously wealthy and the rural poor simply desperate. The countryside, especially in the east of the country, had been ruined by the war in Vietnam, which had spread to Cambodia. Khmer Rouge was what outsiders called Pol Pot's organization. In Cambodia it was known as Angkar, the Party.

Sopheap did not say so, but Nixon and Kissinger had secretly approved an invasion in 1969 and the carpet-bombing of Cambodia, in the ruthless and irrational belief that it would help win the Vietnam War. For the next several years, without any authorization from Congress, B-52s from Guam flew thousands of bombing missions. This outrage, accurately documented by the journalist Seymour Hersh, included the dropping of half a million tons of American bombs and the spending of hundreds of millions of dollars to prop up the American-funded regime of Lon Nol. The blitz only made the Vietcong more resolute, and the bombing created havoc in Cambodia, killing an estimated 600,000 people and driving the peasants into joining the Khmer Rouge.

'The poor people hated the rich and hated the Americans who were killing them,' Sopheap said. 'They were so angry! And when they came to Phnom Penh they did anything they wanted.'

He meant the men in black pyjama-like uniforms, who appeared in the capital in April 1975 and took over, expelling all the residents, looting their houses and sending them into the countryside. These guerrilla soldiers had been living in the jungle, fighting and scavenging, some of them for many years. They were hungry, battle-weary and resentful. A large number of the more recent recruits were in their early teens.

'They liked having power and killing. Pol Pot was not the only reason. The people themselves made the terror.'

'What happened to your family?'

'My father survived because he was a farmer. He was lucky. He knew how to make sugar from palm trees.'

Sopheap's father would have been shot. But in the midst of the terror and starvation, the regime introduced 'dessert day'. Rice soup was all that was available for people, but on dessert day, three times a month, it was decreed that the soup was to be sweetened with palm sugar – cane sugar was unavailable. Sopheap's father was able to provide homemade palm sugar. So he was not shot.

'I was sick,' Sopheap said. 'My body was swollen big. I almost died. It was a terrible time. You've seen the museum and the killing fields?'

The killing fields Sopheap meant were only ten miles from the city. The place was locally known as Choeung Ek. It was one of many. There were 343 other killing sites spread across Cambodia, and numerous torture prisons too, from the Khmer Rouge period, 1974–9. By then the United States was tacitly supporting the Khmer Rouge government, because of our humiliation at having been driven out of Vietnam. By allowing the Chinese to arm Pol Pot, we could hobble the Vietnamese, who were fighting the Khmer Rouge with Soviet artillery along the Cambodia–Vietnam border.

I rode a tuk-tuk through rice fields in brilliant sunshine to a grove of trees where birds were singing. In this peaceful place, formerly an orchard and a Chinese cemetery, 20,000 people were murdered over the course of three years. An open-air museum, it was shaded by tall trees, its largest structure a tower with stepped shelves containing some 9,000 human skulls. Many of the mass graves were still strewn with remnants of the victims' clothes. Most of the prisoners had been beaten to death with shovels, hoes and pickaxes – among the cruellest and most painful deaths imaginable. Splits and cracks were visible in many of the skulls, from the force of a blunt axe head or the blade of a hoe. The skulls, young and old, male and female, said a great deal about who they had been and how they'd died.

When Vietnamese soldiers liberated Phnom Penh – against the wishes of the United States – 129 mass graves were found here at Choeung Ek, one of the graves containing 450 corpses.

The victims were mainly people from the Tuol Sleng prison in Phnom Penh, who had been tortured into confessing that they'd been spies or counter-revolutionaries. Many of them had been Khmer Rouge soldiers who'd fallen under suspicion, or been casually ratted on, or who'd just been unlucky. They were clerks, teachers, landlords – education was equated with wealth ('such people oppressed the poor') – or they were hapless bystanders who'd been pounced on for no good reason. Most were urbanites, termed 'New People', considered inferior to peasants because they hadn't fought and suffered. According to David Chandler in *Brother Number One* (another pirated book I bought on a Phnom Penh street corner), they were mocked with the saying 'Keeping you is no gain, losing you is no loss.' These enemies of the state were driven in trucks the ten miles from the prison, twenty or thirty to a truck – frightened, starved, blindfolded, sick from torture.

WHEN THE TRUCK ARRIVED, THE VICTIMS WERE LED DIRECTLY TO BE EXECUTED AT THE DITCHES AND PITS, a little sign at Choeung Ek said. Because the execution methods were so crude – it was not possible to club more than 300 people to death and also bury them on any given day – a backlog of doomed prisoners built up, and many of them had to wait in locked huts for their turn to die, listening to the screams from the edges of the pits.

A sign on one tree said, THE KILLING TREE AGAINST WHICH EXECUTIONERS BEAT CHILDREN – and it explained that these children, the offspring of the despised privileged class of doctors, lawyers and teachers, were swung by their heels and their skulls smashed against the tree.

Pathways linked the mass graves with the trees and the shrines – small platforms on poles, like bird feeders – where the clothes and sometimes the bones of the victims were stacked. On this hot sunny day, just the sort of day on which the killings took place, these platforms were thick with buzzing flies.

THIS TREE WAS USED AS A TOOL TO HANG A MICROPHONE WHICH MAKE A SOUND LOUDER TO AVOID THE MOAN OF VICTIMS WHILE THEY WERE BEING EXECUTED, another sign said on a tree at the edge of one of the mass graves.

I was stunned and depressed by the visit to Choeung Ek. I had begun to read the Philip Short book, which was not only a biography of Pol Pot but also a chronicle of Cambodia's recent history. One of Short's themes was how, today, the genocide was being marketed to advertise the virtue of the present government, which wasn't virtuous at all. He also emphasized that it was important to look closer at Khmer culture to understand the deep roots of this violence. The apparent anarchy was 'a mosaic of idealism and butchery, exaltation and horror, compassion and brutality that defies easy generalization'.

Writing of 'the eternal Khmer dichotomy between serenity and uncontrollable violence, with no middle ground between', Short said that the killing fields were less an example of Pol Pot's excesses than the sort of behaviour that was endemic in Khmer society. 'The peculiarly abominable form [the ideology] took, came from pre-existing Khmer cultural models,' he wrote. 'Every atrocity the Khmer Rouge ever committed . . . can be found depicted on the stone friezes of Angkor [and] in paintings of Buddhist hells.'

It was self-serving for the United States to call it genocide, Short wrote, for after all, we had helped bring Pol Pot to power. And the existence of these museums of Khmer Rouge slaughter was also a way of suggesting that Cambodia had reformed, which was untrue. The present government was 'rotten' and 'utterly corrupt', and many men in it had been in the Khmer Rouge and had not repudiated their past crimes.

Horrible as the killing fields were, this museum of atrocities distracted attention from the corruption of the present regime. Far from being an aberration, they were an example of Khmer culture run riot. A French missionary had called the terror 'an explosion of the Khmer identity'.

But Pol Pot had lit the fuse. All his life he had the Khmer smile. No one ever knew what he was thinking or feeling. Few people knew his real name. He was born Saloth Sar, and over the years he changed his name at least a dozen times. 'The more often you change your name, the better it confuses the enemy,' he said. What Pol Pot did not say was that the name changes reflected his multiple identities. He'd had a privileged upbringing, some of his childhood spent at the royal palace. His colonial education allowed him to travel to France in 1949, where he was known as a *bon viveur*, if a bit secretive, and eventually as an anticolonial ideologue. He discovered Stalinism. He became a utopian socialist, a leveller, unsentimental, but in the Khmer way, capable of preaching extreme violence.

On his return to Cambodia in the 1950s he allied himself with the anti-French forces and rejoiced in the French retreat. The Vietnam War emboldened him, as the American bombing had, by winning more converts to his cause. Because of his Chinese support, he had powerful reasons to be anti-Vietnamese. He kept to the rural areas, strengthening his army, at a time when the United States was currying favour with China. In his five-year civil war, he fought a weakened, unpopular and crooked government. Half a million people died in this war of attrition. Seeing that the end was near, America's man, Lon Nol, left for Hawaii with a million dollars from Cambodia's central bank. Cambodians were relieved, believing they might at last have a stable and independent government. No triumphant procession by the new leadership entered the fallen capital. Pol Pot waited for days and then slipped into the city in darkness.

As an expression of his weird idealism, Pol Pot declared Year Zero – a clean slate – and abolished money. That alone was the cause of much of the chaos that ensued, because food took the place of currency and was hoarded and fought over. Food became scarcer, and soon starvation and malnutrition were universal. Books were burned and ministerial files dumped in the streets. Phnom Penh was emptied of its population. City dwellers, sent into the countryside, were unprepared for this rustication; most left their homes with as many of their belongings as they could carry; a great number died on the way to remote areas. The whole nation reverted to chaos, a kind of madness and primitivism characterized by machine-smashing and virtual slavery. Hardly anyone laid eyes on Pol Pot, since he was obsessively secretive, an enigma even to his followers.

No personality cult attached to Pol Pot. No pictures of him appeared anywhere. There were no songs, no poems, no sayings, no anecdotes about his life. Turkmenbashi in Turkmenistan was inescapable; Pol Pot in Cambodia was unfindable. No one knew where he lived. He gave no speeches and published very little under his own name. He owned no property. He had no personal wealth. His austerity extended to government events. At one celebration to mark the party's anniversary, only orange juice was served, and the entertainment was Albanian films.

Outsiders demonized and denounced Pol Pot, by this time known as Brother Number One, but no one really knew who he was or what he stood for. In a way he was a classic geek, and like many geeks, a paranoiac.

His ideas remained obscure or oversimplified, but his paranoia percolated into the leadership – to soldiers, the police, prison guards, torturers, to everyone who had power. His reclusiveness and indecision helped create a tyranny that became random and improvisational; no one, neither the frightened populace nor the empowered soldiers, knew what they were supposed to do. Having a weapon helped, for if you had a weapon, you had power. A weapon might be something as simple as an axe or a hoe or a pitchfork. Kampuchea, as the country was known then, became a slave state where, in less than four years, a million and a half people were killed as enemies of the state.

Pol Pot was undone by the invading Vietnamese, who deposed him and installed their own man, Heng Samrin, in 1979. In the same year, wishing to see Vietnam weakened in the so-called proxy war (the Soviet Union was still Vietnam's best ally), the United States supported the right to a seat for the exiled Pol Pot's blood-soaked delegation to the United Nations.

It gave me the creeps to read all this while I was staying in Phnom Penh. Some of the worst of the killing had occurred while I was taking my Railway Bazaar trip, and then writing it, complaining that it had been impossible for me to visit Cambodia. Little did I know what was happening here – but not many people on the outside knew much, or cared.

I had got this far in my reading about Pol Pot when I visited the torture prison at Tuol Sleng, known as S-21. The former Ponhea Yat High School, in a respectable residential area of Phnom Penh, had been converted to a prison – a natural conversion, since large schools of classrooms are designed for confinement.

The building itself looked like any three-storey high school, the same brickwork, the same proportions. Inside, some classrooms had been divided into small wooden or brick cubicles for prisoners awaiting interrogation; other classrooms served as torture chambers. Some torture took the form of shackling a person to an iron bedstead, where he or she was shocked with electricity, beaten with clubs, stabbed and made to confess to crimes against the state.

'The role of S-21 was not to kill but to extract confessions,' Philip Short wrote. 'Death was the finality, but it was almost incidental.'

Obeying an obsessive if ghoulish sense of order, and so as to create a paper trail of traitors, all prisoners at Tuol Sleng were photographed before they were tortured, their names and ages and histories recorded – where they'd lived and worked, details of their families and education, the names of their friends. Far from being mere prison numbers or statistics, they were presented in the round, as utterly human. Their faces were fixed in terror, shocked, fatigued, very ill; oddly serene or deadeyed;

old women, young women, old men, wide-eyed boys, young children. Mothers too, many a woman holding her baby, posed in an agonizing *pietà*, both of them about to die.

Of the 14,000 people who passed through this prison, all were tortured, and all but twelve were murdered. The horror of their plight was evident on the upper floors, where outside the classroom cubicles a veranda was hung with barbed wire. A sign explained: THE BRAID OF BARBED WIRE PREVENTED THE DESPERATE VICTIMS FROM COMMITTING SUICIDE.

Even though I knew that this torture prison had been turned into a museum by a sanctimonious government that itself violated human rights (corruption, embezzlement, torture in police custody, land seizure and extra-judicial killings), I was horrified – who wouldn't be? – by the pathetic faces of the thousands who'd been killed.

One hot day I went through the bare dreary rooms and splintery cubicles, past the displays of doomed faces and the portraits of child soldiers, some as young as ten, and the glass cases labelled INSTRUMENTS OF TORTURE, most of them farm implements – mattocks, axes, clubs, machetes, shovels. Like my visit to Dachau, it was a cruel example of inhumanity, of sadistic and pitiless murder. 'No other country has ever lost so great a proportion of its nationals in a single, politically inspired hecatomb,' Short wrote, 'brought about by its own leaders.'

Though all of this was appalling, the worst moment for me came outside in the sunshine, in the courtyard of the prison, which had been part of the old school's playing field. It was a gallows, three sections, with hooks on each section, looming over three large-mouthed ceramic barrels. The sign on it said, PRISONERS WERE HUNG UPSIDE-DOWN [by their feet, from ropes on the hooks], UNTIL THEY LOST CONSCIOUSNESS. THEIR HEADS WERE THEN DIPPED INTO THE JAR OF WATER. BY DOING SO, THE VICTIMS QUICKLY REGAINED CONSCIOUSNESS AND THEIR INTERROGATORS COULD CONTINUE THEIR INTERROGATIONS.

A week before I visited Tuol Sleng, Vice President Dick Cheney was asked about similar American practices, known by the laughable euphemism 'enhanced interrogation techniques'. These were being used on suspected terrorists in American military prisons. In the torture called waterboarding, which was also used at Tuol Sleng, a hooded prisoner was strapped head-down on a slanted board and such a powerful volume of water poured over his face in a continuous stream that he was briefly suffocated, convinced that he was drowning. And Cheney was questioned about simple submersion, as with the torture jars I was staring at.

What did the second most powerful politician in America think of this way of extracting confessions, this 'dunk in the water'?

'It's a no-brainer for me,' Cheney said, and the president backed him up. 'It's a very important tool.'

The traveller's conceit is that barbarism is something singular and foreign, to be encountered halfway around the world in some pinched and parochial backwater. The traveller journeys to this remote place and it seems to be so: he is offered a glimpse of the worst atrocities that can be served up by a sadistic government. And then, to his shame, he realizes that they are identical to ones advocated and diligently applied by his own government. As for the sanctimony of people who seem blind to the fact that mass murder is still an annual event, look at Cambodia, Rwanda, Darfur, Tibet, Burma and elsewhere – the truer shout is not 'Never again' but 'Again and again'.

Much of my knowledge of recent Cambodian history had come from books, so I decided to find an eyewitness in Phnom Penh.

Heng, a man of about forty-five, spoke English well. Before the Khmer Rouge took over, his father had been a lieutenant in the army and his mother had run a small business in Kampot, about sixty miles south of Phnom Penh, on the coast. They had a good life and a comfortable house. When the Khmer Rouge invaded Kampot in 1972, Heng, who was just a boy, and his parents moved to the capital. Two years later, Phnom Penh fell to the Khmer Rouge.

I asked him, 'In the beginning, were the people afraid or did they think, "This will only last a little while"?'

'My father said that he heard that the Khmer Rouge wanted all the people to be equal,' Heng said. 'Others said the Khmer Rouge soldiers were like wild animals. That frightened us. When the Khmer Rouge took over Phnom Penh they told all the people to go away without taking any property, because it would just be a few days. My parents asked them where to go. Khmer Rouge soldiers said, "Any direction. It's up to you."'

'Were your parents threatened?'

'Yes. If people didn't leave, the soldiers would kill them. My parents decided to go back home to Kampot. It took almost a whole day to travel only fifteen kilometres from Phnom Penh, and we saw corpses almost everywhere by the road. They smelled very bad. It is really difficult to find words to explain all this. When we arrived near Takeo, some thirty kilometres from Phnom Penh, a lady said to my mother, "Please cut your hair." My mother had very long hair. "And throw out your money. If Khmer Rouge soldiers see your hair and money you will be dead."'

'What did Cambodians think of the soldiers?'

'They were so afraid, because soldiers could kill them at any time, anywhere. Khmer Rouge soldiers thought of people as their enemy.' He paused and said in a softer voice, 'Even now, ninety per cent of people are still afraid of soldiers – I mean, government soldiers.'

'Did you or your parents know of what terrible things were happening in Tuol Sleng torture prison or at Choeung Ek killing fields?'

'No, we didn't know anything about that,' Heng said. 'We did not even know the day, the month or the year. You know, there were hundreds of prisons like those throughout the country.'

'What sort of a person was Pol Pot?'

'He had graduated from a French university. If he had been a weak student, he would not have got a scholarship, so it means that he was a smart person. It is very hard to judge Pol Pot. For me, I think the situation during that time is similar to the situation in Iraq. The situation in Iraq before the invasion of American troops was – well, some good things, some bad things. But after America invaded, the situation got much worse.'

'You mean Bush is like Pol Pot?'

'Maybe. But I don't mean Bush is a bad person. The problem was that he did not understand what Iraq people wanted. He cannot govern those people. When Pol Pot took over the country, the situation became chaos. For me, there was almost no single person responsible for Cambodia during that nightmare.'

'Do you think he was heartless, or cruel, or vengeful?'

'I do not think so. I think he was a big boss that had no influence on the staff. I mean, that his people could do anything that they wanted to.'

'What is the best thing you remember from those years?'

'There was absolutely not any "best thing" to remember.'

'What is the worst thing you remember?'

'The worst thing was when the Kang Chhlorp [armed village militia] came to check our house. If they found any rice, sweet potato, sugar or any vegetable, I and my parents would be arrested. That meant the death penalty.'

'If you'd had food?' I asked.

'Yes. If you had food in those times you were an enemy,' Heng said. 'They killed you and took your food.'

The more I knew about Cambodia's infernalities and acrimonies, the more haunted the country seemed and the sadder I got, until, like many fed-up and disillusioned Cambodians I'd met, I just wanted to go away.

24. The Mekong Express

Travel is at its most rewarding when it ceases to be about your reaching a destination and becomes indistinguishable from living your life.

One morning in Phnom Penh, around eight o'clock, I left my hotel, walked along the riverfront on the embankment, A Cha Xao Street, to a certain street corner, and caught the bus to Saigon. The trip was only 150 miles, but it took all day because it involved a slow passenger ferry across the Mekong and the usual delays, hours of them, at the border crossing, two sets of immigration checks, into Vietnam. On the side of the bus was a gaily painted sign: MEKONG EXPRESS. The passengers were mainly Vietnamese and Cambodian, and a backpacking husband and wife from England, all smiles, as well as four middle-aged French travellers, peevish because they had to speak English (almost no Cambodians speak French any more) and pay for everything in American dollars.

Two rivers, the Tonle Sap and the Mekong, converge at Phnom Penh, flowing from the north, and they split again into two rivers, which flow southerly: the Bassac and the continuation of the Mekong. Phnom Penh sits at the western edge of the X that these rivers create, a point the French called Quatre-Bras because of the four wide branching streams.

We crossed the Bassac River on the Monivong Bridge, heading southeast towards the border. Just over the bridge were poor neighbourhoods and the broad, flat countryside of villages, stilt houses overlooking swamps, cows, herd boys, lame dogs and an unbroken expanse of paddy fields. I couldn't read or scribble notes on the bus. I gazed at the labouring Cambodians, who had been unfairly punished for decades by successive regimes and foreign interests, unlucky people still struggling to survive, all the sadder for their politeness.

A few hours down the bad road we came again to the Mekong, waited for the Neak Luong ferry (hardly larger than the three-car Edgartown ferry in Martha's Vineyard), then drove on to it and crossed the turbulent water. Hours later, the road improved near the town of Bavet, on the Cambodian border. We walked through the grandiose gateway – immigration and customs – carrying our bags. No inspection: I could have been carrying a treasure. Then another long walk, across the border to Vietnam immigration and customs, in the town of Moc Bai, as the sun set. And beyond another gateway, a different world.

On this stretch, the look of confidence was immediate. The Vietnamese road was well paved and the houses were in better repair, more substantial in size. There was better lighting, more activity, and finally, like a howl of hope, a great flow of scooters and motorbikes, buzzing outriders beside the bus, building to a bright noisy flow, the riders dipping and weaving, no one wearing a helmet. These motorbikes wobbled along the road, eight abreast, inches apart. The overwhelming density of the stream of bike traffic seemed to bear our little bus onward into the city centre. And for the hour it took to get to the middle of Saigon, the unbroken line of shops, markets and factories gave some credence to the many Thais who had said to me, 'We're worried about Vietnam taking our business.'

Because this was a sentimental journey, and so that I could get my bearings, I asked to be dropped at a certain spot near the Saigon River. Then I walked west to a familiar district: the Continental Hotel, the Rex, the Caravelle, a little park and the main post office.

What I had remembered of the Saigon of 1973 were trashed and empty streets, the colonial façades of the post office and the French-looking city hall, the pinkish brick of Notre Dame Cathedral with its twin spires, some people on bicycles, and at night almost no one out except a few hopeful prostitutes, lingering under the lights at the broken kerbs of street corners. That, and war fear and war weariness, like stinks in the smoke-darkened air.

This was the opposite – mobs of people and honking traffic at ten p.m. Almost the first thing I saw was a great crowd on an apron of pavement, parents and small children, their faces gleaming, in a queue to enter 'Candyland', a bright display of goodies in a department store: children dressed up as elves, contectionery, music, happy mums, smiling dads yakking on mobile phones, everyone well dressed. If there was an image that was the opposite of the Vietnam War, or any war – peace, prosperity, rejuvenation – this was it.

Cambodia was now a dusty memory of subdued chaos, and unlike

Cambodians, who had tended to cling and softly importune, these Vietnamese were indifferent to me. They had other things to do.

That was my first impression. But the next night, while I was strolling
back to my hotel on a busy street, a young man on a motorcycle pulled
up near me and said, 'Mister, you want massage? You want girl? Nice
girl?' and I knew that some things had not changed.

After that, many touts on motorbikes offered me women and massages,
and seemed eager to whisk me away to be massaged, or perhaps mugged.

Saigon, revitalized, hectic, not beautiful but energetic, was a city
driven by work and money and young people, a place of opportunities,
big and bright and loud, yet strangely orderly and tidy. I had seen it
before, under a bad moon; I could say it had been reborn. One of the
greatest aspects of the new Vietnam was its compassion, its absence of
ill will or recrimination. Blaming and complaining and looking for pity
are regarded as weak traits in Vietnamese culture; revenge is wasteful.
They won the war against us because they were tenacious, united and
resourceful, and that was also how they were building their economy.

It was possible to see the effects of positive thinking in their work
ethic and their view of the future. Nominally Buddhist, the Vietnamese
seemed no more spiritual than any other people I met, but they were
practical and efficient and worked well together. In travelling the entire
length of the country, introducing myself as an American (because it was
usual for Vietnamese to ask), no one ever said, 'Look what you did to
us.' Yet war damage was visible all over the place: land mines littering
the jungle, bomb craters, many amputees hobbling in the cities, and –
quietly dying in villages and hospitals – thousands of cancer victims who
had been poisoned by the millions of gallons of Agent Orange we had
sprayed on their trees and on them.

The older Vietnamese remembered everything. I was hoping to meet
one, and I did. Walking in the city one day, looking conspicuous – a
strolling American among hurrying Vietnamese – I bumped into
a grey-haired man who volunteered a hello.

'Where ya going?' he asked. He was Vietnamese, but his accent was
American. Stocky, bluff, coarse in an offhand way, he said he had a
motorbike – did I want a ride anywhere?

I said I wanted to find the bar where they sold 'fresh beer'.

'You don't want to see the war museum and the other stuff?'

'Some other time.'

I didn't say so, but because he looked about my age I wanted to hear his story. He took me to Trung Tam Bia Tuoi, a saloon in a barracks-like building in a fenced-in compound, where we drank beer and ate spring rolls until I could barely stand.

He wouldn't tell me his Vietnamese name. He said everyone knew him as Omar, a name he had bestowed on himself, 'because in *Doctor Zhivago*, Omar Sharif has a wife and a girlfriend – and I do too. Three girlfriends – forty-four, thirty-one and twenty-one. How do I do it?'

But I hadn't asked.

'Blue diamond, you know? Viagra!'

'Did you fight in the war?' I asked.

'Yeah. For the Americans. I was a Marine. Ninth Infantry, in the Delta. Then they shipped me to Danang.'

'I was in Danang after the pullout,' I said. 'Spooky place.'

'Like I don't know that?' Omar said. 'After Saigon fell I was arrested and put in prison. My daughter had cancer from Agent Orange. I wanted to go to the US, but the embassy said I hadn't been in prison long enough, only four months. My brother-in-law was in prison from 1975 to '84.'

'What happened to him?'

'The US looks after people like him. They keep their word. They said "Okay." And gave him a visa. He's in Houston. Another cousin's in Portland. One's in LA. I got forty-seven members of my family in the US, but not me. And now I'm too old to go.'

'Why were you put in prison?'

'They grabbed me because I'd been a soldier with the US. They put me in a camp near the Cambodian border. It was shit. We worked all day and studied all night.' Then he chanted, 'Lenin–Marx–Ho–Chi–Minh, Lenin–Marx–Ho–Chi–Minh.'

He nodded his head as he chanted, holding up a big glass of fresh beer in one hand, a spring roll in the other.

'They said, "Your brain is fucked, boy. Come back inside. We gotta make it better."'

'So you were re-educated?'

'If you want to call it that.' He was laughing tipsily. 'You think you're there for a few days, then it's weeks. Then months. Years for some people. My brother-in-law worked for the CIA. That's why he got nine years.'

All this was after the fall of Saigon, he said, when the embassy was abandoned and the last of the Americans fled in helicopters, with people clinging to the landing slats.

'They found out who I was,' he said of the Vietcong who had occupied the city. 'They said, "Prison for you, boy." It was like *River of No Return*. You know that movie? Good one – Gary Cooper, or John Wayne.'

Neither of them, actually. I checked later and found it starred Robert Mitchum and Marilyn Monroe. Odd that Omar, a professed womanizer, had forgotten Marilyn.

There were still some people in prison, he said. He had begun to glance around the big beer hall, where loud music was playing, a TV was showing music videos, and men were guzzling beer and smoking.

'But it's not like Cambodia. In Cambodia they kill you in prison. Here they make you work and read politics. They don't kill you.'

He became cautious, overly confidential, the way drunks sometimes do, but always in a conspicuous way, talking in pompous stage whispers and making foolish faces when they think they're being discreet.

'Let's move. I've got to be careful.' He swivelled his head at the waiter, who was emptying ashtrays. 'People listen.'

He was now drunker, and like many drunks he became mildly abusive in a matey way, pestering me to have another beer, to drive with him to Cholon to pick up girls. He was also ranting about George W. Bush, who had recently visited Vietnam with Secretary of State Condoleezza Rice. 'She's his girlfriend! I know it! I can tell. I know women!' Meanwhile, the bar had become noisy and crowded, and to complete this picture of disorder, the TV was showing footage of a typhoon that had just killed 1,000 people in the Philippines and was bearing down on Vietnam.

Omar was better-natured the next day, but still self-dramatizing, and occasionally he alluded, with exaggerated facial expressions, to the sinister ways of the current Vietnamese government. He was somewhat unusual in this. Most people shrugged off political philosophy as humbug and simply got on with their jobs.

We were standing outside a little antique shop and I asked a woman who was showing me a carving what she thought of the government.

'Politics!' Omar said. 'Say nothing! People are listening!' He said it loudly enough to be heard on the next block.

On the way to the War Remnants Museum (my suggestion – he'd said 'It's just propaganda'), he told me that he'd been born in Hanoi and brought south as a child, because his father was a soldier in the French army. We swung past the American consulate, where a great crowd of Vietnamese were lined up, waiting for visas to enter the United States. Near them was a monument dedicated to the memory of 168 Vietcong soldiers who were killed on this spot in a skirmish in January 1968.

'Now everyone must respect them for being heroes,' Omar said. 'That's what it says.'

'I'd like the exact wording.'

'We can't stop. There are cops all over the place. They'll ask for my papers if they see you writing things down.'

That was another thing. The Vietnamese who were Omar's age were paranoid and skittish. Younger people didn't know dates or names, didn't care, weren't interested.

The War Remnants Museum was a visual history of Vietnam's road to independence – a bloody road of corpses and land mines that occupied most of the twentieth century and began with the war against the French. 'Vietnam has the right to enjoy its freedom and independence,' Ho Chi Minh had written, and he shouted this to cheering crowds in Ba Dinh Square in 1945. This defiance had the French oiling up their guillotine (also on display), but less than ten years later the French army was humiliated and destroyed at Dien Bien Phu. And then it was our turn.

This ghastly pictorial of torture, massacre, carpet bombing, herbicide, defoliant, terror, dioxin sprayed from planes, Vietcong soldiers pushed out of helicopters or dragged to their deaths, civilian killings and tanker trucks of napalm driven by grinning American soldiers and lettered THE PURPLE PEOPLE EATER – this gallery of horrific condemning photographs, in ten rooms, was all the more shocking for being the work of mostly American or foreign photographers. These men, among them Larry Burrows, Robert Ellison, Sean Flynn, Oliver Noonan, Kyoishi Sawada and Henri Huet, produced much grimmer pictures than the official Vietnamese photographers. In their pictures the American soldier was an isolated, tormented or injured man fighting a rear-guard action, while the Vietcong photographs showed groups of spirited Vietnamese soldiers, manoeuvres, teams of men, few individuals.

Several rooms in the museum were devoted to protests against the Vietnam War, not just in the United States (the Kent State shootings were featured), but also in Britain, Holland, West Germany, Sweden and elsewhere.

Omar said, 'I'm telling you. Propaganda.'

I pointed to a photograph and said, 'That's me.'

It wasn't me, but it could have been: the same wild hair and horn-rimmed glasses, the same winter-pale face, as I picketed the White House in the rain with a few hundred others. And in my memory there arose a vivid, frustrating scene.

You're wasting your time, my embarrassed older brother was saying. *You should have stayed in Amherst.*

Did you hear what Paul just said? his hawkish, mocking wife cried, and she screamed with laughter after hearing me quote a line from one of Ho Chi Minh's *Prison Diary* poems: 'The poet also should know how to lead an attack.'

In early- and mid-sixties America it was regarded as treasonous to be a war resister, but that period was chronicled in detail and gratefully remembered in the War Remnants Museum. I liked being in this room commemorating the defiant ones, the sign carriers, the shouters and chanters against a policy that meant the massacre of Vietnamese and the sending of American soldiers to their deaths. I was reminded that, as a reply, I had joined the Peace Corps, and stayed on in Africa as a teacher. I had nothing to regret.

'Let's get a beer,' Omar said. And at the beer joint he said, 'You're funny, you know that?'

'Tell me why.'

'All that time at the museum. I saw you writing in your notebook.'

'So what?'

'You think people here are interested?' He laughed. 'No one wants to hear about it.' He drank some more, then stared into his empty glass as though he'd seen a spider at the bottom. 'Maybe that's why I like you. It was terrible, man. Terrible.'

He told me he was too old to think about going anywhere else. I didn't want to remind him that everything had worked out for the best.

I said, 'I read somewhere that seven million tons of bombs were dropped on Vietnam.'

'It was terrible.' He was still staring into his empty glass. 'I could go to Bangkok. I could live there. But it would be *River of No Return*.'

He was ageing in a country where young people with no memory of the war – no bitterness and little sense of history – were the driving force. Omar was right. The visitors to the war museums (there was another one, the city museum, which chronicled the fall of Saigon) were mostly foreign tourists, not Vietnamese. Omar, like many others his age, had been consumed by the American war effort, and by the French, whom his father had served. And while he meditated on defeat and betrayal, the young were thinking about the future.

It was possible to see in the photographs that one of the aims of the American generals was to flatten Vietnam, to burn it to the ground in order to flush out the Vietcong – the fury, the revenge, the despair, the irrationality, the nihilism that possess the demoralized warrior when he sees there is no way out. And we failed.

The Vietnamese have had their own revenge in the expression of the most rampant, selfish and opportunistic capitalism. Copyright infringement, Mickey Mouse piracy, fake Rolex watches, knock-off designer goods, bootleg books and CDs and DVDs of popular music and successful films – it was all available, as was the wholesale imitation and manufacture of virtually everything we've ever tried to make. It was an astonishing paradox that, after we had failed to destroy their dream of a socialist paradise, divide their loyalties and visit ruin upon them for our own profit, they had risen – in spite of all our efforts to demolish them – and become businessmen and entrepreneurs. Saigon was one big bazaar of ruthless capitalism, of frenzied moneymaking, of beating us at our own game.

I went to Cholon, just to look. And one day I had a meal at the Hotel Continental – the 'Continental shelf', the veranda where I'd got drunk before Saigon fell, watching the smoke rise from the city's outskirts, had been enclosed and was now an Italian restaurant.

The Vietnam I had seen in 1973 did not exist any more. And for most young people in the south, the war was not even a memory. One reason for this was that in all the years of war, from our first appearance as military advisers in 1961 until the fall of Saigon in 1975, we did not put up a single permanent structure. The French had left some graceful old churches, colonial schools, handsome villas and grand municipal buildings, but in fourteen years and after the billions of dollars spent, the United States had not left behind one useful building. Apart from the land mines and bomb craters and amputees, it was as though we'd never been there.

Over breakfast one morning in Saigon, I read an item in the English-language *Vietnam News* headed 'Today in History': 'In 1976, the Trans-Vietnam Railway is officially reopened after 30 years of the division of the country. Construction of the 1700 km line was completed in 1936.'

In 1973, I had travelled as far north as I could go on a train from Saigon, though some sections had been bombed out. I had reached the end of the line, the dreary and besieged city of Hue, near the coast. After that were some forward fire bases and the demilitarized zone – a no-go area.

After breakfast, I got two train tickets. Mr Lien, who helped me buy them, was fluent in English. He had been born in 1973, in November, the month I'd been here. He was bright, efficient, optimistic and funny – no chip on his shoulder. One ticket was for the sleeper to Hue, where I'd been before, another from Hue to Hanoi, where I'd never been.

25. Night Train to Hue

The typhoon that was big news, a dark ominous blob on a TV weather map four days previously, hit Vietnam the day I left: heavy rain pelting sideways in glittering slashes on the open platform of Saigon Station, crackling on the old blackened cement and drenching the food stalls that had been set up to provision travellers. But I was smiling. Nothing like terrible weather to make a simple departure memorable and dramatic.

Even in the rain and wind and brimming puddles, the station was orderly; the take-away food for sale included rice and chicken, dumplings and sausages, fruit, bottled water, biscuits, beer. I bought my bagful and noticed that there were eight daily newspapers in Vietnamese, no noticeable police presence, no baggage check, no hassle at all, not the slightest intrusion into the traveller's privacy or solitude. My conductor was a polite and attractive thirty-year-old woman in a smart blue uniform. All this order, prosperity and efficiency the Vietnamese had found for themselves after decades of war, in spite of us; we could take no credit for it.

Travel in Vietnam for an American was a lesson in humility. They had lost two million civilians and a million soldiers, and we had lost more than 58,000 men and women. They did not talk about it on a personal level, at least not in a blaming way. *It was not you*, they said, *it was your government.*

In my compartment in the soft-sleeper coach were two conferring twenty-somethings: Mr Pham Van Hai was seeing off his wife. They sat in her berth, which was opposite mine, holding hands.

'She is getting off at Qui Nhon,' Mr Pham said. 'I am not going. She is visiting her family.'

I saw from my map that Qui Nhon was halfway to Hue, the capital of Binh Dinh Province, once a place of heavy fighting. But Mr Pham did not mention that. He spoke of having grown up there, and, as there wasn't much work in Qui Nhon, he and his wife had left to look for jobs.

'That's why we came to Saigon.' No one I had met so far had used the name Ho Chi Minh City. Mr Pham was in property, he said. 'We're very busy. Everyone is looking for property.'

'It's a busy place.'

Mr Pham shrugged and said, 'Saigon is not a beautiful city. But it will be. I've seen Singapore and Bangkok. We need more foreign investment, like them. More companies coming here. We'll make it a beautiful city.'

Property development was booming, he said. Apartment houses were going up, new buildings to meet the demand. He was also involved in construction, so he knew. While he spoke, his wife sat placidly listening. She was tall and slender. She looked athletic in her sweatpants and a sweatshirt lettered *Gymnast*.

'Have a good trip,' Mr Pham said and gave me his business card. He stepped off the train as the whistle blew. That was surely one of the oddities of rail travel here and in many other places, the man leaving his young wife and a foreign stranger in a little compartment, and waving goodbye as they sat on their shelf-like beds, about to spend twelve hours together in congenial propinquity, rocking along side by side, pretty little woman and big hairy foreigner; yet he didn't seem bothered.

Her name was Phuong. She was young and shy and very sweet. Later she told me with pleasure that she was one month pregnant and that she was heading home to tell the family the good news. She made her bed as the train left the Saigon suburbs, and she got under the covers and went to sleep while I watched the last of the city slip past, diminishing from apartment houses to bungalows to huts facing canals and paddy fields, the rain still coming down, and Phuong sleeping with her lips slightly apart and a kind of waxen colour, a beguiling pallor that steals upon the face of someone in deep slumber. I made an effort to look out of the window.

It was all peaceful – the green fields, the children playing among fruit trees, the little stations with red tile roofs, the swamps and cornfields, the pigs snuffling, the chickens strutting in the orchards. I was thinking, Idyllic.

I remembered Saigon as tense and deserted, the countryside grey and fortified; few people were planting anything then, many places off-limits. In my memory Vietnam was very dark, existing in a penumbra of fear – a sea of land mines where idle walking was unthinkable and many bridges were rigged with command-detonated bombs.

That shadowy world was not my imagination. The war – its temporariness and its urgencies – had turned the whole of the south into a sea of mud and rutted roads from the heavy truck and tank traffic. Because of the relentless chemical defoliants we had dumped, none of the trees were very old or very large.

We passed Bien Hoa, where I'd been before, and then the open countryside, hours of it. The big green and empty landscape was the reality of Vietnam; Saigon was exceptional in its dense population and its size and its cacophony. The rest of the country was just banana trees and buffaloes and farmers bent over their rice fields.

I was reading a novel called *The Sorrow of War*, by a Vietnamese, Bao Ninh, who'd been a soldier. The book's setting was a district called the Jungle of the Screaming Souls, near Kontum, a bit northeast of where Phuong was headed. The novel was a love story, but it was also about battle in 1974, the ten survivors (Bao Ninh had been one himself) of a massacred brigade of 500, not long before the fall of Saigon. In other words, a battle that had taken place soon after I had last been here.

Phuong woke up and yawned and saw me reading. She said she didn't know the book. She added, as though as a reason, that she did not feel well as a result of her pregnancy, which was also why she was going home.

'My family will take care of me.'

'What sort of work do you do in Saigon?'

'I am an inspector in a factory,' she said. 'We make leather shoes for women.'

I drew a picture of a fancy stiletto-heeled shoe on a page in my notebook. She looked at it and smiled. She said, 'Yes!' They were exported to Europe and the United States.

With the sort of bluntness that characterizes a traveller in such a country – I would never have hazarded these questions of an American – I asked her how much money she made and the details of her work. She said that she and her fellow workers earned $400 a month. Could that be true? Her husband earned $700 a month. These figures were much higher than the salaries of comparable workers I'd met in Romania and Turkey.

After dark, at Cam Ranh – where I'd also been before, a beleaguered place then – two middle-aged men entered the compartment and took the upper berths. They were labourers; both carried hard hats. They stayed in their berths until dinner was served by the conductor in the blue uniform: each of us got a plastic tray, a box of rice and containers of pickled vegetables.

'You drink?' one of the men said. He offered me his bottle of banana wine. It was brownish, the colour of weak tea. I sniffed it and out of politeness had a small swig that tasted like formaldehyde.

Nha Trang, no less beleaguered in my memory, was the next stop.

'This is a tourist city,' Phuong said.

The rain was heavy here, the typhoon whirling overhead, rain slapping the sides of nearby sheds. Phuong ran into the rain and hurried back to the compartment with two fat ears of steamed corn, one of which she held upright on her lap in her pale hand. She smiled and prepared it for me, peeling its shucks with delicate fingers.

'What do you call this?'

'Popcorn,' she said.

I read more of *The Sorrow of War*, then dozed, waking when the train arrived at Qui Nhon around midnight, and Phuong shook my hand and got off. A big wheezy man entered the compartment and immediately took her berth. He sat drinking beer and staring at me with muddied eyes. I worried about losing my briefcase, so I tucked it under my pillow and slept until dawn.

The choppy sea, whipped by the storm, was only forty feet from the railway line, which skirted the shore; the remnants of the typhoon were soaking the whole coast. I had woken at Danang, where I'd also been before, another besieged city then, where a defiant railwayman had taken me on an engine in the opposite direction to prove a point. In a smiling and slightly crazy way he'd said that there were possibly mines on the tracks, but even so, 'the Vietcong can't stop us'. I had found that very scary, unerasable in my mind because of my fear; and now the opposite, soporific almost, as we rolled past the palm groves, and instead of gun emplacements on the mutilated shore there were beach resorts.

Dripping banana trees, grey sodden dunes, slender sampans drawn up above the tide line, the windows of the compartment streaming with rain. The beer drinker had vanished at Danang. The conductor brought the remaining three of us bowls of noodles. I broke out the tangerines I'd bought at Saigon Station and shared them with the two men – the construction workers – who were now sitting opposite me.

Though they spoke basic English, we didn't say much at first. Oanh, the smaller, more wiry of the two, finished his noodles and drank his banana wine by the capful. His friend, Thanh, then surprised and slightly alarmed me by kneeling and locking the compartment door.

'Why are you locking it?' I asked.

Thanh smiled, touching one finger to his cheek in an I-know-what-I'm-doing gesture, and pulled a plastic bag from his trouser pocket. He sat and opened it, and I caught a whiff of the nutty aroma of dampened marijuana.

Thanh rolled a piece of newspaper, forming a stiff narrow tube about eight inches long. He poked it full of ganja, creating a classic joint, then fired it up, sucked on it a little, inhaled and wheezed with bubbling lungs, his eyes crossing. Then Oanh took a hit, and gurgled happily. And then it was my turn – a blazing spliff at seven in the morning.

When we had finished this dawn ritual, Thanh scattered the evidence out of the window and unlocked the door.

'What is that stuff?' I asked, slurring my speech.

'*Phien*,' he said, pronouncing it *fyeh*.

They were both smiling quietly, sitting contentedly as the train raced along the shore past rain-swept paddies and flooded fields. Some houses were also flooded, their verandas underwater, the water filling the first floor. The coast road was a well-paved thoroughfare with a guardrail and good drainage, much more substantial and better made than, say, the Kamehameha Highway on the coast of Oahu. Apart from a few cars and some men whizzing along on motorbikes wearing plastic capes, there was no traffic. A big jolly hoarding advertising a brand of rice stood where before – at the beginning of a railway bridge and a culvert – I would have seen a gun emplacement.

The news at that moment was of the Iraq War, and so (though I found that news depressing) it was heartening to see this coherence and serenity: life after war, no hard feelings, no blame, the buried past, people looking ahead.

To lighten my load of books, I was transcribing quotations from the Pol Pot biography into my notebook. Recognizing Pol Pot's face on the cover, Oanh tapped it.

'Pol Pot,' I said.

'Bad man,' he said.

He spoke a little in Vietnamese to Thanh. Then Thanh said, 'We fight,' and he tapped Pol Pot's face. He took my pen and wrote *1976* and *1978* in my notebook, and showed me two fingers, meaning two years in Cambodia. He pointed to Oanh. 'Him too.'

Still with the dopey grin of the stoned, Thanh said with gestures and mumbled words that he and Oanh had fought in the first Vietnamese offensive to overthrow Pol Pot and the Khmer Rouge government. This was the so-called proxy war of the Carter administration, when with utter cynicism we stood by, encouraging the Chinese and hoping that Vietnam would be weakened.

I said, 'Did you fight here too? Vietcong?'

'Oh, yes. Sixty-nine and later. Him too.'

Their stoicism and toughness resembled that of many of the men described in Bao Ninh's novel. They had ferried food and supplies down the Ho Chi Minh Trail, they said. Both had been bombed by American planes at a place called Con Meo (Cat Slope). Twelve years they'd been fighting, first the Americans, then the Cambodians; now they were construction workers in Hanoi, putting up new buildings.

'What your country?' Oanh asked.

'America.'

The word surprised him a little and made him smile. He shook my hand. We all shook hands. As with Mr Pham the day before, there was only friendliness in this encounter – no moralizing, no frowns, no scolding. Almost all the Vietnamese I met were like this – not backward-looking and vindictive scolds muttering, 'Never forget!' but compassionate souls, getting on with their lives, hopeful and humane.

In *The Sorrow of War*, the main character, Kien, hears some soldiers in Hanoi talking about a victory in Cambodia. 'But he knew it wasn't true that young Vietnamese loved war. Not true at all. If war came they would fight, and fight courageously. But that didn't mean they loved fighting. No. The ones who loved war were not the young men, but the others, like the politicians.'

The train was pulling into Hue. The last time I'd been here, it had been overrun by angry and frightened American soldiers, and looked like hell. The hell of war – mud and ruin and flames, the whole stinking city on the wane – which is no empty metaphor but actual hell.

Hue I remembered as a blasted, war-damaged and mostly empty town of muddy streets and shuttered houses, one hotel called Morin Brothers, feeble lights, ARVN patrols hurrying in Jeeps on potholed roads, and touts promising ecstasy on drug-and-whore cruises on small boats lit by hanging lanterns on the Perfume River. Prostitutes and soldiers were all that remained of a city shattered and all but destroyed in the Tet Offensive of 1968, when the Vietcong had held the citadel of Hue for twenty-four days, flying their flag over it. And it was flying over it again, but a rebuilt citadel and royal palace, the Forbidden Purple City, which had been mere hyperbole then and was reality now.

I stayed at Morin's again, the hotel by the river, but this was a reincarnated place. The city had been restored and enlarged: the French-built municipal buildings and churches and schools, the chinoiserie on the far bank, the neighbourhoods of small shops, bungalows with walled gardens and courtyards, narrow lanes, bars and small restaurants. The rickshaw drivers' trade had been revived, the so-called cyclos, and their patter too: 'Massage, sir? You want girl? Nice girl! I take you!'

What appealed to me most about Hue was not its royal connection and its Indochinese hauteur or any of its temples, but rather the simple fact of its visible kitchens, the way – because of the heat, but also because it was a tranquil city – I could see people, women usually, cooking the evening meal, noodles in a big pot, or grilled meat, dumplings in a wok, and the families sitting down to eat on low wooden stools. Nothing was more indicative of peace than people unhurriedly eating and having plenty of food: domestic life being lived partly in the open, old women and small children sitting in doorways, watching the rain come down.

There was hardly any distinction between a private kitchen and a public restaurant. The open platform of a shop-house served as both: the woman shredding noodles into a soup pot with vegetables was chatting to her friends, minding her children and serving customers, all at the same time.

Remembering the anxiety I had felt here in wartime, when I had never walked anywhere – I'd been driven fast to every destination – I strolled across the river to the north bank and Dong Ba market to look upon the great piles of fruit and vegetables, the towers of pots and pans, the tea stalls, the slabs of catfish and eels and tuna, the spice bazaar, the stalls selling herbal medications, the shelves of snake wine (each bottle with a coiled cobra pickled inside), the stacks of clothes. Outside, where the market backed on to the river, a willowy girl in a conical straw hat was poling a sampan, standing in the stern and working her steering oar like a gondolier. At the embankment a woman was washing clothes in the river, some men were loading bales on to a barge, and families were settling into big boats for the long river journey to their villages. The boats moved over the river like water bugs, passing the old brewery, the decaying temples, the masses of bamboo lining the banks, the houseboats that were moored in clusters to create a floating village.

All that represented the vitality, richness and colour of old Asia. But along with the snake wine and the powdered antlers for aphrodisiacs and the fragrant bricks of tea was the new Asia of ingenious piracy: knock-off Nikes, fake Tag Heuer watches for $15, Lacoste polo shirts, Zippo lighters and mountains of bootleg CDs. And maybe a new Asia in the way Vietnamese traders incessantly badgered passersby, often screaming 'Buy it!' at me the way the cyclo drivers howled 'Massage!' – persistent to the point of being pests. But who could blame them?

'I worked for the Americans,' one old hawker said. And an elderly cyclo driver told me, 'I was a soldier with the Americans.' I heard this often in Hue.

On a back street, I stopped to rest at an open-fronted shop, sitting on a stool out of the rain, and a woman appeared with a bowl of fish soup and a dish of hard-boiled quail eggs. I drank tea, and soon after the woman's teenage daughter came home from school and translated the woman's questions: Was I married? Did I have children? Did I like the fish soup (which the daughter called *banh canh ca loc*)? And where did I come from?

Ah, yes, American! Welcome! Have some more fish soup!

One thing struck me more than anything else in Hue. Never mind for the moment my memory of the lifelessness and apprehension, the weirdness of war: frenzy one minute and boredom the next, the bureaucracy and clumsy formality, the suspense that was also part of the terror. The difference was so great as almost to erase the memory.

I had been conscious of it since entering the country, though I had not remarked on it or made a note. It was the people's clothes – the whiteness of the white dresses, the starched collars, the decorous *ao dais*, many men in shirtsleeves or in suits, the daintiness of children's tidy outfits, and not their newness but their cleanliness, a crisp and well-turned-out population that spoke with confidence and self-respect; even in the muddiest districts of Hue, the clothes were freshly laundered.

All this was new to me, the Hue of peacetime that did not in the least resemble the Hue of the war. The Vietcong gun emplacements and pillboxes on the old city walls looked more like antiquated follies than leftovers of battle. Apart from the citadel, it was not a rebuilt or restored place but rather a reincarnation, like much else in Vietnam, a whole city risen from the ashes of war.

I was praising the fish soup to a man in Hue who said, 'You should try the eel soup.'

Looking for eel soup, I found Mr Son, whose shop-house, on a corner in the southeast part of the city, was another open kitchen that could have been a family's kitchen, because it contained only two tables and some stools. A hand-lettered sign said CHAO LUON – eel soup. He had no other customers. He also sold beer, whiskey, canned meat and dry noodles; his wife took in laundry. He had fish soup but no eel soup.

'Business is slow,' Mr Son said. 'If I get more customers, I'll find another table.'

'Your English is good.'

'I worked for the American army. That's why.'

'What years?'

'The bad years. Sixty-eight to the time they left. I was a cook at Camp Eagle. First Airborne.' He explained that this camp was about ten miles outside Hue – the US troops stayed away from the city.

When I finished eating, he said that if I came back the next day he would have eel soup for me. It was his grandmother's recipe.

Mr Son was waiting for me the next night. I had looked forward to seeing him, because he was my age and spoke English, and he had been in Hue when I'd last visited, in that haunted and suspenseful period between the American withdrawal in 1972 and the fall of Saigon three years later.

Again I was the only customer. I drank beer and Mr Son sat with me and served me eel soup and explained his grandmother's recipe. She had been a cook in the royal palace from 1917 onward, when an emperor of the Nguyen dynasty had ruled from there.

Madame Son's eel soup: in a large pot, add a quantity of pork bones to a lot of water and simmer with vegetables for five hours. Strain and save the stock. Sauté onions and garlic in another large pot. Add delicate mushrooms, chillies, spices (anise and cardamom), green beans and white beans and chopped eel. Add the stock. Bring to a boil and then simmer for about an hour.

I ate it and we talked about the war. He said it was odd, but few people mentioned it any more. Most people were too young to remember, or had been born in better times. The war, he said, was a miserable time, but he had learned to be a chef then and had enjoyed his work.

'I liked the Americans,' he said. 'They were good to me.'

On a salary of about $30 a month – $300 in military scrip; the US army in Vietnam had printed its own money – he had started at the bottom in the kitchen.

'First, because I could write English, I made lists. "Beans", "bread", "meat", "flour". And I did some easy cooking. Spaghetti is easy. Hamburgers – easy too. The men ate the food.'

He drank tea while I had the eel soup, which was spicy and thick from the beans and the chopped eel.

'Many of those men died,' he said. 'And many of my friends also died.'

'What did you think?' I asked.

'It was terrible.' He made a face. 'And there was nothing here in Hue. Nothing! Just trouble. No people. Fighting now and then, and bombs.'

'The American soldiers had left by the time I got here.'

'They just went away.' He was smiling, not in mirth but at the horror of it. 'That was '72. The end of my work. I didn't know what to do. We all waited, and then it came – the VC.'

'Where were you then?'

'Here, but I didn't stay. I ran. I had a motorbike and hid in the countryside. My house here was ruined. There were no records. No one knew what I had been doing. When I came back to Hue the soldiers found me.'

'Were you scared?'

'Yes. I said to them, "I like peace!" It was true.'

'No prison time?'

'No prison.' He got up and opened another bottle of beer for me. Then, settling again on his stool, he said, 'The years after that were very bad. From '75 to '78 we had no food, no money, no clothes, nothing. It was almost worse than the war.'

Those were the years of the American trade embargo – which lasted until 1994 – when, petty-minded in defeat, we had hoped to make the Vietnamese regret that they'd won the war, and had punished them by withholding aid and food. And we had stood by while China invaded the north and became an army of occupation. Those were the first years of America's friendship with China, the hovering presence and ancient enemy of Vietnam.

While we were talking, Mr Son's elderly father walked in from the street. He was a small, finely made man with a kindly face, a wispy beard and bony hands. He was slightly built but seemed healthy.

'No smoking, no drinking,' Mr Son said of his father.

The man was in his early eighties and, as a lifelong resident of Hue, had seen a great deal – at least one emperor of the Nguyen dynasty at the royal palace, the French colonials, the Japanese and the ructions of numerous battles, of which the massacres and beheadings of Tet in 1968 represented just one episode of many upheavals.

'He looks like Uncle Ho,' I said.

'Ho was a good man,' Mr Son said. 'He grew up near here. Even when he was important he wore simple clothes, not good ones.' He laughed, thinking of it. 'Just like you and me!'

The old man was smiling now. I commented on that.

'My father worked for the Americans. They liked him,' Mr Son said. 'Things got better. They're good now. We're happy.'

26. The Day Train to Hanoi

Even during the war, when I had travelled here, I had thought that if Vietnam hadn't been so beautiful we would not have ravished it, nor would the French have bothered to colonize and plunder it. Its cool, steep, humped-up mountains and jungle-thick valleys and cloud forests sloped past fertile fields to the coastal heat of palmy, white-sand beaches; its people were graceful and hard-working and willing; the warmth of its tropical enveloping climate made it seem a kind of Eden. Of course foreigners wanted to possess the land and its people, even if it meant bombing them to smithereens. But the Vietnamese were tenacious and self-possessed and had triumphed.

Up to this point I had not seen Hanoi, which was as stately as a precinct of Paris, as it was meant to be when it was the capital of French Indochina. The French had been humiliated in battle, had surrendered by the thousands, been taken captive and driven out; but at least they had left long boulevards of imposing buildings behind. And we had left nothing except a multitude of scars and the trauma of the whole miserable business, ten years of terror and seven million tons of bombs.

We had occupied Hue but hadn't improved anything there. The small pink-and-white train station, sitting like a stale birthday cake on its own avenue, was a French colonial confection. It had been a wreck when I'd last seen it. It was back in business, thronged with people, efficient, with a clean waiting room and frequent trains. I got a ticket for the twelve-hour trip to Hanoi, something I had longed to do all those years ago.

Now I was in a seat on a passenger train, rattling north on tracks that ran beside the Street Without Joy, as the retreating French had called it, through sandy hills and grey swamps near the sea. What had been the demilitarized zone along the Ben Hai River, in Quang Tri Province just north of Hue, remained a litter of unexploded bombs and land mines and so many shattered tanks and shell casings that people still scavenged the area for scrap metal.

Dong Hoi was a town of new houses and bright tile roofs for a reason: having been burned to the ground, it had risen again. (Guidebook: 'It was wiped off the map by US bombing.') Here and there among its pink villas and bungalows, people were tending the fires at smoking kilns while others were stacking bricks, the place still being rebuilt. And the same was true of Vinh, a town that had been turned to dust by American bombs and was now rising. Most of the houses I saw beyond the 17th parallel were brand new, the old ones having been burned or blown up.

But amid the newness the old Vietnam endured. Men up to their knees in mud in paddy fields, driving water buffaloes, a kind of harmony reflected in the geometry of their fields, and their conical hats, and the straight lines of their puddled lanes.

Later on, we passed the sudden humps of massive stone mountains with vertical sides and rounded summits. The train guard told me they were called Ouanh Binh. They extended for miles. Seeing a big domed cathedral in the distance, the conductor blessed himself with the sign of the cross to indicate to me that it was a Christian church.

Hearing us talking, another young man said hello and snatched my sunglasses. He put them on and clowned, jeering at me, for his friends.

'CIA! CIA!' he chanted.

'You think so?' I said.

'Yes. You CIA!' he said and poked his finger at me. But he was laughing. He then put the sunglasses on upside down and goofed around some more, and his friends laughed.

While his friends tried on my sunglasses and made faces, the conductor asked me where I was from, and when I told him, he said, 'How do you feel being in Vietnam?'

'Happy that it's prosperous and sad that we bombed it.'

'I think that too,' he said. He wore a rather severe expression, and he knew that no matter where we were on this line to Hanoi there was a bomb crater. And the other visible fact of the trip was that the TV screen in this coach was showing Tom and Jerry cartoons, dubbed in Vietnamese.

The train was full of travelling Vietnamese, and though some got off at the smaller stations, most were headed to the capital. They watched the cartoons, they snoozed, they read, they chatted. Boxes of food were handed out to each passenger, containing rice, pickled cabbage, tofu and something grey and rubbery that might have been meat but could also have been a patch for an inner tube. Outside, whenever we passed a field, people were working, bent over, hoeing or digging or ploughing. Everything I saw was like the embodiment of peace and hope.

Even the young man who had fooled with my glasses made me hopeful. 'CIA!' he called out when I passed his row to stretch my legs. But he was harmless – I often regard teasing as a form of confidence and affection. When we neared Hanoi, this same man helpfully told me some things I must see: the water puppets, the lakes, the Old Quarter, Ho's mausoleum.

Most of the daylight was gone by the time the train got to Hanoi, yet the glaring lamps and illuminated boulevards gave the city a greater dignity, the mystery of night shadows, in which glorious lakes and a huge opera house dominated, and that was when I realized what a wondrous place it was, a kind of Asiatic Paris.

I had no idea. But how was I to know? The noble city had always been represented to Americans as the enemy capital, a rat's nest of villains, and belittled by our propaganda, better off bombed and wiped off the map. That was another lesson in the twisted justification of war: demonized people are more deserving of death, rubbishy cities more deserving of destruction. Talk about them as inferior or taunted or pathologically hostile, and they're no great loss when they're gone.

The Parisian glamour had another dimension. I found a hotel on a back street in Frenchtown, near the well-known but much too expensive Metropole. I went for a late-night walk and realized that among the cafés and restaurants and elegant villas, all this Frenchness, there were also noodle shops and street vendors and hawkers huddled near the joints selling fresh beer and smoked fish. The vast, simple-looking, Europeanized city held another city that was more crowded and complex and Asian, and quite a bit cheaper.

Walking back to my hotel, feeling happy, I paused under a tree to watch the bikes and scooters go past when a motorbike bumped up the kerb some feet away and came straight at me. Her arms apart on the handlebars, a young leering cat-faced woman with long hair and white gloves and thigh-high boots revved the engine and made kissing noises at me.

'Get on! You come me!' She hitched forward to make room for me on the seat.

'I come with you?'

'Me madam. Come my hotel. Get on!'

There is a stereotypical women's fantasy of being swept up by a handsome knight on a horse. This was related to it, a male fantasy you never dare think about: being confronted on a dark street and swept up by a long-haired woman astride a motorbike. Even so, I hesitated.

'You want boom-boom?'

'Yes I do,' I said and laughed in admiration at the suddenness and ingenuity of it. 'But I can't tonight.'

'Forty dollar,' she said. *Fotty dolla*, a kind of Boston accent.

I had to decline, not because I didn't want to, but because I was an older man and happily married and more interested in finding an Internet café to send my wife an e-mail than in hopping on the bike and being driven through the portals of love. This happened two more times as, unbidden, beauties on bikes mounted the pavement and, eagerly smiling, revving their engines, offered to speed me away. Each time they promised the same thing.

'Get on! You want boom-boom?'

Hanoi was a formal city of wide avenues, extravagant topiary and pretentious colonial mansions, picturesque villas with cupolas and mansard roofs, imposing ministerial buildings – every sort of pompous Gallic façade, including the nineteenth-century opera house – and many good restaurants; at the same time it was an improvised city of malodorous neighbourhoods, labyrinthine streets, noodle shops and open-air markets of screeching traders and squashed and stepped-on fruit. It was also a city of stately parks and lakes surrounded by landscaped perimeters. The French capital had been transformed into a Vietnamese capital without any sign that America had been involved. And of course we hadn't been: we had bombed Hanoi and mined Haiphong harbour, and so our history in Hanoi was one of infamy and evil-intentioned outrages directed from the air.

I was continually struck by how most Vietnamese were willing to forgive, or move on, when the subject of the war came up. One exception to this was the memory, by those who had endured it, of what became known as the Christmas bombing of Hanoi. This unambiguously genocidal act of pure wickedness took place in December 1972, just weeks before the signing of the ceasefire, like a final spiteful slap, except that it was not a slap but rather a blitz of firebombs intended to incinerate and cow the Vietnamese.

Nixon had ordered this air strike in mid-December, and for eleven days the sky over the capital was black with B-52 bombers. In their circuit, they dropped 40,000 tons of bombs and aerial mines from Hanoi to Haiphong harbour, killing an estimated 1,600 Vietnamese. Twenty-three American planes were shot down, and we were outraged when the surviving pilots were imprisoned. 'Military targets' was the justification we were given at the time by Nixon and Kissinger, but this lie was transparent propaganda. In one instance, in an old neighbourhood of Hanoi, every house on Kham Thien Street was destroyed, with a great loss of civilian life – nearly all women and children, because their husbands and fathers were away fighting.

On my second day in Hanoi a man mentioned this to me. He was in his mid-fifties, and he recalled it, but all he said was 'Very bad.'

I found photographs of that bombing and others at the Army Museum. Once again, the pictures taken by American photographers were much more shocking than those of the Vietnamese.

In the courtyard of the museum, like an artist's installation, stood the wreckage of American planes, one of them propped upright, as tall as a four-storey building, its nose cone approximating a church steeple. The whole assemblage of fuselages and wings and tails and insignia was given a bulging form. A plaque beside it noted that 40,000 American planes had been shot down over North Vietnam between 1961 and 1973. The message was tendentious in its tone and might have exaggerated the numbers, but there was no mistaking the power of this sculpture as a shrine to downed planes and the futility of that war.

How familiar it all was to me, and would have been to any American of my generation. The helmets and shoes, the medals and paraphernalia of captured US soldiers; the excerpt from President Johnson's diary expressing dismay over the progress of the war, and an accompanying photo showing his distress, his fleshy features and comical nose; the American and European faces in the photographs displayed in the Peace Movement Room – the sort of pictures that are shown in American museums that have areas devoted to the 1960s, images of sign-carrying students, speechifying, picketing and confrontations. That it showed less of the military history of the country than the human dimension, and that it was presented without any gloating, made it all the more upsetting.

A large square of cloth printed with the Stars and Stripes contained the following message in eight languages, including Vietnamese, Chinese, Lao and Cambodian:

I am a citizen of the USA. I do not speak your language. Misfortune forces
me to seek your assistance in obtaining food, shelter and protection. Please
take me to someone who will provide for my safety and see that I am
returned to my people. My government will reward you.

This plea was intended to help an isolated American infantryman or downed bomber pilot lost in Vietnam. Its castaway's tone and its helpless appeal were intended to soften the heart of strangers or even of the enemy. I tried to imagine the effect such a printed message would have today, anywhere in America, if it read 'I am a citizen of Iran' or 'a member of Al Qaeda' or 'a Palestinian national,' and made the same plaintive requests, with an enemy flag unfurled on it.

Most of the museum-goers were Vietnamese. They and the museum attendants, seeing me, greeted me with a smile, asking where I was from.

'America.'

'Welcome.'

I wanted to meet someone in Hanoi who had lived through the bombing. Hanoi was a walkable city. I strolled around for a few days, in the Old Quarter and among the huddled shops and temples and through the big market. I saw the water puppets and Ho's mausoleum and the museum dedicated to Ho's life and achievements.

Rather than eating alone in a proper restaurant – a depressing activity anywhere, sitting and staring – I roamed and browsed and grazed, snacking on noodles and bowls of soup, chatting with people in fresh-beer bars and coffee shops, looking for witnesses.

Invariably, while walking, a motorcycle with a biker babe on board would pull up beside me and demand that I get on behind her.

'You come! Boom-boom!'

This even happened in the area of cloisters and villas and temples and embassies near the National Museum of Fine Arts, where I had gone one day to look at silk paintings and bronzes.

There I found the witness I had hoped to meet, a woman who had been in her early teens at the time of the Christmas bombing. She was now the mother of two girls. Wearing a tissuey silk scarf that accented her fine-boned face and luminous eyes, she was beautiful in the Vietnamese way, slightly built, a dancer's body, svelte, almost skeletal, yet looking indestructible. The delicacy of her fragile-seeming features – and this seemed true of all Vietnamese women I met – was in great contrast to her powerful spirit and her prompt and appreciative manner. This put me in mind of how thirty years of war, successfully defending their country, had given the Vietnamese unshakeable faith in themselves and made them unusually resourceful and alert.

She was Vuong Hoa Binh, the daughter of the late Vuong Nhu Chiem, who had been the curator of the museum, where she worked and where I met her, purely by chance. She smiled easily, she was articulate and she had lived in or near Hanoi throughout the war.

'What is your country?' she had asked.

I told her. She welcomed me. I said, 'Was this museum damaged in the war?'

'It was bombed,' she said. 'The whole city was bombed, of course.'

Her father, the curator at that time, had devised a plan for moving the ancient Buddhas, the stelae, the silk paintings, the porcelains, the gold work and the scrolls to safety.

'He hid it all underground so it wouldn't be damaged by the American bombs,' she said. 'My father supervised the distribution and hiding of it. He put it in many different places, so even if some of it were bombed, the rest would be intact.'

Mr Vuong used the same systematic logic to disperse his family, scattering his five children to five different locations in or around Hanoi, to give the family a better chance to survive.

'If we had been in the same place, he would have lost us all, had a bomb hit us. Hanoi was bombed all the time by B-52s. Yet we all survived!'

'You knew what a B-52 bomber was?' I was impressed that a twelve-year-old Vietnamese girl would recognize a specific aircraft. It was hard to imagine an American adolescent knowing such a thing, so why should she?

'Everyone knew this plane,' she said. 'And we were afraid, even in the bomb shelters.'

'Do you remember the Christmas bombing?'

'I remember everything. I remember the day the bombs fell on Kham Thien Street,' she said, drawing her silk scarf close with her slender fingers. 'It was the nineteenth of December. A thousand people died there that day, and most of them were women and children. Every home was destroyed. It was very terrible to see.'

'You saw it?'

'Yes. My aunt and my mother took me to see the damage,' she said. 'We saw many *cratères* – yes, craters – big holes in the road. And the dead, and the fires. I was so frightened. But my aunt and my mother said, "We must see this. What has been done to us." There's a monument on that street now.'

'Were you living near there?'

'We were just outside Hanoi.' She hesitated, then, seeming to remember, said, 'We didn't have much to eat. In fact, we had very little food all through the war. We were always hungry. Even after the war was over we had so little rice. And it was stale rice – old rice.'

'Because of the destruction?'

'No. Because of the American embargo, and the Chinese invasion.'

We had withheld food from them. I did not say, though Mrs Vuong surely knew, that the Chinese had invaded the northern provinces at a time when we were cosying up to them, and Americans took some pleasure in seeing the Vietnamese being thrashed in their hungry and weakened state.

'We were told that the targets were military bases.'

She smiled sadly at this and said, 'Everything was targeted. The whole city. Especially roads and bridges. Our bridge was bombed by the B-52s' – this was the Chuong Duong Bridge, across the Red River to Haiphong. 'But we repaired it. Factories were especially targeted, no matter what they made. The bombings continued for years. Everything was bombed.'

She meant not only Kham Thien Street but also the railways, the lakes, the pagodas, the mansions, the tenements and huts, the museums, the eleventh-century Van Mien Library, the eighteenth-century Catholic cathedral, the opera house, the ancient university Quoc Tu Giam with its stelae and statues and Confucian temple, the markets and the suburbs – everything. Of the millions of tons of bombs we had dropped, many had fallen on her city. By 1968, when there were half a million American soldiers fighting in Vietnam, the British historian J. M. Roberts has written, 'a heavier tonnage of bombs had been dropped on North Vietnam than fell on Germany and Japan together in the entire Second World War'.

Outside the museum, rain had begun to fall. Hanoi is known for its frequently dreary weather, its cloudy days and its drizzle. Raindrops pattered on the windows and ran down the panes, and the wind sucked at the glass, rattling the casements.

'My mother had a friend whose husband worked at a factory that was bombed,' Mrs Vuong said. 'The woman hurried to the factory as soon as she heard the news. She saw that it was smoking – it had burned. She couldn't see anything. But she wanted to find her husband, even if he was dead. But he wasn't there. Just ruins.

'She walked through the smoke and ashes, and she saw, lying among the cinders, one finger. A human finger with a ring on it. Their wedding ring! She knew then that her husband was dead. She took the finger home and had it buried. She kept the ring. And this year she gave the ring to her son, when he got married.'

'What a story,' I said.

'So many stories from that time,' she said. 'We were poor and we had no food, but we had *esprit*. My brothers wanted to fight the Americans. They wanted to be in the army. Ninety-nine per cent of the boys in North Vietnam wanted to be in the army. To be a solider was the greatest thing. No one hesitated. It was their spirit.'

'So your brothers were soldiers?'

'Another story,' she said, smiling again. 'One of my brothers went to the army recruiter. He came home crying, because he didn't have enough age or weight. He was just a small boy – too young. He kept crying, "I want to be a soldier!" My other brother was accepted. He was so happy to be given a chance to fight.'

'What did your parents think?'

'They were happy. My mother was so happy she went to a lot of trouble to find the right ingredients for spring rolls for him. It wasn't easy in Hanoi then! She had to search everywhere. We had a party. Everyone was happy, my brother most of all, celebrating that at last he was a soldier. He was about seventeen.'

We were standing beside the big windows of the museum, the Buddhas and porcelains behind us, one of the more formal and completely European-looking neighbourhoods of the city outside the window. The rain-steaked panes gave the old French buildings across the courtyard the blur and muted colour of an Impressionist painting.

'It's a beautiful city,' I said.

'Hanoi is losing its beauty,' Mrs Vuong said. 'It was so quiet before. It was smaller. Just bicycles. No motorbikes. Now it's noisy, and the people are not Hanoi people. They're from the countryside. They don't know the city.'

She thought a moment, adding, 'And we are changing. We were poor but we had spirit. I knew my father so well. I knew his life. I knew what he needed. My children don't know what we've been through. I try to tell them. It's impossible for them to understand. I can't explain it to them.'

'But aren't these good times?' I was thinking of the markets that were packed with consumer goods, full of food. I was also thinking of the vitality of the country, the tremendous sense of pride, no visible poverty – nothing like the present-day wreckage of Cambodia and its demoralized people.

'Yes, there's more money, more food, but less spirit. I read books, but my two girls are always using computers. They don't read. They love American films.' And with a kind of wonderment and resignation, she said, 'They want to go to America.'

'It's easy to get there now,' I said, but I was just gabbling. I was thinking of the bombing, the hunger, the death, the severed finger with the wedding ring on it, the party for a soldier, with specially made spring rolls on platters, celebrating the departure of a teenager, off to fight Americans.

'The world is small,' Mrs Vuong was saying.

I said, 'Do you hate me?' and realized as I was saying it that I was becoming tearful, which was a kind of nausea too, I suppose, absurd self-disgust, as my eyes filled.

'No, I don't hate you,' Mrs Vuong said, but that made me feel worse.

She was looking serene, as she had when I first saw her, the small slight figure in the museum, like a dancer. But now she was a little distracted, probably thinking of her daughters in front of computers.

'That was a different time.'

Passing the opera house the night before I left Hanoi, I saw people gathering on the steps for a performance, a play advertised as *Huyen Thoai Cuoc Song (Myth of the Living)*, by the Vietnamese playwright Le Quy Duong.

Finding the ticket office closed, I walked around outside and looked for an explanation. The only English-speaker was a tall, smiling young man in a suit and tie. He had the look of someone who had a ticket. He was beaming from the top of the long flight of steps in front of the floodlit opera house.

'How do I get a ticket to this play?' I asked.

'You can't,' he said. 'It's by invitation only.'

'What a shame. Is it a musical?'

'Some music. Some film. Mixed media.'

'In Vietnamese?'

'No. Body language,' he said.

'I'd like to see it,' I said. 'Who is Le Quy Duong?'

'I am Le Quy Duong,' he said.

'So why not invite me to your play?' I said. 'I'm a writer too.'

He looked amused at my presumption and gave me an envelope with an invitation inside.

His play was, as he said, mixed media, full of gongs and drums, with dazzling lights, mime, masks and floating smoke. The opera house was full. I sat back and tried to divine the creation myth amid the swordplay, the prancing skeletons and the love story. The thing had gusto and was so full of life, so plumped with startling events and sonorous music, that it didn't need explanation.

Afterwards, as I was walking to the lobby, a man said, 'Can you be interviewed?'

'You know who I am?'

'You are the man who . . .' He faltered, then said, 'Le Quy Duong says you speak English.'

'That's me. I speak English.'

I praised the play and then headed into the street, and not twenty yards from the opera house a motorcycle skidded to a halt next to me. The beauty on board revved her engine, hitched herself forward to make room for me, and said, 'You want boom-boom?'

I thanked her and kept walking.

It had been my dream in 1973 to go north on the train and onward to China. But the upheavals! The Vietnam War was only one. In China, the Cultural Revolution had convulsed every part of the country. Travel to these places was impossible. So I had flown from Saigon to Tokyo, where I resumed my Railway Bazaar.

But countries open and close. Time passed. The Vietnam War ended. And soon after Mao died, in 1976, the Cultural Revolution was over. China opened to curious travellers around 1980, the year I sailed down the Yangtze. The US trade embargo, lifted in 1994, was the beginning of Vietnam's economic progress. All the borders were open now.

I got a China visa. I bought a ticket on the overnight train to Lao Cai, the northernmost station on the line from Hanoi, on the Chinese border. This was a simple trip. I left Hanoi at around ten on another night train. Besides the Vietnamese, there were a few backpackers and tourists headed to Sapa, a resort town in the hills above Lao Cai, where tribal people lived – Black Hmong and Red Zao and Tay people.

In a noodle shop in Lao Cai the next morning, as I ate my usual breakfast – a pile of fried rice with an egg on top – a passing motorcyclist asked me if I wanted a ride to the border. I said yes, he put my bag on his lap, and he rode me through town to a building and an archway on the bank of the Red River. I walked through, got my passport stamped and kept walking through another archway, into China.

The frenzy of China was immediate, even in the early morning, in the border town of Hekou. All the trade was going south, over the bridge; the streets were thick with trucks. From Hekou I could still see smoke rising from Vietnamese bungalows. Lao Cai was a country town of friendly folk; Hekou was a modernized town of go-getters.

I boarded a bus for Kunming. The trip took all day, winding amid the jungles of Yunnan Province, where I saw that an eight-lane highway was being built through the villages of the Miao people, in their pink hats and pink aprons, and other tribal people with colourful epaulettes. The motorway under construction was raised on cement pillars that marched across valleys and rubber plantations and bamboo groves. Chinese engineers had gouged a great furrow amid the jungles of southern Yunnan, leaving another blight on the landscape, displacing people, putting up signs, bulldozing virgin forest. Troops had marched through here to go to war with the Vietnamese less than thirty years ago, but in a way this bulldozing, because it would last for ever, was worse than war.

Kunming, a small habitable city I had once visited and written about, was now an ugly sprawl of Chinese-cheesy buildings and four million people. I succeeded in getting to Kunming by land – from Singapore, 2,000 miles. Grown rich on its tobacco crop and manufacturing, Kunming had an enormous Louis Vuitton store and a Maserati dealership and a traffic problem and persistent prostitutes. The Chinese word for hooker is *gai*, chicken.

'Are you a *gai* because you like men?'

'No. I don't like men. I like money.'

China exists in its present form because the Chinese want money. Once, America was like that. Maybe this accounted for my desire to leave. Not revulsion, but the tedium and growing irritation of listening to people express their wish for money, that they'd do anything to make it. Who wants to hear people boasting about their greed and their promiscuity? I left for Japan, revelling in the thought that I was done with China – its factory-blighted landscape, its unbreathable air, its unbudging commissars and its honking born-again capitalists. Ugly and soulless, China represented the horror of answered prayers, a peasant's greedy dream of development. I was happy to leave.

27. Tokyo Andaguraundo

The grey sprawl of Tokyo was an intimidating version of the future, not yours and mine, but our children's. Glittering concrete slabs dwarfed crowds of purposeful people beetling back and forth, arms close to their sides, as though they'd all received the same memo: *Walk fast and look worried*. People become littler as they become alike. Bright lights but no warmth, very tidy, more a machine than a city. I wanted to flee to the countryside. Was there any countryside left in Japan?

From my broom cupboard of a hotel room I saw the domed forehead of Ueno Station. At this massive junction of shiny bundled railway lines I could board a train for anywhere in Japan, including the northern island of Hokkaido. In front of my hotel was a pond in a park, with two shrines on causeways, and some surrounding trees; at the back of my hotel, just past the rear entrance, was a red-light district, a floating world of night-clubs and massage parlours. Bland formality on one side, frivolity on the other, each side offering ways of overcoming loneliness in a city whose true population was more than twenty million.

I hate big cities, probably for the same reasons many city people hate wilderness (which I love), because I find them vertiginous, threatening, monochromatic, isolating, exhausting, germ-laden, bristling with busy shadows and ambiguous odours. And the mobs, and all the shared space. Cities look like monstrous cemeteries to me, the buildings like brooding tombstones. I feel lonely and lost in the lit-up necropolis, nauseated by traffic fumes, disgusted by food smells, puzzled by the faces and the banal frenzy.

When city-slicker utopians praise their cities I want to laugh. They whoop about museums and dinner parties, the manic diversions, the zoos, the energy of the streets, and how they can buy a pizza at three in the morning. I love to hear them competing: my big city is better than your big city! They never mention the awful crowds, the foul air, the rackety noise, the marks of weakness, marks of woe, or how a big city is never dark and never silent. And they roost like tiny featherless birds in the confinement of their high apartments, always peering down at the pavement, able to get around only by riding in the smelly back seat of a slow taxi driven by a cranky cabbie.

Tokyo was like that, a twinkling wonderland of dignified vulgarity that defeated my imagination. At Shinobazu Pond, in front of my hotel, token wildlife, eider ducks and pochards, nosed about the reeds, leafless willow trees drooped at the bank, people strolled from shrine to shrine in Ueno Park and ate ice cream, or else looked preoccupied in ways I found daunting. At the back, narrow lanes of bars, beer joints, noodle shops, massage parlours, love hotels, tattooed mobsters, streetwalkers and clubs catering to every fetish. At some clubs waitresses were dressed as schoolgirls, at others as French maids or nurses or terrifying bitches in black lipstick carrying whips. Sweet-faced girls in sailor suits were also popular as sex workers. Many establishments called themselves lingerie bars, the female staff in undies, and one was actually named Undies Bar. After dark, women loitered in alleys, hoping to be hired for about $37 to sit next to a man in a bar while he got drunk and fondled her. 'And if she likes you,' a man at my hotel assured me, 'she'll fondle you, too.'

All travel is time travel. Having just arrived in Japan, I felt I had travelled into the future, to a finished version of all the cities I'd passed through on this trip. In time, if they made plans, American big cities would evolve to become the same sort of metropolis, just as big, just as efficient and intimidating: Los Angeles and Seattle and New York already had the bones and the general shape of Tokyo, and would soon be just as soulless.

Even long ago, Japan seemed to me the future; it was still so – at least one version, the one in which the worst social problems were solved, poverty was low, literacy high, life expectancy long, ritual courtesies practised with a baffling formality, no homelessness and good public transport. The other future was the dystopia of Turkmenistan, the melancholy of rural India, the open prison of Burma, the social laboratory of Singapore. The price to be paid for success in the future was surrendering space and privacy. Japan's solutions were minimalist: good but narrow roads, rooms designed for midgets, packed subways, tiny restaurants, the whole landscape miniaturized and cemented over.

But for better or worse, a Nipponized future is the likeliest solution to survival in an overcrowded world – an almost robotic obedience, decorum, rigidity, order with no frills, a scaling down of space, agreed-upon courtesies (high-density living requires politeness), the virtual abolition of private cars, an intimidating police presence and no arm-swinging. A big car on a Tokyo back street was a startling event, like the arrival of an aristocrat's carriage on a medieval lane – and it was probably a mobster's car. That was the other certainty: in a controlled city a sophisticated criminal element insinuates itself to connive in keeping order, as the yakuza – the Japanese mob – does in Tokyo, and in Japan generally. 'The one thing that terrifies Japanese people is unorganized crime,' says a criminologist quoted in *Yakuza*, the definitive book on the subject, by David Kaplan and Alec Dubro. 'That's why there's so little street crime here. Gangsters control the turf, and they provide the security . . . Japanese police prefer the existence of organized crime to its absence.'

The other novelty of Tokyo is its inner life, as both a physical fact and a metaphor: the tunnels of the railway under the city, the cavernous underground known by its cognate *andaguraundo*, the shadow life that exists with a crepuscular completeness inside the city. I arrived in Tokyo at night. The city, geeky during the day, weirded out after dark. Night is also a metaphor for the underground: an enclosing and subterranean darkness, and the vast twinkling hoardings and dazzling lighted signs made the darkness darker.

'Go to Shibuya,' a Japanese friend had told me. 'It is very strange.'

Dark alleys and dimly lit bars were a feature of Shibuya, where pretty girls strolled, dressed up in Little Bo Peep costumes. I went and gaped, and what struck me was how these young, cute, overdressed girls greatly resembled the cartoon girls on hoardings and posters and bar signs: pixie faces simplified with white makeup, tousled hair in ringlets, willowy big-eyed waifs with skinny legs and awkward postures – half schoolgirl and half sprite. They were mimicking the pictures Japanese called *manga*, a word that means sketch.

Many of the *manga* booklets I saw catered to male rape fantasies. Such pictorial fantasies are as old as Japanese erotic images, as some of the oldest woodblock prints, the *ukiyo-e* from which *manga* evolved. The word itself was used in *Hokusai Manga*, a sketchbook of the nineteenth-century master Katsushika Hokusai, who was making brilliant landscapes as well as porn as he approached his ninetieth year. Erotic prints of this kind are known in Japanese as *shunga* – spring pictures. One authority on Japanese art, Richard Lane, wrote, 'Scenes of rape are very common in *shunga*.' Hokusai's scenes still have the power to shock, not just episodes of forcible rape, but the rape victim shown sprawled by the roadside, or, in one of the weirder examples, an amorous goggle-eyed octopus performing oral sex on an enraptured naked woman pearl diver.

Manga cartoons, the modern form, are everywhere. In every magazine there's a *manga* section of comic strips: adventure, fantasy, sci-fi, school stories, office stories, heroic tales, samurai epics, ninja dramas, mutant sagas and of course porn. Japanese literacy is probably the highest in the world, yet most books and magazines are thick with cartoons. It seems the Japanese do not outgrow such frivolities, but since in a profound sense there is an infantilizing element in Japanese society, it is a predictable pleasure. A photograph of an actual rape is wicked, but a colourful cartoon rape is permissible. Rape is the most common porn event in the *manga* form, 'funny pictures' of girls being violated. This *manga* involves very young, very submissive, skinny girls – wide-eyed, as in the typical *manga* girl stereotype. Schoolgirls are the object of most men's desire, or so it seems, not only in *manga* but in the back streets of Shibuya, where pouting girls roamed the streets in party costumes and some clubs featured young women in school uniforms.

In daylight the city was busy and efficient, a place of ostentatious deference, bowing and nodding, the pedestrians beetling again, the lingerie bars and fetish clubs empty, the fruit stores and fish markets and noodle shops full. Alarmed by rumours of expensive train fares, I went, the first morning I could, to the Japan Railways office at Ueno with my rail pass and bought tickets to all parts of the archipelago – Sapporo in the north, Wakkanai in the far north, Kyoto further south, Niigata on the west coast. I hardly saw any other tourists. The country was as orderly, polite and well organized as it had been thirty-three years ago, and it was just as alienating.

I could not read a single sign or understand a word, and why should anyone pay any attention to my bewilderment? The small slender race that had tried to conquer half the world by military force, and been thwarted in that ambition, had tried to do the same through manufacturing, and had been thwarted in that by China. Japanese-brand cameras and computers were now made in the People's Republic, and even the $100 latex body suits and sexy lingerie and erotic masks and velvet handcuffs I saw in Shibuya were labelled MADE IN CHINA.

I walked around Tokyo like an alien from another, much simpler planet. Being a Martian in such a huge and daunting city was also like being a child, or someone suffering a strange dream in which all the winking lights and jolly faces on hoardings induced a sense of alienation and melancholy. I only knew how to say please and thank you. Though I sometimes felt (with reason) that I was the tallest human being in Tokyo, I also felt freakish and confused, and so insubstantial as to be almost a goblin, a ghost again. The unusual twenty-first-century city of one language, one people, one culture, one set of rules, excluded me and made me want to head underground.

Because Japan seems to be a world of order and decency and restraint, a book evoking Japanese chaos and rage is like a glimpse of the dark side, the insecurity that lies underground. That book, *Andaguraundo*, by Haruki Murakami, is about the 1995 poison gas outrage on the Tokyo subway. Murakami wrote,

Another personal motive for my interest in the Tokyo gas attack is that it took place underground. Subterranean worlds – wells, underpasses, caves, underground springs and rivers, dark alleys, subways – have always fascinated me and are an important motif in my novels. The image, the mere idea of a hidden pathway, immediately fills my head with stories.

The sarin attack on morning commuters, Murakami has written, was a defining moment in post-war Japanese history, blunt-force trauma to the national psyche. The attack was perpetrated by members of a quasi-Buddhist cult called Aum Shinrikyo, whose guru, a half-blind paranoiac named Shoko Asahara, had turned his believers into commandos. One day, ten of them slipped into the Tokyo subway and punctured sealed packets of the poison on eight trains rolling through the system. One pinprick of sarin is lethal to a human. Twelve people died, thousands were injured, some permanently. All at once Japanese order was violated and the nation made to feel insecure.

Murakami saw it as a seismic event, like the Kobe earthquake the same year. 'Both were nightmarish eruptions beneath our feet – from underground.' Thus the title of his book, *Underground*, a chronicle of the sarin attack that was like 'one massive explosion'. It tells the stories of many of the people involved: the victims, the cultists, the bystanders.

He said he wrote the book because he had lived so many years abroad and 'I have always wanted to understand Japan at a deeper level.'

I did too. That was why I read the book, and it was also why I wanted to see Haruki Murakami in Tokyo. Such a thoughtful man would be the best guide, and seeing him here would also be a way for me to connect in this city of strangers.

Japanese tend not to talk about failure, or to question the system, or to refuse to join the company, or to sit around whistling Thelonious Monk's 'Epistrophy' or 'Crepuscule with Nellie', or to go into self-imposed exile. Haruki Murakami has lived his life as the opposite of a salaryman, following these forbidden ways, and yet this compact, exceedingly healthy man seemed to me (depending on what he was saying at the time) both the most Japanese and the least Japanese person I had ever met. A healthy writer is an oxymoron. Yet Murakami has run twenty-nine marathons and competed in numerous triathlons. One long day he ran a 100-kilometre race. This took him eleven and a half hours.

'You ran sixty-five miles?' I asked. 'How did you feel the next day?'

When he smiles, which is not often, Murakami has a cherubic face. He smiled and said, 'I didn't feel too bad.'

He did not advertise this feat, nor did he go on book tours in Japan. He was so averse to publicity that he had never appeared on Japanese TV or in bookshops, gave no lectures, did no signings, hardly surfaced in Japan at all – though he had taught in the United States and sometimes promoted his books there. But he did not wish his face to be recognizable in Japan.

Another un-Japanese aspect of Murakami's career is that he has chosen to live a large proportion of his adult life outside Japan, in Greece and Italy and the United States (where I first met him). He returns to Japan at intervals to spend time at his house in Oisu, where one of his recreations is playing American jazz records from his collection of 6,000, all vinyl. He is especially Japanese in this respect, in a nation where pastimes or beliefs become consuming passions – whether it is jazz, Thomas Hardy, Elvis, the ukulele or designer labels. Christianity became such a national craze in Japan in the seventeenth century, with mass conversions and baptisms, that the shogun outlawed the religion. Instead of surrendering, the Christian Japanese chose martyrdom, the subject of Shusaku Endo's sombre novel *Silence*.

I got in touch with Murakami. He is the most reclusive writer I know, also the most energetic, and with a lively mind. You would almost take him to be normal. He rises every day at four a.m. ('it used to be five') to begin his day's stint and writes until mid morning; he spends the rest of the day doing whatever he likes, usually running. After ten in the morning he'll shrug and say, 'I've done my day's work.'

Anthony Trollope followed a similar routine. He was woken at four by his Irish servant, with a candle and a cup of tea. He wrote until breakfast time, then went to work at the post office, where he was a senior official. Though elfin (or even phocine) compared to the ursine Trollope, Murakami has Trollopian gusto and good humour and an appetite for work. His curiosity and knowledge of Western culture and American literature are boundless. Besides his twelve works of fiction and the non-fiction *Underground*, Murakami has also translated many American writers into Japanese – among them Faulkner, Fitzgerald, Raymond Chandler, Truman Capote and me (*World's End*).

Murakami rebelled early. In *Underground*, speaking of Japanese conformity, he quoted the Japanese adage 'The nail that sticks out gets hammered down.' He was unfazed. He did not follow the usual route into a company and a job for life. He married his college sweetheart, Yoko, when he was twenty-two ('my parents were disappointed'), worked at part-time jobs ('very disappointed'), lived in his father-in-law's house and started a jazz club, naming it after his cat, Peter Cat.

'It was lots of fun.'

But he had no clear idea of where he was going, except against the grain. His father was a professor of Japanese literature. Haruki did not read Japanese literature. Instead, he read Truman Capote and Chekhov and Dostoyevsky, while listening to Thelonious Monk.

Seven years went by. One day, he was visited by an epiphany. It was springtime, the start of the baseball season. The year was 1978. He was twenty-nine, sitting in Jingu Stadium, watching a game.

A thought came to him (as he told me): 'I'm going to write something. I'm going to be a writer. I had a feeling I was blessed.'

He had never written a word. His major at Waseda University had been theatre arts.

'I went home and started a novel.'

And in time he finished it. Called *Hear the Wind Sing*, it was published in 1979. The story of the epiphany at the baseball game is one that he has told many of his interviewers. It has the elements of a traditional creation myth – a suddenness of spontaneous combustion, a vastation of utter certainty. But its mystical quality is in keeping with the mood of Murakami's fiction, which often has an ungraspable serenity in the narrative shifts, his characters with one foot in Eden, the other in Japan, their motives enigmatic. The other aspect of this story of inspiration in the bleachers – the downdraft of afflatus, a Diamond Sutra in the baseball sense – is that Murakami believes it.

'The book is – what? – not the best. Then I wrote *Pinball*. And then my first good book, *A Wild Sheep Chase*. After that, I've never stopped. It's my passion. It's my love. I have never had writer's block. I've never wanted to do anything else.'

He is Japan's best-known and most widely translated writer. Bursting with health, full of ideas, deeply curious, he is beloved in Japan. Yet he is invisible, never recognized, so he told me; another ghost figure.

The cold day I met him in Tokyo he was wearing blue jeans and a leather jacket, a wool scarf and leather track shoes. Of medium height, mild by nature, watchful and laconic, he radiated innocence as well as toughness. In a profession notable for its self-doubt, Murakami's belief in himself – the sense of his literary vocation being part mission, part love affair – is one of his most remarkable traits. He is so sure of himself you might mistake his confidence for arrogance, but it is mental toughness, of a kind that helps a person run up and down hills for sixty-five miles without letup, rising the next day to continue a long fictional narrative.

'You've probably already written a chapter today,' I said when we met that day. It was ten in the morning.

'Not a whole chapter,' Murakami said and smiled. 'What do you want to do?'

'Just walk.' I had told him once, some time before, in an aside, that I was curious about Japanese implements – cookware, woodworking tools and knives. The paraphernalia unique to Japanese culture – soba bowls and pots, chisels and carving knives – is still made in Japan. Strangely shaped saws, highly specific, for shaping cedar boards, for trimming the edges of chests and tansus, are never seen anywhere else. They are the last designs of traditional tools.

Murakami remembered that I'd mentioned this, and reminded me of it. He said some of these things were sold on a particular street. He showed me the street on a map he'd downloaded from the Internet. It was in a file folder with a set of maps that he planned as a long day's tour of alternative Tokyo – underground in every sense.

Examining this material culture pleased him, because the tools were peculiar to Japan and so well made. Murakami denies that his books have any deep meaning, and he has said he stands against interpretation of his texts, yet hovering over his work, and of *Underground* especially, is the notion that Japan has lost its way.

I mentioned this to him as we walked through the park in front of my hotel, skirting Ueno Station.

'We had pride and anxiety during wartime,' he said. 'Early successes, then defeat. Occupation was hard – US soldiers . . .'

He waved his hand as though to suggest GIs lounging among the cedars and willows at the edge of Shinobazu Pond, and Americans in fatigues and big boots watching us through sunglasses. The reminder of Japan's surrender was a humiliation, but the graceful way Murakami accepted it put me in mind of Borges, who said, 'Defeat has a dignity which noisy victory does not deserve.'

Murakami's way of speaking was abrupt and almost telegraphic. He would say something, and interrupt himself, and lapse into silence. His concentrated silences I took to be proof of his confidence rather than shyness. He had few questions. He was almost absent at times, in a shadow of watchful circumspection.

'We admired MacArthur – we still do. He's like a father figure.'

'Not many Americans think about him,' I said. 'He was fired and forgotten.'

'He helped us rebuild. And we had to work hard to rebuild. The bombing destroyed so much – especially over there.'

He was pointing across a wide busy street towards Kappa Bashi, the street of kitchenware, baskets, lacquerware, knives, strainers, teapots, woodworking tools. He meant the firebombing of Tokyo, which killed more people than the atom bombs. In 1945 Japan was destroyed. Every city except Kyoto had been wrecked. Half the buildings in Tokyo were reduced to ashes. MacArthur's orders, as supreme commander of the Allied powers, had been 'Remake Japan.'

Murakami's voice was so uncharacteristically tremulous and aggrieved I did not mention the obvious – that Japan had drawn us into the war with the unprovoked attack on Pearl Harbor. But clearly his thinking of the post-war struggle put him in mind of the present mood.

'We're in a state of defeat now,' he said. 'We were doing very well – making money. You know the story. Cameras, cars, TV sets. The banks were lending money to anyone.'

And then it ended. He described how the bursting of the *baburu keizei*, the economic bubble, in 1991 and '92 had left people dazed, and in some cases bankrupt. This period of uncertainty was followed by two events in 1995 that shattered the Japanese notion of itself as solid and immutable: the Kobe earthquake and the gas attack, in January and March. Murakami had been travelling for almost a decade, first in Italy and Greece – a Greek island is the setting for the drama in his novel *Sputnik Sweetheart* – then in the United States, where he taught at Harvard, Princeton, MIT and Stanford. The shocking news stirred Murakami, who was far away.

'I wanted to come back, to do something for my people,' he said. He became somewhat self-conscious saying it, perhaps sensing that it sounded vain. 'Not for the country – country is nothing. But Japan's people are its treasure.'

We were walking down the wide street through Kappa Bashi, past shops, but not the ones he intended to show me.

'Before '95, to get rich was everything,' he said. 'And we succeeded, through ingenuity and hard work. We thought that would make us happy.' He had an athlete's upright posture, square shoulders and springy step, and he was moving briskly.

'Did it? Make you happy?'

He didn't answer. He spoke, as he walked, at his own speed. It was a Murakami trait: he wouldn't be hurried or interrupted; he always completed his thought. 'We thought, "Money can solve anything at all."'

We came to a street corner and waited for the signal to cross. For the duration of the crossing he said nothing, but on the other side he picked up where he left off.

'But hard work didn't bring us to a better place. We found that money is not the answer.' He fell silent, noticed that I was scribbling notes, and after a while he resumed. 'We had our goals. We achieved them, but the achievement didn't bring us happiness.'

'So what are the goals now?' I asked.

'Our goal is still to be happy and proud,' he said. 'And we're looking for a new goal.'

'I always thought of Japanese culture as an unchangeable set of traditions and symbols. Like the Yasukuni Shrine.'

The shrine was in my mind because it was controversial (it has been compared to a Nazi monument), because its presence was another victory for the yakuza ('steering Japan backward and to the right', as one observer put it), and because it was mentioned in *Underground*, in a question posed by Murakami to an Aum cultist. 'People who believed in the emperor thought that if you died for him your soul would rest in Yasukuni Shrine and find peace,' Murakami said. That included enshrined memories of the murderers and rapists of Nanking, the torturers of enemy prisoners of war, the looters of Singapore, the sadists on the Bataan Death March, the suicide bombers of Pearl Harbor, the abductors and debauchers of Korean women, forcing them to be sex slaves for the imperial army, and many others regarded by non-Japanese as war criminals.

'The Yasukuni Shrine is for politicians. They want to show their patriotism,' Murakami said when I asked him.

And it was a fact that every prime minister visited the shrine – that repository of the souls of soldiers – in the spring and autumn and on 15 August, the anniversary of the Japanese surrender.

'Before 1945 we were militaristic,' he said. 'After that, we were peace-loving and gentle. But we were the same people. The soldiers who massacred the Chinese in Nanking came home and were peaceful. Let's stop here. Want a cup of coffee?'

The small coffee shop was of traditional Japanese design, all wood panelling and wooden tables and stools. Murakami said he chose it because such mum-and-pop places were disappearing, being forced out of business by the larger, mostly American coffee shop chains. And the coffee was better here too.

'Is this an old place?' I asked.

He said, 'Because of the American bombing, every building around here is less than sixty years old.'

'Do people hanker for the old days?'

'My mother used to say that Osaka is better now,' he said. 'That it's a better world now. A more peaceful one than before.'

'What do you think?'

'We were given liberty. We were given the capitalist system. You know, we never had a revolution in Japan.'

I was also thinking, but did not say: And you were delivered of the notion of conquering Asia and the Pacific, making it part of the Japanese empire. You were saved from that complex fate, and without an empire or an army you were able to concentrate your efforts on becoming prosperous. Murakami might have agreed with that, though he probably would have added: We were A-bombed and humiliated. Which was true.

'You were in college in '68,' I said. 'That was a time of tremendous student protest. Were you in those demonstrations?'

'I was a rebel at Waseda, yes. American soldiers were here on R and R from Vietnam. We held demonstrations. We occupied the university.'

'Are there demonstrations now against the Iraq War?'

'None.'

'Because the government discourages them?'

'No. Student apathy, probably.'

'But there's repression of a cultural kind in Japan, isn't there?'

He nodded. The coffee had come, served by a little old woman in a blue apron and white mobcap. We were the only people in the shop. And it was easy to scribble notes in my notebook at the wooden table.

'Always the feeling you are watched,' he said.

'Did you feel that way – conspicuous?'

'Yes. You have to make up your mind to be different.'

'Your father was bookish,' I said. 'Wasn't that a help to you?'

'My father and I never talked about books. I wanted to escape Kyoto.'

'There's this line in a Henry James essay about England where he says that every Englishman is a tight fit in society. Isn't that also true in Japan?'

'It's true here, but it's changing. I rebelled against it.'

'How?'

'After college I became nothing. My father was disappointed. I was disappointed. Our relationship soured.'

'But you wanted to be a writer.'

'No. I had nothing in my mind.' He stared at me over the top of his coffee cup. 'I was married. I just wanted to listen to music.'

That was when he told me about starting his jazz club, and how for years he indulged himself in listening to music – and also reading. And he had married so young, at twenty-two, his parents thought he was lost. He moved to Yoko's house, where he got on well with her father, who was a shopkeeper and made no demands.

'I loved Yoko. That was everything to me.'

Murakami made these simple statements with a great deal of feeling, such unexpected intensity that I seemed to get a glimpse of both passion and a deep loneliness that love had relieved.

After that, we plunged into the shops of Kappa Bashi. At a place that sold cutlery he showed me the specialty knives, the cleavers and daggers and buck knives of dark tempered steel, and a long, narrow, sword-like knife for slicing big fish for sashimi. On the walls and in display cases were chisels and saws for shaping blocks of ice.

At another shop, selling lacquerware, I bought a pot in the shape of a big square teapot, for pouring soba broth. This same shop sold platters and trays. None of the knives or lacquer items had any application in Western culture, though they were fundamental to Japanese culture. Trays alone were essential items in everyday life here. They were big and small, plastic, wood, lacquered. In a bank, for example, money was never passed from hand to hand by a clerk, but instead always placed on a tray and presented. There were trays for food, trays for cups or bowls, trays for paper cards, for chopsticks, for shoes, for slippers.

We toured tool shops and examined saws and hammers, kitchen-ware shops and basket shops. Some of the designs were ancient, yet they were still sold and used; they had not been displaced by novelties. The Japanese electronic culture of computers and gadgets was probably the most advanced in the world, yet it functioned alongside these old-fashioned tools. In a way, these were remnants from an older world, a reassuring one.

It was the culture that endured in Namiki Yabu Soba, the noodle restaurant where we went next. The formal welcome, the low bow, the politeness – unexpected courtesies in such a hectic city. And while our table was a novelty, the past existed across the room, where a dozen people sat cross-legged on tatami mats.

'This place looks old.'

Murakami smiled grimly. 'Post-war. Like everything else.'

He took out a picture, part of the folder he had prepared for our city tour. The panoramic photo showed twenty-five square miles of Tokyo flattened – not just flattened but scorched, burned to the ground.

'This is what the city looked like on the ninth of March 1945.'

A wasteland, just rubble and cinders, one or two blackened buildings still standing, the river coldly gleaming.

'People went there,' he said, his finger tracing the river, 'but even the river burned. Everything was napalmed.'

As we were hunched over the picture, the bowls of hot soba noodles were brought on trays – a tray for each of us, a tray for the chopsticks, a small dish of pickled vegetables on a smaller tray.

'The B-29s dropped the bombs. It was all planned by Curtis LeMay.'

If I asked any of my well-read friends who had masterminded the firebombing of Tokyo, I doubt whether one of them could have supplied the correct name.

'A hundred thousand people died in that one night, mostly civilians,' Murakami said. He was moving his finger from ash pile to ash pile on the photo. 'It was a wall of flames. We're here.'

His fingertip rested on a featureless patch of ashes.

'People talk about Dresden, but this was worse than Dresden, where thirty thousand people died. There was no escape.'

As I stared at the photo, I was thinking how four years before that bombing was another bombing, Japanese planes flying through morning sunshine, their bombs slamming into the fleet at anchor in Pearl Harbor. But in the documentary *The Fog of War*, Robert McNamara, the secretary of defense during the Vietnam War, said that, based on the bombings he and LeMay had ordered, there was every reason for the two of them to be hanged as war criminals. One of the lame justifications for our bombing of Japan was that none of the Japanese could be regarded as a civilian; all, even women and children, had been war-trained, and so were legitimate targets.

I said, 'A bombing like that is terrible, but it has a purpose in war – to demoralize people, to undermine the government that might have been telling them a different story. It was horrible, but its intention was to make people surrender.'

Murakami considered this. He was a reflective soul, never in a hurry, and always spoke in a thoughtful way. 'Yes, as you say, people here were demoralized,' he said. 'The emperor visited a few days later. It had never happened before. The people were astonished. It was as though they saw a god. He was moved by it. Something had changed. He was so shocked. He made a statement. They began to see that he was human.'

He spoke slowly, as if to help me remember, to let it sink in. But I was thinking of something he had said earlier: *Even the river burned.*

After we left the noodle place, we walked to a market and saw some big white foreigners, *gaijin*, and we talked about aliens, an obsessive subject in racially singular Japan. I felt like a geek, I said, and I preferred anonymity in travel. Yes, Murakami said, it was a fact, all foreigners stood out in Japan.

'But I stood out in America,' he said.

'You were at big universities. Those places are multiracial to an unusual degree.'

'I mean, when I drove cross-country.'

'When was that?'

'In '95, with a Japanese friend,' Murakami said. 'We were stopped five or six times a day driving through Minnesota, South Dakota, Montana.'

'Really?'

'Yes!' The memory of it stirred him. 'I was Japanese in a shiny new Volvo. "Let's see your licence and registration." It happened every day.' Attempting a gruff American policeman's accent, he said, ' "It's just warning ticket." "Why warning? What did I do?" "Did I say you did something? It's a warning." '

I had started to laugh at his mimicking a midwestern policeman, but grimly, because I had heard similar stories from foreigners driving cross-country.

'Utah is the worst! We were stopped all the time,' he said. 'And in South Dakota there's a town called Welcome. I saw the sign. I said to my friend, "Let's stop here." ' He put on a sad face, with an exaggeratedly downturned mouth. 'No one welcomed us.'

He had another story. Once, when he was in Washington, DC, to give a lecture, he went to his hotel to check in. Someone else was ahead of him, so he stood a decent distance from the counter. Then a big white man ('probably a lobbyist') approached and planted himself in front of Murakami. Seeing this, another man indicated Murakami and reprimanded the man, saying, 'He was here first.' The big man said, 'I was here first' – an outright lie.

Still, Murakami said, he had fond memories of America. American cultural artefacts – songs, foods, expressions and place names – are grace notes in his work; his grasp of American society is a unique feature of his fiction.

'Let's go underground,' he said.

We went down an escalator at Kasumigaseki, on the Hibiya line. He handed me a ticket, but when I went through the turnstile I looked back and saw that his ticket had been rejected. Trying it several more times, he held up the queue. People glanced at him and walked around him. He went to a conductor, who studied his ticket and explained a detail of it, indicating the remedy with a white-gloved hand – all railway personnel in Japan, and many workers, wear white gloves.

What impressed me was that all this time, as he was obstructing the turnstile, looking confused among the scores of commuters, consulting the conductor, not a single person said, 'Haruki Murakami! I love your books!' He was not only the best-known and most widely read writer in Japan, but had been writing books for almost thirty years. The author of *Underground*, the story of the subway outrage, was in one of the very stations he'd written about. No more conspicuous than any other Japanese person, he was merely a wraith, unidentifiable as the famous writer.

I remarked on this.

'Yes, no one knows my face. I have never appeared on TV here. They ask, but I always say no.'

'Why?'

'So that I can do this.'

He meant haunt the underground, walk around unobserved, peacefully, in a leather jacket and woollen gloves and a red scarf and blue jeans. He then explained to me how the Aum Shinrikyo terrorists entered the station in pairs, got on the trains, put on gas masks, stabbed the packets of sarin gas with the tips of their umbrellas, then quickly exited the trains. Their actions were timed so that the gas would be released simultaneously, causing the greatest possible harm.

Later, one of the gassed victims said to Murakami, 'Since the war ended, Japan's economy has grown rapidly to the point where we've lost any sense of crisis, and material things are all that matter. The idea that it's wrong to harm others has gradually disappeared.'

And one of the cult members had said to him, 'What I liked most about the Aum books was that they clearly stated that the world is evil. I was happy when I read that. I'd always thought that the world was unfair and might as well be destroyed.'

In this innocent and orderly place, among the passengers streaming through the station in an orderly fashion, no one lingering or looking at others, it was easy to see how anyone who wished to could plant a bomb or be a suicide bomber or, as in the case of the Aum outrage, bring packets of deadly gas on to the trains and stab them open with the sharpened tip of an umbrella. Though they were not obvious as malcontents in this seemingly monochrome culture, there were enough angry people to wreak havoc.

Murakami understood this. He wrote,

We will get nowhere as long as the Japanese continue to disown the Aum 'phenomenon' as something other, an alien presence viewed through binoculars on the far shore. Unpleasant though the prospect might seem, it is important that we incorporate 'them', to some extent, within the construct called 'us', or at least within Japanese society.

We travelled on the Hibiya line to Nakaokachimachi Station, in the Akihabara district.

'Nerd city,' Murakami said.

But it looked exactly like every other place I'd been in Tokyo: tall tombstone buildings, frantically blinking signs, streets choked with traffic, pavements crammed with people, slanting shadows. Walking in a slot among the close buildings, I had a sense of being indoors, which is another weird feature of cities, the way they enclose you, trapping you in their unbreathable air.

'All these guys work in offices,' Murakami said. 'All nerds. So what do we find?'

He was walking along the pavement with his usual briskness, indicating signs and agencies and offices.

'"Pop Life", six storeys of porn,' he said. 'Also massage parlours. See those signs? And video booths over there. And that place, it says "Pure Heart", and that one "French Maids".'

'You have French maids in Japan?'

'No. From *manga*.'

The sexual fantasies of French maids in alluring uniforms, fishnet stockings and stiletto heels, and carrying feather dusters, had originated in *manga* cartoons. That said a great deal about the power of cartoons to influence the inner life of Japanese men, and it evoked something of their solitude, too.

Murakami paused at an intersection and looked around for something to show me. Once again, the crowds hurried past him, the famous writer an invisible presence among his readers.

'Let's look at Pop Life,' I said.

Inside, amid the porn, he whispered, 'What would my readers say if they saw me here?'

Japanese are addicted to euphemisms. Euphemism is a feature of the culture of repression or secrecy; the English, the Irish, the Chinese and the underworld are no less euphemistic. Instead of 'toilet', a Japanese person is more likely to say 'the honourable unclean place' (*gofujo*), and the reply 'I will think it over' (*kangaete okimasu*) means 'No way'. Such euphemisms were discussed in a piece by the Tokyo-based linguist Roger Pulvers which I happened to read in the *Japan Times*. Pulvers wrote, 'The most common euphemism for the horny, randy and raunchy is *ecchi*. This word derives from the first letter, *h*, of *hentai*, meaning abnormal or perverted.'

Ecchi summed up Pop Life. Though Murakami was not easily fazed, even he seemed a bit surprised by what we found on those six busy floors of sex-related merchandise.

'DVDs, lotions, pictures,' Murakami mumbled as we walked around the first floor and climbed the staircase to the next floor, where a whole wall displayed bondage ropes in different colours and thicknesses. '"Bondage" is *shibari*,' Murakami explained as I scribbled. 'But Japanese is subtle and specific. These represent *kin-baku* – tight bondage.'

'Got it.'

The third floor was filled with vibrators, dildos and oddly shaped devices for obscure penetrations. These were arranged according to size and colour and were handsomely boxed. Murakami was fascinated as he picked through the wall display. 'Look, they come with manuals,' he said, squeezing a plastic bag and reading the directions.

An adjoining room was stacked with erotic masks, gag-balls, whips, chains, handcuffs. Also latex outfits and plastic boots.

'"Made in China,"' Murakami translated.

'So they outsource this stuff.'

Murakami held another label. He said, pretending to gloat, 'Designed in Japan!'

The lingerie and the uniforms were hung on clothes racks on the fourth floor. A large sign in Japanese, Korean, Chinese, and English said, 300 OFF IF YOU POSE FOR A POLAROID. Next to it were about a hundred Polaroid shots of Japanese girls – satisfied customers – wearing skimpy lingerie or bizarre costumes, most of the girls smiling as they attempted sexy poses, more playful than vicious, like their scrawled explanations.

'I'm wearing this to a Halloween party,' one caption said. Another: 'I'm wearing this on Saturday.' A third, in fur-trimmed underwear: 'This is a surprise.' A Japanese girl in a French maid's outfit: 'I'm Larry's girl.'

The maid costume cost $85. The rather dreary school uniform was cheaper. There were racks of cheerleaders' uniforms, nurses' outfits, witches' capes, leprechaun getups.

'What's this?'

Murakami translated the label on a red satin jumpsuit. 'Devil Girl.'

Flight attendants' uniforms, soldiers' khakis, even a 'Tea Party Hostess', which seemed to owe something to *Alice in Wonderland*.

'This is a *miko* costume,' Murakami said, holding up a colourful kimono-like robe. 'These women assist at shrines.'

'Is that erotic?'

'Maybe. The *miko* should be a virgin.'

'Sweet Café Girl' was another, like the uniform of a waitress in an American diner or a girl serving customers at a drive-in.

We climbed to the next floor – videos. They were arranged by category on shelves, and many were voyeuristic, 'secret videos', which Murakami translated as *tousatsu*: spy-hole pictures of changing rooms, bathrooms, bathhouses, hot springs, up-skirt shots and sneaky glimpses of naked and semi-naked girls. The other sections, self-explanatory, were labelled BIG BONDAGE and MATURE WOMAN and LOLITA CORNER.

'Here's one,' Murakami said with a crooked smile, lifting a DVD titled *Your Brother's Wife*.

The DVD box featured a photograph of an anxious woman and a tormented man. There was a whole shelf of similar films.

'A different kind of dream,' Murakami said.

Often, later in my trip, thinking about our visit to Pop Life, I smiled at this memory of Murakami in his leather jacket and red scarf, holding the strange little package and musing, *A different kind of dream.*

But the domination dream was the most common. I recognized a theme. Most of the DVDs were fantasies of power – rape, intimidation, submissiveness at its most abject. The uniforms represented maids, serving girls, schoolgirls, underlings – the weak, the compliant, the easily exploited, women who waited and served: these were the roles that inflamed the male imagination in Japan. I saw no mother figures or powerful women, no big blondes, no big-titted babes, no grinning bimbos: only the weak and the vulnerable, sylph-like schoolgirls and pixie-faced sweeties, small skinny sex objects – the sort of girls who were shuffling all over Tokyo, young women whom (as Murakami suggested) only nerds could dominate.

Uniforms are common among Japanese workers, not just waitresses and bus drivers but also road sweepers and shop assistants and train conductors and ticket punchers with their blue suits and white gloves. Because so many people in Japanese society choose or are assigned a role, sex takes the form of role-playing. So does entertainment; so does business with its peculiar suits.

We had reached the top floor and were looking at the guest book with its comments. One statement by a visitor to Pop Life, written in bold characters, stood out in the middle of a page.

'What does that say?'

'"I would rather eat shit than look at these things,"' Murakami translated. 'Okay, we go.'

He pulled out another map. We took the subway to another stop, got out, and began walking. After a lot of trouble – the street numbers were inconsistent – we found the @home Café, where (confirming what I had already nailed as a common fantasy) the waitresses were dressed as housemaids in frilly uniforms and all of them claimed to be seventeen years old. Three of them knelt before us as we entered.

'Welcome home, dear master,' one girl said as Murakami translated. *Danna-sama* meant master, he said. '"Master" sounds better in English.'

'I am Saki, dear master,' Murakami translated as the girl spoke to me, and he added with a knowing smile, 'Like the writer.'

We were given a menu. I said, 'Coffee for me.'

Murakami also ordered coffee. I did a little maths: the two coffees cost $18. Submissiveness had a price.

'Yes, dear master.'

We hung around a while, talking to the obsequious maids, while jovial men at other tables bossed other maids around. Some were having their pictures taken with the maids, the men like masters of the house among their fawning staff.

'This does nothing for me,' I said.

'It isn't much,' Murakami said. 'But there are darker places like this, with harder customers.'

'Wouldn't you rather have a beer?'

We found a quiet bar, one of those top-of-the-building bars that look out on the twinkling city, and we sat in well-upholstered armchairs and chatted. I asked about Yukio Mishima. He was an unlikely novelist – a bodybuilder and the leader of a militaristic ultranationalist group. One morning, upon completing a novel, Mishima and his men, acting on a prearranged plan, barged into a general's office, tied him to a chair, and from his balcony harangued his assembled troops. Then, in the office, while the general watched in horror, they all committed suicide, Japanese style, some hacking others' heads off, the last alive tearing themselves open with knives, their intestines spilling on to the carpet.

'His lover cut his head off,' Murakami said. 'He was a narcissist, and very small – probably compensating for his size. I don't think much of his work.'

'I like *Confessions of a Mask*.'

'When Truman Capote came here, he had sex with Mishima.'

'That's not in Capote's biography.'

'It's not in any book that I know. But it happened.'

We talked about one-book authors, and running, and road trips, and Italy, and Hawaii, and travel generally.

'You were in Tokyo before?' Murakami said.

'Long ago,' I said. 'I felt lost here, and so homesick. I missed my children so much I went to a toy store in Roppongi – Kiddyland, probably still there? – to buy things for them. I carried these toys all the way back to London on the Trans-Siberian Express.'

Murakami listened patiently. He had no children. I finished my beer, ordered another, and we looked through the large windows at the city lights.

'I called my wife from here,' I said, droning on. 'It was a bad line but I could hear her. She was rather unfriendly. I told her how much I missed her. Still, she didn't have much to say. I realized that she was with another man.' I was sipping the beer, remembering. 'So, after the long overland trip back to London, I was exhausted and half insane. I had a book to write. And this guy was hovering around my marriage. I was so jealous and angry. I somehow couldn't get her attention, you know? I said to my wife, "I'm going to kill you."'

It was a dreadful memory. I was deeply ashamed. But here I was in the top-floor bar of a Tokyo hotel with the sympathetic and attentive Haruki Murakami, who knew a bit about life. How many beers had I drunk? Three or four? I was wondering if the pond in the distance had any ice on it this January night. Then I forgot what I had just said. I glanced at Murakami and saw that he was staring at me anxiously.

'Did you?' He was sitting up straight.

'Did I what?'

'Kill your wife.'

'Oh, no. Just threatened to. I threatened the guy, too. Said I was going to kill him if I saw him.'

But Murakami still looked anxious. He said, 'How did you write your book?'

'That's the thing, see? It was the cure. Writing the book fixed my head.'

Murakami nodded and seemed somewhat reassured. He said, 'Pain is inevitable. Suffering is optional. Someone said that. I agree.'

'But, Haruki, you're a healthy guy. All that running. You're in great shape.'

'I say you need to be healthy to see the unhealthy part of yourself.'

'Maybe I should have a Japanese wife, to worship the ground I walk on.'

'You're about sixty years too late,' Murakami said, sipping his beer. He smiled briefly, then looked sorrowful, his face in shadow. He had just remembered something. 'My wife always reads my books before anyone else. She really criticizes. Sometimes I get mad when she criticizes hard.'

I thought of saying, 'She criticizes because she cares,' but resisted it for being a platitude. Anyway, on this point Murakami seemed inconsolable.

We talked about weekend plans. I said I was taking the train to Sapporo and then to the far north, Wakkanai.

'Wakkanai is really boring.'

'Sounds like my kind of place,' I said. 'What are you doing this weekend?'

'Work on my novel,' Murakami said. 'And then run a marathon in Chiba.'

28. Night Train to Hokkaido
Hayate Super Express

The Bullet Train rushed out of Ueno Station, heading north past fifty miles of small grey bungalows packed tight on the flat featureless land, brown mountains in the distance, the low winter sky weeping softly. A few hours later, at Ninohe, in the north of Honshu, snow flecked the ground. At icy Hachinohe I changed to a smaller train, which left ten minutes later, winding past snowdrifts in the fields: bare trees in rows, tall pines at the margin. Every tree looked deliberately planted in the deep snow.

In the afternoon gloom, the snowstorm at Noheji was lovely, like a profusion of pillow feathers blowing across a great glacier-blue bay. The train slid around this coast of lumpy brown islands by the side of the wintry sea where two large swan-like birds were bobbing. Then the town of Aomori and into a tunnel under the Tsugaru Strait to the island of Hokkaido, the train emerging after forty-five minutes to sharp snow-covered mountains like folded linen napkins, and at last the open and unpopulated countryside I had dreamed of, even better because it was heavy with snow that glowed in the thickening dusk.

Changing trains at Hakodate, the transferring passengers – not many of us – were welcomed with elaborate courtesies by a young woman in a spruce-blue uniform, wearing black tights and high heels and a silk scarf knotted at her throat – the embodiment of one of the fantasies from the fourth floor of Pop Life in Tokyo. Nearly every working woman in the public sector in Japan wears a distinctive uniform, and these were the demure and submissive women that inflamed men's passions, objects of desire, driving men mad as they counted change and issued receipts and punched tickets.

A few more hours in the snowy night and we were in Sapporo. The trip that long ago had taken me a full day and a half, with a long cold ferry ride across the choppy strait, was now a swift ten-hour transition in complete comfort from Tokyo, with a tunnel under the sea from island to island. The snow was still falling when we arrived in Sapporo, and it lay deep in the city, drifted and rutted even on the main streets.

Sapporo now had its own subway line and symphony orchestra, a new railway station inside a mall, and rising above the station several hotels. So I rode the escalator from the platform through the shopping area to the hotel lobby, where I was greeted by the inevitable young woman in a grey well-tailored uniform and white gloves and cloche hat, another low bow, all that willingness and submission.

She was another aspect of Japan's culture of cuteness, like the imagery of teddy bears and pussycats, soft and unthreatening and unsophisticated; like the girl dispensing literature about mobile phones in the mall, dressed like a schoolgirl in a pleated skirt and pigtails. Her counterparts were easy to find in the *manga* comics, especially the ones that narrated school love affairs and, after a few pages, turned into full-page illustrations of big splodgy sex acts. These pixie-faced cartoons obviously reassured Japanese men and made them feel less lonely and eager to find similar pixie-faced sales assistants in human form.

I had seen Japanese comic books on my Railway Bazaar trip and was mildly shocked by them, especially by their images of crepitation and vomiting and preposterous sex acts. The singular depictions of farting and puking set them apart in my reading experience. I was reflecting on this in an Internet café in Sapporo when I saw a man across the aisle wearily turning the pages of a thick magazine that was mainly comics, not one strip but a whole cartoon novel.

These comics were a greater elaboration of Japanese life than I had seen before, not going deeper but sprawling, producing a glut of superficiality. By contrast, the bookshops were not well stocked. *Manga* and the graphic novel seemed to represent a dumb, defiant anti-intellectualism, though there were plenty of people who argued that they were art on a par with *ukiyo-e*. But however well drawn, modern *manga* were banal or silly or sheer fantasy, hasty and crude compared with the work of the great printmakers. I found Hokusai's erotic prints much more powerful, indeed sexier, than these ludicrous comics.

The Internet café was the sort of futuristic pleasure-dome time killer vaguely imagined by Orwell or Huxley. Only a few of us were picking up e-mail. Most of the hundred or so booths and cubicles were like sectioned-off open-plan offices, with high walls that even a tall Japanese could not peer over to see whether the person sitting cross-legged, wearing headphones, was looking at photos, playing games, watching videos or scrolling through porn.

Many cubicles had sofas or easy chairs; the renter might be sleeping, snoring loudly, scarfing noodles, slurping miso soup or sipping tea – most of the food in this Internet café in Sapporo was free. In a society where there was so little privacy, a place like this was essential, and it was possible to spend a whole day there for about $20. Many of the users were merely sitting in a plump cushioned armchair reading one of the fat comic books.

But 'comic books' did not do them justice. They appeared in multi-issue sequences, like the Victorian magazines *Household Words* or *All the Year Round*, which printed *David Copperfield* in instalments over many months. *Nana* was one of these – not the Zola novel but thirty-five issues of a Japanese cartoon character and her picaresque and often sexual adventures. Other narratives concerned tough guys, schoolkids, gang-bangers, mobsters, adventurers, sports, fashion, motor racing and of course hard-core porn – rape, strangulation, abduction. Even with declining sales, from a peak of $5 billion a year, graphic novels in some form are probably the future of popular literature – increasingly they are being downloaded to mobile phones. Purely pictorial pleasure, undemanding, without an idea or a challenge, yet obviously stimulating, a sugar high like junk food, another softener of the brain; they spell the end of the traditional novel, perhaps the end of writing itself.

'What time do you close?' I asked the winsome *manga*-like girl with spiky hair at the cash register.

'Never close. All day, all night.'

The well-lit pleasure parlour, with its comics and its computers, its free soup and noddles, its silences and its privacies, was always available; it was filled with people who never spoke to each other.

All this snow in Sapporo made me want to go skiing. Downhill slopes were fifteen minutes away; cross-country trails were under an hour from town. I long ago gave up the slopes, with their snowboarders and cold lift queues. Cross-country skiing is more work, but there's no waiting and no one gets killed by a hotdogger skiing out of control. I travelled by subway and bus to Takino, in the snowy hills south of Sapporo, where some world cross-country championships were about to begin. The pine boughs sagged with snow; the snow was packed solid on the narrow roads.

I wanted something useful to do, to reacquaint myself with a place I had not seen in thirty-three years. Here in the gently falling snow, in a lovely wooded place that seemed the opposite of anyone's stereotype of Japan, I found solitude, pristine drifts, a timber lodge, pine forests where crows were rasping into the emptiness and shaking loose the dust of snow. I rented skis and boots for $12. Apart from a handful of families skiing on this weekday, the trails were empty.

Through the rooky woods, following my map, panting on the steep-nesses, I breathed the sharp icy air and thought, as I had many times on this trip: in 1973 I would have been prowling the streets, bar-hopping, self-dramatizing my youth and loneliness – and now I was skiing, a fresh-air fiend with an eye to going to bed early.

Warming themselves in a stand of pines on one of the bends of Fox Trail were Miss Ishii and Mr Miyamoto. Miss Ishii was from Nagoya and worked in Toyota City, where she translated technical papers from English to Japanese.

'I can read anything, even Shakespeare, but my spoken English is getting worse,' she said.

Mr Miyamoto was from Sapporo. I told him I had been here long ago.

'I was in elementary school then,' he said. 'Sapporo was a city of about a million. Now we have two million.'

'But it's still a good city,' I said.

He made a face. He struggled a bit to speak, then asked Miss Ishii to translate. 'He says, no, it's worse now by far. We had more trees then, more birds, more space. Now Sapporo is big and busy – and for what? Just more shopping. We've lost a lot.'

'But you have all this snow.'

'No. That's another difference. There's less snow. One third the amount we used to have. It's the weather. Back then, minus fifteen was normal. Now it's always much warmer than that. We get to minus ten maybe three times a month.'

'Global warming,' Miss Ishii said parenthetically. She was still trans-lating.

'Global warming is a real thing in Japan. I've seen it, growing up here. It's easy for us to see it because of the seasons and the snow. Before, the weather was colder in the winter. The snow was deeper.'

I said, 'I remember deep snow, over at the place where they had the winter Olympics.'

'It's like this. We used to have four distinct seasons, but now they're confused. We have warm winters and cold summers. Sometimes just a little snow in the winter and a lot in the spring. It's really strange. You were here in 1973. It was different weather then.'

We skied together for a while as the day grew darker. I was also thinking: Back then I would not have found two friendly Japanese to ski with. Mr Miyamoto had a camera around his neck. He boasted that it was old-fashioned – 'Not digital!' Miss Ishii said that in 1986 she had spent an academic year teaching in Tanzania, at Morogoro. She could still say *jambo* and *habari gani* and *mzuri sana*. She was in her early forties, tall and rather angular, with the long, egg-like face of the elegant women in Utamaro prints.

Back at the ski lodge, I asked them about the Japanese who returned after living for generations in Brazil (São Paulo has the largest Japanese community outside Japan). I once read that they found it hard to fit in. One of the Japanese Brazilians, quoted in a newspaper, said, 'We don't work and we make noise. People here don't like that.'

Miss Ishii said, 'In the nineteenth century we were a poor country. The emperor told people to go and find work elsewhere. They went to Peru, to Brazil, to the United States. And some came back.'

'And what happened?'

'Nothing good.'

My last visit in Sapporo was to a bronze bust on a plinth on the grounds of Hokkaido University. It depicted William S. Clark, an American who had helped found the agricultural college that later became the university. A Japanese student had brought me here long ago to tell me that this American had taught the Japanese modern farming methods – techniques that were successful because Hokkaido and his native Massachusetts had similar climates.

'Look, Mister Crack!' the student had said.

Clark had stayed for less than a year, from July 1876 to April 1877, but he was still remembered, and the rousing speech he delivered to students on his departure was part of the university's mission statement.

'Boys, be ambitious!' he'd said. 'Be ambitious not for money, not for selfish aggrandizement, not for the evanescent thing which men call fame. Be ambitious for the attainment of all that a man ought to be.'

I had mocked that a little, but the man deserved credit. In less than a year he had helped create the first modern academic institution in Japan, and after a number of name changes, from Sapporo Agricultural College through Tohoku Imperial University, it became Hokkaido U. A hundred and twenty years after Clark's arrival, Japanese tourists still posed for pictures in front of his bust. I asked some of them why.

'He was a great man. He helped us.'

Now I looked closer at the bust. It was respectful and dignified, but it did not seem very old. I found a university pamphlet that explained its newness: 'The present statue erected in 1948 was modelled on the original which was melted down during the Second World War.'

So the old bronze bust of the inspirational ('Boys, be ambitious!') American William Clark had been turned by the Japanese into a projectile that had thundered down on US soldiers. I recalled an e. e. cummings war poem, how a man, though he was repeatedly told so, would not believe that war is hell. Then the Japanese bought scrap iron from the New York elevated railway, which they used for bombs, and

> . . . it took
> a nipponized bit of
> the old sixth
>
> avenue
> el; in the top of his head: to tell
>
> him

29. The Limited Express
Sarobetsu to Wakkanai

On little trains, as in the simplest noodle shop, a greeting similar to the most formal one in the culture, called *kangei-kai*, was performed for every traveller, no matter how lowly: a deep bow, multiple thank-yous, the ceremonial welcome of *irassahi mase*. Such pacifying rituals of politeness and gratitude, so profuse an awarding of honorifics, seemed archaic in the overfamiliar and insistently casual world of today. But highly structured manners have held Japan together, allowed the mass of Japanese to live at close quarters; in this culture of anonymity and order, they were an acknowledgement that you existed. Such politeness had helped prevent them from killing each other.

So it was on the Sarobetsu Express, shuttling to the far northern coast on tracks that ran at the frozen edge of the immense Sarobetsu Marsh of Hokkaido. It was like a commuter train, only four carriages, no locomotive, just an upright driver in a uniform and peaked cap, visible at the front in his glass booth; and the conductor, the guard and the ticket punchers all troubled themselves to utter the formulas of welcome and to make low bows to the passengers.

Honjitsu wa gojosha itadaki arigatou gozaimasu. 'Thank you for boarding the train today,' Murakami had translated for me.

Wakkanai was boring, Murakami had said, and even the guidebook warned that there was nothing to see there. I imagined a windswept little port town on a snowy coast. It was that, and more, the landscape of my dreams, the true hinterland of Japan. And the trip through the snowstorm in this modest train was one of the most pleasant I'd ever taken. Halfway to Wakkanai the train was almost empty – only four of us in this first carriage. And we few continued into the great snow-covered emptiness of northern Hokkaido, following the course of a dark narrow river for most of the way.

We went by small snowbound stations, like Takikawa, where village streets were filled with packed-down snow, forests and farmland blurred with snowdrifts, icicles hung from house eaves. Some bungalows were up to their roofs in snow.

People lived better here, it seemed. They had more space, with gardens and yards, even in the small city of Asahikawa, which was about a third of the way to Wakkanai. The train wound slowly through the forest, where snowy pine boughs drooped, and at the village of Shibetsu there were farmhouses and barns and silos. What roads I could see were narrow and looked unploughed, no cars on them. On this windless winter day the falling snow built up and bandaged the trees, the pine forests and the birch groves. When the clouds parted and the storm briefly abated, the drifted snow went pink as the sun caught the clouds and slipped into the river valley.

In the miniature towns and villages of rural Hokkaido the people lived in dolls' houses, as in Otoineppu, where the late-afternoon gloom seemed to bring the snowstorm back. And Teshio-Nakagama, about an hour south of Wakkanai, was the snowiest place I'd seen in the whole of Japan, the dolls' houses buried amid rounded drifts, the streets like culverts of snow and some of them snowy tunnels of the sort you'd see in a dumped-on village in northern Maine.

It all seemed blissful until I struck up a conversation with the man sitting a few seats in front of me in the almost empty carriage. His name was Ohashi. He was born near here. He said that this part of Hokkaido was losing population, going grey – ageing faster than the rest of Japan – and that there was no industry any more and even the farms were failing.

'My family has sixty cows. That's not enough,' he explained. 'We had too bad competition from the big dairies.'

Ohashi had found a personal solution. He had faced the fact that he was nearer Russia than Tokyo. He had decided to go to Sakhalin, a short ferry ride from Wakkanai, to learn Russian, and later he studied economics at a college in Kamchatka. The remotest parts of Russia – the farthest from Moscow – were easily accessible from Japan.

'I wanted to leave my family's farm,' he said, 'to live on my own. After my studies, I saw there was no work in Hokkaido for me.'

He got a job in Tokyo with a Russo-Japanese company. Half the workers were Russian, but from the far eastern part of Russia, those same places, Sakhalin and Kamchatka.

'I'm going home for a few days to visit my family,' he said. 'Then back to Tokyo.'

So once again I was reduced to being a romantic voyeur. Where I saw pines and snowdrifts and ski trails and dolls' houses, Ohashi saw only failure, a declining rural economy and old people.

Across the high Hokkaido moorland, the sun disengaged from a puffy storm cloud and suddenly brightened, changed colour, going hotter, the dazzling orange of hot lava, then became a low yellow dome near the frosty hills on the horizon. I watched the diminishing dome: it slid finally into the snow, leaving a glow in the storm cloud, a pinkness, a blush above the ridge of the hills, until it became just a smear of pink, going grey.

After that, the bare black trees were like exposed nerves in the ashy whiteness of the bleak landscape of snowfields at dusk. In this rounded, softened and heavily upholstered world of deep snow, the pine tops changed from ragged lace to bottle brushes to saw blades as the train turned on the meandering river and the angle of the light altered.

Five and a half hours after leaving Sapporo, the train drew into the tiny station of the topmost town in Japan.

It seemed a magical arrival – the little station, the snowy streets, the deep drifts sparkling in the lamplight, frost crystals in the air and a strong odour of the sea. After the passengers vanished I saw no other people. Most of the shops were shuttered, though a few bars were open, and down some alleys I saw winking signs: HAPPY ROOM and FUN PARLOUR and a blue neon sign above a door on a second-floor balcony, LOVE DOLL.

I walked down the snowy street to my hotel and was welcomed with another bow. Over the next few days, headed out to look around, or find a drink, I usually ended up in the neighbourhood of winking signs, and the one that always caught my eye was LOVE DOLL. The words seemed to promise everything: innocence, sweetness, simplicity, comfort, pleasure, warmth. You couldn't find a better pair of words for passive sexual reassurance, and they tugged at my heart as I stood in the snow, looking up at the balcony and the door. I never saw anyone go in or out of Love Doll. That was another enticement. But I kept walking.

Wakkanai was a seaport, after all. Its fishermen sailed their trawlers into the Sea of Japan, and Russians went back and forth to Sakhalin, which was visible on a clear day across the Soya Strait. Russians shopped here. Many of the supermarkets and little stores displayed signs in Russian, carefully lettered Cyrillic. It seemed that I was the only *gaijin* in Wakkanai – I did not see another – but it was obvious that Russians came here for clothes or hardware or fishing gear or sex. One or two casinos with bright lights stood on the main road. But they were empty. Probably it was the weather – snow and strong winds. No boats left Wakkanai harbour while I was there.

Even the bars were empty. The cosiest ones, with oak tables and the owner grilling fish on a *hibachi*, lined the snowy side streets. I never saw more than a few men in each of them, usually old-timers getting drunk on sake and eating sushi.

Hospitality in Wakkanai was almost a burden. In the early evening, sitting in the warmth of a bar, aiming to write up the day's notes, I was always welcomed, offered a drink – at one bar a man presented me with a freshly grilled sardine – and for the next hour or so we'd have the sort of hopeless conversation that a Japanese stranger would have on a winter night in a bar in Eastport, Maine – which Wakkanai much resembled. Alcohol doesn't overcome the language barrier, but it makes it bearable.

'You America!'

'Me America.'

'America very nice!'

We toasted, we drank, we ate sushi; against my better judgement I got drunk and did no writing; and we were soon good friends. This happened in three little snowed-in bars. At the end of the railway line, Wakkanai was a town without an Internet café or a cinema. I didn't mind. The weather was dramatic, the people were friendly, and Wakkanai had its own hot springs.

When the wind dropped and the sun came out, walking in icy Wakkanai, in the crusty snow and across the ploughed-aside heaps that lay like white piping, was like traipsing up and down a wedding cake.

Japan's chewed-looking coastline and angular islands give it a look like no other country on earth, and its lizardy and nibbled shape, more like a set of carvings than a pattern of islands, suggests its cultural complexity. It seems in places as imperial as its past pretensions, a castle set in the sea, an oceanic fortress. Its boast was that it had never been invaded – it was saved from the Mongols by the Divine Wind (*Kamikaze*) that repelled advancing ships in the thirteenth century. That was another reason the American bombing in the Second World War had been so traumatic, moving the otherwise imperturbable Haruki Murakami to tremulous indignation at its violation.

A monument to volcanism, Japan sits on a seam of molten lava and superheated water. It is an archipelago of volcanic cones, and its national symbol, Fujiyama, perhaps the most recognizable volcano on earth, is still regarded as a sacred mountain. Because of these cracks and cones, there is hardly a place in Japan that does not froth with hot springs.

A geothermal shaft of such heat ran under Wakkanai that one re-creation in the frozen town was the community *onsen*, or hot spring. The water was not just scalding hot but laden with beneficial salts and minerals.

For the experience, and because I ached from all the travel, I caught a bus and took the fifteen-minute ride to the spa at the Onsen Dome, on the snowy shore just west of town. It was a Sunday. I discovered that poaching in the *onsen* was the main weekend activity in winter Wakkanai. And like so much in Japan – mealtime, playtime, hospitality, gift giving – it was formalized in a sequence of rituals: the changing room, the shower, the bathhouse, the spa, the hot springs – the progression from pool to pool – and at last the unwinding in lounge chairs afterwards. For some, this post-hot-spring activity involved drinking beer and smoking.

I rented a towel. I was handed slippers and a robe. I bought a ticket. All this was $5 or so. I went to the men's wing of the *onsen*. The main attraction was the large thermal room, with four very hot pools, some of them reddish with minerals, one steaming in the open air on a snowy balcony.

Naked Japanese men – young, old, middle-aged, with smooth and somewhat crêpe-like skin; hairless, bent over, muscular, quite fat, very skinny, all sorts. In some ways it was like the popular impression of a Roman bath, not just a healthy activity but a social one, like a club that was also a big stew, the men walking around and chatting, companionably talking as they sat up to their necks in hot water, a damp towel neatly arranged on their head. The large windows on one side faced the snowy shore and the sea, on the other side the icy Wakkanai hills.

A naked man in a whirling bath smiled at me and said, '*Horosho?*' taking me for a Russian.

Outside on the balcony the steaming pool of hot water was bubbling and throwing up such a volume of mineral salts that they accumulated in a cakey thickness at the rim – this big tureen set in the snow. The air temperature was well below zero, but the water was so hot it didn't matter.

I was sitting in the outdoor pool when the door flew open and two children, a girl and a boy, ran through the snow at the edge and leaped in, laughing and splashing. A young man, who had to be their father, followed them. This was interesting. Though the sections of the spa were divided – men on one side, women on the other – children were welcome on both sides. And the small girl, a water baby of perhaps eight or nine, was absolutely unashamed, playing with her little brother, in and out of the pool, while the father called out and encouraged them.

She was approaching the age, and certainly had the look, of the object of desire in *manga* comics – a big-eyed sprite in pigtails. But no one – the pool held about eight men – seemed to take much notice of her: her beauty, the way she skipped through the snow and jumped into the bubbling pool; her agility in climbing out streaming with water, vapour rising from her cherubic body, her chafed and reddened buttocks, her face framed by damp ringlets, her hooting laughter.

I thought: This is the Japanese at their best – a sunny winter Sunday, their day off, and they choose to spend it at the $5 spa having long soaks, growing red-faced, scrubbing themselves, stewing and all the while talking without urgency. It was like the religious ritual Philip Larkin describes in 'Water':

> If I were called in
> To construct a religion
> I should make use of water.
>
> Going to church
> Would entail a fording
> To dry, different clothes;
>
> My liturgy would employ
> Images of sousing,
> A furious devout drench . . .

And chasing around (Larkin would have approved), the happiest and most human aspect of it, the little girl – naked, pinkish – in and out of the pool, playing tag with her brother in the sunshine and snow and steam among the older men.

Half a day there, scalded by water, penetrated by minerals, exhausted me. I stretched out in the lounge area and rested and drank water, then went back to Wakkanai and the snow, passed Love Doll, and kept going. With a powerful feeling of drowsiness and ease, I slept soundly, buffeted by dreams of crawling through a Japanese obstacle course of tunnels and ladders. Even as I was suffering this ordeal, the words 'This is a dream' were in my head.

In the morning, with my strength back, I wanted to try the hot-spring experience again. Most of all I wanted to recapture the physical and mental bliss I had felt the day before. I made a few inquiries, tramping around Wakkanai in a light snowstorm.

Two people said, 'Go to Toyotomi.'

Toyotomi was about forty-five minutes down the railway line, and the mineral hot springs at its community *onsen*, as well as being relaxing, were said to be beneficial to the skin. I took my bag in case Toyotomi proved to be a good place to stay overnight.

I had seen Toyotomi from the train, snowy streets in lamplight, clusters of houses, a station platform. Snow glow and lamplight gave it a certain grandeur in the night. In daylight it seemed tiny, the houses buried, no cars on the streets, just a village of smoking chimneys.

Only I had got off the train. I stood outside the station wondering where the hot springs might be. A woman sweeping snow nodded at me. I said, '*Onsen*? Taxi?'

'Go there,' she said in Japanese, pointing through the falling snow to an open garage door.

By now, my not speaking the language was no barrier to communication. People spoke to me in Japanese, making helpful gestures, and I instantly understood. The Japanese language was so full of cognates that it sometimes seemed like a version of English, and when someone said *puratto-homu*, I knew they were saying 'platform', just as *byuffe* could not be anything but 'buffet car'.

'*Onsen*,' I said to a man in the garage. He wore a tweed suit and knitted tie and white gloves – the uniform of a rural taxi driver. He spoke rapidly in Japanese.

Somehow I knew from pulses in the air that he had said, 'I can take you there in my taxi for two thousand yen. Another two thousand to come back. The *onsen* itself will cost you about five hundred yen.'

He took my bag and put it on a high shelf.

'Shall we go?' he said.

I realized that I had forgotten to change money in Wakkanai. I had a few thousand yen and the rest in dollars. I showed him my dollars.

'What's the exchange rate today?' he asked.

He made a few phone calls, but no one knew exactly how many yen to the dollar, just the general rate of about 110.

'Where's the bank?'

'We don't have a bank in Toyotomi. It's a small place!'

He stared out of the garage at the falling snow.

'Ah, I know,' he said, still in Japanese, which I seemed to understand. 'There's an American here in Toyotomi. We'll go find the American. The American will help.'

'The American?'

'At the school,' he said. 'Get into my taxi. I won't turn on the meter. Let's find the American.'

In the snowstorm, rolling slowly through the white-packed streets of Toyotomi, he told me his name was Miyagi, that he had been born here, and that summer was a better time to visit, not now in the cold and the snow.

'But the *onsen*,' I said.

'Yes, the *onsen*. Very healthy.'

He drove through the gate of what looked like a municipal building, brick and rather forbidding. It was Toyotomi High School, snow piled to its windowsills. Like every other Japanese building I'd been in, it was very tidy, clean and somewhat spartan.

In a glass enclosure, behind a counter, I saw a Western-looking woman in a black dress. She was the first *gaijin* I had seen in four days in this region. She greeted Mr Miyagi in Japanese. I saw from her nametag that she was Roz Leaver. She was the American. She had a responsive manner, an attractive laugh and a directness that was unusual in Japan. She stood out less for being a Westerner than for being so much heavier than almost any Japanese I'd seen.

'What's the problem?'

I explained that I needed to change some money.

'Right. There's no bank here,' she said. 'I don't carry a lot of money.' She slapped at the pockets of her loose dress. 'I've got about thirty dollars in yen on me.'

She was friendly, said she was glad to help, and she looked imperturbable – apparently unfazed by the snowstorm, by the remoteness of the village or by the Japanese language, which she spoke with convincing ease. She was, she said, from Billings, Montana.

'These guys said to me this morning, "It's cold," and I said, "This is not cold. I can tell you what cold is." '

She had been sent as part of a programme that sponsored teachers to work in different countries – she'd taught in many others.

'I love these students here in Toyotomi,' Roz said. 'They work. They study. No excuses. They're great in the community. And they want to get out of town. Like every kid in small towns all over the world. Hey, like me!'

'Seems a nice place.'

Roz laughed. She had a full-throated laugh that rang in the severe-looking school office. 'This is just a wide spot in the road. What are you doing here?'

'I'm going to the *onsen*. The famous hot springs here.'

She shrugged and blew out her cheeks, so as to seem unimpressed, all the while counting hundred-yen notes on to the desk.

'You must go there a lot,' I said.

Without looking up she said, 'No, I do not go to the *onsen*.'

'It's supposed to be healthy.'

'Look at me,' she said, raising her head and smiling grimly. She jogged her heavy arms and smacked her belly through her dress. 'Do I look like I'm interested in "healthy"?'

She spoke the despised word with a grunt of gusto, while I equivo-cated. One of her co-workers said something in Japanese.

'Don't listen to him,' she said. 'All he does is play *pachinko* and try to hit the jackpot.'

'The water in the hot springs here is said to be good for your skin.'

'I've been in Toyotomi a year and a half and I haven't been near the place. I'm not interested.'

I'd been in Toyotomi less than an hour and it was all I was planning to do. I mentioned this.

'Thing is,' she said, 'I don't take my clothes off for anyone.'

'Right.'

'Unless they're going home with me.' And she peered knowingly at me and seemed to wink.

'That's a good rule,' I said.

'Oh, yeah.' Roz laughed again, her big body shaking, as her colleagues

– four of them, very small and attentive – stood with their hands clasped. From this brief encounter I could tell that her behaviour astonished but also pleased them, since it confirmed their stereotype of a Western woman: the huge appetite, the frankness, the loud voice, the casual posture, but also her strength and her humour. I had only just met her and she was looking me in the eye and joshing me in a way that was unheard-of in Japan.

She pushed the Japanese money over and I gave her the dollars.

'I guess this is enough to get naked with,' I said.

'Good luck,' she said and sized me up.

'How long are you going to be here?'

She brightened again and peered at me and looked hopeful. 'You want to meet later – get some beers?'

'No, um, how long are you going to be in Toyotomi?'

'Oh,' she said, losing her enthusiasm. She gestured with her hand. 'Out of here in July.'

Mr Miyagi the driver said, 'You have money. We go.'

He drove me through the snowstorm and dropped me at the entrance of a group of stucco buildings at the edge of town, the Toyotomi Onsen Spa. It was not a luxury spa or a hotel complex but a community centre at the base of some hills. The buildings were set against the steep sides, some of the picture windows facing slopes where people were skiing, the other windows facing a forested and snowy plain. Many of the windows were opaque with steam.

By now I knew the routine: leave shoes in the lobby, find slippers, buy a 500-yen ticket, rent a towel and look for a locker in the men's section. After that, get naked, take a shower and slip into a steaming pool.

On this weekday morning only one other man was at the spa, sitting up to his neck in the hot water. His face was pink, a damp towel folded on top of his head. He sat in the swirling water at the far end.

The proof that mineral salts were circulating in the pool was the crusted rim, where the salts had collected and solidified in a lumpy mass like a piled-up lava flow.

Scalding water – darker, frothier than at Wakkanai – from Toyotomi's underground spring gushed into the pool from a pipe, and outside, large cottony snowflakes gently fell past the window.

Just the two of us, the old man and me, stewing, sousing, furious devout drenches, then rest intervals to cool off. I felt blissful and sleepy and partly poached. I loved sitting there in the heat, watching the snow twisting down. The old man looked up from the far end of the thirty-foot pool.

'You like?'

'Yes, I like.'

'What your country?'

'United States. Hawaii. Have you been to Hawaii?'

'No. But Saipan. I went there. Very nice. You have *onsen* in Hawaii?'

'No.'

'But you have volcanoes. So you could have *onsen*, hot water from the volcano rock.'

'Good point.'

'Toyotomi is famous for milk and dairy products,' he said, though I hadn't asked. 'Special milk.'

I got out and cooled off; I drank water; I stewed and soused again. After an hour or more, feeling benumbed, I put on my clothes and found a tatami where I lay like a corpse, my muscles glowing, and fell asleep.

Around the middle of the afternoon, Mr Miyagi appeared – suit, tie, white gloves – to pick me up. He drove me to the station, and there I sat drinking hot cocoa from a machine until I boarded the train for the return trip through the pine forests and the villages.

I used to look at woodblock prints of snow scenes in Japan – the Hiroshige images of small, snow-swept, bundled-up peasants carrying parasols in rural villages – and I'd think how improbable the snow seemed, so deep, so thick, like whipped cream, like cake icing, the sugar-coated trees and half-buried huts. But the snow of Japan is remarkable in its abundance, the result of the westerly Siberian airflow picking up moisture from the Sea of Japan, crystallizing it and dropping it in blizzards on the north. Even in their seeming extravagance, almost cartoonish, the Hiroshige prints accurately represent the snow of Hokkaido. As I travelled through the snowstorm on the southbound Sarobetsu back to Sapporo, every hill and village looked sugar-coated.

30. Night Train to Kyoto
The Twilight Express

From the driving snow of wintry Sapporo I travelled into buds and blossoms of springtime Kyoto without leaving the train, rolling into the south of Hokkaido, and through the Tsugaru Tunnel, and along the coast of Honshu to the imperial city of bamboo gardens and wooden temples – a city that, because of its beauty, had not been bombed in the war. It was a twenty-two-hour trip on a brand-new train, about a $100 surcharge for a private berth, but a simple boarding process: show up, get on, no security check, no police, no bag inspector, no warnings, no questions, no metal detectors, no delays. I got to the station ten minutes before the train left, hopped aboard and was formally thanked. Pretty soon we were on the bleak coast of black sand beaches, passing ugly buildings standing in sooty snow-slush.

This was the Twilight Express, with its Pleiades restaurant and Salon du Nord. However xenophobic the Japanese might seem, haughty with ancient pieties in the face of big hairy foreigners, they readily adopted foreign words: Hotel Clubby and Hearty Land and Funny Place were businesses in Sapporo; the Green Coach, or Green-Sha, was the usual description of the first-class car on a train.

Japanese popular culture was penetrated by foreignness. knowing I was about to board the Twilight, I made a list of Japanese magazine titles at a Sapporo Station bookstall. The list included *Honey, Popteen, With, Pinky, More, Spring, Vivi, Tiara Girl, Lee, Orange Pages, Seventeen, Cancan, Lightning, Get On, Mono* and *Trendy*. Though the names were English, the magazines' content was in Japanese. One, named *Men's Knuckle*, advertised 'New Outlaw Fashion', but that was in Japanese, and so was the article 'How to Sex'. This was one of the confusions of the culture. The greatest mistake a visitor could make in Japan was to conclude that the extensive use of these mostly cute English words – Hello Kitty was another well-known brand – indicated that the Japanese were Westernized. This is a bit like concluding that because a Quechua woman in the Andes is wearing a bowler hat, she's an Anglophile.

I was sitting in my compartment, looking through the window at the big breakers curling towards the snowy shore at Tomakomai, the froth hitting the slush and spreading to the tidemark. The sea was grim under a low grey sky as we headed for the long undersea tunnel; fishing boats bobbed at their moorings in all the harbours I saw.

Then the plunge into the tunnel on this day of cold light and clammy air. In 1973, at this point in my trip, I was miserable; I felt I was in the grip of an ordeal. I had almost no money left. I was homesick, and I knew that my wife was angry, our marriage in jeopardy. I felt alienated in Japan, very lonely, travel-weary and fearful. I had the Trans-Siberian ahead of me, and the long slog home, where I suspected I wasn't welcome.

I imagined someone asking, What's the big difference between then and now? I knew that it wasn't all the changes, big and small, in Turkey or India or Singapore or Vietnam. It wasn't computers or the Internet or high-speed trains, not fast food or cheap wristwatches or everyone wearing blue jeans. The greatest difference was in me. I had survived the long road that led to the present. I felt lucky, I felt grateful. I didn't want any more than this in travel, clattering through the tunnel; I didn't want another life. I had a book to read, a book to write, and enough solitude. Most of all, someone missed me and was waiting for me, someone I loved. As Murakami had said of his own love affair with Yoko, that was everything.

I scribbled something about that, and then the train exploded out of the tunnel.

The speed of the train, the shriek of the wheels on the rails, its buffeting on bends, gave me nightmares after that, then interrupted them, and stifled me with dreams of persecution. I dream more when I travel; I dream most in strange beds. After ten hours in my berth on the Twilight Express, I woke up exhausted.

We were approaching the town of Uozu, under black mountains flecked with purplish snow, the Sea of Japan visible on the other side of the line, everything stark and melancholic. The irregularity of Japanese geography – a country shaped like a dissected gecko – and the solemn geometry of its buildings must have a profound influence on the national character and the way the Japanese view the world, thinking (as I suspect): There is no one on earth like us.

The houses were packed together — no room for trees. The villages looked oppressive in their monotony, but this was the practicality of Japan, which was also its severity. A visitor can't be indifferent to any of this; always he has to choose to be an alien or else to go native, making a study of living here, like Lafcadio Hearn, or in our time the scholar Donald Richie. My friend Pico Iyer, traveller and writer, had lived in Nara, near Kyoto, for many years. I wondered how he managed.

Over a breakfast of sashimi, a coddled egg and pink vegetables in Diner Pleiades — huh? — I was thinking how this part of the coast was like a visual echo of Holland. The low-lying land with embankments seemed too flat to be like anything but land reclaimed from the sea.

The flatness of this boggy-looking land was the reason the city of Wajima, about forty miles up the coast, and many small settlements were wrecked by an earthquake (6.9 on the Richter scale) and a flood a few months after I passed through. The earth shook, and the sea rose ('a small tsunami') and sank some of these towns, knocked over buildings, caused landslides and injured many people. I was reminded again that Japan straddled one of the most volatile earthquake zones in the world. Evident here, as the Twilight Express cut inland to Japan's spine, passing under the craggy mountains that were all volcanoes, some cold, some hot.

I had felt disoriented and fearful on my first visit to Kyoto and Osaka, and I had described this confusion in *The Great Railway Bazaar*. I was disoriented on this second visit too, and uncomprehending, but I was calm. Now I regarded my bewilderment as the price of being here. It wasn't possible for a foreigner in Japan to feel like anything but an alien species, not just different but backward, a clumsy yokel from the colour- ful but decrepit past.

After I found my hotel (cheap, near Kyoto Station), I took a train to the district of antique shops, just to look, because I had not found any antiques in Hokkaido, Japanese antique dealers have a reputation for scrupulousness and honesty, which was the main reason I sought them out, to look at authentic pieces — old Buddhas, lacquerware, porcelain, temple carvings. I looked, night fell, I got lost, and I felt a kind of thrill, as though I were descending into the inner darkness of the city.

Recognizing that I had returned to a crossroads near Sanjo Station, I asked two schoolgirls how I could get to the station I'd set off from, Tofukuji.

Using her instant-translation computer, like that of the monk Tapa Snim, one of them, Kiko, said, 'We are going in Tofukuji Station direction. Come with us, please.'

In blue blazers, white blouses unbuttoned at the collar, neckties yanked down, in short pleated skirts and knee socks, they were the objects of desire of many Japanese men, if the pictures at Pop Life were anything to go by. 'Teacher's pet' was a recurring role in Japanese sexual imagery.

As they ascended the escalator, Kiko and her friend, Mitsuko, reached behind them and with the back of their hands discreetly pressed their short skirts against their buttocks. This was to discourage voyeurs riding below them on the moving stairs – the escalators were steep, the skirts tiny, the angle acute. What tragedies and embarrassments lay behind this deflecting gesture? Murakami's women interviewees in *Underground* often mentioned being touched and groped and peered at by men in subways.

Mitsuko, who spoke some English, said, 'I've never been to Hokkaido. I don't have the money. I would like to go to the *onsen* there.'

'So you haven't travelled outside Japan?' I asked.

'I was in Ohio once.'

'Ohio in the United States?'

'Yes. Akron. It was two years ago, for one month. It was foreign exchange. Home stay.'

'Did you like the family?'

'Very nice family. Four children,' and she gave me everyone's name and age.

'What did you like about America?'

'I liked the nature. The trees and birds. Also very big cornfields.'

'And the food?'

'The food,' Mitsuko said and smiled uneasily. 'No rice. But before I went, my family sent a bag of rice for the month. I made rice for myself and the family. They liked it, I think.'

Although the two schoolgirls said they were going to Osaka, they got off the train at Tofukuji Station with me. I asked them why. Mitsuko tried to explain, got flustered, then took out her little computer and tapped the keys. She showed me the window.

I am sending a parcel to Osaka, it said. I read it aloud.

'No, this one.' Mitsuko tapped again and scrolled down.

To bid you farewell, it said.

It was another lesson in Japanese manners. Saying goodbye on a moving train was rude for being overcasual. Bidding farewell properly had to be done on the platform, with salutations and honorifics and mutual bows.

I found my way back to Kyoto Station and my hotel, and walked a bit. I missed the snow of Hokkaido, the dramatic weather – the snowstorms, the large wet snowflakes, the snowy streets. Bad weather seemed to give a point and a meaning to travel, gave a place a backdrop and made it memorable. Kyoto was placid, with mild spring weather.

I looked for an Internet café, to reassure my Penelope back home, knitting her heart out. I hadn't been in touch for quite a while; my BlackBerry did not work in Japan. And I had trouble finding a computer: my hotel didn't have one for guests' use. One of the paradoxes of Japan is that it is so well wired – everyone text-messaging, sending haiku-like exchanges on phones, everyone connected with some sort of computer – Internet cafés were rare. I'd found only one in Sapporo, and there were none in Wakkanai and Toyotomi.

But after a long walk, asking directions, I found a computer, in a cubicle at Top Café. An urgent message awaited me. An editor at a magazine in New York wondered whether I could supply 2,000 words on the subject 'Violence in Africa' for a special issue devoted to that continent.

My Tao of Travel stipulates that such requests should be refused. Concentrate on where you are; do no back-home business; take no assignments; remain incommunicado; be scarce. In travel, disconnection is a necessity. It is a good thing that people don't know where you are or how to find you. Keep your mind in the country you're in. That's the theory.

But I was idle, and the subject challenged me, because even in peaceful Kyoto I didn't think Africa was inherently more violent than anywhere else. So I said yes, and the experience was a disaster. But like most disasters, it contained a lesson.

With free time in Kyoto, I went back to Top Café and paid for a cubicle. The young man to my left was leafing through a *manga* porn comic, the woman on my right slurping instant noodles out of a cup. I began to reflect on violence in Africa. I wrote:

One of the rules of the road in Africa – unwritten but immutable – is that if you happen to bump someone off their bike, or knock them over or flatten their goat, you are to proceed to the nearest police station for safety's sake. Otherwise the crowd that will inevitably gather around the accident will hold you captive, intimidate you and demand all your money. If the worst happens and you kill a pedestrian you must leave the scene swiftly; linger and you will be killed by the crowd, who will then take all your belongings, and your car. I first heard this in 1964 in Nyasaland, and as recently as a few years ago in East Africa.

I stopped typing and thought: Bad government in Africa, beginning with colonial rule, has cheated the people and created a crack that has become a yawning gap. Stepping into that gap are gang-bangers, thieves and meddlers from outside – mythomaniacs, rock stars, celebrities, ex-presidents, politicians, tycoons, people atoning for some personal weakness or debauchery, for their trivial lives or their pop songs. Of course Africa was violent, because it had been destabilized by opportunists of every sort, especially the rock star and the atoning billionaire buddying up to the dictator.

I wrote, giving voice to these thoughts off and on – I took noodle breaks – until the middle of the afternoon. I was so absorbed that I forgot I was in Japan, and was surprised to see a wall of *manga* comics and, up front, the female clerks at the cash register tossing their long hair. I was disoriented by having written so intensely about Africa, but when I scrolled through the piece I could see that it was subtle, felicitous and, best of all, finished. I stood up and, feeling the euphoria bordering on rapture that comes with having completed an assignment, I signalled to an assistant.

'Can you print this for me, please?'

The clerk, a pretty girl, nodded yes. I stepped aside and she slipped past me into my cubicle. Instead of sitting in the chair, she bent over, glanced at the screen, and confidently tapped a few keys.

The screen went dark.

'What happened?' I asked.

Fear took hold of her and rendered her speechless. She tapped some more, and she stared. The screen stared blankly back at her.

Everyone who owns a computer has had this dismaying experience of accidental deletion. It is pointless for me to describe my sense of having been punched in the stomach, while blood drained from my face, anger and grief making me irrational. I felt physically ill.

My look of desolated lunacy alarmed the girl who lost her beauty and became wraith-like in panic.

'You deleted it!'

She could not say sorry. 'Sorry' was what the Japanese said when they brushed against your sleeve in a lift. She was smiling in fear. Blood had drained from her face too.

I struggled with my coat. Fury made me clumsy. I went to the cash register. She rang up zero. She handed me a receipt.

'No charge,' she whispered.

I wanted to cry. I also wanted to drop-kick the computer into Shiokoji Street. Instead, I walked, my throat aching, my eyes burning. I went to my hotel room and, in great pain, working slowly in longhand, began to write a version of my vanished piece.

So that I could vent my frustration, I called Pico Iyer, who lived not far away in the ancient Japanese city of Nara. We met and I raged for an hour or more. He was the perfect listener – sympathetic, serene, uncritical, attentive, computer-hating. When I was finished, he said, 'You don't travel with a computer? Neither do I.'

He used a small notebook and, like me, a preferred brand of ballpoint pen. He had lived in Japan for nine years, though he claimed not to know much about the country and didn't speak Japanese. To me he was the complete traveller – highly educated, humorous, detached, portable, positive, alert, subtle, a great noticer and listener, calm, humane and fluent in his prose. And he had been everywhere. He is best known for his book *Video Night in Kathmandu*, but he had also written a highly regarded book about Cuba. Though he is reserved, his book *The Global Soul* is his most revealing. It is an examination of homelessness, in the sense of being without a country, the condition of living with sentiments of residence but without roots, the state of being 'a permanent alien'. It was an entirely new definition – not an exile or a nomad or an expatriate, but a global soul.

Being slightly built, taking up so little space, Pico was almost invisible – a great quality for a traveller. He was born in India and brought as a child to England, where his father taught at Oxford; he was educated at Eton and Oxford, and afterwards Harvard. Meanwhile his parents had emigrated to California, where his father had taught for a while and then (so I'd heard) become a guru in Santa Barbara.

When we met in Kyoto I said I had to unburden myself. I was nearly always happier travelling alone, but it was a great help to me that at a crucial stage of my solitary trip I had Pico to listen to me howl on the subject of a deleted computer file.

'It's happened to me,' he said. 'I know how you feel.'

I unburdened myself, raging, as we strolled past the temples, gardens, and teahouses of ancient Maruyama Park, for which Kyoto is justifiably famous. I was calmed by Pico's sympathy and by the orderly gardens of Shoren-in Temple, the odour of sanctity in the sacred groves.

Although we spent the entire day and most of the evening walking in this historic district, a parallel narrative was unrolling. We talked about the temples, the shrines, the squat wooden teahouses, the narrow lanes, the Buddha statues and bodhisattvas, the hillsides of spiky pines and fat culms of running bamboo. But we also talked about our common interests: travel, England, marriage, Hawaii and the Pacific, publishers, magazine assignments, book tours, what we were writing now, and, as writers always do when together, of money and other writers.

Walking in our stockinged feet through the Shoren-in Temple, passing from room to room, the successive rooms giving on to beautifully proportioned monks' cells with pictorial screens and views of dwarf pines and stone lanterns, Pico was saying, 'Which of his books do you think are his best?'

'*Biswas*, hands down, and *Mr Stone*, and the essays and journalism of the 1970s. But he's –'

'For me, *The Enigma of Arrival* – look how these *shoji* doors are infinitely expandable. It was how I felt. I understood his sense of loss, and the childhood, the school days. He's alienated.'

'I was going to say he's a horse's arse. He's so cruel to people, so unappreciative. He was awful to his wife. He has no sympathy. I know that sounds superficial. What I mean is, he's a very fearful man.'

'He was kind to me,' Pico said.

I didn't say so, but I could see his affinity with Naipaul, who had once confided to me the misery of being a slightly built Indian among big English louts – how he'd been heckled and abused. As soon as he could afford it, Naipaul had stopped taking underground trains in London, sticking to the isolation and safety of taxis. And Naipaul would have related to Pico's writing, in *The Global Soul:* 'Having grown up simultaneously in three cultures, none of them fully my own, I acquired very early the sense of being loosed from time as much as from space – I had no history, I could feel, and lived under the burden of no home.'

He said, 'Shall we go outside? The garden's really lovely.'

I looked through the low doorway to the gravel path and the Zen arrangement of raked gravel and miniature bushes.

'Sculpted and controlled,' I said.

'That's the whole of Japanese culture. Sculpted and controlled. Look at this sign.' It was in English, and he read it slowly: ' "When you walk a garden there is a case you have to return." '

'Meaning?'

'It would take Borges to make sense of these ambiguities. You met him, didn't you?'

'In Buenos Aires, yes. And that's another thing. Naipaul called him a charlatan. What crap! Borges was twice the writer he is. How was he kind to you?'

'Naipaul had been at Oxford with my father. When I met him, I told him that – oh, I think we go around this upward path.'

'Look at that bamboo on the hillside,' I said. 'It's the running, not the clumping, kind. Bluey green. I wonder what –?'

'I like that, "bluey green". This is a classic garden. I suppose monks lived in this villa. Oh, Naipaul remembered going for walks with my father. He was very touched. He remembered little details.'

'Two lonely Indians in Oxford. Naipaul was depressive then. He constantly mentions that he was going to kill himself at Oxford. I see that as a kind of boasting.'

'Anyway, my father and he hit it off, and – I guess this is the end of the path. Chatwin was a boaster. He was a few years ahead of me at the Dragon School in Oxford. Let's go back to the main road.'

We found a path to another temple, no one around, just a great wooden structure with upright stones inscribed with lines from the sutras.

'I can't take Chatwin's books,' Pico said. 'They don't seem real to me.'

'He tried to make his evasions a virtue, fictionalizing his travels,' I said. 'He laughed and invented places. He invented etymologies. He said the word "Arab" meant "dweller in tents". But it doesn't. Look in an Arabic dictionary. The word means "people who express themselves" – clear speakers. He also said that Robert Louis Stevenson was second rate. Ha!'

We walked further into a park, to Chion-in Temple, Pico said. On the weathered porch, looking down on the city, he said, 'I've spent the whole morning writing about how Kyoto lasted twelve hundred years. The Americans agreed not to bomb it in the war. Now it's being changed out of all recognition because of unchecked urban development.'

'Right,' I said. But my mind was elsewhere. 'The thing that bothers me is that Chatwin never travelled alone.'

'Jan does.'

'So does Jonathan.'

'But Redmond doesn't.'

'Naipaul never did.'

Monks were chanting inside the temple, a brazier was smoking with joss sticks, devotees were praying. The wooden porch was worn smooth and finely grained.

'*Wabi-sabi*,' I said, tapping my toe on the wood.

'That's a really ambiguous expression. Almost meaningless.'

'I thought it meant "weathered and imperfect".'

'Shall we walk down there? I stayed here when I first came to Japan. I went to that monastery – see the little building? I thought I'd stay a year and write about it. I lasted a week.'

'I guess they had you – what? Kneeling, doing sitting positions and Zen meditation?'

'No, mopping floors, cleaning, scrubbing.'

'That's the other big monastic discipline. The Aum Shinrikyo cult was full of moppers and sweepers.'

'The oldest teahouse in Kyoto,' Pico said. 'Also the world's biggest carp. And down there at that temple, ladies of the night and geishas come to make offerings. We can go later. The geisha quarter is nearby. You know about this Jizu figure? Patron of children?'

'I think so. What about sex here, anyway? I saw streetwalkers at the back of my hotel.'

'The women step out of the shadows and say *kimochi*. It happened to me recently.'

'What are you supposed to do? Hey, look at this. The walkway between the buildings. I tried to make one of these in Hawaii.'

'That's a teahouse at the far end.'

'What does *kimochi* mean?'

'Comfort. "You want comfort?" A euphemism for sex.'

'Like "comfort woman" – those Koreans they forced into prostitution.'

'Right.'

Pico was eating sweets out of a bag. 'Want an M-and-M?'

'Thanks. I saw a sign, LOVE DOLL, over a door in Wakkanai. I really regret that I didn't go in and see who was there.'

'No, no. Don't go through the door. My feeling in Japan, seeing something like that, is you never know what you're getting yourself into.'

We were strolling among azaleas, reddish-purple blossoms, and passing through gateways of shaped junipers.

'You did the right thing, not opening that door,' Pico said. 'I've so often gone through the wrong door.'

'I feel better now.'

'You know what they say instead of "I came"? They say, "I went".'

I pointed to the centre of the garden. 'What is the story with that little mound with the bushes on it?'

'Unfathomable Japan. Not like anywhere else. You can't even guess.'

Circling the narrow streets, we passed through a high red gateway and came to Yasaka Pagoda, a Shinto shrine, animistic, venerating animals and the natural world of rocks and trees, where many paper offerings had been attached to the structure.

'Women come here if they want a child, or if they want an abortion, or if they've had a miscarriage. It's the Jizu figure again. They want to catch the spirit of the lost child. It's also frequented by geishas before their nightly gigs.'

'There's one, in a kimono.'

'No, she's too old,' Pico said. 'She's probably in charge of geishas. This is the spiritual centre of the pleasure quarter, haunted by memories of melancholy love.'

The shrine was hung with paper pleas and votive pictures and small wooden panels with specific images. For about $8 I could buy one and hang it. One panel showed a man burdened by a heavy sack.

'Look at that. "It meets a new love and it wishes a deeper edge with the lover."'

'Here's a good one' – a flying boar. ' "It wishes the peace of the world, and the family, and variety."'

'And *variety*?'

Each of us began writing in our notebooks.

'And this one's great. "It wishes that the misfortune not happen."'

'People must be wondering what we're doing,' Pico said.

'We can say market research for our own Shinto shrine – the votive-board concession.'

'It's so peaceful here. It's out of the way. Jan's written about it. She never writes about herself, yet she's had the most amazing life.'

'The untold story of Jan Morris. We'll never know. What's that over there?'

'Love hotel. You can always tell by the name. Hotel King. Hotel Yes. Hotel Happy.'

This was Hotel King.

'I sometimes tell people to stay in them,' Pico said. 'The rates are equivalent to regular hotels and the rooms are nicer. You sometimes can't check in until late, though, after all the lovers have gone home.'

The rates were posted: *All night, 10,500 yen ($95). Short stay, 3 hours, 4,000 yen ($35). Extension, 30 minutes, 1,150 yen ($10).*

The centrepiece in the love-hotel lobby, almost filling the whole space, was a brand-new Rolls-Royce raised on blocks.

'Because it's run by the yakuza. Wherever you see a Rolls or a big expensive car, it's the yakuza.'

At a quarter to six on a weekday evening, twenty-five rooms were taken, only five available, according to the blinking lights. An interior picture of each room and its price was posted on the wall, and the decor varied from art deco to Greek revival to minimalist modern, and one had a fountain.

'It's like a chic restaurant.'

We walked around the geisha quarter, the lanes of teahouses and steak restaurants – steaks were advertised for 17,000 yen ($150). Big black Mercedes sedans blocked the narrow lanes, white-gloved chauffeurs waiting at attention.

Pico led me to a restaurant by the Kamogawa River, and over a meal of sushi and miso soup, salmon and rice, and tuna tartare with avocado, we talked about T. E. Lawrence, India, Hawaiian names, *Pnin*, our families, Jan Morris again, Naipaul again, Borges again, England, Murakami, Wakkanai, hot springs, Henry James, Burma, Vietnam, the meaning of *ecchi*, book tours, monasticism, Xavier de Maistre's eccentric travel book, *A Journey Round My Room*, air travel, school.

'What about Eton?'

'It was the greatest experience of my life,' Pico said.

'But you had to wear all those different clothes. Top hat. Black suit.'

'They had got rid of the top hats. But we still wore formal suits. My closet was full of required clothes.'

'Long ago, I read a book by a Nigerian who went there. *Nigger at Eton.*'

'You know that book? His name was Oneayama. He was a few years older than me, but I knew him.'

'He said they were racist.'

'The usual English schoolboy stuff. They called me "nigger". Any of these Japanese – they would have called them "nigger" too.'

We had agreed to meet the next day in Nara, where Pico lives when he is not travelling. Nara is a small and ancient town, the eighth-century capital of Japan, forty minutes by train from Kyoto, home to some of the greatest temples in the country. In its heyday Nara was also the artistic and spiritual centre, the seat of power, the site of numerous gardens and shrines, temples and parks and teahouses, many of which still existed. When you summon to mind images of an idealized Japan – folding screens full of flourishes, lacquerware, azaleas, graceful multi-tiered pagodas, triple-pitched roofs, stone lanterns, serene or brooding Buddhas – it is in Kyoto and Nara where those images can be found, not in bucolic Hokkaido.

'I've never been to Hokkaido,' Pico had told me. 'And I hardly ever go to Tokyo. When I'm not travelling, I come here to meditate and vegetate.'

The night before I went to Nara to meet him, I woke up several times, my mind teeming with subjects I wanted to discuss with him: the novels of Georges Simenon, English social rituals, Chatwin's Australia, Graham Greene's Vietnam, the charms of Maine, the five volumes of Ford Madox Ford's *Parade's End*, Pico's own book about the Dalai Lama, the Japanese fascination with comic books and much else. He was a friend and a traveller, and with all such meetings, it was like an encounter with a fellow inhabitant of a distant planet. He was not only prolific as a writer but widely read.

I think most serious and omnivorous readers are alike – intense in their dedication to the word, quiet-minded, but relieved and eagerly talkative when they meet other readers and kindred spirits. If you have got this far in this book, you are just such a singular person.

Pico was waiting at the agreed-upon place, near the statue of a monk at Kintetsu Nara Station.

He said, 'I've got a thousand questions to ask you.'

'I have quite a few too.'

'Let's walk. The Deer Park is this way.'

We set off for the northeast part of town, the old precincts where the treasures are, away from the malls and department stores. We cut through Yoshikien Garden and the Deer Park. The de-antlered deer became curious and approached us, pressing damp noses against our sleeves. The deer were not just decorative creatures but important in Buddhist cosmology as 'messengers of the gods', often resting tamely near Buddha's disciples, the *arhats*.

'We were talking about being an alien in England yesterday,' I said. 'I want to tell you about my first week in England, in November 1971 – the humiliations.'

'I'd love to hear it,' Pico said, and after I'd told it all and we'd got most of the way across the park, he said, 'I know exactly what you mean. By the way, this is the garden of Kasuga Shrine. These plants are mentioned in ancient texts.'

I looked at the hedges and shrubs. 'How ancient?'

'The Nara period began around 710.'

'That's incredible,' I said. 'But can you imagine? I'd just come from Singapore to the English countryside. It was dark and cold in Dorset . . .'

And, bless his heart, he listened. And the deer listened, and the crows croaked in encouragement.

'I'm reading Greene's *Lawless Roads*,' Pico said.

'What's not clear in the book is how short a trip it was,' I said. 'Less than six weeks. It's nothing. His Africa trip was eighteen days – and he went with his girl cousin! And he writes as though he's Henry Morton Stanley, who took three years to cross the continent.'

'But Greene makes the most of it. He only needed to spend a short time in a place to sum it up. I've only spent a few days in Tokyo and I wrote a piece about it.'

'It's true. You live in a place and you become blind to it. That's a lovely gate.'

'Nandaimon Gate,' he said. 'I gave a lecture in New Zealand on travel about ten years ago. Quite a large group of people. When it came time for questions, a man stood up and said, "Can you tell us about Paul Theroux's marriage?"'

'Ha! Poor you!'

'I'd flown in from LA. I'd prepared this long talk. I'd been very conscientious. And that was the first question.'

'I can't imagine why. New Zealanders are mad at me because I satirized their governor-general.'

'It's the Australians who are thin-skinned,' Pico said. 'Look at this sign.'

The sign near the gateway said, A PLACE OF PRAYER FOR PEACE AND AFFLUENCE ON EARTH.

He said, 'After Jan wrote about Sydney, they attacked her in all the papers, and they tried to ban her from visiting.'

Among her offences, Jan Morris had described Sydney as a city of louts – in courtrooms, in the Opera House, in the stock exchange, in the ice-skating rink. And in the Sydney Speakers' Corner, where

the arguments were bludgeonly, the humour was coarse, and all around the soapboxes there strode a horribly purposeful figure, wearing a beret tipped over his eyes, and holding a sheaf of newspaper, whose only purpose was to shout down every speaker in turn, whatever the subject or opinion, with a devastating loutishness of retort – never silent, never still, hurling offensive gibes at speaker and audience alike with a flaming offensive energy. Now where, said I to myself, have I seen that fellow before? And with a pang I remembered: the indefatigable ice-slosher, up at the ice-rink.

Pico said, 'They never got over it.'

We passed under the large temple gateway with its overhanging eaves, where an American-sounding woman was explaining the two looming guardian figures to some American-looking students.

'Notice how the arms are crossed,' she said, and we listened. 'Benevolent kings . . . thirteenth century . . .'

'Canadian,' Pico said. 'I like to pick out accents.'

'Maybe Vancouver, but I think California.'

In a whisper, Pico asked a student where they were from. She said vaguely, 'West Coast.'

'I win.'

'You backed into that one. Ah, there it is.'

Standing alone, under a pair of enormous sloping roofs with dragon ornaments and a dormer like an eyebrow, was a gigantic two-storey wooden temple penetrated with white panels. We walked towards it. It was Todai-ji. Pico said it was the largest freestanding wooden structure in the world and that the Buddha statue inside was fifty feet high.

Todai-ji Temple of the Kegon sect was huge and hulking, and because of the rooflines and the porches, not just a pile of timber but a graceful, heavy-browed presence. This eighteenth-century structure was the single most imposing building I saw in the whole of Japan. And inside, the monumental Buddha, cast in bronze, was the largest of its kind in Japan, called the Vairocana Buddha. It matched the temple that enshrined it, and was equally impressive in tonnage and in implied wisdom. The Sanskrit word *Vairocana* meant the Illuminator – this Buddha was associated with 'the sun and the light of grace'. It made me feel like an insect. This was no doubt the intention of Emperor Shomu, who was responsible for it all.

'What about S. J. Perelman – do you like his work?'

I said, 'Very funny stuff. I like it a lot. I knew him in London.'

'I wish I'd met him.'

'These pillars support the roof but not the walls. The walls aren't load-bearing. That's why it's lasted.'

'It burned down several times, though. It was bigger before by about a third.'

'Perelman called me in London after I'd reviewed one of his books. A rave review. He was pleased. "Let's have lunch." '

'Friendly?'

'Very. And a natty dresser. Something of a womanizer. Well read. Widely travelled. Those crazy pieces are based on real trips he made to Shanghai before the war, Java, Egypt, Uganda. He was probably here at some point. He was an Anglophile, but living in England cured him of that. He was strangely anti-Semitic.'

'No!'

'But he was always Yiddling, as he called it, using Yiddishisms to express it. He wrote a piece about Israel in the 1970s for *Travel and Leisure* and they wouldn't print it. Or maybe they made him tone it down.'

'I think he knew Norman Lewis.'

'Another great traveller. I loved *Naples '44* and his book about the Mafia.'

'And *A Dragon Apparent*, about Southeast Asia.'

Normally, 'Look at that statue' is an irritating remark, but I would have missed the statue if Pico hadn't spoken. Although it was off to one side, it was a three-times-lifesize seated figure of an old man with a lined face and piercing eyes, carved in wood, its luminous staring expression somewhat unearthly. He was holding a bulbous sceptre. A red cloth bonnet and red cape gave him the look of the wolf in 'Little Red Riding Hood'. The plaque under the figure gave its name as Binzuru (Pindola Bharadvaja) and explained that he was one of only sixteen *arhats* – ascetics and disciples of the Buddha. And Binzuru was 'the most widely revered of all the *arhats* in Japan', and 'famous for his mastery of occult powers'.

That explained the stare. The small print on the plaque listed instructions for using the statue as a health aid. One was to touch a part of the statue and then, with the same hand, touch a corresponding part of one's own body to promote health or healing.

I touched Binzuru's knee, and my own, to keep my chronic gout away.
'Joseph Conrad had gout.'

'Maybe he got it in Africa, as I did. I was horribly dehydrated on a Zambezi trip. I didn't pee for two days. I was in a tent, half delirious. It damaged my kidneys. After that, I had my first attack of gout in my big toe.'

'Isn't the light beautiful at this time of day?' Pico said. 'What about Hunter Thompson?'

'I saw him when he came to Hawaii. He was always snorting coke or smoking dope or drinking whiskey. He was one of the most timid travellers I've ever known. When he was back in Colorado, he used to call me up at two in the morning. I think he was in pain most of the time.'

'He was someone else whom Jann Wenner rescued. Don't you think Jan Morris was at her best when she was writing for *Rolling Stone* in the eighties?'

Walking downhill along the narrow lanes to the Deer Park again, we evaluated all the men and women who were travelling and writing today, assigning points to those who travelled alone and wrote well, detracting points for attitude, posturing, lying, fictionalizing or being blimpish.

'And that's Kaidan-in,' Pico said, indicating a chalet-like shrine with a meticulously tended garden, the shrubs in bud and some beginning to blossom. As we watched the shrine from its perimeter fence, snow began to fall, the large wet flakes like white blossoms. 'I haven't seen snow here for nine years.'

'I've heard your father was a guru,' I said.

'Wherever could you have heard that,' Pico said, and it wasn't a question. 'It's true. After he settled in Santa Barbara. It was the 1960s.'

'Guru of what?'

'Of the spirit. Of Iyerism, I suppose,' Pico said. 'Lots of theosophy.'

'*Isis Unveiled*? Madam Blavatsky? Walter Besant? Swami Vivekananda?'

'That kind of thing. The house was full of hippies, thirty or forty at a time, some very pretty girls, listening to him and serving him. Joni Mitchell look-alikes. I was at Eton then. I'd come home from this formal English school, properly dressed, and see them in flowing robes. My father was like one of these Tibetan gods, breathing fire, throwing fireballs and thunderbolts. "Get me some food!" "I'm thirsty!" "Do this! Do that!"'

'Was your mother part of the business?'

'No. I think she found it all a strain.'

'You should write about it.'

We had returned to the shopping malls of central Nara and were back in the twenty-first century, away from the *arhats* and the nosy deer and the shrines. We stopped at a Starbucks for coffee.

Pico said, 'No one really knew my father. He didn't write. He was a good speaker. Krishnamurti was down the road, in Ojai.'

'Another California swami.'

'But I give my father credit for being one of the first to take an interest in the Dalai Lama. When the Chinese invaded Tibet and the Dalai Lama fled, no one did a thing. The Chinese just walked in and took over. My father hurried to India, to Dharamsala, in 1960. So I was able to get to know the Dalai Lama when I was very young. That's what I'm writing about now. But the guru story has been told.'

We left Starbucks and meandered towards Nara Station.

'Are you going back to Tokyo?'

'No. Tomorrow to Niigata,' I said.

'Niigata? That's nowhere.'

'There's an international airport there, but a very small one. In Tokyo I got a ticket on a flight from Niigata to Vladivostok. The ferries aren't running because of bad weather in the Sea of Japan.'

'A flight to Vladivostok.' And perhaps thinking of our earlier talk about *A Journey Round My Room*, he said, 'You'd be able to write a whole book about that.'

★

Express trains from Kyoto left every ten minutes for Tokyo. While I waited for the nine a.m. Hikari Express, businessmen crowded the Kyoto newsstands, choosing comic books for the three-hour trip. They hardly looked up when the train passed snow-covered Mount Fuji en route, sitting in the landscape like a vast dessert, the biggest ice cream sundae in the world. I changed trains in Tokyo at noon, crossed the narrow waist of Japan, and arrived in Niigata around two p.m.

The small city was bleak and newish, having been levelled by a tidal wave in 1961. It was also very cold, a freezing wind and sleet blowing from Siberia and across the blackish sea. And as in other provincial towns, the young women of Niigata were fiercely stylish, clicking down the cold streets in tweed jackets, velvet knickerbockers, and stiletto-heeled boots. One of these women sold me a new blade assembly for my battery-powered razor, another sold me a scarf, a third sold me a history of the yakuza. I remained in windswept Niigata for two days and then caught the flight to Vladivostok. The plane left in darkness, four hours late.

You'd be able to write a whole book about that, Pico had said. I considered this optimistic statement soon after we were airborne. The flight took one hour and twenty minutes. Most of the passengers were heavy-faced Russian men in long leather coats, and paunchy women in thick sweaters and big boots, all these people looking misshapen and debauched after the Japanese, sleek as seal pups. Tough Russian youths, too, in greasy nylon parkas, who looked like mechanics; they carried duty-free cigarettes and bottles of Baileys Irish Cream. A Russian blonde in a white leather ensemble sat in front of me. A Japanese man in a thick yellow corduroy suit across the aisle. Next to me an Indian man, very fat, with an earring, sunglasses and a case of samples. No tourists. Thirty minutes into the flight we were given cheese sandwiches and hard sweets. No book in that trip, just this paragraph.

We arrived at Vladivostok, eastern Siberia, around midnight, a world of cold and darkness. The end of the line for most of these people, but for me the beginning.

31. The Trans-Siberian Express

Vladivostok, so far from Moscow – almost 6,000 miles – still retained many of its Soviet trappings: a gesticulating Lenin statue, a decaying GUM store, government offices with patriotic heroes in bronze waving from the roof, and that enduring Soviet trait, stone-faced bureaucracy. It had always been a city of delay and death, and now it was poverty-stricken as well, distant, out of touch and underfunded. Beset by woolly sea fog, and yellow slush and black snow in early February, it couldn't have looked grimmer when it had been the fearsome railway junction for prisoners and slave labourers, victims of Stalin's Great Purge, sent to be worked to death in the far northern mines of Kolyma and Magadan. Some didn't make it that far. The great poet Osip Mandelstam (and many other prisoners) died in a nearby transit prison. His chief crime had been to write a poem in which he satirized Stalin as a ludicrous brute, in lines such as 'His fingers are fat as grubs' and 'His cockroach whiskers leer' and 'All we hear is the Kremlin mountaineer / The murderer and peasant-slayer.'

The new Russia showed in Vladivostok's dreary casinos, the Mercedes dealership, the girlie shows that catered to sailors and the piles of Russian tit-and-bum magazines that were sold by shivering old ladies in ragged overcoats all over town. Ignored and neglected, a decaying city and a navy base at the edge of the frozen world, Vladivostok had become one of the Siberian centres of skinhead gang activity. These chalky-faced and blue-headed thugs in boots and black leather jackets were straight out of *A Clockwork Orange*, even speaking an argot similar to that which Anthony Burgess had fashioned for his characters from Russian: 'droogs' and 'chelovek' and 'glazzies'. But the skinheads were meaner and racist, with Hitlerian views. They swaggered the slushy streets, looking for dusky foreigners to beat to a pulp, and misspelling English graffiti (WITE POWER was one) with spray cans on walls, along with swastikas.

But just when I thought that this icebound city represented nothing more than a glacial point of departure, I was sitting in the hotel bar and the gods of travel delivered to me a horse's arse. He was a honking Englishman, almost unbelievable in his prejudices and pomposities, fresh off the plane from Moscow for a business meeting, monologuing to his Russian friend, who was either very tired or else, like him, drunk.

'What you need to do is to bring back the monarchy,' the Englishman said in the screechy confident voice the English use on foreigners. He thumped his table and looked out on the thawing city of muddy slush, the wind blowing off the steppe.

'*Da*,' the Russian said with no enthusiasm.

'Romanovs aren't hard to find. And Putin is useless, the place is corrupt. Mind you, I like corrupt countries – at least one knows where one stands. Get the tsar back on the throne, if you see what I mean. Get him out and about, shaking hands, a proper figurehead like our queen.'

'*Da*,' the Russian said, but it was more of a question.

'But England's finished. It'll take twenty years to recover from the damage Blair's done. He's destroyed the place completely. They don't give a stuff about the general populace. Blair's wrecked it.'

The Russian seemed to be dozing and didn't reply to the squeaking, grinning voice, the middle-aged Englishman in full cry, wailing about his destitution as an aristocrat.

'We're the fifty-first state. We're just an appendage of America. It's pathetic. But look – Vladivostok! We've flown seven hours and we're still in Russia. It's amazing. This is still Europe!'

I was going to say, *Europe?* But I thought: No, this is too good to interrupt.

'Soviets don't interest me. Soviet history is a bore. Borodino! That's more like it. I was there the other day. Lovely. It's all been preserved. Russia is monumental. Did I say I didn't mind the corruption? I don't mind. It gives an edge to the country. But Britain – you can have it. Viktor?'

'*Da?*'

'Bring the tsar back!'

That was the second night, after I'd recovered from arriving in the dark, at the faraway airport, and quarrelling with the taxi drivers, who demanded $100 to drive me here. When I refused, they drove away, leaving me standing in the snow; but who doesn't have a rapacious-taxi-driver story?

Killing time at the post office on the third day, I saw a young woman of twenty-two or so, rather earnest and plain, wearing a heavy coat, sitting at one of the littered wooden tables, hunched over, making a fair copy of a letter that began, *Dear Sirs! I wish to introduce myself to Philip Morris Company* . . .

'Maybe I can help you,' I said. 'Are you looking for a job?'

My eye fell on another line: *I have unique vast experience to think outside the box.*

'Who are you?' she demanded, scowling at me. 'What do you want?'

'I used to be an English teacher,' I said. That got her attention. 'Mind if I look?'

It was a letter of introduction, to accompany an application for a job at a tobacco company based in Switzerland. The dense full-page paragraph, rather old-fashioned in expression and handwriting flourishes, was scattered with grammatical errors. I made some suggestions, corrected the grammar and advised her to break it into shorter paragraphs, to make it easier to read.

'Thank you,' she said.

'It would help if you got it typed and printed.'

She shook her head. 'That is too expensive.'

'It would make a better impression. I'll pay for it,' I said, and took out some roubles and looked at her signature. 'An investment in your future, Anna.'

She became fierce and snatched up the letter. 'I will never accept charity from you!'

This attracted the attention of the other people at the big post office table – some old women, a young woman with a baby and a bearded old man in felt boots who'd been sleeping on his arms. They looked at me and then at Anna, and they waited for another outburst.

But Anna began to whisper in a harsh voice. She was strangely stubborn and full of warnings. She wanted to leave Vladivostok. She said I should do the same.

'I'm leaving tonight,' I said.

'Leave now. You are not safe here,' she said. 'People will steal your mobile phone. They will find the password. Yes! They have so many ways to do it. You don't know. Why did you come here?'

'To take the train.'

'There is so much crime in this city. You can write me a letter, but maybe someone will steal it out of my mail container.'

'What about this letter?'

'It will be stolen! I want to work. I have sent five letters. But my dream? It is to have my own business. Information technology.'

In this cold and chaotic place, she sat in the stinking post office in her old coat, sending out letters, plotting to leave, as I was. I tramped around the snowy streets as soot drifted from the sky, and I encountered the inevitable pair of American Mormons. One of them, Elder Hogue from Salt Lake City, was buttonholing strangers and passing out invitations.

'What's happening?'

'A film,' Elder Hogue said. 'You're welcome to come and see it.'

I glanced at the leaflet. It was a screening of a film dramatizing one of the great events adumbrated in Mormon doctrine, the visit of Jesus Christ to Central America after he was crucified, in the year 33. Jesus had preached to the Mayans.

'I've seen that film already,' I said. 'Jesus giving a sermon on the pyramid. I'm wondering if it really happened.'

'Surely it happened,' Elder Hogue said, chuckling at my doubt. He had the torpid smile and steady gaze of the evangelist, which was also the expression of the car salesman sizing up a flat-footed customer. I was impressed that, in this terrible place, he looked so presentable and healthy, and he and his fellow missionary were possibly the only people in Vladivostok wearing a white shirt and a necktie.

'How's things in Vladivostok?'

'We're meeting some people,' he said. That seemed ambiguous. I asked him to explain. He said, 'We knock on doors. But it's a sad place. Gangs. Drugs. Corruption. Thievery. I've been robbed. They took my computer. The place is going downhill – just look at it. I've got another whole year.'

'You can set them on the right path,' I said.

'I know we can,' he said, and made a dive at a passerby, an old man who took the leaflet, and Elder Hogue began chatting with him in fluent Russian, framing the Mormon message.

Vladivostok Station bulked against the harbour, a weirdly pretentious example of Russian railway design, with dense walls and great sloping roofs and cupolas and steeples wearing witches' hats, and a clock showing the right time. The whole thing was impressive until I went inside, where its bare interior was echoey and cold. The waiting room was filled with wooden benches, like church pews. Although the station was unheated and rather stark, some of the public rooms had colourful murals of railway scenes.

I was leaning on the banister that led to the outside platform, reading Murakami's *Sputnik Sweetheart*. A young Japanese man approached me.

'I like *Dance Dance Dance*,' he said.

His name was Nobuatsu Sekine. A persevering traveller, Nobu was taking the Rossiya to Moscow and doing a grand tour of Europe. Like me, he had arrived a few days before in Vladivostok.

'What do you think so far?'

'Very primitive. Very dirty,' he said.

He pointed out that the station had no conveniences, no shops, no bar, no newsstand, not even any heat. He was burdened by a heavy backpack and a bulging shopping bag.

'What have you got there?'

'Noodles, beer, bottles of water. You don't have any?'

I said no, it hadn't occurred to me to buy provisions. 'But I have half a pound of powdered green tea from Kyoto.'

'I'll watch your bag if you want to go buy food. There's a market across the street.'

Taking his suggestion, I hurried out of the station and into the night-time snow flurry to the market. I bought noodles, beer, water and chocolate biscuits, and over the next seven days, whenever I saw Nobu, I thanked him for his suggestion. I did not see him often. He was travelling hard class and I was in soft.

We watched an express train pull out of the station for China. It would arrive in Harbin, capital of Heilongjiang Province, the following morning. Most of the passengers were Chinese traders who had come to Vladivostok to sell clothes and household goods and electronics. They were taking nothing back to China but money. They looked delighted to be heading home.

About an hour before the Rossiya left, I found my carriage and introduced myself to the conductor, a woman in a Russian Railways uniform – black jacket with gold braid, black skirt, black boots. She showed me to my compartment, calling it a *kupe*, where a dark balding man with Levantine features was already sitting, talking on the phone.

'Where are you going?' I asked. If he said Moscow, I would have him as a roommate for seven days.

'Khabarovsk,' he said.

'Tomorrow?' I said.

He confirmed this. He said there was no flight there – in most of Siberia the only reliable way to get around was the railway. He added that his English wasn't very good. But it wasn't bad, though he had a heavy accent. His name was Rashid. He was about fifty, a Kurd, originally from Iraq but had been brought to Armenia with his parents in the 1960s. For close to twenty years he had been living in remote Kamchatka, a frozen appendage of far eastern Siberia in the Sea of Okhotsk. He was a businessman in Petropavlovsk. He had four children – he showed me their pictures, stored on his mobile phone.

'You're nearer to Alaska than Moscow.'

'I been Yeleska.' He'd done a circuit, starting and finishing in the Arctic: Kamchatka–Yeleska–Meeamee–Yolando–Deesnee Whorl–Teexah–Yeleska–Kamchatka.

As we were talking, the train whistle blew and we left Vladivostok, heading north to Khabarovsk and then turning left for the long haul around northeastern China.

Seeing that I had pulled out my map, Rashid put his finger on Afghanistan and said, 'I was here, too. And here. And here.'

'What doing?'

'Fighting.'

Moving his finger, he traced his route through towns to the east and south of Mazar-i-Sharif, the places where he had fought in the Soviet army from 1985 to 1987, marching with his battalion, dragging cannons, firing on Afghan positions. He smiled as he read the names of the towns he'd bivouacked in: 'Kunduz! . . . Baghlan!'

'What do you think about that war?'

'Big mistake.'

'For you?'

'For us. For you. For anyone. Afghanistan' – and he smiled again – 'I seenk no one can win in Afghanistan, except Afghanistan people.'

Rashid made a few more phone calls while I sorted out papers. To keep busy, I intended to write notes for a memory of my father. Since his death, I had been unable to write about him without becoming sad; but now, almost twelve years on, I felt it was time. He was a loving father, a private man and a hard worker without any obvious ambition. Although he was a reader of history, of classic novels, he had never read anything I'd written; or, if he had, he'd never mentioned the fact to me.

With a week of solitude on the train ahead of me, I knew I could write a portrait of this kind and somewhat mysterious man.

Suddenly Rashid said, 'Why America doesn't like Azerbaijan?'

'I'm not sure.'

'They are on side of Georgia.'

'There aren't many Armenians in America, but they're powerful. They want the US government to settle the Nagorno-Karabakh problem.'

'Political problem! It's all stupid.' He laughed. He pointed to himself. 'I live in Kamchatka!'

It was like saying he was from another planet, and a glance at the map confirmed it. He said he'd gone to Kamchatka after he'd finished fighting in Afghanistan and left the army. I had the impression that his wish was to get as far away from political follies as possible.

I said, 'Rashid, you're a Muslim?'

'Not Muslim. Zoroastrian. When the sun comes up, I pray.'

'Where else are there Zoroastrians?'

'Plenty in Iraq. Plenty in Turkey. India – many.'

This led to talk of the Iraq War.

'America in Iraq,' he said, shaking his head. 'Yes, Saddam was a problem. He killed my people. He gassed them, he bombed them. Not good. But this American war? It is' – he spread his hands for emphasis – 'disaster.'

He went back to phoning, I went back to reading the history of the yakuza I'd bought in Niigata. Then I was drowsing, and I turned my reading light off. Rashid did the same. Then I heard him clear his throat.

'Who will be next president?' he said in the darkness, over the banging of the train's wheels.

'I don't know.'

'Maybe Gillary,' he said.

'Gillary?'

'Gillary Cleenton.'

'I like Obama.'

'Black one. Good one, I seenk,' he said.

I slept soundly, and the next morning at nine we arrived in Khabarovsk. Rashid gave me a bag of tangerines he'd bought in Vladivostok and stepped into the snow.

As the train pulled out, I went to breakfast. I was the only customer. The ornate wood-panelled dining car, with mirrors and lace curtains, was dirty, the tablecloths spattered and stained with food, the floor littered, the woodwork scummy. One end of the carriage was stacked with beer crates. An unshaven knob-nosed man with wild hair sat at one of the tables, tapping on a computer with black fingernails, a cigarette between his lips.

After a while he surprised me by getting up and handing me a bilingual menu. His hands were grubby. He scribbled my order and went to the kitchen. He was gone a long time. I imagined his dirty hands and drooping cigarette. A submissive old woman, who was probably his wife, brought me a cup of coffee and the omelet I'd ordered. When I asked for bread – *khlyeb*, one of the Russian words I knew – the wild-haired man yelled at his wife and she brought it.

This experience gave me a taste for instant noodles and green tea in my compartment on succeeding mornings, easily prepared using the samovar that is provided on every Russian train – always accessible, always steaming.

The sun was up, the day was bright. Somewhere, bathed in sunbeams, Rashid was murmuring a Zoroastrian prayer. Through the window the land was flat, scattered with emblematic birch trees, some of them bulked with crows' nests. The snow was thin enough so that brown tussocks showed through.

I settled down and began to write about my father, and a few hours later, at a brief stop, the *provodnitsa* introduced herself as Olga. We were, she said, at Birobidzhan.

One station sign was spelled out in Hebrew letters, the other in Cyrillic. The station building was newish, red brick and empty. In the distance I could see a gold-domed church, barracks-like tenements, thick birch logs stacked in railway carriages and a large factory. Even in the glorious snow-gleam, the sun shining in the frost-sparkle, the icy-bright trees, it looked like an open prison. Birobidzhan, at the edge of China, in the heart of eastern Siberia, was the capital of Yevreyskaya Oblast, the Jewish autonomous region. No one got off or on the train.

The proof that Siberia was a simple world simplified even further by snow was the market on the snowy platform at Obluche in the middle of that first afternoon. Old women sold dumplings (*verenike*) filled with cabbage and potato, fried fish, hard-boiled eggs, bottles of water and squares of chocolate. It was the sort of merchandise you'd see on a railway platform in Africa. Little tables of hopeful hawkers, a few roubles changing hands, and they begin packing up as the train leaves, the arrival of the train being the big event of the day.

I soon saw why. Obluche was a place of wooden cabins and snow-bound cottages, huts at the outskirts, like a scene of a nineteenth-century settlement in a Minnesota winter – the small cabins, the picket fences, the thick icicles and the chimneys sending up smoke, and beyond them a great emptiness of snowfields. No footsteps, no car tracks, not another human being nor a vehicle, and China was just beneath the horizon, within walking distance if you had snowshoes.

Even at the larger stations no people appeared, nothing stirred. Bureya was a low town of square Siberian cottages, some prettified with ginger-bread, with smoking chimneys. Where the fences had fallen and the birches iced up, the delicacy of black and white, the land looked like an Andy Wyeth snowscape.

Most days were to be like that, villages of low smoking huts, like Amazar on the Shilka River, hundreds of chimneys sending up white smoke, huddled behind flimsy wooden fences, many miles apart, birch groves, bare trees, a monumental emptiness of snow and sky, the Trans-Siberian moving across the snow like a ship across a frozen sea.

After two days and two nights we had penetrated to an even more desolate region. I had my yakuza book to read, some more Simenons. And I had some writing to do – notes on this trip and the memoir of my father, who, every day as I wrote about him, seemed to recede, smiling pityingly at me.

When I boarded this train in the winter of 1973–4 I had no clear idea how many days it would take to get to Moscow. With delays and blizzards, it ran late, and I ended up spending Christmas on it, feeling miserable and homesick. Now I had my *kupe* to myself. I could not have been more content, sitting in this privacy, watching the cooling gold light from the sinking sun redden the snow and the birch bark, making the world seem so far away. I was released from all concerns, floating across the snowfields.

I made another visit to the dining car. The knob-nosed waiter-chef was a whole day dirtier and grouchier. His fingernails were still rimmed with black; he wore a black cotton hoodie and dark woollen trousers and heavy boots. His thick glasses were smeared with grease. He smoked and tapped on his old computer, but when he took my order he scribbled with a pencil on torn scraps of paper.

'*Salyanka*,' I said. Stew. And, enunciating slowly, '*Ya-ich-nitsa*.' Fried eggs.

With the sort of frustrated intelligence that made him impatient and resentful, he had the look of a Dostoyevskian anarchist or a dissident. But of course he was neither, just an underpaid slob who ran the unpopular dining car with his wife. All this woman ever did was roll paper napkins on a stick to make them into tubes that she placed in vases on the tables to mimic bouquets. Apart from a few drunks, I never saw any other diners. I began to avoid the dining car.

A few days later, I encountered the waiter-chef's wife in the vestibule of one of the cars. It was thick with layers of frozen ice and blown-in snow.

She gabbled at me. I was sure she was saying, 'Where have you been? Come and eat!' But by then I was living on noodles and the smoked fish and sausages I bought on the railway platforms.

Mogocha, one of those platforms, was a sprawl of houses, some big wolf-like dogs frolicking in the snow, a man in a fur hat lifting his boots high because of the deep drifts and a bus chugging down a riverbank and across a frozen river. Many of the cottages had carved and orna-mented blue shutters – a small wood-burning town, looking centuries old, as perhaps it was.

In the past I had sneered at a half-buried place like this and wanted to move on. Now I saw it as not bleak but peaceful, a quiet refuge, muffled by snowdrifts, entirely self-sufficient, too far from Moscow for anyone to care about it, the sort of place I might live in if it weren't so damnably cold.

For hundreds of years this region had been a place of exile. At dusk that day we came to Chernyshevsk-Zabaikalsky. It was as remote and cosy-looking as Mogocha, and it had been a prison for the literary critic and novelist Nikolai Chernyshevsky, who had been exiled there in 1864. His was another typical story of the dangers of expressing an opinion in Russia, but he was a tsarist victim. He had advocated the freeing of serfs and the emancipation of women, and he had argued in many essays that art needed a purpose. After enduring a mock execution, he spent twenty-five years in hard labour and Siberian exile. His crime? 'Subver-sion'. Four months after returning home from Siberia, he died, aged sixty-one. He had written a novel while in exile, called *What Is to Be Done?* (*Shto Delat?*), and it became a socialist tract, which was why there was a brooding silver statue of the man in front of the railway station.

I was reminded here, and elsewhere on this train, of something Nabokov wrote in one of his essays – that much of Russian literature has the smell of the prison library.

Being on the Trans-Siberian was indeed like being on a ship, not any old ship, and not a cruise liner, but an old iron freighter ploughing through a frozen sea, complete with grumpy deckhands, bad food and an invisible captain. And with the same sort of smugness for the passenger inside that I happened to be, warm and comfortable, the deadly elements outside the window, the sleet sometimes lashing the glass.

If there was a Trans-Siberian challenge, the seven nights and days on the long-distance train, it wasn't getting the visa or the ticket or finding one's way to Vladivostok; it was the usual obstacle in travel, the mental challenge. Russians overcame it by staying drunk – the men, anyway. So when I roamed around the train, all I saw were people drinking beer or vodka or else sleeping it off. For a Russian, a train journey of this length was a bender, and because of this, most of them were incoherent.

Nobu was hopping to keep warm on the snowy platform of Ulan-Ude in the early morning. I asked him how he was managing.

'The men in my compartment are very alcoholic,' Nobu said. 'They start in the morning when they wake up. They drink all day.'

He didn't drink. He was snapping pictures and making notes. Now and then we met in a vestibule and talked about Murakami's novels or tried to guess how cold it was outside.

A Mongolian-looking man approached me at Ulan-Ude – squat, round-cheeked, Asiatic. As this was the railway junction for the line to Mongolia and China, I was curious to know his ethnicity. He told me he was a Buryat, and would I like to buy some *manti*?

They were steaming meat-filled dumplings – I knew the word because I'd heard *manti* for dumpling in Turkey and elsewhere.

As he wrapped them, he said, 'You American?'

'Yes, American.'

'Mee-sippi,' he said. 'Al-bama. Flodda.'

'I'm from Boston.'

'Boston Bruins,' he said without hesitating, still wrapping the dumplings. 'You like hockey?'

'New York Rangers,' he said and handed me the package of dumplings. 'Good *manti*. Sank you. Good journey.'

What sent this cheery soul away was the sight of three drunks from the train staggering towards us. It was not yet nine in the morning. They were crapulous and carrying blue cans of beer, one of them with a can in each hand.

'We Marine!' one of them said to me. He told me his name was Fyodor and that they were based on a ship in Vladivostok.

The others began to shout incoherently. They wore tracksuits and slippers. They were going to Nizhni Novgorod, three days west of here.

When they had gone, I saw Nobu taking a picture of Ulan-Ude Station, where, under the station sign, the temperature was given in a lozenge of red lights. It was minus 17 Celsius.

My surprise in this frozen station in the middle of the Siberian steppe was that my BlackBerry buzzed with messages, some of them from Penelope, quite a few urging me to buy Viagra or to have my penis enlarged or to invest in promising stocks. Spam in the wilderness. But a mile out of Ulan-Ude it went dead – as it had been through the whole of Japan – and its only use was as a night light or (as I had used it for months) an emergency flashlight when I woke at night and groped down the carriage to take a piss.

Rolling through deepening snow – the effect of Lake Baikal – I spent the day writing about my father and thinking how nothing had changed on the line since I'd last taken it, thirty-three years ago. The train was still a big clanking antique, the food was still filthy, the trackside villages were still collections of wood-burning bungalows. The railway personnel, especially the women, were diligent about knocking the ice out of the drains with a long-handled axe and keeping the samovar going, but apart from that, there was no service to speak of. They were inattentive to passengers, but scrupulous about standing at attention in uniform by the coach at every stop.

What seemed a sprinkling of snow chips in the late afternoon under a darkened sky thickened to a whirling mass of snowflakes and finally a blizzard that entirely obscured Baikal – quite a storm, since it was the largest lake in the world. Out of the snowstorm at Slyudyanka a mob of hawkers, old men and women in fur hats, lifted bags of smoked fish and jostled in the doorway.

'What is this?' I asked Dimitri, who was in a *kupe* in my coach.

'Is *omul*. Good wiz beer,' Dimitri said.

Omul was a sort of salmon trout found only in Lake Baikal. Prized by

Russians, who made an effort to travel all this way to buy this fish, it was sold cold-smoked (stiff and dried) or warm-smoked (soft and fleshy and aromatic). I bought two bags of each.

The fishmongers in the falling snow at Slyudyanka were a glimpse of old Russia, not just their beautiful fur hats and big bulgy coats and thick mittens, but their dark frozen faces, their deeply pitted noses, as they pushed the bags of fish to the potential buyers on the train. A hundred years ago it could not have looked any different: the same boots, the same mittens and furs and ragged scarves, the same waiting on the platform in the storm for the brief stop of the long-distance train, the same look of urgency.

We stopped again at Irkutsk while I feasted on the fish. Darkness fell, the train ploughed slowly through the night, and in the morning frost-sparkle, four days on from Vladivostok, in another time zone, one of eight on this train trip, the landscape was unchanged: birches and black saplings in the snowfields passing the mud-flecked window.

A settlement of small cottages covered a whole slope of a hillside.

'Dachas?' I asked Dimitri, just a guess, because there was no smoke in the chimneys. As soon as I said it, I thought: It's a surmise, because travellers are always inventing the country they're passing through.

'Yes,' he said. 'People from Krasnoyarsk, they come here in the summer.'

'It's a whole village.'

'Not a village,' Dimitri said. 'A station.'

'What's the difference?'

'No post office. No shop. No school,' he said. He was making a distinction between a seasonal camp and a real settlement.

Dimitri was from Krasnoyarsk, an hour down the line. He had studied mining at the local university. It was a city of mines – I saw many from the train – some of them gold mines, surface diggings. Gold has been mined this way in Russia for more than 300 years.

What interested me about Dimitri was that he was completely satisfied, as a Russian worker, a resident of Krasnoyarsk, a voter and householder and citizen. As we were talking in the corridor of the train, his mobile phone rang.

He answered it, and when he was through talking he said, 'That was my boss. He knew I was on the train. He wants me to work today. It's okay. I like my work.'

He was employed by a company that made mining equipment that was shipped all over the country, even to distant Kolyma and Vladivostok.

Dimitri was about thirty, not tall but muscular. He skied in the hills around Krasnoyarsk, he rode his motorcycle in better weather, he lifted weights. He had his own apartment but was looking for a bigger one, 'maybe when I get married'. He drove a new Toyota Corolla. He wanted a Lexus. He was ambitious but contented, not a boozer, a non-smoker – that rare individual, a sober, happy Russian.

He had no desire to travel, except to Moscow and St Petersburg. He said he wished he spoke English better.

'Your English is fine.'

He tapped his front teeth. 'You say "teef" or "teet"?'

'Teeth.'

'Teef,' he said.

'I have thirty-two teeth.'

'I have feerty-two teef,' he said.

Muttering this mantra, he got off the train with the paperbacks I'd read – three Simenons, the Murakami and the yakuza book. I bought apple juice, yoghurt, salami, bread and smoked salmon from a babushka at the improvised market on the platform at Krasnoyarsk, and I picnicked in my compartment and watched Siberia go past.

Snow, birches, huddled cottages, crows, distant ridges 'eyelashed with firs', trackless snow all day, and then another night in the train. By now I was stuporous in the daytime and spent my nights dreaming, waking exhausted from the variety. Memorial services figured in two dreams, orations (by me) in one, flying (by me) in two, and in a memorable dream I was visited by my dead father, who explained, 'I'm just checking in.'

The previous night, my fifth on the train, we passed through Omsk, where Dostoyevsky had spent four years imprisoned. He'd written about it vividly in *The House of the Dead*.

Staring at the dense pine forest – the taiga – I drowsed all day, intermittently writing about my father, knowing that towards midnight on this sixth day I would be getting off at the city of Perm. We passed Ishim, where there were tyre tracks on the frozen rivers: in winter, Siberian rivers serve as thoroughfares for vehicles. At Tyumen around noon, I bought some chicken from an old woman on the snowy platform, and late in the afternoon, around five, at Yekaterinburg, city of regicide. Guided tours were advertised of the site where the tsar and his family

had been shot in 1918. Yekaterinburg was the first substantial city I'd
come to on the line – it had been named Sverdlovsk on my earlier trip,
when I'd arrived on Christmas Eve, at precisely the same time of day.
Then, watching a boy hoist his dead father in a stretcher off the train,
my depression was complete. This time, I thought: We're on time, we'll
arrive in Perm at midnight, and – as I had not washed for a week – I'll
probably have a bath.

'Perm is a modern industrial city that most travellers could bear to miss,'
the guidebook said. But surely that was just as inaccurate as this same
guidebook's rubbishing my *Great Railway Bazaar* as 'caustic', with travel
guide solemnity and philistinism. My visit to Perm was to be memorable
and enlightening, especially in the snow-muffled silence of the Siberian
winter.

'We were on a secret Pentagon list of Soviet cities to be destroyed!' a
Permian man boasted to me soon after I arrived. Because of its rocket
factories, its cannon plants and its manufacture of explosives, Perm was
closed to foreigners when I passed through in 1973. Perm was another
transit point for Siberian slave labour – had been so since tsarist times –
and out of town had some of the largest and fiercest prisons in the gulag.
Rocket-making, arbitrary incarceration and torture were the industries
in Perm until just the other day when, in February 1992, the prison here
was closed and foreigners were allowed to visit, to attend the ballet, to
eat juicy *posikunchiki* ('pissing dumplings') in the good restaurants, to
wander the snowy streets, to watch the local fatties jump naked into
holes chopped in icy ponds, to drive among the empty hills, the taiga,
the mixed forest, through tiny wooden one-storey villages and to see
the worst gulag, Perm 36 – all of which I managed to do.

Tiny crystals of frost shone in the lights of the main station – not the
same station that Yuri Zhivago detrains at in the second part ('Train to
the Urals') of *Doctor Zhivago*, when he first sets eyes on the city. Perm
looked much the same today: 'It clung to the summit of the hill in tiers,
house by house and street by street, with a big church in the middle of
the top, as in a cheap colour print of a desert monastery or of Mount
Athos.' Much of the action of that mournful fifty-year-old novel of love
and struggle takes place in Perm, called Yuriatin, 'another territory, a
different, provincial world, which had a centre of gravity of its own'.

A city or a landscape that has been described in a novel, even in a distorted way, is made more visible and accessible, even hallowed, with a quality of everlastingness. So I was happy to be in Perm and off the train, but I had become so used to the train's vibrations and my narrow berth, I could hardly sleep in my hotel bed. I was like a startled child in a cradle that had ceased to rock.

In the dark early morning, I met my guide, Sergei, and his translator, Yelena. They'd brought a friend, Viktor Shmirov, an authority on the gulag system and one of its historians. We got into Sergei's car and began driving on the white streets of packed snow, under sulphurous streetlamps.

'Why does the guidebook write that about Perm?' Sergei asked when I mentioned the jibe. 'This city is full of history. Dostoyevsky stopped here on his way to Omsk. The Diaghilev family is from here. Chekhov of course – this is the setting for *Three Sisters*. And Pasternak's book. The city is full of history!'

Dostoyevsky was on his way to prison and had spent only one night here. Sergei Diaghilev fled the city and spent his life in Paris as a balletomane. For Chekhov it was the epitome of stifling provincial cities ('When can we go to Moscow?' the three sisters keep moaning), and Pasternak had been regarded as a literary pariah until fifteen years ago.

I mentioned that *Three Sisters* depicted Perm unfavourably, the stifled sisters longing to leave for Moscow.

'Because Chekhov had a problem,' Sergei said. Sergei's English was not bad, but he preferred to speak Russian. Yelena sat behind me, translating. 'He was turned away from a building because he was wearing the wrong clothes. He never forgave them for this.'

This episode is not mentioned by any of Chekhov's biographers, only the fact that in 1890 he arrived by river in Perm at two o'clock one April morning and left the same day at six in the evening, on a train heading east. He was on his long Siberian trip – eighty-one days from Moscow to Vladivostok, on his way to the penal settlement at Sakhalin. Still, sixteen hours in Perm was enough for a genius like Chekhov to sum up the city as stifling.

'It's like this,' Sergei said. 'What if you went to a city and found a cockroach in your soup?' A big beefy man, he was hunched over the wheel, steering us through the snow. He turned heavily in his seat and faced me, his hands still on the wheel of the slowly moving car. 'You wouldn't like that city, would you? You'd always remember it. "Ah, Perm, that's where I had the cockroach in my soup!"'

'But we have no cockroaches,' Yelena said.

'Five years ago, all the cockroaches left Perm,' Sergei said. 'Was it radiation? Did they sense trouble coming? The professors can't answer this question.'

'And now we are passing Bashaya Smirti,' Viktor said.

'The Tower of Death,' Yelena said and pointed up ahead at a wide grey tower, like a silo with a sloping roof, attached to a grey, ecclesiastical-looking building pierced by small windows.

'There was a wave of repression in the early 1950s,' Viktor said as we made a circuit around the grim-looking tower. 'The Tower of Death was built then for the KGB. People were taken here for interrogation.'

I asked who those suspects might be.

'People regarded as "cosmopolitan"' he said. 'Westernized. Not patriotic. Also what were known as "left radicals". Anti-Stalinists.'

The terrifying tower loomed like an oversized crematorium near the centre of Perm, so I asked the obvious question: 'Did people in Perm call it the Tower of Death?'

'They didn't say it out loud. They whispered it,' Viktor said. 'Under Khrushchev they said it a little louder.'

I mentioned that my favourite writer about the gulag, a man who had been extensively interrogated, was Varlam Shalamov, the author of *Kolyma Tales*.

'This is Shalamov's centenary,' Viktor said, brightening. 'His father was a priest, but Shalamov wasn't religious at all. It's amazing that someone with such a huge experience of prison life didn't become a Christian.'

'Unlike Solzhenitsyn.'

'Yes, and unlike Solzhenitsyn, he did twenty-seven years in Siberia. At the end, he lived in great poverty in Moscow. He died in obscurity.'

Solzhenitsyn was the West's most famous *zek*, or prisoner. Yet in her exhaustive history of the prison system, *Gulag*, Anne Applebaum writes that his prison time was not onerous: '[Solzhenitsyn] was an unremarkable prisoner. He flirted with the authorities, served as an informer before seeing the light, and wound up working as a bricklayer.' And Shalamov's *Kolyma Tales*, which she praises, she also describes as 'among the bitterest in the entire camp genre'.

We had left the outskirts of Perm and were headed northeast, into the snow and pine forests along an unploughed road. Aside from a few cars and heavy trucks, there was almost no traffic. The early morning darkness had lifted; we were travelling through slanting snowfall under a low grey sky.

'I want to tell you a story about the organs of power,' Viktor said, Yelena translating. 'I once had a chance to interview a peasant woman in the northern Perm region. She told me she had never left her village, except once. She had gone to Chernaya, a biggish town. She was very impressed because it was so beautiful. She was sitting quietly, admiring the place, when she heard someone say, "Apoga is coming."'

'She knew the name. Apoga was the chairman of the Emergency Committee of the Cheka.'

The Cheka was one of the previous incarnations of the KGB, now known as the FSB. It has undergone nineteen name changes since 1919, yet it is the same organization, devoted to spying, torture and murder.

'Apoga was a frightening name to the woman. And the idea of seeing him was just terrible. Everyone was scared by the prospect of seeing this man. The woman left as soon as she could – went back to her village and never left again.' Viktor raised his hands. His face was fixed in an expression of helpless pain. 'People could be imprisoned for nothing. That man's name, Apoga, represented terror and fear.'

I said, 'The paradox is that at exactly the same time – the 1950s – we had McCarthy in the US persecuting people for sympathizing with the Soviet Union.'

Sergei was clucking '*Nyet, nyet, nyet*,' before I could finish. 'I've been to America,' he said. 'I know about McCarthyism. The problems were not on the same scale.'

I had to agree, though the motives, the witch-hunts, the betrayals, the stink of fear – of ruined lives and lost jobs and disgrace – that hung over McCarthyism were similar.

'Here's a story,' Sergei said. 'Viktor says people were afraid. It's true. I know it from my own family. My grandmother's family was from Kirov' – Kirov was on the railway line, about eight hours west of Perm – 'and they had eleven children, seven girls, four boys. My grandmother was considered educated, because she'd graduated from primary school with honours.'

Yelena said, 'Is also a joke, Paul.'

'I get it.' I also understood that he kept referring to his grandmother as 'babushka'.

'Her father was a well-known butcher. This man was strong physically, a muscular man. Fifty years later he was still remembered in this province. At the time of the revolution,' said Sergei, 'my grandmother was seventeen. She got married at nineteen, and for eight years all was well. They were in that remote place. The secret police couldn't reach them.

'In the 1920s, Stalin wanted collectivization, so they came to my grandparents. Her father the butcher was a kulak' – a rich peasant, or one defying authority. 'He had a beautiful house that he'd built himself. The inspector wanted the house for his own family. The house was very dear to the butcher.

'"Go to Siberia," the government inspector said.

'What? Until then he had never worried about the powers of government. He was so upset he just lay down and died of a heart attack.

'His two sons – my great-uncles – ran away to fight against this unfair government. My grandmother stayed in the village. But she was scared. She knew the police were looking for her two brothers. At the same time, she was giving bread to her brothers when they sneaked home. The special police wanted to kill them. This was around 1930 or '31. A few years later they were found and shot by the police.

'My grandmother – her name was Matryona – wanted to bury her brothers but couldn't find their bodies. And her grief didn't end there. After the Second World War there was a big famine. As the daughter of a kulak, with primary school honours – ha! – she was made head of a farm. There were no strong men left. She was suffering from hunger.

'In 1946, her son – my seventeen-year-old uncle – went looking for food. They were so hungry they'd go to the fields to look for grains of wheat that had been left behind after the harvest. He found a few grains. And he was seen. He was arrested for theft.

'He screamed at the police, "You are monsters! You have food and we have nothing!"

'For saying that, he was given a twenty-five-year sentence. He spent it in Magadan and Kolyma, washing gravel for gold. There was almost no communication with his mother. In 1954 when Stalin died, he was rehabilitated. He died three years ago and – you know? – he would never speak a word about his imprisonment.

'My grandmother was so afraid of the KGB that when the name was mentioned she made a face. The worst document she'd ever seen in her life was that of her son's sentence. Imagine, twenty-five years. He would have got ten years for theft, but he screamed "You monsters", so he got fifteen more.'

Now we were in the deep countryside, no other cars at all, and the road was buried in snow. The landscape was like a charcoal drawing on white paper – the black woods and the smudged sky and the whiteness of the blizzard.

'There are thousands of such stories,' Viktor said. 'It's a story of terror. People were afraid of anyone in power. The system was cruel. The whole basis of it was that Stalin wanted slave labour.'

All this time, Yelena was translating and I was writing in the notebook on my knee, which was easy because of the pauses between the men speaking and Yelena's translation.

'And you couldn't trust anyone,' Sergei said. 'I had a problem myself. I was on file, someone had betrayed me.'

'What had you done?'

'Told political jokes,' Sergei said. 'But I found out about my file in a roundabout way. I was working for Komsomol' – the communist youth organization – 'in the Political Education Department. It was the eighties. We were dealing with vets from Afghanistan. They had severe stress and trauma, and they found it hard to adjust to life.

'I was stressed too, from the work. I wanted to travel abroad. I put in my application. I was told I'd need a reason. I gave one. They said, "No, Sergei. Sorry, Sergei."

'What? I was very surprised that I was not allowed to go. Five years later, after the USSR broke up, I found out the reason. The KGB gave me the information. That's a funny story. In 1989 I was in Czechoslovakia, the Velvet Revolution, when Havel became president. I was there the whole time. I was running a travel agency.

'The KGB came to me – some guys. They said, "What happened? What's this Velvet Revolution? We don't want the same thing here."

'I decided to blackmail them. I said, "I'll tell you about the Czechs if you show me my file."

'They finally agreed. I looked through my file and I was amazed. It turned out the informant was a girl I knew, a colleague in the Komsomol. After office parties, she wrote reports about who was telling jokes. I had trusted her!'

Big-shouldered, bearish, funny Sergei was hunched over the wheel, squinting into the snowstorm and the road ahead, and reminiscing. I could imagine him with a glass of vodka in his hand, drunk and yakking, being the life and soul of a party.

'Here's the really funny part,' he said. 'At the time, I sincerely believed in communism! I was deputy secretary, responsible for the ideology of the young people. We were believers! I discovered that there were three other spies in my office. And it was an ideological organization!'

'Were you scared when you found out about your file?' I asked.

'Not scared. I was very disappointed. I was disgusted. Here I was, intelligent. I thought our system was the best. But the trouble was, our leaders were old. Brezhnev, Andropov, Gorbachev. Old men!'

'Tell me a political joke,' I said.

'I can only think of Putin jokes.'

I said, 'Surely the jokes are the same, and only the names of the men change.'

'No. There are specific jokes. Brezhnev jokes were different altogether.'

'Such as?'

Viktor chipped in. 'Here's one. A man is talking to another. He says, "Have you heard that Brezhnev had an operation for chest expansion? More room for medals!"'

'It sounds better in Russian,' Yelena added after she'd translated.

Sergei then told a long and bewildering joke about Brezhnev overhearing his neighbours watching a hockey game on television. He said. They said. He said. I wrote it down but didn't understand it.

When I didn't laugh at the punchline, Sergei said, 'Jokes about Brezhnev are kind-hearted. For one thing, he wasn't well. For another, compared to Stalin and Khrushchev, he was good. But Andropov was a problem. He initiated more repression of dissidents.'

'What about the woman who reported on your jokes?' I asked. 'What happened to her?'

'I saw her a few years later,' Sergei said, chuckling at the memory. 'I gave her a few shots of vodka, then told her what I knew. I asked, "Why did you do it?"'

'She just looked at me. "I was doing my duty," she says.'

'So she didn't apologize?'

'Not at all. She said, "I wanted to report everyone who was two-faced." Listen, Paul, I have a huge file. Ha!'

We had gone sixty or more miles into the snow-covered pine forest of Chusovskoy Oblast, the snow blowing across the road in some places, the wind creating sharply pleated drifts. It was another vast but over-simple black-and-white landscape, beautiful and terrifying in its starkness. Just the way the snow danced in the headlights, swirling and funnelling in the gusts, took my attention away from the stories of betrayal. I tried to imagine being a prisoner in this storm, on foot or in the back of a locked truck. There had been millions. Everything that made this place lovely for me, for a prisoner meant only death.

'This is Kuchino,' Yelena said, as Sergei slowed and took a sharp right into very deep snow, going slowly past a village of dark wooden cottages. The half-buried buildings had scalloped, gingerbreaded shutters and wooden ornaments – flowers and squiggles – and some were log cabins, which dated from tsarist times.

Boys and men wandered in the road, dangerously close to our car, peering at us from under fur hats. Their faces were red with cold, snot glistening under their noses, their mouths open as though calling out to us.

'Everyone here is feeble-minded,' Yelena said. 'They were sent here, to the hospital.'

But it wasn't really a hospital. It was an old-fashioned asylum where the patients had been rusticated, and during the day many of them were turned out to wander in the snow. Until they were sent here, they had been locked in a gold-domed cathedral – decommissioned to serve as a madhouse – near the city of Kungur, ninety miles down the Siberian road.

A few miles beyond Kuchino, we came to a steel wall surrounded by trees, and a big gate, and a sign beside it saying that we'd come to Perm 36. A FORMER CORRECTIVE LABOUR COLONY, I read, and the rest was obscured by the falling snow.

One of the patients from the asylum had followed us to the big gate and began pleading in Russian as we drove through.

The compound was so simplified by the snowfall it could have been a Boy Scout camp, but that was a first and fleeting impression. The barbed wire at the top of the high walls and near every entrance told a truer story. So did the small barred windows, the windowless truck in which prisoners were transported, and, when I went inside, the cells, the bunks, the barracks, the torture chambers.

Perm 36 is the only intact gulag prison remaining in Russia. In *Gulag*,

Anne Applebaum writes of Perm 36 as 'a Stalinist-era *lagpunkt* [camp division], later one of the harshest political camps of the 1970s and 1980s'. All the other prisons have been destroyed or were converted to different uses. Perm 36 still exists because of the efforts of former prisoners, gulag historians such as Viktor Shmirov, and, as I learned later, money from the Ford Foundation.

'Not the Russian government?' I asked, though I suspected what the answer might be.

Sergei laughed and said, 'Many of the people in this government were responsible for the prison' – for the fact was that Perm 36, which had operated for more than forty years, had been shut down only recently. Fifteen years ago, this had been a place of torture, forced labour, virtual slavery and death.

'Who was sent here?' I asked as we walked from cell to cell.

'The same people as in other camps. Fifteen per cent anti-Soviet, ten per cent criminals, and all the others – three quarters – ordinary people accused of "misbehaviour".'

'Petty crime?'

'No, no,' Viktor said. 'Missing workdays – say, if you missed three, they'd send you here for ten years. Or lateness. Or taking something from the government.'

'Taking what, for example?'

'A peasant – a hungry peasant – who took three tassels of grain would be arrested and brought here. Like Sergei's uncles. But never mind these things. You have to keep in mind that people were needed. We had a bad economy. Stalin had started a programme of economic moderniz-ation. You know what Churchill said: Stalin found Russia working with wooden ploughs and left it equipped with nuclear bombs.'

'Let's keep moving,' I said. Inside, even with the heat on, the barracks and cells were very cold. They had been repainted, but still they were primitive examples of inhumanity and terror.

'For twenty-four years under Stalin we became powerful,' Viktor said, 'but at the expense of freedom. We had no loans or credit from other countries. We had to do it all ourselves. The only source of labour was the people' – and he gestured to the workshop we were entering – 'Russian people, prisoners, slaves.'

Here at Perm 36 the 'politicals', the criminals, the trady workers, laboured in the machine shop, making small metal Y-shaped connectors to attach wires to electrical terminals. I'd seen them on plugs, on carburettors, on batteries. Viktor said they had to be made by hand, and Perm 36 produced hundreds of thousands of them.

'Government needed labour,' Viktor said, 'so it enacted harsh legislation, creating fear and exploitation. This produced huge numbers of prisoners. And because they were slaves, they were an extremely mobile labour force.'

As we tramped through the snowdrifts to the punishment cells, Viktor said that it was not only these slave labourers who suffered. He recalled that in his own family there was never enough food. 'We were always hungry.'

Perm 36 had gone through a number of phases. After 1953, some prisoners got their freedom, though they had been almost destroyed by their time in the labour camp. Then a power struggle between Khrushchev and his spy chief, Lavrenty Beria, resulted in Beria's being convicted as a spy and shot. Eight hundred of Beria's men were sent to Perm to suffer and work. Because they were canny – most of them had been spies or agents – security was increased, walls were heightened, and the camp was expanded. In 1973 – and I reminded myself that I had rattled past Perm on the Trans-Siberian at that time, feeling sorry for myself – Perm was 'only one of two political camps' in the Soviet Union, Anne Applebaum wrote. Perm was restocked with political prisoners. In the 1980s, Soviet leader Yuri Andropov, a former director of the KGB, had arrested many thousands. 'The prisoners were educated and had been powerful. Some had lawyers!' More camps were built, including others around Perm.

'They built a toilet over there in 1972,' Viktor said, pointing from an iced-up doorway to an outhouse in a distant part of the prison compound. 'It had to serve five hundred and sixty prisoners. They lined up to use it. How did they do it? Yes, quickly.'

Sergei said, 'It was just another tool to humiliate prisoners.'

'Exhaustion, frost, hunger and endless humiliations,' Shalamov had written of prison certainties.

I asked Viktor about the death rate at Perm 36.

'In general, prisoners were worked to death. Six per cent or more died every year. But many were too sick to work. In 1984, only seven per cent of the prisoners here were capable of hard work. The rest were sick or handicapped.'

In the midday snowstorm, under a gunmetal sky, the snowdrifts piled to the windows, the damp rooms and dark corridors too cold to linger in, the outside temperature around 0° Fahrenheit, and crazies from the nearby asylum banging on the high iron gate, it seemed an appropriate day to visit a gulag. I did not want to see it in the summer, surrounded by high grass and picturesque log cabins and wildflowers and tweeting birds. It was most enlightening to see it at its worst, when the broken bunks and the exhibit of prisoners' artefacts – dented bowls and twisted spoons and ragged gloves – were given more meaning by the cold despair I could feel in my bones.

Viktor showed me an exhibit of photographs of well-known Soviet political prisoners: Osip Mandelstam, Isaac Babel, Varlam Shalamov; and they could have included Natan Sharansky, who had served six years in Perm 35, not far away. A leader of the struggle for Lithuanian independence, Balis Gayauskas, had been locked up for thirty-five years. One of his crimes was translating Solzhenitsyn's *Gulag Archipelago* into Lithuanian. He subsequently became head of state security in the Lithuanian government.

'He comes back from time to time,' Viktor said.

In *The First Circle*, Solzhenitsyn had written: 'A great writer is, so to speak, a second government. That's why no regime anywhere has ever loved its great writers, only its minor ones.'

A Ukrainian dissident, Lenko Luk'ianenko, was sentenced to death; his sentence was reduced to fifteen years, which he served here, but before he was released he was given ten more years. A fellow Ukrainian, a poet named Vasyl Stus – 'not a dissident', Viktor said, 'but had the sort of spirit they didn't want' – spent fifteen years here, after being arrested and rearrested. A Nobel Prize candidate in 1980, Stus had lost out to Czeslaw Milosz, a Polish poet who had emmigrated to California, where he wrote lyric poems in the Berkeley sunshine while Stus sat in an isolation or punishment cell translating Rilke from memory and made metal connectors in the machine shop. Stus died in the prison in 1985, 'in mysterious circumstances', Viktor said. But what was the mystery? I saw Stus's horrible little cell and the narrow board of a shelf that was his bunk. I would not have lasted two days.

'I want to explain the slavery of this system,' Viktor said. 'I've been to the US. My friends there would say to me, "We had slaves. It's like American slavery." I said no. Here's the difference. You know Cato, the

Roman? He said, To keep a slave you must give him meat, bread and two bottles of not very good wine every week. Eh?' He let this sink in, and then he said, 'On the Southern plantations, the slaves were fed because they were worth something. They were kept well. They had families and households. They had value.' He smiled grimly and went on, 'Gulag prisoners were slaves who were worth nothing!'

'The word the guards used for gulag prisoners,' a middle-aged Russian woman who was also a historian later told me, 'was dust – *pwl*'. She also said, 'Stalin introduced fear. We lived in fear.' His announced intention in setting up the gulag was 'to isolate those who might possibly doubt our resolution and achievements in the great revolution'.

'And look what we lost,' the historian said. 'Forty million in the purges from 1918 to 1953. Twenty-six million in the Second World War. The best people. It's a wonder we're still here.'

'What little freedom an American slave had was more than that of any gulag slave,' Viktor said.

I went back to the old photographs to look at Varlam Shalamov's tormented, martyred-looking face. I had read his books but never seen his face. Where Solzhenitsyn served up piety, and redemption through suffering, Shalamov was clear-sighted about how everyone involved with the camps – prisoners and guards and party hacks – was debased: the camps represented 'the corruption of the human soul'. 'The camps are in every way schools of the negative,' he writes in one story. 'Every minute of camp life is a poisoned minute.' The prisoner clings to life but without any illusions because 'we understood that death was no worse than life, and we feared neither'. In another story, a fellow prisoner says flatly, 'I'm going to Magadan. To be shot.' All this in temperatures of 60 below. The wonder was that this highly intelligent man had survived, and in *Kolyma Tales* he had created a masterpiece out of the experience. 'A human being survives by his ability to forget,' he writes early in the book, and near the end, in a line that no writer would disagree with, 'It's easier to bear a thing if you write it down.'

Our last visit was to the isolation, or punishment, cells, each a bare cement box with four wooden shelves. I stepped in, and Sergei, in an exuberant fit of macabre humour, slammed the door shut and yelled at me through the door slit. I stood in the semi-darkness shivering, though some warmth was palpable on the pipes bolted to the wall. Trying to conceal my alarm, I shouldered the door open.

Viktor said, 'A former prisoner told me, "I remember every night I spent in that cell. I woke up five times a night. I rubbed my body against the pipes. I did exercises to stop shivering. We had no blanket."'

Many former prisoners told Viktor the same story of the isolation cell. It was a torture chamber, he said as we walked outside into the snow. The prisoners got a quarter of the food the others were given. A *zek*, Anne Applebaum wrote, could be punished for sitting on his bed in the daytime, for not wearing socks or for walking too slowly. And a sick or injured man might end up being held (as in one well-documented case) for two months 'before being taken to the hospital'.

All this history was well within the memory of most people I met. These were the sentiments of a woman activist, one Madam Alexeev, who appeared in a short film about Perm 36: 'To see that this is not a labour camp but a museum is to realize what an incredible step we've taken from our years of slavery.'

True, but the film had been underwritten by the Ford Foundation, and many of the prison guards, the floggers, the torturers, the spies, the men hissing the word 'dust' at the suffering slave labourers, the hacks and political flunkies who had made this prison possible, were in the Russian government now – including Russian president Vladimir Putin, who had headed the KGB when Perm 36 had been a place of great suffering and death.

In the lowering darkness of late afternoon we drove back to the city of Perm on the empty roads. The snowstorm had not abated. The landscape seemed much bleaker and colder for my having seen the slave labour camp hidden in the hills.

For all the upbeat talk of Perm as the setting of *Doctor Zhivago* and Chekhov's *Three Sisters*, I still could not ease my mind after I'd seen the gulag. Many places in Perm, some of them innocent-looking, were associated with repression or imprisonment. Sergei only depressed me more when he said things like 'Dostoyevsky walked down this street on his way to prison in Omsk!' and, at the Kama River, 'Look at this river – barges brought prisoners here from Moscow, before the railway! Even in tsarist times.'

And long afterwards, too. In *Hope Against Hope*, Nadezhda Mandelstam recounts her experience of misery and suffering passing through Perm on a barge with her husband, Osip. The Perm Public Library had mounted an exhibit about Pasternak, which was also a recounting of repression, imprisonment and book banning – the 1957 novel had not appeared in Perm until more than thirty years later.

And the churches, too, every one that I saw – lovely eighteenth-century onion-domed buildings, not just in Perm but in Kungur, down the Siberian Road, and the Belogorsky Monastery high on a hill outside the village of Kalinino – had served as either a prison or a madhouse, many of the rooms used for torture or solitary confinement. Some of these handsome buildings had functioned as prisons until 1990.

'See the bullet marks?' Sergei said.

He traced his gloved fingers on the deeply pitted brickwork of the Belogorsky Cathedral wall as we stood averting our faces from the sharp freezing wind. The wind was so strong it tipped my body, and I had trouble standing upright. This hilltop in the Urals was the coldest place I'd been in Russia. The whole wall was plastered with blown snow and ice, but the gouged bricks were unusual.

'After Stalin took over this church in 1930 and made it a prison, the police lined up seventy-four monks against this wall, five at a time, and shot them.'

Later, a Russian told me in passing, 'You know why people were imprisoned and tortured in churches? Huh? Because of the thick walls and the strong construction. They were soundproof. No one outside could hear the screams.'

The next day, more memories of misery at the Peter and Paul Cathedral, the oldest stone building in Perm – and another former prison, like Belogorsky, and St Nicholas in Kungur. Up to their knees in snow, nine children stood looking hopeful – most of them skinny and pale-faced adolescents who were very cold – with their hands out, begging as the snow fell on their heads.

'They are from poor families,' Yelena said.

But after the experience of Perm 36, even their sadness was an anti-climax. We went to the ice caves outside the city of Kungur; they were dungeon-like, like a deep freeze three miles deep, just darkness, tumbled boulders and slimy stalactites. The entrance was protected by clanking steel doors, making me think that these caves, too, might have served as a prison in earlier times.

On another day, in another snowstorm, I saw some naked, fattish, middle-aged couples in Speedos jumping into a hole that had been cut through the ice in a lake. Barefoot in the snow, they gasped from the cold, their skin blotchy pink, their body hair prickling with ice.

That frosty night at Perm's Tchaikovsky Theatre, I sat, drowsy with champagne from the lobby bar, and watched the ballet *Sleeping Beauty*. In the audience were children, families, old women, stuffed shirts, old couples holding hands and local beauties in stylish boots, tight sweaters and fur hats. The atmosphere could not have been sweeter, nor the music more beguiling. Yet my mind, ruminative with the melodies and the wine, wandered back. I imagined this same theatre, perhaps the same ballet, fifteen years ago: the lovely sets, the costumed dancers, the music, the warmth and well-being – and up the road the prisoners regarded as slaves.

'Next to the right to create, the right to criticize is the richest gift that liberty of thought can offer,' Nabokov wrote, with Soviet prisoners in mind, adding that the American living in freedom 'may be apt to regard stories of prison life coming from remote lands as exaggerated accounts spread by panting fugitives'.

Perm 36 represented forty years of the starved and dying, half frozen, benumbed in their plank bunks, shivering in rags, waking up from a state of near mortification every few hours in the cold, turned into slave labour, reduced to dust, because of something they said or wrote.

'This is *posikunchiki*,' Yelena said, helping me to some dumplings in a restaurant in Perm on our last evening, a farewell delicacy. 'They squirt when you eat them. "Pissing dumplings".'

Sergei poured vodka. He raised his glass. 'Friendship!'

We ate dumpling soup (*pelmenye*), Tatar buns with spinach (*potchmak*) and mushroom stew in pots (*garshochki*). We toasted one another with vodka, saying that we would stay in touch, that we'd meet again in warmer weather – and I drank, and drank again, and drunkenly agreed to return, and made more extravagant promises, as travellers do just before they move on.

It was still snowing as the overnight train, the Kama Express, named for the river, left Perm for Moscow. This was around noon. I was bewildered by the thought that a habit of travel I'd acquired was now ending – the long backtrack that had begun many months before in London and become a way of living, as long journeys do. We were crossing the Urals, the Asiatic dividing line; now, out of Asia, I felt restless, inattentive, thinking only of the way home.

This train was luxurious by Russian standards: I had a private compartment (cushions, lace curtains, tassels), I drank my Kyoto green tea, and the *provodnitsa* brought me biscuits. Throughout the afternoon, hawkers in the driving snow on unshovelled railway platforms sold dried fish and handicrafts and home-knitted wool shawls, the cottage industries of an earlier time, my whole railway experience a throwback, complete with belligerent drunks and demanding beggars at many stations.

Before Kirov – formerly Vyatka – where Sergei's babushka had suffered political repression, I was standing at the window looking at the passing birch forest when a man setting his luggage down asked where I happened to be from. When I told him, he smiled, almost in pity. I knew what he was thinking, so I asked him for his opinion.

'Do Russians talk about us fighting in Iraq?' I asked.

'Russian people don't pay much attention. Yes, they talk about it sometimes.' He said no more about that, implying: I'm not going to insult you by repeating what people say. 'It's not really in the news. We have our own wars.'

I was surprised by how good his English was; though it was heavily inflected, he was fluent and direct.

'We were in Afghanistan,' he said. 'It's unwinnable. Because there's no government. Iraq, though . . .' He nodded almost approvingly. 'The effect has been to put the oil price up. This is good for us. Now I must say goodbye. Have a good trip. This is my station.'

He got off at Kirov. Night had fallen. At some stations after that, people rushed out of the darkness in thick fur hats and big felt boots selling fish on sticks jammed through their gills. Though we were less than ten hours from Moscow on the main line, it might have been a scene from the earliest years of the Trans-Siberian.

The night passed quickly. I was roused by a rapping at the door – 'Moskva!' I woke and yawned and, as always, took a vitamin pill and shaved with my battery-powered razor and brushed my teeth. Then I walked into Yaroslavl Station, jostled by the crowd – people bright-eyed with fatigue, yawning, sleepwalking along the platform through the falling snow.

After the usual give-and-take with a taxi driver – half quarrel, half negotiation – and a slow trip along unploughed city streets, I found my hotel. The desk clerk wouldn't admit me because I was too early. I went outside and walked. As I passed a sushi bar in the pre-dawn snowfall, a woman on a stool leaned at the window and beckoned to me – a prostitute, still alert and willing in the early morning. She represented a new Russian tendency: having been relieved of the burden of unsmiling dogma, they seemed restlessly preoccupied with the worst excesses of the West, not just the flesh, but money and crime, the joyless greed and promiscuity I had seen in the new China too.

I walked for several hours, enjoying the emptiness of the city, looking magical in the snow. After I checked into the hotel and had a bath, I went on a walking tour with a woman who was a historian of the city. I wanted to know how it was different from the Moscow I had seen in 1973.

'It's a completely different place,' she said. 'Though 1973 was better than 1988, when we had nothing.'

The country had collapsed in 1988, and for the next few years food was scarce and consumer goods were almost unobtainable, she said. This woman's children liked cheese. She made cheese at home in her kitchen, squeezing milk through a cloth bag. She wanted to buy bunk beds for them. She was put on a six-month waiting list.

'You know the joke?' she said. 'A woman wants to buy a car. She is given a voucher and told, "It will be delivered in ten years." "Morning or afternoon?" she asks. "Why do you want to know?" She says, "Because the plumber is coming in the morning." It was like that.'

But the economic tide turned in 1995. Putin kept his promises and things improved. My guide didn't say so, but it was well known that the Russian government was filled with crooks, embezzlers and opportunists.

We strolled around, from Beria's house ('he buried bodies on his grounds') to Gorki's house (oceanic theme, sea creatures and coral) to the mansion that housed the Union of Russian Writers on Porvaskaya Street, which is mentioned as Rostov's house in *War and Peace*.

'Our history is that of the government fighting against its own people,' she said as we crossed New Arbat Street. She helped me buy tickets for performances at the Moscow Conservatory, and then she said goodbye.

I went to a Mahler concert and in the middle of the lugubrious music remembered the long days I'd spent on the train passing Siberian birches and snowfields. The next night I sat through half of a Poulenc opera, and when I asked for my coat the woman spoke fiercely in Russian, and I knew she was saying, 'But it's not over yet!' It was over for me. Tchaikovsky the next night: passionate and dramatic, and I reflected on the forbidding place that Russia had been that first time: the closed cities, the repression, the gulag, no magazines to speak of, hardly any restaurants. And here were sushi bars and pizza parlours and Mexican restaurants and coffee shops and newsstands selling *Time* and the *International Herald Tribune* and bookshops with my own books in them, in Russian and English. In one of those stores, I was chatting up a Russian woman, telling her my travels. I told only half of what I'd seen, because she would never have believed me. Yet she wasn't impressed. She just said, 'Why do you travel alone?' as though I was out of my mind.

And why was I still here? I felt I was killing time, especially in Russia, which, in spite of all the talk of change and reform, seemed exactly the same place as it had ever been: a pretentious empire with a cruel government that was helpless without secret police.

I was at the conservatory in the L. L. Bean boots that I had been tramping around in since Japan, listening to Tchaikovsky, *Variations on a Rococo Theme*, with a wonderful cello soloist, and in the mythomania that all travellers indulge in, I was thinking that it was like the closing theme music to my trip: cue the violins.

32. Night Train to Berlin and Beyond

In the morning darkness and lamp-lit iridescence of the Moscow outskirts, on the fast train to Berlin (via Minsk and Warsaw), I remembered my story about the American girl in India, how I had added a thought to my Tao of Travel. It was about a true journey being much more than a vivid or vacant interval of being away. The best travel was not a simple train trip or even a whole collection of them, but something lengthier and more complex: an experience of the fourth dimension, with stops and starts and longueurs, spells of illness and recovery, dawdling and hurrying and having to wait, with the sudden phenomenon of happiness as an episodic reward.

Some travel didn't involve locomotion, but instead periods of residence and reflection, a weightless orbiting, as when I became almost invisible and seemed to dissolve, ghost-like again, in an agreeable location, an aromatic version of home, days of work and thought when I remained monkishly in my head, unaware of the exotic – days when I would emerge from my hotel room into a crowded Asiatic lane as though I'd been beamed there as 'matter transfer' by a hot light, surprised to see a bazaar and rickshaws and skinny street vendors, pretty girls staring, and I would laugh: *What am I doing here?*

I'd come to see that travel for me was no longer a fun-seeking interlude, not even the roundabout detour of heading home, but a way of living my life: a trip without an end where the only destination was darkness. The beauty of it was that I was doing it in the simplest way, as a homeless person with a small bag and a briefcase of papers, rubbing across the world, travelling light. The epitome of this was the elderly father of the Jain I had met in Jodhpur, who, after a long career as an accountant, said goodbye to his family and set out on foot to spend the rest of his wandering life seeking enlightenment, or a monk like Tapa Snim in Mandalay, his whole material existence tucked into a bag slung over his shoulder, travelling from country to country to solve holy riddles in his head about the Buddha as a pinecone tree.

In the dining car of this Berlin train, I was making notes on the flyleaf of the book I was reading, one I had bought in Moscow for the onward journey. It was *Venus in Furs*, but it did not live up to its lurid cover or its reputation as an erotic classic. I ordered bread, fried eggs and tea (I could still say *khlyeb* and *ya-ich-nitsa* and *chai*).

The rock-faced Russian men pigging it over a messy breakfast at the next table noticed my book. Gesturing with big fingers and smiling, they indicated, How about a closer look at the cover?

The book was passed from horny hand to horny hand, the fat fingers poking at the bosomy torso wrapped in a fur stole. Before they went back to their sausages and their vodka, the men regarded me with widened lips and welcoming teeth.

'You woodka.' They were not so much offering me a drink as ordering me to take one, the inevitable Russian challenge.

I took one. They bullied me to repeat it. We toasted peace and friendship. Five shots later, my brain was inflamed. The sun came up, glanced on the snow, slashed through the window and stung my blood-shot eyes.

'Fryendsheep!' Oleg was saying. His friends were Valery and Alexey. They were steelworkers going to Minsk. They had the dangerous and half-domesticated look of men who'd just been given bad haircuts.

'To money!' I said, attempting a joke.

'No money!' Oleg said. 'Money – sheet!'

'To the little children,' I said.

'What you are saying?'

'To love,' I said.

'Love,' they said.

'Bush is *rediska*,' Oleg said with the suddenness of a drunk.

'*Rediska?*'

'Is a bad fruit,' Oleg said.

A radish, I guessed, a mildly denigrating euphemism.

'Peace,' I said, and was glad when at last the vodka bottle was empty. I was helplessly drunk at nine-thirty on this sunny morning as the train drew into Minsk's bright, cold and dazzling snow, its pistachio-coloured station. I had to lie down. I slept and woke and read the rest of *Venus in Furs*, written by the man whose name Freud chose to define the desire for pain. *Oh, a man must feel like a God when he sees others before him trembling*, I read, and thought of the paranoiac Stalin and his gulag.

'*Kontrol!*' a Polish border guard shouted at Terespol Station as she flung my door open that night. Black leather coat, boots, black gloves: she could have stepped from Sacher-Masoch's novel.

After a peaceful night, '*Kontrol!*' again, and I looked out of the window into the edge of Germany and the first snowless landscape I had seen since Vladivostok.

In the next compartment, a young English couple and their small child were headed for a skiing holiday in the Alps. They asked where I'd been. I'd just come from Perm, I said, and I mentioned the gulag.

'I'd do all right in a gulag,' the wife said, sniffing confidently.

'How so?'

'I like being on my own.'

I got off at Berlin. It was a whole city now, and rebuilt. The wall was down, and fragments of it were erected as freakish monuments. More sushi bars and pizza parlours and Mexican restaurants and coffee shops, and couples strolling in the sunshine. I went to three museums, and at nightfall, instead of checking into a hotel, I went back to Berlin Hauptbahnhof and caught the Paris Express.

In the most comfortable compartment of the many night trains I had occupied on my trip was a wide bed with a soft duvet, a writing desk, and a bathroom as large as any in a Japanese hotel – with a shower stall and a swing-out sink. I took a hot shower, drank some beer and went to bed. I woke to green bushes, and trees in bud, and a silvery fog like threadbare silk fraying to scraps and ghosting over the green hedges and plough marks of neatly ruled fields.

The mild morning in Paris was a gilded evaporation of dissolving fog, like a mist of decomposing angels, the sun burning through its essence and beautifying the ornate backdrop of biscuit-coloured buildings, revealing the city to me once again as a luminous stage set.

For the sake of symmetry, and because I was hungry and had time to kill, I checked my bag at the Gare du Nord and walked across the street to the Brasserie Terminus Nord. I ordered the same meal that I'd eaten that early evening, months and months ago, before taking the Orient Express to Budapest – *bouillabaisse*, green salad, a half bottle of white burgundy. Afterwards, I walked a little, and thought: Once a city's boulevards have been marched on by triumphant Nazis, they never look quite so grand again. Then I took the Eurostar to London.

I fell asleep and woke after nightfall in Kent, at the far end of the

Channel Tunnel, intending to finish this book, which I'd written every day of the trip. In the darkness tonight no images of the past were visible to disturb me. The landscape was shrouded with a veil of forgiveness, and bad memories were buried – like many I'd endured on my trip – in the dark backward and abysm of time. Nothing to remember but my last meal. At the end of my day's notes I wrote the one word, *Done*.

It's true that travel is the saddest of pleasures, the long-distance over-land blues. But I also thought what I'd kept fretting about throughout my trip, like a mantra of vexation building in my head, words I never wrote. Most people on earth are poor. Most places are blighted and nothing will stop the blight getting worse. Travel gives you glimpses of the past and the future, your own and other people's. 'I am a native in this world', aspiring to be the Man with the Blue Guitar. But there are too many people and an enormous number of them spend their hungry days thinking about America as the Mother Ship. I could be a happy Thai, but there is no life on earth that I am less suited to living than that of an Indian, rich or poor. Most of the world is worsening, shrinking to a ball of bungled desolation. Only the old can really see how gracelessly the world is ageing and all that we have lost. Politicians and policemen are always inferior to their citizens. No one on earth is well governed. Is there hope? Yes. Most people I'd met, in chance encounters, were strangers who helped me on my way. And we lucky ghosts can travel wherever we want. The going is still good, because arrivals are departures.